Philipp Blom

Veronica Buckley was born and educated in New Zealand, and later studied at the Universities of London and Oxford. Christina, Queen of Sweden, was the subject of her first much-praised biography. She lived in Paris while writing *The Secret Wife of Louis XIV,* and now lives in Vienna.

ALSO BY VERONICA BUCKLEY

Christina, Queen of Sweden:
The Restless Life of a European Eccentric

The Secret Wife
of Louis XIV

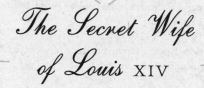

The Secret Wife of Louis XIV

FRANÇOISE D'AUBIGNÉ, MADAME DE MAINTENON

VERONICA BUCKLEY

PICADOR

———

FARRAR, STRAUS AND GIROUX

NEW YORK

www.picadorusa.com

Picador® is a U.S. registered trademark and is used by Farrar, Straus and Giroux under license from Pan Books Limited.

For information on Picador Reading Group Guides, please contact Picador.
E-mail: readinggroupguides@picadorusa.com

Designed by Michelle McMillian

The Library of Congress has cataloged the Farrar, Straus and Giroux edition as follows:

Buckley, Veronica.
    The secret wife of Louis XIV : Françoise d'Aubigné, madame de Maintenon / Veronica Buckley.—1st American ed.
        p. cm.
    Includes bibliographical references and index.
    ISBN 978-0-374-15830-9
    1. Maintenon, Madame de, 1635–1719. 2. Favorites, Royal—France—Biography. 3. France—Kings and rulers—Paramours—Biography. 4. Louis XIV, King of France, 1638–1715—Relations with women. 5. France—Court and courtiers—History. 6. France—History—Louis XIV, 1643–1715. I. Title.
    DC130.M2B9   2009
    944'.033092—dc22

                                                                2008016210

Picador ISBN 978-0-312-43005-4

Originally published as Madame de Maintenon: The Secret Wife of Louis XIV in Great Britain by Bloomsbury Publishing

First published in the United States by Farrar, Straus and Giroux

First Picador Edition: September 2010

10 9 8 7 6 5 4 3 2 1

FOR PHILIPP
—SO WENIG FÜR SO VIEL

I said to her one day, after the King's death, "Madame, I've brought you a book to write the story of your life in. Because you know they'll write your life one day, and they won't tell the truth, so you should write it yourself, Madame." And she said to me, "My life . . . has been a miracle."

—MADEMOISELLE D'AUMALE

CONTENTS

ELEVEN   The Course of True Loves   180

TWELVE   The Poisons Affair   207

Part Two

THIRTEEN   Madame de Maintenant   225

FOURTEEN   Uncrowned Queen   256

FIFTEEN   La Vie en Rose   282

SIXTEEN   La Vie en Bleu   311

SEVENTEEN Crusaders   337

EIGHTEEN   Castles in Spain   374

NINETEEN   All Passion Spent   406

           Epilogue   429

           Notes   431

           Bibliography   475

           Index   485

ILLUSTRATIONS

1. *Les petites Antilles ou Les îsles du vent.* Copperplate engraving by Jacques-Nicolas Bellin (1703–72), 1764. Paris, Bibliothèque Nationale de France. Copyright © Bibliothèque Nationale de France.

2. *Beggars Receiving Alms at the Door.* Etching, burin, and drypoint by Rembrandt van Rijn (1606–69), 1648. London, British Museum. Copyright © Trustees of the British Museum.

3. *Le château de Mursay* (1550–1630), ancienne demeure de Madame de Maintenon, près de Sciecq (Deux-Sèvres). Private Collection. Copyright © LL/Roger-Viollet.

4. *Portrait dit autrefois de Paul Scarron* (1610–60). Oil on canvas, French School, seventeenth century. Le Mans, Musée de Tessé.

5. *Portrait of Ninon de Lenclos* (presumed). Oil on canvas, attributed to Pierre Mignard (1612–95). Marseilles, Musée des Beaux-Arts. Copyright © Roger-Viollet.

6. *Portrait of Madame de Sévigné.* Oil on canvas by Claude Lefèbvre (1632–75). Paris, Musée Carnavalet. Copyright © The Bridgeman Art Library.

15. *Vue de l'Orangerie, des escaliers des Cent-Marches et du château de Versailles, vers 1695.* Oil on canvas, attributed to Jean-Baptiste Martin, l'Ancien (1659–1735). Versailles, France, Châteaux de Versailles et de Trianon. Photo copyright © RMN/Franck Raux.

16. *Portrait de Philippe d'Orléans, Monsieur, frère du roi Louis XIV.* Oil on canvas. Copyright © Roger-Viollet.

17. *Portrait of Elizabeth Charlotte of Bavaria, duchesse d'Orléans (la princesse Palatine).* Oil on canvas, after Hyacinthe Rigaud (1659–1743). Versailles, France, Châteaux de Versailles et de Trianon.

18. *Portrait of Jean-Baptiste Colbert (1619–83), ministre.* Oil on canvas by Claude Lefèbvre (1632–75). Versailles, France, Châteaux de Versailles et de Trianon. Photo copyright © RMN/Gérard Blot.

19. *Portrait of François-Michel Le Tellier, marquis de Louvois (1641–91), Secrétaire d'État pour la Guerre, Intendant Général des Postes, Surintendant des Bâtiments Civils, Arts et Manufactures.* Anonymous print. Versailles, France, Châteaux de Versailles et de Trianon. Photo copyright © RMN/Gérard Blot.

20. *The Battle of Blenheim in 1704.* Watercolour, English School, eighteenth century. Private Collection. Copyright © The Bridgeman Art Library.

21. *Portrait of François de Salignac de la Mothe-Fénelon, archévêque de Cambrai.* Oil on canvas by Vivien Joseph (1657–1734). Versailles, France, Châteaux de Versailles et de Trianon.

22. *Portrait of Jacques-Bénigne Bossuet.* Oil on canvas by Hyacinthe Rigaud (1659–1743). Paris, Musée du Louvre.

23. *L'Evesque de Meaux, Secrétaire du Conseil de la Sainte Ligue.* Dutch caricature, attributed to Dusart and Gole, 1691. Paris, Bibliothèque Historique du Protestantisme. Copyright © The Bridgeman Art Library.

24. *Madame de Maintenon, Veuve de Scarron.* Dutch caricature, attributed to Dusart and Gole, 1691. Paris, Bibliothèque Historique du Protestantisme. Copyright © The Bridgeman Art Library.

25. *A Missionary Dragoon Forces a Huguenot to Sign His Conversion to Catholicism.* Engraving by Gottfried Englemann (1788–1839), after an original drawing of 1686. Paris, Bibliothèque Nationale de France. Copyright © The Bridgeman Art Library.

26. *Portrait of Françoise d'Aubigné, marquise de Maintenon.* Oil on canvas by Pierre Mignard (1612–95). Paris, Musée du Louvre. Copyright © Peter Willi/The Bridgeman Art Library.

27. *Portrait of Louis XIV.* Drawing on papier gris and pastel by Charles Le Brun (1619–90). Paris, Musée du Louvre, D.A.G. Photo copyright © RMN/Jean-Gilles Berizzi.

28. *La maison d'éducation pour jeunes filles de la noblesse créée par Madame de Maintenon en 1686.* Anonymous engraving. Yvelines, France, École militaire spéciale de Saint-Cyr. Copyright © Roger-Viollet.

29. *Portrait of Louis de Rouvroy, duc de Saint-Simon, memoirist.* Nineteenth-century lithograph by François Delpech, after a French portrait of 1715. Copyright © Roger-Viollet.

30. *Portrait de Philippe, duc d'Orléans, Régent de France (1674–1723) et Minerve, sous les traits présumés de Marie-Magdeleine de La Vieuville, comtesse de Parabère, sa maîtresse (1693–1750) (détail),* 1717–18. Oil on canvas by Jean-Baptiste Santerre (1651–1717). Versailles, France, Châteaux de Versailles et de Trianon. Photo copyright © RMN/Gérard Blot.

31. *Portrait of Louis-Auguste de Bourbon, duc du Maine.* Oil on canvas, after François de Troy (1645–1730). Sceaux, France, Musée de l'Île de France. Copyright © Lauros/Giraudon/The Bridgeman Art Library.

ACKNOWLEDGMENTS

There are several people whom I would like to thank by name for their help during my research for this book. Mlle Françoise Gillard of the Comédie-Française; M. Dominique Lelys, for guidance on the colonial period in the French West Indies; and M. Jean Raindre, for most kindly guiding me through the Château de Maintenon, its library, and the Noailles private family archive.

I must also extend my thanks to the staff of the following archives and libraries: Archives départementales des Yvelines; Bibliothèque municipale de Versailles; Bibliothèque-musée de la Comédie-Française; Bibliothèque nationale française; Bibliothèque historique de la ville de Paris; British Library; Manuscripts Department, Library of the University of Amsterdam; Österreichische Nationalbibliothek; Senate House Library of the University of London.

Special thanks are owing to my dear sisters, Anne Buckley and Bernadette Cantin-Buckley, for reading the manuscript.

Finally, I would like to thank my editor, Courtney Hodell, and my agent, Victoria Hobbs, *sine qua non*.

The Bourbon Family Tree

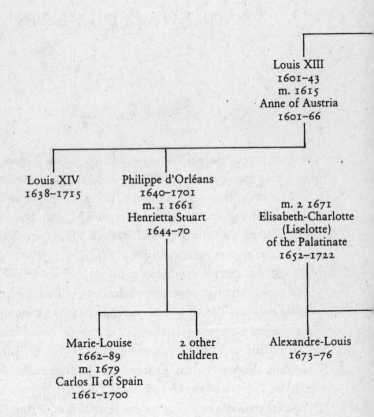

Louis XIII
1601–43
m. 1615
Anne of Austria
1601–66

Louis XIV
1638–1715

Philippe d'Orléans
1640–1701
m. 1 1661
Henrietta Stuart
1644–70

m. 2 1671
Elisabeth-Charlotte
(Liselotte)
of the Palatinate
1652–1722

Marie-Louise
1662–89
m. 1679
Carlos II of Spain
1661–1700

2 other
children

Alexandre-Louis
1673–76

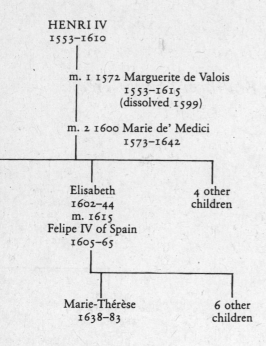

HENRI IV
1553–1610

m. 1 1572 Marguerite de Valois
1553–1615
(dissolved 1599)

m. 2 1600 Marie de' Medici
1573–1642

Elisabeth
1602–44
m. 1615
Felipe IV of Spain
1605–65

4 other
children

Marie-Thérèse
1638–83

6 other
children

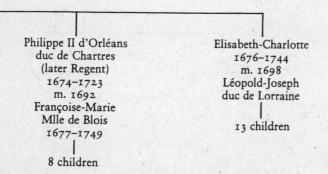

Philippe II d'Orléans
duc de Chartres
(later Regent)
1674–1723
m. 1692
Françoise-Marie
Mlle de Blois
1677–1749

8 children

Elisabeth-Charlotte
1676–1744
m. 1698
Léopold-Joseph
duc de Lorraine

13 children

The Bourbon Family Tree

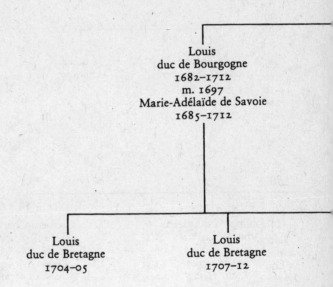

Louis
duc de Bourgogne
1682–1712
m. 1697
Marie-Adélaïde de Savoie
1685–1712

Louis
duc de Bretagne
1704–05

Louis
duc de Bretagne
1707–12

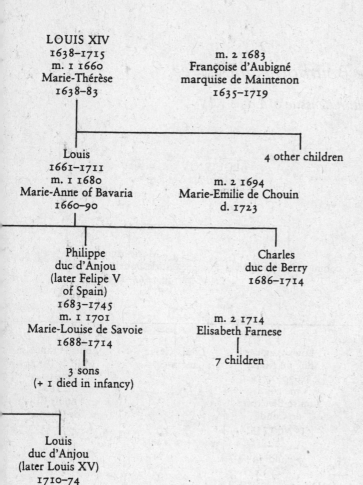

LOUIS XIV
1638–1715
m. 1 1660
Marie-Thérèse
1638–83

m. 2 1683
Françoise d'Aubigné
marquise de Maintenon
1635–1719

Louis
1661–1711
m. 1 1680
Marie-Anne of Bavaria
1660–90

4 other children

m. 2 1694
Marie-Emilie de Chouin
d. 1723

Philippe
duc d'Anjou
(later Felipe V
of Spain)
1683–1745
m. 1 1701
Marie-Louise de Savoie
1688–1714

3 sons
(+ 1 died in infancy)

Charles
duc de Berry
1686–1714

m. 2 1714
Elisabeth Farnese

7 children

Louis
duc d'Anjou
(later Louis XV)
1710–74

The Bourbon Family Tree

Illegitimate issue of Louis XIV

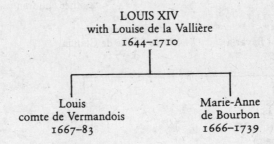

LOUIS XIV
with Louise de la Vallière
1644–1710

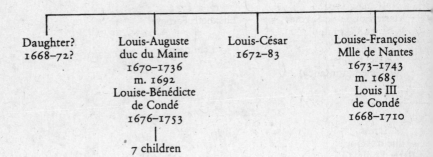

Louis
comte de Vermandois
1667–83

Marie-Anne
de Bourbon
1666–1739

Daughter?
1668–72?

Louis-Auguste
duc du Maine
1670–1736
m. 1692
Louise-Bénédicte
de Condé
1676–1753

7 children

Louis-César
1672–83

Louise-Françoise
Mlle de Nantes
1673–1743
m. 1685
Louis III
de Condé
1668–1710

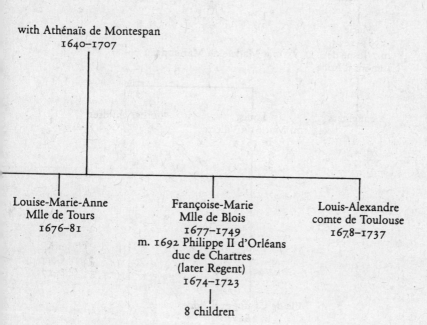

with Athénaïs de Montespan
1640–1707

Louise-Marie-Anne
Mlle de Tours
1676–81

Françoise-Marie
Mlle de Blois
1677–1749
m. 1692 Philippe II d'Orléans
duc de Chartres
(later Regent)
1674–1723

8 children

Louis-Alexandre
comte de Toulouse
1678–1737

The d'Aubigné Family Tree

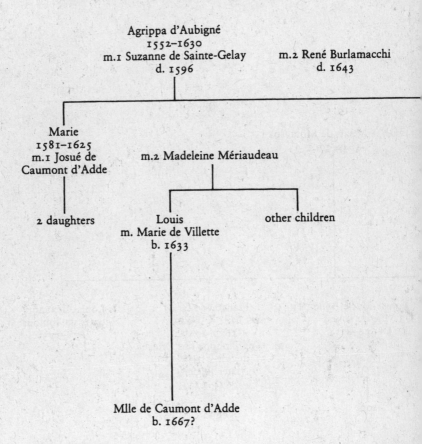

Agrippa d'Aubigné
1552–1630
m.1 Suzanne de Sainte-Gelay
d. 1596

m.2 René Burlamacchi
d. 1643

Marie
1581–1625
m.1 Josué de
Caumont d'Adde

m.2 Madeleine Mériaudeau

2 daughters

Louis
m. Marie de Villette
b. 1633

other children

Mlle de Caumont d'Adde
b. 1667?

see overleaf

see overleaf

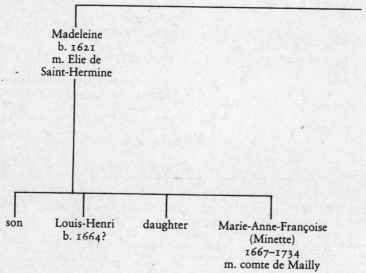

Madeleine
b. 1621
m. Elie de
Saint-Hermine

son

Louis-Henri
b. 1664?

daughter

Marie-Anne-Françoise
(Minette)
1667–1734
m. comte de Mailly

The d'Aubigné Family Tree

Agrippa d'Aubigné
1552–1630
m.1 Suzanne de Sainte-Gelay
d. 1596

continued from previous page

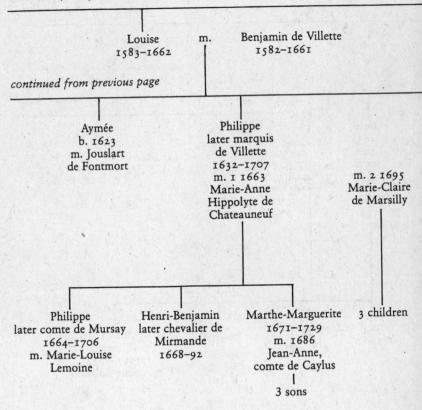

Louise
1583–1662

m.

Benjamin de Villette
1582–1661

continued from previous page

Aymée
b. 1623
m. Jouslart
de Fontmort

Philippe
later marquis
de Villette
1632–1707
m. 1 1663
Marie-Anne
Hippolyte de
Chateauneuf

m. 2 1695
Marie-Claire
de Marsilly

Philippe
later comte de Mursay
1664–1706
m. Marie-Louise
Lemoine

Henri-Benjamin
later chevalier de
Mirmande
1668–92

Marthe-Marguerite
1671–1729
m. 1686
Jean-Anne,
comte de Caylus

3 children

3 sons

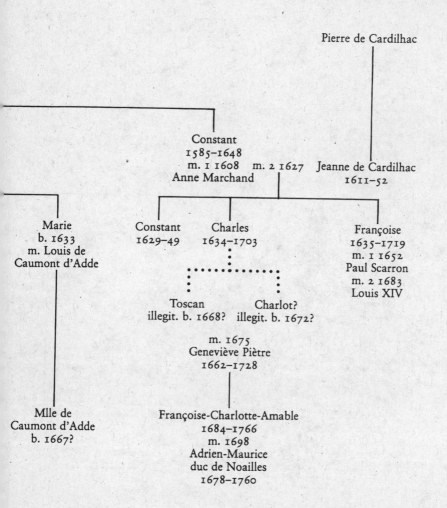

Pierre de Cardilhac

Constant
1585–1648
m. 1 1608   m. 2 1627   Jeanne de Cardilhac
Anne Marchand   1611–52

Marie
b. 1633
m. Louis de
Caumont d'Adde

Constant   Charles
1629–49   1634–1703

Françoise
1635–1719
m. 1 1652
Paul Scarron
m. 2 1683
Louis XIV

Toscan   Charlot?
illegit. b. 1668?   illegit. b. 1672?

m. 1675
Geneviève Piètre
1662–1728

Mlle de
Caumont d'Adde
b. 1667?

Françoise-Charlotte-Amable
1684–1766
m. 1698
Adrien-Maurice
duc de Noailles
1678–1760

Part One

Prologue

*T*here is a palace twelve miles from Paris, set in a forest rich with game, a Renaissance château of vaulted ceilings and marble floors, graced with elegant terraces leading down to the river Seine. Here, on a bright September morning near four hundred years ago, a fine little boy was born. He was his mother's first child, though she had been twenty-three years married. She rejoiced, and the nation rejoiced with her, for she was a queen, and her squalling little boy the long-awaited heir to the fleur-de-lys throne of the Bourbons.

There is a fortress in western France, inland from the rough Atlantic coast, a medieval donjon of cold grey stone, surrounded by swamp and woodland. Here, on a bleak November day, another child was born, a sister for two little ragged boys. Their mother was young and beautiful and the baby whole and strong, but the mother did not rejoice. She sighed, or wept, perhaps, though there was no one with pity to spare for her, for her home was a prison, and its stone walls deaf.

ONE

Doubtful Origins

There were no chains or balls of pitted lead. There were no shrieks from racks or wheels of torture. It was a long and narrow cell, without much air, without much light, damp, bare, its window barred. Bundles of drab belongings lay piled in the corners, with half a dozen mugs in brown clay and a few chipped bowls, sticky with the leavings of the last grey meal. Hard sleeping-benches lined the walls, spread with dirty blankets, and in the middle of the floor, wittily, defiantly, stood a gaming table served by a couple of rickety chairs. Next door, a bigger but equally bleak room for the indebted and the destitute, then a dreary sickroom, and one chilly little private cell, available to anyone in exchange for a silver coin. Below, there was "the cave," a dank cell like the first, and like the first, serving both men and women. And beside this, the dungeon, where the least fortunate coughed and sighed through the days and nights of lives with no more hope.

Thus the home of Sieur Constant d'Aubigné de Surimeau, only son of the famous Agrippa d'Aubigné, poet and Protestant warrior, friend of kings, angry, disinheriting father. With the fifty-year-old Constant in his grim confinement were his wife, Jeanne, aged twenty-four, their little boys, Constant, aged six, and Charles, just one year old, and a

baby girl, newborn in the prison, in the sickroom perhaps, or in the little private cell, struggling to life on the narrow bed or on the rough
floor. They named her Françoise.

It might all have been very different. Constant had stood to inherit,
in whole or in part, three substantial estates, in addition to the lucrative
governorship of an important Protestant town in his native region of
Poitou, in western France. All this would have come to him through
the efforts of his father, whose constancy in faith, bravery in battle,
and shrewdness in outwitting his in-laws had won him a premier place
among France's Huguenot gentry. Agrippa d'Aubigné had made his
name in the previous century, during France's "spectacularly un-
Christian" wars of religion; he had been the close friend and comrade-
in-arms of the Protestant Henri of Navarre, later King Henri IV, first
Bourbon King of France. After more than fifty years of pitched battles
and acts of savagery on both sides, the matter had been more or less resolved in 1594, when Henri agreed to accept Catholicism as the price
of the French crown. "Paris is worth a mass" was his legendary remark on this occasion; cynically setting aside his unpredictable wife
into the bargain, he had then married the solid and solidly Catholic
Marie de' Medici.

Apart from his capture of the crown itself, the signal achievement
of Henri's life was beyond doubt his promulgation of the Edict of
Nantes, four years after his accession to the throne, in 1598. This famous Edict, at the time one of the most advanced pieces of legislation
in Europe, guaranteed a limited toleration of Protestantism within
predominantly Catholic France. Members of the Protestant RPR, the
Religion Prétendue Réformée ("so-called reformed religion"), as hostile
Catholics referred to it, were thenceforth permitted to train pastors, retain their temples (though not more than two in the same district), conduct services, get married, baptize their children and educate them, all
within their own Huguenot sect; moreover, Protestant men could once
again purchase civil service posts or commissions in the King's army,
two vital methods of social and economic advancement. On the surface a peacemaking measure between two factions long at war, the
Edict of Nantes contained a grain of revolutionary significance for

France: it recognized that religious and political allegiance could be two separate things. After 1598, a Frenchman could officially be both a Protestant and a loyal servant of his Catholic King.

Nonetheless, Henri's farsighted Edict was too soon, or perhaps too weakly enforced, to overcome the country's religious divide, and far from integrating the two communities, it finally dictated their formal separation. Most of France remained officially and exclusively Catholic. The Huguenots were accorded 120 "places of safety," towns with an already Protestant majority, mostly in the south and west of the country, where their cult might be freely practised. And it was to one of these, his own staunch western province of Poitou, that the disgusted Agrippa d'Aubigné had retreated after the King's apostasy to the "stinking" Catholic Church. Here, over the next twelve years or so, he had raised three children (Marie, Louise, and Constant), buried his wife, fathered an illegitimate son (Nathan), and produced a series of poems and tracts of high literary merit, "my spiritual children," as he termed them. On the clever and spirited Constant, "my eldest and only son," Nathan notwithstanding, Agrippa lavished "the care and expense," as he said, "that might have been spent on the son of a prince." The boy was taught "by the best tutors in France, all enticed away from the best families by the doubling of their wages."

Agrippa's efforts were to no avail. Constant proved an unwilling pupil and a most ungrateful son. By the age of twenty he was squandering his talent and his property in the time-honoured ways. "This wretch," wrote his father, "first abandoned his books, then took to gaming and drinking, and then managed to undo himself completely in the stews of Holland." Returning to France, Constant had compounded his reputation, first by marrying without his father's consent, and then by killing a man in a duel; the latter, however, an *affaire d'honneur*, occasioned him no penalty. It was only in 1613, when he abducted a girl admired by one of his friends, that Constant was arrested and, at the age of twenty-eight, condemned to death.

He escaped execution by agreeing to enlist in the army, a Protestant army then in rebellion against the Queen Mother, Marie de' Medici. King Henri IV, royal friend of Agrippa's youth, had been assassinated in 1610, and his widow Marie was now Regent of France on behalf of her son, the twelve-year-old Louis XIII. On Henri's death, his widow had at first confirmed his great religious Edict, but in the ensuing three years, guided from afar by the Pope and from closer at hand by her own court favourites, the malleable Marie had begun a general suppression of Protestantism within the country. In practice, the terms of the Edict had never been fully observed, but now the protective walls of the Protestant "safe places" were crumbling, and the soldiers deputed to guard them were well in arrears of pay. Huguenots on their deathbeds were being accosted by Catholic priests threatening hellfire, funerals were being disrupted, and Huguenots going innocently about their business were being harassed in a thousand petty acts, in direct violation of the Edict.

More important than all the daily frictions of Catholic-Protestant life, however, was the Queen Mother's increasingly apparent enthusiasm for the cause of the Spanish Habsburgs, which loyal Frenchmen of both confessions eyed with distaste and anxiety. The Habsburgs in general, and the Spanish in particular, were among France's bitterest enemies. It was their fanatical King, Felipe II, the "stately Catholic," who had kept the fires of France's internal religious wars stoked for decades, providing "Indian gold"—money from his mines in South America—to Catholic extremists in France. Fears of outright war between France and Spain had remained alive right until Henri's death. Naïve politically, his widow, Marie, had failed to grasp that the death of her powerful husband had greatly weakened the country's standing; France was no longer viewed in Europe as a steady bulwark against Spanish Habsburg influence. A Habsburg herself on her mother's side, Marie was even seeking to forge an alliance with the Spaniards by a double royal marriage: her daughter Elisabeth was to marry the Prince of Asturias, heir to the Spanish imperial throne, and even more alarmingly, her son, France's boy-King Louis XIII, was to marry the Spanish King's daughter. In these two impending marriages, Marie saw a double celebration of alliance between two equal powers, while the Spaniards, and many Frenchmen, too, saw instead the doubly sure

Spanish capture of a weakened but still useful dominion, and its certain continuance thereafter in the Catholic religion.

In 1613, just in time to ensure Constant d'Aubigné's reprieve from execution, the boy-King's cousin, the prince de Bourbon-Condé, decided to oust Marie and capture the Regency for himself. He set himself at the head of an army manned by anxious Huguenots concerned for their fate if France should fall under the control of fiercely Catholic Spain. Condé himself was Protestant less by conviction than by political convenience, but he was Frenchman enough and nobleman enough to resent the power of the German-Italian Marie de' Medici, sprung from a despised branch of parvenu merchant bankers and manipulated by her papist puppet masters in Madrid—which provided a good excuse, at least, for an ambitious and greedy prince more than ready to capitalize on the genuine fears of his Protestant compatriots.

It was in Condé's army of Huguenots that Constant now enlisted, apparently following arrangements made by his father. After desultory warfare of three years or so, during which both royal marriages defiantly took place, peace was finally concluded in 1616. The peace brought freedom for Constant, and a payoff of a million and a half livres for the prince de Condé. The provisions of King Henri's Edict were reaffirmed, Protestant security assured, and the encroachments of Rome on French-style Catholicism once again repelled. But a year or so later, the bridegroom-King, now aged fifteen and already two years into his legal majority, decided to take the reins of the kingdom into his own hands. He banished his mother to her country château and incarcerated the prince de Condé with his lovely young wife in the fortress of Vincennes, where the pair consoled themselves with the procreation of a family of distinguished troublemakers. To his alarmed Huguenot subjects, the young King declared baldly, "I do not like you," then set about undermining them financially and, spasmodically, by armed assault.

Constant transferred his allegiance to the newly ascendant Catholic extremists without a moment's remorse—not even for his Protestant father, who was now, for the fourth time in his life, under sentence of death as a traitor. Indeed, far from appealing to his new comrades to spare the aged Agrippa, the "wretch" of a son pocketed his 8,000-livre "conversion fee" and set off to lead an armed attack on his father's fortified redoubt of Dognon in their native region of Poitou. But the old soldier proved too tough for them; he repelled the attack, disinheriting the apostate Constant once and for all and renouncing him as "henceforth a bastard." Constant's place in his father's affections was taken by Agrippa's actual illegitimate son, Nathan, a steady young man of some seventeen years. The fortress of Dognon and the governorship of the nearby town of Maillezais, two jewels in Constant's expected inheritance, were sold to a more reliable Protestant, and with the proceeds in his purse and Nathan at his side, Agrippa betook himself to a gentlemanly exile in Calvinist Geneva, acquiring, at the age of seventy-one, a rejuvenating new wife into the bargain. "Father, forgive them" was the coincidental lesson of the day, recited by the officiating minister, "for they know not what they do."

The disowned Constant lived a year or so on the 8,000-livre price of his apostasy before adding a double murder to his sins. Learning that his wife, an heiress whose money he had himself frittered away, had arranged to meet a lover, he stormed into the auberge of their tryst, where he found the young man seated on the privy, and there he stabbed him, not once, but thirty times. He considerately permitted his wife to say her prayers before dispatching her, too, with a restrained six blows of the same dagger. Murder being considered a reasonable revenge for outraged seventeenth-century manhood, for these two deaths Constant paid no penalty at all. Even his father forbore to censure him for this, though he soon enough had other cause to do so.

In 1622 Constant made a second attempt to recapture his lost inheritance of Dognon; once again he failed, and this time found himself imprisoned in the Protestant "safe town" of La Rochelle, on France's Atlantic coast. Once out, he wrested control of his father's former town of Maillezais and shrewdly turned it over to the Catholic party at court. Their gratitude was insufficient, it seems, for by 1624 Constant was at Geneva, weeping on his father's knees, "furiously writing prose and verse against the papacy," and vowing to take up arms again in the

Protestant cause. Agrippa, trusting more to hope than experience, gave him money; Constant departed for Paris, but was back again a few years later, in need of more.

The old man did his best to persuade his son to take to soldiering again. It was February of 1627; Protestant armies were on the march all over Europe, battling the Catholic Habsburgs for the crown of the Holy Roman Empire. The war was entering a critical phase, and France's Huguenots were again in open revolt, this time against the repressive policies of the now twenty-six-year-old Louis and his *premier ministre*, Cardinal Richelieu. Agrippa felt that Constant could provide a useful extra sword for the Huguenot bastion of La Rochelle, in the family's home region of Poitou. Instead, the son declared a preference for England, where the late King James's favourite, the "duc de Bouc-quinquant" (Buckingham) was preparing an invasion fleet in support of the La Rochelle Huguenots. To England and its Protestant King Constant did go, but not before stopping in Paris to relay his own Catholic King such information as he possessed concerning France's Huguenots and their military plans. A succession of conversions and betrayals followed, and by the end of the year Constant found himself once again in prison, this time in Bordeaux, on the order of the Catholic duc d'Épernon, governor of the region.

No one could pretend that he had not brought his misfortune upon himself, unless the blood of a born adventurer can be blamed for reappearing in a second generation. Constant had inherited enough of his father's bold temperament to get himself repeatedly into trouble, but not enough of his strength of mind to get himself out of it. After years of pardons and second chances, Agrippa at last turned his back on "the treacherous soul and leprous body" of his only legitimate son, and abandoned him completely.

Constant was down, but not out. The ups and downs of a wayward life had detracted nothing from his habitual charm and plausibility. The prison governor at Bordeaux, Pierre de Cardilhac, was delighted to have so entertaining a prisoner under his dismal roof. He allowed Constant an unusually long leash, and even gave him leave to play the viol and the lute in one or two concerts in the town. He had, moreover, a very young and very pretty daughter, herself apparently kept on a leash of equally flexible length.

Pierre de Cardilhac was a distant cousin of the duc d'Épernon, at whose orders Constant had been imprisoned; indeed, he owed his post to this connection. Quite suddenly he received a letter from the duc, ordering him to have his daughter married "before Sunday" to the prisoner d'Aubigné. Constant had been in the prison not yet three months; he was forty-two years old, and the girl was just sixteen. The assumption must be that she was already pregnant, or at least that she had been seduced by Constant. No birth was recorded, however, and the hasty wedding ceremony itself remains the only possible evidence of it.

In the short life of Constant's bride, Jeanne de Cardilhac, there had been much less drama than in his own, although there would be compensation, and more than enough, in the years that lay ahead of her. Her family background was modest by comparison with his, though in quality of birth they were more or less equals. Her father, formally a "gentleman landowner," does not in fact seem to have owned any land at all, and his present position as prison governor, "lieutenant commander of the Château-Trompette," was a minor post by the standards of the day. Though Jeanne brought no property to the marriage, she was attractive and intelligent; Constant was later fond of declaring that he had "fallen in love" with his jailer's daughter. The marriage contract does not seem to have been graced by any exchange of money, or indeed any dowry at all, except an early freedom from prison for the bridegroom and a precocious strength of character in the bride.

The ceremony took place on December 27, 1627, with conditions attached, both positive and negative: Constant's sentence was quashed, but Jeanne was forbidden to see any member of her family ever again—further evidence, perhaps, of an illegitimate pregnancy. Unwelcome in their native district, nonetheless the couple could not go far, being without money; Constant even had debts outstanding. To repay them, if he did repay them, he fell back on his old habit of gambling, and adopted the new habit of counterfeiting coins. From Bordeaux, the pair moved a hundred miles north, to Niort, and in 1629

Jeanne gave birth to her first son, named Constant for his father, who was by now involved in open conspiracy against the state. Though his political principles were no stronger than his religious convictions, he was keen to make money, and to that end was busy recruiting men for the mercenary army of Gaston d'Orléans, brother of King Louis XIII, and at twenty-one years of age already an experienced rebel.

Though Marie de' Medici, mother of Louis and Gaston, had been recalled from exile in her country château, the government of France was by now dominated by the King's brilliant prime minister, Cardinal Richelieu. Three years before, Richelieu had arranged an advantageous marriage for Gaston—advantageous, but unwanted—and the young duc had responded by plotting to have Richelieu assassinated. The plot had failed; Gaston had saved his own skin by denouncing his accomplices, and was now up in arms once more against the Cardinal and his own brother, protesting the increasing centralization of power in France at the expense of the great local princes, including, of course, himself. Though this rebellion failed, too, sending his fellow conspirators to the scaffold, Gaston was pardoned, to carry on plotting further, equally unsuccessful campaigns. Recruiting-master Constant was arrested yet again and incarcerated in a first prison, then in a second, where in 1634 Jeanne gave birth to their son Charles, and then in a third, at Niort, where, on November 24, 1635, their daughter, Françoise, was born.

The little girl was one of the least welcome things in the world: a daughter in a poor gentry family. Even if Constant should be released, even if they could move to some other district, away from their disgrace, and find some steady way of life, perhaps even reclaim a part of their lost inheritance, Françoise would be as a millstone around their necks. Her brothers would somehow make their way—the Church, perhaps, for the introspective elder boy, the army for his outgoing brother; either one of them might be apprenticed in the law or find a place with a merchant house in one of the great cities. But the girl would be only a liability, draining the family purse for a paltry dowry to persuade some man to transfer her to his own account books. In the meantime, she would passively reflect the family's standing, wherever they might find themselves. In an age of fervid social consciousness, the dependent daughter was the readiest weather-vane for the fortunes of the family as a whole, and every gown, or last-year's gown, would tell the tale: the d'Aubignés still belonged, or they belonged no longer, within the blessed circle of gentlemen's families.

To start their baby girl on her difficult journey, Jeanne and Constant took at least a first sensible step: they engaged two promising godparents, both nobles with definite links to the d'Aubigné family. The godfather, François de La Rochefoucauld, seigneur d'Estissac, was a cousin of sorts to Constant—in fact, Agrippa's great-nephew. The nine-year-old godmother, Suzanne, was the daughter of Charles de Baudéan, a boyhood friend of Constant's (Constant had served as a page to Charles's father) and a distant relation, now governor of the town of Niort. Though Suzanne was to make a prestigious marriage, and her mother was to interfere determinedly, for good and ill, in the baby's later life, the godfather would live out his days in the provinces, and his expected influence would come to nothing at all.

The baptism took place four days after the birth, in the church of Nôtre-Dame in Niort. The child's name was a tactical choice, as her elder brother's had been: Françoise was named for the governor's wife, as Charles had been for the governor himself. Constant père did not attend the baptism; the prison regime at Niort being less liberal than he had known in Bordeaux, he had not been given leave. It is not certain whether his family returned to him once the ceremony was concluded. The baby was provided with a wet-nurse, as was customary, and it may be that she was taken to live with this woman, in or near Niort, for her first two years or so. In any event, by the end of 1638, soon after her third birthday, she was living with her Aunt Louise, Constant's surviving sister.

Jeanne had departed the year before for Paris, with the two boys in tow, seeking to overturn a part of Agrippa d'Aubigné's will. The old warrior had died in 1630 at the age of seventy-eight, and Constant's lost inheritance had been bestowed on his two sisters. The greater part of it, Agrippa's château of Crest near Geneva and, above all, the very fine estate of Surimeau, had been left to the elder sister, Marie, who had since died. Surimeau was in the Niort region; it had woods and meadows and a valuable mill, and contained within it the second estate, smaller but very beautiful, of la Berlandière. Long before, old Agrippa had craftily winkled Surimeau away from its legal owner, his brother-in-law, and now, in similar mode, Constant's own brother-in-law, Josué de Caumont d'Adde, was winkling it away from him. Allowing a few begrudged parcels of its land for his son, Agrippa had bequeathed most of the property to Marie and her heirs, in default of whom it was to return to the d'Aubigné family. Marie was no more, though her two daughters were still living, but their "ugly, vulgar spendthrift" father had no intention of returning the inheritance to the family of his late wife. Neglectful of his elder daughters, he had married again and was now bending or breaking the law to ensure all rights to Surimeau, including those reserved to Constant, for the children of his second wife. And he had a certain right on his side: the estate had technically belonged to Agrippa's first wife, not to Agrippa himself; moreover, after the last Huguenot uprising, Agrippa had been convicted of treason, so that his property in France was not legally his to dispose of. Nothing was quite clear, and in this lack of clarity Jeanne had mounted a plucky challenge to her brother-in-law Caumont d'Adde.

This required her to bring a case before the Parlement of Paris, a lengthy and expensive business with no certainty of success. It was no doubt her sister-in-law, Louise, who had agreed to finance the undertaking. On their father's death, eight years before, Louise had been shocked to learn of Constant's exclusion from the family fortune, and had set aside from her own inheritance the substantial sum of 11,000 livres, amounting to several years' income, for the benefit of her brother and his family. Now she had taken in his little daughter to live with her as one of her own children.

Louise and her husband, Benjamin Le Valois, seigneur de Villette, lived at Mursay, a pretty château a mile or two from Niort, with a small farm and its own peasant-worked lands attached. The estate, made over to Louise by Agrippa twenty-five years before, had provided her husband with a way of life perfectly suited to his uncomplicated temperament. Hampered by his Protestantism in a time of Catholic favouritism for every official post, and lacking the ambition in any case to make a successful career, Benjamin in his thirties had taken readily to the life of a country gentleman. It was not high living—the land around Mursay was swampy and he was obliged to do plenty of physical work himself—but a regular income, a steady domestic life, and the consolations of his religion had made him a contented man.

Louise and Benjamin de Villette, now in their fifties, had four children of their own, two older girls and a boy and girl nearer in age to Françoise. Their elder daughters, Madeleine and Aymée, aged seventeen and fifteen in 1638, when three-year-old Françoise came to live with them, played the roles of big sister and governess to their little cousin, but it was the boy, Philippe, aged six, rather than five-year-old Marie, who became her daily companion and a fast childhood friend.

The château of Mursay, complete with moat and turrets and a fairy-tale forest, was a paradise for an active child; memories of the years she spent there were to remain a source of delight to Françoise for the rest of her life. She was treated no differently from the other children; her clothes were hand-me-downs from the three sisters, just as they had been between the sisters themselves. Her wooden shoes were her own, however, made expressly for her, deliberately too big and stuffed with straw until she should grow into them. Françoise's daily needs were attended to by Aunt Louise herself, and from the elder girls, sitting at a table in the warm château kitchen, she learned to read and then to write, and it was fortunate that the girls knew how, since even many of the teachers in the *petites écoles* of the time did not. In the 1640s, writing, as distinct from reading, was still an expensive skill to acquire; parents had to provide the necessary "little lap desk, a knife, some paper, an inkwell and some powder," and as yet it was of hardly any practical use for country boy or girl alike. But as well as writing, Françoise learned, from cousin Philippe, the even rarer skill of arithmetic, "the nine arabic numbers, as well as the roman numerals, and [counting up] to a thousand," then calculation of the cost of household purchases, the values of the different coins, and so forth. Of arithemetic, she was a keen pupil, or perhaps her cousin taught her particularly well; whatever the case, all her life she would retain a habit of regular accounting, keeping notes of incomings and outgoings, adding up expenditures even in her letters. A bright and precociously mature child, she no doubt learned a good deal as well from her Aunt Louise, whose own methodical temperament was in perfect accord with the orderly and frugal dictates of provincial gentry Protestantism.

Life at Mursay was lived in modest comfort. There was money and moral approval enough for all necessities, but not for any luxury. In a rare criticism of Mursay, Françoise was later to note that no fire was ever set in the bedrooms, a hardship for her if not for the other girls, for she felt the cold keenly: the need for a "good big fire"—"I love a big fire more than any other luxury"—is a frequent refrain in the pages of her adult correspondence. Despite their fervent Protestantism, Louise and Benjamin did nothing to turn their very young niece away from her baptismal faith, except to provide her with a daily example of kindness and generosity and quiet personal effort—in short, an example of practical goodness, without the crucifixes and holy icons so beloved of contemporary Catholicism. Françoise absorbed the lesson thoroughly, and through it learned to value the principles of Christian living above any technicality of faith or form of worship. In her adult life, through years of bitterly contested religious disputes, she would hold to this unfashionably tolerant view.

On Sundays, while the de Villette family attended the service at Niort's Huguenot temple, Françoise was deposited in the prison with her father. It is a moot point whether these visits were of benefit to either of them in the development of filial or parental love. Françoise's own memories have her often left standing in a corner of the cell, in silence, while Constant played cards with the jailors, now and then interrupting the game only to berate the little girl for her mother's continued absence and his own poverty. She did sometimes play with the daughter of one of the jailors, the gloating little owner of a minia-ture tea service, which the prisoner's daughter could not match with a single toy of her own. Françoise, however, at five or six years old, was able to make a spirited response to this undeniable inequality of worldly goods: "I'm a lady, though," she would remind the little girl. "You're not." Constant apparently did now and then have a tender word for his daughter; at least he supposedly said of her, once, that "this innocent little thing is my only consolation." But a letter of Françoise's adult life, written to her Uncle Benjamin, tells a more likely story: "You were my father, really, when I was a child," she wrote. "I owe more to you than to any man in the world."

If she had found a father in her uncle, Françoise was equally fortunate in finding a mother in her kindly aunt. Jeanne herself was still in Paris, where she had begun very boldly by seeking to have her husband set at liberty. To this end, she had managed to secure an audience with Cardinal Richelieu himself via a Dr. Citois, a native of her own Poitou region and now personal physician to the Cardinal. *Son éminence rouge* had refused to release Constant, remarking that Madame d'Aubigné would be much happier with her husband in prison than if he were to be set free, but he had agreed to speak to the King about having him transferred to a prison in Paris, so that the family might at least be reunited. They had painted "a very black picture" of Constant at court, added Citois; Jeanne should give up hope of any further favours.

So the battle had begun, and it was to last five years, with writ followed by suit and suit followed by countersuit. Jeanne sought, and gained, a formal financial separation from Constant; her claims might be better pursued, it seemed, if she were legally his creditor rather than his dependent, and she spent her last good sum on buying up his debts. She became a regular supplicant at the Paris law courts, striding over, then trudging over, and finally shuffling over, worn and discouraged, to the grand *palais de justice* from her nearby lodgings in the rough-and-tumble courtyard area of the Sainte-Chapelle. Plan after plan came to nothing: brother-in-law Caumont d'Adde had proved as determined as he was unscrupulous, and he was more than a match for Jeanne, struggling more or less alone in Paris. In the spring of 1642 he gained a vicious reinforcement in the person of his son-in-law, who arrived in Paris to prod things along, "painting some good colourful portraits" of Jeanne, as he himself admitted, to discredit her in the courts.

Several times he turned up at her lodgings, threatening to have her children declared bastards and herself a criminal and a whore if she refused to withdraw her case. "Since then, she's been ill," he reported with satisfaction. "But she's agreed to write to her husband about it, and she will. She'll do anything to escape my tyranny . . . I'm very pleased to see that Monsieur and Madame de Villette appear to be sound asleep . . ."

It was not so. Louise and Benjamin continued to support Jeanne— "The smallest gift to those in need is much more valued than the greatest gift to those living in plenty," she wrote gratefully to them. But in the lawsuits themselves, they seem to have had no hand, and in fact had been advising her for almost a year already to abandon them. Carrying on, they felt, would help her "more morally than legally." Benjamin visited Jeanne in Paris at least twice, travelling by coach or on horseback the three hundred miles of rough road from Niort, and from time to time she also saw the baronne de Neuillant, wife of Constant's friend Charles de Baudéan and mother of Françoise's godmother; with Madame de Neuillant, Jeanne even went to court at the Palais-Royal, presumably to solicit the help of some powerful person, though if so, nothing came of it.

Louise remained in Niort with the children and the farm. Though a financial pillar for Jeanne, she could also be critical of her. Always kind but also naïve, Louise adored her wastrel brother, regarding him as one of the world's perennial unfortunates, more sinned against than sinning. Jeanne was sufficiently aware of her own dependence on Louise to avoid risking any criticism of Constant in her letters. "I feel so sorry for him," she wrote, carefully saying nothing of her own deprivations. "I wish with all my heart that I could be with him, as he wishes. I'm sure it would bring him relief and consolation."

Whether he wanted his wife's company or not, Constant certainly wanted money: in the summer of 1642 he had not even been able to pay for medicines for six-year-old Françoise, who had fallen ill with a serious case of ringworm. The apothecary had been paid by her Uncle Benjamin, who, evidently not trusting his brother-in-law to pass the money on, had obliged him to sign a little declaration: "I acknowledge that I have received . . . the sum of seventy-two livres, which Monsieur de Villette has kindly provided as an outright gift to accommodate the urgent needs and expenses incurred by illness of Françoise d'Aubigné . . ." Jeanne, not yet aware of the payment and so not yet embarrassed by it, apologized to her sister-in-law simply "for the trouble this poor itcher is causing you. It was so very good of you to have taken her in. God grant she may be able to repay you for it someday . . ." And she signed the letter with a more than conventional declaration of subservience and fidelity: "I trust that one day I will be able to be with you as much as possible, rendering you my services, my most honoured sister. Your most humble, most faithful, and most obedient servant, J. de Cardilhac."

To this letter, Constant replied, through Louise, by return of post. He told Jeanne that he had had enough of waiting for her to return, and had himself initiated a case against her in the local Niort court. She had been paid the money from the Caumont d'Adde family, he insisted, 14,000 livres of it, and she was living off it in Paris, "having abandoned, against all the demands of justice, her imprisoned husband and her daughter, six to seven years old," the latter being in consequence "in great danger of being turned from the Catholic, Apostolic, and Roman religion, and spiritually corrupted" at the hands of the Huguenots who had taken her in. This danger was causing "greater concern" to Constant, or so he had declared, with fantastic hypocrisy, in his deposition to the court, "than all the other afflictions that I am now suffering." Louise herself added that she had taken her brother's part, that Jeanne had been too long away, that she was wrong to hold Constant's "bit of misbehaviour" against him, and that her own behaviour itself could scarcely be justified.

Jeanne's response this time was swift and spirited. She suggested that Louise "cast aside your sisterly passion and imagine yourself in my place." It was true that she had received a small sum from the sale of Agrippa d'Aubigné's château in Switzerland, but this had long since been spent. For the past eighteen months, she wrote, she and the boys had been living "on the providence of God and nothing else," or, more specifically, on less than five hundred livres. "I haven't a penny to my name," she insisted, "and I owe money to everyone, to three quarters of the people in the house we were in, to the baker, and others . . . I've had to sell all my furniture, and cheaply, too, in a single lot, since the landlord refused to let a stick of it leave the house until the rent arrears were paid, and we're now in a convent, living on the generosity of an honourable and virtuous lady, but only until Michaelmas. That's the only help I've had that I felt I could accept. It's true that other people have offered to help me," she conceded, "but only under certain conditions . . . You call it a bit of misbehaviour on your brother's part to leave his wife and children in a situation like this . . . It's time I learned my lesson . . . In future I'll take care of things myself . . . You should approve of all this. I know that I have God's blessing. He sees into my heart . . ." There followed a brusque, conventional signature: "Your most obedient and humble servant, J. de Cardilhac"—with the afterthought, perhaps a little anxious: "And my brother's humble servant, too."

Jeanne does not seem to have been exaggerating. The Paris courts soon declared her bankrupt, and Constant dropped his case; even Caumont d'Adde's son-in-law went home to Niort, though he did not give up: for the rest of Jeanne's life he was to harry her, though unsuccessfully, for the money she had received from Agrippa's Swiss château. The five-year battle had cost her almost everything, not least her dignity. She had refused to prostitute herself to some wealthy "protector," as her reference to "certain conditions" suggests, but she had not been able to avoid the next-to-last lady's refuge of "taking in" work—doing small pieces of embroidery and basketwork for the better-off people of the town. This was a double humiliation to her genteel soul, since, in addition to an admission of poverty, it was a degradation to the ranks of those who laboured with their hands.

Jeanne had never received much formal education, but her letters reveal a woman of intelligence and moral strength. She was now thirty-one years old, to all intents and purposes alone with her two sons, aged eight and thirteen. The three of them would be safe at the convent "until Michaelmas," that is, for three months, until the autumn of 1642. In the meantime, and perhaps afterwards as well, her only consolation,

it seemed to her now, would be found in her religion. Given her girlhood in the prison and her years with the irreligious Constant, it is curious that Jeanne should have found her way to the writings of one
of the most farsighted churchmen of the day, "one of our Catholic authors, the late Bishop of Geneva," as she called him, in fact none other
than the great humanist François de Sales, later a saint in his own
Church and a fount of practical wisdom for Christians of every kind.
Perhaps it was the same "honourable and virtuous lady" who was paying for her keep in the convent who had directed her towards him; in
any case, his words were of comfort to her now—though one piece of
advice she must have read ruefully: "Widows should not take up lawsuits," wrote the virtual widow Jeanne, relaying the Bishop's advice.
"He says it generally has bad consequences."

Jeanne and the boys remained in the convent well beyond Michaelmas, and might perhaps have stayed for years had it not been for the
death, in December 1642, of Cardinal Richelieu, who five years before
had declined her request to set Constant at liberty. King Louis XIII,
anxious to distance himself from the unpopular policies of his late
prime minister, announced a flourish of political amnesties. Prisons
were opened around the realm, among them the prison at Niort, and
Constant breathed the air of freedom at last. He paused long enough to
collect his unwilling seven-year-old daughter from Mursay, then took
the road for Paris, and it was there, in the early months of 1643, that
Jeanne and the boys and their father, and Françoise, came together to
be remade as a family.

And in the same city, at the same time, the royal family itself was
being remade. The death of Louis XIII in May, at the age of forty-one,
had left a little boy just four years old on France's Bourbon throne. In
political terms, at least, the new King Louis XIV was perched most
unsteadily.

TWO

America!

The d'Aubigné family had been remade with limited success. In theory, Jeanne had been pleased about it; her husband was finally a free man, and her daughter had been returned to her. But the daughter's appearance had struck no chord of love in Jeanne's maternal breast. Since her infancy Françoise had been more or less another woman's child, and she came into the family home now as a stranger. And if the child was unknown, the husband was only too familiar, the same man that he had always been, untempered by his time in prison: high-spirited, hot-tempered, still spouting grandiose schemes, hopelessly unreliable, and, above all, without a penny in his pocket. If there had ever been love between husband and wife, or even a sexual bond, it had long since dwindled away. Custom and religion and simple lack of alternative kept Jeanne beside Constant now. As for Constant, he stayed beside Jeanne when it suited him, wandering away from Paris periodically, in search of work, perhaps, more likely in search of his daydreams. How the family lived for the next year or more remains unclear, but it is certain in any case that they did not live well. Constant must have been a charmer to the core; despite his reputation, he was still able to borrow money, and at the end of 1643 he even received

1,000 florins, bequeathed to him, when old Agrippa was past knowing of it, by his widowed stepmother in Geneva, herself perhaps
prompted by Constant's illegitimate half-brother, Nathan.

With his elder son and namesake, now fourteen years old, Constant
seems to have had no rapport. Five years of hardship and anxiety had
worsened the boy's naturally melancholy turn of mind. He was withdrawn and lethargic; though close to his mother, who was very protective of him, he does not seem to have made any emotional connection
with any other family member, including his rediscovered little sister,
whose apparently engaging personality might have been expected to
draw him out of himself somewhat. By contrast, the younger boy,
Charles, formed an immediate bond with her. Just one year older than
Françoise, he slotted neatly into the place left vacant by her favourite
Mursay cousin, Philippe. The two became a pair, learning their lessons
together and covering for each other in their childhood scrapes.
Charles, the absolute opposite of his brother, blessed or cursed with
their father's ebullient temperament, was restless and adventurous,
given to the moment. His natural charm and persuasiveness captivated
Françoise, and she loved him fiercely, as she was to do through sixty
years of profligacy and irresponsibility on his part, and forbearance
and generosity on her own.

She had need of her brother's affection, since none was forthcoming
from her mother. Reunited with her only daughter after an absence of
years, Jeanne had taken an immediate disliking to her, kissing her
"only twice," we are told, "and only on the forehead"; they were the
last kisses she was ever to bestow on her. Françoise was now a bright
and black-eyed eight-year-old, very pretty, with curly dark hair. Her
often serious expression was apt to give way to sudden flashes of humour, but she could be stubborn, too, a trait which did nothing to
endear her to her mother. A supposed Protestantization in the house
of her Aunt Louise was the readiest excuse for the disciplining of
Françoise; she was certainly slapped, and probably pushed and pulled
about now and then, but her tough little spirit stood firm. "My mother
brought us up very strictly," she was later to say. "We were never al-

lowed to cry if we fell over or burned ourselves with a candleflame or had any other kind of little accident."

She was diligent at her lessons and a willing helper in the house, though rather untidy, it seems, which may have been enough to provoke her mother when the charges of incipient Protestantism wore thin.

Françoise appears to have received her earliest religious education by a kind of osmosis rather than by any direct instruction. She had lived five years at Mursay in a staunchly Huguenot home, with regular family prayers and readings from the Bible; from this, by the age of eight, she would have been familiar with the best-known biblical stories and New Testament parables, at least. There had been, of course, no Catholic symbolism at Mursay, no holy pictures or statues or rosary beads, and few stories of saints or martyrs. Louise and Benjamin had not obliged her to attend their temple services, but neither had she been taken to the Catholic mass, so that by the time she arrived with her father in Paris, she was Catholic only formally, by her baptism. Her mother, observing this with dismay, decided to put things back on the right footing. She took the child to a Catholic church, an environment wholly unfamiliar to her, with its residual smells of incense and its images of torture on every side. In years to come, Françoise would relate how she had refused to make the conventional gestures before the altar, turning a defiant back on it. Jeanne had slapped her there and then.

There is no reason to read any precocious religious heroism into this incident. A strong-willed child was being forced to do something that she did not want to do by an equally strong-willed mother. The church must have seemed a bizarre and alarming place to Françoise; the images no doubt frightened and repelled her. It is not known whether there was any service in progress during this first visit, but if so, she would have heard only the alien sounds of Latin chants and recitations, nothing familiar, not even a hymn, and certainly nothing to reassure her. There was no bond of trust or affection between mother and daughter that might have softened the effect of so much unwelcome novelty; no wonder, then, that the result should have been contention.

Jeanne, so forbearing with her unhappy elder son, had no patience to spare for her daughter. The little girl, a child in perfect health, clever, helpful, warm-hearted, even beautiful, might have been greeted by her mother with joy, as a lost treasure now found again. Instead, as the youngest and, perhaps, the most vulnerable member of the family, and possibly, too, as a sudden embodiment of her mother's younger self, she appears to have served as a whipping-boy for Jeanne's many fears and frustrations. There was nothing to be gained by remonstrating with Constant, and Jeanne also recognized a measure of culpability in herself: writing of "the difficulties which his bad behaviour has caused," she said, "I have always accepted them and I will endure them as long as it pleases God, since I've well deserved the treatment I've received"—a reference, perhaps, to her own "sin" as a sixteen-year-old in allowing herself to be seduced by her father's prisoner. Guilt over the past, whether warranted or not, was thus added to present misery and anxiety for the future. It is not surprising that Jeanne needed an outlet for the weight of all this; it is only sad that she found it in bullying her wholly innocent daughter. "She did not like to talk about her mother," the adult daughter's secretary was to record, decades afterwards.

Wherever he had been in the previous twelve months, by the spring of 1644 the child's father was back in Paris, soliciting the *Compagnie des îles d'Amérique* for some honourable and lucrative post on an island of the distant Caribbean. The company, arrogating this power to itself, had granted him the governorship of any one of the islands that he could claim for France. Once installed, he intended to turn planter and make a late fortune for himself in bananas or indigo. At sixty years of age, the irrepressible Constant had decided to try his luck in America—already the land of opportunity.

Since Columbus's great voyages of discovery 150 years before, hundreds of fleets had set out from Europe for the promising New World, not only to the vast continental regions of North and South

America, but also to the trail of little islands in the Atlantic Ocean and the Caribbean Sea, the latter known to the French as *les Camercanes*. All of these islands, and indeed half of America, were still semi-officially in Spanish possession, though of this the Spaniards themselves had been unable to take full advantage. Eager above all to exploit the gold and silver of the southern continent, they had made only desultory efforts to colonize the less immediately profitable Caribbean islands. This had left the islands and the local sea routes open to the depradations of other Europeans, state-sponsored or otherwise.

Constant owed his present opportunity, suitably enough, given his temperament, to the efforts of one Pierre d'Esnambuc, a *flibustier*—one of the original pirates of the Caribbean. In 1626, d'Esnambuc had obtained Cardinal Richelieu's support for the establishment of a "Gentlemen's Association for the Colonization of the American Islands," more generally known as the *Compagnie des îles d'Amerique*. Pocketing a unilateral declaration of his own governorship of the island of Saint-Christophe (St. Kitts), he had promptly sailed off to found France's first Caribbean colony and, as he hoped, to enjoy a life of easy wealth. Now, nineteen years later, it was Constant's turn. The *Compagnie* was hopeful, and Constant, no doubt, ebulliently optimistic: some previously unwanted patch of land, four thousand miles away, was bound to provide a good living and a good life from now on for the whole d'Aubigné family.

The reaction of the family itself to this news is unknown, but it can be imagined. For the younger children, it must have presented itself as a tremendous adventure. For their brother, it was most probably a source of deep anxiety, if indeed he was not already past caring where he went or what became of him. Jeanne's feelings are likely to have been mixed. It was not an altogether wild idea; fortunes were indeed being made in the islands, and the family did not need a fortune, after all; any decent living would do, after what they had already endured. There were risks, of course—but then, what were the risks? As it was, they had nothing to lose, no money, no home, no position, no prospects. The sea voyage had its dangers, that was true; the climate in the islands might be injurious to their health; but poverty and the cold northern winters were not likely to help any of them on that count. On balance, Jeanne's attitude was probably one of cautious agreement.

One way or other, the journey was arranged. It was Jeanne herself who paid, on April 19, 1644, 330 livres "in good silver écus" for the passage of the five d'Aubignés, plus two servants and one *engagé*, an indentured labourer, on the *Isabelle de la Tremblade*, to the island of "Gadarbeloupe." Payment for the labourer's passage had in fact not yet been made: for this Jeanne was to buy for the captain "six hundred [pounds]" of tobacco on arrival in the islands. How she had raised the initial money is uncertain: the Ursuline nuns at Niort, presumably thinking more of a Catholic d'Aubigné future than the Protestant d'Aubigné past, had lent her eighty-three livres; perhaps something was still remaining from Agrippa's widow's bequest; perhaps Louise and Benjamin helped. In any case, at the beginning of September they set sail from the port city of La Rochelle, the old safe town where years before the Huguenots had battled in vain against Richelieu's besieging Catholic forces.

The family and their servants were quartered between decks on the *Isabelle*, with the engagé further below in the squalid cargo hold with sixteen of his fellows. The ship was overcrowded, even for those, like the d'Aubignés, who were permitted up on deck, and even there, passengers and crew were obliged to share what space there was with livestock squealing and clucking night and day. Those with the foresight to bring along a supply of "roots or leaves of angelica, cloves, or rosemary" were able "to counteract"—somewhat—"the evil smells of the boat."

Though they themselves had had to borrow to pay their passage, the d'Aubigné family were still better off than almost everyone else on board. There were a few other "gentlemen" in more or less the same position as Constant; at La Rochelle he had already made friends with three of them: Jean Friz de Bonnefon, "squire and lord" of Cardeluz; Michel de Jacquières, lord of Herville, recently married, his wife apparently left behind in France; and the engagingly named Merry Rolle, lord of Gourselles. Like Constant, it seems, not a man of them had an acre of land to his name, but together they made a quartet of goodfel-

lows, one for all and all for one, at least while the going was good. They
had come to some agreement about proceedings once they reached the
islands, and intended to throw in their lots together.

The d'Aubignés' servants, possibly a married couple, were to work
for the family as valet and maid. Their engagé was one of many on
board, all "thirty-six-monthers," whose passage had been paid by a future "master" for whom they were to work for three unwaged years.
Though the duration of his servitude was limited, on a day-to-day basis the thirty-six-monther was not much better off than a slave. His
master effectively owned him, and could flog him, rent him out, or sell
him as he pleased. "Some of the engagés go native," recorded Maurile
de Saint-Michel, a priest dedicated to "the difficult and dangerous undertaking of converting the savages," who was on his way to the islands
at the same time. "They hide in the forests, and live from the forest
fruits, and they only come out at night to steal things. I know several of
them who've chosen that life rather than live like slaves with those
who've paid their passage out." There were even a few women among
the engagés, but most of the *Isabelle*'s women passengers were simply
poor girls, newly released from the workhouses, some of them former
prostitutes, making a sad way as colonial brides to be married off to
some lonely settler, as yet unknown, on an equally unknown island.

The food, apart from the freshly slaughtered animals, was mainly
salted cod and dry biscuits. Though it was not unknown for ships to
carry their own boxed gardens with them, making fresh vegetables
available at least some of the time, the *Isabelle* apparently did not do so,
since many of her passengers were quickly stricken with scurvy. As the
first cases appeared only days out from port, this may have reflected
the poverty of their usual diet on land as much as any deficiency at sea,
but in any case it cannot have added to the captain's popularity, given
that the ship's provisioner was his own godfather. Being on a French
ship, the passengers were at least spared the "detestable pudding"
dished up as standard on contemporary English vessels, "a composi-
tion of pounded biscuit or flour, lard, raisins, salt and pepper . . . tied
up in a cloth and cooked in the same pot as the soup . . . then served
[with] old cheese grated over it, which produces a most intolerable

stench." If they went without pudding, the d'Aubignés sometimes went without drinking water as well. Too little of it had been stowed, and what there was was soon brackish and dirty. Fortunately, Constant had thought to include with the family's provisions a thirty-pint barrel of brandy; perhaps it was this that kept them going.

"Most of our passengers were sick," wrote Père Maurile. "Some of them had the fever, and the rest were paying their painful tribute to Neptune . . . giving up the food from their own stomachs to feed the fish." No doubt one or two seasick d'Aubignés also spent days lying, like Rabelais's antihero Panurge, "all of a heap on Deck, utterly cast down and metagrobolised."

Françoise, in fact, only barely survived the journey. She fell ill with one of the many fevers that beset her contemporaries on land and sea. She became worse; she seemed to be dying; eventually it appeared that she was dead. Her stiff little body was wrapped in a sheet and placed on the gangplank to be tipped over the side into the deep. A few prayers were muttered, and Jeanne approached, apparently to place a final kiss upon her daughter's forehead. The kiss was never given, for Jeanne detected a sudden sign of life, some warmth perhaps, an opening of eyelids or a faint pulse—enough, in any case, for a cry and a few shouts to announce an emergency on board. Françoise was retrieved, the sheet cast off and her body rubbed frantically with warming alcohol, and she revived. "One doesn't return from that far for nothing," a flattering bishop was to remark on hearing the story decades later.

In early November 1644, the *Isabelle* anchored at Fort Royal on the island of Martinique, where a handful of French soldiers manned a stout little fort. A few days later she pushed on for the settlement of Pointe-Allègre on Guadeloupe, a hundred miles to the north; here, nine years before, a small colony of French cotton and tobacco planters had been established.

Given Constant's position as prospective governor of one of the islands, the family was met at the harbour by Guadeloupe's governor, Charles Houël, who conveyed them to his official residence, a good place, very probably, since the island could already boast a number of spacious planters' houses. Constant might have enjoyed a sojourn with Houël, who was something of an adventurer himself—in years to come, he would appoint himself director of Guadeloupe's fabulously lucrative sugar industry and buy the island outright. But Constant did not stop now to trade daydreams with him. Leaving his family behind, he set off with Merry Rolle and Bonnefon and Jacquières, and their engagés, for the tiny neighbouring island of Marie-Galante. Named by Columbus himself in 1493, for his ship the *Maria Galanda*, it was more of an islet than an island proper, measuring less than ten miles across. As yet uncolonized by any of the great powers, Marie-Galante· was reputedly inhabited only by "Irois," Carib Indians armed with nothing more menacing than a few bows and arrows. These, it was assumed, could be easily disposed of by a few good men from the garrison on Martinique; it was even possible that, as elsewhere in the islands, the natives might prove cooperative. In the governor's residence on Guadeloupe, Jeanne and the children waited.

It was late in the rainy season, hot and humid. Everyone, except for Charles, was miserable. Ten years old, extroverted, adventurous, and above all a boy, he had quickly made himself at home in the exotic surroundings. With a freedom denied his sister, he wandered off every day to amuse himself with new friends, other boys from planters' families, "black Caribs" of mixed blood, and even some slave boys. There were probably no Indians among his friends; new diseases and outright violence had starkly reduced their numbers. Only twenty-five years before, French sailors arriving on the island had been greeted by "naked savages painted red and armed with bows and arrows," but by the time of the d'Aubignés' arrival, there were few Indians to be seen in Pointe-Allègre or any of the other coastal settlements. Between African and European, however, it was a freer time than Guadeloupe was later to know. In these years before the island's first sugar plantations, the slaves were still marginally outnumbered by the French, and relations between the two were not yet rigidly regulated, as they were later to be. Charles's little society was no doubt as irrepressible as any other group of ten-year-old boys, going where they pleased, climbing trees and shooting birds in the dense tropical bush, bragging and scuffling and getting into mischief in the dusty streets of the town. In the heat and disorder of colonial Guadeloupe, Charles, in his father's image, was putting his best efforts into enjoying himself.

His elder brother might have done the same, but Constant, now aged fifteen, spent his days instead indoors with his mother. Jeanne did not press him to any activity, and could hardly have succeeded if she had done. She simply watched as he slipped from listlessness and melancholy into a debilitating depression. With her husband away, with Constant beyond help and Charles out of the house all day, she turned her unwelcome attention to nine-year-old Françoise. On the pretext of protecting the girl from unspecified "dangers," Jeanne forbade her to set foot outside the door, even to stand in the coolness of the garden. Françoise spent the weeks shut up in the suffocating house, set to reading pious books and writing letters home to relatives—only those whom her mother nominated, however, and only those with money to spare. Charles was officially writing letters, too, but in practice his sister wrote his for him, an exchange, fair or not, for the forbidden fruit that he picked for her from the orange trees just outside the door. "I loved oranges," said Françoise, "and so abundantly did they grow that they had to be swept off the paths before one could stroll along them."

Constant père returned to Guadeloupe after a month or so, with unusually bright news. The tiny island of Marie-Galante was perfect for a plantation; he had already procured, though not necessarily paid for, a substantial piece of land, and had even bought a few slaves. They were going to grow tobacco and bananas and indigo, and he was going to grow rich. Only one detail remained to be attended to: the Irois who lived on the island had turned out to be not Indians after all, but "thirty-six-monthers" of the English-speaking kind, indentured Irish labourers escaped from the British West Indian islands. They were opposed—indeed, aggressively opposed—to the idea of French plantations on the island they had come to regard as their own.

A lesser, or perhaps a wiser, man would have abandoned the enterprise altogether, but Constant transplanted his family to the tiny island regardless. With them went Merry Rolle and Jacquières and

Bonnefon, and their various engagés and servants. There was of course no settlement on Marie-Galante, or at least no French settlement; presumably some arrangement had been made with the Irish, permitting them to stay. Constant remained just two or three weeks with his family there, and though he made no progress in providing for them materially, the simple fact of his being present gave them some respite, real or imagined, from their habitual insecurity. Jeanne, in particular, relaxed, and even began addressing Françoise, with an affection that was not to last, as *"petite d'Aubigné"* or *"Bignette."* Constant himself for once had time and inclination to spare for his daughter. Intelligent beyond her nine years, she was now, apparently for the first time, an object of some interest to him. He chatted with her and teased her about her Catholicism, demanding to know "how a clever girl like you can believe all those things they teach you from the catechism." "They" was of course the child's own mother, who evidently had made some progress in retrieving Françoise from the erroneous Protestant path.

Soon after the new year of 1645, Constant set sail for La Rochelle. The Irish setback on Marie-Galante had in no way discouraged him; by the end of March he was in Paris, soliciting formal governorship of the island from the *Compagnie des îles d'Amérique*. What he told the company's commissioners is unknown, though he seems to have played down the "Irois" question; the document granting his request is in any case revealing of the near-dictatorial powers of a colonial governor of the day:

> Assured of your loyalty, courage, good conduct, and experience, we commit and depute to you . . . the governorship of the said isle of Marigalante . . . to undertake on the said isle all that you shall judge useful for the service of the King and the progress of our affairs, and to maintain union and concord among the people and ensure that justice is properly done among them . . . We require all captains, officers and soldiers and other inhabitants of the said isles to obey you in everything pertaining to this charge.

The business accomplished, Constant set about arranging the further advancement of his own interests. He took ship for England, en route adopting the Protestant faith yet again, to make preliminary enquiries about the value of Marie-Galante to the English crown. A journey back across the Channel, with an abjuration to Catholicism on landing, allowed him to pursue further negotiations with the *Compagnie* and other interested parties in France. Back to England he sailed, then back to France, each time purchasing religious conversion with his passage. The to-ing and fro-ing continued for nine months. It is surprising that one or other of the two sides did not grow tired of dealing with him, since it is unlikely that he could have kept all his travels secret. Perhaps in Constant they simply recognized one of their own kind: a born opportunist, long on persuasiveness and short on principles, ready to see the good in anything that turned to his own financial advantage. And after all, if they were paying him a little for his pains, it was nothing they could not afford to lose. Risk was part of the colonial game. And if in the end he delivered them nothing, they had had at least the pleasure of the gamble.

In December 1645 Constant finally set sail back to the Caribbean, carrying with him an agreement to deliver to the English both Marie-Galante and the French-held northern and southern coasts of Saint-Christophe, whose centre was already in English hands. To the French themselves he was to deliver either Marie-Galante or, if this proved impossible, any other island he pleased. Incorrigibly optimistic, he was probably expecting to make a clean sweep of all three islands, making both parties happy and himself very rich. He was too gregarious a man to keep his plans entirely to himself, and he can be readily imagined on his journey back to the Indies, sitting on the grubby deck, brandy bottle in hand, entertaining fellow passengers with tales of future wealth and glory. If younger men shook their heads at the sixty-year-old's daydreams, one or two at least must have listened with sly admiration for the old man's unquenchably youthful sense of possibility.

Whatever Constant's plans at this point for Marie-Galante, his family, had they known of them, would not have been enthusiastic. Jeanne and the children were no longer even on the island, having fled in the previous October, chased out by the increasingly hostile Irish. The family's "protector," Merry Rolle, had been the first to give up and go, swiftly followed by his noble friends. The engagés and slaves had seized their chance to escape, leaving Jeanne no choice but to leave, too, although, revealing the origin of her daughter's own stubbornness, she had stuck it out to the end, and was the very last of the French to leave. They took ship for Martinique, and docked at Fort Royal, scene of their first arrival in the islands a year or so before.

Here Jeanne found a letter waiting for her, written in the late summer of 1645, when Constant was still in France. It was a buoyant missive, as always, and full of news: Jeanne was to settle in, presumably on Marie-Galante, in high style. All would now be well; their worries were at an end; from now on there was going to be money and to spare. Surprisingly, she took this on trust; perhaps, like the company commissioners, she felt she had nothing to lose. Though Marie-Galante was now out of the question, a good colonial life might be lived just as easily on Martinique. So Jeanne did as her husband had instructed, borrowing heavily against his expectations. She found a fine, large house in the northern settlement of Le Prêcheur, away from the rough garrison town of Fort Royal, and staffed it handsomely, adding to her two servants at least twelve, and perhaps as many as twenty, newbought slaves.

Le Prêcheur was a lovely site, luxuriant with tropical vegetation, its close heat moderated by the trade winds, and ringed by nine little coves of black sand, the ancient gift of Mount Pelée, the island's dormant volcano. In her beautiful house, supported by her husband's promise of continuing money, Jeanne found some quietude at last, and her daughter reaped the benefit of it. For the first time, Françoise was permitted a measure of freedom, and she took advantage of it by wandering outside, listening to the birds, even joining with her mother's slaves in the chants and rhythms of their traditional songs and dances.

She and Charles did have some lessons to do, set for them by their mother. Jeanne cannot have had many books to hand, but she did have one that was read and enjoyed by all literate people at the time: a pop-

ularized version of Plutarch's *Parallel Lives* of the great Greeks and
Romans. It is not surprising that Jeanne should have taken care to
carry a copy with her on her long journey; Plutarch's practical wisdom,
in its way, was not so far from that of her much admired François de
Sales. Both accorded well with her own untheatrical morality: "Never
do anything you'd be ashamed to do in front of the people you respect." "If you want to be happy, consider those less fortunate than
yourself." So she urged her young ones, guided by the ancient moralist
as by the modern. Jeanne seems to have begun by reading the Plutarch
stories to the children herself, and thereafter it became more or less
their only reading. They do not seem to have minded. Even Charles
was happy to sit still for an hour or two every day, drinking in the old
heroic tales; he and his sister learned passages by heart together outside
in the garden, with the sun slanting through the palm tree fronds.
Given the many "good works" of her later life, Françoise might have
been expected to respond more to the down-to-earth lessons in living
woven through the *Lives*, but during her childhood it was their heroic
aspect that appealed to her above all. "My brother insisted that his heroes were more extraordinary than any heroine. But I said that a
woman like that has done more to make herself heroic than a man. We
argued it out between us." So she was to say long afterwards, revealing
that even as a ten-year-old, and despite her mother's uneven love, she
had possessed a keen sense of her own intrinsic value.

She revealed a keen aesthetic sense, too. "There is an extreme pleasure to be had in gazing at the celestial constellations in the beauty and
serenity of a tropical night," wrote Père Maurile. Françoise loved to
look out through the sultry darkness at the black sea, with the stars
brilliantly reflected in it. "I imagined," she said, "that these reflections
must be diamonds, since I'd heard people say you could sometimes
find diamonds in the sea."

In March or April 1646, an intrepid young Frenchman visited the
family at their lovely abode in Le Prêcheur: he was Esprit Cabart,
chevalier seigneur de Villermont, just eighteen or nineteen years of age,
the son of a parlementary lawyer in Paris, traveller, entrepreneur, man
of letters, art collector, gourmet, colonial governor, and possible spy—

most of this as yet in embryo, but already a stark and unflattering contrast to the listless Constant, unable to move beyond the four walls of his own house, and only one year younger. Cabart de Villermont was a sociable young man, but discreet and reliable, too; officially in the Caribbean to seek out interesting plants for the royal gardens, he was in fact looking into the slave trade, currently dominated by the Dutch and the English, with a view to a French involvement in this profitable traffic. His visit to the d'Aubignés was not simply a matter of chance, the usual banding together of gently bred compatriots in faraway places; rather, he appears to have known the family already, perhaps through his acquaintance with a relative of theirs in Paris, the baron de Saint-Hermant, a cousin or perhaps brother of Jeanne's friend Madame de Neuillant. While his ship was being refitted in Fort Royal, he stayed with the family in Le Prêcheur, a most welcome guest to them all, Constant perhaps excepted. For the children, he had adventurous tales to tell, and was young enough to tell them thrillingly; for Jeanne, being mature beyond his years, he provided a sympathetic ear, sensible conversation, and above all a link to home; in the future, he would be of good practical service to her.

Cabart de Villermont left Le Prêcheur probably sometime in April 1646, unwittingly signalling the end of the d'Aubignés' good days on Martinique. One evening—"I had just put my doll to bed, and drawn my veil over her for a mosquito net"—fire broke out in the grand house. Jeanne rushed to save her books, a revealing priority, and afterwards chided her tearful daughter: "What, girl! Weeping for a house!" she exclaimed. Françoise does not seem to have replied, "but I was crying for my doll," she later admitted. "The fire was gaining the place where I'd left her."

The books were saved, but the doll was lost, and with her went the house, presumably most of the family's possessions, and all their borrowed money other than that made flesh in their living slaves. They seem to have moved at this point into the house of a Monsieur Delarue, a native of Niort like themselves, who took them in out of kindness, or perhaps for some small rent, and there they waited, and waited, for Constant.

Where he was now, they had no idea. They had had no news of him since the letter written from France in the previous summer, urging Jeanne to borrow freely to set up house on Marie-Galante. But between then and now they had fled Marie-Galante, borrowed a fortune, and lost everything in the fire. At the beginning of June 1646 Jeanne penned a bitter letter to Louise at Mursay, making reference to the unrelenting family of Caumont d'Adde, still pursuing their now useless lawsuits against her. Jeanne no longer cared. "Let him eat up the property of widows and orphans as he likes," she wrote. "I don't want to talk about him any more." As for Constant: "I shall say nothing to you of him or his behaviour, since I don't want to lessen your goodwill towards him. Let me simply say that I intend to send your elder nephew back to start out in the army somewhere. He's just wasting away here, wasting his time, and his health; the air is bad and the food is bad, too. As for the younger one, I'd like him to get a place as a page; he's a really lovely boy, even if I do say it myself, and since their father doesn't deign to think of them, I'll have to be mother and father both. If you hear of anything suitable for them, please be so kind as to let me know . . . I can see I'll be here for some years yet . . . Bignette will be writing to you. She forgets everything—it's so hot here, and the food is so bad . . . She has no pleasure, poor child, except to hear news of you . . ."

Reading this letter, secure in her château at Mursay, Louise cannot but have felt the gradual wearing down of her sister-in-law's once determined spirit. Cabart de Villermont's visit had evidently prompted Jeanne to do something about her sons' professional lives, but her listless phrases—"If you hear of anything suitable for them, please be so kind . . ."—do not suggest any very active pursuit of a position for either of them. There was no news, no money, and quite suddenly, it seemed, no hope. After months of incautious optimism, she gave in at last to despondency.

It was to be sixty years before Françoise felt able to tell the story, to other little girls of the age that she had then been, of the wretched time the family spent in their last weeks on the island of Martinique. If Constant was oblivious, and Charles managed to escape to the bush or the beach, it was Françoise who bore the brunt of her mother's grimly altered state of mind. Occasional empathy with the "poor child" notwithstanding, Jeanne, strained and isolated, vented her daily frustrations on the daughter she could not love. Françoise records her mother on one occasion cruelly brushing her hair until she drew blood from her scalp, then forcing her to stand outside to battle the tropical insects which settled on her bleeding head. It was the act of a woman overwhelmed by anxiety, lashing out at the nearest thing; but all the same, as Françoise's secretary would one day comment, it was "a very hard thing to do to her daughter."

The girl had already given signs of an exceptional resilience, to which Jeanne's own strong will had no doubt contributed. There was a natural toughness in her, as natural as her warm heart and her quick mind. But cruelty, and from a mother's hands, is a powerful catalyst in the forming of a character, and it was probably during these last days on Martinique that the first glint of iron entered Françoise's soul.

Rescue came for them all in the form of a letter from Constant, written at the governor's residence in Basseterre on the island of Saint-Christophe. The letter seems to have reached them in Le Prêcheur later in this June of 1646. Why Constant had taken so long to seek them out can only be guessed at. He had left La Rochelle in December 1645, presumably arriving in the islands towards the end of February; in the four intervening months he would have had time enough to sail to France and back again—perhaps he did. It is possible that he had been on Saint-Christophe all the time, making secret arrangements for the takeover of the English-held centre of the island. But even unreliable Constant would not have been very likely to leave his family unprovided for and unenquired after on an island only 150 miles away. If he had, it was probably Cabart de Villermont who had recalled him to his responsibilities, informing him, if he did not know already, that they were at Le Prêcheur on Martinique and waiting for news of him. Cabart de Villermont had encountered him in May or June in Basseterre, where Constant had established himself as a high-ranking guest of Governor de Poincy.

At Le Prêcheur, belongings were packed, money was scraped to-gether, and passage booked on some ship or boat to Saint-Christophe. They arrived sometime in July, it seems, and took up abode, all four of them, and probably their servants, too, at the governor's spacious residence.

For Jeanne, the sense of relief was tremendous. First, Constant was found; he was well, he had prospects, or at least appeared to have. They were at last living comfortably—indeed, more than comfortably, in a beautiful mansion with servants everywhere, with good furniture and good food on the table every day, and money to pay every bill. An ele-gant form of charity it may have been, but for now this was not Jeanne's concern. The d'Aubignés were welcome here; Constant and the governor got on very well; his plans were interesting and, for a time at least, seemed feasible; and—most importantly in the governor's eyes—he carried the imprimatur of the all-powerful *Compagnie*.

And Basseterre was delightful, a fine little town of modern streets and squares, and a busy port with every modern convenience. The d'Aubignés excepted, everyone had money to spend, the fruit of thriv-ing tobacco plantations across the island. The governor was Robert de Longvilliers de Poincy, the second in what was to be a centuries-long family line of important officials in the Caribbean. He was a young man, and he enjoyed living in high colonial style. Every visitor of any vague distinction became his guest; every evening saw a sumptuous repast served in his beautiful dining-room, and no one was happier that this should be the case than the ingratiating Constant and his re-juvenated wife. Even Cabart de Villermont spent two months with them, gracing the governor's liberal table and adding a touch of de-light, no doubt, to Jeanne's primary feeling of deliverance.

And she was transformed: still only thirty-five and now charming and beautiful once again, she was the star of every candlelit dinner and every sunny breakfast. No complaints about "bad food" issued from her pen now; the governor's table was a byword for extravagance, and the local fare was more than equal to his demanding standards. There was poultry: familiar chicken, plus pigeon and dove and "two or three types of parrot, very good for eating," as well as "an infinity of other

birds, not at all like ours." There was meat: *agoutis*, "a kind of rabbit,"
or perhaps *acouli*, "a kind of cat, but very good to eat," tenderized in
papaya juice or spiced with sauces made of pimento or the clovelike
touri. There were freshwater and salt fish of all kinds, as well as crab,
turtle, shark, and sea cow, "though the natives can't bear to eat this
since it's much too fatty, but foreigners will" (it was a standard treatment for venereal disease). The local manioc plant provided both
bread and wine. Vegetables included sweet pumpkin and, previously
unknown to the European d'Aubignés, potatoes, both white and red,
boiled or roasted. For dessert, there were cashew nuts—"We made
a really delicious wine from these, very good for stomach-ache"—
and an endless supply of citrus and other local fruits: guava, papaya,
banana—"We made wine from this; it tastes just like cider"—and
pineapple—"We made a very good wine from this, too." And for those
with an especially sweet tooth, there was the ubiquitous sugarcane—
"We ate lots of this; it fattened us up and kept us regular."

For six months the d'Aubignés lived in comfort at Basseterre, *en
famille* and without worry for the first time in years, indeed for the first
time ever. But it was for the last time, too. At the end of the year, Constant sailed again for France, leaving his family in the care of Governor
de Poincy, who by now had, frankly, had enough. Why Constant had
gone, no one was certain. When he would return was less certain still.
The governor's polished manners grew markedly less suave as the
months wore on, as the rainy season came, as no word arrived from
Constant, and as the first anniversary rolled around of this hopeless
gentry beggar family sponging off him in his own proud house.

Jeanne was no fool, and the children, too, were old enough now to
feel their own humiliation. If the boys did not care, Françoise did. She
was a perceptive eleven-year-old, and every turning downwards in the
governor's tone stabbed as a little pin into her sensitive skin. How
Jeanne gathered the money together is uncertain—there was a young
lady by the name of Rossignol who may have helped—but in July
1647, after more than three years in the Caribbean, they all set sail
home for France, a two-month voyage once again, this time tossed by
storms and, much worse, overcast by a sense of desperation. "When

the sea waves rise," wrote Père Maurile, " beating furiously against the hull of the ship, reducing all on board to a fearful silence, in this we see the power and the anger of God . . ."

It is romantic, at least in retrospect, whether or not it seemed so to Jeanne and her family, that on the high seas on their voyage back to France, they were almost captured by pirates. It was an all-too-common danger in an age of disputed territories and overstretched navies, with every cargo worth a fortune and every loyalty up for sale. The very island they had come from had boasted a retired buccaneer as its first colonial governor; his retirement had merely opened the field for another half-dozen to take his place. Facing them now, Jeanne showed a glint of the old mettle: she dressed Françoise and Charles in their best clothes, the more nobly to confront whatever should befall them, and about her daughter's waist she wrapped a wooden rosary, an amulet against the fate worse than death that was certain to befall her if she should survive the anticipated journey to some unknown land in the East. But after her miserable Caribbean years, the prospect of life as a white slave seemed not so bad to eleven-year-old Françoise; eyes fixed on the pirate ship, she whispered to her brother, "At least if we're captured, we'll never have to see *maman* again."

They were not captured, but remained with maman, and early in the autumn of 1647, on a fine day, perhaps, or perhaps with a chill already in the air, they docked at La Rochelle.

THREE

Terra Infirma

*Y*ou're a fine fellow not to have written to me for two months. Have you forgotten who I am, and the place I hold within the family?" A letter from a lady to a gentleman, written, not without irony, at this time, but it is not a letter from Jeanne to Constant. It is a letter from the marquise de Sévigné, aged a lovely twenty-two, to her cousin, the comte de Bussy-Rabutin, teasing him for his unaccustomed neglect of her. It had been many more than two months since Jeanne had heard from Constant, and Madame de Sévigné, writing from the comfort of her country château, would have been grieved to see that other neglected lady disembarking from the ship at the port of La Rochelle in the autumn of 1647, worn and weathered, laden with the remnants of a life of half-gentility, shepherding her three sunburnt children in winter clothes now much too small for them. The youngest child, nearing twelve years of age, was a pretty brunette, with huge black eyes looking out from a brown face. Three or four years later, when it was pale once again, the marquise would come to know this pretty face well.

La Rochelle was a fine city of white stone, wealthy with shipping and trading. A Protestant safe town, it had once been self-governing, almost Hanseatic in spirit, but its proud independence and much of its prosperity had come to an end in 1628, after the prolonged siege by royalist troops which Cardinal Richelieu had led in person and which the English Duke of "Boucquinquant" had so dismally failed to raise. Four-fifths of the people of La Rochelle had perished in the siege; those who survived had found their religious freedoms intact, but their civil and political rights, as Protestants, thenceforth greatly restricted.

Since those days of religious warfare, during which Constant had proved so accommodating to both sides, La Rochelle had recovered much of its population and all of its vitality, and money was again passing easily through the hands of the town's busy residents. If the d'Aubignés had made no fortune in the islands, others were certainly doing so. The quays were laden with sacks of tobacco and indigo, and successful traders, waving and yelling instructions, pushed past Jeanne and her little crew now towards their goods and their profits.

The family's immediate need was for somewhere to sleep. Like all port cities, La Rochelle was full of cheap lodgings, and Jeanne quickly found one: a single attic room for the four of them to share. It was a very far cry from their twenty-odd slaves in Martinique and the governor's residence on Saint-Christophe, but it was shelter, and it would serve—it would have to serve—until Jeanne should get word to Constant and he should come for them.

Constant, however, was never to come for them, for he was dead, and he had lain four weeks already mouldering in his grave. And as in life, so in death: no one was quite sure where he was. He had died in the Rhône province of Orange, said one report; at Constantinople, said another: there he had been planning to be circumcised and convert to Islam, for reasons now lost, and perhaps best left in obscurity.

The last word heard from him had been entirely typical: a letter asking for money—not for his family, however, who went unmentioned, but for himself, "some little allowance, paid once a year . . . I'm going as far away as possible from everyone who knows me . . . I'll send you the address . . . I'll be going by the name of Charles des Landes." This letter, to his half-brother Nathan in Geneva, had been written from Lyon in June of 1647, and from Lyon he had made his way to Orange, or rather back to Orange, where he had lived for a few months longer in the house of the widow Deslongea, a name suspiciously similar to the alias which he himself had been on the point of adopting. It seems that he was intending to settle, with or without the widow, in Provence or the prosperous Languedoc, but on the last day of August, in the widow's house, he had died.

It was not until two and a half years later that Jeanne would receive confirmation of her husband's death from the "Pastors and Elders of the Reformed Church of the town of Orange," and it was the pastors and elders who had buried him, too, "according to the rites of the Reformed Religion, which he had practised in private and in public in our congregation during the whole time of his sojourn in this town, which however was only about four months." Constant had evidently made an umpteenth tactical abjuration in order to remain in Orange, which, though only fifteen miles from Avignon and perched alongside the Rhône river, was not at this time part of France. It was a tiny, independent principality, an ancient fief of the Holy Roman Empire, ruled by the Dutch prince, William II—crucially, for Constant at least, a Protestant.

Constant's choice of this little bastion of reformed religion is significant, for it lends credence to the assertion of his brother-in-law Benjamin that, since his return from the Caribbean early in 1647, he had been travelling back and forth to England, changing religion on each voyage, as he had done before first setting off for the islands in 1644. One especially well-informed contemporary, the memoirist Gédéon Tallemant des Réaux, recorded in his journal on October 1, 1647, at about the time of the family's arrival back in La Rochelle: "I knew for a reasonable certainty that d'Aubigné . . . went over to the English in the islands and not long ago he was sent to England by their commander in those distant countries." Even Cabart de Villermont, Jeanne's adventurous young friend, noted that Constant "went to England on an English ship. He changed religion and they went in pursuit of him; then he came to Paris and changed religion and there was another pursuit." Precisely when these events had occurred, Cabart de Villermont did not record, but the "pursuits" are interesting: it seems more than likely that Constant's repeated bargaining of French against

English interests had finally been discovered, or had finally become too dangerous, or too much of a nuisance, for him to be allowed to carry on. A French subject, he could hardly have been tried for treason in England, but in France he could be, and it would not have been by any means the first time. The Protestant principality of Orange would then have provided a refuge for Constant from the French Catholic forces who were hunting him down. Settling under an assumed name in some larger, sparsely populated region, "as far away as possible from everyone who knows me," would have been a sensible plan thereafter for this tired, penniless sixty-two-year-old, with the noose tightening around his neck.

Constant's intrigues, then, appear to have been catching up with him as he met his undramatic end. Whether Jeanne knew anything about them or not is unknown. For her, in any case, they would have been no more than a footnote now to the huge fact that he had disappeared, leaving them to confront a frightening future, and more immediately a long French winter, with hardly a penny to their name.

A hundred years later, when Jeanne and her children were past all mortal help, there would be many who claimed that their families came to their aid at this desperate time. Jeanne's own relatives, forbidden to see her since her marriage to Constant twenty years before, supposedly now stepped forward to assist. There was "a thorny discussion" between the Catholic relatives on Jeanne's side and the Protestants on Constant's, with each side wanting the spiritual credit for helping the widow and her orphans, but neither wanting the expense of it. The problem was compounded by the only thing of any substance that Constant had left behind him—apart from the widow and orphans themselves, and probably a certain amount of debt—namely, his dreadful reputation. He had been a felon and a traitor many times over, he was a wanted man, and there might also be creditors trying to reclaim their money. Neither side of the family was eager to be seen to be too closely connected to him.

Louise and Benjamin de Villette would undoubtedly have come more quickly to the rescue had they not feared implication in Constant's former intrigues with the English. It is hard to blame them, given what was happening in England at this time. A parliamentary army had risen against the King; the royalist forces had been defeated, and Charles I himself was now a prisoner. The Puritan cavalry commander Oliver Cromwell seemed about to take power in the land. The English Puritans were Calvinists, like France's Huguenots, like old Agrippa d'Aubigné, who had fled to Geneva under sentence of death, and like Uncle Benjamin and Aunt Louise, now pacing anxiously at Mursay.

For things had been stirring in France as well. With the King only nine years old, the regency was still in the hands of the Queen Mother, Anne of Austria (herself in fact a Spaniard, with her misleading title reflecting her mixed Habsburg origins). Every noble and commoner knew nonetheless that the real power in the land was the prime minister, Cardinal Mazarin, an unpopular Italian, "subtle and full of trickery," who had exhausted both province and town with taxes and, perhaps even less wisely, "reduced the bourgeoisie of Paris to despair" by rescinding their rights to certain housing rents and demanding extra money from the wealthiest among them. The Paris *parlement*, whose membership was almost identical with that of the city's despairing bourgeoisie, had been regarding the situation with official "impatience." Mazarin needed the extra money from them, for while the other powers of Europe were seeking peace after thirty years of war, France fought on, determined to batter a weakened Spain back behind her own frontiers and off the imperial stage for good. But France's generals could not be relied upon. Many of them were powerful lords in their own right, with their own regional armies, whose men felt more loyalty to them personally than to king or country. The lords resented Mazarin's concentration of power in his own hands, and they found ready support among peasants and townsmen weighed down by the burden of the Cardinal's taxes.

To add to the general sense of instability, the greatest of all the regional lords, the old prince de Condé, had just died, leaving a brilliant and demanding son to uphold the family's reputation as troublemakers of the first rank. The prince de Condé now was the twenty-six-year-old Louis de Bourbon, victor of the legendary Battle of Rocroi, where he had forced the Spaniards to doff their laurels as Europe's mythically invincible soldiers once and for all. Condé, a cousin to the King and first among the "princes of the blood," was as popular as he was powerful, and he was unhappy, particularly with Mazarin, who had recently denied him an admiralty to which he had felt himself entitled. Thirty years before, Condé's cynical father had made use of the country's Huguenots to serve his own interests against a little king and his regent mother, and there seemed no reason now why the restless son might not do the same. Once again, allegiance to Protestantism had come to imply disloyalty to the crown, with the daily fear of harassment, imprisonment, or worse.

Louise and Benjamin's hesitancy in helping their desperate d'Aubigné relatives is thus understandable, but Jeanne and the children paid a searing price for it. In La Rochelle, in their attic room, they spent three cramped, cold, hungry months in real degradation. There was no fire, for Jeanne had no money to buy wood. At times there was not even money for food. Eighteen-year-old Constant, paralysed by depression, spent his days now, as he had long done, lost in his own grey world. It fell to Charles and Françoise to get the family's bread, and they got it by going out into the streets, begging coins from strangers. Three times a week they would knock at the doors of a convent or almshouse, and ask for a crust of bread and a bowl of soup— "the pittance," which a Père Duverger remembered giving to them at the gates of his Jesuit college. Provided they came only every other day, they were not turned away.

It was a worse time than most to be going begging. The beginnings of political rebellion and a series of poor harvests had dragged the country into recession; in the rural areas, malnutrition was widespread, and many towns were inundated with country folk bereft of the smallest means. The d'Aubignés, though Catholic themselves, were fortunate at least in being in La Rochelle, still predominantly Protestant despite decades of interference from the Catholic hierarchy. In dozens of other French towns, beggars were being rounded up by the thousand and forced into the new *hôpitaux*, prison-style work-

houses founded by the *Compagnie du Saint-Sacrement*, a secret group
of powerful Catholics intent on constraining what they perceived to be
the ground forces of social disorder, "gallows meat, from which come
thieves, murderers, and all sorts of other good-for-nothing rascals."
The medieval ideal of compassionate Christian almsgiving was fast
giving way to an aggressive new mixture of controlled charity and the
disciplining of the poor. Françoise and Charles, at twelve and thirteen,
were easily old enough to have been set to work sewing or labouring
twelve hours a day in one of the grim *hôpitaux*. Had they known it, the
shame of begging might have had its own sharp compensation in the
freedom of the cold city streets.

Charity is a bitter bread, but the soup they received at the convent
gates was in fact not always so bad: lots of fat in the water, and salt and
herbs, thickened with bread. If they were lucky, instead of the fat there
was collar of beef or bacon rinds or sheep's innards or tripe. On fasting
days, which included every Friday, the soup would be meatless, but all
going well, there would be peas or beans, with onions and chives and
butter; otherwise, only cabbage, or only leeks, or only turnips.

Thus, with cabbage and fat and sheep's innards, Jeanne and her
children were kept alive until the last days of Advent, the bleak mid-
winter, when Louise and Benjamin finally relented, or found strength
to risk a Catholic reprisal. Thin, dirty, their clothes turning to rags, the
four poorest of poor relations closed the door at last on their pitiful attic in La Rochelle. By Christmas, they were safe in the château at Mursay.

With log fires downstairs, clean beds upstairs, and warm food and
kind words every new day, things had taken a decided turn for the better for the d'Aubigné family. Jeanne was at last able to make some
plans for a settled future, and she made them very quickly indeed.
Within a week or so of their arrival, a delighted Françoise learned that
she was to remain at Mursay, while her mother, with heroic determination, returned to Paris to take up her lawsuits yet again. Charles was to
go to the city of Poitiers, some forty miles from Niort, to serve as page
to a Monsieur de Parabère-Pardaillon, governor of the region and a
relative of Jeanne's friend Madame de Neuillant; he was as happy to go

as his sister was to stay. As for Constant, once he had fattened up and recovered his spirits, he was to take up a lieutenancy in the navy along-side his cousin Philippe; unlike the army, where a young officer's com-mission could cost tens of thousands of livres, the navy was a cheap way for a boy of good family to begin a promising career. What Con-stant himself felt about a professional life at sea is not known; he may have dreaded it, or he may have been past caring. Whatever the case, it did not eventuate. The comfort of Mursay and the hopeful new prospect of a good career proved too little, and too late, to help him. A few days into the new year of 1648, Constant was found drowned in the moat surrounding the château—not an accident, it seems, but suicide.

"All her tenderness was for her elder son, who drowned himself at Mursay," Françoise's secretary was later to write. "She didn't love the others." Perhaps. There is no knowing whether Jeanne felt more now for her two surviving children, or how deeply they were affected by their brother's death. At twelve and thirteen, Françoise and Charles were old enough to understand what had happened and to feel some loss, though neither had been close to him. Constant's emotional life had been lived through his mother, and in large measure hers had been lived through him. To her withdrawn, helpless burden of a son she had extended a daily kindness that she had shown to no one else. He had been able to lean on her unreservedly, and at an age when he might have supported the whole family, he had lived as her dependant. She had protected him and provided for him, as his father had so singularly failed to do for her. In Jeanne's own staunch Catholic terms, her son's suicide meant that his soul now writhed in infinite pain, lasting to all eternity, though no doubt she prayed for him, prayed for some impos-sible exception. But the daily suffering of her firstborn had engendered more or less the only tenderness in Jeanne's untender life, and his death put an end to it for good.

It is a pity that tough old Agrippa d'Aubigné had never known his daughter-in-law, for in some respects she was more like him than any of his own flesh and blood. Inured to hardship and misfortune, she did not give up now. She packed Charles off to the Parabère family in Poitiers, where he settled in with wonderful ease, and she herself set

out for Paris with her friend Madame de Neuillant, to resume her endless lawsuits. Françoise, as planned, remained behind, ensconced, as
she saw it, in paradise.

Three years and more had passed since she had left her happy life at
Mursay, but she slipped back into it without difficulty. Her two eldest
cousins were now on the point of marrying, and Aunt Louise placed
her in the formal daily care of her own maid, a Madame de Delisle. The
governess this time was Françoise herself rather than Madame, who
was in fact illiterate. Françoise took great pleasure in teaching her to
read and write; there was a lesson every day, but if the teacher had mis-
behaved at all, the pupil forbade the next day's lesson. Madame de
Delisle had thick greasy hair, which Françoise dressed for her every
day—"and I wasn't revolted," she later remembered. "I loved her with
surprising tenderness. I've always loved the people who looked after me."

Unsurprisingly, she had no regrets for her mother, though at first
she did miss Charles. But as before, his place was quickly taken by
Louise and Benjamin's youngest, Philippe. Now almost fifteen,
Philippe was enjoying a last year of relative leisure at home before taking up his commission in the navy. He was quick to revive his childhood friendship with his "American" cousin, and if it was her choice
rather than his to sit feeding vegetable skins to the rabbits or to wander
over to the horses and give them their oats, her exotic stories of life on
the high seas made him willing enough to oblige her.

With Aunt Louise, Françoise made regular journeys to nearby
Niort, where together they distributed victuals and linen to the poorer
folk in the town's *hôpital*. It was Françoise's special task afterwards to
stand on the drawbridge of the Niort fortress and hand out food to the
beggars waiting there, a piquant duty for a girl so recently a beggar
herself. She was well able to appreciate the irony, and the warning, in
the situation; though just twelve years old, she had already experienced half a dozen substantial reversals of fortune. Her temperament
was active and outgoing; unlike her brother Constant, she had not
been beaten down by bad luck and hard times. But she was equally unlike her brother Charles, whose hyperabundant exuberance allowed
him to live quite happily from day to day, learning no lesson from his

father's example and brushing off his mother's concerns. Françoise's character was more determined, but it was more sensitive, too. The strains of their early years, barely grazing her brother's thick skin, had cut deeply into her own. An uncertain material life, compounded by her father's absences and her mother's antipathy towards her, had left a deep well of insecurity where a bright self-confidence might have been. Adversity had not broken her, but it had left its mark. She was not afraid of hard work or punishments or loneliness; she had not even been afraid of pirates. She had, as she was always to have, great sympathy for the poor, and an empathy with them, too, an empathy in fact too strong for her own well-being. It was only too easy for her to imagine herself standing on the other side of the drawbridge, out-at-elbow once again, pushed aside and shouted at by better-fed townsfolk, begging her bread with a cold and dirty little hand. It was this that Françoise was afraid of, and it was this that she was to fear always, through a lifetime of generosity to others. She was afraid of poverty, and of its ugly sister, humiliation.

The paradise regained at Mursay was not to last. Unknown to Françoise, as to her aunt and uncle, she had been selected to serve as a pawn in the vital seventeenth-century game of getting ahead at court. The strategists were her mother's friend, the baronne de Neuillant, and her daughter Suzanne de Baudéan, Françoise's own godmother, now aged eighteen. Though the baronne was wealthy and clever and Suzanne was beautiful, they were not an attractive twosome: one contemporary described them plainly as "the meanest and most avaricious pair the world has ever seen." Madame de Neuillant had high ambitions for Suzanne, and they were not likely to be realized, she knew, in the depths of the western provinces. For a daughter of the aristocracy, success meant only one thing: marriage to a son of the aristocracy, preferably higher up the ladder than oneself and, naturally, as rich as possible. To attract the attentions of a suitable young man—or an old man, if it came to it—Suzanne needed a position at court.

Her uncle, the baron de Saint-Hermant, Madame de Neuillant's brother, held the prestigious office of *maître d'hôtel ordinaire* within the royal household, ensuring the correct provisioning and service of the King's table. This was a foot firmly in the palace door, but in these years of the regency, with the King himself only ten years old, a young lady's promotion at court depended on the attention of the powerful and usefully devout Queen Mother. In Françoise, Madame de Neuillant now recognized an excellent means of ingratiating herself with the Queen Mother and putting her daughter forward: here was a little Catholic girl, officially an orphan, since her father was dead, living on the charity of a Huguenot aunt, swallowing all manner of Protestant heresy along with her daily bread. Madame made a formal application to the Queen Mother, requesting permission to take the girl under her own wing and return her once and for all to the faith of her fathers.

The letter served its turn; the pious Queen Mother assented, and a royal lettre de cachet was dispatched to claim Françoise. Although there is no record of Jeanne's involvement, given her friendship with the baronne and her own devout Catholicism, she had probably agreed to the plan. Louise and Benjamin were not consulted, and against a royal instruction, in any case, there was nothing they could have done. Françoise's own wishes were not considered at all. In November 1648, an effective kidnappee, she climbed resentfully into Madame de Neuillant's carriage and was whisked away from beautiful, heretical Mursay. The "meanest and most avaricious pair the world has ever seen" duly received their reward. Suzanne was appointed *demoiselle d'honneur* at court. She swiftly met the requisite handsome prince (in fact a duke) and married him, to his lasting regret. "Everyone knows what money-grubbers she and her mother were," an acquaintance recorded, "and how her husband suffered it all in silence."

The disruption to Françoise's own life towards the end of 1648 was symptomatic of a more dangerous disruption in the country at large. For social and, perhaps, religious reasons, she had been wrenched out of her pleasant girlhood at Mursay to an unfamiliar and less kindly world. On the wider stage, the matter was above all political. The concentration of power in the King's hands, set in motion by Henri IV and hugely advanced by Cardinal Richelieu, had been

Mazarin's paramount policy since the beginning of his premiership five years before. For him, as for Richelieu, "the King's hands" were effectively his own.

But it was not just an egotistical power-grabbing that was now at issue. Regional *parlements* all over the country, opposed to the principle of absolute monarchy, were resisting Mazarin's attempts to subject them to the sole authority of the King. The Parlement of Paris was the most resistant of them all. Encouraged, perhaps, by the revolutionary events across the Channel in England, where Oliver Cromwell's victorious parliamentarians were soon to have King Charles I on trial for his life, the Paris *parlementaires*—a word newly coined to reflect their newly threatening identity—had finally ceased their customary acquiescence in whatever the Cardinal wanted (in the King's name), and had begun to make demands of their own. They wanted the right to assemble the lords and high officials to decide affairs of state without the King. They sought the abolition of the intendants, loathed high and low as the King's representatives and claimers of revenues supposedly due him, even in regions where the royal authority was not recognized. Effectively, the Paris parlementaires wanted to turn the country into a constitutional monarchy, or even a confederation.

With Mazarin distracted by the ongoing war with Spain, and invasion from the Spanish Netherlands a daily possibility, the parlementaires had grown ever more daring. But in August 1648, a brilliant victory over the Spaniards at Lens by the mercurial prince de Condé gave Mazarin a breathing space to turn the tables on them. Within a week, he arrested three of their leaders in a clumsy pounce on their way home from the victory service at the cathedral of Nôtre-Dame. One escaped; one of the prison carriages broke down, and a helpful passerby recognized the parlementaire Broussel, despite his captors' attempt to disguise him as a bankrupt en route to the debtors' jail. "They had been intending to have them tried straightaway," the Dutch diplomat de Wicquefort reported on the same day to his princely masters in Germany. Mazarin and the Queen Mother were at once seen to be behind it all, and the crowds assembled for the victory celebrations swiftly turned into a furious mob. "Within half an hour the whole town more or less had risen up and dragged chains out to block the streets. The people were calling for Monsieur Broussel to be brought back. They were calling him their father and saying some really insulting things about the [King's] ministers."

The rioting did not stop. Incited by regional parlementaires and fuelled by successive bad harvests and general resentment against Mazarin's high taxes, it gradually spread through most of the country, no longer a riot but a real uprising, and eventually civil war. This was the first Fronde, *la Fronde du Parlement*; it lasted more than six months, and led in the end to the King's troops besieging their own capital.

The ten-year-old King himself had been spirited away from the city in the middle of a January night, together with his mother, his nine-year-old brother Philippe, his gouty and complaining uncle, the duc d'Orléans, and, of course, Cardinal Mazarin. With the royal family safely out of the way, though "doing without everything" at their unprepared château of Saint-Germain fifteen miles away, the siege of Paris began. As dawn broke on the very next morning of January 6, 1649, the prince de Condé led the royalist troops to their positions outside the town, with his own twenty-year-old brother, Conti, "a jealous, unthinking, undersized hunchback," leading the rebels inside.

For more than two months, no provisions were allowed into Paris, though messengers went back and forth: the Queen Mother instructed the parlementaires to disperse; the parlementaires refused, and instructed the Queen Mother to send the King back; the Queen Mother refused. The parlementaires took a bold step further: "Since Cardinal Mazarin is known to be the author of all the disorders of the State and of our present misfortune," they wrote, "the Parlement has declared and declares him disturber of the public peace and enemy of the King and his State. He is enjoined to leave the Court this day, and within one week to leave the kingdom. This time having elapsed, all subjects of the King are enjoined to hunt him down." "In the whole Parlement of nearly two hundred persons," de Wicquefort reported, "there were only three who disagreed with this, and some even suggested there should be a price on his head of 100,000 écus." But although the decree enjoining him to go was announced "to the sound of trumpet" and printed and relayed everywhere, the determined Cardinal stayed put.

In early March of 1649, the Queen Mother agreed that four days' provisions might be permitted into the city, in order to give the parlementaires strength to sign a peace treaty. Compromises were to be made on both sides, with a few more on the parliamentary side; when the final treaty was delivered from Saint-Germain, it was found to have been signed on the King's behalf by his mother and his uncle, and also by Cardinal Mazarin. This unexpected insult left the Parlement in no doubt that Mazarin would thereafter be as powerful as he had ever been. After months of fighting and hardship, they had effectively returned to a shamefaced status quo ante. Sighing over lost principles, but anxious, too, about lost profits, one by one they quieted their martial rhetoric and slipped back into their business clothes. They signed the treaty a few days later.

A two-month siege of their capital had sufficed to dispel the political principles of the parlementaires, and Madame de Neuillant's interest in Françoise had faded with equal swiftness. For a few weeks after capturing her in November 1648, she had taken the trouble to parade her around the province in a carriage and six, posing as her rescuer from heresy. But once everyone of influence had seen the girl and congratulated the baronne on her recapture for the true faith, and with Suzanne's marriage concluded, Françoise had effectively served her purpose. Madame did not want to keep her at home; she had another daughter there already, a second girl to feed and clothe and marry off, and besides, Françoise was wilful: though formally Catholic, she would not take the sacraments and would not even join in the family's daily devotions. As with the incident with her mother at the altar of the Catholic church in Paris, this probably reflected more stubbornness than determination to take any particular religious stand. Thirteen years old, penniless, and now friendless, Françoise seized on the power of refusal, recognizing it as her only power.

She wanted to go home to Mursay, but, though Madame de Neuillant was as eager to be rid of her as Françoise was to be gone, this would have been too clear an admission of sectarian failure on the baronne's part. Clearly, the girl could not stay, but neither could she be sent back. At length the baronne resolved the problem in the time-honoured way. For a gently bred Catholic girl with no money of her own and no husband on the horizon, there was only one suitable place: Françoise was duly deposited inside the gates of the local convent.

It was not so very terrible a fate. The Niort convent was part of the Ursuline order, still fairly new in France and even rather fashionable. The Ursulines were teaching nuns, devoted to the education of girls, a still innovative idea at a time when fine needlework and a smattering of music was the best the most fortunate could hope for. Even among the well-to-do, few parents bothered to teach their daughters anything more challenging than basic literacy and a handful of vaguely Christian principles, mostly pertaining to modesty in the company of men. The successful running of a household was commonly left to the chance of finding good servants, and the management of a landed estate, the eventual responsibility of many gentry women, remained to most a mystery. One lady of the time congratulated herself on having acquired a fine Venetian mirror in exchange for "a lot of wretched fields that did nothing but grow corn." There was no tradition as yet of the skilled foreign governess with her geography and history books and her built-in second language. Girlhood was generally spent in servitude or indolence, according to social standing.

Against a background of this kind, the quiet Ursulines in their graceful black habits could almost be counted radicals. At the turn of the century, they had been no more than a loosely organized community of devout laywomen committed to female education, but by the time of Françoise's girlhood, the Ursulines had become a formal religious order, living in convents under the triple vow of poverty, chastity, and obedience, with an added fourth vow, still rare among nuns, of dedication to the education of young girls. Though the sisters lived strictly, their teaching methods were progressive, drawing on the highly successful and often brilliant techniques developed by the Jesuits in recent decades. As far as possible, each girl was taught according to her

talents and inclination, from a conventional but flexible repertoire of
subjects: "reading, writing, needlework, housekeeping, and all sorts of
arts useful for a respectable woman of the gentry." All of this served
the overarching purpose of Ursuline education: preparation for Christian motherhood. It was the surest way, the sisters believed, to ensure
the salvation of mankind: "Young girls will reform their families, their
families will reform their provinces, their provinces will reform the
world."

There were about thirty girls resident in the Niort convent, all, like
Françoise, *demoiselles* (young girls of good family), and some hundred
more who came each day for lessons at no charge. On Sundays, poor
girls of the district arrived for training in the domestic arts that would
secure them a living in service. Every girl, rich or poor, received instruction in Catholic beliefs and Christian living: nothing exegetical
or theological that might encourage any real thinking—one mother superior, indeed, had recently been reprimanded for her too-enquiring
approach and instructed to "confine her intellect to simple things"—
but enough to make her a dutiful wife and mother, and a good benefactress of her community, if she had the means, or a faithful servant
within it, if she had not. The better-off girls received training as well
in the social graces they would need in years to come as the wives of
prominent men.

The daily regime of the thirty pensionnaires was modelled on the
nuns' own community life, and it is a straightforward story, as one contemporary recorded:

The girls got up at 6, washed and dressed (a nun would help the
little ones), a good deal of attention was paid to hygiene, such as
washing of hands before meals and a mouthwash after meals.
Mass was at 7, breakfast and recreation at 7.30. Lessons began at
8.15 and lasted until 10. Dinner was at 10.30, preceded by
prayers. Lessons were resumed at 12.15 until 2, when Vespers
were said and the girls had a bite to eat. At 3 there was catechism
teaching for a quarter of an hour, followed by needlework for an

hour. Then there was reading and again catechism until 5 when supper was served and bedtime was 7.

Françoise was at first resistant to these highly structured charms of convent life. To a rebellious thirteen-year-old, the place seemed a prison of petty regulations, and the nuns themselves infantile. Regarding their newest charge as a child still, they promised her a holy picture if she would agree to "convert" formally and make her first Communion. "Well of course with a holy picture on offer, I was bound to agree," she noted mockingly. Reconsidering their approach, the nuns sent for a priest to persuade her by rational argument, "but she gave as good as she got, with the Bible in front of her," familiarity with the scriptures being a hallmark of Protestant upbringing. Françoise stood her ground with some pride, but it brought her little comfort. With the winter setting in, she was miserable day and night in the freezing stone convent cells. Only an intangible heat emanated from the little furnace of resentment inside her, and every thought of the callous baronne, and of the lost kindness of Aunt Louise, kept it burning.

Confined and dispirited, at length she fell ill, and the illness proved a turning point. She was given into the charge of one of the younger nuns, a Sister Céleste, who nursed her carefully and kindly back to health. The little dual-heretic, not really Protestant and not yet quite Catholic, could not help responding to this new motherly tenderness of which she was so much in need. Sister Céleste, intelligent and perceptive, understood the girl's strong but sensitive nature, and set about to win her over by sympathy and a gentle persuasion. As Françoise returned to her lessons, she remained in the young nun's special care, and Sister Céleste made judicious use of her position. Françoise need not tire herself by studying the catechism, said Sister Céleste, though perhaps she would enjoy reading these beautiful poetic psalms. She need not do any sewing of shirts or aprons, but she might like to help with the colourful embroidery for the priestly vestments. She need not even attend mass if she did not care to, though all the other girls would be there, and she might not want to be the only one left out. Beloved Aunt

Louise had vanished, but here in her place was Sister Céleste. Within a few weeks Françoise was more or less in love.

"I loved her more than I can say," she related long afterwards to the young girls then in her own care. "I had no greater pleasure than to sacrifice myself in her service." It is the language of the martyr and the lover, peculiarly apt for a clever and lonely thirteen-year-old desperately in need of some kind of tenderness and some kind of faith. "Sacrificing herself" for Sister Céleste became the object of Françoise's daily life. There were not many demands for heroism within the confines of an Ursuline boarding school, but Françoise did her utmost to turn straw into gold: there was extra laundry and sewing and ironing to be done, the little girls had to be put to bed, others needed help with their lessons, there were things to be gone without—candles, fruit, sleep—so that Sister Céleste might have more of them.

It was a customary practice among the Ursulines to have the older and brighter pupils helping with the younger ones; Françoise was one of these *dizainières*, with ten girls in her charge, under the general supervision of one of the nuns. She seems to have excelled at it; the sisters were more than satisfied with her, and, more surprisingly perhaps, "the girls liked me very much"—her own claim, but borne out by many subsequent affections. From the Ursulines, Françoise had learned two great pedagogical truths: that empathy is a powerful teacher, and that gentleness can be more persuasive than force. In later life she was often to appeal to these same principles, though it must be said that her actions did not always match her words. But for the moment, the nuns' methods resonated perfectly with her own needs, and they produced as well a small local victory for the Catholic Church's educational army: "Little by little," said Françoise, "I became a Catholic."

Little by little, life with the Ursulines had turned from misery to happiness. But even this austere idyll was not to last. At the end of her first three-month term, it emerged that Françoise's fees to the convent had not been paid. The "meanest and most avaricious" Madame de Neuillant had declined to pay them, observing coolly that she herself was no relation to the girl, after all. With impressive effrontery, she had forwarded the bill to Louise, whose generous heart was for once overcome by its own devout Protestantism: she simply refused to pay for her niece's Catholic education. The nuns expended some effort going back and forth between possible benefactors who might allow Françoise to stay, but it was to no avail; no one seems to have considered that she might stay on as one of the hundred or so day-girls, who paid no fees at all; probably her higher status as a demoiselle perversely worked against her in this respect. So, with the spring blossoms budding in the convent garden, she was finally escorted through the great wooden gates. She left Sister Céleste weeping behind them.

"I thought I'd die of grief," Françoise recalled. "For two or three months I prayed night and day that God would take me. I didn't know how I could live without seeing her." Her passion for Sister Céleste, and the young nun's reciprocating fondness for her, took the only course now open—a voluminous correspondence. But moral support was not much help. Françoise was back, unwilling and unwanted, with Madame de Neuillant in Niort.

Fortunately, she was not the only child in the governor's grand house. The youngest of the baronne's children, a girl named Angélique, was about her own age; a "late child," she was not much loved by her worldly mother. Though very distantly related, and only by marriage, the two girls called each other cousin in the manner of their region, and to this pair was often added a third in the person of Angélique's actual cousin, Bérénice de Baudéan. Each day they would be sent out, with little masks on their noses to protect them from sunburn, to drive the governor's turkey cocks as far as a little fountain on his grounds. "They gave us big sticks to keep them from going where they shouldn't," Françoise related, "and a wicker basket, with our lunch in it, and a little book." The little book was required reading for every gently bred young person in the kingdom: Pibrac's *Quatrains*, already more than sixty-five years old and surely less than thrilling for a trio of thirteen-year-old girls:

> *Changeable are the blessings of health*
> *Quivering is the voice of fame*

Fortune never remains the same
Virtue alone is our only wealth.

This and another 125 similarly worthy verses were set for the three to learn by heart, a dozen or so daily, a stodgy dessert after their lunch of bread and cheese. They digested both in the same place every day, a natural grotto overlooking the governor's meadows, before shepherding the turkey cocks back home.

Françoise, as the poor relation, had extra work to do, doling out hay for the six carriage horses that had once carried her triumphantly around the district. She was back in wooden clogs, just as she had been as a tiny girl at Mursay, though Madame de Neuillant shrewdly gave her shoes to put on whenever there were dinner guests. Although she was now a widow, the baronne had suffered no loss of standing in the district—her late husband's governorship had been deftly taken up by her son. Their grand house was full of servants, and also of visitors on every kind of public and private business, and despite the baronne's efforts, there was not much that passed unnoticed. "The girl was a relative of hers," noted one gentleman from Paris, "but Madame de Neuillant gave her next to nothing to wear. She was so stingy that the girl had only a single brazier for warmth in her room." Françoise remained in the house for the next eighteen months, and for the whole of the eighteen months she was kept firmly in her place—shivering in a cold bedroom or working in the stables, and when at dinner, at the bottom of the table, in which humble place she sat every day in silence, being forbidden to speak.

But though she said nothing, she listened to everything and watched everything, and there was plenty to see and hear. It was the governor's residence, after all, and anyone in the region with pretensions to influence or culture sooner or later arrived at the door. As often as not they stayed to dinner, an afternoon meal at this period and the main repast of the day, with various courses of meat, fish, and fruits, and ample opportunity for serious talk or witty stories or simple gossip. And if Françoise noticed all that was going on about her, as the

months passed, she in her turn began to be noticed, too, in her metamorphosis from a hesitant girl into a beautiful young woman.

At fourteen years of age, Françoise was already fully grown, a lovely
brunette "with very beautiful black eyes," womanly in her figure, intelligent, and, though she said next to nothing, an evident appreciator
of lively and witty conversation. Her clothes were hand-me-downs
and her skirts often too short for her, and her hands were rather rough,
it seems, an unsurprising blemish, given her daily work. But this could
not detract from the charm which she exuded from her poor relation's
end of the table. The governor's visitors shook their heads that such a
lovely girl, being penniless, should have so bleak a life before her. But
the women liked her for her modest appearance and quiet, graceful
ways, and the men were drawn to her for simpler reasons.

Among the very first of her admirers was Antoine Gombaud de
Plassac, more generally known as the chevalier de Méré, a native of the
Poitou region himself and a frequent visitor at the governor's residence
in Niort. When he first met Françoise, in 1649, he was in his early forties and quite a glamorous figure, a former soldier and now a man of
letters, supporting his mother and five of his seven siblings on the
earnings of his (unremarkable) poetry, and on friendly terms with the
various luminaries of Parisian literary society. The chevalier had a
touch of the rake about him, too: he was an enthusiastic gambler, unfortunately with very little money to stake, but to help him with this
passion he had engaged the services of a brilliant young mathematician, still in his mid-twenties: none other than Blaise Pascal. The
chevalier was interested in probability—more precisely, the probability of winning at cards—but in its purest mathematical form the subject proved equally absorbing for the profoundly religious Pascal. He
began a correspondence about it with Pierre de Fermat, and between
them the genius pair swiftly solved the chevalier's problem, at least on
paper. They carried on to establish the principles of probability theory
together, and the chevalier continued a more confident gambler—
though, perversely, never any richer.

Françoise was flattered by the chevalier's attentions to her, and soon accepted the designation of his *écolière* (pupil) in French literature, Spanish, and Italian—"She understood Spanish and Italian very well"—and probably some of the classics: the chevalier, an able scholar, knew Greek and Latin, in the manner of a gentleman of the day, and also, unusually, Arabic. The lessons, often conducted by letter, were interspersed with fulsome expressions of praise for the pupil, who was still only fourteen years old. "If you were simply the loveliest and most delightful person in the world . . ." the chevalier began. "But you have so many other more precious qualities that, when one writes to you or speaks to you, it's hard not to be rather afraid of you. I find in you something so rare and pure, I can't imagine that even the finest man there's ever been would deserve your attention." The chevalier, it is clear, was more than a little in love with Françoise, but his admiration of her inner qualities, that "something so rare and pure," was genuine, too. Beyond the secondhand clothes and weathered hands, he saw the diamond in the rough, and he was determined to polish it.

"I would really like her to be your écolière, too," he wrote to his friend, the duchesse de Lesdiguières. "She's worthy of whatever good training she receives . . . She's not only very beautiful, with a beauty one never tires of, but sweet-natured, appreciative, discreet, reliable, modest, intelligent . . ." The duchesse, famed in Parisian society for the elegance of her manners, had thought of taking "this young Indian girl" with her on a journey to southern France. "If you had taken her away with you," the chevalier declared, "she would have returned—a masterpiece!"

Thirty years later, when the promptings of passion had long given way to the fond recollections of a proud teacher, the chevalier de Méré would write, and publish, a letter reminding Françoise that he had been "the first to give you proper instruction, and if I may say so, without wishing to flatter you, I never saw a more delightful girl than you, for your personal charms as well as for the warmest heart in the world, and the cleverest head."

It may have been the chevalier's admiration of her niece that now reawakened Madame de Neuillant's determination to get rid of her.

Evidently, the girl was grown up; she was attractive; it was time to marry her off. The chevalier himself, an obvious candidate despite the thirty-year difference in their ages, had not stepped forward, nor was he likely to. His impractical father having mismanaged a fine estate to the edge of bankruptcy, the chevalier was obliged to live more or less on his wits, and lacked the means to found a gentry family.

Françoise, of course, had no dowry of her own, and besides, the baronne still had her own daughter Angélique on her hands. There was no use having the pair of them competing in the same small town of Niort for the same small circle of men. With the autumn approaching, she packed both girls into her carriage, "between the hard-boiled eggs and the brown bread," and set off for Paris, Angélique to acquire some polish at court with her sister, and Françoise to be disposed of, not in marriage, however, but once again in a convent.

The Ursuline house stood outside the medieval walls, towards the southern limits of the city, in the rue Saint-Jacques. Deposited at the gates, Françoise showed her mettle. Outraged by Madame de Neuillant's rejection of her and frustrated by her own powerlessness, she gave the baronne no farewell, but hurled herself inside "before anyone could tell me to get in." But all the same, the gates were locked behind her.

If Madame de Neuillant had expected this second convent spell to cure Françoise of her headstrong "Protestant" ways, at first there seemed no chance of it. She began by refusing to speak—so determinedly, in fact, that the nuns concluded that the girl must be mute. Conferring with the baronne, they discovered the deception and increased the pressure. Françoise responded by going on hunger strike. The nuns remained unmoved; fasting, they pointed out, was standard mortification of the flesh, part of the usual repertoire for them all. They themselves often ate only the leftovers from the girls' own meals. Françoise reconsidered. Resistance was evidently futile. A tactical appearance of defeat was bound to be the quickest way out. She adopted a submissive pose and, on the highly unorthodox assurance that Protestant Aunt Louise would not be damned to everlasting fire, she finally agreed to make her first Communion.

Before communicating, she made an outwardly humble confession and afterwards wrote a letter, not very humble at all, to her brother Charles, gloating that she had "beaten you to it, even though you're a year older than me." She had the grace to admit, all the same, that the gloating itself was unfortunate evidence of a lack of any real "conversion" to a life of Catholic piety.

Although from now on there was to be no going back to the Huguenot ways she had learned at Mursay, Françoise was never to be a thoroughgoing Catholic in the manner of her mother or even Madame de Neuillant. She was a believer and would remain so; indeed, she could hardly have been otherwise in this century of staunch belief, where even Newton and Galileo and other men of the daring new natural sciences could remain devout. She believed in God, and accepted, at least outwardly, the Catholic forms of practise, but she was never to be able to swallow the orthodoxy whole. Sitting with Charles, discussing the anguishing subject of hell, and perhaps thinking of their elder brother, she had remarked, "I think God will change His mind. He won't leave the damned in the flames forever."

Less than a month after making her first Communion, Françoise was released from the convent into the pulsing city of Paris. A few streets and a world away, in the cul-de-sac Saint-Dominique, behind the Palais d'Orléans, stood the bourgeois house of Madame de Neuillant's brother, Pierre Tiraqueau, baron de Saint-Hermant. The baronne had been renting the third floor of this house for some time, and it was here that a happier Françoise was now transferred. Although her skirts were still too short and she had to bed down with the servants, she had won a first solid victory against the powers of chance and force which had until now served her so ill. Here, in the baron's overflowing house, she had found a small space of her own.

FOUR

Burlesque

Paris . . . is . . . one of the most gallant cities in the world; large in circuit, of a round form, very populous, but situated in a bottom, environed with gentle declivities, rendering some places very dirty, and making it smell as if sulphur were mingled with the mud; yet it is paved with a kind of freestone, of near a foot square, which renders it more easy to walk on than our pebbles in London.

So wrote the English diarist John Evelyn, a cautious admirer of the great city that was now Françoise's home. It was early in the autumn of 1650, and she was just turning fifteen.

If the city she had come to was noisy and dirty, it was at least, if only temporarily, a city at peace. The Fronde had ended, or so it seemed, and Françoise's own arrival in Paris had been preceded, only weeks before, by the return of the twelve-year-old King and his royal court, a likely incentive in itself for Madame de Neuillant, with Angélique to marry off, to settle in the city once again. The King had been warmly received in Paris, but, despite the Queen Mother's apparent victory over the parlementary *frondeurs*, behind the scenes it was the opportunistic prince de Condé who was in fact pulling the strings. "All the same, the anti-Mazarin faction shouldn't rejoice just yet," the physician Gui Patin wrote presciently to a friend in Lyon. "There's very little reason to trust this prince . . . We'll see some thunderbolt falling on someone's head this winter."

The court had been reestablished, not in the Palais-Royal, as before the Fronde, but in the vast, fortress-like palace of the Louvre. Still under construction after a hundred years of building, the Louvre contained, in addition to all its noble apartments, a beehive of *ateliers*— studios for the scores of artists and craftsmen working to complete the palace, inside and out, and for others of their fraternities enjoying royal patronage. The Louvre's south façade, spreading alongside the Seine, faced the île de la cité, cradle of ancient Paris and a crossroads now for the life of the modern city. At the eastern end, the old palace of the Capeit kings had already disappeared, though two grand vestiges remained in the prison of the Conciergerie, and in the Gothic jewel of the Sainte-Chapelle, a dazzling reliquary for Jesus' crown of thorns, sold to the French King four hundred years before by the shrewd Emperor of Constantinople for three times the cost of the chapel itself. And at the island's eastern edge, lowering across the river, stood the cathedral of Nôtre-Dame, a massive assertion of the power and the weight of the Catholic Church at the very heart of France. In the shadow of Nôtre-Dame, black-gowned Sorbonne scholars battled the muscular forces of the new empirical science with the rusting weapons of the middle ages. And in between them all, in the fetid alleyways and crooked medieval streets, still serving equally as thoroughfare and rubbish dump, the "little people" of Paris plied their daily trades: butchers and bakers, blacksmiths and ironmongers, apothecaries, tailors, signwriters and scribes, potters and printers and prostitutes. Thoroughfare and rubbish dump, too, was the city's wide river of the Seine, and its banks were alive with everyday commerce.

Most of the great gates to the city still functioned, manned by armed but bribable customs officers and closed at midnight by the raising of rickety drawbridges. But the medieval walls encircling the "round form" of old Paris were gradually being broken down and broken through. Beside the walls, beyond them, even on top of them, sprawled the stalls of petty traders and the shacks of new arrivals from the countryside, tramping in with their sacks and carts, their provincial accents and provincial habits. As urban life pushed outwards and country life pushed in, the old walls which had confined the city for centuries strained to contain the uncontainable. Paris was bursting at the seams.

Native-born Parisians looked haughtily down on the newcomers from the countryside, though their city was as yet no oasis of urbanity: all its dwellers, rich and poor, lived more or less equally prone to dirt, violence, and sudden illness. The city's infamous stinking mud competed with every kind of waste, animal and human, to smear unwary shoes and stockings. Family chamber pots were routinely emptied into the unlit streets, already strewn with the refuse of a thousand cottage industries. Water, barely clean, was actually rationed; ordinary folk received about one quart per day, with inevitable results for personal health and hygiene. The city was full of animals: horses and mules for transport and cartage, cows and pigs and every kind of poultry for food and feathers and skins: flocks of sheep still grazed the Champs-Élysées, making those grassy fields "most unpleasant for those on foot, particularly if there's been a bit of rain."

The Parisian *manière* was scarcely more refined. The troubles of the Fronde had disrupted the already slack policing of public order, and gangs of young men, many of them still in military service, swaggered unchallenged about the town, harassing the young women and threatening everyone else. Gentlemen might carry spare footwear when making private visits, but many still needed handbooks of gentility to remind them "not to spit inside"; at home they beat their children and servants, and their wives, too, with impunity. Though a little better informed, perhaps, and less bound to the rituals of land and season, the native Parisians were not so very different in habit or temper from their country cousins. All gave substance and spice to the thick potage of a great city in the making.

Within this melee of three or four hundred thousand souls, Françoise found herself a definite country cousin, and a poor cousin at that; but nonetheless she was safer than most from the dirt and danger of life on the unruly streets. The comfortable house of the baron de Saint-Hermant stood outside the medieval walls, towards the southern limits of the city, in a newly residential quarter still under development. The baron held the prestigious position of maître d'hôtel ordinaire within the royal household, overseeing service at the King's table. In consequence, he was entitled to live at the Louvre itself, a mile or two away, but if he did, he left at home his wife and daughters, one of whom, Marie-Marguerite, was about Françoise's own age. Marie-Marguerite seems to have been quite a knowing city girl compared with the provincial Françoise; she certainly read poetry and, scandalously, "novels," with or without the approval of her publicly pious aunt, Madame de Neuillant. The two girls struck up a friendship all the same, and it was in the company of the confident Mademoiselle de Saint-Hermant that Françoise now encountered at firsthand the sophisticated salon world of which she had heard from Cabart de Villermont in the Caribbean islands and the chevalier de Méré in Niort.

A friend of the Saint-Hermant family, Cabart de Villermont was now living just a step away from their house in the cul-de-sac Saint-Dominique, and it is most likely he who first invited the girls, perhaps with the baronne along as chaperone, to spend an evening of dining and conversation at his large house in the suggestively named rue d'Enfer (Hell Street), next to the gardens of the Palais d'Orléans. The house, known as the Hôtel de Troyes, was not in fact his at all. He was no more than a lodger there, his many entrepreneurial plans having as yet borne no financial fruit, a forgivable failure in a man still not quite twenty-three years of age. His landlord at the Hôtel de Troyes, the abbé Paul Scarron, was a good deal older, already over forty, and though not rich, he was famous, or rather infamous. Author of countless clever and scurrilous verses, a scholar and a wit, a man of gentlemanly birth but no money, a failed priest, renowned ladies' man, and general disgrace to his family, Scarron was also horribly crippled, the victim of a virulent rheumatism, brought about, some said, by his youthful debauchery. His life as an abbé, never much more than an excuse for an annual stipend, was long behind him, and he was now best known for his writing—some of it literary, much of it decidedly risqué—and for his regular evening salon, a mecca for every Parisian in search of culture or conviviality.

Scarron's lively salon had grown, paradoxically, out of his own disabilities. As it became ever harder for him to move about and visit others, his friends had taken to coming to him, and for some years past, he had been keeping a more or less open house. Aware of his host's modest means, each guest was accustomed to bringing his own food or wine or firewood with him, and in this way Scarron had been able to develop his big yellow drawing-room into a veritable *salon parisien*, with good conversation and a good meal guaranteed to all comers. The original circle of friends remained, now forming a sort of human hub, with scores of others circling around them, residents of Paris or visitors from elsewhere, believers and freethinkers, people interested in books or art or general gossip, and, since witty conversation was always in fashion, courtiers and high society people, too. Sooner or later, everyone, even the Jesuits, beat a path to Scarron's open door.

It is at first surprising, given the host's reputation, that Marie-Marguerite and Françoise were permitted to attend these salon evenings, with or without a chaperone. Most Parisian salons, and certainly Scarron's, were places of very free speech and a good deal of intrigue in politics and love. "Monsieur Scarron's house was full of young people, who only came because they could do as they pleased there," noted one disapproving lady. Admittedly, Cabart de Villermont was living in the house, and Françoise's old admirer from Niort, the chevalier de Méré, was a regular visitor, too. But the most important consideration was probably Madame de Neuillant's wish to get Françoise married and off her hands as quickly as she could. She may have been thinking of Cabart de Villermont himself as a possible match; he was a promising fellow and only seven years older than Françoise, and he was particularly well regarded by Jeanne d'Aubigné, who had finally abandoned her fruitless legal endeavours and was now living quietly in the village of Archiac, near Niort.

Whatever the reason, it was shortly after the New Year of 1651 that Françoise made her first entry into the yellow drawing-room in the rue d'Enfer. Despite her beautiful face and a grace of movement natural to her, it was on one basic level a clumsy entry, since Madame de Neuillant had not troubled to have any new clothes made for her, and she walked through the door in one of her old dresses, perhaps her only decent dress, which was, in any case, much too short for her.

The occasion for this first meeting between Françoise and Paul Scarron is not known. It was a salon evening, perhaps, crowded with clever and elegant people, where even in a gown of proper length, a fifteen-year-old provincial girl, no matter how pretty, would certainly have felt intimidated. Or it may have been a quiet morning visit, with Françoise the only newcomer, stepping self-consciously into the room in her plain country shoes. Whatever the occasion, the sudden, first sight of Scarron in person proved too much for her. Overcome by horror or pity, she broke down at once in tears.

"My body, it's true, is most irregular," Scarron himself admitted. "Pregnant women aren't even allowed to look at me." The celebrated poet, toast of the Paris salons, was seated in the middle of the room, his twisted body propped up and strapped into a large wheelchair, with a wooden tablet affixed on which he rested one clawlike hand. His own description of himself, set in a preface to one of his published verses, shows the dreadful impression he must have made, and reveals as well his infamously sardonic wit:

This is for you, dear reader, since you've never seen me . . . I used to be a well built man, though I admit I was never very tall. Anyway, now I've shrunk more than a foot. My head's a bit too big for my size. My face is quite full, considering how scrawny my body is, and I have enough hair that I don't have to wear a wig . . . I can still see pretty well, though my eyes are a bit pop-out; they're blue, and one of them's darker than the other . . . My nose is generally quite stuffed up. My teeth used to be nice pearly squares, but now they're the colour of wood, and soon they'll be the colour of slate; I've lost one and a half on the left and two and a half on the right, and there's a bit of a gap between one or two others, they're a bit nibbled away . . . Since my legs are at an acute angle to my body, and my head is permanently bent down to my stomach, I'm a sort of human Z. My legs have shrivelled up, and my arms as much as my legs, and my fingers as much as my arms. In short, I'm a shrivility of human misery.

Françoise recovered herself sufficiently to step forward and be introduced. "To look him in the face, she had to lean over so far she was almost on her knees"—so reported a witness of the two of them together. What they said at this first encounter is unrecorded—probably no more than a few amused civilities on his part and some quiet replies on her own. The girl's family name may have recalled one wry tale to Scarron: years before, her impossible father, Constant d'Aubigné, had borrowed the precise sum of 1,148 livres from Scarron's father; needless to say, it had never been paid back. If Scarron remembered this now, he would also have seen at a glance that the daughter was in no position to redeem the father's sins, and in fact it seems that for the time being, he gave no further thought to her at all.

Nonetheless, the meeting was fateful for them both. In the tearful fifteen-year-old, Scarron had found a far better opiate than any his apothecary had yet procured for him, and for her, from the bulbous blue eyes of this wreck of a man, the light of a bright, still distant star shone out.

Legend has it that Scarron's misery had been set in motion by a carnival prank of his own devising, a dozen years before, during his tenure as canon to the bishop in the provincial town of Le Mans. Bored with the usual carnival masks and costumes, and perhaps feeling hampered by his own cleric's soutane, he had thrown off his clothes altogether and jumped into a vat of honey, then ripped open his mattress and rolled around in its white feathers before tearing out into the streets to harass every pretty girl who passed. It had all been too Boccaccian for the locals. They chased him to the river, where he spent the night hiding in the damp rushes. He caught a chill, then a fever, and the calvary of his rheumatism had begun.

Two years later, Scarron had abandoned his post and returned to

Paris, perhaps to attend his dying father—a famously pious parlementary counsellor nicknamed the "Apostle," who had gone about his
business for decades with tomes of Saint Paul tucked under his arm—
or perhaps to seek medical advice for his own deteriorating condition.
If the latter, it was only the first of many hopeless attempts to find a
cure: the spa at Bourbon, to take the waters; the Charité hospital for
gelatine baths; mercury pills, which brought on spasms of the muscles
and nerves and eventually, so the rumour went, impotence; and no
doubt every other lotion and potion from the near-useless chests of
seventeenth-century medicine. Scarron's malady was incurable, and
the unknowing treatments of the day may even have made it worse.
When discouragement became absolute, he would have himself carried to church, to pray for a miracle.

On his return to Paris, bearing his pain and deformity courageously
and with his sense of humour intact, he had settled first in the suitably
named rue des Mauvais-Garçons (Bad Boys' Street) in the lively
Marais quarter, and then in the quieter rue d'Enfer. The move was
arranged by Scarron's own "Sister Céleste," one Angélique-Céleste de
Palaiseau, aged in her late thirties, a professed nun and, appropriately
enough, one of Scarron's former mistresses. Abandoned by a later se-
ducer and literally left holding the baby, she had turned to Scarron for
help, and he at least had not let her down. The child had been adopted,
and Céleste had entered a convent, where she had lived quite content-
edly until the convent itself, following the nuns' too ambitious property speculations, had gone bankrupt. The nuns had dispersed, and
Céleste had found herself once again with Scarron, this time as his
nurse, an office which she apparently discharged with great care and
kindness.

It is not known whether Françoise struck up any kind of friendship
with this second good-hearted Sister Céleste. During these first
months of 1651, she does not even seem to have seen very much of
Scarron himself, and the first impressions created at their meeting, of a
pretty country girl on the one hand and a pitiful invalid on the other,
remained for the time being unchanged. In the spring, Françoise set
off for Niort with Madame de Neuillant, returning to her country

house, as was her wont, at the end of the winter social season. Marie-Marguerite de Saint-Hermant remained with her family in Paris, but she and Françoise wrote regularly to each other, and, the *lettres provinciales* being elegant and amusing, Marie-Marguerite took to carrying them along with her to the salon evenings at the rue d'Enfer, where, "admired by all," she read them aloud to the assembled company, in the custom of the day.

The letters revealed a very different Françoise d'Aubigné from the pretty little nobody of the previous winter. Scarron was probably as surprised as anyone else, though the letter he now sent to Françoise suggests otherwise, perhaps with more gallantry than truth:

> Mademoiselle, I had my suspicions that the little girl who walked into my room six months ago in a dress too short for her, and who burst into tears (I can't imagine why), was every bit as bright as she seemed. Your letter to Mademoiselle de Saint-Hermant is so witty that . . . I'm annoyed with myself for not taking more notice of you before. To tell you the truth, I would never have believed that anyone could have learned to write so well in the islands of America or in the Ursuline convent at Niort. You took more trouble to hide your light under a bushel than most people take to show theirs off. But now that you're discovered, I trust you won't refuse to write to me as well as to Mademoiselle de Saint-Hermant . . .

Françoise did not refuse, egged on, perhaps, by her experienced schemer of an "aunt," the baronne de Neuillant. Françoise's letters to Scarron have not survived, but some of those which he wrote to her were kept, and they reveal a gradually more galant tone as the correspondence progresses. Most probably, this meant no more than that Scarron was feeling freer to indulge in his usual flirtatious banter; perhaps it provided an outlet for the fantasies of a once notorious lover of the fair sex, now hopelessly infirm. As the summer went on, the "little girl" became a "young girl," and at last a tormenting "absent beauty." "I should have been more wary of you the first time I saw you," he wrote, "but how could I have guessed that a young girl would end up troubling the heart of an old fellow like me?"

It is not at all likely that Scarron had really fallen in love, despite his impassioned tones. The last time he had seen Françoise, she had been for him no more than a "little girl in a dress too short for her." Moreover, a man in his physical condition would have been wary of making genuine epistolary love to any fifteen-year-old, even if she did seem bright. Instead, ten or twenty charming letters had turned the relationship between them into a conventionally circumscribed flirtation, typical of the period, with Scarron in the role of declared "lover," and a mutual admiration of elegant turns of phrase on either side. It was a game, and it is a measure of Françoise's advancing sophistication, and of her enjoyment in this gallantry at a distance, at once provocative and safe, that she had learned to play it so quickly and so well. Scarron's own letters give a hint of it: "You say," he writes, "in that teasing way that makes me really desperate, *You only love me because I'm pretty.* Well I certainly don't love you because you're ugly." Evidently not: by now Françoise was receiving, with apparent equanimity, rhapsodic verses about her "white, plump, naked body, lying on the bed with her legs spread out."

And at the end of the summer, when she returned to Paris, things began to change in earnest, not because of any new or stronger sentiment between them, but through the realization that each might be of practical benefit to the other, not just for the pleasure of a harmless flirtation, but solidly, and in the long term. "Come back, in God's name, come back!" Scarron had implored melodramatically, and in the autumn of 1651 she had done so, tagging along with Madame de Neuillant on her customary return to Paris for the season of banquets and ballets. And from this point, Françoise and Scarron apparently saw each other every day.

If further proof were wanted that Scarron's flirtatious correspondence with his "little tigress" was, at least at the start, not meant to be taken too seriously, his astonishing plan to go to America surely provides it. Barely able to move, totally dependent on others for his most basic daily needs, the incorrigibly hopeful poet had persuaded himself that his health could be regained in the sultry heat of the Caribbean islands, and throughout the period of his correspondence with Françoise he had been steadily making plans to go. Cabart de Villermont had encouraged him, naïvely or irresponsibly, with exaggerated stories of cures brought about spontaneously by the climate, the food, and the general way of life there; the desperate Scarron was only too willing to believe him. America's lesser seductions of fortune and freedom enticed him, too. Like Constant d'Aubigné and so many others, he viewed the new island colonies as a collective El Dorado where the smallest investment could multiply fantastically, "where the earth yields wealth without labour, no cash, no taxes, no usury, a land of peace and abundance, with fresh fruits all year round, and the finest fish cheaper than fish-hooks, and sugar cheaper than water, and the daughters of the Incas to make love to . . ."

And as a final temptation, the islands were far away in every respect from the restrictions and anxieties of Paris, "my own dear town, where so many good people are about to become destitute, thanks to the civil war." For, throughout France, the Fronde was being enflamed into a further bloody phase by the irrepressible prince de Condé. On September 5, 1651, his thirteenth birthday, King Louis XIV had attained his legal majority; Cardinal Mazarin, still in exile, had been invited back into the royal fold, and Condé himself pointedly excluded from any place in the new government. Over the following weeks, from his own fief in Bordeaux, he had begun raising an armed force against the King, with the declared aim of driving Mazarin out of the country once and for all. In Paris, a supportive parlement had put a price on the Cardinal's head and, even more alarmingly for him, it seems, had set about selling off the 40,000 books in his prized library, "the fruit of seventeen years of collecting," as his despairing librarian wailed unavailingly. Scores of the city's artists and intellectuals, fearful of the violence or threadbare from lack of steady patronage, began to pack up and leave, many waiting, all the same, until after the January book sale. The librarian himself at last turned his collar against the cold new wind and set off to seek shelter in Stockholm, lugging thousands of the

Cardinal's books along with him for the Swedes' acquisitive young Queen.

It is not known whether the scholarly Scarron turned up to see, or to profit from, the despoliation of Mazarin's great library on January 8, 1652. In the early days of the Fronde he had evinced no strong feelings for or against the Cardinal personally. A few tame ditties poking fun at "Julius Mazarin, no Julius Caesar" had been more or less the extent of his political activity, but more determined spirits, mimicking the popular burlesque style of his literary verses, had begun to circulate witty and far more vicious attacks. The innocent Scarron was held to blame, and was viewed thenceforth as a prime *agent de guerre de plume* against Mazarin and, by implication, against the Regent Queen Mother and the young King.

The pension of "five hundred écus per annum,in good and loyal coin" which Scarron had held as self-styled "Honorable Invalid to the Queen" was now cancelled, and a genuine loathing of Mazarin on his part was not long in developing. Indignation at the injustice done him and anxiety at his sudden impoverishment combined in a bilious fermentation; the result was the outrageous *Mazarinade*, a tirade of 396 savage lines slandering "Richelieu's monkey," a thief and a rat whose only real distinction was his service as "personal urinal" to other cardinals. "Take off for Italy," Scarron screamed, "with your two hundred dressing gowns and your shitty underpants, and burn the bridges behind you, because if they catch you, they'll cut off your balls, one after the other, and spread your guts across the pavements, and hang your cock as bait on the end of a fishing rod . . . Bugger you, you bugger, buggering and buggered, buggering boys, buggering goats, buggering the state, buggering the world . . ."

Unsurprising, then, that in the early days of 1652, with the Cardinal likely to reassume power, Scarron was looking to get out of Paris while he could, and nothing closer than South America seemed a haven safe enough: "In a month's time," he wrote to his poet friend Sarrazin, "my miserable fate will find me en route for the West Indies . . . I've subscribed a thousand écus to the new Indies company. It's going to establish a colony three degrees from the equator, on the banks of . . . the

Orinoco. Adieu, France! Adieu, Paris! Adieu, my friends! Adieu, ti-
gresses in the guise of angels! . . . I'm renouncing burlesques and
comedies for a land with no false piety, no inquisition, no murderous
winter, no crippling swellings, no war to starve me to death."

The "new Indies company" had been formed for the heady mixed
purpose, common enough at the time, of gold-digging, missionary
work, and plain derring-do. Its members were headed for the Guiana
port town of Cayenne, on the northern coast of South America. Scàr-
ron had been drawn into the enterprise through a salon friend whose
pious cousin was one of the company's founders, but his decision had
been by no means hasty. Swayed by Cabart de Villermont and the delectable frangipani tarts of his Antilles-trained cook, he had been considering the voyage for some time before Mazarin's expected return
had added the strain of urgency, and though he might quip to his
friends about it, it held all his serious hopes, with the thousand in-
vested écus, raised from the sale of his prebend in Le Mans, represent-
ing almost the sum of his worldly goods.

But, paralysed, strapped into his wheelchair, he could not make the
journey alone, and Sister Céleste, it seems, had declined to make it
with him. Instead, she intended to retire, for the second time, to a convent; the disappointed invalid had the grace to help her pay her way
into a decent place. He had then approached an old friend, asking him
to find him a wife, "a badly behaved woman," he added incorrigibly,
"so that I can call her a whore without her getting upset." No such
woman materializing, his thoughts had at last turned to Françoise.

It was late in the winter of 1651–52. Madame de Neuillant, normally in Paris at this season, had followed the court to Poitiers, where
her younger daughter Angélique had found a place as demoiselle
d'honneur to the Queen Mother. Françoise had been deposited en
route at the baronne's house in nearby Niort, escorted by a suffering
chevalier de Méré, who by now, according to the amused Scarron, had
"damned his soul" through his "desperate" love for her. "She's caused
me some sleepless nights," the chevalier himself confessed.

It seems that Françoise was still in Niort when she received Scarron's proposal, and it seems, too, that the proposal was not exclusively

one of marriage. Perhaps to allow her an honourable way of declining, if the idea of an intimate life with him should prove too repugnant to her, Scarron had offered Françoise two alternatives: he would provide her with a dowry to enter a good convent, or if she preferred, she could become his wife.

His motive was clear enough: he needed a nurse, regardless of any voyage to South America. He liked her; she was intelligent, and she enjoyed his wit and his sociability. What was more, she was of a practical bent: she would care for him and run his household admirably. Helpfully, she was also poor, used to having next to nothing; her tastes were simple; she would make no fanciful demands. And though she was young and beautiful, there were no other serious suitors. Many men admired her, and she might easily have become a kept mistress, but her girlish sense of propriety, and also, it seemed, a hardy grain of pride, had so far kept her from this. Scarron had not much to offer her, but it was more at least than she currently possessed. He knew this, and it gave him the courage to propose.

The letter of proposal, and Françoise's response, if indeed she wrote one, have not survived. But there can be no doubt that she considered it all in a very hardheaded way. Though she enjoyed Scarron's company, she cannot have harboured any romantic illusions about this pitiful man, more than old enough to be her father, who could do little more than scratch his back with a little stick and scribble with one crabbed hand. The offer of a convent dowry was probably not meant to be taken seriously; the average dowry for Françoise's convent in the rue Saint-Jacques, for instance, was around 10,000 livres, and Scarron certainly did not have this kind of money to spare. Without a good dowry, Françoise would have been obliged to live as a lay sister, effectively a convent servant, with heavy manual work her daily occupation, or else a lowly *fille séculière*, caring for the sick and poor of the parish.

Her alternatives were alarmingly few: she could perhaps attempt to return to her uncle and aunt at Mursay, assuming she would be welcome there again as a dependent poor cousin; but legally she was still a minor, and would be so for nine more years. A spiteful word from

Madame de Neuillant could have her plucked once again from her Huguenot family and deposited in a convent, or some dreadful *hôpital*. What else then might she do, if she was not to return to begging in the streets? She was pretty, and very young, and ladylike, and a virgin: there was clearly the alternative of becoming the mistress of some well-to-do gentleman, at least for a time. But if religious scruples did not deter her, the longer-term prospects of such a life would have given Françoise pause: in time, with no legal protection, she could be too easily discarded and left alone, or perhaps with a brood of illegitimate children, an older woman, as her own mother had been, battling for bare survival.

Marriage to Scarron would be, in any case, marriage. She would at least have the status of a wife, not of a mistress, and never of a pathetic *vieille fille*, never an old maid, never that "very low figure in the world," struggling to get by on charitable handouts, with people sniggering and condescending to her. With Scarron, she would be spared any unwanted *vie intime*; he would not, indeed could not go this far. And he was a gentleman, after a fashion, though he did have to earn his living. His father had been a parliamentary counsellor; he himself was an *homme de lettres*, despised by some, perhaps, but still admired by many. He was friendly with famous people, including people at court; he had, or he had once had, a pension from the Queen Mother. He had connections and talent and plans: the Antilles might be less of an El Dorado than he supposed, but there was no more hunger in America than Françoise had known already in France.

Above all, marriage to Scarron was sure to be a temporary affair. He was already more than forty years old, and his health was as poor as it could be; she would certainly be a widow before ten years had gone by. Widowhood, like marriage itself, would confer a certain standing, and perhaps even a pension. Scarron might eventually have some little sum to settle on her; she knew of his family's two small estates in the country, their ownership disputed, it was true, but still, they might be his in the end. And she would still be young, probably no more than twenty-five, with a measure of respect due her as his widow, and some connections among the well-to-do, and another new life still possible ahead of her. All in all, as she later confessed succinctly, "I preferred to marry him than enter the convent."

Thus was the marriage concluded between two vulnerable, sensible people. Neither of them had anything to lose by it, and each had a good deal to gain. Though many people gossiped, no one made any protest. Only the Queen Mother dared to say aloud what was whispered or pondered elsewhere: "What on earth will Monsieur Scarron do with a wife?" she declared on hearing of the match. "She'll be the most useless piece of furniture in the house."

∽≈∾

FIVE

Marriage of True Minds

*I*t was Cabart de Villermont who now took charge of proceedings. Friend of both bride and bridegroom, he quickly became a quasi-father of the bride as well, managing all the administrative matters attendant on the marriage, and escorting Françoise from Niort back to Paris, not to the house of the baron de Saint-Hermant in the cul-de-sac Saint-Dominique, but back to the Ursuline convent in the rue Saint-Jacques, where she was to spend the month or two before her wedding day. Cabart de Villermont had been accorded power of attorney by Françoise's mother, "the lady Jeanne de Cardilhac, widow of the high and mighty Monseigneur Constant d'Aubigné, chevalier, lord of Surimeau and other places," who, despite her impressive legal title, was at this point living on the charity of a parliamentary counsellor in Bordeaux, in whose house she was staying as a guest of the family. She had given her agreement to the marriage immediately. A woman better placed might have hoped for something less brutally businesslike for her only daughter, but Jeanne nursed too many memories of a precarious life lived on precarious means. Security, even a modest security, could not be other than her foremost concern.

Why Françoise had returned to the convent, rather than to the baron's house, is uncertain, but she does not seem to have raised any objection. She did not return as a pupil, in any case, but rather as a young lady taking temporary lodgings there: no girl over the age of fifteen was admitted as a pupil with the Ursulines, "for fear they should bring a worldly mentality into the convent." For the nuns themselves, however, things were not quite so straightforward. Given Scarron's reputation, the impending marriage had not been mentioned to them, and once they realized that their young charge was visiting the infamous house in the rue d'Enfer, they declared she would have to go. Françoise managed to keep her bed and board through the intervention of a reliable Jesuit known to all parties, and it was not until the wedding day itself that she finally left the convent.

It was April 4, 1652. Cabart de Villermont accompanied the couple to the great tribunal of the Châtelet de Paris, where the marriage contract was signed "before the King's notaries . . . between Monseigneur Paul Scarron, gentleman, and the demoiselle Françoise d'Aubigné." The gentleman was nearing forty-two years of age; the demoiselle was sixteen. They promised "to take each other in legal marriage, to be solemnized in the eyes of our Holy Mother Church . . . to be united as spouses and to hold all goods, moveable and immoveable, in common, according to the custom of this town, jurisdiction and county of Paris." As her dowry, Françoise was to provide one third of her inheritance from her late father—in effect one third of nothing, which nothing was to be added to the common marital property. In private, her fiancé detailed her dowry as "two big eyes, very mischievous, one very pretty blouse, one pair of beautiful hands, and a great deal of intelligence." For his part, Scarron was to provide her, if she should survive him with children, with "one thousand livres to be taken from the value of his possessions, moveable and immoveable," and all of his possessions if she should survive him alone. Each thus agreed to endow the other with his own worldly goods, not that either possessed much in the way of worldly goods, but the contract was duly signed nonetheless "in the year one thousand six hundred and fifty-two, the fourth of April, after noon."

With the legal formalities completed, the couple moved on to the

solemnization of the marriage "in the eyes of our Holy Mother
Church." This probably took place at Scarron's own house in the rue
d'Enfer. He had a small chapel there, where a local priest came to say
mass for him and, perhaps, to hear his confession now and then.
Though not devout, he was a genuine believer, and in any case the
marriage could not have been completed without a Catholic ceremony.
Scarron was wheeled to the altar with his young bride beside him, sustained by the smallest community of friends and family. On the bridegroom's side, there was only Cabart de Villermont, and on the bride's,
just the baron de Saint-Hermant and one other relative of his own. Her
mother was not there, nor her brother Charles, nor beloved Aunt
Louise or anyone from Mursay, nor Madame de Neuillant, nor even
Françoise's friend, the baron's daughter Marie-Marguerite: she was at
court, "setting the courtiers' hearts on fire," with far grander wedding
plans in her head.

Scarron, of course, had a wide circle of friends, and it is curious that
none but Cabart de Villermont was with him on his wedding day. Almost certainly Scarron himself had chosen to keep the ceremony as
private as possible. "He liked teasing people, but he didn't like it if
anyone teased him," remarked his young friend, the writer Jean Regnault de Segrais. Scarron the pitiless satirist was, on his own account at
least, a sensitive man, anxious to avoid the satire of others. Twisted
and trapped in his wheelchair, taking to wife a beautiful sixteen-year-
old, the master of burlesque had become a burlesque character himself. Even the priest felt obliged to ask him, in the middle of the
wedding ceremony, whether he was "in a condition to exercise the
rights of marriage." "Why, Father," replied Scarron slyly, "that's between Madame and myself."

"He really was just like a Z, there's nothing more true," said his
friend Jean de Segrais. "At the time of his marriage he couldn't move
anything but his tongue, and one hand." It was rich food for the gossips. How far could "the rights of marriage" be exercised, even with a
lovely young virgin as temptation, when you could move no more than
your tongue and one hand? "He couldn't even turn from one side of
the bed to the other," glowered the frustrated and envious chevalier

de Méré. Contemporaries concluded, smirking or repelled, that the couple's *vie intime* was probably not "white," in the euphemism of the day, but a rather sordid grey. "Scarron said of his wife, 'I'm not going to do anything stupid to her, but I'll teach her plenty.'"

So reported Jean de Segrais, and it may have been true. But it may also have been nothing but a bit of sad bravado in response to a very insensitive question. Françoise's devoted care of Scarron, which did not flag over the eight years that their marriage was to last, suggests that in any case, he did nothing, or asked nothing, that she did not accept. Sexual intercourse itself was probably impossible; many of Scarron's acquaintance spoke of his impotence, and he was not the man to have lived in chastity if he had not been obliged to do so. And there was certainly no pregnancy, which might otherwise have been expected for the healthy young woman that Françoise was. Not least, a child would have meant considerable financial gain for them both: the "small farm" which Françoise had heard talk of did exist, and was in the hands of Scarron's half-siblings; he stood to gain four thousand livres from it, by his own reckoning, though the siblings reckoned it at three thousand (and Scarron's lawyer at five). But for this, as the memoirist Tallemant des Réaux noted, "someone would have had to give his wife some children."

Segrais himself, only in his twenties at the time, admitted to having broached the subject with Scarron, as he relayed in company more than forty years later: "*You can't satisfy a woman just by marrying her*, I said to him. *You have to give her at least one child as well*. And I asked him whether he was able to do it. And he said to me, laughing, *Are you telling me you'd like to have the pleasure of doing it for me? I've got Mangin here who'll take on the job whenever I say*. Mangin was his valet and a good fellow. *Mangin*, he said—I was there when he said it—*Will you give my wife a child?* And Mangin said, *Yeah, all right, if it's God's will*. We told this story a hundred times. Everyone who knew Scarron laughed like mad."

Satisfaction, sexual or maternal, was in any case a low priority for Françoise in the first six weeks of her marriage. Her immediate concern, apart from the daily care of Scarron himself, was the impending voyage to America. Though no written record remains of her feelings about it, her agreement to marry Scarron, with the voyage already in the planning, implies that, on balance, they were positive. Having returned to France as a twelve-year-old, she was not exactly an old hand at colonial life in the islands, but all the same, she had spent three years there, she had weathered the sea voyage there and back, and she knew something of the climate and the food, the people, and the general way of life. She seems to have enjoyed the modest prestige of the *connaisseuse* which this afforded her, engaging Jean de Segrais with reminiscences of her "Indian" life, eating pineapples under the palm trees—"their taste is a cross between apricot and melon, and their flower is like an artichoke"—and alarming him, too, with stories of the less idyllic aspects of the place: "She and her mother were sitting outside one day, eating their curds and whey, when along came a snake, five or six feet long, and they fled, leaving everything for him to swallow up."

A convoy of boats was due to sail on May 18, 1652, from Paris to Le Havre, the first stage of the voyage to the Caribbean, and sail it did, with "seven hundred men and seven dozen girls, going forth to multiply, according to God's command." Scarron and Françoise, however, expected to be among them, were not on board. The reason is unknown, but it was as well for them that they were not, since the expedition deteriorated step by step, from comedy to farce to tragedy.

It was accompanied at first by crowds of Parisians, rowing down the Seine in their own little boats, waving and throwing flowers to the colonists. But one of their vessels, loaded with a stash of arms and ammunition, was suddenly declared to be secretly en route to Cardinal Mazarin; its passage was blocked, and its innocent crew dragged back to the city as treacherous anti-frondeurs. A little further along, the expedition's missionary leader, too daring or too trusting in the Lord, attempted a dangerous crossing from one vessel to another; shortsighted, misjudging his footing, he fell into the swift spring river and was drowned. Near Rouen, one boat was smashed to pieces on hidden rocks, and when the fleet arrived at Le Havre, the seagoing vessels were found to be not yet ready. In the ensuing weeks of idleness, the colonists caused petty havoc, selling off items intended for the settlement, eating steadily through their provisions for the voyage, and developing a keen dislike of the new expedition commander struggling to keep them all under control. They put to sea at last without salted meat or vegetables, with no oil or candles, nor even a fishing-net. Those who survived the voyage set upon one another immediately on landfall, and those who survived this savagery were massacred shortly afterwards by a band of Cayenne Indians. Cardinal Mazarin notwithstanding, Scarron and Françoise had done well to remain in France.

For a few months over the summer of 1652 Scarron continued to talk of America, but he took no further serious steps. In missing the boat he had saved his life, but lost his whole investment. But there was money coming in from his new comedy *Don Japhet*, written in the months before his marriage and made popular in Paris with the help of its star, the famous actor Jodelet. And a sudden windfall in June, when the courts finally awarded Scarron the disputed family lands, dispelled all immediate financial worry. Early in October 1652, with cash in hand and his new wife in tow—or rather in tow himself, for while Françoise travelled by coach, he followed behind, propped up in a litter chair—he set off southwards for the beautiful valley of the Loire.

The newly gained family properties lay near the small medieval town of Amboise, and here Scarron and Françoise remained, possibly still thinking of America, for the next three months. Nothing is known of what they did there, except that they both grew steadily more bored. By now it was wintertime, with nothing to be done outdoors, and little enough indoors, since it was not the season for visitors to the countryside. Françoise at least had a household to run, but for Scarron, for whom a large and convivial company was now life's principal pleasure, it was an especially dreary exile. He managed to do some writing, in fact of his *Virgile Travesti*, an irreverent parody of the ancient *Aeneid*—"It's a good enough work to stand that kind of treatment," he had remarked—but his heart was not in it, and the work progressed slowly, his despondency emerging instead in pieces of a less considered vulgarity: "Money will always be money," he wrote, "and poetry good for wiping bums."

Though out of sight of the great world, he and Françoise were at least not out of mind. In Paris they were still mentioned in the fashionable daily news-sheets, even if with more fabrication than information. In November, Jean Loret, Scarron's friendly rival in scurrilous verse, published the following in his *Muze Historique*:

> *It isn't true that he can't move,*
> *As people are objecting:*
> *A little further time will prove*
> *His lady is expecting.*

It was not true, and it is not known whether Scarron was more flattered or humiliated by it, or whether Françoise blushed, or felt indignant. But the scuffs and brawls of literary life in Paris were not sufficient to keep them from wishing to return; for Scarron, in fact, they were among the city's prime attractions. Of far greater concern was Cardinal Mazarin's likely revenge for the purple-prosed *Mazarinade*; for some time, Scarron even feared he might be hanged. At the beginning of February 1653, following the King's declaration of a general amnesty for all frondeurs, Mazarin returned to Paris in triumph; ignoring the King's amnesty, he proceeded to take reprisals against those who had opposed him by armed force. But the pamphleteers escaped his vengeance, too small fry, it seems, for him to bother with. The consequent sudden easing of Scarron's fears, coupled with the tedium of life in the provinces, persuaded him to return. By the end of the month he had made a first and, as it happened, a last farewell to his house in the country, and set off back to Paris.

They did not return, however, to the house in the rue d'Enfer, which had, perhaps, a new tenant. Instead they took up lodgings with Scarron's elder sister, also named Françoise, who lived in the lively and not overly respectable Marais district, in a very comfortable house in the rue des Douze-Portes (Twelve Doors Street). Scarron liked to call it, however, la rue des Douze-Putes (Twelve Whores Street) "because there are twelve whores living there, if you count my two sisters as one," as he said to Jean de Segrais. His sister was in fact the long-standing mistress of the duc de Tresmes, who was also the owner of her house. The duc himself, recently widowed, lived with his twelve legitimate children around the corner in the rue de Foin, where his property backed, without apparent irony, onto a Minims convent. In the rue des Douze-Portes, Françoise Scarron had her own young boy, fourteen-year-old Louis, whom Scarron referred to as his nephew "in the Marais fashion." Despite his quip about "Twelve Whores Street," Scarron's other sister, Anne, was by now no longer living in Paris.

Françoise Scarron was fifty years of age when her brother and his young wife came to stay with her. She was an attractive woman—even the duc de Tresmes's late wife had liked her—still pretty, with "a pleas-ant temperament, a lively mind, and the ability to succeed in every-thing she undertakes," or so at least thought the erudite Claude Saumaise. "She likes men," said her brother more succinctly, "and my other sister likes wine." Be that as it might, Scarron liked her, and cer-tainly preferred her to the duller-witted Anne; despite the seven years between them, he and Françoise had always been a close pair, and a few years before, he had made a will leaving to her "each and every piece" of his furniture, silver plate, and money in gold and silver.

The young Françoise seems to have liked her namesake, too, show-ing no prudery towards this openly kept woman with her illegitimate son. Neither did the association hamper her swift entry into Parisian society; she was very soon spotted at the celebrated *samedis* (Saturdays) of one of the city's grandes dames, Madeleine de Scudéry. Though this lady was forty-six years old and Françoise just seventeen, they took to each other at once, and Mademoiselle de Scudéry, an engaging por-traitist of the people about her, soon immortalized her new friend in her *Clélie*, a lengthy romance of ancient Rome which she was then preparing. Françoise appears as a wise young beauty named Lyriane, and she is described as follows:

She was tall, with a good figure, and a fine, even complexion. Her hair was of a very attractive light chestnut colour, her nose was pretty, her mouth just the right size, her manner sweet, refined, spirited, but modest. And to make her beauty more perfect and more striking, she had the most beautiful eyes in the world, shining, soft, passionate, full of intelligence. At times they had a sweet kind of melancholy which was altogether charming. And at times they were full of enthusiasm, which would give way to joy. The gifts of her mind were no less: wide-ranging, gentle, pleasing, well formed. She spoke precisely and naturally, agreeably and without affectation. She knew the ways of the world, and a thousand other things which she made no show of. She didn't play the beauty, though she possessed every advantage for the role . . .

Like Françoise and Scarron, Madeleine de Scudéry lived in the Marais district, with many of the city's more liberal and licentious souls. Despite her lively salon and the romantic nature of some of her writing, she was a devout Catholic who lived on chastely intimate terms with her newly declared "admirer," the twenty-nine-year-old historian Paul Pellisson, himself a Calvinist. She had been orphaned as a small child and, like Françoise, had been brought up by an uncle and aunt. But the young Madeleine's education had been markedly different from that of Françoise, in fact from that of almost every girl in France. Her uncle had possessed a substantial library of classical and modern texts, in which Madeleine had been encouraged to read widely. As a result, she was one of the few well-educated women of her day, a doyenne of the bluestockings later derided to great public amusement by Molière in his play *Les Précieuses ridicules*. "They weren't really the way he presented them, though," remarked Jean de Segrais, who knew Madeleine de Scudéry. "He made that up because he knew it would look better on stage."

A genuine intellectual, Mademoiselle de Scudéry was also a modest and warmhearted woman with a sound practical intelligence—her uncle had insisted she learn the principles of household management alongside her Latin and Greek. But the latter had proved more useful to her: with no beauty and no fortune, she had been obliged to earn her own living as a professional writer, mixing new social ideas—most radically those concerning the position of women—with her knowledge of the classics.

Apart from the popular version of Plutarch's *Parallel Lives* which she had read with her brother in their tropical garden on the island of Martinique, Françoise knew little of the classics. But Mademoiselle de Scudéry's social or, as they were considered, moral questions—May a woman refuse to marry? Can women produce real art and literature?— were already of interest to her, and in later years she would explore some of them herself with the seventeen-year-olds under her own wing. And in the meantime, she was definitely learning, not Latin and Greek, however, but more of the classics in her own language, and some in Italian and Spanish, too. Her teacher was not Mademoiselle de Scudéry, but Scarron himself, who was delighted to find an excellent pupil in his pretty young wife. Building on the foundations laid in Niort by the admiring chevalier de Méré, he set to making a graceful little house of culture and learning, not unbalanced by erudition, but well lit and appropriately furnished for a budding *salonnière*.

Françoise's tastes were not deeply intellectual, but she enjoyed this broadening of her mental horizons, and was grateful for it. Importantly, as she realized, it gave her a familiarity with the conversational ways of the city's cultured classes, many of whose brightest stars were now appearing regularly within her orbit. With her skirts at last of proper length, she had no wish to emphasize her humble origins by any socially inept remarks. "Take every chance you can," she later advised, "to learn whatever you need to avoid looking ridiculous in the eyes of the world"—a response, perhaps, to the warning given by her first teacher: "If you've made yourself look ridiculous even once, it's very hard to redeem yourself."

But there was little chance of it. "She was very mature and extremely bright," said Jean de Segrais, "and she rendered Scarron very good service. He consulted her on all his writings, and was very happy to take her advice." Scarron—"I've always been a bit lazy"—was rather slapdash in his work, and especially disliked revising; for him, the first draft was generally the last. In such circumstances, another, cooler eye would have proved very helpful. During these years of the mid-1650s, his prime literary effort was the second part of his *Roman Comique*, a satirical meandering through contemporary society which his long-standing friend Cabart de Villermont claimed to have inspired. Scarron had apparently begun translating a highly controversial work by the philosopher Pierre Gassendi, who, despite being a priest, was seeking to prove that the natural world operated mechanistically, without the intervention of God. Cabart de Villermont, correctly assuming that this was hardly the way for Scarron to ingratiate himself with the court and regain his pension, persuaded him instead towards an original comedy, "so that in a way the public has me to thank for this amusing work, though I didn't write it."

Whatever Cabart de Villermont's contribution to the beginning of the *Roman Comique*, Françoise's assistance continued as the weeks and months went by. And gradually, and no doubt unexpectedly, the literary discussions and the lessons she was receiving forged a bond between the unlikely husband and wife. Scarron's work became, if unevenly, something of a collaboration between them, and the endless giving on Françoise's part, the bathing and dressing and feeding, became a smaller part of their relationship. Scarron had begun giving, too, the only thing, perhaps, that he could give, but it was a valuable gift, and Françoise appreciated it, and the new daily reciprocity gave dignity to them both.

At the end of February 1654, after a year as guests in the rue des Douze-Portes, Scarron and Françoise moved into a house of their own. It was a new house, not very large, and the rent they paid of 350 livres per annum was not enough to secure it for themselves. Instead, they shared it with the notorious Claude de Bourdeille, comte de Montrésor, who had only recently been pardoned by Cardinal Mazarin for the part he had played in the Fronde. Montrésor had darker doings to his credit: he had twice plotted to assassinate Mazarin's predecessor, Cardinal Richelieu, and had fled into exile, losing all his estates, and eventually returning only to imprisonment in the Bastille. Now nearing fifty, politically uninvolved and financially barely solvent, he had begun a quiet new life in the Marais. The three shared the house with a handful of servants: Anne, the cook; Madeleine, the maid-of-all-work; and the laundry-maid, another Madeleine. Scarron's obliging valet Mangin had taken his leave, and in his place there was Jean; and eighteen-year-old Françoise, for the first time in her life, had her own personal maid, named Michelle.

Though comparatively modest, the new abode in the rue Neuve-Saint-Louis was a definite step up for Françoise. The unimposing street door opened into a courtyard, which faced the kitchen and scullery, storerooms, stables (though they had no horses), an outbuilding for the coach (though there was no coach), and a staircase leading to the upper floors. On the second floor, Françoise had four rooms of her own: one not much more than a passage, then a dressing-room, a pretty little sitting-room hung with red and yellow brocade, and her bedroom, large and nicely furnished with tapestries on the walls and a Venetian mirror, and, as if there were not already Madeleines enough in the house, a good gilt-framed painting of the saint of that name. There was a big bed with high bolsters, twelve little chairs and four armchairs, all covered in yellow damask, with a *cabinet de toilette*, a dressing-table, and some little pedestals for flowers and ornaments. The fireplace was simple but large, with not one but two andirons to support good big logs, allowing her at last the "good big fire" she had always longed for.

Scarron's bedroom was on the third floor, a smaller room than her own, but also well furnished, with tapestries and paintings on the walls, and a four-poster bed upholstered, like Françoise's, in yellow damask. Here Scarron lay alone night after night, sleepless and crying out with pain, "praying to the Lord, if he would increase my torments, to increase my endurance and my faith as well." By day, no cry was ever heard. "I support my ills quite patiently," remarked the invalid himself, with more than truth.

Scarron's yellow bedroom opened onto the landing, and from there directly into the drawing-room, furnished, like the rest of the house, in yellow—Scarron's choice, and perhaps a reflection of his terrible need for optimism and gaiety. "That yellow damask furniture would have been worth five or six thousand livres," remarked Jean de Segrais, clearly impressed. In the centre of the drawing-room was an immense round table, encircled by twelve good chairs. The rest of the furniture was of beautiful nutwood, lined, unsurprisingly, with yellow baize. Several hundred books of classical and modern masters filled the shelves of two large bookcases. A pretty *sofa de repos* reclined in a corner, heavy curtains draped the windows, and on one wall hung a marvellous, sensuous new painting by Nicolas Poussin, *The Ecstasy of Saint Paul*, which Scarron had bought two or three years before, in an art-loving ecstasy of his own.

All in all, the little house in the Marais was more than comfortable, suggesting to the casual visitor that Scarron was doing rather well with his verses. But those better acquainted with the household could have told a different story, for apart from the valuable Poussin painting, almost all the furniture had been purchased with money lent by generous friends. Others were providing the logs for the "good big fire" for the lady of the house; wines and cheeses and pâtés arrived with every second visitor; the very bread and salt was bought, as often as not, with strangers' coins.

Scarron was used to it, and so were his friends; it had been customary, before his marriage, for guests to bring a "contribution" to his salon evenings at the rue d'Enfer. He joked about his new *"hôtel de l'impécuniosité"* at the rue Neuve-Saint-Louis, but Françoise was not much amused. As with her aunt and uncle at Mursay, as with the governor on the island of Saint-Christophe, as with Madame de Neuillant in Niort and her brother in Paris, and with Scarron's sister in the rue des Douze-Portes, she was once again living more or less on charity. Though sensible enough to appreciate the gifts, she did not give way to effusive demonstrations of humility or gratitude. "The best way of conducting oneself, if one wants to avoid attracting dislike or trouble, is to fear no one and to despise no one, and to be pleasant at all times," the chevalier had advised, and Françoise took the message to heart, maintaining an outward composure; but all the same, the humiliation of her daily dependence scratched quite sharply at her smiling public face.

With the formal end of the Fronde in the summer of 1653, the city's cultural life had revived. The lively salon of the rue d'Enfer had been reborn in the rue Neuve-Saint-Louis; old friends were returning, and every day Scarron's pretty wife drew curious new people to the house. Most of them came in the evening, when, thanks to their own generosity, the table was always well spread, with plenty of wine to ensure a general conviviality.

The Parisian salon at mid-century was one of Europe's glories, a sparkling mix of minds and manners, elegant, provocative, sensual, intellectual, and, above all, great fun. Everyone was welcome; poverty was no bar. In an age of rigid class distinctions, the salon was a free-flowing social river, its only elite the brilliant and the beautiful. There was no competition from the universities, where learning was confined to law and medicine and theology—no politics, no fine arts, none of the exciting new natural sciences, and of course no women. Neither was there much competition from the royal court; the years of the Fronde had seen the court at once everywhere and nowhere, the Louvre deserted as often as not, and the great palace of Versailles as yet no more than a humble wooden hunting lodge, and the glint in a little boy's eye.

There were other salons, of course: even the legendary Madame de Rambouillet, doyenne of the *salon français*, now almost seventy and in fact an Italian, was still welcoming guests at her beautiful hôtel. But Paul Scarron's salon in the big yellow drawing-room was by now the best of them. "It's the one where people talk the most nonsense," as he himself noted, "nonsense" being literature, philosophy, politics— though with less enthusiasm now—and, of course, plain gossip. And Scarron himself, despite his pitiful physical state, was a very good host: well informed, always amusing, drawing attention to his sufferings only to make fun of them. "It's one of the miracles of the century that

a man in such a condition could laugh the way he did," wrote Tallemant des Réaux, master of anecdote and one of the younger salon
regulars.

"Scarron's house was the meeting place for all the most cultured
people from the court, and all the clever people in Paris," said Jean de
Segrais, a constant visitor and himself both cultured and clever, supporting six siblings, as he did, on the earnings of his poetry. And along
with the poets came the powerful: the great military commander
Maréchal Turenne, and Nicolas Fouquet, superintendent of the King's
finances, a man with the kingdom's wealth at his disposal and a generous patron of the arts. There were the brilliant, all the grand names of
France's *grand siècle*: Corneille, La Fontaine, and the great Racine, still
in his teens; the young Italian composer Lully, phenomenally talented
and phenomenally arrogant; the painter Mignard, just returned after
more than twenty years in Italy, enraptured by the portrait potential
in the face of his young hostess; and of course the bluestocking
Madeleine de Scudéry, very tall and very thin, and "so extraordinarily
ugly that I'm afraid to describe her for fear of upsetting my more sensitive readers," as the writer Furetière noted coyly. She came with her
devoted admirer Pellisson, no oil painting himself, being "a little man,
with a very big hump on his back by way of recompense, and one leg
longer than the other, blind in one eye and not seeing overly well with
the other, the scarlet rims of both providing their only brilliance,
but"—thankfully—"with a most attractive mind."

And there were the noble, among them the duchesse de Montpensier, *la Grande Mademoiselle*, cousin to the King, who during the
Fronde had famously fired a cannon at the royal troops from the top
of the Bastille. "She has killed her husband," Cardinal Mazarin had
vengefully declared, thenceforth waylaying all Mademoiselle's future
suitors. There were the brilliant and noble: the duc de la Rochefoucauld, frondeur extraordinaire and future author of the famous *Max-
imes*, a man of the world with, according to his friend Segrais, a perfect
understanding of the human heart. With him came his intimate friend
the comtesse de La Fayette, one of France's first novelists, and the
marquise de Sablé, herself an author of fine maxims and hostess of an

important salon. There were the brilliant and beautiful, first among them Madame de Sévigné, coquettish and unlamenting (her unaffectionate husband had recently been killed in a duel), and already writing her delightful letters; and the courtesan Ninon de Lenclos, "Our Lady of Love," now in her mid-thirties but still with her three orders of lovers in tow—the payers, the martyrs, and, lastly, the favourites, who neither paid nor suffered long.

And along with all these glittering people came their many, many friends and admirers. Some came searching: young men came looking for literary advice or inspiration or publishers; the satirist Jean Loret came looking for gossip for his weekly gazette; the comte du Lude came looking for Madame de Sévigné; the comtesse de la Suze came looking for any available young man, "since my husband makes love to me as if I were a tree-stump"; and the portly poet Saint-Amant came looking for dinner, with his doomed *confrère* Tristan l'Hermite hanging on his arm, looking for one last drink. Isaac de Benserade came looking for help with his libretto for Lully's new opera, and he came, it is said, preceded by wafts of the many perfumes which he wore to conceal, insofar as was possible, his naturally fishy smell.

Others came accompanied: Monsieur de la Sablière, with his young wife, sweet and shy, soon to be immortalized in a glorious portrait by Mignard; the marquise du Plessis-Bellière with her parrot; the duc d'Elbeuf with his celebrated pork pâtés; and the maréchal d'Albret with his cheeses "as good as cheeses can be." Cardinal de Retz came with his new red hat, and the abbé Fouquet, brother of the great minister, came with vengeance in his heart: he had lost his mistress to the Cardinal, and had vowed to cut up his body and salt it—having killed him first—but neither opportunity arose in Scarron's yellow drawing-room.

Some of the guests were rich, some fabulously so; some, like their host himself, had no money at all to speak of. No one minded, provided someone could make a joke of it, and there was always someone who could. Wit—*l'esprit*—or at least a keen enjoyment of it, was the only real entry fee to the Parisian salon.

Françoise had wit, an abundance of it, as was remarked by everyone who came close enough to hear her quiet voice. She did not seek the limelight in the way of most of the other women, with the confidence of their wealthy background and their easy familiarity with the salon world. Unlike them, she had still a good deal to learn. Scarron's lessons were expanding her knowledge of books and ideas, but the manner of the salon, the ways of cultured society, could not be assimilated at second hand. A warning from the chevalier echoed every evening in her ears, already assailed by countless things new to them—"One foolish statement will erase the impression of twenty sensible ones"—and she made up her mind to say nothing at all rather than risk making a fool of herself by speaking out of turn. Her exhortation in later life, to a young girl about to enter the same kind of world, reveals how she managed now in the brilliant circle to which her marriage had given her entrance: "Don't talk too much. Listen instead. Don't ever appear surprised; it looks provincial. Don't reveal your ignorance by asking for explanations. You can learn a thousand things without anyone realizing you didn't know them already . . ."

If knowledge meant confidence, money meant confidence, too. The Sévignés and Sablières arrived, of course, in their own private carriages, the women dressed in beautiful gowns, with fans and jewels, taking silver coins for the servants from embroidered silk purses. Françoise had no means of competing with elegance at this level, but her response was masterful. Unable to perform à la mode, she played instead a tactical counterpoint, dressing with deliberate simplicity and disdaining even the plainer jewellery she might have worn. It was a shrewd stratagem for a girl not yet nineteen, and it worked: in her perfectly tasteful, simple frocks, she charmed everyone. What need to gild the lily when it was so young and pretty, with such a lovely figure and such a natural grace? To the women, it looked like modesty; to the men, it looked like innocence. Both found it irresistible.

"Don't try to keep up with the great ladies," Françoise later advised the impoverished young demoiselles in her care. "You'll only make yourselves ridiculous . . . If you can't afford to dress as they do, take precisely the opposite path: choose perfect simplicity. Don't let people think you're spending every penny you can on clothes. Show that you

have courage enough to place yourself above this weakness of our sex."
That "this weakness" was in fact a strength—the strength, at base, of
money—Françoise knew very well. Unable to meet it directly, she
chose instead the path of subversion.

Scarron was more than happy with the quiet simplicity of his wife's
appearance. Despite his raucous verses, he was a fastidious man, preferring a neat and sober dress to any extravagance of style, and he
could not have obliged her, in any case, had she asked for silks and
satins. He was equally happy with her capable management of his unusually demanding household and, to his surprise, perhaps, with her
comportment among his guests. Dignified, tasteful, charming without
being flirtatious, never putting herself forward but noticing every re-
quirement, she had swiftly become the perfect salon hostess.

"And what I admire in such a young person," wrote the chevalier de
Méré to his friend the duchesse de Lesdiguières, "is that she won't accept any attention from men unless they're well behaved, and consequently I think she can be in no great danger, though the handsomest
men of the court and the most powerful men in finance are attacking
on all fronts. But if I know her, she'll resist plenty of assaults before
surrendering, and if she allows so many men to flock around her, it's
not that any of them will succeed with her, but rather that she knows
how to keep them at bay."

To some extent, Françoise's new role of virtuous society hostess
came naturally to her. She was observant and self-controlled, she had
long been accustomed to putting other people's needs before her own,
and inexperienced as she was, she was generally reserved with men.
But these natural bricks were held together by a mortar more con-
sciously constructed: the modest dress, the careful listening, and soon
a degree of pseudo-piety as well, all came together through a keen calculation. By appearing to withdraw from the fray, Françoise made herself noticed, and eventually admired. If she could not sparkle as the
other ladies did, she would glow with a softer light all her own.

On the fast days of Lent, with Scarron and his guests tucking into
their beef in defiance of the religious laws, Françoise, "in the middle of
the *ragoûts* and sauces," ate nothing but herring and butter and a bit of

salad. "I made the ragoûts for them myself," she noted. "And I have to admit I felt very pleased with myself for not eating them." Visiting the minister Fouquet at his grand offices to request a pension for Scarron, she dressed in so unflattering a style "that her friends were ashamed to take her there." Fouquet was impressed by her modesty, though perhaps also a trifle disappointed—he was a noted admirer of the fair sex—but he duly awarded Scarron the pension, and Françoise was thenceforth included in Madame Fouquet's outings to the park in her fashionable carriage.

"What I don't like so much about her, I have to say," continued the chevalier, "is that she's too attached to her duty, despite everyone trying to correct this fault in her." "But I wasn't doing these things for love of God," said Françoise later. "It was for love of my own reputation." She was horrified to receive a visit from a friend one Good Friday: "He shouldn't have come," she said. "He should have thought I'd be passing the day in pious reflection. I wasn't, of course, but he should have thought I was."

If Scarron knew the depth of his wife's careful façade, he made no mention of it. Her calm, pleasing, rational manner, her reputation for speaking truthfully, of "never turning her wit unkindly against anyone," was one of "my idols," as he wrote. Her apparent restraint concealed passionate feelings—humiliation, jealousy, fear perhaps, and maybe ambition, too—but it protected her and gave her confidence, and it earned her the respect and even the admiration of a worldly crowd by no means easy to impress, who simply took it at face value. If Françoise paid the price of the deception in a certain loneliness from time to time, there was enough that was genuine to allow her some real friendships, and to keep the façade standing as time went by. Her own construction, built out of need and anxiety in the uncertain days of her first youth, it was to serve Françoise very well, and she was never to abandon it.

SIX

End of the Beginning

I'm not going to attempt to describe the King's entry for you. I'll only say that neither I nor anyone else could tell you how magnificent it was. I can't imagine a finer spectacle, and the Queen must have gone to bed last night very happy with the husband she's chosen.

Thus Françoise, writing to her friend, Madame de Villarceaux, of the ceremonial entry into Paris on August 26, 1660, of the resplendently handsome twenty-two-year-old Louis XIV.

If the Queen was happy with her new husband, she had no cause to congratulate herself about it. Far from having any choice in the matter, Marie-Thérèse had simply served as a traded chattel in the time-honoured way of all princesses, happy and otherwise. "I bring Your Majesty peace and the Infanta," Cardinal Mazarin had declared, neatly summarizing the conclusion of his negotiations the year before with the Spanish. The Peace of the Pyrenees had brought an end at last to twenty-four years of warfare, alternately fierce and desultory, between France and Spain. Behind the declarations of eternal friendship was a clear loss for the Spaniards: the peace had cost them a great deal of land and the handing over of their King's daughter to her first cousin, the King of France.

If the augmentation of his realm had flattered Louis's already substantial political ambitions, his equally substantial vanity had been deflated, if only temporarily, on acquaintance with his new wife—pious, dumpy, and none too bright. Even her French was galumphing. "She has very white skin," reported the courtier Madame de Motteville in her defence, "and though her face is long, it's round at the bottom, and her cheeks, if a bit fat, are nonetheless pretty, and if she only had more height and better teeth, she might be classed among the most attractive persons in Europe."

"I'm not going to attempt to describe it all for you," Françoise continued, although she did in fact give a long and exuberant description of the scene. She made no further mention of the new Queen, however; already, on her entry into the capital, as she was to do for the rest of her life, Marie-Thérèse had passed more or less unnoticed.

Françoise's letter to Madame de Villarceaux is a delightful series of pages, the voice of a twenty-four-year-old in high spirits, leaning over the balcony at the house of a friend, passing cheeky comments and pointing out her personal friends riding along in the vast entourage: "Rouville was in borrowed plumes. I wouldn't have gone at all if I'd been him—the King knows he can't afford that sort of thing . . . I don't know which of the gentlemen looked best. They all looked marvellous. If I had to award a prize, I'd give it to the horse that was carrying the seals . . . Cardinal Mazarin's retinue wasn't the worst: it was led by seventy-two mules . . . Beuvron was trying to catch sight of me, but he was looking in the wrong direction. I was looking for Monsieur de Villarceaux, but his horse was so frisky, he was twenty feet away from me before I recognized him. He looked very fine, not so magnificently dressed as some of the others, but certainly one of the most dashing. He rode very well . . . We called out to each other as he passed."

Madame de Villarceaux would have been glad to know that her husband had looked so fine and ridden so well, though she might have been less pleased at the eagerness with which he and Françoise had no doubt called out to each other. Villarceaux had been one of Françoise's keenest admirers since his own approach to Scarron some years before, seeking to establish an acquaintance, and his admiration had not passed unreturned. Louis de Mornay, marquis de Villarceaux, gentleman of the royal household, was a recognized "favourite" of the courtesan Ninon de Lenclos, and in fact the father of her infant son, but this, in his view and also in hers, did not necessarily preclude an intimate relationship with Françoise as well. Tallemant des Réaux recorded that "Scarron laughed at those who hinted, ever so gently, that his wife had become Villarceaux's mistress," but Scarron was aware that the marquis had been writing billets-doux to his wife, and he did take the considerable trouble of going to Ninon's house to discuss the matter with him privately. As for the long-suffering Madame de Villarceaux, some years older than her husband, she came frequently enough to Paris to have, perhaps unwisely, befriended Françoise, but in general she maintained a discreet distance at her château, consoled by her fabulous personal wealth.

Villarceaux was in any case by no means Françoise's only admirer. The chevalier de Méré was still about, and sundry self-styled poets were rhapsodizing over her, with others providing a chorus of more prosaic sighs. Among them, "the handsomest men of the court and the most powerful men in finance, attacking on all fronts," as the chevalier had noted, were the young comte du Lude, hedging his bets between Françoise and thirty-four-year-old Madame de Sévigné; the marquis d'Hequetot, scion of the Harcourt dynasty, one of Europe's most ancient; the duc d'Elbeuf, trailing a frondeur's reputation and a new wife unwillingly behind him; the marquis de Marsilly on his two crutches, broken-legged from musket-shots received in battle; the handsome Alexandre d'Elbène, supported rather differently, by an inherited fortune of stupendous proportions; and Scarron's physician and alchemist La Mesnardière, triply resigned to failure, more or less, in medicine, chemistry, and love. The King's counsellor de l'Orme had reputedly offered 30,000 écus (some said 300,000) in return for the lady's "final favours," but this would-be "payer" had received short shrift.

Françoise kept them all on a high-tension leash, a technique she is said to have learned from Ninon, Our Lady of Love herself; but one man, with an appropriately victorious name, certainly stood higher in her favour than any of the others. This was César-Phébus, comte de Miossens, known as the maréchal d'Albret since his moment of glory during the last days of the Fronde, when it had fallen to his charge to arrest the rebel prince de Condé. Now in his mid-forties, d'Albret was an *homme galant* of exemplary cast: he had already skewered three men, including his own best friend, in duels fought over affairs of the heart. Villarceaux was shortly to find Ninon reclining in his arms and, presumably with a thought to the duels, to resign her there forthwith. Whether d'Albret was also Françoise's lover, as was rumoured, is unknown. "Up to this point, I don't think she's taken the plunge," wrote Tallemant des Réaux of this time. But the lady was certainly tempted: "Beauty can be a kind of misfortune," she later sighed. "It makes you liable to lose your reputation, and possibly even your soul."

There were other temptations, too, which she may not always have resisted. Despite teasing comments from Scarron about her fondness for Ninon, with whom she often shared a bed in the custom of the time, Françoise had no sapphic tendencies, at least not naturally. But she passed half her days in a highly suggestive environment, marked by erotic language and gesture, with men looking admiringly at her and some propositioning her outright. It is not at all improbable that over years of living in this kind of atmosphere, the demands of her own sexuality grew stronger, and that during her "months on end" in bed with Ninon, there were moments, and perhaps hours, of tenderness or sensuality or even lovemaking between them.

Ninon had had ample recent opportunity to investigate the pleasures of sex with women. In the summer of 1656, a moral crusade led by the pious Queen Mother and the stringent men of the *Compagnie du Saint-Sacrement*, the *"cabale des dévots,"* had cleared hundreds of prostitutes from the streets of Paris, and Ninon, though not technically a prostitute at all, had been swept up with them and locked away in the prison-convent of the Madelonnettes, near her own quarter of the Marais. To the shock of the Visitation nuns who staffed the place, vast parcels of rich food and wines had arrived daily from prominent men wishing to ease the pangs of Ninon's incarceration, and the nuns' alarm had been mightily increased when dozens of young courtiers began scaling the convent walls and charging about the grounds, demanding her release. Ninon had been swiftly transferred to the more distant convent of Lagny, twenty miles from Paris, in a town suitably fortified against attack by wartime enemies or impassioned *galants*. Here she had languished for a year, until the maréchal d'Albret, with a too hopeful guarantee of reform on the lady's part, had procured her release in the summer of 1657.

The convent of Lagny was not a reform institution like the Madelonnettes. There were nuns, of course, with varying degrees of vocational devotion, but it housed as well many girls and women, generally of good family, who were there simply because they had nowhere else to go. They lived more freely than the nuns, and among them Ninon had quickly become a star. "A woman's virtue is nothing more than the art of appearing virtuous," she had instructed them, no doubt presenting a more attractive option than the joyless sisters, obliged to follow every last letter of their bleak law. Ninon was a libertine, a professional breaker of rules. It was her job to know all there was to know about lovemaking, about the many different ways of eliciting pleasure, for herself and for her partners, about the forbidden sexual positions which had recently made their way into France along with table forks and ice cream and other exotic Italian phenomena. "I can play the man if I choose to," she had more than once declared. Writing from Lagny to a homosexual friend, she had remarked, "I'm taking a leaf out of your book, and beginning to love my own sex."

None of it is certain, but it is clear in any case that Françoise and Ninon were not obliged to share a bed, like the very poor, or like friendly cousins on a brief visit. They lived only minutes from each other; no long, cold carriage ride would have dissuaded either one from returning home after an evening spent at the other's house. "They had no reason to sleep in the same bed"—for months on end—"unless they found pleasure in it." Scarron's teasing may in fact have hinted at a genuinely sensual involvement between his free-living friend and his wife, and if so, it may even have been something of a relief to him. An affair between Françoise and Ninon would have struck less brutally at his already humbled manhood. A woman lover was a different kind of competition, and there would at least be no illegitimate child to humiliate and grieve him further.

Other than this, despite occasional jibes from her husband, Françoise's relationships with women were almost certainly innocent. She enjoyed women's company, and by now could count among her friends some of the city's most beautiful and distinguished ladies. Even the extraordinary Queen Christina, visiting Paris in the autumn of 1657 after abdicating her snowbound Swedish throne, was moved to request an introduction to Paul Scarron's enchanting young wife. Scarron himself, having regaled the Queen in advance with gallant declarations of eternal devotion, expected handsome financial advantage from the meeting, but his only reward in the end was a witty backhanded compliment: "I might have guessed it would take a Queen of Sweden to make a man unfaithful to a woman like that," Christina is reported to have said.

Though Françoise was proud of her new social connections, she was aggrieved, and perhaps resentful, when her own modest means restricted her movement among them. "My wife is most unhappy," wrote Scarron to Uncle Benjamin at Mursay, "having no money and no coach to go where she wants, when she has been offered the great happiness of accompanying one of the Mancini misses . . ."

The quintet of Mancini sisters, lively to the point of scandal, were the nieces of Cardinal Mazarin. Marie Mancini, the young King's first love, had asked Françoise to attend her on her journey to western France, where she had been more or less exiled after the arrangement of Louis's marriage to the Spanish infanta. Though obliged to decline this honour, Françoise was able to console herself with the even more illustrious Marie-Madeleine Fouquet, lovely young wife of the King's *Surintendant des Finances* and herself magnificently well born. Madame Fouquet had become quite attached to Françoise since their first outing in the park together in her elegant carriage. "I find my wife so full of Madame's attractions that I fear something impure may be going on between the two of them," wrote Scarron to the maréchal d'Albret, in the certainty of their innocence. And elsewhere, ironically: "I'm afraid that *débauchée* Madame de Montchevreuil is going to get her drunk and have her way with her before sending her back to me"—Madame de Montchevreuil being known for her almost tiresomely good behaviour.

Tallemant des Réaux records the daughter of a court florist, "well known for her love of women," visiting Françoise, then indisposed "with a touch of colic," with a bouquet in one hand and a large purse of coins in the other. "She'd been looking for an excuse to spend the night with her for ages, and in the end she simply got into the bed beside her and kissed her. Madame Scarron leapt up and chased her out." Françoise had no wish to be taken for a lesbian, and even less to be taken for a prostitute.

Scarron himself, meanwhile, had been growing ever less able to pay court of any kind to his wife. Years of near paralysis, together with an overindulgence in pâtés and cheese and frangipani tarts—"I've always been a bit greedy"—had fattened him to the extent that he was now even breathing with difficulty. His illness was so advanced that for months he had been spending most of the day in bed, in a state of exhausted half-sleep. His wonderful salon had declined with him, and Françoise had begun to take whatever chance she could to slip away to other Marais gatherings, often at Ninon's house or at the grander residences of Fouquet or the duchesse de Richelieu.

By the late summer of 1660, it was apparent that Scarron was nearing his end. "The bloody doctor's got me hexed: He says I'll be dead by Friday next," he wrote during a rare lucid hour. "So I'm writing my will." And so he did, in a last flourish of burlesque:

> To my wife I bequeath the freedom to wed,
> For fear she end up in an illicit bed.
> It's true in that way she's endured a long Lent:
> I'd have serviced her better if I'd been less bent.
> To fat Saint-Amant, a good parcel of cheeses,
> To the fop Benserade, as much scent as he pleases,

To my dearest friend Loret, some wine, quite a lot,
To that idiot doctor, my chamberpot.

If the doctor had been banished, Scarron's friends were still, as ever, more than welcome in his yellow house. They did not desert him now, so that his final days were spent as he had always loved to spend his days—in warm and congenial company. Feeling the approach of death, he admitted that, a hesitant Catholic, he could not decide whether or not to accept the last rites. The maréchal d'Albret and rich Alexandre d'Elbène, steady atheists both, dismissed the idea, but Françoise insisted and, perhaps for her sake, Scarron agreed that a priest should be sent for. D'Albret and d'Elbène remonstrated; Scarron changed his mind: there would be no final embrace in the arms of Holy Mother Church. In the end it was Ninon, Our Lady of Love, who brushed past them all with a priest in tow. "Come on, then, Monsieur, come on," she admonished him, "do your duty, and don't take any notice of what my friend says. He doesn't know any more about it than you do."

Scarron took the sacrament, with wife and friends weeping around him. "I'll never make you weep as much as I've made you laugh," he told them, sadly and truthfully. Outside, colporteurs paced about beneath the windows, calling out the news of his impending death, but if Scarron heard them, he was past caring. He had strength enough to dictate an epitaph for his own waiting grave, then, true to ironic form, he produced a lengthy bout of hiccups, before finally breathing his last. His body was carried the following evening to the nearby church of Saint-Gervais, and buried with minimal ceremony. Though it was not customary for a wife to attend her husband's funeral, Françoise was present—indeed, it seems she was the only mourner there. Where Scarron's body came to rest is unknown: perhaps in the common grave for the poor, perhaps beneath a flagstone in the nave of the church. Wherever his grave, it was never to bear the irreverent epitaph he had prepared for himself:

This man knew every pain there was,
He sighed and groaned and choked,

And suffered death a thousand times
Before he finally croaked.
So keep it quiet as you go by,
Don't even make a peep:
This is the first in many nights
That Scarron's got to sleep.

And despite his facetious last will, Scarron had in fact died intestate, leaving only debts. More than a hundred years later, the parish of Saint-Gervais was still demanding payment from his distant heirs for the cost of the poet's burial.

Jean de Segrais, though a good friend of Scarron's, had not joined those keeping vigil at his deathbed. Segrais had been travelling with the King on his wedding journey, and had not heard that Scarron was failing at last. He arrived back in Paris only days afterwards, and "the first thing I did was go to see him, but when I reached the house, they were carrying out the chair he always used to sit in. They'd just sold it as part of his assets."

Scarron's "assets" were effectively the contents of the house in the rue Neuve-Saint-Louis. On the very day of his death, with his body still in the yellow bedroom, creditors had demanded that the house be sealed so that nothing might be taken out, and in the days that followed, everything was sold to repay what might be paid of his debts. Those of his friends who had furnished the house with their own loans or gifts were too generous now to make any claims to the curtains and books and tables being carted off to auction, though various Scarrons emerged from the countryside to behave with less restraint.

Françoise, dressed in widow's black, had left the house in the morning of the seventh of October, just hours after Scarron's death and before the bailiffs' arrival. She took with her, presumably, some clothes and whatever small items she possessed of any value, notably a drawing of herself recently made by Pierre Mignard. Several friends had invited her to stay with them, but Françoise accepted instead an offer from Scarron's cousin Catherine, the maréchale d'Aumont, of her own furnished rooms at the Petit-Charité convent of the Hospitalières, near the Place-Royale in the heart of the town. These rooms, which Madame d'Aumont retained permanently for her own periods of religious retreat, were similar to the lodgings Françoise had taken at the Ursuline convent in the weeks before her marriage. The arrangement provided her with a safe and respectable home that she could treat as her own, coming and going as she pleased and inviting whatever guests she chose to see her there, and she apparently took full advantage of these freedoms, bringing in "a furious number of people, which wasn't at all to the nuns' liking." In any event, it was not intended to be more than a temporary home, possibly until November, when, at twenty-five, she would reach the age of legal majority and be entirely her own person de jure as well as de facto, though, with her father deceased, it is not clear who might otherwise have stepped in to take legal charge of her during the intervening months.

Françoise did mourn Scarron, but not deeply, and not long. She was always to speak of him with compassion, but their relationship, after all, had been more friendship than marriage, and she could hardly have wished him a longer life of ever more awful suffering. His death had freed her from one great anxiety—the wearying daily care of the invalid himself—but it had also left her in something of a limbo in terms of her own situation. Once again, she was without any real home, with almost no money to hand. Sensibly, she engaged a lawyer in an effort to protect her "widow's portion," if indeed it proved to be any amount at all, from Scarron's circling creditors. On October 23, 1660, she wrote to Aunt Louise at Mursay:

> I have been so overwhelmed these last few days, and Monsieur Scarron's death has occasioned me so much grief and so much business to attend to, that I haven't even had time to write to ask you for a copy of my baptism document, which is absolutely necessary. Please send it to me as soon as you possibly can . . .

Aunt Louise must have complied directly, for sometime in November, Françoise was able to write to Uncle Benjamin of a modest financial success:

> Monsieur Scarron has left ten thousand francs in assets, and twenty-two thousand francs of debt. Twenty-three thousand are due to me by my marriage contract, but it was drawn up so badly that although my claim has priority . . . I'll still have to pay some of the debts . . . Anyway, after all our representations, it seems I'll get four or five thousand francs outright.
>
> That's all that remains of this poor man . . . From all this you'll see that I'm not destined to be happy, but I suppose we have to view this kind of thing as a trial sent from the Lord, and resign ourselves . . .

Françoise could not resign herself, all the same, to the idea of living on charity yet again. Madame d'Aumont's kindness had given her a roof over her head, and she had no doubt been grateful for it. But Madame d'Aumont's kindness quickly began to run out of control; she began sending food to the convent, then wine and candles, then clothes, making sure at the same time that every detail of her thoughtfulness was broadcast loudly. Finally, when a cartload of firewood from her turned up in the convent courtyard, Françoise stormed outside and sent it straight back. And when the bill fell due for the *chambres de retraite*, she insisted on paying it herself, though possibly with money borrowed elsewhere, and decamped forthwith for her old Ursuline convent at the rue Saint-Jacques.

By early December she was settled in there, and relaxed enough to include pieces of ordinary Paris gossip in her letters to Mursay. "They've staged a comedy at the Louvre about the King's marriage. Everyone was delighted by it. It's a pastorale. They show the King on stage . . . I couldn't go, of course." It was her state of mourning which had prevented Françoise from attending; neither she nor any of her friends was deterred by the fact that the pastorale was the work of the ambitious young Philippe Quinault, who five years before had stolen an entire act of Scarron's for a play of his own. "I'll never make you weep as much as I've made you laugh," Scarron had said. Eight weeks after his death, the memory of him, and loyalty to it, was already fading. "But what is there that time does not dissolve? as Scarron used to say," sighed Madame de Sévigné.

In one respect, at least, the same phenomenon was shortly to work very much to Françoise's advantage. Scarron's pension as Honorable Invalid to the Queen, rescinded after his virulent *Mazarinade*, was about to be reinstated, thanks to the efforts of two friends from the yellow salon days whose positions at court allowed them regular conversation with the Queen Mother. The ladies painted a glowing picture of the virtuous young widow who might so easily be drawn by poverty and her own beauty into "gallantry," namely a life of sin with one or other, or one and others, of the city's wealthy men. The poor little thing, the ladies sighed, had even been a pupil at the Ursuline convent in the rue Saint-Jacques, which Her Majesty had herself declared open in 1620, in the days of her own beauteous youth. The Queen Mother, tough-minded but very pious, did not take much persuading. "But I've forgotten how much the pension was," she said. The amount had been five hundred livres per annum. "Two thousand livres," said a quick-thinking courtier; the ladies nodded in sage agreement, and passed the Queen Mother a quill.

"Virtue alone is our only wealth." So Françoise had chanted years before, with her thirteen-year-old companions, chasing the turkeys on the baronne de Neuillant's farm in Niort. For once, the old Pibrac quatrain had been tangibly substantiated.

The Queen Mother's pension was wonderful news for Françoise. For the first time in her life she had her own sure income, and the four or five thousand of her "widow's portion" could be tucked away for future eventualities. Two thousand livres was by no means a fortune, at least among the gentry, but it was comfortably more than she had ever had before. During her marriage, her personal allowance had been only five hundred francs, about 130 livres, per year. Now she would have enough to live the life of a lady, in a house of her own, with a "good big fire" and two or three servants, decent clothes, and pleasant outings. If not luxury, it was comfort, and importantly, it was enough to keep her within the orbit of the rich, and even the very rich, with whom she had been able to socialize during the years of her marriage.

Above all, it was hers, her own money, guaranteed from the royal purse, still charity of a kind, perhaps, but not understood as such in the terms of the day. A royal pension had more the status of a reward, for virtue or merit or services rendered to the Crown. At base, too, it was a way of maintaining the social order, with well-bred people provided with public money so that they might continue to live as well-bred people: a circle serving the interests of all those within it, with those on the outside remembered, often enough, only in emergency, or possibly at prayer. For Françoise, the Queen Mother's pension was certainly not charity: it was money of her own, to which she was entitled. It gave her the independence she had craved, and a steadier measure of social respect, and hand in hand with these, it gave her self-respect as well.

SEVEN

The Merry Widow

Françoise was now in a very agreeable position: a pretty widow of modest but independent means, twenty-four years old and in perfect health, with plenty of friends and admirers and no one to worry about but herself. In the eyes of contemporaries, it was all most enviable, indeed a near perfect situation, as the *comédiens* of the day reflected: "I'm a widow, thank God," declares the playwright Dancourt's Madame Patin to her brother-in-law. "You've no right at all to tell me to behave myself." Molière's young widow Célimène starts up a salon of convivial friends, most of them men. "I love being loved," she admits with a winsome smile. And offstage, Madame de Sévigné, who knew the pleasures of young widowhood from personal experience, was consoling her niece with the reminder that "the name of widow is the name of liberty."

If Françoise was free from men's control, and now also free from want, she was free as well from responsibility. There were of course no children, and even her mother had no claim on her now: Jeanne had died quietly in Niort, not long after her daughter's marriage. No record of Françoise's reaction remains, but given the cold relationship between them, the news is unlikely to have affected her deeply. Brother

Charles was still alive, the image of his incorrigible father, drinking and whoring from one town to the next, but at least keeping more or less on the right side of the law. Five years before, Scarron had obtained a post for him as standard-bearer in a cavalry regiment, and had sent him 4,000 ill-spared livres to purchase all the necessary appurtenances. Charles had probably not heard the recent news of his sister's royal pension, since otherwise he would certainly have been in touch with her at once, as he was later to be whenever he needed a few extra thousand, or a horse, or a house, or a well-paid job with no work attached to it. And Françoise, whether out of sisterly affection or a sense of duty or simple weakness for an appealing rascal, would always be ready to oblige him.

But for now, she could suit herself, and she did so first by renouncing her plain dresses and setting out for the fashionable boutiques which lined the Cours-la-Reine, an elegant boulevard running alongside the Seine. Here, accompanied by her well-to-do friends, she purchased all the fancies and vanities which lack of money or excess of pride had forbidden to her before: colourful fabrics for new gowns, shoes and headdresses, silk purses and lace hankerchiefs. Her manner, too, became swiftly less retiring. She spoke more, and laughed more, and flirted more openly, and ate more than herring on the designated fast days.

In all of this she was encouraged by her old friend the maréchal d'Albret, who, following the chevalier de Méré and Scarron, seems to have become her third instructor in the art and science of living à la mode. Despite the "furious number of people" she had received in her rooms at the convent, Françoise could have held no salon there, nor did she think of doing so elsewhere now that the centerpiece of Scarron and his wit had disappeared. Instead, she spent her afternoons and evenings at other Marais salons, at Ninon's comfortable house in the rue des Tournelles, or at the grand hôtels of the d'Albrets or the duchesse de Richelieu, and sometimes even out in the country, at the fabulous Fouquet château of Vaux-le-Vicomte, a jewel of baroque architecture and the most beautiful château in France, built by the great Le Vau, with interiors painted by Charles Le Brun and magical fountain gardens by the master of landscape, André Le Nôtre. The minister Fouquet had gathered there every writer and artist of merit or promise; the rich and the beautiful also flocked to Vaux-le-Vicomte, and Françoise, a favoured friend of Madame Fouquet, was invited along with them all.

But it was in Paris, at the d'Albret house in the rue des Francs-Bourgeois, with the maréchal César-Phébus indulging in his usual flirtations and the maréchale Madeleine in her own peccadillo of too much wine, that Françoise met a number of younger women who were to form a special new circle of friends for her, and who would remain linked to her, for better and for worse, for the rest of their eventful lives.

The youngest, cleverest, and most ambitious of them all was Anne-Marie de La Trémoïlle-Noirmoutier, a cousin of Françoise's broken-legged admirer, the marquis de Marsilly. "Quite tall, a brunette with blue eyes, not a beauty, but attractive," Anne-Marie was barely a year out of the mild convent where she had spent her days "piping the praises of God." Though just eighteen years old, she had already "something majestic in her whole bearing," as well as "plenty of intelligence and a very nice speaking voice," both of which she was to use to impressive effect. Anne-Marie had been recently married off to a suitable count, and hence was introduced to Françoise now as the comtesse de Chalais—she would earn eventual notoriety as the princesse des Ursins.

Like Françoise, she was a native of the Poitou region, but little familiarity could have existed between them in their early years, even had there not been a seven-year difference in their ages, since Anne-Marie belonged to the highest echelons of the aristocracy, to which the "high and mighty Monseigneur Constant d'Aubigné, chevalier, lord of Surimeau and other places" would barely have had tradesman's access, even if he had been out of prison. The illustrious family of La Trémoïlle were political animals born and bred. Anne-Marie's father had been a leader of the royalists during the Fronde, and later an ally of the prince de Condé, risking execution for treason. Her mother's father was a Counsellor of State; her father-in-law had been a conspirator in the attempt to assassinate Cardinal Richelieu—he had been among the last of the French nobles beheaded by order of their King. Anne-Marie had grown up in the middle of intrigue and even danger; the love of politicking was in her blood.

She herself was later to admit that, in these days of her youth at the d'Albrets' salon, she had been exceedingly jealous of Françoise, as the latter's niece recorded: "Maréchal d'Albret and all the other gentlemen always had important things to discuss with [Madame Scarron], while Madame de Chalais was left with the young people. And all the time, [Madame Scarron] was wishing they'd think a bit less of her good sense and leave her alone to have a bit of fun, instead of keeping her in a corner talking court business as they did. I think that shows the difference between these two women . . . [Madame Scarron] was not a natural intriguer; she was a delightful person, made for society."

She found a taste of it, at least, in two of the "young people" with whom Anne-Marie de Chalais was always being left. Both were cousins of the maréchal d'Albret, both living in his house on the rue des Francs-Bourgeois, and both incessantly "fighting like cats." They were Judith de Martel, "frighteningly tall," and Bonne de Pons, "as lovely as the day; the maréchal found her extremely attractive—and so did plenty of others." Though well-born, Judith and Bonne had no money of their own, but their Marais life was nonetheless a good one, the broad-minded maréchal allowing them an encouraging degree of latitude and the tipsy maréchale seldom being in a state to remonstrate. Somewhere within their mutual loathing, the two cousins had found one subject at least of agreement: both maintained a genuine affection for Françoise. Though she enjoyed the company of each of them, it was Bonne, "a bit mad, always herself, never stopping to think, full of imagination, always amusing," who was to become the closer friend.

And along with Bonne and Judith and Anne-Marie de Chalais, there was a fourth young woman whom Françoise met now at the rue des Francs-Bourgeois, a woman who, unwittingly and, as it turned out, to her own grave disadvantage, was to faciliate the Widow Scarron's rise from pretty *salonnière bourgeoise* to the greatest lady in France.

"She met Madame de Montespan at d'Albret's house—she never moves from there." So recorded the duchesse de Montpensier, with a touch of condescension befitting a cousin of the King. The twenty-year-old Madame de Montespan, formally Françoise-Athénaïs de Tonnay-Charente, marquise de Montespan, was a cousin of d'Albret by marriage and a frequent guest at his house, along with her brother, the comte de Vivonne, aged twenty-four, and her two sisters, vain and snobbish Gabrielle, marquise de Thianges, at twenty-six the eldest of the family, and brilliant Marie-Madeleine, future abbess of Fonte-vrault, just fifteen years old. All four were exuberant sprigs of the ancient Rochechouart de Mortemart tree, one of the grandest in France, and all four were confidently aware of their own impressive lineage. "Before the sea appeared in the world," ran their dynastic motto, "Rochechouart bore aloft the waves."

They were an appealing quartet nonetheless, known for their quick family wit, the celebrated esprit Mortemart, and all of them physically attractive, Madame de Montespan indeed a stunning beauty, "blonde, with big azure blue eyes, a small rosy mouth, and very good teeth . . . of medium height, and a good figure, though with a tendency to plumpness"—not necessarily a disadvantage for a woman, all the same, in an age of voluptuous sensuality. Whether or not the marquis de Montespan appreciated his wife's attractions, he did not generally accompany her to the d'Albrets' salon, but despite this, she had so far remained a woman "of respectable conduct and a good reputation." At the d'Albrets, as everywhere she went, Françoise-Athénaïs was a star attraction, if a trifle unrestrained: wonderfully beautiful, always dressed magnificently, enchanting every listener with her famous wit, and screaming with laughter herself—"You could have heard it two hundred feet away." She had recently discarded the Françoise of her given name in order to identify herself more emphatically with the Athénaïs—Athena, Greek goddess of wisdom, war, good quality fabrics, and everything else worth paying attention to.

Though very grand and often contemptuous of lesser mortals—including, it is said, the "parvenu" royal family of Bourbon—Athénaïs was not above paying attention to Françoise. She enjoyed her quick wit and conversation, and even her style, but in the pretty Widow Scarron she saw no competitor for her own natural place at the centre of the d'Albrets' salon, or indeed of anywhere else. An easy familiarity developed between the two, and they were frequently together, the resplendent glories of the one complemented by the subtler glow of the other.

A description of Françoise survives from about this time, in which it seems that her hair has darkened since the "light chestnut" which Madeleine de Scudéry had recorded eight years before, and her mouth has become rather more sensual and her figure more womanly. She is here observed by a man, rather than by the chaste Mademoiselle de Scudéry, but the difference also reflects the natural blooming of a beautiful young woman between seventeen and twenty-five years of age:

> Her appearance was charming. She was rather tall and well proportioned, with a lovely oval face, her complexion fine if a little too brown, big black eyes, the loveliest in the world, her hair also very black, her mouth quite large with nice teeth and very red lips, an elegant nose, a beautiful bosom, pretty arms and hands, and a livelier mind than all the other women, obliging, amusing, yes, a very appetizing little Christian.

In short, apart from her circle of women friends, the Widow Scarron was the subject of a good deal of admiration, and many men of high standing would willingly have taken her as a kept mistress. As far as is known, however, no offer of marriage was forthcoming: among her current rather grand acquaintance, her few thousand livres would have been no more than the price of a moderate night's gambling, and she had no name, and no connections other than all her friends themselves possessed already. She was proud of her reputation as a woman who had never "taken the plunge," and she was fiercely attached to her independence. And her present life was good: it was a life of gadding about to beautiful places in beautiful clothes, and after all the grey and anxious years, she was revelling in it. "Widowed a day and widowed a year are not the same thing at all," wrote Scarron's old friend La Fontaine, adding a new fable to his soon-to-be-famous collection. "A pretty young woman may go about in mourning dress for a while, but only until she finds something better to wear." What matter if the nuns at the Ursuline convent found Françoise's behaviour "not to their liking"? She paid her bills there. She could come and go as she pleased. And she was having a wonderful time.

Françoise's resistance to becoming a mistress was buttressed by two, possibly three principles: she wanted to pay her own way in life; she did not want anyone looking down on her; and she may also have been held back by religious convictions regarding the sinfulness of extramarital sex. This last, if it existed for her at all, was certainly the weakest of the three. Life as a mistress was a social norm, however pious or shocked its public detractors might be. For a decade or more, Françoise had been surrounded by women who thought nothing of *galanterie*, with many of them actively seeking it as an obvious means of keeping body and soul comfortably together. Among her best friends she counted the celebrated Ninon de Lenclos, literary-minded and well-to-do, choosing whatever lover she pleased—including the husband, the son, and later the grandson of her own friend, Madame de Sévigné. Admittedly, Ninon had spent a year confined in a convent by order of the Queen Mother, but now she was out and about, undimmed and undaunted. Françoise's sister-in-law, Françoise Scarron, had been the mistress of a duke for decades, and the mother of his son as well. There was a mistress standing, as she had done for centuries, at the very top of society's tree, in the person of the King's own *maîtresse déclarée*, her position openly acknowledged and according her vast privilege and influence. A wealthy wife who bore another man's child might be disgraced—there was the question of property inheritance, after all—but a husband who fathered children outside marriage could rest comfortably by his ancestral fireside, and recognize them or not, as he pleased.

Françoise had made it clear that the restrained behaviour of her married life was not "for love of God," but "for love of my own reputation." It was part of a plan, and the plan had served its purpose: she had made her roundabout way into the charmed circle of good society, and she now had the means to stay there. False perfection was no longer required; she was accepted on her own attractive and solvent terms. Consequently, she could at last afford to take a risk.

"A widow is a most dangerous thing. She knows very well how a woman can please a man, and consequently she presents a great temptation to them." Thus François de Sales, bishop and soon a saint, whose practical guidance Françoise would one day seek—though not yet. Rumour would later have it that in this first year of her widowhood, she began a dalliance of some kind with her friend and mentor, the fifty-year-old maréchal d'Albret, and it is not impossible. But it is much more likely that the mutual attraction which had been felt for some years already between herself and the marquis de Villarceaux, "one of the most dashing" men among all the King's retinue, now blossomed into a real love affair.

Villarceaux was in his early forties, dark and handsome, a fine sportsman, rich (thanks to his wife), and well placed at court. Having served his term as "captain of the King's pack of seventy hunting dogs for hare and fox," he was now lieutenant-captain of the King's light horse. His reputation as an unscrupulous lover of the fair sex preceded him everywhere, aided by his own fluid pen, which turned out reams of "private" pages detailing his many conquests—many of which made an inevitable way into other than private hands. Villarceaux was not above outright seduction, and had even been known to resume his pursuit of a deflowered demoiselle once she had been safely married off to some unsuspecting old general or duke. Ninon had taken a revenge of sorts on behalf of all her deceived sisters: she had kept Villarceaux at bay for a twelvemonth or more, and then had obliged him to put down hard cash, with the result that by the time she had surrendered to him at last, he was madly in love with her.

"Three months in love with the same woman would be an eternity to me," Villarceaux had written to a gentleman friend, stealing a well-known phrase from Ninon herself, but this bravado notwithstanding, he had remained devoted to her, to her periodic annoyance, for six or seven years. No doubt the son they had had together ensured an ongoing bond between them, though Ninon had at first not wanted this encumbrance to her profession: it was Villarceaux who had persuaded her to have the child rather than risk her life with the same abortifacients that had killed another celebrated courtesan only months before. This suggests that he was not absolutely heartless, but nonetheless, for a *débutante*, Villarceaux remained a dangerous man. To engage in galanterie with him now, Françoise must have been feeling very confident, or very much in love.

Although she was generally reticent about her personal feelings, it seems that she had taken Ninon into her confidence, or at least that Ninon had ferreted out the truth. There was even a rumour that Ninon herself had attempted to set things in motion between the two *innamorati*. The reliable Tallemant des Réaux recalled that "Madame Scarron went that spring [of 1661] to the country with Villarceaux and Ninon, whose apparent purpose was to corrupt her." It seems quite likely. Despite their son, Villarceaux had never been a "favourite" of Ninon's, but always one of her "payers," indicating that whatever the gentleman may have felt, the lady had never been in love with him herself. "Ninon wasn't at all concerned at what was happening between Monsieur de Villarceaux and Madame Scarron," wrote Ninon's close friend Antoine Bret, "even though he was still her lover, and that sort of thing would normally end a friendship between two women. They were both at fault with regard to her, but she forgave them both. She put her friend's fears at rest and reassured the marquis, too. She was content to be their confidante, and she certainly felt no shame in taking on that role."

Ninon was now forty-five, Françoise already twenty-five and still, most probably, a virgin. Ninon may well have thought it high time to take the girl in hand before the bloom was off the rose: no one was going to be sighing after a forty-year-old ingénue; she herself had lost her virginity at fifteen, and after all, no woman could live without love, whether or not she charged for it. Like Françoise, Ninon had known years of hardship; indeed, her father, like Françoise's, had been convicted of murder—in his case, that of a rival lover of his own married mistress—and had been exiled from Paris, leaving his fifteen-year-old daughter to fend largely for herself. Thence, making good use of her wit and charm and of the unusually liberal education which her father had provided for her, Ninon had earned her way to her present prosperity; in recent years she had even grown respectable. Perhaps, at this point, she was envisaging a *vie de courtesane* for her young friend, who certainly possessed all the natural requirements of beauty and manner. But for the moment, discretion was all. "A woman's virtue is nothing more than the art of appearing virtuous," Ninon had pronounced in the convent at Lagny. And since her release, she had kept rather more to herself, still receiving her gentlemen, but without any public show. In Paris, as always, there were simply too many eyes and ears, so she and Villarceaux packed the young widow into a carriage and set off for the privacy of the country.

They called a halt in Rueil-en-Vexin, some ten miles outside the city, at the château of their friend Charles de Valliquierville, a wealthy old frondeur now devoting all his time to the pursuit of the fashionable occult sciences. Though his château stood at a barely decent distance from Madame de Villarceaux's own, it was here that Ninon and Villarceaux had arranged so many of their own trysts during the preceding years. Now they had returned, bringing with them a young lamb, or rather not so young, as an overdue sacrifice on the altar of illicit love.

It seems that the lamb had both priest and priestess, and that Ninon may even have remained with the lovers to oversee Françoise's deflowering. Whatever the case, for a time the three were regarded as an inseparable society trio, and by some even as a ménage à trois. "Don't the three of you make love together? Weren't you yourself the first to initiate her? Didn't you arrange things between her and Villarceaux?" So Ninon was questioned by her good friend Charles de Saint-Évremond, no angel himself, now exiled in England for having poked fun at the recent royal marriage. Ninon declined to answer, but she did confirm to Saint-Évremond that "I often let Villarceaux and her use my yellow room," adding disingenuously, "Of course I can't give you any details about what went on. I didn't see anything with my own eyes."

Two others who may have chosen a tactical blindness at this point were the marquis and marquise de Montchevreuil, friends of

Françoise's for some years already and, in fact, Villarceaux's cousins. Like Charles de Valliquierville, they had a house in the Vexin country-side, indeed only a mile or two away, and the nearness of the two houses allowed the love affair to blossom further. In moral terms, the Montchevreuils had a solid reputation—it was Madame de Mont-chevreuil whom Scarron had accused ironically of "having her way with" Françoise—but they were, insofar as château proprietors can be, "as poor as church mice." If they were aware of the relationship be-tween Villarceaux and Françoise, it is probably this comparative poverty, and the fact that their own children were too young to be aware of things, which persuaded them to keep their cousin's mistress under their roof; certainly it was said that Villarceaux helped them fi-nancially during this summer. Whatever the Montchevreuils' reason-ing, Françoise was happy enough to pack up her belongings at the Ursuline convent and install herself with them, and in so doing, she es-tablished one of the firmest friendships of her life.

"Montchevreuil was a very good fellow, modest, decent, but really dense. His wife . . . was tall, skinny and sallow, with a stupid laugh and ghastly long teeth, ridiculously pious and affected. Give her a wand and she'd have been the perfect wicked witch." It is true that no one claimed the marquise was a beauty, nor the marquis a wit or a scholar; he was rather a steady and capable man, perhaps reminding Françoise of her Uncle Benjamin. It is also true that the marquise had a reputa-tion for extreme piety, which at times became too much for her less zealous companions. "She would start talking about vespers two hours in advance. She was worried that her husband and Madame Scarron wouldn't go." She was right to worry: the pair were not above staying behind, on impious principle, playing cards conspicuously in the drawing-room.

All the same, a "ridiculously affected" woman is not likely to have appealed to Françoise, whose preference was always for a straight-forward manner. And it had been the delightful Marie-Madeleine de Fouquet, wife of the King's Surintendant des Finances, who had intro-duced her to Madame de Montchevreuil in the first place: Madame de

Fouquet would certainly have had no need to befriend an impoverished minor aristocrat had she not had some good personal qualities to
recommend her. "There is nothing so fine as a sincere heart," the chevalier de Méré insisted. "It is the foundation of wisdom"—and in this case,
no doubt, the foundation of friendship, too. If not a couple to sparkle in
salon circles, the Montchevreuils proved good friends to Françoise, and
she in her turn was to repay them manyfold, in later life rather grandly,
but for the moment in the simplest ways, as she herself related:

> There's no greater pleasure than obliging others . . . My good
> friend Madame de Montchevreuil was constantly ill or confined
> to bed. And since I was perfectly well I took charge of her house-
> hold. I did all the accounts and whatever needed doing. One day
> I sold a calf for her . . . It was a lot of trouble and I got very dirty
> doing it . . . I had the children with me all the time, one of them
> learning to read, another one learning the catechism . . . The lit-
> tlest girl was still a baby; her hips were not quite straight, and
> there was a particular way of swaddling her that only I could
> manage. She had to be changed often; they used to come to me
> even when we had visitors and whisper to me that the baby
> needed changing, and I would excuse myself and go and do it,
> then return to the visitors . . . But there you are, that's what you
> do when you want to be loved.

"The pleasure of doing good, in my opinion, is the purest and noblest
pleasure of all." This, too, she had learned from the chevalier. But all
the same, Françoise's first thought, of obliging others, rings somehow
less true here than her last, of wanting to be loved.

The affair with Villarceaux did not outlast the summer. Perhaps the
gentleman found that three months in love with the same woman was,
as he had boasted, eternity enough; perhaps the lady was humiliated
by whispering and knowing glances where once she had encountered
respect. "No one has ever established a good reputation by enjoying
herself," she later sighed. "A good reputation is a wonderful thing to

have, but it costs a great deal. The first sacrifice it demands is pleasure. And what I wanted more than anything was a good reputation, to be respected: that was my personal idol."

For a woman, a good reputation meant, far above all else, a reputation for virtue, specifically sexual virtue. "A debauched girl has no more claim to respectability than a corpse has to the rights of living men," growled the moralist François de Grenaille. Ninon de Lenclos was thoughtful and generous and clever and amusing, but she had slept with a lot of men, and there were many, many houses where, in consequence, she could never be openly admitted. Françoise had been, to all appearances, a faithful wife for eight years, and she had been widely praised for it, particularly in the circumstances of a marriage bereft of physical love. Marriage in itself had given her some status, but it was her own stubborn virtue, in the face of constant temptation, which had wrapped itself around the penniless prisoner's daughter in her too-short skirt, and hoisted her up onto her pedestal. The affair with Villarceaux had threatened to topple her, until she made up her mind not to fall.

Whether she or he decided to end the affair is unknown. If the decision was his, the pain of rejection may have hardened Françoise's resolve; if hers, the death of Uncle Benjamin during that summer of love in 1661 may have been the first occasion to give her pause. "You were my father, really," she had written to him only months before. Father or not, the good Huguenot countryman, not to mention his God's-law-abiding wife, would have been appalled to learn of their niece's liaison with Villarceaux. In any event, as Françoise herself said, "I wasn't seeking the esteem of anyone in particular; I wanted everyone to think well of me." If other lovers succeeded Villarceaux, nothing is known of them; no contemporary diarist or gossip lets drop any name; no sighing admirer hints of being "treated kindly." Françoise had too much pride, the scarred interior pride that follows scorching humiliation, to risk her reputation again. From now on, every other man, and every other need of her own, would serve only as an offering to her "personal idol," her own god of respect.

François's friend Bonne de Pons, "a bit mad" but "as beautiful as the day," had narrowly missed becoming the King's mistress, and she was quite annoyed about it. In 1661, at the age of sixteen, she had been taken to court with the wine-loving maréchale d'Albret, and while there had engaged the interest of the twenty-three-year-old King, one year married and already desperately disenamoured of his podgy Spanish wife. The maréchale's friends, "perhaps pushed by the maréchal," persuaded her to pack her niece swiftly off home before anything untoward could happen, and so, on the pretext of an illness on the part of the maréchal, she went. Bonne's dismay was great when she found her uncle-cousin d'Albret in perfect health, but he managed to console her, "or so the gossips say," by taking her as his own mistress instead.

By the time she had managed a return to court in the mid-1660s, Bonne's hopeful bark had sailed: the King had already chosen a mistress, Louise de la Vallière, another sixteen-year-old virgin, sweet, shy, and attractive despite a small bust, uneven teeth, and a slight limp, these last to Bonne's sure disgust. Both the King and Louise had at first been so uncertain of each other's feelings, and of their own literary skill, that each had turned to the marquis de Dangeau, a mutual friend at court, for help with the requisite poetic billets-doux, with the result that the obliging marquis had spent months on end writing love letters to himself before the two lovers could proceed.

Despite the remonstrations of his pious mother and five public sermons from the thundering Dr. Jacques-Bénigne Bossuet, his official "counsellor and preacher," the King had maintained Louise in her position for more than six years, during which time she had borne him three children, of whom one daughter had survived. While retaining her semi-official place as maîtresse déclarée, Louise herself had not survived long as the exclusive recipient of Louis's affections. "The King . . . is only too susceptible to illicit passions which have been so much talked about that I shall have to make some mention of them here," the diplomat Spanheim recorded in his memoirs. "He has had fleeting passions for various lovely ladies at court . . ." "During all these affairs," continued the duc de Saint-Simon, "the King never stopped going to bed with the Queen, often late, but without fail, so much so that to make himself more comfortable, he spent the after-dinner hours between two sheets with his mistresses."

Every night, as he came to the Queen's bedroom to say good night, as he did religiously, and only religiously, the King encountered, sitting with his wife, the most gorgeous of her six ladies-in-waiting, Françoise's friend from the d'Albrets' salon, Athénaïs de Montespan. She had won her coveted position in 1663, with the aid of the King's brother, Philippe d'Orléans, an extravagant cross-dresser known at court simply as "Monsieur." As lady-in-waiting to Queen Marie-Thérèse, Athénaïs had gained a certain prestige and also a stipend of her own, but neither of these had been enough to satisfy her own sense of grandeur, or her need for money.

Though her Mortemart family had been noble for centuries, it was no longer rich, and in Monsieur de Montespan, Athénaïs had married, or had been married off to, a marquis of modest means. Though a young man and from a suitably ancient line, his discouragingly rustic Gascon temperament, and more especially his Jansenist connections, had precluded his advancement and consequent enrichment at court.

The Jansenists were a rather grim sect within the French Catholic Church—the great Blaise Pascal, a firm adherent, had almost abandoned his study of mathematics to escape the sinful pleasure he derived from it—but more importantly, their unorthodox views on theological questions had left them politically suspect: in the civic life of the state, interwoven as it was with religious customs and requirements, no one could be certain where their loyalties lay. Stepping beyond the bounds of orthodox Catholic doctrine, the Jansenists believed that man could not attain salvation by any effort of his own, but only by the grace of God, unasked for and unmerited, as the sympathetic John Milton wrote at this very time:

> *Man shall not quite be lost, but saved who will;*
> *Yet not of will in him, but grace in me*
> *Freely voutsafed.*

The Jansenists further held that those who were to be saved by God's grace had been predestined for salvation since their birth, indeed since the creation of the world, so undermining the whole vast edifice of Catholic teaching, based as it was on the bargain of good behaviour in this world against salvation in the next.

The Jansenists' denial of this ultimate quid pro quo made them political radicals, too, for all the layers of France's social pyramid were effectively justified by the Church's authority, with *le petit peuple* at the base, the divinely appointed King at the pinnacle, and everyone else ranged accordingly in between. The Jansenist doctrine of predestination raised the daring, indeed outrageous idea that the grubby-faced peasant might in fact be one of God's elect, while his landlord, or his bishop, or even his king, might unwittingly be already doomed to everlasting hellfire. It was altogether too dangerous. Jansenist schools and convents were subject to interference, closure, and even destruction, but the sect was robust, and it persisted. The most that could be done by Church and court was to block the professional advancement of those with Jansenist tendencies, thus denying them money, influence, and political power.

This was the stone wall which Athénaïs's husband had confronted. Still only in his twenties and with his fortune yet to make, the marquis de Montespan had consequently decided to take the only real option open to him, that of purchasing a commission in the army. Since he had gambled away what little cash had been at his disposal, Athénaïs had herself been obliged to sell her best diamond earrings in order to help him on his way. But, news of his unimpressive martial exploits arriving at her door, she decided now, if indeed she had not done so before, to abandon her husband and make a career for herself as mistress to the King. To this end, melding détente with subversion, she began to inveigle herself into the Queen's good graces, making sure to be the last to attend her each night as she awaited the King's arrival from the apartments of his fading violet, Louise de la Vallière.

The King saw through Athénaïs at once, and even made fun of her attempts. "She's desperate to make me fall in love with her," he said to Louise, and they laughed together at all her little tricks. The Queen suspected nothing. "She was fond of Madame de Montespan; she viewed her as a good woman devoted to her duties and to her husband. Imagine her dismay . . ." Louise, though no fool, fatally underestimated Athénaïs's determination and her charms, and in her naïvety, as the courtier Primi Visconti relates, actually brought about her own downfall: "She so much enjoyed Madame de Montespan's elegance and her witty turns of phrase that she couldn't be five minutes without her or without saying something nice about her to the King. This of course made the King curious to know more about *La Montespan*, and he quickly came to prefer her to her friend." In the end, the King would return from his day's hunting, go directly to Louise's apartments to take off his boots and change his clothes, "hardly saying hello to her," and then pass straight into Athénaïs's apartments, "and there he would remain all evening."

In May 1667, with Louise once more expecting, the King "expressed my affection" for her by declaring the little estate of Vaujours a duchy, bestowing on her the title of its duchess, "and I have recognized a daughter I had by her." Both Louise and Queen Marie-Thérèse understood this apparent promotion as the dismissal that it really was. Louise was instructed to leave Saint-Germain and return to Paris, and, as Primi Visconti remarked, "though La Vallière complained about this, she had no one to blame for it but herself."

The King had changed a good deal from the hesitant lover of half a dozen years before, relying on a courtier to write his love letters for him. In that same year of 1661, his prime minister Cardinal Mazarin had died, croakily bewailing his imminent separation from an embezzled fortune of thirty-five million livres. As Louis admitted, "Only then did it seem to me that I was King: born to be King." Though he had formally attained his majority at the age of thirteen, Mazarin and the Queen Mother together had continued their joint regency long beyond this time, effectively governing France for almost eighteen years.

The Cardinal's death had given twenty-two-year-old Louis a free ruling hand at last, and he had immediately asserted what he saw as an unequivocal personal authority. Perhaps recalling tales of his father

sending his regent grandmother Marie de' Medici off to her Loire valley château, he had swiftly banished his regent mother, Anne of Austria, to her own political exile. He had then announced his intention
to rule the country on his own, without a prime minister, an intention
"to which everyone swore absolute loyalty," as one of his courtiers
recorded, "and which no one believed he would be able to carry out."

Louis had more confidence in himself, as he made all too clear in his
Mémoires, written for the eventual guidance of the little dauphin.
"The ministers of kings should learn to moderate their ambition,"
Louis declared. "The higher they elevate themselves above their proper
sphere, the greater the danger that they will fall." Before long, surintendant Nicolas Fouquet, Mazarin's expected successor as prime minister, had been arrested on trumped-up charges of corruption, and
escorted, by the legendary musketeer d'Artagnan, to an effective
show-trial, where he was condemned to life imprisonment.

Though searches revealed an extraordinarily large number of letters from court ladies thanking him for the regular monies he had been
sending to them, Fouquet's only real crime was to have presented the
young King, unwittingly, with a challenge to his new sense of himself as the country's absolute ruler. A man of great power, Fouquet
was also deeply cultured and a noted patron of the arts—Françoise's
husband, Scarron, had been one of his many beneficiaries. His magnificent château of Vaux-le-Vicomte, thirty miles from Paris, had over-
flowed with every treasure that talent or influence could provide:
beautiful furniture, paintings and sculptures, rare manuscripts, even
the finest food, for his chef was the famous François Vatel, toast of
every dining table in the land (later to skewer himself in shame at the
late arrival of the oysters for a banquet chez the prince de Condé). To
embellish his château, Fouquet had employed the best of the very best:
architect Louis Le Vau, painter Charles Le Brun, and André Le Nôtre,
garden designer extraordinaire.

In August 1661, five months after Mazarin's death, Fouquet had
staged a fabulous fête at Vaux-le-Vicomte, and everyone at court, including the King, had attended. The gardens, the music, the lighting,
the banquets, and, not least, the *première* performance of Molière's

comedy *Les Fâcheux* (The Nuisances)—all the delights and splendours of the evening had sealed Louis's attitude, jealous and vindictive, towards his surintendant. Newly come into his own, the egocentric King had no intention of being upstaged, politically or socially, by anyone, least of all by one of his own ministers. "He had come to work with me as usual," Louis wrote to his mother soon after the fête, "and I chatted with him over one thing and another, pretending to look for various papers until, through the window of my room, I saw d'Artagnan in the château courtyard . . . I dismissed Fouquet, and he went out at just the moment that poor d'Artagnan stopped to greet Monsieur Le Tellier, so he missed him. He thought he'd been given a hint to get away, but he caught him in the square by the church . . ." Fouquet was condemned, his too-marvellous château was placed under sequestration, and his lovely young wife, Marie-Madeleine, Françoise's friend, swiftly disappeared from court and city circles.

Louis's determination to have no rivals is perhaps mitigated by his youth and the novelty of power to him, though it does suggest a meanness of spirit not found in any truly great prince. Less excusable is the behaviour of the *intendant des finances* Jean-Baptiste Colbert, whose unscrupulous ambition had been a driving force behind his superior's fall from grace. Colbert was "brilliant," though not altogether "amiable," which should have given Louis pause for thought. Taking advantage of the King's inexperience, forty-two-year-old Colbert had been able to dazzle him with an array of fabricated accounts, supposedly proving malfeasance on Fouquet's part. "I left him to investigate the things I hadn't leisure to look into fully," Louis wrote, naïvely. Colbert had been Mazarin's foremost protégé, and despite Louis's determination to rule alone as an absolute monarch, there is no doubt that, with Mazarin dead and Fouquet condemned to life imprisonment, Colbert quickly became prime minister in all but name.

From the very beginning of Louis's "personal reign" in this year of 1661, Colbert made himself indispensable to the King, and from this followed a swift accrual of power over the finances of the kingdom, its trade, its law and administration, to a large extent its armed forces, and, not least, the royal household, arbiter par excellence of the nation's influence and wealth. Never presenting himself as more than the King's loyal servant, within a handful of years Colbert had become, in effect, the real ruler of France. Louis, young, inexperienced, superbly proud, sensed the truth uneasily: "Colbert had his own interests at stake," wrote the abbé de Choisy. "He wanted Fouquet's place, and he did whatever he could to discredit him among all the men of business." "Colbert's ferociously active on the King's behalf," added Primi Visconti. "You'd think the treasury was his personal property . . . Once he told the King off about his own spending."

In that same month of May 1667, having demoted Louise de la Vallière from mistress to duchess, the King of France sent an unfriendly letter to his mother-in-law, the recently widowed Regent Queen of Spain. He informed her that, with her husband dead and with full payment of her daughter's dowry still outstanding, parts of the Spanish Netherlands had now been "devoluted" to Marie-Thérèse—effectively, to himself. Without waiting for a reply, he then declared the peace between France and Spain, the eight-year-old Peace of the Pyrenees, sealed by his own marriage, to be at an end.

Louis's supporters portrayed this as necessary to keep France safe from invasion from the north via the Spanish Netherlands, but others saw it as his first step in a determined enterprise of national and personal aggrandizement. Diplomacy had its uses, but for Louis, as for most of his contemporaries, force of arms, under more or less any circumstances, was a legitimate assertion of political authority: in other words, might was right. Besides, as he recorded for the benefit of his little son, "When you act in contravention of a treaty, it isn't really contravening it, because no one's taken it literally. If I hadn't broken the Peace of the Pyrenees, I would have been negligent in my duty to the state: the Spanish would have been first to break it if I hadn't."

Thanks to his capable war ministers, Le Tellier and his son Louvois, and to Jean-Baptiste Colbert, now *contrôleur-général* (de facto prime minister), Louis currently had at his command a fully functioning Ministry of War, "perhaps the first genuine one in any European state," and a newly expanded army of 80,000 men. A fortnight after his letter to the Queen of Spain, they were marched off to Flanders under the leadership of the veteran Maréchal Turenne, friend of Scarron in the old yellow salon days, to wage their "War of Devolution." With the towns of the Spanish Netherlands weakly defended, and the Spanish themselves, with their empire in terminal decline, unable to pay for reinforcements, the French troops encountered so little resistance that they laughingly dubbed the campaign *la promenade militaire*.

The King himself had gone along for the stroll, as had Marie-Thérèse and Athénaïs. Though *la belle* Montespan had set off on the journey as the Queen's lady-in-waiting, she returned to court in the middle of August with a higher, if secret, honour: though the King retained a place in his heart for his former maîtresse déclarée, by now Athénaïs had definitely pushed Louise into second place. Surprisingly, the normally bashful Louise had declined to shrink away into oblivion, returning from Paris to Saint-Germain without waiting for Louis's permission. "Madame de la Vallière is quite reestablished at court," Madame de Sévigné reported to her daughter in Provence. "The King received her with tears of joy, and Madame de Montespan received her with tears . . . guess why? *One* has held tender conversations with each of them. It's all very difficult to understand. We must hold our tongues."

In October 1667, the half-wanted Louise gave birth to a half-wanted son. Pathetically, she named him Louis, and in recognition, his father declared him comte de Vermandois. Lawyers and parlementary counsellors began to dig and delve to construct a legal precedent, and in February 1669 the little boy was legitimized. In November of the same year, at the age of just two years, he was named Admiral of France—with contrôleur-général Colbert, now Secretary of State for the Navy as well, assigned to assist him temporarily in his duties.

EIGHT

City of Light

Françoise, meanwhile, had been enjoying what she herself declared to be the happiest time of her life. Apart from day trips into the surrounding forests and summer sojourns in the country, she had spent these years in Paris, where she had rented a house in the rue des Trois-Pavillons in her familiar quarter of the Marais. This had ensured an easy continuation of her social life, with Ninon, the d'Albrets, Madeleine de Scudéry, the duchesse de Richelieu, and Madame de Sévigné all her neighbours. Though her house was small, she lived comfortably there with a handful of servants, including her lady's maid, Nanon Balbien, a capable and trusted girl who was to remain with her all her life.

Françoise was now thirty-three years old, still dark-haired and lovely, an established and popular figure in the brightest Paris circles. After the sartorial blooming of her early widowhood, she had settled into a quiet elegance of dress, her preferred colours a discreet green or blue, and her chosen luxuries characteristically tasteful. She wore particularly beautiful linen, always perfectly matched and snow-white, a clear mark of social standing in a time of dirty streets and rudimentary laundering. Her shoes were of the best quality, and her gowns of fine muslin, "a very fashionable fabric at that time for persons of middling fortune." At home, she burned wax candles rather than the cheaper and less fragrant tallow, "and that wasn't very common in those days." With these indulgences, and her usual "good big fire," and toys for the Montchevreuil children, and a modest charity, she had still something left at the end of each year from the two thousand livres of her royal pension.

In 1666 or thereabouts, around the age of thirty-one, she had taken a personal "confessor," according to the custom of the Catholic nobility and gentry. She chose the abbé François Gobelin, a former soldier and Sorbonne doctor of theology, apparently "highly esteemed," but all the same a limited man, more of a stickler for pious detail than a leading light of intellect or spirituality. Françoise's engaging of Père Gobelin may suggest a twitch of devout feeling on her part, but in the main he seems to have fulfilled a social obligation for her, without needing to be taken too seriously on the religious front. Certainly his steady advice, sounding away on page or in person, did nothing to change her behaviour where she had not already decided to change it herself. Throughout their relationship, which was to last a quarter of a century, it was Françoise, not the reverend père, who was to keep the upper hand.

In these early days at the rue des Trois-Pavillons, he had attempted to persuade his "appetizing little Christian" to adopt a less tempting attire. Françoise was not an elaborate or coquettish dresser in the way of most women of her circle, but her beauty and a natural sense of style ensured her attractiveness, whatever she wore. She seldom went décolletée, except on days of exceptional heat: "Why, you have a really beautiful bust," exclaimed the surprised duchesse de Richelieu on just such a summer's day. "You've always covered it up so very carefully, I'd always assumed there must have been something wrong with it." Père Gobelin complained of the luxuriance of her gowns. "But, monsieur," she protested, "I always wear the most ordinary fabrics." "Perhaps," he replied, "but, my dear lady, when you kneel down, there's such a vast expanse of gown at my feet, spreading out so very gracefully, I really have to say it's excessive." But Françoise's fashionable muslin gowns became no less luxurious.

Having failed where her dress was concerned, Père Gobelin had then attempted to change her social behaviour. Observing how entertaining she was, and how much she enjoyed the attention this brought her, the abbé, himself no doubt a master of the art, instructed her "to try to bore everyone" instead. Françoise responded wickedly by adopting a complete silence when in company, restraining herself so determinedly that "it quite turned her off piety." So little did Père Gobelin succeed that "I've heard her say that if people hadn't been likely to talk about it, she wouldn't have bothered even going to mass on a Sunday."

She is not likely to have been much prompted towards piety by the second priestly presence in her Marais life, the eccentric abbé Jacques Testu. Lanky, garrulous, given to tipping jugs of water over his head to clarify his thinking, the forty-year-old abbé was a notorious womanizer—and an optimist, placing his hopes of a bishopric on Ninon's conversion from courtesan to Carmelite. "The diocese would have to be full of young women, of course," Ninon remarked laconically. Abbé Testu was aghast at the strictures being placed on Françoise by the earnest Père Gobelin, and he turned up at her house to protest. "Really, Madame," he told her, "you're dealing with a fanatic." But she kept Père Gobelin on; at base he was a good man, and his limitations, paradoxically, were an advantage: she could follow his advice or ignore it, according to her mood. In consequence, her attempts at a more devout life were half-hearted and short-lived, and she spent her days, not at church or in private prayer, but dining in congenial company, or driving about in the fashionable quarters, or going to plays and operas in "excessive" muslin gowns.

For most people in Paris, these years of the 1660s were a golden time, despite their harsh beginning. A bad harvest in 1661 was soon forgotten in a cornucopia of cheap bread for the poor and new entertainments for those with money to spare. The city itself was changing, building and regulating its way to a confident, modern livability.

In his capacity as surintendant of the King's Buildings—one of his many lucrative posts—Colbert had initiated a massive programme of royal and public construction. The huge old medieval gates of Paris, and its ancient walls, already crumbling at the time of Françoise's arrival fifteen years before, had finally been demolished to make way for wide new streets and even more houses. New churches and, for the rich, grand *hôtels particuliers*, city versions of their country châteaux, were replacing the sombre dwellings of an earlier age—the new high gateways, allowing the family coach to drive in directly from the street, were an especially prized contemporary feature. With some twenty-two million people, France could already boast the largest population of any country in Europe; now, with an estimated 600,000 inhabitants, France's capital had become Europe's largest city.

In 1666, the King himself went for a walk in the streets of Paris to observe the city at first hand, and subsequently ordered a bevy of swans to be brought from abroad to grace the river Seine—anyone caught trying to steal their eggs was to be fined three hundred livres. Trudging the streets in the King's wake, Colbert and his protégé, Gabriel Nicolas de La Reynie, reached a different decision, equally aesthetic in its practical way, about beautifying their burgeoning city: they instituted a set of tough regulations to clean it up.

Residents and business proprietors found themselves liable to a new "mud tax," payable twice yearly on fixed days; those failing to pay saw their furniture seized by the city bailiffs the very next day. The new post of rubbish collector was added to the city payroll, and Parisians were obliged to make their own pragmatic contribution to public cleanliness: apart from the mud tax and a fine, newly instigated, should they be caught throwing anything out of their windows into the street, they were now required to appear on their doorsteps "every morning at seven o'clock in summer and at eight o'clock in winter, carrying out their household refuse as the church bells ring; and all the mud and dirt on the pavement in front of their houses is to be swept into a pile at the end of the building for official collection"—by the new rubbish men, who were themselves fined if they failed to do the job properly.

A new regulation was applied to the city watchmen, whose carts full of human excrement were thenceforth required to be closed when in motion—with the result that the streets "are now so clean, the horses are almost slipping on them." A new police force, the first of its kind in Europe, was formed to combat crime and vice: police archers rounded up the destitute and locked them away in workhouses and convents; "bohemians and gypsies" were sentenced to the galleys; and, apparently crucially, students were confined to colleges at all but a handful of specified hours. In an attempt to prevent murders and thefts, even the wearing of masks was forbidden, with a few fashionable ladies, occasionally including Françoise, continuing to defy the new law.

Within a handful of years, Paris had shaken off its thick medieval crust of filth and disorder, and was setting the tone in modernism and elegance for the whole of Europe. There was even street lighting. In other French towns, those who ventured out in the dark were obliged to rely on flickering hand-held lanterns, or the candlelight from an occasional tavern, or that most ancient help of travellers by night, the moon. But in Paris, with a new "light tax" to complement the mud tax, street lanterns burned until late into the night, so that "up till two or three in the morning, it's almost as light as day." The King had a medal struck with the device *Securitas et Nitor* (Safety and Light), and Paris, *la ville lumière*, was born.

Though the new regulations had certainly cleaned things up, they had not really succeeded in dampening anything down. Tinkers and fruit-sellers still thronged the streets with trays of half-legal goods for sale. Displaced communities of beggars and thieves had swiftly regrouped elsewhere. Cabarets and gambling dens obeyed the rules when the police were about, and otherwise lustily ignored them. In the beautiful gardens of the Tuileries palace, newly opened to any "decently dressed" member of the public, prostitutes wandered freely about, offering French lessons to foreigners, though "they're much more skilled in love than in grammar," as one Italian noted, unnecessarily, in a journal of his visit to Paris in the middle of the decade.

If the city's hardy public life had carried on through its own perennial strength, its more delicate cultural and intellectual flowers had been reinvigorated from above by a brisk shower of royal attention and money. The liberal arts, Louis declared, "are the finest ornaments of the State," and he vowed, "It is the King's mission to revive them." A large pot of gold was made available to just that end, prompting a wave of flowery verses comparing Louis to that most celebrated of all patrons of the arts, the Roman emperor Augustus.

Though some prominent individuals, notably Fouquet, had continued to prop things up during the lean years of the Fronde, there had been no steady royal patronage since the death of the cultured Cardinal Richelieu twenty years before, and the newly available money created terrific excitement among the city's artists and scholars, each one hoping to see his name on the precious *liste* of recipients-to-be. Colbert commissioned Fouquet's decorator, Charles Le Brun, to choose the happy painters and sculptors. Among the writers, Molière, the King's favourite playwright, was one of the first to be named; he gave his thanks in typically flippant verse, berating his sleepy artistic muse for being still in bed at six o'clock in the morning:

> *My lazy Muse, I'm scandalized*
> *To see you still in bed:*
> *Get up! And to the Louvre at once*
> *To bow your grateful head.*

Louis may have viewed the revival of the arts as "the King's mission," but as always, the work of carrying it out was left to contrôleur-général Colbert, his "labouring ox." Happily, Colbert, who claimed to have Scottish ancestry, was more than equal to the task. "I am so constitutionally inclined to work," he had written to Cardinal Mazarin, "that I cannot bear the very thought of idleness, or even of moderate work."

It was just as well for the artists and scholars who benefited from the new, strategically named *gratuités*. Unlike pensions, accorded until further notice and generally for life, the gratuités for these "trumpets for the King's virtues" had to be renewed annually: beneficiaries proving insufficiently enthusiastic about the King's character or martial exploits or dancing were liable to find their names scratched from the list, with countless dramatically unbalanced plays and factually dubious histories the result. But if Louis regarded the liberal arts as "ornaments of the State," the farsighted Colbert recognized them as among its most vital structural supports, less a reflection of France's grandeur than a crucial aspect of its creation and maintenance. At home and abroad, propaganda—written, painted, sculpted, sung—was essential for the reign of unparalleled glory that he was determined to build for his egocentric young master.

There were no objections from Louis himself. Delighting in the details of Colbert's strategy—the ballets and operas, the amusing Molière plays, the grand entertainments, the military campaigns and building projects—he lacked the capacity to understand the plan as a whole, and to redirect it as circumstances changed. A natural authoritarian, his self-importance inflated by years of deference and flattery, intelligent but never deeply thoughtful, and woefully lacking in education owing to his war-disrupted childhood, Louis understood only those parts of Colbert's plan that accorded with his personal tastes. Unable to analyze, he criticized instinctively; unable to brook restraint, he thrust aside whatever stood in his way. Before the decade was out, Louis had come to view anything that he wanted himself as conducive to *la gloire de la France*, and to justify it accordingly.

For the moment, what he wanted was new plays and operas, and the fruit of his desires enriched the people of Paris, both the "decently dressed" and the greater body of the (literally) unwashed. In the 1660s, the Parisian theatre was still a place where people of every class rubbed shoulders. Attendance at a play was often more like a political meeting than an opportunity to enjoy a comedy or drama. Actors were constantly heckled, whether for the characters they played onstage or for their personal behaviour offstage. Opposing groups were hired to whistle at them, or to boo or applaud; sometimes fights broke out. The strutting young lackeys of the rich were more troublesome than anyone else; some theatres tried to bar their entry. Despite it all, the 1660s was a wonderful period for the playwrights of Paris: Racine, still in his twenties, wrote the first four of his great tragedies; Molière wrote twenty-one comedies; even middle-aged Corneille, now past his prime in art as in life, produced ten new plays; and dozens of lesser men churned out hundreds of lesser works which have since drifted back into the wings.

It was an even livelier time for the opera, already dominated by the King's temperamental favourite, Giovanni Battista Lulli, recently naturalized as Jean-Baptiste Lully. Dancer and impresario as much as composer, Lully was ruthlessly ambitious in all three fields; what he failed to achieve by talent and industry he managed by tantrums and intrigue. Now in his thirties, he was busy gestating a plan to strangle the theatre of his supposed friend and collaborator, Molière, by denying him the music and ballet which were as much a part of contemporary plays as they were of the opera. The King, besotted by Lully's talent and intimidated by his rages, declined to involve himself in this battle of the artistic giants, and so ensured Lully's eventual victory.

Lully might have won in any case, since by the middle of the decade the Paris public had already begun to prefer the opera to the theatre. Satirical moralist Jean de La Bruyère explained the trend succinctly: "It's the machinery," he said. "Plays don't need chariots and things flying about, and the opera does. Quite simply, the audience loves a spectacle." For one English visitor, all the same, the spectacle was not consolation enough: during his evening at the Paris opera, he complained, he was obliged to endure "some gentlemen singing along from start to finish."

Louis's enthusiasms and Colbert's energies were revitalizing the court as well, with a series of increasingly lavish entertainments to delight the happy *invités* and to vaunt the young King's taste and splendour. In the midsummer of 1668, Françoise attended the latest of these, the most magnificent to date, given at Versailles, fifteen miles outside the city. As yet, this royal estate was no more than a charming country house with a few statues in a modest park. Louis had been considering demolishing it to make way for something grander, but, dissuaded by Colbert, he had abandoned the plan, so that when Françoise and her friends drove up to the marble courtyard on that June evening of 1668, they saw before them a near-perfect royal *maison de plaisance*.

If they had hopes for its survival, the scale of the evening's entertainment might have given them pause for thought. The King had dubbed it *le Grand Divertissement*, and it was to surpass anything that Fouquet at Vaux-le-Vicomte or any prince anywhere else had ever done before. The fête was ostensibly a celebration of the treaty of Aix-la-Chapelle, which had put an end to France's promenade militaire, the War of Devolution, "a magnificent confirmation of the rights of the Queen," but for Louis it served, too, to boost his still private determination to dismember, in the longer term, the failing Spanish Empire.

Versailles being comparatively small, the number of guests had been limited to about 3,000, which apparently included "every person of quality, male and female, from Paris and the neighbouring provinces." Nine lavishly decorated dining-tables had been set up in the garden, but these were for selected ladies only, since it was to the ladies in general, if secretly only to their uncrowned queen, that the evening had been publicly dedicated. The exultant Athénaïs sat, with tactical modesty, at Table 4, in company with Françoise and Madeleine de Scudéry. The crowned Queen was naturally seated at the first table beside the King, but, despite her prominent place, she was, as always, outshone from all sides. What little grace Marie-Thérèse might have possessed had vanished in the seven months of a new pregnancy. Though she had borne four children since her marriage eight years before, only two had survived, the dauphin Louis, now aged seven, and his sister Marie-Thérèse, just one year old.

The King had gallantly intended that he himself should bear the entire cost of the evening's festivities, and to this end had "strictly forbidden every sort of ornament and gilding," as the chronicler Montigny recorded for the benefit of the next day's news-sheets. "But how can you regulate fashion?" he jotted rhetorically—"ornament and gilding" were, naturally, ubiquitous. Payment for the fête had in any case been left to Colbert, in his endlessly useful capacity as Superintendent of the King's Buildings. Versailles being a royal building, and Colbert being its Superintendent, it was up to him to keep the costs of the evening down, as well as to arrange all the various settings and sittings—not forgetting the fireworks. Of these, as Madeleine de Scudéry recalled, there were first a thousand little cannons firing off "in heroic harmony, if I may so put it," and then "a thousand things shooting from rotundas, fountains, parterres, bushes, and a hundred other places, and at last from the top of the water tower—so many brilliant stars, they could have dimmed the sun."

Louis may well have attained his hope of surpassing anything that had ever been done before, for the whole scene was utterly fantastical. The outdoor ballroom, octagon-shaped, illuminated by "an infinite number of chandeliers," was decorated with exotic orange trees and fountains spouting water "like a deluge of pearls." Along the garden paths towards it, statues of antique gods and heroes stood, "all coloured and lit up," at every crossing. Small though it was considered as yet, the park contained an amphitheatre large enough to seat all 3,000 guests, and facing this was a theatrical garden, constructed especially for the evening. Here the marvellous Molière and his troupe performed their new play, also constructed especially for the evening: *George Dandin, or The Confused Husband*. It is the tale of a rich peasant who makes a fool of himself by marrying a woman from a higher social class—terribly amusing for the "persons of quality" in the audience, and a reminder to the servants handing out refreshments not to think of getting above themselves. During the interval, the ballet scenes of a new Lully opera were performed, with the composer himself taking a prominent part in the dancing.

The King danced, too, not onstage, however, as he often did, but in the ballroom, accompanied by musicians perched on four little amphitheatres, "and you know he is the most graceful dancer in the world," said Madeleine de Scudéry, without undue flattery, since it was well known to be true. And, evidently feeling the need to make some mention of the other royal personage present, she added diplomatically, "As for the beauty of the Queen—well, you know about that already."

By the time Françoise stepped back into the carriage awaiting her in the marble courtyard, the dawn of a bright summer day was breaking.

It was not her own carriage, of course; as yet, a luxury of that scale remained beyond her pocket, and she had still to rely on the kindness of friends to ferry her about from place to place. The journey back to Paris took three hours or so on the new paved roads, ample time for her to reflect on the evening's pleasures, and on the distance she had travelled from her aunt's little château of Mursay.

NINE

Duty Calls

rançoise had not been back to Mursay since 1662, following the death of her beloved Aunt Louise. There she had reestablished her particular friendship with cousin Philippe, who had once taught her arithmetic at a table in the château kitchen. Philippe was now aged thirty-six; he had married soon after his mother's death, and he and his wife, Marie-Anne, had two little boys, Philippe, aged four, and Henri-Benjamin, still only a few months old. During her visit to Mursay, Philippe had given Françoise a number of d'Aubigné family documents supposedly proving her title of nobility, but now, in July 1668, she decided to rescind them in order to avoid a new tax specific to those of noble birth. It was a good indication of her current ambitions: protecting her financial position was evidently more important to her than taking a step up the social ladder. Provided she could continue to live in decent comfort in her own little Marais house in the rue des Trois-Pavillons, she was content to remain simply Madame Scarron—or rather, Madame d'Aubigné Scarron, as she was beginning to call herself, adding the lustre of her grandfather's still respected name to the more equivocal sound of "Scarron."

In August 1668, Queen Marie-Thérèse, to her delight, gave birth to her second son, Philippe, and in September, to her horror, Athénaïs realized that she herself was pregnant by the King. Though they had by now been lovers for more than a year, Athénaïs was so distraught by the realization that she went on a frantic diet in an attempt to conceal the truth: "She became thin and sallow, and so changed, she was almost unrecognizable." When the baby arrived, in the late spring of 1669, it was swiftly spirited away, so swiftly, indeed, that not even its sex is known for certain.

A royal *bâtard* was of course no novelty. Louise de la Vallière had borne the King children, too, but Louise had been unmarried; there was no Monsieur de la Vallière to lay legal claim to them or to complain of the King's adultery. Moreover, the King himself had recently taken an untactical public stand on the matter: in 1666, he—or rather, Colbert—had established a new council for the "Reformation of Justice," effectively the Paris police force, whose complex remit included "the fight against debauchery" and "the tracing of unfaithful wives." Unwisely, perhaps, Louis had installed at the head of the new council Colbert's protégé, the exceptionally diligent Gabriel Nicolas de La Reynie, whose energetic efforts in his new post had been receiving a great deal of public attention.

Matters were made worse a few months after the baby's birth with the unexpected arrival at Saint-Germain of Athénaïs's husband, the marquis de Montespan, back from his latest unsuccessful military campaign, this time against Algerian pirates. The marquis turned up at the palace in a large black carriage, with horns mounted on the top of it to emphasize his outraged state of cuckoldry. The King's relationship with Athénaïs had been suspected for some time—"Praise the Lord!" her father-in-law had declared. "Here is Fortune knocking on my door at last!"—but officially, at least, it was still secret. The marquis had the effrontery, or the courage, to lecture the King about adultery and to warn him of an eventual divine punishment. Athénaïs was terrified, and Louis outraged. Two days later, he made his response: he gave orders to have the marquis arrested, before setting off for a spell of autumn hunting at the Loire Valley château of Chambord.

While the marquis fumed in his Bastille cell, Athénaïs and Louis reconsidered. Neither had the least intention of putting an end to their affair. Athénaïs was clearly very fertile: she had presented the marquis himself with a son and a daughter before they had been even two years married; indeed, she was already pregnant again. Beyond that, such contraceptive methods as were known were certainly not of a kind to be contemplated by the King: he was not going to practise withdrawal; he was not going to wear any fish-skin condom; he was not going to allow his "fabulous" Athénaïs to risk her life with poisonous abortifacients. In short, there were bound to be more children. A longer-term solution must be found.

It was Athénaïs who found it, and she found it in Françoise. Living outside the court, reliable, refined in her manner but practically minded, and above all absolutely discreet, she seemed the perfect person to take charge of a secret household for unwanted royal children. Word had spread of her capable deputizing for Madame de Montchevreuil several years before, but it was probably "mad" and "beautiful" Bonne, like Athénaïs now a lady-in-waiting to the Queen, who suggested a potential saviour in their mutal friend, Madame Scarron. Bonne had married in 1666; she had a two-year-old daughter of her own, and Françoise had already proved a fond honorary aunt to this little girl. The offer was duly made.

Françoise hesitated. She was happy as she was, in her little house in the middle of the Marais. She did not want the intrigue and work and deception that a sensitive appointment of such a kind would involve. She sought advice from Père Gobelin, who advised her to verify one or two aspects of the matter. Athénaïs's two pregnancies, in the absence of her husband, had not passed unnoticed, but, despite the marquis's melodramatic appearance at Saint-Germain, it had not yet been finally accepted that her lover was the King himself. Louise de la Vallière's determination in refusing to leave the court had in one respect paid off: she had remained the official maîtresse déclarée, still appearing frequently in public with the King, still living in her apartments next to his own.

Louis's wish to keep the court guessing had met, it seemed, with some success. The father of Athénaïs's illegitimate children was rumoured to be one of his own favourites, the duc de Lauzun, *maréchal de camp* and *colonel-général* of dragoons. Just a few years older than Louis, Lauzun had served for many years as the King's unofficial comrade-in-love, arranger of his many brief affairs, provider of fast horses, and general guard outside bedroom doors. Lauzun came from Gascony, a region supposedly peopled by a rabble of puffed-up fast talkers, crafty, showy, and dishonourable, and though this may have been no more than a snobbish Parisian cliché, it was one that Lauzun's own rather wild behaviour had done nothing to contradict.

For Françoise, as Père Gobelin realized, a near connection with Lauzun could only be disadvantageous. Until now, she had maintained a reputation for probity; her very income from the court depended on it; her name should not be publicly linked with that of the disreputable duc. Père Gobelin's view was that if Lauzun was in fact the father of Athénaïs's children, Françoise should decline their charge. If the King was their father, on the other hand, the usual constraints did not apply; in this case, she should agree. After all, the King's children by Louise de la Vallière were in the official care of Madame Colbert, wife of the ubiquitous minister and certainly a lady of considerable standing. Françoise duly requested confirmation of the children's paternity, and it seems that a letter from Louis himself was soon in her hands, requesting her, or rather commanding her, in his usual *chevaleresque* way, to accept the charge. She did so at once.

Jupiter had a son . . ."

It was a dramatic, not to say melodramatic, beginning. Within the château of Saint-Germain, Athénaïs was nearing the end of her labour. Beneath the terraced windows, Françoise waited, masked and cloaked, in an unmarked coach. At the stroke of midnight the baby arrived, a healthy boy. No one dared take time to wrap the usual yards of swaddling cloth around him; he was simply covered in a piece of linen and tucked inside the cloak of the duc de Lauzun, who had sneaked in, some say, by way of the Queen's own bedroom. However he had come in, he very quickly got out again, and made his way down to the waiting coach, "scared to death" that the baby would begin to cry. Françoise took the little bundle from him and clambered in, and the coachman whipped his horses all the way back to Paris. By the time they reached the city, an early summer sun was rising on the last day of March 1670, and the first morning in the world for Athénaïs's little boy, Louis-Auguste de Bourbon.

"Dont abuse my secret," Madame de Sévigné wrote a fortnight later to her cousin, the comte de Bussy-Rabutin. "I wouldn't want the whole of Paris knowing it." But this secret was no more than a reconciliation between the two of them: she had refused to lend him money, and he had taken his revenge in an unflattering public portrait of her; now she was once more declaring her fondness of him. The normally well informed Madame de Sévigné had heard not a whisper about the new arrival at Saint-Germain.

Françoise's work had in fact begun some time before the baby's arrival. In anticipation of his needs, she and her maid Nanon had moved from the rue des Trois-Pavillons to a larger house in the rue des Tournelles; courtesan Ninon and confessor Gobelin thus became more or less their next-door neighbours. By now Françoise was also supervising the care of Athénaïs's first child to the King. He, or more probably she, had been tucked away with a Mademoiselle des Oeillets, one of Athénaïs's chambermaids and an obliging mistress of the King whenever the later stages of pregnancy left Athénaïs herself less inclined to love. Conveniently, Mademoiselle des Oeillets lived in the Marais, too, in the rue de l'Echelle, and here Françoise had been appearing daily to ensure the smooth running of this secretly important household.

Back at her own new house in the rue des Tournelles, she had been recruiting servants to assist with the care of the new baby. Most vital of all these was, of course, the wet-nurse, by preference a youngish mother in robust health, prepared to abandon her own newborn in order to feed a richer woman's baby. The medical men of the day regarding all bodily fluids as intermixing, sex and breast-feeding were held to be mutually exclusive, at least for those who could afford to separate them, lest the mother's milk become tainted with semen. With the priests declaring a husband's right to marital intercourse above all other family needs, well-to-do Catholic mothers were expected to avoid breast-feeding, and poorer Catholic mothers to avoid sex.

In *La Maison réglée*, a popular "good housekeeping" guide of the day, the former Versailles steward Monsieur Audiger listed the duties, as he saw them, of the contemporary wet-nurse:

> The duty of a wet-nurse is to take good care of the baby. She must keep his linen clean . . . and never let him cry at night or during the day, but must put him at once to the breast . . . To keep her milk, the nurse must take breakfast in the morning and have a little bite in the afternoon; she must take only a little wine with her meals, and must abstain from seeing her husband. And she must be constantly cheerful and lively and in good humour, and sing and laugh all the time to amuse and distract the baby . . . The swaddling mustn't be too loose or too tight, and the nurse must take care that the pins don't prick him . . . She may have a servant to rock the baby . . .

Madame de Sévigné, herself the mother of two children, was more succinct in her requirements, stating simply that "a wet-nurse must be able to produce milk like a cow." Françoise would have known what to expect, in any case. She had had plenty of practice caring for babies at the home of the Montchevreuils. After meeting with several potential nurses, she chose the capable but, as it turned out, rather greedy Madame Barri, at a generous fixed wage, "and other little sums, very frequently."

Françoise's charge increased almost immediately. In order to allay suspicion of the baby boy's identity, she decided to take in two other children with him: the first, two-year-old Toscan, is believed to have been an illegitimate son of her brother Charles, apparently deposited at the rue des Tournelles in a picnic basket—with Athénaïs's help, the undeserving Charles had been given an infantry commission, and had readily taken to at least one traditional aspect of seventeenth-century soldiering.

The second child whom Françoise asked for was Bonne's little Louise, "and Madame d'Heudicourt gave her the child without any trouble, since they were good friends, and she knew how fond she was of children." There was no particular hard-heartedness in Bonne's handing over of her two-year-old daughter. As a lady-in-waiting to the Queen, she would certainly not have been looking after the child herself; Louise would have been in the care of a nurse, very likely hardly seeing her mother at all. In 1671, cousin Philippe in Mursay welcomed a daughter of his own into the world. A child of the Huguenot country gentry, Marthe-Marguerite was not put out to nurse, nor, as yet, did Françoise ask for her, but in due course this little girl, too, was to find her way into her care.

Françoise's friendship with Bonne de Pons, now la marquise d'Heudicourt, had so far been most advantageous: it had probably brought her the position of governess itself, and also, in little Louise, a good means of keeping it secret. Bonne was a good friend and reliably amusing company, but there was a streak of mischief in her which led her to frequent indiscretions and, now and then, to serious troublemaking. Since her marriage to the marquis d'Heudicourt, the King's "Master of the Wolf-hunt," she had been known as "the big she-wolf," suggesting that her legendarily easy virtue contained something of the predatory, too. And early in 1671, two years after Françoise had taken on her charge as governess, Bonne let slip her never more than flimsy social guard.

She had been having an affair, and her de facto uncle, the maréchal d'Albret, had chided her for her indiscreet conduct of it. D'Albret was at this time in high favour at court, and it is no doubt the risk to himself that had roused his ire, since marital fidelity, on his own or anyone else's part, had never before figured among his concerns. Bonne countered with accusations of her own: d'Albret was a hypocrite; he had rallied smartly to Athénaïs, "like a good courtier, and taken her part, and become her best friend and advisor," abandoning Monsieur de Montespan, who was his own cousin. And what about his own affair with Françoise? Bonne proceeded to say "the most awful things you can imagine about him and Madame Scarron."

But this was by no means the main cause of d'Albret's anger. Not content with saying bad things about her friend Françoise, Bonne had been writing worse things about her friend Athénaïs, revealing to her lover, and to another inquisitive suitor, the secret of the household at the rue des Tournelles. It had taken eighteen months for these compromising letters to find their way into Athénaïs's hands, and when Françoise was told of them, she refused to believe it. Bonne would never be so disloyal to her friends or to her King, she insisted. Unless she saw the letters with her own eyes, until she saw Bonne's own handwriting, she would maintain her innocence.

At Athénaïs's urging, Françoise was summoned to court, and here, for the first time, in February 1671, she was presented to the King in person. Louis showed her the letters; astonished, she acknowledged Bonne's guilt, and agreed to sever all contact with her forthwith. Bonne was banished to her husband's château in the country, and departed "in absolute despair, having lost all her friends . . . and accused of every treachery under the sun." For failing to keep his niece in check, d'Albret was paid the backhanded compliment of an appointment as governor of Guyenne, an effective demotion from the court life in which he delighted to a stint in the dreaded provinces.

"I was quite distressed to have to abandon Madame d'Heudicourt," Françoise wrote to her cousin Philippe, "but I could not support her any further without doing real harm to my own reputation and to my fortune." Herself too recently arrived in court circles, Françoise had not the courage to forgive her friend outright and risk her own dismissal. Besides, Bonne's guilt was clear. And if Françoise could not support her, she did not abandon her entirely. "Send me news of that poor woman," she later told Philippe, "and tell her that nothing can lessen my fondness of her. If I saw her she'd see that I love her with all my heart."

Bonne's daughter, Louise, remained with Françoise, and life at the rue des Tournelles continued much as before, apart from a probable relief on Françoise's part: the secret was clearly out, and the burden of concealment now weighed less heavily on her own shoulders. It is not likely in any case that she had ever managed to carry out her charge in perfect secrecy. Though the real nature of the household could not be publicly admitted, the truth cannot have been kept for long from all the curious inhabitants of so closely linked a world. Most probably, the "secret" was an open secret, unrecognized because unspoken. Provided it was not officially known, it was accepted as being not known at all; there would be no public scandal, and Athénaïs's husband could take no formal steps to reclaim her children, who were, in legal terms, his own.

Françoise herself related that, during these governess years in Paris, she would frequently have herself bled by a physician in an attempt to reduce her blushing whenever friends questioned her—or teased her, perhaps—about her whereabouts and how she was spending her days, indicating that they knew very well what was going on. She did her best to keep up her usual social rounds, but the to-ing and fro-ing, and the work itself, were gradually wearing her down. "It's quite hard to get to see you," the chevalier de Méré wrote to her. "We're beginning to think you're neglecting your old friends . . ."

The beau monde may have known the truth of the matter, but the public at large did not, and Françoise found herself "climbing up ladders to hang curtains and do all sorts of other things, because I didn't want workmen coming into the house. I did everything myself; the wet-nurses did nothing whatsoever, for fear they'd spoil their milk . . . I spent whole nights up with the children when they were sick . . . and then I'd get dressed up and go out visiting . . . I grew thinner and thinner . . ."

And her house grew fuller and fuller. With Françoise herself, and Nanon and three small children and the nurses and the rest of the servants, and a vastly increased amount of cooking and laundering, it had become a hive of busy, blustering, squalling humanity, never still, never quiet, never quite under control, but kept going nonetheless with money from the King and constant effort from Françoise. In June 1672, Queen Marie-Thérèse bore the King a third son, who was named Louis-François; this child, of course, remained at court. But six days later, Athénaïs also bore Louis a son; this newborn, Louis-César, by contrast, had to be deposited elsewhere.

Athénaïs's husband had long since been released from the Bastille; at his château in Gascony he had held a mock funeral ceremony for his departed wife, put his children and servants in mourning, and declared his permanent outrage at the King's theft of Athénaïs by adding a set of cuckold's horns to the Montespan family crest. He was clearly not going to accept the state of affairs in the spirit of a dutiful subject. Athénaïs's two sons by Louis could not yet be publicly recognized. Little Louis-César was going to have to be added to the four children already in the rue des Tournelles, and Françoise was going to have to move to a bigger house.

In the autumn of 1672, a suitable place in the rue Vaugirard was duly purchased by the King, and for the first time in all the twenty-two years of her Paris life, Françoise found herself living outside the Marais. The rue Vaugirard was on the edge of the district of Saint-Germain, the grandest of Colbert's grand new residential developments and, usefully, a district which housed most of the city's foreign visitors; there were thus fewer locals to observe the comings and goings in Françoise's own household. One visitor especially was anxious to remain unidentified: in 1671 the King had lost his second legitimate son, Philippe, not even three years old; the following year, baby Louis-François had died, aged only four months, along with his five-year-old sister, Marie-Thérèse, and their unknown half-sibling, who had in the meantime joined Françoise's little brood. Françoise had been deeply moved by the death of this child in her care, "far more than the real mother," who had apparently never troubled to visit at all. But if Athénaïs was little affected, the King had found his paternal feelings belatedly roused by the deaths of so many of his children, so quickly.

He began to take an interest in his two illegitimate sons at the house in the rue Vaugirard, and at the end of 1672 he took to visiting them there.

The younger boy, Louis-César, was still an infant in swaddling clothes, but Louis-Auguste was three years old, an attractive, curly-haired child, affectionate and precociously intelligent. Though hidden away from the lustre of the court, he far outshone his twelve-year-old half-brother at Saint-Germain. Young Louis, the unprepossessing dauphin, was only too clearly his mother's son, fattish, timid, and slow to learn. The King, determined to respect and love him as heir to the Bourbon throne, had hampered him all the same with two ill-chosen governors, brutal even by contemporary standards, who had flogged and ranted the boy into a hatred of all learning and a reluctance to take a stand on anything but the value of a good hunting dog. "The dauphin became like an idiot," wrote Primi Visconti. "No one could make any conversation with him. People even said that the little marquis de Créquy had secretly introduced him to a certain immoral practice, and when the dauphin's deputy-governor realized this, he hid himself with a big stick behind the dauphin's bed, and when he saw his hands moving under the covers, he jumped out and started beating him . . . The dauphin was only young, but he offered money to any army officer if he'd get rid of his governor for him."

By contrast, the innocent, three-year-old Louis-Auguste promised to be everything a prince should be. With the dauphin retreating into a sullen silence, his little half-brother swiftly became the King's favourite son. As for Françoise, she adored the child. He became her little "*Mignon*," her sweetheart; so she was to call him for the rest of her life.

Surrounded by children, naturally responsive to them, yet with no child of her own, into this little boy she poured all the love and longing of a mother in all but name. To each of the children she was warm and attentive, but there is no doubt of her special tenderness for him, a tenderness conjured, perhaps, out of her own mother's long-ago lack of tenderness for her. The child responded with an equal love, and his love, too, was to be lasting. At the age of thirteen he is found writing

to her enthusiastically "in between mathematics and some Bible reading. I've just been to the château of Glatigny and I was thrilled to see
my dogs: Roland, Commère, Rodrigue, Medea, Jason, Hebe, Cyrus,
Nigaud, Nanon, Finette, Morette, Charmant, and Belle-Face. Now
you know more about my hunting pack than my schooling." Three
years later, from a first army post, he would write that he felt towards
her as a son towards his mother, adding, "I couldn't bear it if you
didn't love me . . ."

The King saw it all on Françoise's discreet visits with the children
to the Louvre and Saint-Germain, and also during his own increasing
hours at the rue Vaugirard. At first he had not much liked Françoise—
"He couldn't stand her," said the abbé de Choisy bluntly—regarding
her as too clever, too contained, and, worst of all things, a possible
prude. But having seen her affectionate manner with the children, he
had gradually warmed to her. "She knows how to love," he remarked
one day. "It would be something to be loved by a woman like that."

Whether or not he was already thinking of making her one of his
many casual mistresses, he was prepared to make public his new esteem for her: in March 1673 Françoise saw her pension increased from
two to six thousand livres. "A king must distinguish persons of quality
and merit," wrote the King, and perhaps he had as yet acknowledged
to himself no deeper reason for his sudden tripling of Françoise's pension. Perhaps, but already it was whispered at court that the King was
finding the governess "so delightful and such good company that he
can hardly bear to be away from her . . . It's true that two thousand
livres wasn't much of a pension, but still, this sudden increase does
seem to raise the hope of other blessings . . ."

Françoise was beginning to be known at court, not just by reputation,
through her well-born Marais friends, but in herself, as a regular visitor. Bringing the children to visit their parents, no matter how discreetly, she had been seen, and discussed, by the courtiers as well as the
servants. She was also beginning to be known as something of an authority on court affairs, all the various and vital activities and person-
alities of "that country," as it was known to its habitués. Over supper

in her magnificent house in the Marais, Madame de Sévigné lapped up all the gossip to record for her daughter in Provence: "Madame Scarron is charming," she wrote, "and her mind is marvellously penetrating. It's a pleasure to hear her talking about all these dreadful goings-on in *that country*, which she knows well—how desperate Madame [Bonne] d'Heudicourt felt . . . the trials and tribulations of all the ladies at Saint-Germain, not excluding the most envied of them all [Athénaïs]. It's delightful to hear her chatting about all that. Sometimes the conversations go much further, into religion or politics."

Françoise's star had evidently begun to rise. She had made the acquaintance of the King, she had tripled her earnings, and through her efforts, in 1672, her undeserving brother Charles had been appointed governor of the Dutch city of Amersfoort, captured by the French during the promenade militaire of 1667. "But I don't regard this as a permanent establishment," she wrote to him. "It's a step towards something else. So make of it what you can, for the service of a man who must have charmed you even more than he's charmed me, since you've seen him in military mode. It seems to me it's a pleasure to serve a hero, especially a hero we see at first hand . . . Out of this honour, my dear brother, you must work miracles. Apply yourself, be careful and precise in your work," she urged, well knowing Charles's tendency to be nothing of the kind. "Don't be harsh with the Huguenots there," she warned, unwittingly prescient of troubles to come. "It's gentleness that draws people. Jesus Christ gave us that example . . . And remember, if you're not devout enough to become a monk, there's nothing better on this earth than to make people think well of you."

TEN

L'Arrivée

With the King giving the example of galanterie, it's easy for the young courtiers to become his devoted disciples. The court loves love: gay, delightful, unconstrained love. Any man unhappy in love is ridiculous. The fashion is for conquests and intrigues, not sighs and gloomy resignation . . . A young lord carries on several affairs at once. Fidelity to one's beloved is rare, inconstancy the rule . . . But to cross the accepted limits, to go to excess . . . this His Majesty does not permit. He wants to keep the court half-way between the austere piety of his mother's day and the licentiousness of the more intemperate courtiers. When occasion requires, the King knows how to be dignified and respect the conventions, but at Saint-Germain . . . life has a certain freshness, a spontaneity, a natural elegance . . . The fashionable word now is *flexible*, marvellously appropriate to describe the young courtiers' behaviour. It evokes an ease of manner, and a touch of informality, too. It's the opposite of pompous ceremony and rigid etiquette.

Thus the *mode de vie* at the court of the thirty-four-year-old Louis XIV in the palace of Saint-Germain-en-Laye, twelve miles to the west of Paris. This had been the court's principal residence since 1666, when Louis had turned his back for good on the unfinished Louvre.

Saint-Germain's Gothic origins had long since been obscured by sacking English armies and the gentler legions of architects from Italy, and it now stood as a graceful Renaissance edifice set in splendid formal gardens in the new French style, designed by the great André Le Nôtre for the King's then favourite, Louise de la Vallière, and completed in this very year of 1673. Running through the parterres and copses, a stone terrace, nearly two miles long, gave views of the beautiful valley of the Seine and, away in the distance, the great city of light. Impressive though the palace was, the King had been unable to resist remaking it to his own, more ebullient taste. To that end, teams of builders and craftsmen were now at work inside and out, directed by the famous pair of Louis Le Vau, designer of Fouquet's Vaux-le-Vicomte, and Jules Hardouin-Mansart—and, whenever he cared to interfere, by the King himself.

Françoise knew Saint-Germain well. It was from beneath its windows, in the middle of a March night in 1670, that she had spirited away the newborn Louis-Auguste, her "Mignon"; since then she had returned many times with the boy and his brother, to allow them to be petted by their father, and sighted by their mother, who otherwise made no effort to see them.

In June 1673 Athénaïs had borne the King a daughter, named Louise-Françoise, though the King called her *Poupotte* (Dolly) or *Maflée* (Chubby), signs of an indulgence of which she would be quick to take advantage. Athénaïs was still aged only thirty; in the last three years she had borne three children. Now, her latest little arrival persuaded the King that he could not keep his unacknowledged offspring in hiding indefinitely; he decided to have them legitimized and brought to court to live openly as his own.

A legal precedent existed already in the person of the comte de Vermandois, the King's illegitimate son by Louise de la Vallière, so that in December 1673 Louis-Auguste, now aged almost four, became the duc du Maine, eighteen-month-old Louis-César the comte de Vexin, and newborn Louise-Françoise Mademoiselle de Nantes. But, though declared the King's legitimate sons, the boys were to have no claim to the Bourbon throne. All three children were to remain in the official care of Madame Scarron; she was to give up the house in the rue Vaugirard, and come to live with them at the palace of Saint-Germain.

She was not particularly inclined to go. No doubt she had been feeling pangs of homesickness for the happy time of theatres and dinners with her friends in the Marais, coming and going as she pleased, before her life had been taken over by curtain-hanging and wet-nurse supervision and tending sick toddlers all through the night. She was now aged thirty-eight: youth had disappeared, and a long life could not be guaranteed. She had a good pension of 6,000 livres, enough for quite an elegant life in a good house of her own, entertaining friends, dressing in gowns of Dutch velvet—"I saw some samples the other day; it's on sale in Amsterdam; if it's not too much trouble, perhaps you could bring me some . . ."—with money left over for the inevitable debts of brother Charles, and for "our relatives constantly asking me for help." She had made a start already on what was to prove a long career of financial assistance to d'Aubignés, Scarrons, de Villettes, and assorted other cousins any number of times removed.

But then there was Mignon, the little duc du Maine, still her darling, still precocious, still delightful, but now suffering cruelly with a deformed leg, twisted and shortened in the spasms of a serious fever. If she declined to move to Saint-Germain, she would possibly never see him again, and she loved the boy, with a deep need of his presence, as if he were her own son.

As for him, unable to walk, enduring constant pain, he had grown more dependent on her, rather than less, as the months since his illness had gone by. In the spring of 1673, with Bonne's Louise in tow as well, she had taken him on a strenuous two-hundred-mile journey to Antwerp to consult a physician there; it seemed he might be able to help the child by straightening his leg and enabling him to walk. Since the King's Louis-Auguste did not yet officially exist, he and Françoise had travelled in disguise, she as the unknown marquise de Surgères and he as her son.

The journey had proved to worse than no avail. The treatment had been disastrous. Mignon had been several times placed in a stretching contraption, "like a prison rack," and his leg pulled and twisted, while Françoise sat beside him, mopping the perspiration from his forehead, her own heart rent by his screams. At the end of it all, his shorter leg had become longer than the other, and far from being able to walk, he could barely stand upright. Though it had not been her sole decision to take Mignon to Antwerp, she was partly responsible for the journey and, arguably, for its dreadful outcome and the child's continuing suffering. Guilt, then, and perhaps a determination to cure him yet, were added into the balance as she considered what to do.

In the end it was Père Gobelin who convinced her. Beneath its sparkling surface, he said, the court was a dark den of iniquity; the children would have a much better chance of growing up good Christians if their debauched mother's influence could be kept to a minimum, and his own, through Françoise, increased. In fact, Athénaïs had little influence over the children, never having taken much interest in them. On the other hand, if Françoise were to leave, there was no telling what unthinking or uncaring person might be installed as their new governess. Moreover, thought Françoise, like her marriage to Scarron, her duties at court would not be likely to last long. It was the custom of the day for well-born boys to remain with their governess only until the age of seven, when they were transferred to the care of a male tutor for their formal education. Mignon was already almost four. Whether Françoise liked it or not, he would be removed from her care in three short years. But by then, perhaps, his leg would be healed, and in any case she would have done all she could for him. As for the non-royal children, Charles's five-year-old boy, Toscan, could be sent to the country, while Bonne's Louise, the same age, could go with her to Saint-Germain. Françoise spoke again to Père Gobelin. He urged her to go, and at the end of 1673, she did.

Despite being the premier royal residence and the official seat of government, Saint-Germain was not large. The many visiting counsellors and diplomats who came to see the King could not be housed there overnight, and were obliged instead to make the daily journey from Paris in their velvet-lined but unsprung coaches. There was not even room at Saint-Germain for the courtiers, who compensated for this by building themselves elegant houses nearby, so that by the time of Françoise's arrival, in January 1674, a fine new town was springing up beside the palace. Even the King's apartments, though recently remodelled, were admitted to be small. Only Athénaïs had space enough, with a magnificent suite decorated by the celebrated François d'Orbay. Here, in her boudoir, she would lie for two or three hours every day, "stretched out naked on the bed, to be massaged with pomades and perfumes." The balconies surrounding her apartments overlooked the beautiful gardens designed for the discarded Louise de la Vallière, which might have given the confident Athénaïs occasional pause for thought. No longer loved by Louis, Louise nonetheless remained at court, a useful diversionary tactic for a King who preferred his private life to remain something of a mystery as far as his courtiers were concerned.

La belle Montespan was seldom alone in her spacious suite. Apart from the King and her children, when Françoise brought them visiting, she shared it with a literal menagerie of other creatures: exotic birds of all kinds and colours, some of them flying around freely, goats and lambs with ribbons about their necks, piglets in costumes, mice scurrying about pulling tiny brass carriages, one screeching monkey, and even a small bear. At "dinner," an early afternoon repast, Athénaïs presided at a table for ladies only, normally a prerogative of the Queen. Afterwards, she would hold court seated in a proper chair, "with a back and arms," while the princesses and duchesses perched on lowly stools around her.

Athénaïs was intelligent, generous, and sincerely religious, but her ascent to the absolute summit had brought out the less attractive aspects of her character. Wallowing in a bizarre luxury, she had become indulgent and petulant by turns, with her pets, her servants, her children, her friends, and even with the King himself. All day and half the night, her loud voice could be heard, screaming with laughter if it suited her mood, otherwise arguing with the King or shouting at her servants, as often as not with a clout for good measure. Despite her noble Mortemart ancestry, Athénaïs's passions were those of the newly rich: gorgeous dresses, huge jewels, sumptuous carriages, and the constant, flagrant waste of money—all sustained by the King, whose passion for her, after seven years, showed no sign of flagging.

The uncrowned Queen, it seemed, needed a palace of her own, and construction had duly begun on her fabulous château at Clagny near Versailles, which was now costing the King, or rather, the public purse, 300,000 livres every year, to say nothing of the "excessive expense" of her apartments at Saint-Germain. Even the prince de Condé, *le Grand Condé*, the King's own cousin, whose royal pension soared above all others, received only 150,000 livres, though admittedly he had a million or so from his estates as well. Françoise's proudly earned 6,000 livres was a pittance by comparison, and most courtiers could barely have imagined how a country priest could keep body and soul together on four or five hundred a year, or a labouring townsman feed his family on half that sum. Athénaïs did not forget the obligations of charity, but she was not above betting half a million livres on the turn of a card; it was too daring, too dazzling, too much plain fun, and if she should lose, the coffers could always be refilled. "She'd play the entire evening . . . throwing the price of a ship or a château onto the table without a second thought," while the King watched ambivalently, justifying the greed and extravagance of his irresistible mistress with a political gamble of his own—that his courtiers' addiction to dice and cards was an antidote to plotting and Frondes.

The worst game, or the best of all, was *le hocca*, a high-stakes lottery introduced from Italy, where it had long been outlawed. The Parlement of Paris had prohibited it, too, though the parlementaires themselves, on their visits to court, were not always immune to the temptation of playing. "Le hocca is forbidden, on pain of imprisonment, but still they play it in the King's own house!" Madame de Sévigné declared. "It's nothing to lose five thousand pistoles before dinner; it's absolutely cut-throat." In an effort to stamp the game out, police commissioner La Reynie added to the prison term a fine of 3,000 livres, then 6,000, but the potential winnings were simply too high,

and apart from anything else, le hocca had simply become "the fashion
at court," as La Reynie complained to his master, Colbert. "This
means it will certainly spread to the bourgeois in Paris, and then the
tradesmen and artisans. It will create more disorder than ever." Touchingly, the commissioner employed a local mathematician to create a series of geometry games to replace the desperate fashion for gambling.
They do not seem to have achieved quite the same popularity.

Françoise was not a gambler—the stakes would have been much too
high for her, even if she had been inclined to join in—but she did take
part in the other amusements of Athénaïs's alternative court. Typically, the King and his mistress, with a select group of courtiers, would
pass the early hours of the evening at board games or cards (Françoise's favourite was the two-handed piquet), or listening to some
new poem or play. Their maestro, Molière, had departed for good only
months before, spitting out his last words with bright consumptive
blood during a performance in the title role of, perversely, *La Malade
imaginaire* (The Hypochondriac). But other writers had emerged, and
Lully was still there, inventing dances and composing songs, begetting
children and seducing young men, all with the same obsessive energy,
a wonderful source of gossip and entertainment for opera-lovers and
everyone else. There was a great deal of talk, of course, especially over
supper at the end of the evening, and here Françoise shone, as she had
done on so many evenings in the salons of the Marais. The King observed her admiringly, but also with a touch of anxiety; Athénaïs so
clearly enjoyed batting words back and forth with the governess that at
times he felt almost redundant. In the end he asked her not to continue
talking to "your clever friend" after he had gone, fearing, no doubt,
that the conversation might turn, unflatteringly, towards himself.

It turned often enough from the amusing to the merely tiresome,
and this Françoise enjoyed much less, though court protocol demanded a high degree of tolerance for plain silliness. One game played
among the duchesses and princesses was a version of musical chairs,
with the gentlemen trying to push the ladies off their seats. Françoise's
lack of enthusiasm must have been evident, or her reputation for good
sense too intimidating, for the courtier elected to dethrone her drew

back with an exaggerated cry. "Ah, no! Not Madame Scarron!" he exclaimed. "I'd sooner try to pinch the Queen's bottom."

There was not much likelihood of it. Having lost, as she did routinely, at her own favourite card game of *hombre*—"Half the court was
living off her losses"—Marie-Thérèse would have spent the rest of the
evening within her own apartments, kneeling sadly in silent prayer. In
the early days of their marriage, Louis had wished her to hold a ladies'
court of her own, as his mother had done, but "her stupidity and her
bizarre French soon put an end to that idea." The court was now wherever the King was, and the King was invariably with his mistress, until
he came to the Queen to say goodnight—"the King never stopped going
to bed with the Queen, often late, but without fail"—but this cannot
have been much consolation to the lonely Marie-Thérèse, who had not
even her children to comfort her—five of the six were by now dead.
Overly pious even as a girl, in the fourteen years of her marriage she
had sunk ever more deeply into an extreme, very Spanish Catholicism.
The King's many infidelities had grieved and humiliated her. Louise
de la Vallière had at least been discreet, but Athénaïs was flaunting
her favoured status openly. "That *whora* will kill me!" wailed Marie-
Thérèse.

The King observed the forms, and for him the forms were sufficient: in public, the Queen took first place. But Marie-Thérèse, thirty-
six years old, wanted more than formality. Far from her homeland, still
struggling with the capricious French language, disdained or ignored
by all the courtiers, she had been sufficiently naïve to hope for love,
and in her unreasoning heart she hoped for it still.

Extraordinarily, the same hope was being nursed, and for the same
man, in the heart of another foreign princess, more recently arrived at
court. Towards the end of 1671, the King's widowed brother, Philippe,
duc d'Orléans, "Monsieur," had married for the second time, his bride
the nineteen-year-old Princess Elizabeth Charlotte of the Palatinate,
known to her own, much missed Rhineland family as "Liselotte."
To the snobbish French courtiers, Liselotte was all that a German
princess ought to be: a hefty, badly dressed lover of chocolate and

sausages. "She's no beauty," wrote Primi Visconti, "and in fact, when Monsieur saw her for the first time, he turned to his courtiers . . . and muttered, *Oh! how can I go to bed with her?* For the first three days she ate nothing but an olive and didn't say a word . . . But she was soon talking . . . even more than necessary."

No woman, in any case, could have satisfied the promiscuously homosexual Monsieur, though Monsieur himself had met his marital duty manfully. From his first marriage, two daughters survived, and by the time of Françoise's arrival at court, Liselotte herself had a son, Alexandre—"so terrifically big and strong, he's much more of a German than a Frenchman; everyone here says he takes after me, so you'll gather he's no oil painting"—and she had recently conceived a second. Though not beautiful, Liselotte was at least no fool; utterly unaffected, shrewd and witty, with an earthy, self-deprecating humour, she had endeared herself surprisingly strongly to both husband and brother-in-law.

Where Monsieur was concerned, she had understood the state of the case at once. Accepting their mutual duty to produce a few dynastic scions, the pair had agreed to demand no more of each other, and in consequence became, at least for most of the time, relaxed and affectionate friends. As for the King, though he could not admire Liselotte for any womanly charm, he did enjoy her company. Their mutual passion for stag-hunting, not shared by the Queen or any of Louis's mistresses, brought them regularly together, and he was constantly amused by her pithy observations on the vanity and hypocrisy of the court. But, like the Queen, Liselotte dreamed of more from the King, and the very impossibility of her dream embittered her towards the women he admired, and more than any of them, towards Françoise. "The King invites me every Saturday to Madame de Montespan's *medianoche*," Liselotte informed her Aunt Sophie in Hanover, and every Saturday at this midnight supper she encountered the governess, beautiful, amusing, and most frustrating: being neither vain nor hypocritical, nor flirtatious, nor frivolous, she provided none of the usual easy targets for Liselotte's pungent wit. The solid princess was reduced to disparaging the Widow Scarron for her humble background and modest position at court, the only respects in which Liselotte herself indisputably had the advantage.

It was unfortunate, for in fact the two had much in common, and they might have formed an alliance of good sense to counter the costumed piglets and other follies that infected so much of court life. Neither was a natural courtier, each lacking the instinct to manipulate and dissimulate, so necessary to hold one's own in "that country." Françoise either said what she thought or said nothing at all; Liselotte simply said what she thought, and added a rude joke. Both women were clever without being intellectual, both witty, both fond of children; both missed the quiet pleasures of family life in the country—stocky Liselotte even missed "running and jumping about"—metaphorically, perhaps. Not least, both held to a straightforward, practical Christianity, dismissive of rosary beads and statues, unimpressed by the melodramatic lives of the Catholic saints and martyrs. Though both were now formally children of Rome, Liselotte was Lutheran by birth and unsubtle temperament, and Françoise at least half-Huguenot, by upbringing and by nature, too. "If people hadn't been likely to talk, I wouldn't even bother going to mass on a Sunday," she had said, and Liselotte would no doubt have agreed. "Catholic sermons are too long," she sighed, jolting awake at the end of one of them. "They work on me like opium. The minute one starts, I fall asleep, and it's the same whenever nuns start singing."

Above all, both Françoise and Liselotte were outsiders, suspect in times of conflict for their earlier Protestant lives, never quite fitting in among the silky courtiers born and bred, never quite sure of their place in the pecking order. As the wife of Monsieur, Liselotte ("Madame") supposedly held precedence after the women of the King's immediate family, but in the attitudes of the court it was not so simple: Liselotte was obliged to make unofficial way for Louise de la Vallière, still maîtresse déclarée, and for Athénaïs, always pushing her way into the front row, and now and then even for Madame Scarron, treated with rather more deference than she was strictly entitled to.

But if this was true, Françoise herself took no reassurance from it. Certainly, her graceful and contained manner encouraged the courtiers

to behave towards her with respect: no one was going to push her off
her chair or try to pinch her bottom, or berate her or make fun of her in
public—though from time to time Athénaïs issued instructions to her,
each one a tiny humiliation, as if she were a maidservant. Her place at
court, all the same, was not secure; at any moment she could be dismissed by Athénaïs, or even by the King. But then, it was not her ambition to spend her life at court. She had her 6,000 livres a year, and
with that, she could be comfortable anywhere. The pension could be
revoked, of course, but so vindictive a step was unlikely. All that mat-
tered, while she remained at court, was that she should continue to receive the respect which she so prized, and without which she could not
thrive. While Liselotte willed her to slip down a rung or two, Françoise
battled, mostly with herself, to keep a steady footing. "You're very particular about what's due to you," she said to her Mignon, in an unreflecting reprimand. "Look at the King: he is relaxed and polite; he
never makes a fuss about what's due to him." "Ah, but Madame,"
replied the clever little boy, "the King is sure of his position, while I
cannot be sure of mine."

Secure in himself at court, Louis was by now equally secure in his
kingdom. No threat remained from ambitious princes seizing the
advantage in a country weakly governed. The civil wars of the King's
early youth had brought the lesson firmly home, contributing in no
small part to his determination to maintain an absolute monarchy. After ten years of personal rule, with the Fronde almost twenty years in
the past, he was confident of his own power and popularity. In 1667, he
had instructed the Paris and provincial parlements to confirm all his
royal edicts as the law of the land, and they had supinely accepted the
instruction without a murmur.

"The old parliamentary resistance has fallen out of fashion," wrote
Colbert. "It's all so long ago now that people scarcely remember it." As
for the princes, they were sufficiently occupied, it seemed, in money-
making and social politicking at the newly vibrant court—the antidote
to plotting and Frondes that Louis had hoped. So it was not to distract

his nobles and safeguard his own position at home that the King and his minister now decided to engage in a foreign war. Rather, it was a matter of national prosperity, at least for Colbert—and for Louis, a matter of national pride.

Colbert was a convinced "mercantilist" in the fashion of the day, a believer in strict protections for his own nation's commerce, and constant, no-holds-barred attacks on everyone else's. As Minister for Finance and Secretary of State for the Navy, he was perfectly placed to manage both sides of the equation, with ultimate control of tariffs and taxes and all the nation's shipping, not only the vessels and galleys of the war fleet but, lucratively, the merchant fleet as well. Both fleets were as yet small in comparison with those of other powers—the Swedish, for example, or the English, and especially the Dutch—but things were soon to be different: Colbert had already set in train a massive programme of naval expansion. With this completed, he believed, France was bound to emerge the victor of these ongoing "money wars," since France was by nature endowed more bountifully than any other nation in Europe. Only France was large enough, its people numerous enough, its towns sufficiently inventive, its climate and lands sufficiently diverse and fertile, to provide every need of its own, and still have produce and goods to spare, to sell beyond its borders.

All dreams and rhetoric: in a man less powerful than Colbert, it would have been recognized at once for the wishful thinking that it was. France in 1672 was rich only in potential, and its insignificant navy was the least of its commercial problems. Its population of twenty-two million was boasted of as the largest in the whole of Europe—"Monsieur Colbert said that a King's wealth lay in having many subjects; he wanted everyone to get married and have children"—but, if the largest, it was also among the most backward.

A hundred years and more after Flemish and English farmers had begun the productive enclosure of lands, the peasants of France, some three-quarters of the population, were still working according to the wasteful "fallow field" system of the Middle Ages, effectively leaving a third of the country's arable land untilled. Their tools were medieval, too, commonly made of wood and wicker; a lucky man might possess a

solid wheat scythe imported from the Habsburg lands. Far from producing surplus goods for trade, France was nowhere near providing
even for its own consumption: the poorer Frenchman, as often as not,
was clothed in Spanish wool and ate from English tin, while his richer
compatriot wore elegant fabrics from Leiden and dined from plates of
German or South American silver, before retiring to bed in sheets of
English linen. France's soldiers went into battle armed with Swedish
muskets charged with Flemish gunpowder, supported by Danish cannon pulled by horses shod with good Flemish iron. Copper for French
coins came from Japan; one tiny southern town produced the only steel
in the land, and after two centuries of valuable coal-mining in England
and the nearby Spanish Netherlands, the French had made no effort to
exploit their own reserves of this most promising of minerals. The
very cheese eaten in France was, much of it, Dutch. And all of it,
cheese, gunpowder, copper, linen, everything, passed through the
busy hands of the merchants of Amsterdam, whose enterprise and industry had created a golden age for their own United Provinces of the
Netherlands.

France had no banks, no stock exchange, nor even a proper national
exchequer. The needs of the state were financed spasmodically by
loans from *banquiers* (actually merchants) to the King, commonly at
25 percent interest. The ensuing huge liabilities were frequently reduced by devaluation of the currency—a tactically shrewd step, perhaps, but strategically naïve, since it encouraged the better off to keep
their wealth "sleeping" in elaborate silverware and other expensive
household goods, so reducing the amount of money in general circulation and hampering trade throughout the country. France was rich in
land and in people, and it should have been rich in fact, but in 1672, the
tiny, windblown, half-drowned Dutch Republic, with its paltry million and a half souls, was very much richer, indeed by far the richest
country in Europe.

It was more than Louis could stand. These plain Dutch *boers*, with
their great black-and-white cows spurting the best quality milk and
their disconcertingly productive farms and market gardens, these
shop-soiled townsmen, jangling the coins of fifty different countries in

their pockets, consulting one another everlastingly in their citizens' councils, had not even a king to call their own. It was an affront to the princely houses of Europe that they dared to call themselves a nation at all. Disgusted by their Protestant pride and ambition, and "tired of these [commercial] insolences," intoned Jean Racine, Louis's dutiful poet-turned-historiographer, "the King resolved to punish them."

In reality, the pride and ambition belonged above all to Louis himself. The French could not remotely compete with the vast network of international trade masterminded from Amsterdam. Even the produce of France's Caribbean islands, the indigo and tobacco in which Françoise's wayward father had planted his hopes, and the laboriously cultivated sugar, prospering at last on her own childhood islands of Martinique and Guadeloupe, were bought and sold by the Dutch.

As if all this were not injury enough, the little republic had added two grave insults to *la grande nation*. First, the Dutch had instigated an alliance with England and Sweden to contain French ambitions in the Spanish Netherlands, then slipping from the grasp of a weakened Spain: at the Treaty of Aix-la-Chapelle in 1668, this "Triple Alliance" had been able to pressure France into handing back to Spain much of the territory it had only just conquered. And subsequently, they had declined to accept a French invitation to a dual partitioning of the Spanish Netherlands. Louis had regarded this latter affair almost as a question of noblesse oblige, and was shocked to be repulsed by the upstart pseudo-nation, but the Dutch had preferred to avoid having a clearly aggressive France as their immediate neighbour. "When a Prince is wounded in his reputation . . . this is the subject of a just war," wrote the English polemicist Henry Stubbes, hitting the French nail precisely on the head. Colbert's worries about cheese and gunpowder aside, Louis's offended pride proved a more than sufficient *casus belli*.

The ground for war had been prepared by secret diplomatic overtures to others who stood to lose by the Dutchmen's vibrant trading successes, notably their two partners in the Triple Alliance. Sweden's herring men and England's cloth and timber men were more than pleased

to anticipate a reversal of the United Provinces' too-happy trading fortunes; the Swedish government agreed to stand aside and let France
have its way, and the English lent the power of their substantial navy to
assist the small French fleet.

Since the end of the Thirty Years War in 1648, concluded very
much to their advantage, the Dutch had neglected matters of national
defence to pour all their resources into trading, so that by 1672 their
army had declined to a mishmash of poorly trained soldiers and casual
militias, standing to desultory arms in a series of crumbling fortresses.
In consequence, when Louis rode off northwards on May 12 of that
year, he was anticipating a second promenade militaire in the mode of
his 1667 War of Devolution. Confident of a victory that would dazzle
the Dutch into permanent submission, and determined to reinforce it
by his own majestic presence, he even allowed a flicker of glory to illu-
minate a stunned Queen Marie-Thérèse, who found herself declared
Regent of France for the duration of His Majesty's absence—to no
great harm, since Colbert remained behind with her.

Leading the 120,000 French troops, apart from the King himself,
were Maréchal Turenne and the prince de Condé, his two best generals, as well as the little Maréchal de Luxembourg and the brilliant
Sébastien Vauban, still only a captain at almost forty years of age, but
soon to prove himself without peer throughout Europe in the vital art
and science of military engineering. Their pockets lined with papers of
alliance with the Archbishopric of Cologne and the Bishopric of Münster, whence a further 30,000 troops had been contributed, the French
planned to march through these territories neighbouring the Spanish
Netherlands, and thence into the United Provinces. By the second
week of June 1672, they had captured six towns, avoiding pitched battles and opting instead for the expensive but more predictable siege
warfare, the "most theatrical form of warfare," that Louis so enjoyed.

Despite the poor state of his nation's defence forces, the energetic twenty-two-year-old Prince Willem of Orange, newly appointed
Captain-General, had managed to harass and drag together a Dutch
army of 20,000 men. They stood waiting now, with trenches dug and
defensive walls thrown up, at Ijssel on the south bank of the Rhine, in

Netherlands territory, with the French, under Condé, pressing up towards them. But at the ford of Tolhuis, Condé unexpectedly diverted his army across to the north bank of the river, in German territory near the fort of Schenk, so bypassing the young prince and his troops altogether. A small band of Dutchmen, hidden behind hedges, engaged them on the other side, and though Condé himself was badly wounded, the French sustained few losses.

Condé in fact had gone across the river in a boat, and the King had been miles away in Doesburg, but a handful of inexperienced young cavalrymen had charged excitedly into the water on their horses, and though most of these had lost their lives, the drama was ripe for exploitation. The crossing of the Rhine at once acquired legendary status in France, providing the subject for countless paintings and tapestries extolling the martial exploits of the newly acclaimed *Louis le Grand*. "I can't understand how they managed to cross the Rhine swimming," a breathless Madame de Sévigné wrote to her cousin five days after the great event. "To plunge into the river on horseback, like dogs hunting a deer, and not to be drowned, or killed once they got to the other side, it staggers me just to think of it."

In Vienna, the Holy Roman Emperor Leopold I was also staggered just to think of it, and his shock was mixed with outrage. Though he had agreed to remain neutral in any Franco-Dutch conflict, he viewed this French Rhine crossing now as an act of aggression on his own imperial territory. Abandoning his promise of neutrality, he determined to support the Dutch, who were already seeking out others willing to join them in driving the French out of the Netherlands and back into their own country. They found a feeble ally in Leopold's Habsburg cousin, King Carlos II of Spain, and stronger support in the "Great Elector" Friedrich Wilhelm II of the rising Prussian state of Brandenburg. But this new coalition was months in the making, and in the meantime the French were making alarmingly swift progress. Once on the north bank, they advanced along the river, capturing all the riverside towns, and finally Arnhem, where Condé, swathed in bandages and frustration, was deposited to recuperate. There was now nothing to stop the French from marching on Utrecht, and then on to the priceless wharves and warehouses and businesses and banking houses of undefended Amsterdam itself.

This had been Condé's plan, and it would almost certainly have made a swift and brilliant end to a swift and brilliant campaign. But the prince's command had perforce fallen to his rival, Maréchal Turenne, who decided instead to backtrack part of the army and besiege the city of Nijmegen. The alert Prince of Orange took advantage of the time thus gained to move his own small army to Amsterdam, and there, on June 20, 1672, the great dykes to the Zuidersee were opened, flooding the city and the plains around it, causing great loss to the local people, but putting a definitive end to any French plan to capture the capital. Further opened dykes left French troops helpless all over the country: the Dutchmen's last and only real defence, their *waterlinie*, had saved them. Though troops under Louis took Utrecht on June 30, and Turenne's men took Nijmegen on July 9, the initiative had been lost. After the dreadful spring and summer of this, their *rampjaar*, their year of disaster, the Dutch took heart at last, and dug in their heels in stubborn resistance.

Thereafter the military situation became ever more difficult for the French, and victory ever more unlikely, though the King was loath to accept the truth. The young Prince of Orange, now declared Stadthouder (governor) of the United Provinces, agreed to peace negotiations. Louis's response was outrageous: all the territories the French had conquered, regardless of their retreats forced by the flooding, were to be confirmed as France's possessions; all Dutch fortified garrisons were to be replaced by French garrisons; Dutch tariffs on French wines were to be rescinded and a huge indemnity paid; Frenchmen were to be permitted to travel at will in the United Provinces, subject not to Dutch law but to French; the Protestant burghers were to pay for the upkeep of Catholic priests in their own land; and, as a final slap in the republican Dutch face, an embassy must be sent each year to the French court, bearing a medallion expressing "the depth of their contrition, their subjection to [Louis's] royal authority and their eternal gratitude for his gracious clemency"—terms "as brutal and uncompromisingly vindictive as any that European powers have inflicted on each other in the course of their history as nation states." The proud and prosperous United Provinces of the Netherlands were to become, in effect, a vassal state of France.

Unsurprisingly, Louis's terms were rejected, and the fight went on. In September 1672 a combined preliminary imperial and Prussian force of 40,000 men, under the command of the great generalissimo of the Thirty Years War, Count Raimondo Montecuccoli, advanced into the Rhineland. The French armies, separated and discouraged, with increasing supply problems for their frequent sieges, gradually found themselves on the defensive. By November, the Regent Queen of impoverished Spain had even managed to send more reinforcements— "men for the Dutch and money for the Germans"—which at last gave Louis pause for thought, though an honourable retreat, much less an admission of defeat, remained for him impossible.

After seven further months of effort on both sides, months of hunger and disease and destruction, the French achieved one major victory at Maastricht, an important town in the Spanish Netherlands, which capitulated on June 29, 1673, after thirteen days of siege masterminded by the brilliant Captain Vauban. The following day, Louis entered the city in triumph. "What do you think of the conquest of Maastricht?" wrote a breathless Madame de Sévigné to her cousin. "The King alone had all the glory of it." But the capture of Maastricht was not enough to revive France's military fortunes. In September, pressed hard by the coalition, the French were forced to retreat from the United Provinces, retaining, of all their vanquished towns, only the lately captured Maastricht.

It had not been an entirely happy year for France's military reputation, as Louis was forced to reflect from the safety of Saint-Germain. The Dutch war was becoming a general war. A few weeks after the New Year of 1674, his cousin Charles II, King of England, signed a separate peace with the United Provinces, thereby withdrawing from France his crucial naval help. With Louis's own Marine still pitifully small, this was heavy news indeed. Behind the scenes, the astute young Prince of Orange had been working to detach Protestant England from Catholic France, and though the quietly Catholic Charles II had wished to continue supporting his French cousin at the expense of his Dutch nephew, his staunchly Protestant parliament had refused to vote him the means to do so. Charles was powerless within the confines of his constitutional monarchy, as Louis was disdainfully aware. His own monarchy, by contrast, was absolute, and his toothless parlement, since the defeat of the Fronde, nothing but a waste of good commercial time for its busy bourgeois members.

France's autumn withdrawal from the Spanish Netherlands, with only Maastricht to show for sixteen months of fighting, was a clear defeat, though Louis chose not to see it in that light. By the middle of the winter, in a tacit admission of the strength of resistance in the Netherlands itself, his troops were on the march to the east, to the region of the Franche-Comté, still held, if only just, by the failing Spanish Habsburgs.

The Franche-Comté, the former "Free County" of Burgundy, which bordered Switzerland and the Alsace, belonged, in Louis's view, within France's own natural frontiers. The prince de Condé had in fact captured the region already, during the War of Devolution in 1668, but the terms of the treaty concluding that war had obliged the French to return it to Spain. Now Louis was determined to get hold of the Franche-Comté for good, and he wanted to be recognized as having captured it in person. Accordingly, he sent Condé north to hold the Dutch at bay, Turenne to the east to confront the Emperor's forces, and two other generals to the south to deflect any possible Swiss reinforcements for the coalition. This left him with only the troops of the Franche-Comté itself to deal with—5,000 mercenary soldiers, plus a scratch band of 5,000 barely trained local militiamen. Louis himself led an army of 25,000 experienced men, including elite troops, and he took the precaution of sending the duc de Navailles ahead with a smaller force to carry out the preliminary work of invasion: scouting the terrain, establishing supply lines, bribing or executing local leaders, and terrorizing everyone else. This accomplished, Navailles was packed off to join the prince de Condé, leaving the way clear for Louis himself to take the credit for the region's capture.

On May 2, 1674, the King set up camp outside the town of Besançon, in the centre of the Franche-Comté region. The plan was simple: the unfortunate town was to be besieged, with as much noise and smoke as possible, after which it was to make an abject capitulation, opening its portals to the triumphant King of France. Captain Vauban was on hand to manage the siege itself. Queen Marie-Thérèse was on hand as well, and Athénaïs, and scores of courtiers from Saint-Germain, all in attendance to watch the spectacle and gasp in amazement at the explosions and the collapsing city walls.

Louis was an experienced entertainer. In his frequent ballets at court, he had often appeared as Alexander the Great and any number of other military heroes. Now he was to appear, in this "most theatrical form of warfare," in his own personal role of Louis le Grand. As always, his magnificent metteur en scène rose to the occasion: "[U]nder Vauban's direction, siege warfare came to look ever more like a ballet choreographed down to the last detail, or a stage tragedy with a foregone conclusion." As at Saint-Germain, as at Versailles, so now at Besançon. Throughout the siege, the King was constantly visible, "encouraging the troops." The town held out for thirteen days, then capitulated to Louis as cued, to the applause of half his court. He then went home, leaving the other towns of the Franche-Comté to be captured less theatrically by his generals. The last one fell on July 4: little Faucogney, defended by just thirty soldiers and two hundred townsmen, who declared to the French envoy inviting them to surrender that they were all "resolved to die for the King of Spain." They did.

On July 13, 1674, a week of festivities began at Versailles, to celebrate the capture of the Franche-Comté at last. The last magnificent banquet was held in one of the château's interior courtyards, where, "on a parterre strewn with flowers, an octagonal table had been built around an immense triumphal column." "Kings should enjoy giving pleasure," wrote Louis.

ELEVEN

The Course of True Loves

No place at the octagonal table had been set for Louise de la Val-lière, nor was she to be seen anywhere at Versailles on that splendid July evening. After seven years of alternating hope and hu-miliation, she had given up at last. To keep the courtiers guessing, as the King had been anxious to do, she had been permitted to remain his acknowledged maîtresse déclarée, while enduring a steady demotion in her real standing at court. She had even been foolish enough to receive the King privately during the later stages of Athénaïs's three pregnan-cies, when Louis routinely sought to console himself with casual af-fairs. But by the beginning of 1674, even desperate Louise had accepted that the King's heart would never again be hers. Religious by temperament, she made up her mind to put a belated end to her shameful situation in the classic way of the discarded royal mistress: she decided to enter the convent.

No one was surprised at the decision in itself, and Louise's friends can only have been pleased at this long-delayed step towards personal dignity. But the court on the whole was shocked by the choice of con-vent she had made. Far from a genteel refuge stocked with comforts, as the Ursuline convent might have been, the Carmelite convent which Louise had chosen was the most doctrinally rigid and the most austere of all. Its regime of absolute self-abnegation—endless hours of prayer, unheated stone cells, bare feet, minimal food and sleep, even self-flagellation—was regarded by most at court as only for the perversely religious. Even Louise herself seems to have quavered at the brink, using various weak excuses to postpone her departure: "Her chambermaid threw herself at her feet and begged her not to do it. How could anyone resist that?" asked Madame de Sévigné, with a rhetorical smirk.

Behind the scenes, the pliable Louise had been prodded along the path of repentance by two ambitious and powerful courtiers: Jacques-Bénigne Bossuet, bishop, religious orator extraordinaire, and harsh tutor to the young dauphin; and the marquis de Bellefonds, *maréchal de France* and *premier maître d'hôtel* of the King's household. Both were known *dévots*, staunch Catholics of the most unyielding kind, born again, as it were, to lives of absolute commitment to God's will, or at least to their own understanding of it. Committed to the "conversion"—the religious rebirth—of France, they viewed the court as their most vital field of operation. From the court flowed half the power in the land, and Bossuet was determined that, sooner or later, that half would be increased to the whole. He was a fanatical proponent of absolute monarchy, ordained by God: the divine right of a king to rule, challenged by no one—though advised, of course, by the wisest and most righteous men in the kingdom. The "conversion" of the King was thus Bossuet's worldly and otherworldly goal; through him, the whole of France could be regained for God, and Bossuet would one day lead to the heavenly gates a repentant nation of twenty-two million souls.

Louis's late mother, devoutly Catholic, "who had great influence on the King" and "whom he respected so much," had set the first torch aflame, but since her death, in 1666, it had had no obvious bearer. Her expected successor, pious Marie-Thérèse, had proved sadly unfit for the task, with no attractions to draw the King into her orbit, and no intelligence to draw anyone else. Now timid little Louise was to raise the heavy torch aloft. After so many years of tacit accommodation to the

King's desires, this sacrifice of herself, of her life at court, of all pleasure and all comfort, even of her two young children, was to jolt the
King into a reconsideration of his own sinful way of life—his uncontainable, adulterous sex life.

Athénaïs, at least, saw the stratagem for what it was. Louis, an instinctive if unreflecting Christian, had been periodically rattled by
doubts of his own salvation. At thirty-five, in superb health, he could
still brush aside his fear of the final reckoning, but Bossuet's influence
was nonetheless strong, and every day his cabale des dévots grew more
determined. The King was already inclined towards him because of his
support for the still contentious principle of absolute monarchy, in
which he himself, naturally enough, believed unequivocally. Apart
from anything else, the idea of it suited Louis's egocentric temperament: he had even admired the despotic rule of the Turkish sultans,
until he had been reminded that several of them had quite recently
been strangled.

The King needed no one, wanted no one, to tell him what to do,
least of all his mistress. "I command you all," he had told his ministers,
"if you should see that any woman, whoever she is, is getting the upper
hand and dictating to me, even in the slightest way, you are to alert me
at once, and I'll have got rid of her within twenty-four hours." If
Bossuet were to convince the King, if the King were to be "converted,"
it would mean the end of Athénaïs's own reign; she might herself be
locked away in some convent, dead to the world. The Carmelite idea
was altogether too dangerous: Louise would have to be stopped. Athénaïs dispatched Françoise, rational, unintriguing, unaligned with any
party, to persuade her to change her mind.

It was too late. Too many people had been informed for Louise to
retract her decision now; she would only look foolish, as if she had
been threatening the King in some impotent way. Françoise remonstrated. There were other convents, less harsh, less lonely, where she
could continue to see her friends and her children—she must think of
her children as well. Louise brushed it all aside. She had taken steps already along her new path of piety: beneath her silk court gowns, she
was wearing rough and scratchy pieces of hair shirt. As for her chil-

dren, they were the fruit of sin; her suffering at the separation, and theirs too, would serve as some expiation of the wickedness of their engendering. Neither Madame Scarron nor anyone else was going to deter her. She had lived a life of fornication, and now she had repented, like that greatest of all repentant fornicators, Mary Magdalene; like her, Louise hoped, she would one day attain forgiveness. To that end, she had determined to pass what remained of her life in penitence, beginning with an act of self-humiliation—a public apology to Queen Marie-Thérèse.

Françoise was aghast. "A public apology?" she exclaimed. "How unseemly!" But Louise insisted that, as her sin had been public, so her repentance should be, too; and indeed it was, with Louise kneeling at the Queen's feet, asking her pardon, watched by a crowd of scandalized or gleeful courtiers, the King tactically absent. The Queen raised Louise to her feet and kissed her. Athénaïs coolly invited her to supper the same evening.

The following morning, Louise bade farewell to the King—he shed a few tears, "but she's dead to me now"—and to her two young children, whose bewilderment and distress are best left undescribed. She was followed to Paris by dozens of courtiers, and for more than a year they continued to visit the Carmelite convent, watching through the grille as she knelt at prayer or took Communion, or merely walked from one place to the next with the lowered eyes and contained movements of a chaste bride of Christ. Though the dévots had pushed her further than she might otherwise have gone, Louise's conversion was nonetheless sincere; she wanted to live her life of penitence, undisturbed by pointing and staring people from a world she had rejected. But she had become a celebrity. At court, the dévot marquis de Bellefonds circulated her private letters, relaying her daily struggle to subdue the last remnants of her will. Louise asked permission to move to an isolated convent in the country, but this was denied. "She's too useful an example," replied the mother superior.

When the fuss had subsided and Louise had finally made her profession of vows, she continued to receive occasional visits from a very forgiving Marie-Thérèse, permitted, as the Queen, to penetrate be-

yond the convent grille with a few accompanying ladies. Athénaïs
came along once, determined to prove Louise's misery in her cold and
hungry reformed life. She spoke at length and loudly of "Monsieur's
brother" (the King), insisting that Sister Louise must surely have some
message for him—"I'll be sure to pass it on for you"—and maliciously
sent out for the ingredients of a favourite sauce, forbidden to Louise,
which she made herself, then ate "with an admirable appetite." "Are
you sure you're comfortable here?" she asked Louise, disingenuously.
"I'm not at all comfortable,", Louise replied with dignity, "but I am
content."

Françoise, by contrast, while comfortable enough in her little apartment at Saint-Germain, was not content at all. With Louise out of the
picture at last, Louis had begun to turn his attention towards his children's quiet governess. His passion for Athénaïs had not lessened, but
her volatile temperament and her many pregnancies had encouraged
him to engage in a series of casual affairs. Surrounded by willing maid-
ens and matrons who "would have given themselves to the devil to
have the King's love," he had found it only too easy, and with the gorgeous Athénaïs long and securely captured, Louis the passionate
hunter-King was now training his sights on a more elusive prey. At
almost forty, three years older than the King himself, Françoise remained a definite beauty, and, though not overtly voluptuous in the
way of Athénaïs, she still possessed the contained sensuality of her
young womanhood, with her reluctance to join the troupe of would-be
royal mistresses only increasing her appeal.

Françoise did not want to become Louis's mistress. She did not
want to be blown hither and thither in a gale of honours and emotions,
only to be pushed out at last, discarded and humiliated, into a cold
convent cell. She was doing very well with her 6,000 livres per year; her
position was not grand, but it was reasonably secure, as secure, at least,
as any servant's position at court could be. Naturally, she did not want
to risk offending Athénaïs, on whose goodwill that position largely
rested. And above all, Françoise was proud; though modest in her de-

meanour and careful to make no claims for herself, nonetheless, in her heart she felt herself to be superior to the overdressed, overpainted cat-fighters jostling daily for the King's attention.

For six months or more, since her January arrival at court, Françoise had been battling to resist his advances, but the battle had been as much with herself as with the handsome, persuasive Louis, at thirty-five a man at the peak of his powers, not least physically. "The Queen must have gone to bed last night very happy with the husband she's chosen," she had written suggestively after seeing him for the first time, and though that had been in 1660, in the intervening four-teen years Louis had lost none of his appeal for her. Tall among his contemporaries, strongly built and with a natural grace of movement, a fine horseman and an exceptionally good dancer, his presence majes-tic, his face manly and framed by a virile abundance of curly dark hair, he was, in appearance at least, the very model of a modern monarch. He spoke little, often wittily, never in anger, and always to the point. A great admirer of "the ladies," he also enjoyed female company even without the promise of sex. And although indifferently educated and not especially clever, he had an instinct for talent and sincerity in both women and men, believing firmly, at the same time, that women should confine themselves to family and religious activities (and illicit sex where required) and should above all refrain from meddling in anything remotely political.

The quietly spoken, womanly, capable governess of the royal bâ-tards thus suited his inclinations very well, and it swiftly became clear that he suited her own. By the beginning of March, four years after be-ginning her charge and two months after her arrival at court, the strain of resisting both the King himself and her own strongest feelings had made her quite unwell. "My sufferings . . . You've been so thought-ful . . . I'm feeling better . . . I hope I won't fall ill again . . . My deli-cate health . . . I shall have to take more care of myself . . ." So she mumbled to Père Gobelin, in a sort of code which he understood only in part. He knew very well that Françoise had not caught cold or come down with a fever or broken a leg. He realized that her illness was *moral*, in the term of the day; he saw that she was distressed in mind, and that naturally, this had affected her health.

The situation was difficult. The King's habits were only too well known, and after all, he was not just any man. Françoise was his subject, his servant, and his employee; most people at court would have considered her honoured to become his mistress as well. The very priest she had appealed to had told her as much: "He didn't understand at all," she told Père Gobelin. "He said there was nothing sinful in it. I'm sure you would have thought differently." Only two months after arriving, she had been ready to leave the court, "to remove myself from a situation very far from assuring my salvation . . . If a pious and sensible person advises me to stay, I'll do so, whatever it costs me, but if I had my own way, I'd leave . . ." Ah, no, Père Gobelin had replied, there were the children to think of, there was their future as Christian souls; this was the reason she had come to court, against her will, in the first place. Understanding the King's designs on Françoise, but failing to understand, from her roundabout phrases, that she herself had been tempted, he counselled her to stay at her post, warning her at the same time to keep away from Louis if she could.

It is true that the children were important to Françoise, though probably only Mignon could have kept her at court. "If he were walking, I'd be happy with them all," she wrote. "He's always ill, though not in danger of his life, but that doesn't comfort me much; it's terrible to see someone you love suffering . . . I wept about it all through mass today. Nothing could be more stupid than loving a child so much when he isn't even mine . . . It's really foolish of me to stay in such a disagreeable situation . . ."

The "disagreeable situation" was being made worse by the involvement—or, as Françoise saw it, the interference—of Mignon's mother. After years of more or less ignoring her children, Athénaïs had begun to take an interest in their upbringing. Needless to say, her erratic views did not accord with those of their steady governess, and daily disagreements between the two swiftly became the norm. It was not that Athénaïs had experienced any sudden surge in maternal affection;

rather, she had noticed the attention the King had been paying
Françoise, and, reluctant to challenge either of them directly, she had
given vent to her anxiety by niggling about the children, counter-
manding instructions, and generally getting in Françoise's way wherever she could.

Françoise had managed to endure the "situation" until it touched
the question of the children's health—indeed, given the medical practices of the time, of their physical safety. Athénaïs had been talking
to the physicians. The duc du Maine, she decided, was to return to
Antwerp for more stretching treatments on his afflicted leg, and his little brother, the two-year-old comte de Vexin, sway-backed or round-
shouldered, was to have thirteen cauterizations along his spine in an
attempt to flatten the offending curve. Françoise protested the gro-
tesque propositions regarding "my little princes." "How could you
know better than I what's best for my children?" challenged Athénaïs,
and Françoise lost her self-control at last. That evening, she wrote an
impassioned missive to Père Gobelin:

Madame de Montespan and I had a dreadful argument today. I
cried and cried, and she told the King all about it, from her point
of view, anyway . . . I can tell you it's not easy at all being here
with this sort of thing happening every day . . . I've thought a
thousand times about becoming a nun, but I'm afraid I'd regret
it . . . I've been wanting to leave here ever since I arrived, but
I'm afraid I'd regret that, too . . . Please, I beg you, think of my
peace of mind. I know my duties here are one path to salvation
for me, but I'm sure I could get there more easily from somewhere else, and I can't see why God would want me to put up
with Madame de Montespan. She's incapable of friendship, and
I can't do without it. Every disagreement we have is another reason for her to hate me. She complains of me to the King, undermining his respect for me, saying whatever she likes, so that now
he thinks I'm some kind of madwoman. I dare not appeal to him
directly; she'd never forgive me if I did, and anyway, I owe too

much to her, I couldn't say anything against her, so I won't ever be able to do anything about it. I suppose I'll be dead sooner or later in any case . . .

Thus, with stoic melodrama, Françoise concluded her complaint. Père Gobelin urged less melodrama and more stoicism, and in the end, stoicism triumphed. A fortnight later, she informed him as follows:

I spoke to Madame de Montespan yesterday morning . . . We had quite a heated conversation, but frank on both sides. Then I went to mass, and afterwards dined with the King . . . The upshot of it all is that I shall try to reconcile myself to things here for the time being . . . but I'm quite determined to leave at the end of the year . . . God will guide me to do whatever is best for my salvation.

Whatever was "best for [her] salvation," there was increasingly little chance of her leaving the court at all. It was infuriating to have to deal with Athénaïs's tantrums and interventions, but at the same time, only the court could provide salvation in another, worldly sense. "[Françoise] was born with nothing," as her secretary was later to write, "and staying at court with the King was her only means of getting away from that. She said that many times."

And that was not all. "Keep away from the King if you can," Père Gobelin had warned her. But she could not. It was not just that she was living at the heart of the court, seeing the King and speaking to him every day. It was not just a question of staying in the background, avoiding his glances, pretending not to notice certain gestures and hints and, if it came to the point, refusing him outright. All of this she could have done, as Père Gobelin well knew; in a battle of moral strength with the King, Françoise would surely be the victor. What Père Gobelin had failed to realize, and Françoise had not dared to say, was that the enemy was not in fact the King himself, in all his strength, but rather her own weakness. At the age of thirty-eight, for the second time in her life, she had fallen in love.

Athénaïs had sensed it, and, as her ever more aggressive behaviour over the children revealed, she had sensed the King's response as well. In July 1674, she had taken spirited action in her own defence, by presenting Françoise with an offer of marriage from the duc de Villars-Brancas, an embarrassing and decrepit old hunchback who had buried three wives already. "She and Madame la duchesse de Richelieu are trying to marry me off," wrote the supposed fiancée to her confessor. "It won't succeed . . . As if I hadn't already enough trouble in my present enviable state without looking for more in a state that makes three-quarters of the human race miserable."

No more was heard of the duc de Villars-Brancas, but in the same month of Françoise's indignant refusal, the King presented her, for no apparent reason, with 100,000 francs (about 35,000 livres), of which, perhaps to assuage her conscience, she distributed 1,000 to several convents. In September he accorded her a lucrative thirty-year monopoly on the manufacture of oven and furnace hearths for the baking and dyeing trades. In October he gave her another 100,000 francs outright, then another 50,000, then yet another 50,000. Unsurprising, then, that somewhere in the first few days of November 1674, she apparently overcame her religious scruples, or her fear of discovery or rejection or dismissal, and became Louis's mistress at last.

It is a measure of Françoise's discretion, and of the King's preference for secrecy in his private life, that no one seems to have discovered the fact, at least not at once. "We've had a horoscope read for my younger son," wrote an unaware Liselotte to her aunt. "It seems he's going to be the Pope; to be honest, I think it's more likely he'll turn out to be the Antichrist." Primi Visconti noticed only that the going price for the office of gentleman of the bedchamber, with the right to attend the King as he answered his evening call of nature, had risen to 60,000 écus, with one or two hardy souls prepared to pay 100,000. "So you see how the French value everything that comes from the King, even the most repugnant things."

Though almost eveything at court had its price, Françoise was not a woman to be purchased. Years of virtuous widowhood had made that clear; the gifts of francs and oven monopolies might as easily have insulted as persuaded her. She had at first been startled by the King's admiration, then disbelieving, then flattered, and finally responsive. "A good reputation is a wonderful thing to have," she had said, "but it costs a great deal. The first sacrifice it demands is pleasure." If she had determined to make that sacrifice at the age of twenty-five, now, at thirty-nine, she had changed her mind. From the summit of glory, the demigod King of France had turned towards her with a delightful invitation on his lips, and she had accepted. "Virtue alone is our only wealth," came an echo from her girlhood. "Not so," she replied. Pleasure was wealth, too, and the love of a King was wealth, and she would rejoice in them both while she could.

On November 10, Françoise wrote brightly to her brother Charles:

> You may have heard that I'm buying an estate . . . It's Maintenon, fourteen leagues from Paris, ten from Versailles, and four from Chartres. It's beautiful and grand, and will bring in ten or eleven thousand livres a year. So if the worst comes to the worst, you'll always have somewhere to retreat to . . . I hope I'll be able to see you before the end of the winter. I'm feeling very well indeed . . .

Two days later, Athénaïs gave birth to her fifth child by the King, a daughter, Louise-Marie-Anne, Mademoiselle de Tours, swiftly dubbed "Toutou."

If Françoise thought, for a few glorious weeks, that she was on the point of replacing Athénaïs as the King's maîtresse déclarée, her illusions did not last long. The courtiers' gossip and her own clear eyes reminded her daily that she was in fact just one more link in the daisy-chain of court flowers plucked by Louis. "The King fucks them, the Lord saves them," declared Madame de Sévigné's cousin, the comte de Bussy-Rabutin, newly released from prison, as he observed yet another cast-off royal mistress making her way to the convent, and avoiding a second spell in the Bastille only by his oblique flattery of the King's masculine pride.

That Françoise had not plotted to become Louis's mistress, as was common, and even expected of more or less every eligible woman at court, but had given in at last, after a year or more, may have been a mark in her favour as far as her "salvation" was concerned, but it made no difference now. The King had made a conquest of her, just as he had made of so many before her. The first excitement once past, Françoise's deep-seated pride, her sense of herself as beyond such things, above such things, was wounded to the core. She could not pretend to be so special, after all. She had lowered herself, and become just one more pretty skittle in a common row, like every other sexually obliging woman at court.

Humiliated, she watched as the King continued with the many amours he regarded as his due: young Anne Lucie de la Mothe; mature and lovely Lydie de Rochefort; the "divine nymph" Marie du Fresnoy, daughter of a laundress, elevated to the King's bed via that of his minister Louvois; lively Olympe de Soissons, niece of the late Cardinal Mazarin; Anne de Soubise in a particular pair of emerald earrings, indicating her husband's absence and her own availability; red-haired, blue-eyed Isabelle de Ludres. "I am sure, Madame, that those eyes have caused plenty of damage," Louis said to her suavely, while Athénaïs spread the improbable rumour that Isabelle's body was covered in scabs. "Not as much as I would wish, Sire," Isabelle replied. She was soon satisfied. "He liked almost all women," Françoise's niece later wrote, "except his own wife."

As Françoise watched one mistress succeed the next, so the maîtresse déclarée watched as well. The casual affairs Athénaïs tolerated, and at times even encouraged, regarding them as kind of a safety valve for the King's powerful appetites, and at the same time no real challenge to her own position. In due course Athénaïs was promoted to the position of surintendante of the Queen's household, a deep humiliation for Marie-Thérèse, but a triumph for la belle Montespan herself. The troupes of virginal demoiselles d'honneur and sophisticated dames d'honneur, two traditional royal harems, were thenceforth to be chosen by her. She took care to fill them, as far as possible, with the least attractive blossoms of France's noble family trees.

But Françoise remained her chief rival. Unable to dismiss her, Athénaïs took to battling with pettier weapons. She began to argue again over the care of the children: the King took Athénaïs's part, but gave Françoise a present of four hundred livres to have some new gowns made for herself. In February 1675, overhearing Athénaïs berating Françoise in public for her lowly birth and her marriage to the disfigured Scarron, the King responded in the time-honoured way of rewarding a favoured commoner: he raised her to the nobility, naming her marquise de Maintenon, after the pretty estate she had recently bought, leaving Athénaïs "berating Louis for pandering to her pride."

In a last-ditch attempt to distract the King from the new marquise de Maintenon, Athénaïs cast at his feet a pair of lovely but manipulable rosebuds: her own niece, Mademoiselle de Thianges, who was, however, too much of a huntress herself for Louis's machismo temperament, and, more successfully, the marquise Marie-Angélique de Fontanges, just seventeen years old and perfectly suited to the purpose at hand, being "a sweet and simple girl," according to Primi Visconti. "As beautiful as an angel, and as stupid as a basket," was the assessment of the less indulgent abbé de Choisy, who ought to have known: a connoisseur of female beauty and intelligence, he had glided through many a drawing-room, and into many a lady's boudoir, convincingly disguised as a woman himself.

Madame de Sévigné would no doubt have agreed with his assessment of La Fontanges. She reports having watched the young marquise and her mentor dancing at a court ball. Despite her heavy figure, Athénaïs had danced well, but the lovely Marie-Angélique, "all dressed up by Madame de Montespan," lacked rhythm, it seems, as well as mental powers. "She wanted to dance a minuet . . . but her legs wouldn't do what you know they have to do; the courante went no better, and in the end all she could manage was a curtsy." "Her astonishing beauty made the King get carried away without thinking, and almost in spite of himself," said Choisy. "No amount of good qualities can make up for stupidity," wrote the chevalier de Méré, shaking his head from the sidelines.

Though Athénaïs was evidently more convinced of the King's interest in Françoise than Françoise was herself, both seem to have been equally anxious about it. Humiliated that she had not replaced Athénaïs, after all, as first in the King's affections, Françoise had retreated altogether from his bed, but if the maîtresse's laurels were not to pass to her, she was still unwilling for Athénaïs to keep them. In consequence, taking a leaf out of Athénaïs's own book, she decided to try to distract the King with a sexually appealing but otherwise less powerful rival, a pretty young girl who could tempt Louis away from Athénaïs's embraces, but who lacked the maturity and discretion to replace Françoise herself in his esteem and confidence.

At thirty-nine, a grandmotherly age at court, Françoise could not easily compete with an ever-replenishing flutter of freshly seduceable girls, but real friendship, real intimacy with the King, perhaps even real influence over him—these she could aim for. And if they brought with them physical love, so much the better, but not if she must share the King with half a dozen others. She had known little enough of love, had so rarely dared seek it, had given herself to the King at last, and had been repaid with his infidelities—she wanted him to desire her, but more importantly, she wanted him to need her, to esteem her. Not least, in assuming the role of alternative supplier of casual mistresses to the King, Françoise would be striking a blow at Athénaïs's ability to manipulate him.

In the longer term, if she could not seduce the King, Françoise could persuade, or guide, perhaps even control him, while his basic sexual needs were attended to by some pretty demoiselle. Naturally, cleverness of any kind would be a disadvantage: a simple, sweet, manipulable girl would suit her purpose best.

Athénaïs having already selected the ideally dim but luscious Marie-Angélique as her own pseudo-rival, Françoise fixed on nineteen-year-old Olympe de Piennes, lately arrived at court with two pretty little sisters and a stern old aunt. Olympe was exceedingly beautiful, and, unlike Marie-Angélique, an excellent dancer as well; indeed, during her performance in a carnival ballet, she had captured the hearts of half the King's courtiers, including the dissolute old gourmand duc de la Ferté:

"For her sake," Primi Visconti relates, "the duc abandoned his gluttony and drinking, and from a big, fat, greasy man he became a skinny little well-behaved fellow, but he was wasting his time; he was married, and the girl was spoiled for choice where lovers were concerned."

The determined Françoise, "who had been paying her a lot of affectionate attention," issued an invitation to Olympe, together with her aunt and sisters, to visit the apartments set aside for her use at Liselotte's palace of Saint-Cloud, near the lovely Paris park of the Bois-de-Boulogne. They came, and found prepared for them a sumptuous repast, at which Olympe's personal servant turned out to be— the King himself. While Françoise sequestered the aunt and sisters in polite conversation, Louis took Olympe away for a few private words of his own. She was subsequently observed driving to and fro between Paris and the court, though it was noted that she was always home by midnight.

The King's many dalliances were, naturally, prime matter for gossip at court, and they seem to have misled the ambitious Bossuet and his dévots into imagining a decline in Louis's eight-year-long passion for Athénaïs. Towards Easter of 1675, they opened a new front in their campaign against his sinful way of life, flamboyantly typified in his too-public affair of double adultery with Madame de Montespan. A ferocious sermon, delivered by the court's second orator extraordinaire, the Jesuit Louis Bourdaloue, condemned Athénaïs outright as a "stumbling block" on the King's path to salvation.

But it was Bossuet's stern private lecture, threatening hellfire or the loss of France to the Huguenots or, worst of all, perhaps, a slipping in his subjects' esteem, that brought Louis at last to his repentant knees. "Madame de Montespan had had a dream that all her hair had fallen out," wrote Primi Visconti. "Her maid came to tell me." And a few days afterwards, to enormous scandal, a humble local priest refused la belle Montespan herself the Easter absolution and Communion required of all its adherents by the Roman Catholic Church. Bossuet ad-

vised that she be sent away from court, and shortly after Easter she retreated to, of all places, Françoise's new château of Maintenon.

Françoise went with her. "Madame de Montespan and I were always the best friends in the world," she later told her niece. "She used
to speak to me quite openly and tell me whatever she was thinking. We
never expected our friendship to end because, although we certainly
had some fairly lively quarrels, that didn't change our feeling for each
other." At this point, their "feeling for each other" probably included
a good measure of mutual consolation; both had retreated rather
bruised from their various battles with the inconstant King. Athénaïs
did not know that he and Françoise had become lovers, but she was
keenly aware of the possibility of it. In fact, it seems that by this time
Françoise had drawn back from the King, not through any pious remorse, but rather through remorse at her own foolishness in joining
the already too-large ranks of royal mistresses.

For the recent attacks of the dévot battalion she had shown no sympathy, as her confessor Père Gobelin had noticed. In annoyed tones,
she had dissuaded him from visiting her at court, though he was anxious to do so. "No, it wasn't me who asked you to come here," she
wrote. "Of course I can't stop you, and naturally I'm more concerned
for your convenience than my own pleasure . . . but you know I'm not
mistress of my own time here . . . As to the devotions you've suggested for Lent, I'd like to follow them, but really, I can't possibly, I
haven't a moment to spare in the morning, and it's all I can do to get to
mass every day. As for what you say about my dress, it's not as easy as
that; I'm not wearing anything colourful as it is, and if you want me to
wear less gold on my gowns, I'll have to have new ones made especially . . . Père Mascaron preached against the King today; it was quite
out of place, exceeding the bounds of good taste . . ."

The dévots' victory was in any case brief. In the weeks following
Athénaïs's separation from the King, Bossuet paid several visits to each
of them, determined to keep them on the straight and narrow road which
he had laid down for their salvation. But a bare month after Easter, the
primrose path was already beckoning. In July, the King returned from
Flanders, and Bossuet agreed that Athénaïs might return to court,

"provided she was accompanied at all times by three or four *prudes*"—women of unimpeachable respectability. "From now on," wrote Madame de Sévigné in early July, "her friends will be advising her to do just what Bossuet says." But by the middle of the month, Bossuet's directions were passing completely unheeded. At a reception hosted by Queen Marie-Thérèse and chaperoned by a roomful of dévots, the separated lovers met for the first time in more than two months. They greeted each other, shed tears, exchanged a few words in lowered tones, bowed to the guests, and retired to the nearest bedroom.

Françoise was not present to witness this startling victory of passion over piety. She had left the court at the end of April, not to escape her "disagreeable situation," but pursuant to a victory of her own, in the matter of little Mignon's crippled leg: despite his mother's wishes, he had not returned to the "prison rack" at Antwerp, but instead had set off with his governess to the healing waters of the Pyrenees spa town of Barèges, far to the south near the Spanish border. It was a rough coach journey of almost two months—"It took less time to get to America"—and Barèges itself proved "a place more frightful than I can tell you; and what's more, even in July it's freezing." But despite frequent migraines and "dreadful company," Françoise felt well during her six-week sojourn in Barèges, "since I have less trouble and aggravation here than elsewhere," as she told her brother Charles.

"Elsewhere," at Saint-Germain, the trouble and aggravation had not passed unnoticed. "My dear, here's a turn of the cards that will surprise you," a riveted Madame de Sévigné relayed to her daughter the following month. "The bosom friendship between Madame de Montespan and her travelling friend [is] an absolute aversion . . . It's all bitterness, it's dislike, it's white, it's black . . . There's been a rumbling underground for six months or more, and now it's starting to come to the surface. The friend's friends are all very upset about it . . ."

Françoise, no doubt also "very upset about it," had in any case managed a temporary escape. "It seems a thousand years since I heard anything from the court or from Paris," she wrote to Père Gobelin only a week after her departure, "and I assure you I haven't been bored for a moment. Monsieur le duc du Maine is the most delightful companion.

He needs constant care, but I'm so fond of him that it's a pleasure for me to give it." At Barèges, Françoise took daily spa-water baths in her room, and "our prince," now five years old, was also bathed and massaged every day, with the joyful result that "he's walking, not very vigorously yet, but it seems that eventually he'll walk normally. You can't know how tenderly I feel towards this child, but you know enough to guess how tremendously happy I am about this."

En route back to court from Barèges, she spent a happy fortnight in her native Niort, staying at the Ursuline convent with Sister Céleste, kind-hearted rescuer of her early days there, and at the château of Mursay with her cousin Philippe and his wife Marie-Anne. Françoise greatly enjoyed the company of Philippe and Marie-Anne, whom she had not seen since her visit to Mursay in the summer of 1668, seven years before. Their two boys, Philippe and Henri-Benjamin, had grown beyond recognition; they were now aged eleven and seven respectively, and their little sister, Marthe-Marguerite, was almost three years old. Françoise was delighted with the three children, particularly the girl—"my little angel"—and determined to do whatever she could to advance their prospects as they grew older. Philippe and Marie-Anne were naturally pleased, and showed their well-placed cousin "every sort of consideration and friendship." Young Philippe, too, not far off his naval apprenticeship, was already old enough to appreciate the possibility of influence at court; within the next few weeks he wrote several letters to Françoise, enclosing information about himself to be passed on to the marquis de Louvois, Minister of War.

In October 1675, Françoise arrived back at Saint-Germain. Hand in hand with the little duc du Maine, limping along beside her, she made a triumphal entry into the King's apartments. "People bring up children too delicately here," huffed a jealous Liselotte. "If I were master, they'd all be sent to my aunt in Osnabrück."

Athénaïs, though no doubt relieved to see her five-year-old son walking at last, was also less pleased with the praise accruing to the new marquise de Maintenon because of it. Françoise's six-month absence had allowed Athénaïs's relations with the King to settle back into much their old pattern, with herself the undisputed queen of Louis's affections and, as *La Sévigné* noted, "calmly taking precedence of all the duchesses." But beneath the happy surface, things were no longer the same as they had once been. Though still sexually enamoured of Athénaïs, Louis was growing tired of her constant tantrums and demands, her wild extravagance—in a single evening she had lost, then rewon, four million pistoles (forty million livres) at cards—and her jokes, in company, at the Queen's expense: "Remember, Madame, she is your mistress," he had at one point to remind her.

"The King's attachment for her is still extreme," wrote Madame de Sévigné later that summer."It's certainly enough to annoy *le curé* [Bossuet] and everyone else, but perhaps it's not enough for her. There's a sadness behind her outward triumph." If Louis was still attached to Athénaïs, his heart was certainly not hers alone. "They're all good enough for him," noted Liselotte, "provided they're women: peasants, gardeners' daughters, chambermaids, ladies of quality, as long as they can pretend to be in love with him." Athénaïs still had confidence enough to sit down to cards with Marie-Thérèse, draped in nothing more than a dressing gown, with the poor Queen herself "only too happy to be invited at all, and often enough sent on her way with the sort of wink you'd give to dismiss a servant." But, beyond any doubt, her star was waning at last. "They say she's happy," began Madame de Sévigné, "but *one* is speaking of Madame de Maintenon now as his first or second friend."

For two further years, the Queen wept and prayed and gambled at hombre, all to no avail, while Françoise became lethargic, fell ill with migraine, bewailed her "situation" to Père Gobelin, and sought periodic sanctuary at Maintenon. During a second visit to the southern spas in 1677, she even stooped to using seven-year-old Mignon to further her cause: a long series of charming letters to the court, penned by the little boy but clearly dictated by herself, kept the King's attention on her throughout the four months of her absence. As for Athénaïs, she began to overeat seriously and even, it seems, to drink. These indulgences had the effect which eight pregnancies had been unable to achieve: already struggling with a strong family tendency to embonpoint, she was soon of a very generous circumference. The courtier Primi Visconti, seeing her struggling out of her carriage in her long skirts, caught sight of one of her legs, "and it was almost as fat as my own torso," he declared, adding gallantly, "though it's true I have lost quite a bit of weight recently."

In April 1677, Athénaïs had borne a sixth child to the King, a daughter who was named Françoise-Marie, and soon created Mademoiselle de Blois. The little girl was born at Maintenon, where Françoise and Athénaïs had retreated together while the King was away with his armies in the Netherlands. "I've had Monsieur le duc du Maine [Mignon] and Madame de Montespan here for six weeks," Françoise had written to her cousin at the beginning of the month, "so you can imagine I have plenty to do." The three had remained at Maintenon until the middle of May, a sojourn of some three months, which suggests that the friendship between the two women remained strong, despite their "lively quarrels" and the court gossip relayed by Madame de Sévigné. The new baby's name was perhaps an indication of the friendship—Athénaïs's four previous known children by the King had all been named either Louis or Louise—but it may equally have been a rather tactless indication of the King's own continuing interest in Françoise: their previous daughter, born during the days of Louis's secret visits to the Paris house, had been named Louise-Françoise. In August 1678, separated, reconciled, separated, and reconciled again, Athénaïs gave birth to the last of her children with the King—not at Maintenon, however, but in her own château of Clagny, near Versailles. The newborn comte de Toulouse was named Louis-Alexandre, so completing, with his brothers Louis-Auguste and Louis-César, Athénaïs's trio of little heroes.

One love story of these years, at least, had ended more or less happily, albeit in the "state that makes three-quarters of the human race miserable." Early in 1678, at the age of forty-four, Françoise's brother Charles had finally married. His sister had been correct in regarding his governorship of the town of Amersfoort as a temporary establishment. Following further efforts on her part, albeit not noticeably on his own, he was now governor of an entire region, that of Cognac, in southern France.

Charles, so like his father in so many ways, had mimicked him in marriage as well, taking a bride almost young enough to be his grand-daughter. The new Madame d'Aubigné was Geneviève Piètre, only daughter of a provincial counsellor, and just fifteen years old. Charles had said nothing at all to his sister about the marriage until it was a fait accompli. Françoise had pretended not to care, but in fact she was deeply offended, having been for a year or more in the process of ar-ranging a marriage for Charles herself, in fact no fewer than five times. Charles had apparently been happy to leave things in her hands, spec-ifying only the (large) size of dowry he expected, but in the end he had made his own impulsive match.

Geneviève was neither rich nor pregnant, and Françoise was baffled by the step Charles had taken. "I hope you didn't get married just for the sake of getting married," she wrote to him a few days after the event, with her new sister-in-law *en visite* at Saint-Germain, "and I hope you'll try to make a reasonable person of your wife." First impressions had not been good. "She seems very spoiled to me," Françoise continued snappily. "The middling classes always bring up their children worse than anyone else."

Her letter, hectoring and disappointed, reveals as much about her-self as about the unpolished fifteen-year-old Geneviève. There is good sense in it, and much affection, but also anxiety about social standards, and above all an assumption of authority which must at times have rankled with Charles, the more so, perhaps, since he had been relying for years on his younger sister for his very daily bread. For whatever reason, Françoise evidently regarded herself as entitled to advise, if not dictate to Charles how he and his wife should set about their mar-ried life, "and if you don't take my advice," she warned, "you'll be sorry one day, because she won't be fit for decent company."

Don't let her get up late—she's a slug; she's been having break-fast at eleven . . . Don't let her go out alone, don't let her mix with low types, and don't let her play the grande dame, either, or you'll both end up looking ridiculous . . . She spends two or three hours a day in front of the mirror, painting her face, but that's just her age . . . She's modest and pious—that you should encourage . . . Her manners are atrocious, and she speaks like a fishwife, but that's the least of our problems; she'll soon learn to speak proper French . . .

It is revealing of the earthy nature of this brother-sister relationship that Françoise also felt free to give Charles advice about his sex life:

> If you want to be happy, try not to get tired of your wife. Don't behave crudely in front of her, and don't let her behave crudely in front of you. I advise you not to sleep together all the time— you have two nice bedrooms which will suit you both perfectly. Don't take any notice of what anyone says about it; nothing matters except your own happiness. Don't let her get dressed or undressed when there are men present, and don't get undressed in front of her yourself, if your valets are in the room . . . Don't ever talk about your wife in public . . .

And she added:

> You'll find it strange that a woman who's never been married herself should be giving you so much advice about marriage, but honestly, with everything I've seen—people make each other miserable, and it's through the tiniest things, but when these things happen day after day, in the end they really loathe each other. I do so want to see you happy. There's nothing I wouldn't do to help you.

It is curious that Françoise describes herself here as "a woman who's never been married," despite her eight years of admittedly unusual marriage to Scarron. This is probably a reference to the absence of sex between them, though in the rest of the letter she seems to be speaking of something that she has experienced for herself as well as observed in many other marriages: the need for a certain reserve, a kind of self-containment in daily life, not less than the politeness shown to others known less intimately. "Try not to get tired of your wife. Don't behave crudely in front of her . . ." If you want to be happy, she is telling her brother, you and your wife must respect each other.

Whether Charles ignored his sister's advice, or whether it was simply no good, he did not manage to avoid "getting tired" of young Geneviève. Five years later Françoise was transferring money to "that poor creature Garé," one of his several mistresses.

I n London, in the same year of 1677, another couple had entered the marital state, and though no one had expected it, least of all themselves, it was to make this particular couple quite happy. In November, the Catholic-leaning English King Charles II had married off his niece, Princess Mary, to the daring young Dutchman Prince Willem of Orange. Like Geneviève Piètre, Mary was just fifteen years old, though unlike Charles d'Aubigné, Calvinist Willem was still a youthful twenty-seven. The marriage sealed an alliance between England and the United Provinces, a perilous alliance for the Catholic French, which would eventually lead England to the dual reign of William and Mary and a firmly Protestant crown at last.

It was one more frustration for the King of France. More than five years after his affronted pride had led him to attack the United Provinces, there was still no sign of peace. Louis had been forced to make concessions, handing over conquered towns in the Spanish Netherlands in exchange for several southern territories. There had been victories: the previous year, the great Dutch admiral Ruyters had been vanquished at Stromboli, and France's armies had gained 15,000 Hungarians, eager to brandish their own exotic swords at their hated Habsburg Emperor. And in April 1677 Louis's brother, the flamboyant Monsieur, had beaten the Prince of Orange at Cassel, despite having come late to the battle—when the first shots were fired, "he was still sitting in front of the mirror, adjusting his wig." This had been a bittersweet victory, all the same. "The people of Paris went wild with joy," wrote Primi Visconti. "They really love Monsieur. But at court they'd rather he'd lost the battle for the King's sake . . . since the King's never been in anything but sieges. They say he'd give ten million to have been at the crossing of the Rhine in person . . ."

But neither Stromboli nor Cassel nor any number of poorly defended Dutch towns had been enough to give France a final victory, and put an end to the fighting for good. Spreading far beyond the Netherlands, Louis's second unprovoked game of soldiers had metamorphosed from a promenade militaire into a series of tough campaigns lasting six years, costing tens of thousands of livres, laying waste to towns and farmlands, and, crucially, breeding a deep mistrust of Louis himself that would, in due course, bring his kingdom to near ruin.

In August 1678, peace negotiations began at last in the Dutch city of Nijmegen. They continued until the end of the year, and involved not only France and the United Provinces but also England, Spain, Sweden, Denmark, six German states, and the Holy Roman Empire. The French were confirmed in their possession of some conquered territories, including rich Flanders and the much-desired Franche-Comté.

On the strength of this, Louis unilaterally declared the war a complete victory, and to commemorate it, he presented his premier architect, Jules Hardouin-Mansart, with a commission of unexampled magnificence: *la Galerie des Glaces*, the Hall of Mirrors, at Versailles. The elaborate ceiling, painted by Charles Le Brun, was to convey the glory, such as it was—or rather, such as it was to be considered—of Louis's military conquests in the Netherlands. The palace of Saint-Germain was declared too modest to house the court and the person of Louis le Grand. The principal royal residence in future years was to be Versailles, and to this end, orders went out for tens of thousands of workmen to rebuild and extend and embellish the "little hunting lodge" to the required level of splendour.

> *The brazen throat of war had ceased to roar;*
> *All now was turned to jollity and game,*
> *To luxury and riot, feast and dance . . .*

With peace come at last, the court returned to its customary ways. And for the figure at its shining centre, almost all was well. On September 5, 1678, the King celebrated his fortieth birthday, receiving an excellent report from his physicians, at least. "This year had been exactly as one would wish for a life so precious as his own," they recorded, though one malicious princess, rejected, it seems, after a brief affair, had found the King's "sceptre" rather smaller than it might have been.

"The Queen of Spain is weeping and wailing," wrote Madame de Sévigné a year and a week later, in the middle of September 1679. But, though she had hardly less reason to weep and wail, it was not to the neglected Spanish Marie-Thérèse that Madame de Sévigné was now referring. The kingdom of Spain itself had just gained a new queen, by courtesy of the King of France, and on the last day of August, at the château of Fontainebleau, she had endured a prolonged ceremony of official congratulations on her ascension to the rarefied ranks of the crowned heads of Europe.

"The Spanish ambassador arrived in a magnificent coach," wrote Primi Visconti, "but it was the same one he'd arrived in ten years before: Paris was scandalized . . . His wife spoke a mixture of Roman, Genoese, Milanese, Spanish, and French. No one could understand it."

The unhappy new Queen of Spain was Marie-Louise d'Orléans, a lively, attractive, and accomplished girl, the elder daughter of Monsieur by his first marriage to the famously beautiful English princess Henri-etta Stuart. Like her mother, who had been obliged to marry her own cousin, and her uncle, who had been obliged to marry his, Marie-Louise was being sacrificed for the sake of fair diplomatic winds—in this case for French envoys travelling to the Spanish court at the severe monastery-palace of El Escorial near Madrid. For them, despite a residual splendour, the imperial capital was a definite hardship post, isolated, backward, "horribly muddy in winter and unbearably dusty in summer." The court itself was no more pleasant: the food was bad and the government worse, the economy stagnant, the provinces rebel-lious; obscurantist priests blocked every new idea, while a horde of black-clad grandees, like ravens clawing at a battle carcass, despoiled what was left of a once great empire.

For a century, Spain had been the greatest power on earth. Its extraordinary empire had spanned the globe, from the Netherlands to West African Guinea, the Philippines far to the east and farther to the islands of the Pacific, and, above all, half the continent of America, captured, astonishingly, by fewer than a thousand conquistadores. No other nation had ever achieved half so much. But soldiering and plundering had not been enough to manage such vast territories, nor even, in the end, to maintain prosperity at home. A rigid social order, a marked disdain for trade, and a "soporific mental climate" had slowed all progress in the land, then gradually turned it backwards. By 1679, even in the populous capital of Madrid, there were "very few tradesmen or merchants, but an extraordinary number of monks and nuns." For thirty or forty years already, Spain had been declining.

For seventeen-year-old Marie-Louise, this had all been as nothing compared with the horror of her impending marriage to the Spaniards' wretched King, a pitiful specimen of humankind who had so far hobbled and scrabbled his way through nineteen years of "living death." Carlos II, the last of the Spanish Habsburgs, was the ghastly result of generations of inbreeding—such a lost cause, even within his own family, that he had never been taught even to keep himself clean. "The King of Spain is shorter than average, rather thin, and he limps a bit." So the French ambassador had begun his report, diplomatically, before getting into his stride. "He has received no education, has no knowledge whatsoever of letters or of science, and indeed can barely read or write. His face is extraordinarily long and narrow and fleshless, and his features all out of proportion, so that he looks quite bizarre . . . By nature and by upbringing, he has no understanding of anything, no feeling for anything, and no inclination to do anything." Thus poor, drooling Carlos, "the centre of so many hopes," uncombed and unwashed, his speech impeded by an abnormally large tongue, his bones crippled with disease, "a rachitic and feeble-minded weakling, the last stunted sprig of a degenerate line." His Spanish subjects had dubbed him *El Hechizado* (The Bewitched), attributing his many maladies to sorcery. Carlos himself believed the same, confusedly submitting to exorcisms in an attempt to make himself whole.

"A daughter must obey her father, even if he wants to give her a monkey for a husband," says Molière's Dorine to her despairing young mistress in *Tartuffe*. In fact, Marie-Louise's own father might have relented, or at least Madame de Sévigné thought so: "The people are saying, Oh, Monsieur is too kind-hearted; he'll never let her go; she's too distressed." But for once, paternal authority had not proved supreme. The father now was brother to a King; it was for the King to dispose of all his subjects, and by no means least a strategically useful princess. A fortnight after the celebrations at Fontainebleau, Marie-Louise was "still pleading for mercy, throwing herself at everyone's feet." Two days later: "The Queen of Spain was an absolute fountain today . . . I don't know how the King of Spain can maintain his pride in the face of such desperation." The King of France, at least, had remained unmoved, and before the month was out, Marie-Louise was sent on her way. "Madame," her uncle had said to her, "I trust this is farewell forever . . . They say she wept excessively . . ." Liselotte, her stepmother, was kind enough to accompany her for part of the journey.

"The Queen of Spain was rather too thin when she lived in France, but she's started to fill out since she's been in Spain," wrote the French ambassador a few months afterwards. It was only too truly spoken: the formerly vivacious Marie-Louise had begun a sad descent into deepest depression and a morbid obesity. And in the end, Louis's wish for his niece was to be granted: Marie-Louise would never set eyes on France again. She was to die at the age of just twenty-seven, reputedly poisoned by her mother-in-law because of her childlessness, but in fact more probably through the appalling effects of grief and distress on her once lovely young body. More than a decade later, Carlos would demand that her corpse be exhumed for him to gaze upon, and he would do so, lost in tears and, very possibly, near to madness.

The once great empire of Spain was mired in troubles, but there was something rotten, too, in apparently healthy France. If Louis was concerned about the disorder in his own adulterous "personal house," in his house of state the trouble was only just beginning.

TWELVE

The Poisons Affair

*I*t began with an ordinary execution, the grim public beheading, after multiple tortures, of a convicted murderess, killer of her father and two brothers, would-be killer of her sister, her husband, her daughter, and her lover. So skilful had she been that it had taken ten years for her crimes to come to light, and so skilful was the executioner now that the stroke of his sword seemed to pass her by, so that for a moment her head still stood on her shoulders, before toppling slowly sideways. The body of this petite and blue-eyed "enemy of the human race" was subsequently burned on the scaffold, and her ashes scattered to the winds; spectators later returned to steal her bones as souvenirs of the day. "It's over at last, la Brinvilliers is in the air . . . and we're breathing her in, so that we'll all catch the poisoning fever and astound ourselves." Thus Madame de Sévigné to her daughter in Provence, writing with more prescience than she knew.

The victim and culprit now "in the air" was Marie-Madeleine Gobelin d'Aubray, marquise de Brinvilliers, wife of Colonel Antoine Gobelin, heir to the tapestry fortune, and daughter of Antonin Dreux d'Aubray, Counsellor of State (deceased). The marquise's high birth and her many noble connections had inflated public interest in an already gripping case, and though it might have helped her—preliminary interrogations had had to be held outside Paris, since the accused was related to half the city's magistrates—the enormity of her crimes and the King's personal interest in the case ensured that all was pursued to the ghastly end. Though wealthy by birth and marriage, the hedonistic marquise had been perennially short of money; this, and a lover's revenge, and in the end little more than habit, had been her apparent motives.

Worse than any other factor was her chosen method of dispatch, more frightening than any other to the seventeenth-century mind: the marquise had murdered by poison, an ever-present weapon, or so it was believed, since in an era of dirty water and tainted food, and fevers and infections of every kind, most poisons were exceedingly difficult to detect. A few remedies existed, provided the problem was identified in time—even lemon juice or a beaker of milk could prevent the working of some concoctions—but many supposed antidotes were worse than the poison itself. Physicians were next to useless, a later than last resort; though now and then an autopsy might satisfy the lawyers by proving guilt, nothing at that stage could help the victim.

The marquise had poisoned her elder brother with "an elaborate raised pie . . . filled with cocks' crests, sweetbreads and kidneys in a rich cream sauce," her younger brother through simple bread and wine, and her father through some thirty doses of various powders and fluids administered by a servant accomplice. Monsieur d'Aubray's subsequent "extraordinary fits of vomitings, inconceivable stomach pains and strange burnings in the entrails" had evidently not been uncommon ailments at the time; at any rate, his death had at first been attributed to the gout.

By tradition, the most sophisticated poisons came from Italy, as did the most sophisticated poisoners. The marquise had been no exception in this respect; she had had her Italian, too, a former inmate of the Bastille whose nationality alone would have been enough to convict him, in public opinion if not in law. The investigators had dismissed this man, but had been alarmed to uncover a connection between the marquise and the King's own apothecary, who had been sent to Italy, or so the marquise had said, at the instruction of Nicolas Fouquet, the King's former surintendant, to study the making of poisons. Though the marquise had admitted this under savage torture, the police had accepted it as perfect truth, and from it they had deduced a plot to kill the King and liberate Fouquet from his long imprisonment in the fortress of Pignerol. From this point, one overly suspicious misconstruction had led to the next.

For almost three years, the investigations had remained, for the most part, underground, with the police, aided by paid informants known as *mouches* (flies), tracking down ever more suspected poisoners. In March 1679, a Parisian woman named Catherine Montvoisin, alias *La Voisin*, had been arrested in a second spectacular murder case. She had been betrayed by one of her accomplices, one of the many suspects, among them several wealthy people, who were by now being held in the Bastille. The King, though not seriously alarmed for his own safety, was concerned nonetheless at the amount of "evidence" being turned up, particularly against prominent people, including some who frequented the court. Convinced that "no man with four millions to his name would ever be found guilty," he had set up a special commission, *la Chambre d'Arsenal*, to investigate and try all the cases—Parisians quickly dubbed it *la Chambre ardente*, "the burning commission," a reference to the inquisitional courts of the previous century where doubtful Catholics had been tried for heresy. At its head, the King had placed his energetic police commissioner, Gabriel Nicolas de La Reynie, introducer of the city's "mud" and "light" taxes, tracer of unfaithful Parisian wives, and warrior against general debauchery and corruption. His duties included "the repression of blasphemers and the sacrilegious, divines, witches, alchemists, [and] the fight against abortion," a wide remit in an age of little discernment between religion, magic, and natural science.

Among the high-born and the educated, as among the poor, the same mixture of mud and light prevailed. The Queen herself, deeply devout in the Spanish mould, loved having her fortune told. Her cousin, the less devout duchesse de Montpensier, la Grande Mademoiselle, was currently consulting an astrologer for advice about mar-

riage. The beautiful Princess of Würtemberg had allegedly prosti-
tuted herself to gain the ultimate alchemical secret of the philosopher's
stone, with hundreds of serious proto-scientists devoting life and fortune to the same search. And "every person in Lyon believed," as Jean
de Segrais reported, "that the abbé Brigalier had made the devil appear, and among people of quality, too."

Medical practice was hostage to the same muddle of beliefs.
"Madame de La Fayette is drinking soups made of viper stock," wrote
Madame de Sévigné to her daughter in that summer of 1679. "They're
absolutely bringing her back to life; you can see it just by looking at
her. She thinks they'd be very good for you. You take a viper, cut off its
head and tail, cut it open, skin it, and it's still moving. Even after an
hour or two, you can still see it moving." Françoise, avoiding viper
stock, took her medical woes instead to the prior Trimont de Cabrières,
a famed healer of the incurably sick. He had been brought to court under the dual protection of the devout Cardinal de Bouillon and the
brutally cynical Minister of War, the marquis de Louvois, both of
whom believed in his powers unreservedly.

And there were poisons everywhere, not just in kidney pies and
wine, but available, for very little money, at any number of shops and
booths all over the city. Toxic substances were sold and indeed produced by all kinds of people: by chemists and apothecaries, of course,
but also by grocers, midwives, perfume-sellers, gardeners—anyone, in
fact, who had a mind to do so, since there was no regulation to speak of.
There were hundreds of poisons in circulation, in small doses barely
considered poisons at all, lotions and potions and powders, some supposedly for external use on skin or hair only, some to be used internally,
to induce abortions, or for *les clystères*—colonic purges, the favoured
panacea of all Molière's stage physicians and every other medical man
besides. Most were variants of stock substances: the sulphuric acid vit-
riol, silver-white antimony, corrosive sublimates, bits and pieces of
toad or snake, certain plants, and, of course, arsenic.

La Reynie's battle was consequently being fought uphill, with the
public by no means necessarily on his side. A pair of boulevard playwrights had taken advantage of the tremendous interest in the whole

affair to present a lively new play on the subject: *La Devineresse ou les Faux Enchantements* had opened in September 1679 at the Hôtel Guénégaud, home of the late Molière's still active troupe. The rumour ran that La Reynie himself had had a hand in the writing of it, but if so, he signally failed to take its message to heart. The play tells the story of the wily Madame Jobin, who makes a fortune by duping the ladies and gentleman of Paris with fortune-telling, love potions, and charms. "In my job," says Madame Jobin, "chance is the most important thing. All you need is presence of mind, a bit of boldness, a taste for intrigue and a certain knowledge of the world, and you need to have people of quality seen visiting you, and keep abreast of what's going on, especially all the little love affairs, and above all, you need to talk a lot to the people who come to see you. You're bound to say something that's true, and you only need to get it right once or twice to find yourself the latest fashion."

This confession of the fictional Madame Jobin is remarkably close to that of the thoroughly real memoirist Primi Visconti, who had been waylaid at Louis's court by his apparent talent for reading palms and telling fortunes. Though it was all "just a game" to Primi Visconti, it had made him wildly popular among the more frivolous members of the upper crust. Like Madame Jobin, he had done no more than take notice of things and pick up all the gossip. "Though I pretended not to be listening . . . I'd remember all the whispers," he wrote, "and I'd mention a few things, really only guessing . . . [and] they'd all be astonished by my penetration . . . Before long I was receiving invitations to the most illustrious houses . . . The whole of Paris was dying to see me." La Reynie certainly knew of Primi Visconti; in fact he made plans to arrest him, but "the King stood guarantee for me," and the court's favourite fortune-teller remained at liberty.

In fairness to La Reynie, whether or not he had a hand in the play, or indeed even saw it, the affair had long since gone beyond love potions and fortune-telling. The Parisian woman lately arrested, Catherine La Voisin, had been charged not only with the murder of several husbands, but also with attempted murder (by poisoning and bewitchment), and with inducing abortions with potions and "metal implements." La Voisin was a widely known *devineresse*, but fortune-telling and casting spells had emerged as the least of her activities, and so it had proved with the many, many others who had been arrested in her train. La Reynie's investigations were revealing a layer of criminal activity previously unsuspected, at least by his rather earnest self. Among the privileged as among ordinary folk, witchcraft and poisoning—and, above all, abortion—appeared to be entrenched practices of daily life. "Men's lives are up for sale as a matter of everyday bargaining," he relayed in dismay. "Murder is the only remedy when a family is in difficulties. Abominations are being practised everywhere—in Paris, in the suburbs, in the provinces."

Even before the La Voisin affair had broken, La Reynie and his police had been actively hunting down the perpetrators of these "abominations," which included all manner of sacrilege—black masses, casting spells with holy words, attempts to commune with the dead— all punishable by hanging or beheading. Even blasphemy could incur the penalty of a cruel tongue-piercing and condemnation to the galleys for life. All suspects were tortured, not in order to obtain a confession of guilt, which, among the untitled and the poor, was more or less assumed, but in order to extract information about their supposed accomplices. It was a hideous and also largely useless practice, as the president of the Paris parlement himself had observed, noting that it was "rare that it has extracted the truth from the mouth of a condemned man." Tortures permitted in French prisons included the rack, with arms and limbs stretched to breaking point; the *brodequins*, a kind of press with screws which gradually crushed the limbs; and the water torture, with gallons of water forced down the victim's throat, causing terrible pain. On his own tourist visit to the Châtelet prison, the English diarist John Evelyn witnessed a man charged with robbery who was "to have the question, or torture, given to him." Evelyn describes the torture in detail, adding, "There was another malefactor to succeed, but the spectacle was so uncomfortable, that I was not able to stay the sight of another."

La Voisin herself had been subjected to the water torture, and the transcript of her interrogation is "interspersed with her shrieks and pleas" for pity. She had eventually produced the names of thirty-six people apparently in league with her. These thirty-six had been tortured in their turn, producing further, ever less likely names, and so the investigation had spread. In February 1680 La Voisin was condemned to be burnt alive, then tortured further in case she might recall any other accomplices not yet named. In the last week of the month, she was taken by cart to the Place de Grève for execution.

She did not go quietly. Pushing away both priest and crucifix, she refused to offer the required penitential prayer en route at the cathedral of Nôtre-Dame. Arrived at the foot of the scaffold, she would not get down from the tumbrel, and had to be pulled out by the guards. Chained in irons to the stake, five or six times she kicked the flaming straw away, swearing violently, until at last the fire enveloped her. "They say the repercussions will surprise us all," Madame de Sévigné remarked.

The King's two most powerful ministers, Colbert and the war minister Louvois, may have been less surprised than others. As the tortured prisoners gave up ever more names, Colbert could not help but notice how many of them were connected to his own wide clan of officials and protégés. Undetected by the single-minded La Reynie, Louvois, Colbert's premier rival, had been manipulating the investigation to ensnare as many as possible of Colbert's friends and his own enemies. *Le clan* Louvois had been at odds with *le clan* Colbert since the beginning of Louis's personal reign in 1661, and though the Colberts had on the whole had the better of things to date, their lustre was just beginning to dim through the signally underhand efforts of the "fat and sweaty-palmed" Minister of War.

The most prominent of Louvois's targets now was François-Henri, duc de Luxembourg, maréchal de France, one of the four Captains of the Royal Bodyguard, "the chiefest places in trust about the King's person," and in fact a former favourite of Louvois himself. Despite his high position, Luxembourg was an easy target, being the object of general dislike, at least among the men. "His low stature was not the worst of his defects," wrote the diplomat Spanheim. "A deceitful little hunchback" was Primi Visconti's more direct opinion.

As governor of Holland after the French invasion of the 1670s, Luxembourg had proved himself to be nasty and brutish as well as short, treating the local people with great cruelty and permitting his soldiers to pillage, and worse, as they pleased. But in due course he had tasted defeat as well, and this had wrought vengeance on his own head. In 1676 he had been unable to raise the siege of the beleaguered German city of Philippsburg; he had blamed his long-time ally Louvois for failing to send reinforcements, and from this point the grudge-bearing Louvois had become his determined enemy.

Early in 1680, following allegations made by a supposed magician by the name of Lesage, Luxembourg was arrested on charges of sacrilege, sodomy, incest, counterfeiting money, and several attempted murders, including that of his rich but otherwise unappealing wife, "the ugliest person alive." Any one of the charges would have been enough to sentence the duc to death. But, though he was known to be a superstitious man, fond of magic books and fortune-telling, and though there may have been some truth in the talk of homosexual liaisons, his only real mistake was to have fallen out with Louvois, who now proved ready to hound his former friend to disgrace, into exile, or even to the block.

Luxembourg did not wait for the guards to come for him, but defiantly set off for the Bastille in his own carriage. En route he encountered Athénaïs, and both stepped down to confer in private. The duc's bravado had not lasted long, for he was by now weeping "very hard." A second time he broke his journey, to pass a few moments in prayer, but, unable to decide which saint might most suitably intercede for him, he left the church, still weeping. Eventually confined in a "most disagreeable" cell overlooking the prison's stinking moat, he was briefly interrogated by La Reynie, before demanding to see a priest. The priest was denied him, though, in compensation, La Reynie sent him a copy of *The Lives of the Saints*.

For two days Luxembourg attempted a hunger strike, sitting sullenly in his cell, but on the third day he changed tack and began a constant snapping at his jailer to *"Shut that window! Light the fire! Get me some chocolate!"* Madame de Sévigné, well informed as always, and disgusted with the duc's petulant behaviour, relayed the whole story to her friends in the country. "He's not a man," she wrote, "not even a little man; he's not even a woman; he's just a little womelette." But when his trial finally came about more than three months later, Luxembourg behaved with exemplary dignity. His defence clear and his personal innocence evident, he was quickly acquitted, though his manservant, more muddled in his testimony, was condemned to the galleys, and his jolly personal astrologer, apparently in need of a chastisement that would wipe the smile from his face, spent the rest of his life shackled to the wall of a dungeon. Once released, the duc took care to ally himself as closely as possible with Louvois's rival, Colbert, in fact turning to Françoise to help him arrange a marriage within the Colbert family.

Luxembourg had been too proud, or too determined to prove his case, to take advantage of a hint from the King to leave France before he could be arrested, but other highly placed persons, similarly warned, decided not to wait at home for the inevitable knock at the door. The comtesse de Soissons, née Olympe Mancini, a niece of the late Cardinal Mazarin and one of Louis's occasional mistresses, enthralled all of Paris with her dashing midnight escape, leaping up from her gaming table to grab a few large and beautiful jewels and the marquise d'Alluye, her large and beautiful best friend, before galloping off to Brussels, pursued by armed horsemen sent by Louvois.

Bereft of his quarry, the minister was obliged to content himself with trying to create a sinister reputation for the comtesse in Brussels, whose "naturally superstitious" people were alarmed to see a bevy of "devils" (black cats released by one of Louvois's men) surround her as she knelt at mass. The comtesse was about to be accused of the murder of her husband, though no one actually believed in her guilt. She had gained nothing financially from the comte's death, and in every other respect, as was widely known, he had been a more than accommodating husband, at one point even taking pains to reconcile his wife with a lover, one of many, with whom she had quarrelled.

Within a week, the comtesse's sister, Marie-Anne, duchesse de Bouillon, found herself facing a similar charge: she had supposedly attempted to procure the murder of her own husband, the duc de Bouillon, in order to marry her current lover, the duc de Vendôme. Adored by her indulgent husband, who raised no objection to her many affairs "provided he got his share," the rich, liberal, and "singularly seductive" duchesse was equally adored in Parisian society, where worldly heads nodded approvingly at her restrained practice of receiving only one lover at a time.

An inveterate unblusher of this mettle was not likely to be intimidated by the upstart policeman La Reynie, with his fantastical ideas of conspiracy against the King's life; far from taking flight as her sister had done, *La Bouillon* stood trial with fabulous defiance, turning up at the Chambre ardente with husband on one arm and lover on the other. As anticipated by the riveted Parisians, she proved more than a match for the commissioners. Had she offered a sack of gold to the magician Lesage to get rid of her husband? She had not, and there was her husband now, waiting for her with a train of carriages outside this very door. Had she tried to poison her servants, who knew too much about her amatory affairs? She had not, and in any case all of Paris knew about her affairs. Had she ever seen the devil? La Reynie asked her. "Yes, I have," she retorted, "and he looked just like you." With no evidence, the case against the duchesse collapsed within the day. The multiply cuckolded duc was so proud of his wife's triumph that he begged permission of the King to publish an account of it for all the courts of Europe. Permission was not forthcoming.

The duc de Luxembourg and the two Mancini sisters had provided good entertainment for the gossips, and throughout the first months of 1680 many other noble names were pronounced, enlivening the proceedings further. Though alarmed at first, the King was not convinced of any real crime in the highest circles, but he was dismayed all the same by the uncovering of so many occult practices at his own court, indeed very close to himself. According to La Reynie, some of the accused had spoken a good deal about Madame de Montespan. "All those involved in this must be brought to task, whatever their rank," wrote Louis to Colbert sternly.

The extent of the affair and the involvement of so many rich and powerful people seemed almost impossible, and had La Reynie been able to view it all with less horror and more perspicacity, he might have seen that in fact it was. Colbert, no doubt concerned to protect his allies, protested that those giving testimony had been facing "all the terrors of torture and death," adding sensibly, "One is naturally ingenious in these extremities." But the police commissioner did not hear, or did not heed, the minister's warning. A supporter of the monarchy during the civil wars of the Fronde, La Reynie had retained a strong, not to say fervid devotion to the King, and this, combined with a consciousness of his own family's long tradition of civic service, gave him an exaggerated diligence in his task now. In his determination to leave no stone unturned, he pushed the investigation to its limits, and then beyond.

Primi Visconti describes the court in 1680 as being in a state of terror. "You couldn't trust your friends any more," he relayed. "All it took was a letter to La Reynie, from anyone at all, and at once you were thrown into prison. Lots of innocent people spent months locked up before being interrogated." And, injustices aside, police efforts were in some cases positively counterproductive. "Lots of people who knew nothing about poisoning started to learn all about it," continued Primi Visconti, "and it's different here in France: elsewhere people use it to take revenge on their enemies, but here they use it against their father or mother . . . or to arrange a new marriage for themselves. There have been more poisonings since the Chambre was set up than there were before. As soon as anyone gets a stomach-ache, he says he's been poisoned, and they arrest all the cooks and servants."

Poisoning and witchcraft fever swiftly spread outside of Paris, startling many innocent provincials. The marquis de Jorné was arrested after sending a servant to buy bookworm powder for his library. The duc de Nevers was locked up by his own anxious family after cheekily baptizing a pig. Madame de Sévigné's family in Provence came down with a collective dose of gastric trouble: "Where on earth did you get the idea that you've all been poisoned?" wrote the marquise. "How ridiculous!" As her witty cousin remarked, "If all the bad cooks in Paris were seized, the prisons would soon be overflowing."

By the end of August 1680, the King's concern about Athénaïs had developed into a real fear, "and I can assure you," added Primi Visconti, "that a great many ladies spent sleepless nights, and a lot of men were even more worried, since it now seemed they were going to go after the homosexuals. Colbert didn't approve of the tribunal. He thought it was . . . bringing the nation into disrepute." Perhaps it was Colbert who persuaded Louis now to order the transcripts of certain interrogations—notably those mentioning Athénaïs's name—to be left as loose sheets rather than being bound together in volumes. These were delivered into his own hands, the same hands which, almost thirty years later, would destroy them.

Athénaïs was by now entangled in a series of accusations against members of her own Mortemart family. Under torture, La Voisin had confessed that she had been approached by the duchesse de Vivonne, Athénaïs's sister-in-law, for help in poisoning her husband—the duc de Vivonne, doomed by his family's bodily heritage, had in recent years grown grotesquely fat and, presumably, less attractive to his wife. At the same time, Athénaïs's cousin, the marquis de Termes, a fanatical seeker of the legendary philosopher's stone, had abducted an alchemist lover of La Voisin, keeping him prisoner for months in a fiery laboratory in the tower of his château.

The name of Madame de Montespan had elicited riveted attention from La Voisin's torturers. Their determination to know more had, in some measure, kept La Voisin alive, and she had seized the advantage by spinning out her story as long and as vividly as she could. After her death, her daughter had carried it further still, and though Colbert gauged her a "cunning and ingenious" girl, and even the credulous La Reynie admitted her to be of "a strange cast of mind," her testimony was accepted as the truth. Madame de Montespan, she said, had been visiting her mother for five or six years, seeking her help to retain the King's affections. La Voisin had provided her with love potions, and these Madame de Montespan had mixed with the medicines for the King's regular clystère purges.

When the power of these appeared to weaken, La Voisin had taken to casting spells on the King, and had then paid a priest to celebrate a series of black masses sacrificing babies to the devil, in which a naked Madame de Montespan herself had supposedly participated. When all proved vain, and Athénaïs had resigned herself to losing her position as maîtresse déclarée, she had decided to take her revenge on the King, and La Voisin had supplied the means in phials of poisoned love powders.

The King had been away in Flanders, on a summer tour of his newly gained provinces, when the first of La Reynie's letters concerning Athénaïs arrived. By Christmas 1680 there was no more to be extracted from La Voisin's ingenious daughter, but another woman, screaming as her legs were crushed in the brodequins, cried out that she had given love potions to Madame de Montespan to give the King. To her priest she later confessed that it had all been a lie, "to free herself from the pain . . . and out of fear of the torture being reapplied." "The Chambre ardente," wrote Primi Visconti, "was like an inquisition . . . of people's consciences." Though only La Reynie really believed the women, behind all the overblown accusations there was a grain of truth just large enough to undo Athénaïs once and for all.

Françoise, less frivolous by nature than Athénaïs, or perhaps less desperate for the King's love, had made no visits to fortune-tellers and bought no doubtful love potions. She had begun this "year of terror" at court with a promotion to the post of *deuxième dame d'atour* (second lady-in-waiting) to the Princess Marie-Anne of Bavaria, newly betrothed to the nineteen-year-old dauphin, and in fact yet to arrive at the French court. Mignon and his brothers were now of an age to leave the care of their governess for the stricter supervision of a male tutor, and Athénaïs's youngest children had been sent away to Paris, to the house in the rue Vaugirard that had once been Françoise's own, to be cared for there by other nurses and governesses.

In consquence, Françoise had been briefly without a post at all, until the King had pronounced her dame d'atour, which justified her presence at court, and at the same time brought them more often together. It was possibly Françoise rather than Louis who had felt the need of some new public justification for her presence, for it was apparently in this month of January 1680 that she resumed her affair with him, reclaiming him from the vapid Angélique de Fontanges, who was by now in any case quite unwell. She had endured serious haemorrhaging following the birth, and swift death, of a baby fathered by Louis—"wounded On His Majesty's Service," as Madame de Sévigné remarked.

Prodded by her conscience, perhaps, Françoise took advantage of her renewed influence over the King to nudge him a little closer to the neglected Marie-Thérèse, with the result that by the end of May, in an astonishing turnabout, Françoise was much loved by the King, highly esteemed by the Queen, and absolutely detested by Athénaïs. By the summer, Françoise was away at the southern spas with Mignon. By the autumn, she had returned to court, to general, glowing praise, and Athénaïs had begun to topple from her pedestal at last.

The Chambre d'Arsenal had been disbanded in October, though it was to resume in the spring of 1681 and continue for more than a year. No one but La Reynie had much faith in it by now. "[P]eople viewed [it] as a private court for two or three people to carry out their personal vendettas," wrote Primi Visconti. Jean de La Fontaine recorded his opinion for posterity in one of his already beloved fables:

> It's all prejudice, intrigue, favouritism,
> Nothing to do with justice, or next to nothing.

In less than two years of existence, the *Chambre* would investigate 442 people, arrest 218, imprison 65 for life, condemn 36 to be hanged or burnt alive or broken on the wheel, send scores to the galleys, and torture one woman to death. For all that, "[t]hey never found so much as a malicious thought against the King." Some professional criminals had certainly been involved in the affair—black masses, for example, or sticking pins in wax dolls, appeared to be the prerogative of specialists—but much of it was no more than a superstitious outgrowth of the quasi-magical religious beliefs of the day. More or less everyone believed that spirits walked the earth, that the devil could be conjured, that a prayer could be distorted into a curse, and that the curse would work.

The rest was a question of entrenched, if ugly, social norms: violent acts of revenge or desperation, abandonment and killing of babies, abortions procured with dangerous potions or dirty metal tools. As to the last, so many had been discovered among both ordinary women and ladies of rank that Louis called a halt to all further investigations. Abortion was a particular problem in France, noted Primi Visconti, "whether it's because of the climate, or because the husbands are all away at the wars, and the young girls fall in love so quickly . . . [but] the King didn't want to press this matter any further, given that the whole kingdom was infested with the practice."

Though many innocent people suffered, some did benefit in the end from the changes brought about by *"l'affaire des poisons."* Some genuine criminals, hired blades and dispatchers of unwanted babies, were swept off the streets for good. New laws regulating the sale of toxic substances left Parisians safer than they had been before. And in a definite public health advance, apothecaries were thenceforth barred from making medicines out of toads and snakes.

Françoise recorded nothing of what she thought of the whole poisons affair, or if she did, she was careful to destroy it later. But it settled her fate as surely as it settled that of the *misérables* forced into exile, or to prison, or to the stake. Athénaïs's involvement, whether criminal or not, had finally debased her bright gold coin for good. It had cost her the King's trust, and with it his esteem and, in the end, even his passion for her. Louis had been stricken by the sordid and scandalous revelations as by a final, shocking insult after years of lesser injuries inflicted through Athénaïs's pride and greed. Françoise, by contrast, seemed a tranquil haven after the storm, discreet, undemanding, above suspicion, with no taste whatsoever for the foolish superstitions which had tainted almost every other lady at court. Besides, of all Louis's available mistresses, she was probably the only one "incapable of abusing her closeness to the master."

Athénaïs's loss was Françoise's fabulous gain, and though the King privately rebuked his impertinent courtiers, he did not contradict their witty acknowledgement of her new standing: by the end of 1680, the humble Widow Scarron had been gloriously transformed into the lady of the moment, Madame de *Maintenant*.

Part Two

THIRTEEN

Madame de Maintenant

No Spring, nor Summer beauty hath such grace,
As I have seen in one Autumnall face.

In the month of November 1680, Françoise turned a mellow forty-five, "still attractive in her person," as the abbé de Choisy confirmed. Louis, handsome and vigorous, was now forty-two, and his solid sister-in-law Liselotte just twenty-eight, the contrasts a source of indignation to her, keenly resenting as she did the King's evident preference for "the old Maintenon woman" over her much younger, hearty dumpling self.

Liselotte was in love with the King, but even those immune to his charms were puzzled by his choice. "No one knew what to think of it," wrote Primi Visconti, "because Madame de Maintenon was old. Some thought she was the King's confidante, some that she was just a servant, and some supposed the King had chosen her, as a clever person, to write a memoir of his reign . . . Lots of people pointed out that some men are actually more attracted sensually to old women than to young ones."

The worldly chevalier de Méré, so warm an admirer of Françoise in the springtime days of her girlhood, might have had a pertinent word

or two to say, had anyone thought to consult him at his quiet estate in
Poitou: "The most beautiful women are more dangerous than ever
once their youth is behind them," he had written. "If they have lost in
one respect, they have gained in another, and what they have gained—
in grace or in accomplishments—makes them loved even more."
Forty-year-old Athénaïs, outraged and still scheming, may have recognized, in the poised and undemanding Françoise, the respite that
Louis needed after her emotionally extravagant self. As the abbé de
Choisy observed, "Madame de Maintenon was good-natured and
obliging, whereas the King never could stand up to Madame de Montespan in person." But it was Madame de Sévigné in Paris, with the advantage of detachment from the daily life of the court, who probably
came closest to divining the truth: "She has shown him a new country
which he has never known before—normal friendship and conversation, without constraint or pretence, and he's charmed by it . . .
[Madame de Montespan] is terribly jealous of the trust and friendliness between them . . . You can defeat passion, but against intelligence
and conversation . . ."

"The King doesn't like to see a man so much in love that he's a slave
to his passion," wrote Primi Visconti. Louis was sensually drawn to
Françoise—indeed, he seemed devoted to her: "He gives her more care
and attention than she receives from any of her other friends," wrote
Madame de Sévigné. But Louis was confident nonetheless that he had,
and could retain, the upper hand in their relationship. With Françoise,
there would be no scenes, no demands, and no challenges to his authority. She was, as the abbé de Choisy had said, "good-natured and
obliging," though neither Louis nor the abbé suspected the tactic behind this continual complaisance. As Françoise confessed to her secretary many years later, "I'm naturally impatient, but the King never
suspected it, though I was often at the end of my tether . . . I'm naturally frank, and in the early years of my favour, I was always having to
pretend to agree with him. At times I'd be upset . . . but I never said
the least word to show it. Sometimes I was really angry . . . God alone
knows what I suffered . . . But the King would come into my room,
and there would be no sign of any problem. I would pretend to be in a

good mood. I put all my effort into entertaining him, to keep him away from women, and I couldn't have done that if I hadn't been always obliging and good-tempered. He would have looked for his pleasure elsewhere, if he hadn't found it with me."

Françoise's self-control, so marked a contrast with Athénaïs's unpredictable moods, ensured the King a relaxed and pleasant environment, and bound him ever closer to her. She well understood the attraction for him of her oasis of calm amid the constant demands of court and state, but if there was calculation in her determined mastery of her impatience and frankness and even anger, there was a measure of instinct, too. Françoise wanted first place in the King's affections, but not, as Athénaïs had done, in order to play the *sultane* at court, nor even, like so many others, to garner what money and prestige she could from a more fleeting liaison. Françoise wanted Louis to love her, and her need for his love was profound. Many friends were fond of her; many men had desired her; Scarron had loved her, in his half-fulfilled, circumvented way; the marquis de Villarceaux had loved her, perhaps, but not for long, and not exclusively. Neither mother nor father had given her a sound emotional sense of herself, and from her stable life at Mursay she had been wrenched into a situation of hardship and humiliation. Françoise needed love, and respect, and security. Louis, it seemed, could provide them all.

From her own point of view, it was hardly a difficult bargain. She was physically drawn to him, flattered by his attentions, fed and clothed by the pension he had awarded her. He was the King, and if he strayed among pretty maids-in-waiting, if he could be autocratic and even selfish, his presence and his favour were compensation enough. From being in love with a handsome prince, from accepting his fluctuating attentions, Françoise had progressed easily to wanting him exclusively for herself, not sexually, perhaps—this seemed impossible—but in deeper emotional terms. And in her apparently steady and undemanding self, she provided the same emotional constancy for him—the uncertain little boy-King, worshipped, ignored, coerced, overruled, and diplomatically traded into a morbid marriage, played upon endlessly by subtler minds, both male and female—now a King nearing the pinnacle of his reign, but still at times uncertain, shielding himself from his own doubts with an attitude of firmness, even inflexibility.

So Françoise kept her dissatisfactions to herself, and whatever it may have cost her, the pretence worked. While Athénaïs fumed and Liselotte wept her big, neglected tears, it became ever more clear that Louis simply could not do without his Madame de Maintenant. "His Majesty often spends two hours of an afternoon in her room, chatting with an ease and friendliness which makes it the most desirable place in the world." So Madame de Sévigné conveyed the news to her daughter in Provence. "The other day the King spent three hours with her—she had migraine . . . The King spends only a few moments with Madame de Montespan . . . Madame de Maintenon's favour grows higher and higher, and Madame de Montespan's diminishes even as you watch."

Though now "old," or at least in middle age, Françoise remained a beauty, her skin firm and fresh, her figure fuller and more voluptuous, without the heaviness which so bedevilled Athénaïs, her chestnut hair showing no streak of grey, and her eyes, "the most beautiful eyes in the world," still glowing with warmth and sparkling with intelligence. Though the King's desire for her was still strong, by now she felt confident enough to refuse to sleep with him when she did not want to. "Not all the ladies responded to the King as he wished," observed Ezechiel Spanheim approvingly. "They didn't want to ruin their virtue, or their chance of a good marriage . . . As for Madame de Maintenon," he continued, with only partial truth, "this was primarily a friendly and trusting intercourse, and a particular esteem for the lady, rather than the effect of any more tender passion which her charms might inspire, if she or the King were of a more appropriate age . . . Her father was mixed up in some bad things," Spanheim added. "He took her to live in Canada, in America."

If Louis had his own frustrations to endure, at least Queen Marie-Thérèse was happy. For the first time in many years, she was receiving "a kind of attention and consideration and tenderness that she was by no means used to, and it made her happier than she had ever been.

Moved to tears, she would exclaim, in a sorry transport of joy, *God has sent Madame de Maintenon to give the King's heart back to me!* Never quick on the uptake, Marie-Thérèse evidently did not see that her apparent benefactress was also serving, at least occasionally, as her husband's mistress, nor did she realize that Françoise's real aim was not "to give the King's heart back to [her]," but to keep it away from Athénaïs, and—perhaps—in the end, to secure it for herself.

"Perhaps" to secure the King's heart for herself—it is as much as can be said with any certainty. After eight years of living at court, close to the King, Françoise was by now, beyond any doubt, of central importance to him. She was his favourite mistress; it was with her that he spent the greatest part of his leisure hours, in amicable conversation, if not in lovemaking. The abbé de Choisy felt that she allowed him "to relax from the cares of state," but it seems, too, that she had also begun to use these private hours with the King to persuade him to her own way of thinking, and in so doing, to further her own interests. She had already been promoting her preferred physician, Guy-Crescent Fagon; in time she would manoeuvre him into the post of personal physician to the King. For the marquis de Montchevreuil, her loyal friend from the Marais days, she had arranged the position of governor to the now ten-year-old duc du Maine, her Mignon. "I've told [your manservant] that he could mention my name to Colbert whenever he needs anything," she had written to her brother early in 1679; and in the summer of 1680: "I'll speak to Monsieur Colbert . . . and you'll be paid your salary." Madame de Sévigné went so far as to say, at this time, that "Madame de Maintenon is the machine directing everything"—an exaggeration, no doubt, but a reflection all the same of her perceived influence at court.

Yet even in moments of superoptimism, Françoise can hardly have believed that she would hold any lasting sway over the King. Louise de la Vallière in her bleak convent; Angélique de Fontanges in her early grave; Athénaïs, with her six royal children, in the mortification of her unvisited apartments; the Queen herself, in her pathetic dependence on the crumbs from a servant's table; and a host of lesser mortals who had pleased the King for a year or a day—all gave warning of the transience of his affections, indeed of the transience of all the glories of the earth.

What use to Louise was her beauty now, what use Angélique's coach and eight grey horses? What use was even a crown to Marie-Thérèse, the laughing-stock of every chambermaid who served her? Françoise, with intelligence to burn, saw only too clearly the eventual writing on her own silk-covered wall. It was this which in earlier days had made her draw back from the King's embrace, and it was this which now persuaded her that to be his mistress, or his confidante or even his counselor, was not enough—either for her or, so she persuaded herself, for him. For the moment, she had the upper hand, as Louise and Athénaïs and others had had before her. She was like them, it was true, but she was different, too. Where they had relied on their hold on Louis's heart, she would forge a stronger bond with him, a bond that would ensure a lasting, indeed an everlasting glory, for him and also for herself. She was not going to be counted as just one more royal mistress. Her goal was far, far higher. Françoise had decided to save the King's soul.

The decision did not reflect any genuine new-found piety on her part. Rather, it revealed her need for a serious aim in life, and no doubt, too, a tactical accommodation to the increasingly dévot tone of the times, with its accompanying elevation of her own public reputation. The new plan revealed as well Françoise's understanding of the King's own rather simple religious sense: for Louis, the public conventions were to be observed; the private requirements were to be striven for; the Lord was to be feared, though sin could be forgiven if repentance were sincere; salvation, achievable only through the Catholic Church, was the ultimate goal of every person in the land. Louis certainly expected salvation, though since his first manhood, his appetite for illicit sex had kept him in a near-constant state of potentially damning sin; of this he was perfectly, and sometimes anxiously, aware. But where the champion preacher Bossuet had failed, after years of threats and thundering sermons, Françoise intended to succeed. From now on, her work would be to draw Louis away from the sinful sexual liaisons that were endangering his immortal soul, and send him back to the bed of his legal wife.

By the late summer of 1681, she was confident of at least a temporary success, and conveyed as much to her cousin Philippe at Mursay. "The King has no galanteries now," she told him, "and you can say so, without fear of appearing badly informed." There remained, all the same, the question of her own relationship with Louis. Was not this itself a galanterie? Ironically, suspicion of herself continued to be deflected by Athénaïs, still officially maîtresse déclarée, so that, as Louis had intended, the courtiers remained unsure of what was happening in the vital realm of the King's amours. But Françoise knew the truth, and her equivocal responses to Louis's expectations of sex—supposedly refused for reasons of piety—reveal her compromised conscience.

Perhaps she should have known better. But even intelligence to burn, and a wide experience of the ways of the world, had so far proved too little for real self-knowledge on her part. Françoise's own relationship with the King was an intractable flaw at the heart of her noble project. She was aware of this, uncomfortably, but she lacked the moral strength, or more probably the religious faith, to take the necessary steps for change.

Far from being a dévote in the hard-line Bossuet manner, Françoise was no more than a believing Christian at a time when all but the rarest folk were believing Christians. Her mixed upbringing and her preference for the pragmatic over the mystical had made of her a formal Catholic with definite Protestant tendencies, but she took no interest in the ongoing religious battles of the day between Catholic France and the interfering Pope, or Catholic France and its own grim Jansenist sect, or Catholic France and the Huguenots. Though she certainly possessed some "Christian" virtues—self-control, a keen sympathy for the suffering, and a distaste for frivolity and extravagance—these were more aspects of her character than the hard-won results of any religious endeavour. Françoise's faith had never been a matter of great importance to her personally. The confessor she had chosen for herself, Père Gobelin, a sincere but manipulable man, had always been an in-adequate spiritual guide for her, and he was quite out of his depth with regard to her extraordinary position now.

A letter of this time to Père Gobelin reveals the singularly unex-cited beat of Françoise's religious heart:

> I pray for a moment when I get up; I go to mass every ordinary day, and twice on holy days of obligation; I recite the office every day, and read a chapter of some good book; I say a prayer when I go to bed, and if I wake in the night, I say a *Laudate* or a *Gloria Patri*. I think of God often during the day, and offer my acts to Him; I ask Him to take me away from court if I can't make my salvation here, and for the rest, I don't know what sins I can be committing. My temperament and my good intentions prevent me from doing anything really bad; I like to please people and to be well regarded, and that puts me on my guard against my other passions—and anyway, they're not really faults, just nor-mal human traits: I'm very vain, and frivolous and lazy, and I'm very free in my thoughts and judgements, and I'm cautious in what I say, out of ordinary prudence. So, that's how it is with me; send me whatever instructions you think most suitable for my improvement.

It is hardly the letter of a dévote in the Bossuet mould, or of a sinner determined to repent and save her immortal soul. It is in fact the letter of a woman who is scarcely taking the thing seriously at all. Françoise's behaviour, as she outlines it herself, is completely unobjectionable. She has no faults, "just normal human traits"; she is incapable of doing anything "really bad." She says her morning and evening prayers, and goes to mass like everyone else; the very foibles of which she accuses herself, with cheeky irony—vanity, frivolity, laziness—are precisely those she is well known never to have had. In the religious terms of the day, it is a shocking letter, revealing either an utter unawareness of the then supposed natural human tendency towards sin and the constant need for humility and repentance, or, more probably, an alarming spiritual pride. In psychological terms, it reveals Françoise's condescension towards her chosen confessor, and her boredom with the petty restraints being placed in the name of salvation on ordinary, decent people going about their ordinary, decent lives. "As for my clothes, I'll change them," she adds. "I'll stop wearing gold. I don't care one way or the other. It won't bother me. I'm spending too much anyway . . ."

A deeply religious Françoise, abandoning her sinful relationship with the King, might have taken the veil, like Louise de la Vallière, or at the very least retired to the life of a virtuous chatelaine at Maintenon, succouring the poor and promoting good works, the proverbial lady bountiful in the comfort of her own demesne. But it was not religious conviction that motivated her now. What she wanted above all was what she had always wanted: lasting respect, what she herself called *bonne gloire*. As the saviour of the King's immortal soul, she would possess something that not even the highest in the kingdom had ever possessed, not Athénaïs, not Colbert, not even Bossuet. Louis's path to salvation would be Françoise's path to glory, and on the way, conveniently, she could save her own soul as well. If luck or providence had brought her thus far, so very, very far from where she had begun, only a glint of real ambition could take her any further.

Françoise was not a natural strategist—her rise from unwanted prisoner's child to "the machine directing everything" could never have been planned, in any case—but she knew how to take advantage of the opportunities that came her way. And the winds at court were changing; Bossuet and his dévots had been gaining ground. The King needed to capture the moral high ground from the pleasure-phobic Jansenists and the politically suspect Huguenots; the extravagant costumes of debauchery, once worn with pride and flair, had begun to look rather tawdry. The shock of the Poisons Affair had prompted a return to more conventional intercourse with the supernatural. The retreat into good behaviour was not uniform—"The duc de Vendôme has lost 10,000 écus at billiards against a prelate (a leading light of the Church!)," announced Madame de Sévigné, with feigned horror—but the general trend was indisputable. Piety was becoming fashionable.

Françoise seized the chance to place herself at the forefront of the new trend. With a new determination, and arguably some hypocrisy, she took a first step to align herself publicly with the dévots. Under the apparent patronage of "a lady of great virtue," recognized immediately as herself, she published a little penitent tract supposedly written by Louise de la Vallière on the occasion of her entering the convent. It was in fact the work of the duc de Beauvillier, son-in-law of the minister Colbert and a known follower of Bossuet, but for Françoise's purposes now that made no difference—indeed, she consulted neither Beauvillier, the actual author, nor Louise, now Sister Louise of Mercy, under whose name the tract was being published. Bossuet added an introduction to these *Reflections on the Mercy of God*, advising his readers that the "lady of great virtue" would have thought it an injustice "to deprive the faithful of a work so useful to sinners wishing to convert."

Père Gobelin, earnest and simple, had proved unable to guide his self-satisfied lamb into a properly penitent fold. But clever Bossuet had miscalculated, too. Surprised and impressed by her difference from the flaunting, grasping Athénaïs, he had accepted Françoise on her own public terms. Her undoubted intelligence, her dignity of manner, her discreet behaviour, the modesty of her dress, her apparent lack of interest in honours and riches, all gave to the outsider—to Bossuet, bound up in his own vast ambition and confident of his personal judgement—the appearance of a natural piety, and he began to consider Françoise, with her evident influence over Louis, as a perfect pawn in his own strategic game of converting the nation through the conversion of the King. The Queen herself, "a saint, but not very bright," was useless for his purposes. Françoise, though less of a saint than Bossuet suspected, was likely by contrast to prove very useful indeed.

For all his brilliance, he failed to understand Françoise, mistaking the persona she had constructed for herself, out of social necessity and personal preference, for the face of a profound religious faith. And she, less brilliant but more perceptive, saw his mistake, and quietly decided to make use of it for herself. In her terms, Bossuet and his dévots would serve as an advance guard for her own eventual securing of the King's salvation—an advance guard, and a protective guard, too, for in the jealous, intriguing environment of the court, Françoise needed allies. "Did she think the first volume of her life was always going to remain unread?" wrote Madame de Sévigné. "And the story's been retold so maliciously, doesn't she realize how that must have harmed her?"

Françoise realized very well, and warned her talkative brother to "be careful what you say about me . . . Don't talk about my good fortune; don't say anything about it, good or bad. They're enraged against me, and as you say, they'll do anything to do me harm." Regardless of her present standing with the King, she remained vulnerable to those who were whittling away at her pedestal now with the sharp little knives of her humble birth, her poverty, her marriage to the cripple Scarron, her entry to the court as a paid servant. Athénaïs, luckless catalyst of her own downfall, stood first and most furious among Françoise's detractors. "She was almost unhinged by the King's preference for Madame de Maintenon," wrote the abbé de Choisy. "She regarded her as so far beneath her."

Louis had added cowardly insult to injury by sending Françoise herself to convey to Athénaïs the news of her demotion: "She told her, in the clearest terms," the abbé de Choisy recorded, "that the King no longer wished to have any particular liaison with her, and that he advised her for her part to think of her salvation, as he intended to think of his own. It was such a harsh thing to say that Madame de Maintenon had several times begged the King to reconsider, and even suggested that he might have difficulty holding to his decision, but he pressed her so firmly that in the end she did it." As the abbé had observed, "the King never could stand up to Madame de Montespan in person . . . He certainly feared her more than he loved her."

The discarded Athénaïs, "suffocating in black bile," had both the means and the motive to act against Françoise. She had staunch support from the duchesse de Richelieu, an apparent friend from Paris salon days who, however, "was only fond of Madame de Maintenon as long as she was poor and unknown. She resented her current good fortune. As far as she was concerned, Madame had stolen her own rightful place as confidante to the King." But if Françoise was anxious, she was not cowed. "If my enemies fail, we'll laugh at them, and if they succeed, we'll endure it with courage," she insisted to Charles. "We're in a good situation, after all," she added, revealing a sound gift of perspective, "when you think of how we used to live."

And in the meantime, she was not without defence. She herself was vulnerable, but Bossuet—unless the King were to dismiss him outright—was virtually unassailable, and from now on she drew closer to the preacher and his dévots. They would encircle her pedestal, and she would do whatever she herself could do to keep her place on top of it, and reach up even higher.

The King wasn't ashamed to make her [second] dame d'atour to the new dauphine, but, not daring to go all the way, he . . . put the maréchale de Rochefort in the first [dame d'atour's] place. She didn't mind being in such unequal company . . ." Thus the duc de Saint-Simon, writing of the first days of 1680.

Until that point, the post of deuxième dame d'atour had not even existed. It had been created especially for Françoise, giving her not only a formal justification for remaining at court, but also a certain authority there. Like most such posts, there was little real work attached to it: Françoise was to supervise the dauphine's hairdressing and part of her wardrobe, not with any effort of her own hands, but through the selection of maids and, now and then, the placing of orders for furs or silks. Within the dauphine's household, she would be subordinate to the unproblematic Madame de Rochefort, first lady-in-waiting, and also, less happily, to the dauphine's dame d'honneur, the malicious duchesse de Richelieu. Rumour of Françoise's new post had evidently been about for some time. Six weeks before the announcement, perhaps concerned that an apparent overconfidence on her part would displease the King, or perhaps not yet convinced about the post herself, Françoise had cautioned her brother not to believe it. "I am not a dame d'atour," she insisted. "When the dauphine's household is announced, I'll let you know. Until then, take everything you hear about it with a pinch of salt. This rumour is being spread by people ill-intentioned towards me."

The dauphine was the wife of the King's only surviving legitimate child, nineteen-year-old Louis de France, known to the court as "Monseigneur." His marriage to the twenty-year-old Marie-Anne-Christine-Victoria of Bavaria, sister of one of the seven Electors of the Holy Roman Emperor, reflected the growing power of the Austro-German Habsburgs at the expense of their Spanish cousins. "The light of her intelligence and her charming manners . . . compensated amply for the lack of a certain, shall we say . . . beauty," reported the diplomat Spanheim, "and facilitated her entry into the dauphin's good graces." "The dauphin accepted his wife the way he'd accepted his lessons as a boy," remarked Primi Visconti, with wry perspicacity. "He was brought up in fear."

His expected throne aside, however, the dauphin, dim-witted and with no personality to speak of, was not well placed to expect more in a wife. Even Liselotte, by her own admission no oil painting herself, had told him that "even if I saw him naked from head to foot, he couldn't lead me into temptation." "He was a terrific eater," reported the duc de Saint-Simon. "One day he spent the whole day eating, and . . . after supper he went up to change, but he didn't come down . . . In the end they found him half-naked and unconscious in his room . . . They forced an enema into him. It took a long time to work, but after two hours there was a prodigious evacuation—up and down." The bride was clearly going to need all the resources of her charming manners.

The dauphine had been accompanied on the last stage of her journey from Bavaria by Françoise and Bossuet, "and if she thinks all the men and women at court are as bright as those examples, she'll be very disappointed," remarked Madame de Sévigné, with painful truth, at least as far as the girl's mother-in-law was concerned. "They were all talking about the new dauphine one day in the Queen's apartment," said Primi Visconti, "and the duc de Montausier said to the Queen, *What a mind! It will take a good deal of time to take the measure of her. Though of course in the beginning, people said the same even about Your*

Majesty. And he stopped suddenly, realizing what he'd said. The courtiers started to laugh. Of course the Queen didn't understand a thing."

And if the young dauphine had cause to be disappointed in her husband and her mother-in-law, her celebrated father-in-law quickly disappointed her, too. "After a bit," Primi continued, "the dauphine changed her manner with the princesses and duchesses who formed her circle. She began to praise their gowns and to talk of nothing but fabrics. She'd been warned not to talk about anything else. The King's attentions to her had been diminishing because she had begun to inform herself about court affairs." To his own displeasure, Louis had found that he had underestimated the new dauphine's intelligence, though his low opinion of her feminine charms may have been more generally shared. "She is a brunette, of middle height and a noble demeanour," added Primi with determined gallantry. "She has good skin, pretty hands, and pretty eyes, and that makes the rest of her features bearable."

At first the young dauphine had been pleased to find Françoise a member of her household, regarding her with friendliness and interest. But through the insinuations of Madame de Richelieu, her dame d'honneur, and the malice of Liselotte and her husband, Monsieur, she had gradually grown mistrustful of Françoise, and even perhaps to fear her somewhat. Françoise managed to have her protégé, the physician Fagon, appointed to the dauphine's household, but the dauphine herself began to keep increasingly to herself, with only her Bavarian maid for company. Toothache, then fever, then a possible pregnancy, soon confirmed, then fever again, all provided more than enough in the way of excuse to allow her withdrawal from court life, to the extent of absenting herself almost completely from court activities. Eventually, the King's intervention put a stop to the little cabal. "Madame la dauphine has come out of her rooms and goes about in public . . . The Court is very gay . . . the King is very pleased, and the royal family is very close," wrote Françoise to Charles, omitting to mention that she herself was feeling satisfyingly vindicated, and that Madame de Richelieu and her "little cabal" were not feeling very satisfied at all.

———

Françoise was now a person of some importance at court, her new standing declared to all by the sombre black gowns she was obliged to wear as deuxième dame d'atour to the dauphine. She had been sorry to abandon the greens and blues and other, brighter colours she had long preferred, but she was happy enough with her new manner of dress, in that it gave her an added distinction at court, and indeed wherever she went. To dress entirely in black indicated sobriety, certainly, and in this case, a measure of formal authority, but at the same time it implied wealth: black cloth was expensive, the necessary dyes being difficult to produce and to apply. In her rich new rustling gowns, Françoise presented an impressive figure to the world, and to this she added her own touch of quiet elegance in the form of a diamond cross at her neck; for the time being, this was to be her only jewellery.

No impressive figure in black gown and diamond cross was likely to wander the court alone. Françoise possessed her own retinue of servants, including two longer-term favourites, her maid Nanon Balbien and an African page named Angola, on whose behalf Françoise was currently engaged in speculation in commodities—namely, oats. "I asked you to buy the oats as an investment of Angola's money," she wrote to her estate manager at Maintenon. "I'm told there's nothing safer than buying oats now, and selling them later. It's a large-scale plan. Do help me with it."

As for Nanon, she had by now been with Françoise for almost twenty years. "And she thought just as much of herself as her mistress did," snapped the snobbish duc de Saint-Simon, resentful of the overlooking of his own, bluer blood. "She dressed just like her, and did her hair in the same way, and imitated her affected speech and her manners and her piety. She was a sort of little fairy godmother, and all the princesses were delighted if they had the chance to speak with her or give her a kiss, even though they were the King's own daughters. And all the ministers working in Madame de Maintenon's apartment always bowed to her, very low."

Nanon and young Angola were capable and reliable, but an ambitious dame d'atour needed a different kind of following, too. She

needed more highly placed people of her own, people who could protect her against her enemies at court, people who, preferably, owed
their positions to her, and whose progress would advance her own reputation. Françoise needed a clan.

Her recent alliance with the court dévots had brought her two
promising younger friends, thirty-year-old Jeanne-Marie, duchesse
de Chevreuse, and her sister, twenty-three-year-old Henriette-Louise,
duchesse de Beauvillier. Daughters of the King's minister Colbert, the
two duchesses shared a keen dislike of Athénaïs and her sultanesque
ways, a dislike which the recent marriage of their youngest sister,
thirteen-year-old Marie-Anne, to Athénaïs's fourteen-year-old nephew,
had done nothing to lessen. The marriage had cost the King "fourteen
hundred thousand livres": 600,000 for Marie-Anne's dowry, which
Colbert, apparently, was unequal to paying himself, and 800,000 to repay the debts of Athénaïs's incorrigibly extravagant family. The two
elder sisters were only too pleased to attach themselves to Françoise, as
Athénaïs's obvious if undeclared enemy, "and she, for her part, was
not at all averse to the King's seeing persons of such quality choosing
her over Madame de Montespan."

Apart from Colbert's daughters and their two husbands, there
were of course the Montchevreuils, the tall, skinny marquise with
her "ghastly long teeth" and the "modest, decent . . . dense" marquis.
Through Françoise's efforts, they were now well entrenched at court.
"Madame de Montchevreuil was a woman of some merit," wrote Françoise's niece, "if one accepts the word *merit* as meaning no more than
virtuous. She was a rather pathetic figure, and not very bright at all,
but she was most attached to Madame de Maintenon, and it suited
Madame to be able to introduce someone unexceptionable at court,
someone who had known her in the days of her obscurity."

Françoise had arranged the marquise's appointment as governess to
the dauphine's maids-in-waiting. "The position wasn't so much in itself, but there were great distinctions attached to it: she was regarded
as the fourth lady in the dauphine's household . . . and the most illustrious names in the kingdom were employed there."

The marquis had been for four years already governor to fourteen-year-old Mignon, the duc du Maine. Françoise had at first offered this post to another old friend from her salon days, the poet Jean de Segrais, but Segrais had declined, having no longer any need to earn his living. He had recently married "a very rich cousin, who wanted to marry a poor man, so that he wouldn't be able to look down on her." "And besides," as Segrais himself said, "I was getting a bit deaf . . . Madame de Montespan's sister said that shouldn't have deterred me, since I was supposed to be talking to the prince, not listening to him. But I said to her that, in that country, you needed to have good eyes and good ears as well."

Montchevreuil, not so dense, in fact, was managing the job very well, though Françoise could not prevent herself from giving him periodic advice about it: "You need to reason with him—he's been used to that since he was in swaddling clothes. Keep all his tutors under control; they don't care about anything except their own particular subject. Good reasoning will be of more use to him than a bit more Latin. Let him see what happens to the money he gives to charity; that will help him learn to govern . . . Excuse me for saying all these things—if it's not good advice, at least it's well intentioned. You know how extremely fond I am of our duc."

The long-toothed marquise, by contrast, was not doing so well with the maids-in-waiting. As Françoise's niece reported the case, they would have been quite a handful for even the shrewdest and firmest governess. "Mademoiselle de Laval—the talk going around about her! Mademoiselle de Biron—she was too plain to get anything in the usual way, so she got it all by intrigue. Mademoiselle de Tonnerre was mad. She was eventually hounded out of court. Mademoiselle de Rambures wasn't beautiful, but she had the kind of amusing talk that men like. She set her cap at the King, and then afterwards at Monseigneur, and he fell in love with her well and truly. Mademoiselle de Jarnac was plain and in poor health, so there's not much to say about her." It was all too much for the simple marquise. "She's too good for this country," sighed Françoise, implying, no doubt, that Madame de Montchevreuil was simply too naïve. "She loves these girls as if they were her own daughters, and she gets involved in all their little interests. She thinks they're all going to behave perfectly. Then of course she's disappointed when they don't. I do what I can in the way of moral support . . ."

Bonne de Pons was back, the marquise d'Heudicourt, now aged thirty-eight, still "a bit mad," though chastened somewhat by her years of glum provincial exile and, sadly, no longer "as lovely as the day." "Madame d'Heudicourt is here," wrote Françoise to Charles. "She's ill, and more decrepit than an ordinary sixty-year-old." Following her banishment from court, years before, for leaking the secret of Athénaïs's illegitimate sons, Bonne had been trying to negotiate a return. Françoise had set things in motion by obtaining the King's permission to reestablish personal contact with her erring friend. There seems to have been no formal reconciliation, but little by little Bonne had been accepted back into the courtly fold.

Madame de Sévigné had been disapproving, "How ridiculous!" she puffed. "In her state of health! She looks as ugly as the devil, and she can't even stand up without leaning on a big walking-stick. She's far too fond of that country." Bonne had left her uninteresting husband behind in his provincial château, but had brought with her a new little daughter, "as lovely as an angel, and always hanging about the King's neck." Her elder girl, Louise, now thirteen years old and still in Françoise's care after ten years or more, was soon to be married to the marquis de Montgon; she would prove a loyal protégée as a well-placed *dame de palais*.

Bonne no longer had any influence at court, and indeed was entirely dependent on Françoise's protection, but she was more than welcome regardless. "She never opens her mouth without making me laugh," Françoise told her niece, "though it's true that in all the years I've known her, I can't recall her ever having said anything that I wished I'd said myself." Bonne was "such good company, so imaginative, so full of jokes, that she and Madame de Maintenon were soon as close as if they'd never been apart." "I simply can't resist her," admitted Françoise.

Irresistible Bonne, young Louise, and the worthy Montchevreuils, however, were not enough in themselves to form the kind of clan that Françoise wanted to establish. She needed more people, and she began to look about her in earnest. Charles d'Aubigné and his wife, Geneviève, were the obvious next candidates, but the pair of them, unfortunately, were out of the question. After three years of marriage, and three years of advice from her sister-in-law, Geneviève was still undressing in front of valets, and had not yet even learned "to stand up straight, and walk like a lady." Françoise's efforts to have her taught "proper French" had merely exchanged one defect for another: instead of speaking "like a fishwife," she was now sounding "like an affected little idiot, with all sorts of silly mannerisms. In the name of God, can't she speak naturally!" tutted Françoise in exasperation.

As for Charles, a most unflattering account of him was just about to appear in print in the bestselling *Caractères* of the satirist Jean de La Bruyère:

> Here he comes: the closer he gets to you, the louder he shouts. He walks into the room: he's laughing, he's yelling, he's roaring. You block your ears, it's like thunder. What he says stuns you no less than his voice itself. He never shuts up, and if he ever quietens down it's only to mumble some smug or idiotic thing. He takes no notice of the time, of the people about him, of the normal proprieties . . . He's hardly sat down before he's annoyed everyone. He's the first to the table, and he takes the top place, with women on both sides of him. He eats, he drinks, he tells stories and jokes, he interrupts everyone else. He has no discretion whatsoever . . . He dictates everything . . . If there's gambling, he has to win, and he laughs at everyone who loses . . . There's no kind of self-satisfied stupidity he's not capable of. In the end I give up and go. I just can't stand him any more.

In short, Charles and Geneviève were much too embarrassing. "No, don't move to Paris," an anxious Françoise wrote to her brother. "It would look odd for you to be living nearby and not to have anything much to do with me. Of course, that's just my advice. It's not an order . . ."

There were, of course, Charles's two illegitimate sons, still apparently in Françoise's care and, it must be said, doing better than they were likely to have done in the care of their father. Charlot, now about twelve, though looking much younger, was living at Maintenon, "perfectly healthy, shorter than ever, and cleverer than ever as well. He's delightful, a real character. He hasn't grown an inch." Françoise saw him frequently and reported to Charles that in due course, "he'll have to go to college, and then into the cadets. They're marvellous, especially the Poitevins [where he'll go]. They won the prize for military exercises." In the longer term, Charlot might prove suitable.

And there was Toscan, who had been cared for in Paris together with Athénaïs's little princes, and who would now have been aged about thirteen. Six or seven years before, when Françoise had first left Paris to reside formally at court, he had been sent, or so it seems, into the care of nurses in the country, and her letters confirm that she had subsequently provided various sums of money for his maintenance. Françoise had been supporting a great many children over the previous decade or so; by 1680, indeed, there were as many as ten boys of Toscan's age living at her charge in the village of Maintenon. It is not clear whether or not Toscan himself was even still alive, but it is certain that in the spring of 1681, "a boy of twelve or thirteen, of quite a good family" had begun to demand more of her attention than the other nine. "He's showing every possible sort of bad tendency," she wrote to Père Gobelin. "He's a liar, he's lazy, he gambles, he steals"—in short, a gamut of vices, each already revealed, irredeemably, by brother Charles and father Constant. "Whether I humour him or punish him, I haven't been able to get anywhere with him . . . What can I do? Where can I send him?"

Where Toscan was sent, if indeed he was Toscan, is unknown, but in any case the boy had not promised well for Françoise's clan-building purposes. More acceptable, or better behaved in public at least, were her de Villette cousins from Mursay. The girls were all married, and two of them *mères de famille*; they could not easily be dislodged from Poitou. Their brother Philippe, however, her childhood favourite, was a definite prospect; he was by now a senior naval officer with an impressive record to his name. In 1676, the King himself had written to congratulate him on his distinguished conduct in battle against the Dutch near Sicily, and Françoise's own praises had swiftly followed: "I was in transports of joy at the news of your successes . . . You know how women love brave men . . . I'll do all I can to keep your name on people's lips, but it's best if you carry on the way you've been doing, since I don't have that much influence, and you've done more to recommend yourself than all the ladies in France could do for you . . . Oh, while you're in Sicily, could you get me thirty yards of green or crimson damask? I think the green would be better value . . ."

Two months later, Philippe's twelve-year-old son had been slightly wounded in battle off the coast of Rome and subsequently promoted to ensign. Françoise wrote an excited letter to his mother: "I've told the King . . . and I'm sure that, once your first moment of concern for the boy has passed, you'll realize how pleased you are to have brought a little hero into the world."

Encouraged by his cousin's enthusiasm, and placing too much confidence in her influence at court, Philippe had begun to rely on her to push his career a few steps higher. Françoise had proved more willing than able to help. In the summer of 1679, she had approached the marquis de Seignelay, Colbert's son and his deputy at the naval secretariat, to request promotions for Philippe and also for two of his young nephews, already serving in the navy. The Saint-Hermine brothers, in their middle teens, were the sons of Philippe's eldest sister, Madeleine, who forty years before had taught Françoise to read and write at the big kitchen table at Mursay.

Her efforts on their behalf, as on Philippe's, had produced only modest results: the younger Saint-Hermine boy might, perhaps, be made an officer; Philippe himself might, perhaps, have command of a vessel, "but Seignelay said . . . you've been treated very well indeed already. He said you've already had one command, and you got it before your superiors, and your ship was bigger than theirs, and you've also been given a pension sooner than you should have been—in a word, he said you should be perfectly happy with what you've got." As for the elder Saint-Hermine brother, Seignelay had been polite enough "to refrain from informing the King about him, out of consideration for me, but apparently he's an absolute good-for-nothing, lazy, incompetent, and undisciplined. The officers he's served with haven't been satisfied with him at all. After all Seignelay said, I felt quite relieved they hadn't hanged him . . . This isn't much for you," she had concluded to Philippe, "but we're not in the strongest position. You have an exaggerated idea of influence in general and of mine in particular. It's not my fault. I do what I can . . ."

It was indeed not Françoise's fault, and her Mursay family were not by any means in the strongest position. No amount of capability or heroism or influence at court was going to be enough from now on to ensure the advancement of Philippe and his brave young son, let alone his two nephews, for they were all Huguenots, disqualification enough to outweigh any other merit. For reasons of national security, Louis had decided that a single religion was henceforth to be observed by all his subjects, and that religion was to be Catholicism. No Protestant town or community or family was to remain to threaten the nation's political stability with any possible sympathy for France's Protestant enemies. Absolute loyalty to Louis was to be required, and that loyalty was to include a perfect agreement with all his aims and all his values. Since it was clear that most Protestants would not abjure their faith voluntarily, they were to be pressured into doing so by the narrowing of the professional paths open to them.

In the spring of 1680, the King issued an instruction that "all naval officers professing the so-called Reformed Religion are to be gradually removed from the service." Those agreeing to convert to Catholicism were to be retained, with the King himself helping to pay for the cost of their conversions, "either by supplying more missionary priests, or by paying the heretics a direct conversion fee."

It was 1680, a propitious time for a purge of Louis's navy. The six-year-long Dutch war had been concluded at the end of 1678; for sixteen months France had been at peace. So the anti-Huguenot instruction came as only a partial surprise. Since the beginning of Louis's personal reign in 1661, the terms of Henri IV's great 1598 Edict of religious toleration had been subject to ever more stringent interpretation. As in the days of Constant d'Aubigné's tactical abjurations of faith, Huguenots were once again being excluded from official appointments and from the practice of certain crafts; restrictions were being placed on their transfers of money, on their status in the law courts, even on their rights to marry and to educate their children. Spurred on by his priests, Louis had begun a slow throttling of Protestant life in the kingdom. His Huguenot subjects, a million people or more, were by now "choking in little gulps."

Fifteen years before, after repeated pressure from the King, the Protestant vicomte de Turenne, one of France's great generals and a friend of Françoise's from the days of Scarron's salon, had finally made his own abjuration, so depriving his Huguenot confrères of their best protector. Though, at the time, Turenne had brushed aside accusations of unprincipled ambition, his conversion to Catholicism had raised him from honourable maréchal de camp to the rare and glorious rank of maréchal de France. Françoise's ambitions for her cousin Philippe were not so exalted, but it was clear to her, in any case, that, as a Huguenot, he could not progress much further than he had already done, and that her younger Huguenot cousins, her "nieces and nephews" just starting out in life, were unlikely to be able to advance at all.

In consequence, she had been pressing Philippe towards Catholicism since as early as February 1678, two years after his impressive conduct in the sea battle near Sicily: "There's no knowing what the King would do for you, if you would convert. He really seems to want to do something for you." But Philippe's confessional integrity, or plain stubbornness, had proved unassailable, and the anti-Huguenot instruction of April 1680 seemed to have brought a halt to his professional advancement once and for all.

Frustrated, Françoise made up her mind that if Philippe refused to help himself, she could at least do something for the younger generation of de Villette cousins, her "nieces and nephews" from Poitou. These eight grandchildren of Aunt Louise and Uncle Benjamin were now between nine and sixteen years of age; the four boys were already serving in the navy, with the four girls living quietly with their families in the Poitou region. If Françoise was to "do something" for them, they would have to be nearer at hand, and more importantly, they would have to abandon their Huguenot faith and formally accept Catholicism. In this way, she could ensure good professional prospects for the boys, good marriage prospects for the girls, and, in the longer term, an influential clan of blood relatives for herself.

Philippe had made clear his own refusal to abjure his faith, and it was unlikely that his sisters would be any more willing. Attempts to persuade them would be merely wasted breath. A firmer stratagem was going to be needed. Most of the young cousins were within easy reach. Françoise decided to kidnap them.

Early in the summer of 1680, only weeks after the April anti-Huguenot instruction, she again approached Seignelay at the naval secretariat. With his assistance, she arranged for Philippe to take command of a ship assigned to a routine voyage to her old island of Martinique, there to wave the French flag in the faces of the other colonial powers. Philippe was relieved. It was more than he had expected, though the ship was "only a thirty-six-cannon vessel," named—with appropriate irony, though he did not know it—Les Jeux (Games). Later in the summer he set off for the Caribbean, accompanied by his younger son, twelve-year-old Henri-Benjamin. It was a long voyage out and an equally long voyage back, and in the months of Philippe's absence Françoise intended to act.

The capture of Henri-Benjamin, sailing the high seas with his father, would have to be deferred, and the elder, "good-for-nothing" Saint-Hermine boy might perhaps be overlooked altogether, but that still left six: Henri-Benjamin's brother, sixteen-year-old naval ensign Philippe de Villette, and their sister, nine-year-old Marthe-Marguerite; Louis-Henri, the younger Saint-Hermine, also aged about sixteen, and his younger sisters, one whose name is unrecorded, and Marie-Anne-Françoise, known as Minette; and a girl of about the same age, Mademoiselle Caumont d'Adde, granddaughter to the vicious old Caumont d'Adde who had hounded Jeanne d'Aubigné over her inheritance.

Young Philippe, at least, was likely to be an easy catch. Even at the age of eleven, following Françoise's 1675 visit to Mursay, he had understood the advantages of having a relative at court, and had written requesting her help, and also the help of the Minister of War. Since then, he had been only too happy to visit her at Saint-Germain and Versailles, where his minor battle wound and his reputation as "a little hero" had ensured him a good reception. Nevertheless, when it came to abjuring his faith, he proved quite stubborn—"but we need not be deterred by that," wrote Françoise briskly. And indeed, by early December 1680, with Philippe père still safely distant in the Caribbean, she was able to write to Charles, "Our little nephew is now Catholic; I have him here with me. He's becoming a real courtier. I hope the King will do something for him; he's very presentable. I'm now expecting [Louis-Henri de] Saint-Hermine, and I'll be doing my utmost to convert him, too."

Françoise had placed responsibility for Louis-Henri's capture on Charles's own rather shrugging shoulders. How he managed it is uncertain, but within a fortnight the boy had been deposited at court, bringing with him, however, a much less compliant attitude than his cousin. "Monsieur de Saint-Hermine arrived today," Françoise relayed to Charles, "and I think he'll give me a bit more trouble . . . But I did like Minette when I saw her . . . If you could send her to me, I'd be very pleased. There's no other way than by force, since the family are not going to be happy at all about Philippe's conversion. So you'll have to get her to write to me, saying that she wants to become a Catholic. You send me that letter, then I'll send you a lettre de cachet which you can use to take Minette to your house, until you can send her on . . . Do attend to this. I really want this little girl, and you'll be obliging me as well as doing a good deed."

Charles duly obliged with a convincing lie to the local Huguenot authorities about a Christmas visit to court for his little cousins, Mademoiselle de Saint-Hermine and her sister Minette, and Mademoiselle de Caumont d'Adde. The capture of the youngest girl, Marthe-Marguerite de Villette, was left to her Aunt Aymée, now Madame Fontmort, who agreed to the plan with no apparent hesitation. Whether troubled by a strong religious conscience, or simply in periodic need of a "conversion fee," Aymée herself had already switched between Protestantism and Catholicism no fewer than three times. "God, who knows everything, doesn't know what religion my sister is," her brother had commented wryly. Perhaps equally significantly, Aymée had no child of her own; in any case, she evidently lacked the empathy to imagine the distress of her sisters Madeleine and Marie, and of Philippe's wife Marie-Anne, as their children were whisked away by their highly placed and high-handed relative.

Aymée simply invited Marthe-Marguerite to visit her overnight, and once safely distant from Mursay, they made their rendezvous with the two other girls, minus Minette: "They were astonished and upset to see me," Marthe-Marguerite was later to write. In the week before Christmas 1680, wicked aunt and wailing nieces all arrived in Paris. Here, on December 21, Françoise met them, and two days later she penned a lengthy missive to her distraught cousin, Marie-Anne de Villette:

> Although I'm quite sure, Madame, that you give me your daughter with a good grace, and that you are overjoyed at my nephew's conversion, I realize at the same time that you will be in need of consolation, and that's why I'm writing.
>
> Monsieur de Mursay [Philippe de Villette] made his devotions yesterday . . . I see nothing but good in him; I've discovered no defect other than that he talks a bit too much. I don't yet know what I'll do with him. He seems to want to give up the navy, and lots of people think that would be for the best, but whatever happens, don't worry, I'll look after him as if he were my own son. He's learning to dance, and he'll have to learn to ride as well, if we keep him on land. The King is filled with kindness for him, and I hope he'll grant him a pension . . . Since Huguenots can't hope for anything, we have to ask on behalf of Catholics.
>
> . . . I went to Paris on Saturday to see Madame [Aymée] de Fontmort and my nieces. I found them all looking very unattractive, which I wasn't at all pleased to see. Mademoiselle de Saint-Hermine was barely recognizable; Mademoiselle de Cau-

mont d'Adde has got very thin, and your daughter [Marthe-Marguerite] was as yellow as wax. I took her away with me. She cried a bit, when she found herself alone in the coach, then for some time she said nothing at all, and then she started singing. Since then she has told her brother that she was crying because of what her father told her when he left [for the Caribbean], that if she changed her religion, and went to court without him, he would never see her again. She calmed down when I mentioned you, and of course she's used to me now. When I told her that she'd grow to love me, she told me that she loved me already. I spent today reading with her and teaching her tapestry; she has a dancing-master, who tells me she's doing very well. She likes the food here better than with her aunt in Paris.

. . . How sorry I am for you, my dear cousin! How distressed you must be, caught between husband and children! Your heart must be torn in two . . . I feel so very strongly about those I love that I can understand better than anyone how painful it must be for you. Take consolation in God, and in my friendship.

. . . Monsieur de Seignelay told me today that Monsieur de Villette will be back here in February. I hope that the fondness he has always had for me will prevent him from getting too carried away, and that he will realize, in his anger, that what I have done is a sign of the friendship I have for my relatives. I'm really disappointed that I didn't get Minette . . .

It was the first in a series of staggeringly unapologetic letters to "my dear cousin" in Niort, whose own swift and anguished protestations have not survived. "Your letter makes me feel so sorry for you," Françoise wrote only two days later, "or rather your situation makes me sorry for you." Marie-Anne's "situation," and the reason that she was "caught between husband and children," was that, though her husband was a Huguenot, she herself was Catholic. Under the terms of their marriage contract, their children were required to be brought up as Huguenots. In her heart of hearts, Marie-Anne may indeed have

been "overjoyed," as Françoise suggested, to see her son already converted, but she must have been anxious in the extreme as to what her
husband would say on his return from sea a month or two hence.

Françoise had clearly persuaded herself that by seizing the children
and inveigling them into Catholicism, she was acting to everyone's
general benefit. In one sense, it was true: as Huguenots, there was no
advancement possible for them, professionally or socially, whereas as
Catholics they could take full advantage of the influence she now possessed in her close connection with the King. The Saint-Hermine and
Caumont d'Adde families seem to have seen things more or less in this
light: though there is no extant correspondence with them on the subject, if Françoise can be believed, they reacted "obligingly." No doubt
they were less attached to their Protestant religion than cousin
Philippe de Villette had already proved himself to be—perhaps
Françoise even imagined that their own response might persuade
Philippe to adopt a more pragmatic attitude—and the whole affair cer-
tainly reveals the lack of importance she herself attached to some of
the greatest religious and political questions of the era: Liberty of con-
science within the state, or religious conformity? Did Holy Mother
Catholic Church provide the only route to salvation, or was she the
prophesied "scarlet whore of Babylon" and the Pope himself the
Antichrist, as Luther and Calvin and Knox had all insisted? Would
Protestants be damned to everlasting flames, or would it be the
Catholics weeping and gnashing their teeth in hell for all eternity?

Unlike her staunch old grandfather, Agrippa, and revealing a trace,
perhaps, of her calculating father, Constant, Françoise viewed these
matters above all politically: religious contention had torn France apart
in her grandfather's day, and had torn Europe apart during her own
childhood; it must not be allowed to do so again. The Catholic Church
now had the upper hand in France, and it was best for everyone, she
felt, to accept that and make their way along its clearly marked paths.
She had herself been captured in the Church's name in a practice by no
means uncommon, and for her all had turned out better than could
ever have been expected. Why should others not be "rescued" in the
same way, since in the end, it was all for their own good?

Françoise also wanted to build up her own clan at court, and in the longer term, who would be more loyal than the flesh of her own flesh? The boys would make their way in the army or the navy, and at court she would have the girls, or one of them, at least, to mould and shape—perhaps, though she did not say it, in the image of that phantom little girl that she herself would have liked to be. She was not impartial in her treatment of her three "nieces"; having failed to "get" Minette, the one above all that she had "really wanted," she settled for Marthe-Marguerite as her special protégée, depositing the other two in a Paris convent under the general supervision of their Aunt Aymée.

Marthe-Marguerite remained at court with her brother Philippe and, for a few weeks, her cousin Louis-Henri de Saint-Hermine. As Françoise had anticipated, he had indeed been giving her "a bit more trouble," and in the middle of January 1681 she was obliged to send him off to Père Gobelin in Paris, for him to try his conversionary luck with the recalcitrant young man. "Don't tell him any more than you have to about invocations to the saints and indulgences and the other things that are so shocking to Protestants," she warned. But only three weeks later, Père Gobelin had given up, too. Louis-Henri and the girls in Paris had proved less obliging than their parents, "to the infinite glory of Calvinism," as their cousin Marthe-Marguerite later accorded. "They're all leaving on Sunday," Françoise informed Charles. "They put up a good resistance and then made a dignified retreat—I'm convinced they'll repent of that . . . By the way, do look after Madame [Aymée] de Fontmort. She took this action only for God and for me. Her family are going to be absolutely furious with her. Do please do what you can to help her. She's a very good woman, and clever and brave, and she'd have some good advice for you and your wife, too . . ."

By mid-February, most of the damage had been undone. Only Philippe and Marthe-Marguerite remained at court. Philippe, already a young man, was quite happy, making his way energetically as one of the King's musketeers, having given up the navy definitively. But his nine-year-old sister had settled less easily, writing dozens of notes to her mother in Niort, and showing signs of apparent stress. "I've been making her take medicinal powders and herbal tea, and she is looking much better for it," Françoise reported to Marie-Anne. "All her hair is falling out; I don't want to shave her head in case it grows back brown, so I'll just cut it very short when she goes to stay in the convent."

In March 1681, Philippe returned from his eight-month-long trick voyage to the Caribbean, and as Françoise had feared, "the fondness" he had always had for her did not prevent him from "getting . . . carried away." He was outraged. "My father's letters to Madame de Maintenon were full of bitterness and reproaches," recorded Marthe-Marguerite in later years. "He accused her of ingratitude to his mother, her Aunt Louise, and of injustice and cruelty towards himself, but she had the authority of the King behind her, so there was nothing he could really do." "I'm not even going to reply to your demand that your daughter be returned to you," Françoise wrote to him with perverse indignation. "Judge for yourself whether I'd be stupid enough to give her back when I've had to use force to get her."

There was indeed nothing that Philippe could do. The King had taken a further, long-considered step towards the complete Catholicization of the realm, drawing up a new instruction which would require Huguenot parents to transfer all their children under the age of sixteen to the custody of their nearest Catholic relative. Those who refused would see the children taken from them by force in what was effectively a legalized kidnapping. And in the meantime, there was always a lettre de cachet, a royal command which no one could gainsay. It was just such a command that the baronne de Neuillant had used more than thirty years before to capture Françoise from Mursay. Françoise herself, though willing to resort to the same means, had not needed to do so. Where Madame de Neuillant had required force, she had succeeded by duplicity. "Madame de Maintenon had only asked to see the [Saint-Hermine and Caumont d'Adde] girls. She had promised not to make any effort to convert them, and so the Huguenot Council had felt they couldn't refuse her request."

"I feel so very strongly about those I love . . ." she had written to Philippe's wife—so strongly that she had made callous use of some of them, lied to others, abused their trust, and stolen their children, with the sole apparent regret that she "did not get" one last little girl. But as she insisted to Philippe, "If the King lives, there won't be a single Huguenot left twenty years from now," which events were to confirm, almost literally.

Françoise had stooped to unscrupulous methods, reflecting, no doubt, a hardening of her ambition to wield some influence of her own at court. But in the end, she was proved right. One by one, her Huguenot cousins came back to her, and one by one, they converted. In 1686, five years after his tirade of letters "full of bitterness and reproaches," Philippe himself was to accept the inevitable and become Catholic, ending his days as a marquis and a lieutenant-général of the King's armies. His son, Philippe, also a lieutenant-général, became the comte de Mursay, and Henri-Benjamin the chevalier de Mirmande. Stubborn Louis-Henri de Saint-Hermine became a lieutenant-général, too; Marthe-Marguerite became the comtesse de Caylus; Minette, captured at last, became the comtesse de Mailly. In short, all the boys advanced professionally, and all the girls married well.

⁓

FOURTEEN

Uncrowned Queen

The year 1678, with the annexation of the Franche-Comté, marked the flood tide of Louis's military glory. It was no longer endurable that his magnificence should be inadequately housed. It was decided that Versailles should become the permanent seat of both the Court and the Government.

So the work had started, and it was costing a king's ransom. Colbert had been complaining for years that "this house is more . . . for the pleasure and diversion of Your Majesty than for his glory . . ." But on May 6, 1682, Louis finally took possession of Versailles. It was a day of piqued pride for him, all the same: he learned that the Arkansas region had been renamed Louisiana in his name—and that the Mississippi had been renamed the Colbert River.

"Taking possession of Versailles" meant formally moving the premier royal residence from the château of Saint-Germain, where Louis himself had been born, to his father's former hunting lodge, heretofore a place for country fêtes and fireworks. Saint-Germain was admittedly small, but Colbert had not been protesting without reason: there were several other larger places that might have served in its stead. To date, the royal residence in Paris had been Catherine de' Medici's Tuileries palace, begun well over a century before and, like so many royal residences, still unfinished: an obsessive tinkerer where buildings were concerned, Louis had himself demolished the impressive windows and the oval staircase which had been its most distinguished features. To the east of the city there was the château of Vincennes, large, certainly, and very imposing, but more of a fortress than a palace, and still serving as an aristocrats' prison—the prince de Condé himself had been conceived in one of its many cells. There was Fontainebleau, "about fourteen leagues from the city," with its marvellous hunting forest: "It abounds with stags, wolves, boars . . ." But Fontainebleau was already perfect, and it was too obviously someone else's creation, the Renaissance jewel of François I.

And of course, as Colbert had kept reminding the King, in Paris itself there was the gigantic palace of the Louvre, but as the King had kept reminding Colbert, it would be altogether too much trouble to install the court there. For generations a place of courtly entertainment rather than a royal residence, and already full of artists' studios, presaging its eventual metamorphosis from palace to museum, it would certainly not have been an easy place to house hundreds of courtiers with any dignity or comfort. Colbert himself admitted that the royal apartments were no better than "rats' holes"; the King's own bedroom was apparently so dark that even at high noon the servants would be groping their way about trying to put things in order.

Colbert was committed to maintaining Paris as the centre of power, and for years he had been urging the King to fix and finish the enormous Louvre. At first the King had complied, though without much conviction. A covey of architectural wizards had been brought in to present their plans, most famously the great Gian Lorenzo Bernini, reluctantly venturing from his beloved Rome to chilly Paris—nothing but "a heap of chimneys," to his sophisticated Italian eyes. As might have been predicted, Colbert had found Bernini too "artistic," Bernini had found Colbert too practical, Louis had found Bernini arrogant, and Bernini had found Louis the same: the result was the gradual abandonment of the Louvre to lesser mortals.

In later days it would be said that it was not the Louvre but the city of Paris itself that Louis had rejected, reminding him, as it must have done, of his precarious boyhood during the years of the Fronde. "Paris being the capital of the kingdom and the seat of the King, it is certain that it sets the pace for all the rest of the country," Colbert had insisted to his son. But in absolutist France, it was not Paris or any other city, but simply wherever the King was, that set the pace. Where the court went, so went the life and soul of the country. The difficult, gloomy, unfinished Louvre was undoubtedly a factor in Louis's decision in favour of Versailles, and certainly, apart from demolishing it completely, which was several times considered, it could never have been remodelled according to his taste. But also, the Louvre was an urban palace, inescapably planted in the middle of the "heap of chimneys" and everything else that made up the ever-expanding city, and Louis was quintessentially a man of the country, physical, sporting, loving the open spaces, knocking down walls and throwing open windows wherever he went. Early and prolonged anxiety about political disorder had overlain his natural egotism with a mania for control, but, the planning and plotting behind him, he was happiest outside, a good horseman, a passionate hunter, but also a connoisseur of the delights of a simple afternoon stroll in park or garden.

The Tuileries palace had a garden, a very fine garden, in fact, which Louis had once planned to extend with avenues of trees stretching to "the heights of Chaillot"—two miles or more through existing crop fields, whose owners had been warned to expect no compensation. But even with its garden, the Tuileries was still in the city, subject to disturbances, perhaps, but more surely, subject to competition from other centres of political or artistic ambition. Paris "sets the pace for all the rest of the country," Colbert had written, but Louis wanted to set the pace himself. A court based in Paris would inevitably be surrounded by satellites of power and interest: too many great men had their own great houses there. There were too many rich men, too many men who wrote books, men with their own ideas about statecraft, men with their

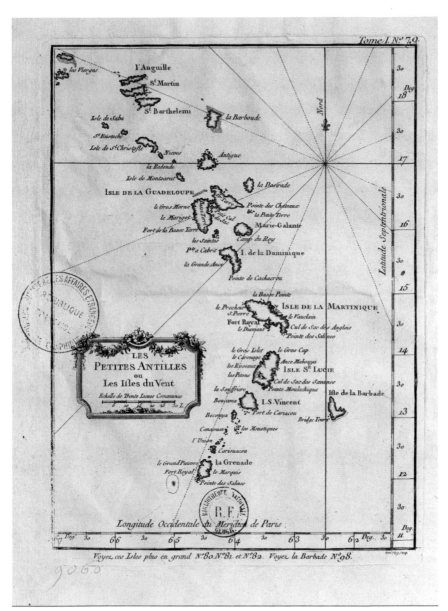

1. The Lesser Antilles, *les îles Camercanes*, where Françoise lived between the ages of eight and twelve, in alternating ease and hardship. She almost died of fever on the outward journey, and narrowly escaped being captured by pirates on the voyage home.

2. Rembrandt's *Beggars Receiving Alms at the Door*, 1648. In the same year, Françoise and her brother Charles spent the autumn months begging for food in the streets of La Rochelle.

3. The Château de Mursay, near Niort, in western France. Françoise lived here as a tiny child, and again in the last years of her girlhood, with her Aunt Louise and Uncle Benjamin de Villette and their family.

4. Paul Scarron, burlesque poet, *salonnier*, and long-suffering invalid, whom Françoise married at the age of sixteen. "My body, it's true, is most irregular," he admitted. "I'm a sort of human Z."

5. Ninon de Lenclos, "Our Lady of Love," the most celebrated courtesan in Paris and a lifelong friend of Françoise's. Her "three orders of lovers" comprised the payers, the martyrs, and the favourites, who neither paid nor suffered long.

6. Marie de Rabutin-Chantal, marquise de Sévigné, keen observer of court life and an admirer of Françoise. "You are one of those people who should never die," wrote her adoring cousin. Through her celebrated letters she gained a different kind of immortality.

7. Louis XIV as a young man. "The Queen must have gone to bed last night very happy with the husband she's chosen," wrote Françoise on seeing the King for the first time. Married at twenty-two, Louis promised to be faithful to his wife once he reached the age of thirty, but proved unable to keep his word.

8. Athénaïs, marquise de Montespan, the King's "greedy, proud, ambitious and temperamental" mistress. Her wit and beauty kept him captive nonetheless, and she bore him seven children.

9. Louis de Mornay, marquis de Villarceaux, one of Ninon's "prayers" and Françoise's lover in the early days of her widowhood. "[He is] one of the most dashing [among all the King's men]," she wrote to his neglected wife.

10. Françoise as governess, with Louis and Athénaïs's eldest two sons, the dark-haired duc du Maine and the blond comte de Vexin. "Nothing could be more stupid than loving a child so much when he isn't even mine," she wrote of the little duc du Maine, her "Mignon" (Sweetheart).

11. Louise de la Vallière, the King's first mistress, who bore him four children. "Of a tender, reflective and modest nature," as the diplomat Spanheim noted, by her affectionate promotion of La Montespan she brought about her own downfall.

12. Marie-Thérèse, Louis's devout Spanish first cousin and his Queen, "a saint, but not very bright," as Françoise's secretary observed, and all the court agreed. "The King liked almost all women," wrote Françoise's niece, "except his own wife." Only the eldest of her five children survived infancy.

13. Versailles as Françoise saw it in 1668, attending her first royal fête. A charming country *maison de plaisance*, it was deemed too modest for the court of Louis le Grand.

14. Versailles under massive reconstruction in the early 1680s. Françoise was living here at court. "There are twenty-two thousand men and six thousand horses at work here every day," wrote the marquis de Dangeau.

15. Part of the completed château of Versailles in the 1690s. Françoise's apartments were near the King's, on the first floor of this southern wing, overlooking the *parterre du midi* and the orangery.

16. Philippe, duc d'Orléans, the King's brother, known simply as "Monsieur." An extravagant homosexual, he nonetheless married twice and dutifully fathered six children. Louis denied him any political power and was annoyed when he proved a bold and effective military commander, riding into battle with his wig always freshly powdered.

17. Elizabeth Charlotte, "Liselotte," *la princesse palatine.* Though married to the King's brother, she nursed an unrequited passion for Louis himself and jealously referred to Françoise as "the old turd."

18. Jean-Baptiste Colbert, marquis de Torcy, Comptroller-General and Secretary of State for the Navy. His vast competence and capacity for work effectively made him the governor of France. A determined nepotist, he regarded the kingdom "almost as a family business."

19. François-Michel Le Tellier, marquis de Louvois, Colbert's bitter rival and a ruthless Minister of War. When told of the imminent marriage of "the greatest King in the world" to "the Widow Scarron," he threw himself at Louis's feet and burst into tears, begging him to reconsider.

20. The Duke of Marlborough's (mostly mercenary) soldiers at the Battle of Blenheim, 1704. It was a major victory for the English and their allies during the War of the Spanish Succession against France. Louis had engendered the thirteen-year-long conflict by placing his grandson on the contested Spanish throne.

21. François de Salignac de la Mothe-Fénelon, Archbishop ("the Swan") of Cambrai. "I've never seen anything to match his expression," said the duc de Saint-Simon. "You had to make an effort to stop looking at him." Françoise tried to travel a new spiritual path with Fénelon, but the venture brought her to the brink of ruin.

22. Jacques-Bénigne Bossuet, Bishop ("the Eagle") of Meaux, the court's champion hellfire-and-brimstone preacher. He and Françoise sought to manipulate each other to gain influence over the King.

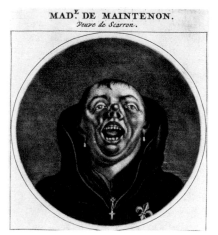

23. Bossuet portrayed in a Dutch caricature following the Revocation of the Edict of Nantes in 1685. The Edict had guaranteed civil and religious tolerance towards France's Protestant Huguenot minority. Bossuet strongly supported its revocation.

24. Françoise portrayed by the same Dutch caricaturists. Though she did not support the Revocation, she urged her Huguenot relatives to convert to Catholicism in order to ensure their professional advancement.

25. After 1685, Catholic dragoons were instructed to cause as much trouble as possible for those Huguenots who resisted conversion. "With methods like these," wrote a disgusted Fénelon, "one could convert all the Protestants to Islam."

26. Françoise as Santa Francesca of Rome, painted at Louis's request. Her ermine cloak indicates royal status and hints at her secret marriage to the King, never otherwise publicly acknowledged.

27. Louis in middle age. By 1690 the glorious period of his reign was over and France's *grand siècle* was drawing to its close.

28. La maison royale des Dames de Saint-Louis, Françoise's school for poor girls of noble birth. From a grand and imaginative beginning, it descended into a conventional Catholic boarding school, but Françoise always loved Saint-Cyr and retreated there after the King's death.

29. Louis de Rouvroy, duc de Saint-Simon. He despised Françoise for her humble beginnings and resented her influence at court, describing her secret marriage to Louis as "the most profound humiliation for the proudest of Kings."

30. Philippe, duc d'Orléans, Liselotte's son and the King's nephew. After a dissipated early youth, he displayed energy and intelligence as Regent following Louis's death.

31. Louis-Auguste, duc du Maine, Françoise's "Mignon." Pushed by his ambitious wife, he became involved in a plot against his cousin, the Regent, and was eventually imprisoned. "[His disgrace] was Death's first strike at her," wrote Saint-Simon of Françoise. She lived just three months longer.

32. Françoise in old age. Shortly before her death, at the age of eighty-three, she received a personal visit from the Russian Tsar, Peter the Great. "He pulled back the curtains at the foot of my bed so as to get a better look at me," she wrote to her niece. "Naturally, he was perfectly satisfied!"

33. Louis *en armure*. Sans teeth, sans hair, sans taste, he maintained his majestic demeanour to the very end of his life, a few days before his seventy-seventh birthday.

own courts of artists and society people, too many little Fouquets altogether.

Louis could never have controlled them. To ensure his preeminence as ruler and as patron, as dictator of high culture and director of the nation's future, he needed a court isolatable from any other centre of power, isolatable geographically, perhaps, but more importantly, isolatable conceptually, and he had decided that the pretty maison de plaisance at Versailles, set in unpromising marshland, "the most sad and barren of places, with no view, no water, and no woods," was going to provide it. "It will not be possible to create a great house in this space," Colbert had warned, "without a complete upheaval and without incurring a prodigious expense." Louis had been undeterred, receiving architects and decorators every Thursday morning, annotating their plans with his own hand—"and don't do anything until I get there." As for the "prodigious expense" Colbert had warned of, that was his problem.

And so it had begun. There had been work going on at Versailles, particularly in the gardens, almost from the start of Louis's personal reign, after Cardinal Mazarin's death, in 1661. But from the later 1670s, following the King's decision to make his premier residence there, the scale of the work had increased phenomenally. Expenditure was huge: within three years of the official move in 1682, construction at Versailles was eating up six million livres a year, almost 6 percent of the kingdom's entire revenue, though rumour had it to be much more: as Primi Visconti relayed to a friend, "I heard Monsieur [the King's brother] say that the King has already spent a hundred million francs on it, and there's not the tenth part of it done yet." Years before it became the building of the century, Versailles was the building site of the century, the disorder and expense both greatly inflated by the lack of any overall plan, and by the King's tendency to impulsive alteration and even demolition. With the court already in residence, there were still, as the marquis de Dangeau recorded, "22,000 men and 6,000 horses at work here every day."

The working day for most of the 22,000 men began early: for the construction workers, at five in the morning in the summertime (until seven in the evening), and at six in wintertime (until six). But they had two good pauses during the day, from nine to ten in the morning (when they ate their "dinner," the main meal of the day) and from two to three in the afternoon. Sundays were days of rest, and the Church dictated many more holy days, up to half the days of the year, on which no work could be done—and of course no money earned. The vast scale of the Versailles project encouraged exceptions, all the same: local priests sometimes permitted work after mass on a Sunday morning, against the objections of the masons' and plasterers' guilds and, perhaps surprisingly, at times even of the King himself. Those not working on the actual construction of the buildings, notably the architects and other designers, but also some of the craftsmen, often carried on through the night. "We have two teams of fine carpenters at Versailles, one working in the daytime and the other at night," reported Colbert, general supervisor, as usual, of everything and everyone involved.

Colbert's customary attention to detail ensured that wages remained stable for all workers throughout the many years of their labour on the great project, though his less than perfect mastery of economics meant that their money periodically lost value in terms of what it could buy. The technicians and master craftsmen—engineers and surveyors, carpenters, masons, gilders, and so on—were in fact paid fairly well, around 1,000 livres per year. Skilled workers such as plumbers, tilers, locksmiths, or general carpenters earned only about thirty livres per year, wages which in fact had been fixed at the same level for centuries, though they were greatly augmented by middleman takings from labourers whom the skilled workers brought in with them. Labourers were paid by the day or for a particular job: digging or carting might earn a man two hundred livres per year, of which certainly half would be spent on bread—not food, but simply bread—for himself and his family. Meat was a luxury: Louis's men at Versailles would have worked a ten- or twelve-hour day to pay for two pounds of beef.

"Consider how many poor workingmen I've fed by giving them work on my buildings," the King recorded in his *Mémoires*, in a piece of too hasty self-congratulation. In fact, by contemporary standards,

Louis's workmen were generally held to be poorly paid, their wages kept down by a great number of even lower-paid soldiers seconded to augment their ranks, and this at a time when, even on average wages, a vast number of working people were "teetering constantly on the edge of starvation." The workmen at Versailles may have had some idea of the pay scales of their masters, or perhaps they were simply too remotely high to make much sense to them: Colbert's annual salary as Surintendant des Bâtiments du Roi, for instance, was 21,000 livres, though this represented only a part of his income, since, like many others in the King's service, he held a number of high-level posts simultaneously. The *premier architecte* at Versailles earned 6,000 livres per year, the equivalent of Françoise's pension, while *maître jardinier* Henry Dupuis earned almost three times that sum—less two hundred livres one particular year, when he had his wages docked for not doing the job to royal satisfaction. Among the workmen, and the maîtres, for that matter, if they knew of it, the forty million livres lost (and luckily, rewon) by Athénaïs in that single evening at cards must have passed for the stuff of legend.

By now, Athénaïs herself was passing into legend. She remained Louis's maîtresse déclarée and surintendante of the Queen's household, though now obliged to ride two carriages behind the King. For a while she retained a sumptuous apartment at Versailles (twenty rooms on the second floor, while the Queen herself had only eleven on the third), but Françoise's ascent was unmistakable. Her own apartments had been among the very first to be built, and though she had insisted they should not be too large or too grand, they were nonetheless on the second floor, near to the King's, in the château's new south wing. From her windows she overlooked the orangery, its exotic trees still as yet concealed beneath the magnificent double stone staircase, but soon to be on full display: palm trees and citrus trees (twenty-two varieties), pomegranates, cloves, and oleanders, all kept warm during the winter months with fires of English coal.

Françoise might have envied them: most rooms inside the château had no fireplace at all, and those which did were frequently filled with dirty smoke. Always susceptible to the cold, she had requested wooden shutters for the windows of her apartments, but Louis had refused, insisting that shutters would disturb the appearance of the south façade. "So we can perish in symmetry," Françoise noted wryly, rugged up in the little niche, just big enough for a few armchairs and a set of padded screens, which she had constructed in one of her rooms—the warmest shelter available within the palace of an aesthetically purist king.

Louis did relent a little, all the same, permitting her to add double frames (painted gold) on the inside of the windows, so keeping out at least some of the draught—and indeed the smell, for just beyond the orangery lay the *pièce d'eau des Suisses*, so called for the Swiss Guards who were digging the lake at this very time. It was a matter of removing water before water could be added: the ground, swampy and stinky, had first to be drained, and many a good Swiss soldier lost his fever-racked life in the process. By bizarre contrast, at the little Trianon palace, built in the same years within the château's great park, the sweet fragrance of tuberoses was "so overpowering that no one could stand in the garden, even though it was enormous."

Beneath Françoise, on the ground floor of the south wing, Liselotte and her husband, Monsieur, had their own fine apartments, not quite so blessed with the orangery view, though equally cursed with the swampy stench. By now they had agreed that their mutual dynastic duty might be considered fulfilled. Their first son, Alexandre, "so terrifically big and strong," had died at the age of just three, but there remained eight-year-old Philippe, duc de Chartres, and six-year-old Elizabeth, marquise de Chartres, who together now provided their mother with her principal comfort and interest in an otherwise rather lonely life. The talented Monsieur, barred from any serious work by his autocratic brother, had been reduced to a life of more or less continuous partying with his many "Italian" (homosexual) friends, and Liselotte had been reduced to keeping herself warm at night "with six little dogs wrapped around me," as she admitted to her aunt. "No blanket will keep you so warm as a good little dog."

The royal family and their attendants in the south wing of Versailles were gradually joined by dignitaries and courtiers and servants in a new north wing, then in two huge flanks on the eastern side of the château, facing the town, and finally in the vast semicircle of *écuries*, officially stables, but in fact the abode of the 120 royal musicians and numerous other court followers content to bed down with the grooms and pages, or even beside one of the King's six hundred horses— "which are better housed than I am," as the Elector of Hanover was to remark. Versailles was never really finished, but while Louis lived there, it eventually contained 452 bedrooms, some of them squeezed onto hasty mezzanine floors, 226 apartments of varying sizes (the King's own numbered forty-three separate rooms), plus various corners and cupboards, altogether housing some 3,000 people, at least part of the time. Spreading out from the château itself were dozens, then scores, then hundreds of further buildings, with the little brick pieds-à-terre thrown together by the keenest courtiers in earlier Versailles days gradually giving way to handsome stone hôtels particuliers, and all the shops and taverns and trades and services of a busy new town sprouting around them.

For it was not just the premier royal residence that Louis had moved to Versailles. The seat of government had moved as well, and in absolutist France, with its deliberately weakened regional powers, this meant the whole apparatus of a fast-expanding state—the ministers, the military men, the diplomatic corps, counsellors and administrators at every level, city planners, senior churchmen, and all the aristocratic hangers-on, not to mention the tailors, milliners, jewellers, armourers, the moneylenders of high and low degree, and everyone else who created the appearances which the *grands seigneurs* so desperately needed to keep up. When the King was in residence, some 10,000 people thronged the courts and corridors of Versailles—and this did not include the workmen, 36,000 of them at their peak, still labouring inside and outside, and sleeping in temporary shelters thrown up for them in the château's vast grounds.

The grounds, in fact—a large domaine comprising a series of gardens (*les Jardins*), the open park and mile-long canal (*le Petit Parc*), plus the hunting forest (*le Grand Parc*)—were probably the most successful aspect of the whole gigantic project. Overseeing it all was the King's *premier jardinier*, André Le Nôtre, now seventy years old and the indisputable master of the elegant, geometrical *jardin à la française*, which, though no one cared to remember it now, was in fact, like so much in the grand French style, essentially Italian. Le Nôtre had begun work on the gardens in the 1660s, modelling them on those he had already designed at the château of Vaux-le-Vicomte, the country seat of the imprisoned minister Fouquet. Though twenty years had passed, few trees had been allowed to grow to a natural maturity in the marshy Versailles soil; instead, the impatient King had insisted on massive transplantations from other parts of France. On ground quite bare a week before, complete fluffy forests appeared, torn from Fouquet's former parkland and stuck into the earth by a new mechanism of pulleys and levers. In one year alone, some three million hornbeam trees were dug out of the Lyon forest to provide instant hedges for Le Nôtre's charming bosquets, secluded groves for concerts and dancing, and for lovers' trysts. No one at Versailles seems to have worried about depriving the Lyonnais of a major source of firewood, though recent winters had been so harsh that the water and wine at the King's own table had frozen, and the beautiful porcelain tiles enveloping the little Trianon palace in the park had begun to crack in the frost (Louis held Colbert responsible).

The King himself did not feel the cold at all, which may explain his lack of empathy with those, like Françoise and Liselotte, who did. Louis's bedroom windows were kept open all night, regardless of the season. His perverse love of even the coldest fresh air may also explain the absence of any real ballroom or banqueting hall in the huge new château: most of the grand entertainments were expected to be held outdoors. Even the splendid long Galerie des Glaces was more of a reception hall, almost a throne room, than a place for dancing or staged performances. Le Nôtre's gardens, with their bosquets and allées great and small, were in effect "an open-air extension of the palace," designed to provide ever-changing *scènes de théâtre* for the glittering social life of a royal court.

The results in any case were wonderful. The domaine, though "a place naturally without water," as the English philosopher John Locke recorded after his visit there, "hath more *jets d'eau* and waterworks than are to be seen anywhere, and looking out . . . one sees almost noe thing but water for a whole league forwards . . ." Locke was referring to the Grand Canal, more than a mile long, which stretched out from the end of the formal gardens. Three hundred men had spent twelve years digging it out, working in tragic relays, with many of them dying from malarial fevers contracted from the mosquitoes that flourished in the marshy soil. "The water is putrid," wrote Primi Visconti in 1680. "It infects the air; in August this year everyone fell ill, the dauphin, the dauphine, all the courtiers, everyone. The King and I were the only ones who didn't." Françoise had escaped as well. She was away in the eastern region of Lorraine, with the King, in fact, inspecting Vauban's defensive fortifications on the country's eastern border, though Visconti had forgotten this. Far from being feverish, Françoise was able to report to her brother that, in health and in spirits, spending every day in the King's company, she was "feeling very well indeed."

During the day, the Versailles gardens were open to the public—a first guidebook for sightseers had been printed as early as 1674, and Louis himself was now penning his own *Manière de montrer les jardins de Versailles*, though admittedly this was meant only for the most distinguished visitors, who in addition were provided with "fifteen rolling chairs upholstered in damask of various colours," in case they should be feeling less than royally energetic: the whole domaine measured almost thirty square miles. But even without any rolling chairs of their own, "the public" loved the gardens, and they came in droves. Anyone reasonably well dressed and reasonably well behaved was admitted. "The King . . . has ordered that all the fences around the groves are to be removed. All the gardens and all the fountains are to be for the public," the marquis de Dangeau recorded. Louis's *maître jardinier*, Henry Dupuis, oversaw the work, as he was to oversee the planting and pruning of the royal gardens for more than forty years. As the Versailles gardens became established and the numbers of "the public" increased, the King often made a tactical escape to the newer grounds of Marly, where "he preferred to watch the gardeners working."

But in fact there was nothing that could keep him for long away from Versailles. Beyond the thrill of the chase, beyond the pleasures of his many mistresses, building was Louis's passion, and if his planning was erratic, his ambition overall never wavered. He was determined to make of his Versailles the best, the most beautiful, the most impressive edifice in France, indeed in Europe. There was solid competition: from his cousin, the prince de Condé, a wealthy and enthusiastic embellisher of his already graceful château of Chantilly, just north of Paris; from his brother, Monsieur, duc d'Orléans, with his famous garden fountains at Saint-Cloud (a marvel in France, Bernini had conceded, though barely acceptable in a proper Italian garden); and even from the ghost of his deposed minister Fouquet, dead in his cell in the fortress of Pignerol, still haunting Louis's imagination through his magnificent château of Vaux-le-Vicomte, designed for Fouquet by Le Vau, Hardouin-Mansart, Le Brun, Le Nôtre—in short, everyone subsequently captured by Louis himself for Versailles. Not least, in his vast new residence Louis was at last overtaking his own uncle and father-in-law, the "Planet King" Felipe IV of Spain, with his country château of Buen Retiro and the Segovia palace of Alcázar. Louis had never seen either of these acknowledged splendours of contemporary royal architecture, but descriptions of them by his ambassadors, and perhaps even by Felipe's timid daughter, Queen Marie-Thérèse herself, had roused his jealousy: in the Alcázar especially, the glittering *Sala de Espejos*, with its Rubens ceiling, had been a definite spur to Louis's own Galerie des Glaces thirty years later, with its ceiling by Charles Le Brun.

"The King admits himself that there are faults in the architecture of Versailles," wrote Liselotte. "To save the old château, he's had to add new buildings all around it, covering it with a cloak, as it were, and that's ruined everything . . ." Without any beauty of her own, Liselotte had revealed, all the same, that she was not devoid of aesthetic sensibilities. The little hunting lodge, now spreading out unendingly on its swampy ground, was turning into a vast architectural jumble, with one designer after another struggling to maintain the old and construct the new under the eye of the demanding and interfering

King. Yet, in the same chaotic metamorphosis, Louis's Versailles was on the way to becoming the premier palace of Europe, and his court the arbiter of taste and splendour for the whole continent.

By the time of the formal move there in the spring of 1682, the "putrid" canal at least had been completed, with the impatient King insisting on using it even while the last work went on. Small ships and launches had been transported to it from the ports of Le Havre and Marseilles, and for pleasure trips *à l'italienne* there were two gondolas, carted (with their four gondoliers) across the Alps from Venice. Most remarkably, the Grand Canal was also serving as a harbour for miniature versions (maximum draught just over a yard deep) of all the new ships of the *Marine* which Colbert was gradually building up into a force fit to challenge the mighty Dutch navy. In this way, the King was to be kept abreast of developments of the fleet into which he, or his minister, was pouring so much money. For a time, it seemed that the canal might even be linked to one of France's great rivers, so making it part of the country's internal navigational network. But in the end, it remained above all a place for pleasure—including ice-skating on the frozen winter water—and for courtly display.

The King preferred its summer delights, gliding up and down the canal in his own splendid *galère*, painted in his royal colours of blue and gold, with red damask sofas inside to recline upon and forty-two red-faced rowers outside to power it. At six every evening—the King was a punctual man—he would set off in the galère with Françoise and Athénaïs both, while Marie-Thérèse, attended by assorted princesses, followed sadly behind in a lesser bark. Maîtresse secrète and maîtresse déclarée were courtiers enough to maintain appearances during these excursions. "Let's not make fools of ourselves," Athénaïs had said to Françoise. "We can keep up a front of perfect agreement. That won't oblige us to like each other any more than we do. We can take up the cudgels again when we get back." "They weren't visiting each other's apartments any more," Françoise's niece reported, "but wherever they met, they greeted each other and conversed so cordially and so animatedly that anyone who saw them without being in the picture would have thought them"—as Françoise had once described them—"the best friends in the world." "Madame de Montespan and I went for a stroll together today, arm-in-arm, both laughing a great deal," Françoise wrote to the marquis de Montchevreuil. "We're not on any better terms, for all that."

A thénaïs's final defeat began with a death, the sudden and quite unexpected death of Queen Marie-Thérèse. At the age of forty-five, she had appeared to be in good health, and in fact, like Françoise three years before, had just completed a five-week tour with the King, inspecting Vauban's impressive military fortifications in France's eastern provinces. Louis, rarely sympathetic to those who could not enjoy the rugged, pounding travel of an unsprung coach for hours on end, had noticed for once that the journey had been tiring for the Queen. Within a week of returning to Versailles, she had come down with fever, and four days later, as Liselotte relayed to her aunt, "in the afternoon at three o'clock, she died, and all through the ignorance of the doctors, who've killed her as surely as if they'd plunged a dagger through her heart. She had a boil under her arm, and they pushed it through her veins back into her body. And in the end, last Friday, they gave her something to make her vomit, and the boil burst internally."

The doctors themselves recorded that the Queen had died of "a cruel and malignant fever," and prescribed a week of "morning drops in a few spoonfuls of wine and half an ounce of *thériacquedans* [an opium extract], also in a bit of wine," to prevent the King from succumbing, too, after which ministrations, apart from a stomachache and a bitter taste in the mouth, both treated with more wine, he remained "in perfect health." An autopsy performed on the Queen's body revealed that "all her lungs" were gangrenous. In Paris, the Mercure Galant news-sheet reported Louis's own rather pathetic epitaph on his unremarkable wife: "In the twenty-three years during which I lived with the Queen, she gave me not a single anxiety, nor did she once oppose my will."

Marie-Thérèse, long-suffering in life, had at least not suffered long in death. "She died quite quickly and easily," as Liselotte reported, inspiring more attention and more praise in a single week than she had done in the previous forty-five years. In Paris, chansonniers wandered the streets singing sentimental songs about her, to which the cultured police commissioner La Reynie, looking up from his Aristotle, listened with indulgent condescension: "Let them," he said. "The people must have something. They seem really touched by the loss of the Queen. Of course the words are ridiculous, but the people like them; they express their kind of feelings." At court, the response to the news was as Marie-Thérèse herself, slow as she had been in most respects, would surely have foreseen: "With too little intelligence and too much devotion," noted the diplomat Spanheim, "she could only have made the court less gay and less lively . . ."

On hearing the news, a shocked Françoise had turned at once to retire to her own apartments, but the duc de la Rochefoucauld, taking her "quite violently" by the arm, had "pushed" her instead to Louis. "This is no time to leave the King," he told her. "He needs you." The duc's loyalty to his sovereign evidently outweighed his personal feelings, as suggested, perhaps, by the violence of his gestures, since, as Françoise's secretary was to record, "he didn't like her at all." She remained no more than a few moments with the King before being escorted out by the war minister Louvois. He took advantage of the opportunity to express his own dislike of her, instructing her to go to the dauphine, who was pregnant and who had just been bled, and tell her not to go to the King, but to stay in bed instead. "The King doesn't need your demonstrations of friendship," said Louvois nastily, "and the state needs a prince."

Forbidden by tradition to remain under the same roof as his deceased spouse, the King set off the same day for his brother's château of Saint-Cloud, and Françoise set off for Fontainebleau, where Louis encountered her four days later, he with his mourning already behind him, and she so greatly afflicted, to all appearances, that he could not resist teasing her about it. "And I can't promise that she didn't respond like the maréchal de Gramont," wrote her niece, the maréchal having famously concluded, observing the lukewarm grief of a newly bereaved countess, "Oh well, if *you're* not upset I don't see why *I* should be."

"Madame de Montespan wept a lot," continued Françoise's niece. "Perhaps she was afraid she'd be sent back to her husband . . . I saw Madame de Maintenon from close at hand, and her tears seemed to me sincere." But although she may have shed some tears sincerely for the otherwise unregretted Queen, most of Françoise's tears were in fact for herself. In recent months, it was true, Marie-Thérèse had been singing her praises, grateful for the increased attention from her husband which Françoise had prompted. But the prompting had been for reasons of Françoise's own: since Athénaïs's fall from grace, Marie-Thérèse had been a vital part of her personal rationale for remaining at court, her real work not the superintendence of the dauphine's wardrobe, but the superintendence, as it were, of the King's salvation. Louis was to be kept from sinful sexual liaisons (her own excepted), and sent back to the bed of his legal wife.

This noble work was now bound to be compromised. The King would surely press Françoise to be more obliging than she had lately been, or he might return to Athénaïs, or take a new mistress, or even a new wife, and what would become of her influence then? "You're quite right to think that the Queen's death has distressed me," she wrote to Charles a few weeks after the event. "No one has more reasons to be so, and I'm aware of them all, and very forcibly."

Liselotte felt she had reason of her own to miss the Queen. "In all my troubles she always showed me the greatest friendship in the world," she wrote two days after Marie-Thérèse's death. But in later years, she recalled having to exaggerate her feelings, just as Françoise may have done. "We were all very concerned, very worried," she wrote, "because we were going to be travelling in the same carriage as the King, to Fontainebleau, and we all thought he'd be downcast and impatient and in a bad mood, and that if we didn't look sufficiently grief-stricken, he'd be telling us off. We were agreeably surprised to find him so lighthearted. It put us all in a good mood."

As Françoise's niece observed, the King was in fact "more touched than afflicted" by the Queen's death. Of all the women he had ever known, as he himself remarked, she was the only one he had never loved. Liselotte felt that he had been "very moved to see her die," but added spitefully, "Madame de Maintenon found a way of consoling him, though, and within four days."

Liselotte was not far from the truth. The Queen had died on Friday, July 30. On Monday, the King met with Françoise at Fontainebleau, and by the following Saturday, she was already writing to her importunate brother, "No, you can't come and see me, and if you knew the reason why, you'd be overjoyed, it's so advantageous and so marvellous." If the King had found consolation already, as Liselotte saw through eyes more green with jealousy than red with any weeping of her own, Françoise had evidently found it, too. Her letter expresses her extraordinarily good spirits and a high confidence for the future. Charles had been complaining about his wife's failure to produce a child. His sister dismissed this out of hand. "You've got the vapours, that's why you're looking at things so bleakly," she wrote airily. "The misfortune of having no children is common enough in the world, and I think you're too sensible to be worried about your name dying out . . . You're old [Charles was forty-nine], you have no children, you're not in the best of health. What you need now is rest and ease and piety. All these things are already at your disposal, and I'll contribute with pleasure. If you want to buy an estate, I know of a good one. If you prefer to eat up all your money at Cognac, don't hold yourself back. You have more than 30,000 francs a year for the next six years. After that, if I'm still alive, we'll have something else, and if I'm not, you'll have Maintenon."

"We'll have something else." What Louis had said to her, what "advantageous and marvellous" thing, can only be assumed, but it is likely that during these days at Fontainebleau, less than a week after the death of his wife, he had informed Françoise of his intention to marry her. A few days after her letter to Charles, Françoise wrote to Marie de Brinon, a former Ursuline nun whom she had met some time before through the Montchevreuil family, and who had become an increasingly close friend. Madame de Brinon was now superintendent of a school for poor girls in which Françoise had been taking some inter-

est, providing money and clothes, and also a number of the girls themselves, bereft of means or prospects, who had come to her notice in the
parish of Maintenon or who had been recommended to her protection
through people at court. Françoise thought highly of Madame de
Brinon and trusted her discretion, though not absolutely, it seems. She
admitted that she had been unable to sleep, and hinted at some great
change afoot for the King—"I ask your prayers for the King. He has
more need of grace than ever, to endure a state contrary to his inclinations and habits"—but insisted at the same time, in reply to a now lost
enquiry on Madame de Brinon's part, "There's nothing at all to say
about the matter of Louis and Françoise. That's just foolishness.
Though I'd like to know why the lady wouldn't be willing. I would
never have thought she'd be the one to rule it out."

It was a cautious letter, disingenuous even, and perhaps a touch
embarrassed—hence the reference to "the lady," deflecting her own
feelings somewhat—but Françoise need not have worried. Before she
had even sent it from her modest rooms at Fontainebleau, the King had
insisted she be reaccommodated in the late Queen's own apartments
there.

On the first day of September 1683, a full month after Marie-Thérèse's
death, Bossuet delivered a grand and lengthy eulogy for her at the Paris
cathedral of Saint-Denis, final resting-place of the royal bodies of
France. There being only too little to say about the Queen herself,
Bossuet was reduced to reciting her family history and the circumstances surrounding her path to "the most illustrious kingdom that
ever existed under the sun, and the most glorious throne in the universe," praising the "happy simplicity" of her temperament and, in
the absence of any other beauty, the "striking whiteness of her skin,
symbol of the innocence and candour of her soul," and fibbing that
France's people had attributed all the King's military victories to the
power of their late Queen's prayers.

Even in full flight, Bossuet was unable to change the minds of his
flock of courtiers about the unachieving Marie-Thérèse. His effort

was pronounced a fine eulogy all the same, and the dauphin, if no one else, appeared to be genuinely moved. Twenty-two-year-old Louis, pudgy and slow, was Marie-Thérèse's only surviving child, "because, according to one of the physicians here, the King never gave the Queen more than the dregs of his glass. And it's true: one often notices that debauched men have very few children," noted Liselotte, overlooking Louis's nine recognized illegitimate offspring, and various other little rumours besides.

Louis recorded no comment on the side-swipe that Bossuet had taken at him towards the end of the eulogy: "All salvation comes from this life, and we know not when our hour will come. *I come like a thief in the night*, says Jesus Christ. And He has been as good as His word. He came, surprising the Queen at a time when we thought her in perfect health, and at her very happiest . . . Misled by our pleasures, our amusements, our health . . . our flatterers . . . and by our false penitence followed by no change at all in our behaviour"—Athénaïs was still, to all appearances, in her accustomed place—"we shall arrive all at once at the end of our days . . . *Like a thief in the night*, the Lord has said—an ungracious comparison, you may say, but what does that matter, provided it gives us all a good fright now, a good fright which will lead us to salvation. Tremble, fellow Christians! Tremble every moment, in the sight of the Lord! . . . The scythe that has cut off the Queen's days is raised above our own heads . . ."

And as if to confirm the threat, the very next day, out chasing deer in the forest of Fontainebleau, proudly dressed in his favourite blue and red hunting costume, the King took a bad fall from his horse. "Kings aren't centaurs," he is said to have remarked, but a letter about it from Françoise to her brother indicates the gravity of the accident. "We've hardly got over the loss of the Queen and here we've been, fearing for the King's life. We thought he'd broken his arm, but it's only half broken, and he's doing so well that, thank God, it seems we needn't fear anything further. This accident has opened his eyes . . ."

The fall had not in fact "half broken" the King's arm, but rather, as his physicians recorded, had "completely dislocated the left elbow."

The elbow was set by a Doctor Félix—regarded, extraordinarily for a physician of the day, as an exceptionally capable man—and the lump rubbed with a warming ointment of rose oil, egg yolk, vinegar, and plantain water, then wrapped morning and evening with a hot poultice of strong wine, absinthe, and myrrh. Louis's forearm, bruised and swollen, was massaged with "a pomade of ox hooves, washed several times to get rid of some of the smell, and afterwards with another pomade made of orange blossom." The anticipated further treatment, "according to the correct method," was a bleeding, "but His Majesty was *so cruelly distressed by this* that we could not manage it, and we decided instead that a complete abstinence from meat for four or five days, and an almost complete abstinence from wine, would achieve the same result, and it seems to us that it has done so." The royal elbow was subsequently encased in a plaster of wax and resin, and thus the King gradually recovered, spared the infection and gangrene that were the too frequent accompaniments of an injured limb.

He was not, however, spared the sight of the grim death, just four days after the accident, of his extraordinary first minister Colbert, at the age of sixty-four. From his doubtful beginnings as manipulating nemesis of the minister Fouquet, Colbert had ended, after twenty years of herculean work, Comptroller-General of Finances, Secretary of State for the Navy, "a very fine capture since the navy included warships and galleys, ports and arsenals, coastal fortifications, control over the sea-going navy as well as the interior waterways . . . plus the colonies and foreign trade . . . And he was also surintendant des Bâtiments du Roi, another key sector: all the royal demesnes and control as well over all kinds of urban development and land management. And then he bacame surintendant of the King's household," not to mention that "waterways and forests, the mint, bridges and highways, tax collection, provincial administration, all landed in Colbert's pockets." Thus history's reckoning of the man who had, in effect, created the various glories of Louis's reign to date. It was not enough, all the same, to prevent Colbert's dying in atrocious suffering, from stones obstructing his kidneys. And if the King had admired his apparent successes, the cost of them had been decidedly unappreciated in the country at large—to such an extent, in fact, that Colbert's body was buried at night, in secret, for fear of rioting by the ungrateful taxpayers of Paris.

"We shall arrive all at once at the end of our days . . . *I come like a thief in the night*, says Jesus Christ." If Bossuet needed support for his ministry of fear, he had it now in the sudden deaths of the Queen and of Colbert, and in the King's own alarming accident. But Louis, for one, had already been persuaded. To begin with, he had indeed had a fright: the death of Marie-Thérèse, the very same age as himself, had startled him into a realization of his own mortality. And helpfully, the sins of debauchery had become less interesting of late: the lovely Athénaïs was, by general admission, less lovely than she had been, and beautiful, basket-silly Angélique was dead—at the age of twenty, if further weight were needed for Bossuet's already heavy argument.

"But the King couldn't do without women," as the abbé de Choisy observed, and as Louis himself well understood. "Better to marry than to burn," as the apostle Paul had insisted, and as the King no doubt believed. Not that marrying Françoise was any sort of last recourse for him, if the diplomat Spanheim is to be believed. Observing the two firsthand, he writes of "the attachment to her that the King displays openly . . . the visits he makes to her, the long conversations he has with her . . . And she is a most intelligent, sweet, amiable woman . . ." Only reasons of state, it seemed, and "the King's excessive passion for glory" prevented Françoise, "with no land and no fortune . . . formerly living on charity," from becoming his wife and Queen.

It is true that, concerned to avoid the possibility of civil strife in the future, Louis did not want to raise up a second royal family, but, as the abbé Choisy pointed out, at almost forty-eight, Françoise was in any case "beyond the age of having children." It might have been useful for Louis to remain officially available for a second strategic marriage with some European princess—for a time, French courtiers talked of the Portuguese infanta—but a feint of this kind could not have been maintained indefinitely. There was in fact no reason of state why a marriage with Françoise could not have been openly acknowledged, and she herself crowned Queen. It would even have served to declare a great spiritual victory, the triumph of virtue over worldly considerations of kingdom or caste. But Louis's new-found interest in saving his soul had not progressed so far. For "the greatest of all men," the public humbling of his princely self, even for eternal advantage, was simply impossible.

Louis had trouble enough announcing his intention of even a secret, morganatic marriage with Madame de Maintenon. The horrified reaction of his war minister, Louvois, admittedly one of Athénaïs's circle and certainly no friend to Françoise, gave a good indication nonetheless of what he might expect from almost everyone else at court, and everyone else at every other court, besides. The King had approached Louvois in confidence, "as if the thing hadn't yet been quite decided, and asked his opinion of it. *Oh Sire!* Louvois had gasped, *Has Your Majesty really considered this? The greatest king in the world, covered in glory, to marry the Widow Scarron? Do you want to bring dishonour on yourself?* And he threw himself at the King's feet and burst into tears. *Sire, pardon the liberty I take. Relieve me of all my posts, throw me into prison, but I will never look upon such an indignity.* And the King said to him: *Get up! Are you mad? Have you lost your mind? . . .* And the next day Louvois could see from Madame de Maintenon's cool and awkward manner to him that the King had had the weakness to tell her everything. And from that point onwards she was his deadliest enemy."

Louvois was present, all the same, at the nuptial mass, which was conducted at midnight, as was customary in order to avoid a long fast before Communion, and in almost total secrecy, which was not customary at all. "It was rumoured that the King had secretly married her . . . At first it was dismissed as nonsense . . . but then . . . most people came to believe it, imputing it to the King's piety, a penitence for his sinful liaisons . . ." The ceremony took place, it seems, during the night of October 9–10, 1683, in a chapel at Versailles, and was conducted by François de Harlay de Champvallon, the sixty-year-old Archbishop of Paris, himself in well-known need of salvation from the

many women who had been keeping him for years from closer attendance to his priestly duties. Apart from the grudging Louvois, the only
other certain witnesses were the King's Jesuit confessor, Père François
de la Chaise, and his faithful valet, Bontemps, "the best valet ever," in
the abbé de Choisy's view, "rough on the outside, but refined on the inside." "He had the King's entire confidence in every intimate or personal matter," said the duc de Saint-Simon. Though the dauphin was
not present, he had been informed of the wedding, as had the marquis
and marquise de Montchevreuil, Françoise's friends from the long-ago
days of her affair with Villarceaux, and her trusted maid, Nanon Balbien, "as capable as anyone else of keeping a secret, and with senti-
ments far above her station in life."

But at the momentous hour of the ceremony itself, it was only from
Bontemps that Françoise can have received much moral support. Louvois's antagonism had long been apparent, and the two priests, as she
knew, regarded the marriage as a matter of the King's religious duty,
and no more. True, or nearly true as this might have been, it was humiliating for her to be reminded of it in the presence of the stern confessor and the hypocritical archbishop. In all their talk about salvation,
they might have acknowledged some love for her, as there surely was,
on the King's part, and some respect for her, as she felt there ought
to have been, on their own. Bontemps at least behaved towards her
with respect, extremely so, in fact, and on his own initiative, with the
King's acquiescence, he began to address her from now on as "Your
Majesty"—though only when in private.

It had indeed been weak of Louis to relay Louvois's insults to
Françoise, as if they shed new light on a matter still under discussion,
or were something they could laugh about together, or if she needed
reminding of the discrepancy between her position and his. But he had
told her the story, very probably, not for her sake, but rather for his
own. If he was vastly her superior in terms of rank, in human terms, in
intellect and character, it was she who was the stronger. This he knew,
and it made him uneasy. Egocentric and vain, shrewd enough to see his
own shortcomings, Louis had not the humility to turn them to spiri-

tual or personal advantage. There was room for a little modesty, but
only in things that he did not care about: the courtiers might laugh at
his anonymous bad poetry, and he would laugh to see them, and the
natural order, as he understood it, would remain undisturbed. But in
his own house, as within his own kingdom, he must be master, and his
wife, of all people, must acknowledge that. A reminder now and then
of how the world perceived them would maintain a useful dent in her
pride, and add a little prop to his own.

And there would be no public acknowledgement of their marriage.
It would remain a secret, morganatic, dynastically ineffectual—as if it
could have been otherwise, given Françoise's age—and giving to her
no powers, no income, no patronage, no new standing at court, nothing, in fact, but the same clear conscience gained by Louis with the
regularization at last of their mortally sinful liaison.

Françoise was, in any case, in no position to have asked for more,
nor indeed to have rejected the King, if she had wished to do so. "I preferred to marry him than enter the convent," she had said of her marriage to Scarron thirty years before, and this would have been a likely
alternative now, if, having known him for eleven years, having been his
mistress, off and on, for nine, she had declined to marry Louis. And
after all, as she had written to Madame de Brinon, why would the lady
not have been willing? No greater worldly honour was ever likely to be
bestowed upon her. "When I think of all your gifts," the chevalier de
Méré had written to her when she was just a girl of fourteen or fifteen,
"it seems to me that the greatest princes . . . could never be happy
without you . . . Alexander and Caesar would have preferred you to all
their conquests." Now she was a woman in middle age—old, in fact,
by her own reckoning—and she knew something of the world and its
Alexanders and Caesars. She had met and talked and lived with le
Grand Condé and la Grande Mademoiselle and Louis le Grand, and
she knew that even "the greatest princes" concealed weakness beneath
their fighting armour. In short, the King's uneasy need to keep her in
her place was in part a response to the personal strength which shone
through Françoise's modest demeanour. "The King loved dignity,"
said the duc de Saint-Simon, "but only for himself."

Louis was a natural autocrat, admiring and rewarding competence in others, but brooking no real opposition. As a young man of twenty-two, at the start of his "personal reign" following the death of Cardinal Mazarin, he had swiftly banished his still powerful mother to a cold political exile. His Queen, Marie-Thérèse, far from posing any threat to his authority, had not even been capable of maintaining a sphere of her own in entertainment and fashion, as Athénaïs had done so splendidly. Now, at the age of forty-five, after more than two decades of unchallenged rule, Louis had no intention of allowing any alternative court to emerge under the aegis of a new "Queen Françoise," cleverer by far than Marie-Thérèse, less self-absorbed than Athénaïs, more astute, perhaps, than Louis himself. He did not want any woman about him interfering in public affairs, not because she would not be able to do so effectively, but rather, he feared, because she would.

As for the Widow Scarron herself, she was honoured, greatly honoured, by her marriage to so great a king, but if she took pride in her extraordinary new position, this she would keep to herself. She would not be seen to be claiming more than others would regard as her due. She would not seek to be crowned Queen. Were she to do so, the court would see only the Widow Scarron, a woman come from nothing, from doubtful blood, from beggary, perched on a throne in borrowed finery, a figure of outrage—or worse, of ridicule.

In her marriage, Françoise had been confronted with a bitter truth: more fit to be Queen than any other of Louis's women, more naturally fit by far than the poor late Queen herself, she could not ascend the throne without losing the one thing she wanted above all else: the respect of those about her. In her heart, she felt entitled to be Queen, but rationally, she knew that it would undermine thirty years and more of work and discipline and risk and amazing good luck. It would relegate her, at a stroke, to those who sought to live above their natural station, to a courtly version of Molière's famous *bourgeois gentilhomme*. "Will you look at Madame High-and-Mighty, playing the lady," says the playwright's Madame Jourdain, "and both her grandfathers were linen-drapers." "Did she think the first volume of her life was always going to remain unread?" Madame de Sévigné had written, rhetorically. Françoise, of barely noble birth, born in a prison, the child of a murderer and traitor to his country, widow of a crude and disfigured beggar-poet, living on charity—"and the stories have been retold so maliciously," Madame de Sévigné had continued. As Queen, Françoise would be a laughing stock.

So there would be no coronation, and the marriage would remain a secret. Suspicions there might be, but they were not to be confirmed. "Madame de Maintenon would never have agreed to make it public," her secretary was to write in later years. "That would not have been conducive to the glory of so great a King, which was more important to her than her own." This at least was to be the version of events which it suited Françoise to circulate, for the roundabout purposes of her own bonne gloire.

And in the meantime, there were one or two supposed compensations. She was at last permitted to ride with the King in his own carriage: with Françoise a dame d'atour, there was nothing officially to prevent it, and Louis turned a blind eye to the humiliation inherent in the deception. He had insensitivity enough to propose a little promotion for Françoise shortly after their marriage, on the death of the unfriendly duchesse de Richelieu: *La Richelieu* had been the dauphine's dame d'honneur, "and after her death . . . the dauphine asked this favour of the King as something she wanted passionately," wrote Françoise's niece, with Louis evidently unable to comprehend how a plea to serve as lady-in-waiting might be offensive to a Queen manquée. "Owing to her modesty, Madame de Maintenon repeatedly refused this honour, regarding it as above her," added Marthe-Marguerite, improbably and, possibly, ironically. And every morning Françoise received a sulky homage from the dauphin in the form of a compulsory visit, which both endured in almost complete silence. "He'll quite happily go three or four hours without saying a word to anyone," sighed Liselotte, and it seems that he made no particular effort now to converse with his unwelcome new stepmother.

Athénaïs was receiving daily visits, too, only marginally less reluctant, on the part of the King. From maîtresse déclarée, still her acknowledged position, she had become an effective red herring *royale* in her grandiose apartments, deflecting suspicion from Françoise through Louis's regular appearances between mass and dinner in the early afternoon. The trick seems to have worked, with even the most hawk-eyed observers, including Athénaïs herself, never sure whether or not the King had married the former governess. Like all courts, Versailles was full of "open" secrets, known by everyone though never actually declared, but even so, a real secret might be genuinely kept if those who knew its truth were few and discreet. Those best placed to glean private information were, naturally enough, the valets and maids, involved as they were in lighting the midnight corridors and guarding the doors and serving the intimate suppers and changing the bed linen. A trustworthy servant, like Françoise's Nanon or Louis's Bontemps, was worth a fortune to a highly placed man or woman in need of secrecy, and many a clever servant made a small fortune out of that inescapable fact of courtly life.

"I knew I had nothing to fear from her ambition," Louis had once written of his regent mother. "He knew that Madame de Maintenon was incapable of abusing her intimacy with him," wrote the abbé de Choisy now. Françoise's reward, a few months after the wedding, was to see Athénaïs demoted from her twenty sumptuous rooms flanking the King's to a former large bathroom on the ground floor—refurbished, it must be said, "to make it habitable in winter"—with the grand staircase leading from this up to Louis's own apartments blocked off. Other than symbolically, however, Françoise was not the beneficiary of this change. Louis himself seconded the twenty vacated rooms for his own collection of paintings and objets d'art, including gifts from the King of Siam and the Emperor of China, "and one most remarkable pearl." It is not known whether Athénaïs ever took the long way up to see it.

FIFTEEN

La Vie en Rose

hink about your pleasure and your salvation; they're not incompatible." So Françoise wrote to her brother Charles, shortly after her wedding and six years after his own. Charles, however, had already given up hope, if indeed he had ever entertained any hope, of melding the two, and his indulgent sister was already sending money to one, at least, of his mistresses.

But Françoise was happy and excited. "I'm dying to see you," she wrote to her friend Madame de Brinon the day after her wedding, "but I can't say when that will be. I've hardly had time to turn around, and even now I should be asleep . . ." "The greatest of all men," for whom "most of the court ladies would have given themselves to the devil," was her very own husband, and he was handsome and virile and devoted to her; and, more or less unexpectedly, he was faithful. Even Athénaïs, as she herself lamented to a sympathetic nun, "hadn't touched the tip of his finger since the comte de Toulouse was born [six years ago]." "The good sister could have done without knowing the details," remarked the abbé de Choisy, though he was interested to hear them from her nonetheless.

Françoise had no such complaints. "You ask whether it's true that the King has married Madame de Maintenon," Liselotte wrote to her Aunt Sophie. "I can't honestly tell you. Few here doubt it, but I think that as long as it hasn't been declared, I won't believe it. And knowing as I do how marriage is conducted in this country, I think that if they were married, their love wouldn't be as strong as it is now—unless perhaps keeping it secret adds a bit of spice that they wouldn't have if it was all out in the open."

While Athénaïs was demoted to the redecorated downstairs bathroom, Françoise now moved into a fine new suite overlooking the central, "royal" courtyard at Versailles. Allotted her own stables alongside the palace, she at once appointed a young nephew of Scarron's her personal equerry. Before long she had also been accorded spacious private apartments at Saint-Germain and the châteaux of Compiègne and Marly, as well as the late Queen's rooms at Fontainebleau and, of course, her own château of Maintenon. Even the beautiful little Porcelain Trianon in the park at Versailles, with its thousands of blue and white tiles, built as a love-nest for Louis and Athénaïs, was soon demolished in favour of a new, larger Marble Trianon, complete with Ionic columns outside and Chinese-style furnishings inside, where the new royal couple could retreat together from the press and fuss of the court. Here, Françoise's own ground-floor apartment, with its enormous floor-length windows, opened out into a secluded garden, as if the rooms themselves were part of it.

The new Marble Trianon was the venue for occasional, very select gatherings—the duc de Saint-Simon sulked for years at never being invited, and took his revenge in his famous memoirs in diatribes against Françoise and the King—but most court gatherings in these years were held in the palace itself, in the apartments of one or other wealthy courtier, or in Louis's own splendid rooms. In the wintertime, three evenings every week were devoted to *appartements*, private parties with entertainment, generally a concert or a single scene from a new play or opera. The appartements had been recently instituted by the King in a fit of homesickness for the royal court of his youth, where his stately mother had held regular cultural and social evenings for her favoured courtiers. On Queen Anne's demise, the mantle of hostess-royal had passed to Louis's wife, Marie-Thérèse, but, lacking the grace to carry it, she had felt it slipping at once from her rounded shoulders. Now there was Françoise, who would undoubtedly have managed it all superbly: "She was so charming and witty, she was really made for the delights of society," as her niece said. But Françoise was only an uncrowned queen, and though the King might have allowed a new precedent to emerge, he chose instead to assign his wife a supporting role, and play the host himself.

The thrice-weekly appartements were wildly popular, with every courtier striving to be at the centre of attention—apart from Liselotte, who found them "unbearable." On three further evenings of the week, a fully staged theatrical performance was given, either a comedy or an opera with ballet. Liselotte found these no more enjoyable than the appartements. "It's the same stuff all the time," she huffed. "Nothing but bits of old Lully operas. It's all I can do to stay awake." Better by far, she felt, were the Lutheran songs of her girlhood, "and I can still sing them out good and loud, the way we used to do, driving along in the coach." Every Saturday evening the King gave a ball, often in the *grande galerie*, the magnificent Hall of Mirrors, first illuminated in all its candlelit glory in November 1684. "Add to that the brilliance of the court in full dress and the sparkle of the precious stones . . ." But this spectacular evening brought Liselotte no pleasure, either. "I don't like these French dances," she grumbled. "These interminable minuets are unbearable . . . Don't they do German dances in Germany any more . . . ?"

Not built for dancing, her ear attuned only to simple hymns or country tunes, Liselotte could not even console herself with the extravagant suppers provided at every court entertainment, since the dishes, though wonderfully varied, were simply not to her taste. "I much prefer English food to French," she insisted, unaccountably. "I just can't get along with this stuff here. I don't like ragoûts, and I don't eat broths or bouillons, so there's only a little bit that I can eat: leg of lamb, for example, roast chicken, medallions of veal, beef, salads. In

Holland I also ate gulls' eggs, in fact I ate so many of them that I made myself sick, so now I can't even eat those . . ." The King's *appartement* suppers were generally served in the fashionable *ambigu*-style, with all the dishes, sweet and savoury, provided at the same time. Each guest took what he fancied with his own knife and spoon. Those who considered themselves *très à la mode* would use a fork as well, though Louis himself disdained this newfangled Italian implement.

The French were meat-eaters of the first order. "In any other country," wrote an astonished German visitor, "if they ate the same number of capons and hens and chickens in a year that they eat here in a day, the species would just about die out." This might have pleased the carnivorous Liselotte, had it not been that in France, "roast or fried meat is never cooked through, and as for duck and other river birds, they are eaten quite bloody." Elegant dishes of the day included capon (evidently not yet died out), with oysters and capers, pigeons in fennel, roast rabbit stuffed with cheese and truffles ("but I don't like rabbit"), goat roasted in cloves, and lamb's tongue fritters in citrus marinade, the tongues skinned "in the usual way." Frogs were on the menu, too, though only the legs and the base of the spine, "skinned and washed thoroughly," boiled into a broth ("but I don't like broths"), or fricasseed with chicken, or dipped in batter and fried, this last served under the misleading name of "frogs in cherries," the "cherry" being the little button of bone that was all that remained of the wide, flapping foot.

Salads ("I can eat salads") contained not only the usual lettuce or cucumber or celery, but also chicory, spring violets, bellflowers, parsley stalks, or beetroot and anchovies ("but I can't stand fish"). They were served along with the roasts, as were the sauces, now fashionably buttery where they had once been full of vinegar, with the new Italian chilli-pepper tomato sauce in discreet little pots on the side. And of course there were fresh peas, *petits pois*, recently introduced from Italy via the King's indispensable valet, Bontemps, and now the absolute rage at every elegant table. Served with cucumber, asparagus tips, artichoke bottoms, or, classically, cooked in a pan with butter and lard and seasoned with salt and spices, "but lightly, so as not to overwhelm their natural taste," and mixed with cream just before serving, petits pois were becoming "the emblematic vegetable dish of the age." Ten years later Françoise could write, "The saga of the peas is still going strong. People talk about nothing but their impatience to eat them, the pleasure of having eaten them, the anticipation of eating more of them. There are ladies here who finish their supper with the King, and a very good supper, too, and their bowl of peas is waiting for them to eat before they go to bed. How on earth their digestion survives it . . . ! I don't know how I'm going to stand it. I'm getting depressed for lack of rational conversation."

Desserts at the King's suppers were either traditional—fresh or preserved fruits, including a selection from four hundred varieties of pear, now mostly lost—or the new Italian sorbets and ice-creams, made of fruit, sugar, and snow kept cold in underground ice rooms.

Warm drinks included coffee from Venice, which the King didn't care for at all. "But coffee will go out of fashion, like Racine's plays," remarked Madame de Sévigné, mistaken, as it transpired, on both counts. There was tea purchased from Holland and, controversially, hot chocolate, brought from the Americas via Spain. Twenty years before, the Sorbonne's Faculty of Medicine had approved its use as beneficial to health, particularly for insomniacs, but by now Madame de Sévigné was warning her pregnant daughter not to touch a drop of it. "Last week it gave me colic and kidney pains for sixteen hours at a stretch," she declared. "Aren't you afraid it will burn your blood? . . . The marquise de Coetlogon drank so much chocolate last year when she was expecting, that she gave birth to a little boy as black as the devil . . . You know, I feel personally aggrieved against chocolate," she added, ". . . because I love it."

For those who preferred cool drinks, there were fruit juices flavoured with flowers or nuts or spices, and, of course, wine. The standard Greek and Cypriot wines had recently fallen from grace, and the preferred accompaniment to the creamed peas and frogs' legs and bloody duck breasts was now champagne, as yet a reddish still wine, pressed from the black pinot noir grape, which occasionally—and most annoyingly—fizzled.

And there was eau-de-vie, brandy, once used only for medicinal purposes, but so widely drunk now by poorer folk and causing so much havoc among them that it had been rechristened *eau-de-mort*. In between swigs, workers and streetfolk grabbed for the leftovers of these huge royal suppers at special markets set up on the mornings thereafter, while the fortunate who had attended them hopped into their coaches for a day-trip to Paris to investigate the delights of the newly opened *Procope*, the city's first Italian ice-cream parlour.

"The winter has passed in so many delights," wrote Françoise to Charles in the spring of 1684, after six happy months of married life. "What a cavalcade of ladies after dinner and after the ball this evening . . . Versailles is astonishingly beautiful, and I'm thrilled to be here. There are all sorts of lovely things planned: balls in the King's apartments, plays at Monsieur's, promenades everywhere, midnight suppers in my rooms—well, you know, the King wants us to enjoy ourselves." Confessor Père Gobelin received the leftovers, whatever of piety could be slotted in between social appointments in the life of his lamb gone astray. "I'm really desperate to save my soul," she assured him at the same time, unconvincingly, "but pride and laziness prevent me. You must tell me how to fight such enemies. I must go. I'd like to write more, but there are people talking to me . . ."

It was all simply wonderful. France was at the pinnacle of her glory, and Louis le Grand, Françoise's own husband, revelling in the fullness of his mature manhood, was at the pinnacle of his. In 1686, in Versailles's dazzling Hall of Mirrors, he received a vast delegation of ambassadors from the kingdom of Siam, each one wearing a pointed headpiece of gold which touched the Savonnerie-carpeted floor as he bowed to the great French monarch, whose splendid name had reached "the extremities of the Universe"—or at least Siam. The ambassadors launched into a prolonged harangue declaring eternal friendship between the Siamese (who were afraid of Dutch encroachment in their region) and the French (who were eager to disrupt Dutch trade there). A handy missionary priest undertook to interpret.

Every last courtier enthused about the gold and silver and the ex-

otic screens and porcelain and the Japanese cabinets, all displayed at
the end of the galerie, which the Siamese had presented as gifts to the
court—everyone, that is, except lonely Liselotte, and the sulky war
minister Louvois, "who never thought much of things he'd had no
hand in."

Apart from the appartements and the balls and banquets, Françoise
had a special, private reason for feeling happy and excited in the first
months of her marriage. Though she herself was "beyond the age of
having children," her twenty-two-year-old sister-in-law, Geneviève,
after seven years of marriage, was finally expecting a baby. Françoise
responded to the news with the barrage of fond advice that her brother
and his wife had by now come to expect. "You'll easily believe how delighted I am about Madame d'Aubigné's pregnancy," she wrote to
Charles. "Women know more about these things than the physicians
do, and the less fuss she can make about it, the better. She should wear
loose clothing, so that the child can be more comfortable, and she
should eat well, so that it's in good health, and if she has any cravings,
let her have what she wants . . . Adieu, my dear, dear brother. I love
you more than my prickliness lets me say."

"The baby clothes should have arrived by now," she wrote six
months later, "on this first day of March" in 1684. "They're not very
magnificent. You know I'm rather proud of going to the other extreme.
I'm very much looking forward to hearing the news of Madame
d'Aubigné's delivery, and I don't really mind what the baby's sex is."
After six further weeks, with the baby still to make its appearance, she
was sending Charles words of anxious encouragement: "Don't be concerned about this delay: heroes are always at least ten months in their
mothers' wombs. All the same I'd be glad to see her over this business,
which is always dangerous."

The baby arrived safely on April 15. Despite her insistence on "not
really minding" about its sex, when it was pronounced to be a girl,
Françoise's delight bubbled over, and she declared at once her intention to take the child for herself. "I already feel a kind of tenderness

towards my niece. Do make sure she's not an only child, so that I can have her when there's another one to amuse you." she instructed, before continuing with her habitual string of advice:

> I've heard you're very much occupied with her, and that you go into her room more than once a day. That's fine, but don't kill her with too much playing: let her sleep, in her cradle as much as possible. Look after her eyes, and don't let anything happen to mark her face. I'd rather she died than had any deformity. They tell me she's well made. You mustn't hold her more than is necessary; babies are best off in their cradles, they lie straight, especially during the first three months, before they start playing. It's really the nurse who should be looking after her for now, and you must treat the nurse well, and let her do more or less as she likes . . . My compliments to the new mother. She can't look after herself too carefully. Women's health depends on avoiding difficulties in childbirth. She shouldn't be in a hurry to get back on her feet too quickly . . . Tell the nurse it's my heiress she's nursing.

In fact, the baby's arrival seems to have brought more happiness to the excited aunt than to either of the parents. Only six weeks later, Françoise was obliged to send placating words to Charles, who had taken offence at his wife's difficult new "mood." "I'm sorry to hear about this," she wrote. "I had thought a child would bring your wife and you closer together. But the stronger one must support the weaker; your intelligence and your age should make you patient. Give her every honest pleasure, and don't leave her alone, as I've heard you do . . ." And, once again, the temptation to advise her incapable brother proved too strong for Françoise to resist:

> If you don't mind my saying so, men are a bit tyrannical. They like every sort of liberty, and don't allow any at all to their wives. A man locks up his wife while he's running about, and thinks

she's only too happy to see him when he feels like coming home. This is dangerous with most wives, and unwise with all of them. Men find their wives in a bad mood, when they've simply been bored all day. Personally, I wouldn't dream of entertaining a man who paid no attention to my own pleasure . . . I've seen how several families live, and I know very well how people should live together to keep the peace.

But she could not keep her attention turned for long from the newborn baby itself:

Mademoiselle [Marthe-Marguerite] de Mursay here is turning out quite pretty, and she'll be a very good dancer. Her brothers are very good fellows, but despite everything I do for them, I feel there's a certain little girl, two months old, who's more important to me, and I very often think of the pleasure I'll have in finding her a husband, if my life, and my favour, last another twelve years. Since I can't do anything else for her, I've done something for her nurse's husband, and you can assure the nurse that I regard her as the nurse of my own daughter. Let her enjoy every comfort, so that her milk will be good.

Geneviève remained moody, Charles remained uncomforted, and Françoise remained principally interested in the baby. "Don't give in to your natural melancholy," she urged her brother three weeks later. "You live in comfort and ease, that's the best thing in the world; we're often envious of positions that we wouldn't like if we had them . . . If you or Madame d'Aubigné need anything, or want anything, feel free to ask me, and let me know when the first tooth comes through, so that I can send the nurse a present. You've said nothing about your daughter's baptism; have you given her a name? Who were the godparents? What's her name? She should have a pretty name."

As was customary in this age of frequent infant deaths, the baby, though already three months old, had not yet been given a name, but the aunt's urging now prodded the parents into making a decision. Charles and Geneviève had the child baptized and named her, unsurprisingly, Françoise. They could hardly have done otherwise for "my heiress."

> The King has agreed that the ladies at court should establish a charity at Versailles, to take care of the poor as they do in the Paris parishes. Madame la duchesse de Richelieu will be the superior . . . There are a number of people we don't know what to do with: some cripples, who can't earn their own living . . . and there are also some innocent girls selling themselves on the streets.

Thus Françoise to Père Gobelin in the early months of her marriage. The Versailles charity was a new initiative, a response to the too-rapid growth of a quiet village backwater into an unruly, overcrowded town servicing the expanding court. Though Françoise was to play a subordinate role here, she was by no means a beginner as far as charity work was concerned. In particular, for more than twenty years already, she had been sponsoring scores of boys and girls, orphans or simply children from poor families, feeding them, clothing and housing them, and always providing some kind of training so that, in the longer term, they would be able to fend for themselves in life. Her letters are replete with references to donations and alms and pensions, not only for children but also for older people fallen on hard times, though her kindly gaze was sometimes tempered by a sceptical glint: "It often happens that in the very same places where people are crying misery, you can hardly find anyone who wants to work," she observed to her friend Marie de Brinon. "However, the able-bodied can be helped simply by giving them a means of earning their living . . ." Many of these "able-bodied" she had been employing on her own estate at Maintenon, where, as well as a farm, there was a large linen "manufactory." And the stream of smaller kindnesses she had undertaken for those without means was more or less never-ending: "Please give the curé five hundred francs for the parish elderly"; "I'm sending you sixty louis for that little adopted girl"; "I've bought one woollen gown for young Jeanneton, and ordered another."

"It would take too long to record all the details of the things she did to help the poor," wrote a later secretary. Françoise's personal income, which included a 48,000-livre pension from the King, was by now in the order of 90,000 livres per annum, and every year, some two-thirds of this sum was distributed to her many charitable concerns.

In individual terms, however, the greatest beneficiary by far of her charity was still her wastrel brother Charles. There was barely a week without a letter to him, and barely a letter without a promise of money or some other help: "I'm sending you the fifteen pistoles that you owe the prince"; "I'll look for a house for you, and pay half the rent"; "If the furniture that you have of mine is any good for [either of your residences], you're most welcome to keep it"; "I'll send you a manservant; you're quite right to want a tall one; short ones are no use at all." In a single year, as she reminded him, she had provided his wife with no less than 2,661 livres' worth of clothes: "one brown satin skirt, embroidered, 330 livres; one pink muslin skirt, ninety-four livres; one flame-coloured bodice, thirty-eight livres; four pairs of shoes and two pairs of slippers, forty livres . . . —and this is not to reproach you, or to ask for repayment, but only to show that money goes quickly for people like you . . ."

If Charles had sensed the exasperation in his sister's tone, it had done nothing to change him. He was an incorrigible spendthrift, or rather, an incorrigible acquirer of things for which he could not pay. Three months after her letter about money going quickly, Françoise was alarmed to learn that he had been involved in a rough altercation with creditors in Paris, one of whom had turned up at Versailles to complain to her in person. The resultant letter reveals not only her frustration with Charles, but also some anxiety for herself:

I'm really sorry to be going on at you all the time, but who's going to speak frankly to you if not me? I have been informed of some dealings you've had which are neither fair nor honest. It's too late to be bargaining over prices once you've been arrested— you just have to pay up. Paris tradesmen aren't afraid of violence; they make even the greatest men pay. It's understandable if you don't always have the whole sum you owe to hand, but in that case you come to some arrangement with them and pay what you can, and once they see you mean to pay in the end, they'll stop harassing you. This sort of thing damages a family's reputation. You really have to stop doing it, without making any more trouble. It's doing more harm to you than it is to them.

Though Françoise did not say it, and though Charles would hardly have cared if she had, his impossible behaviour was doing harm to her as well, embarrassing her at court and reminding people of the unflattering "first volume of her life." No number of woollen gowns for poor girls was going to make up for the gossiping and sniggering of better-born courtiers, and no amount of effort for the new Versailles charity was going to change the attitude of its resentful directress, "Madame la duchesse de Richelieu," who, as had already been observed, would have preferred Françoise to remain an object of charity herself.

Queen without a crown, perched on a pedestal built on sand, Françoise needed something solid, something unignorable, to impress the snobbish and disparaging people around her, and to engage their respect once and for all. She needed a domain of her own. With local charity dominated by the antagonistic duchesse de Richelieu, she turned to the only other avenue open to an ambitious and respectable woman of the day: she turned to education. Here, at least, she could feel secure.

For several years already, she had been involved in a project for the education of poor children, particularly girls. In 1681, with the help of her friend Marie de Brinon, she had established a small school, first in the town of Montmorency and later in Rueil, both a few miles distant from Paris. From the outset, the vivacious Madame de Brinon had served as the school's superintendent and headmistress. Intelligent and energetic, a former Ursuline nun, she had been devoted to the school, as indeed she was to Françoise. Mixed in with her enthusiasm and her steady religious principles was a touch of the renegade, which amused Françoise and endeared *La Brinon* to her, though at times it cast doubt on her administrative capacities. "You can't think highly enough of her, and you can't love her too much," she had relayed to Père Gobelin. "But you have to watch her; she comes up with wild ideas. Afterwards, she'll reconsider, like a lamb, but you have to keep her on a tight rein at first."

Things had begun humbly at Montmorency and Rueil, with most provisions begged or borrowed, at least as far as Françoise could bear to solicit them: "We mustn't lose the least bench or the smallest straw chair; everything will be of use to us; and then we'll have to ask for less, which is the best thing of all as far as I'm concerned . . . In this country you must do nothing but wait for the right time, without letting it be seen that you're even dreaming of wanting something for yourself." So she had urged Madame de Brinon from her sickbed at Versailles, to which she had frustratingly been confined with a haemorrhoid crisis.

The little school had met with such success that, early in 1684, it was moved to larger premises in Noisy, near Versailles. This brought the project much closer to Françoise, and, though day-to-day responsibility remained with Madame de Brinon, Françoise maintained a directorial hold on everything. With every Saturday morning's post, enthusiastic directions went flying from Versailles to Noisy: "Keep what wood you need and pay for it. I don't want any trace of cheating; that sort of thing gets back to the King, and we have to make sure he has a good opinion of us." "It's not that I'm looking to save money; I want to save time, and establish a way of doing things, once and for all." "We mustn't forget anything, since we'll be spied on, by those who wish us well and those who don't." "I don't know where to place the sacristy . . . We mustn't spoil the symmetry from the outside . . ."—an ironic consideration, given her despairing sigh about having to perish from the cold in symmetry in her own rooms at Versailles.

Madame de Brinon had been assisted at Noisy by three former Ur-

suline nuns of her own choosing, and though Françoise had been satisfied with this choice in educational terms—"It's true that I like the Ursulines . . ."—the sisters' physical care of the girls was failing to meet
the expected standard, as a visit of one little pupil to Versailles had
made only too clear: "I'm sending her back to you," wrote Françoise to
Madame de Brinon in February 1684. "I'm most disappointed at
what's happened here, which all the servants and [the physician] Monsieur Fagon know about. [My maid] Nanon . . . wanted to do her hair;
she had to cut it like a cap, and as the hair fell from her head it was moving, there were so many lice in it; her face was so covered with them
that some even went into her mouth . . . . I hold you to blame for the little care you're taking with all these beggar-girls . . ."

In the very next month, March of 1684, the King had agreed to the
establishment of the new Versailles charity under Madame de Richelieu's direction, and Françoise realized that in order to set her own
stamp on things, she would have to aim higher than the little school at
Noisy. Reviewing the facts, she quickly concluded that the limitation
lay not in herself or her ideas, nor even in Madame de Brinon's faulty
administration, but rather in the choice they had made of their working material. Beggar-girls, whether crawling with lice or not, would
never be much more than beggar-girls—laundry-maids or scullery-
maids, perhaps, milkmaids if they were lucky. A very pretty and clever
one might reach the pinnacle of service and become a lady's maid,
dressing in her mistress's cast-off gowns and keeping her hands soft
until she married some coachman or valet.

It was useful work, to give these girls some schooling; it gave them
a means of keeping themselves and saved them from the worst, as
Françoise knew from her own harsh experience as a hungry, dirty
beggar-girl herself. An extraordinary mix of talent and effort and luck
had raised her up from this pitiable place, but such an ascension was
unlikely to be repeated. The little school at Noisy, even with improved
administration, would never be more than an example of charitable
work; Madame de Richelieu could easily do as much in Versailles.

Françoise wanted something more prominent, something impressive and influential, something that no one else had done. She would

need more money, much more money, and much more, too, than "the least bench or the smallest straw chair" that she and Madame de Brinon had begged and borrowed for the little school. The idea of a school was right, given "the talent that I have for the education of children," as she had written to the wife of her cousin Philippe, in supposed justification of the capture of her sons and daughter. For this larger, more influential school, beggar-girls would not do. Françoise needed girls with real potential for eventual prominence and influence. She needed demoiselles.

And after all, if she had been a beggar-girl, she had been a demoiselle, too. Her treacherous, murderous father had also been "the high and mighty Monseigneur Constant d'Aubigné, chevalier, lord of Surimeau and other places." "I'm a lady": so she had insisted, even as a six-year-old in her father's prison cell.

Here before her now was a chance, of a kind, to remake her own poor-but-noble girlhood. The country was full of impoverished aristocrats and their dowryless, futureless daughters. *Here* was work for her; here would be her domain. Here she would provide what should have been provided for her: care and kindness in a suitable environment, a proper education, pretty gowns to wear, and a good dowry when she came to marry. She had missed every bit of it, but her new protégées, her little demoiselle second selves—they would have it all.

Today the King signed the letters patent for the establishment of the community of Saint-Cyr . . . Madame de Maintenon will have the general direction of it . . . The *demoiselles* and the *dames* must prove a nobility of three grandparents, or a hundred years . . .

Thus the marquis de Dangeau, on the sixth day of June 1686. Work had begun on the building two years previously, with Louis's instruction to Jules Hardouin-Mansart, one of his own Versailles architects, to locate a suitable site for it. Mansart chose a large terrain near the village of Saint-Cyr, a few miles to the west of Versailles itself. There was a great deal of underground water at the site, he said, a necessity for an institution intended to house several hundred people. Françoise objected to the site for the very same reason: in her view, the underground water would make the place constantly damp, and it would be impossible to keep the cellars from flooding.

She lost the argument, and in the spring of 1685 construction began on the swampy terrain. Water was pumped out of the ground by huge new machines, and work proceeded at the frenetic pace now usual for buildings of a royal stamp, so that in only fifteen months the 2,500 workmen, reinforced by a contingent of soldiers, had brought Mansart's drawings and diagrams to life. "It was all built so quickly, there were lots of mistakes made: they didn't even leave time for the greenwood to dry out," said the abbé de Choisy, but though the building remained without much decoration, in the end it was no less impressive for that—even Liselotte was obliged to admit that it was "a fine big building." A restrained château in creamy stone, it was curiously suitable for an institution of Françoise's own: all that was needed was there, with nothing extraneous to disturb its quiet harmony. Her own room, next to the simple chapel, overlooked the gardens of fruit trees and flowers, but also, in keeping with her practical temperament, it adjoined the girls' dormitories and the rooms of the teaching dames.

The building of Saint-Cyr had cost 1.4 million livres, a quarter of the annual construction costs of Versailles. A further 100,000 livres per year were provided for its maintenance; another 100,000 or so would be raised annually from the estate granted to it.

Though overruled about the actual site of the new school, Françoise had involved herself in every other possible aspect of its development. Battling a cold and laryngitis and rheumatism in her draughty Versailles rooms, in early April 1686 she wrote to Père Gobelin of "the great increase in the amount of work I have to do," but her tone is more excited than complaining. "Madame de Maintenon entered into the smallest details with a capacity and patience very much exceeding her sex," noted the abbé de Choisy admiringly, "but in this case it was necessary. There were so many difficulties constantly arising . . ."

A less sympathetic observer regarded Françoise's overactivity simply as evidence of a *maladie des directions*—essentially, a need to control everything, with its usual concomitant unwillingness to delegate any real responsibility to anyone else. Certainly, her letters in the months before the opening of the new school reveal an attention to details that might have been left to others among the thirty-six teaching staff and thirty-four live-in servants now being employed for Saint-Cyr: "Sister Martha is to share a room with the other sister from Montoire . . ." "Sister Madeleine can sew . . ." "I agree with you about our baker; the bread is always baked on the outside and soggy in the middle." "I'm not sure about the cows. If you have cows, you'll need grazing land, and cowherds to look after them, and someone to watch the cowherds, and any number of other things which will make a pint of milk very dear." "You're right, there are too many girls in the green class. Put the four biggest ones in with the yellows." "No, make all the greens yellow, and all the yellows green. I know that sounds bizarre." "The dames have no winter skirts. We'll need four or five hundred by October . . . They mustn't be more than four or five inches below the garters. They don't show. They're only for keeping warm. If they're short they'll stay clean and they'll last several winters." "One of the upstairs rooms will have to be separated into two for those two 'mothers superior'; they'll never be able to maintain proximity *and* saintliness."

But if to some this seemed a frittering away of precious time that might have been otherwise spent, Françoise could not have agreed. She loved all the small tasks of charity, and loved as well the simple fact of being active and unconstrained. By far she preferred this to the false and repetitive commerce of so much of life at court. As she remarked to her secretary on returning from an elegant dinner with ladies and gentlemen of the court, "Now *that* was a waste of time."

The King had involved himself with the new school as well, frustrating his architect Mansart with his frequent insistence on changes to its design. Françoise, knowing Louis's passion for building and well used to his determination to have his own way, had accepted without comment his intrusion into her pet project. "The King is very much occupied with [the building of] Saint-Cyr," she had written in February 1686. "He has made alterations to the choir and to several other places." By the spring, with the building almost completed, he had become more concerned with the school's constitutions. Madame de Brinon had produced a first draft that was subsequently pulled to pieces by the illustrious quartet of Françoise, the King, his confessor Père de la Chaise, and Paul Godet des Marais, later Bishop of Chartres, who was to become an increasingly important figure at the school and in Françoise's personal life. "We're working very hard on Saint-Cyr," she assured Madame de Brinon in April. "Your constitutions have been examined. We've cut some of it and added to it and admired it." Away from centre stage, in Paris, Père Gobelin, appointed religious superior of the school, had been requested to cast his pedantic eye over the document. "Do keep working on the constitutions," urged Françoise. "You know there are always a thousand grammatical faults in whatever a woman writes," she conceded, before adding tartly, "but if you don't mind my saying so, there's a certain charm in it that's very rare in men's writing." Finally, what was left of Madame de Brinon's constitutions were turned over to the virtuoso duo of the historiographers-royal, Jean Racine and Nicolas Boileau-Despréaux: "They're correcting the spelling," reported Françoise.

In the summer of 1686, the doors of the Maison royale de Saint-Louis at Saint-Cyr were opened to 250 demoiselles, its very first beneficiaries. For each one, documentary evidence had been required of at least four generations of nobility on her father's side—"We can't include the mothers," Françoise had admitted to Madame de Brinon. "There are too many mésalliances"—an indication, perhaps, of long-ago passions unconstrained by caste, or perhaps of merchants' daughters bringing handsome dowries into the families of the poorer aristocracy. Poverty and perfect health were the two remaining requirements: one unhappy girl, arriving on June 10 after a journey of three hundred miles, was sent straight home again for having "something wrong with her eye."

Those who remained included quite a number from Françoise's home region of Poitou, every last one, despite her yellowed linen and provincial accent, boasting an irreproachably aristocratic name: ten-year-old Jeanne de Chievres-Salignac from Barbezieux; a trio of young "Valentin" cousins from Rouillac—Marie Valentin de Montbrun, aged fourteen, Marguerite Valentin de Boisauroux, also fourteen, and Philippes-Rose Valentin de Montbrun-Boisauroux, aged just ten. And among all the *breton* and *provençal* and *languedoc* sounds were the clompety accents of two lone little Dutch girls, twelve-year-old Anne-Thérèse Vandam d'Andegnies, and her nine-year-old sister, Marie-Henriette-Léopoldine.

Not all the girls had sisters, of course, nor even cousins. Most of them were alone, and very far from their families. At Saint-Cyr they were treated kindly, and almost certainly better in material terms than they had been at home, but if this was not enough for some of them, Françoise was unsentimental. "Not all mothers are as loving as yours, my dear," she said in reproach to one homesick little girl. "I myself was never kissed more than twice by my own mother, and then only on the forehead, and after long separations." In a perverted kind of psychological projection, Françoise's girls were to be both protected from and subjected to the trials of her own early life: they were to have the material security and sense of noble privilege that she herself had not known, but they were not to have the stable emotional warmth that she had more sorely missed, and whose lack she had never really overcome. It was an inconsistency that was to be revealed in almost all the structures of life at Saint-Cyr, including what she herself would teach the girls.

Saint-Cyr was in fact a very unusual place. To begin with, it was not a convent—the only educational institution for girls in all of France that was not. Its thirty-six teachers, the dames of Saint-Louis, took simple vows of chastity and obedience, but they were not nuns bound by the solemn vows of formal profession. They did not wear habits, but dressed instead in the style of the more serious ladies of the court, in good quality gowns, modest, certainly, but also elegant.

The girls themselves, 250 of them between the ages of seven and twenty, were even dressed rather splendidly. They were divided into four groups, according to age, with each group's gowns and ribbons a different colour: red for the youngest girls, then yellow, then green (Françoise's favourite), and for the eldest girls, the King's royal blue. Far from the beggar-girls' woollen dresses, or even Françoise's own genteel muslins from the days of her young widowhood, the gowns of Saint-Cyr's demoiselles were of beautiful silk, rustling along the cool white floors with the sound of fine ladies in the making.

"Ladies," or at least gentlewomen, the girls were certainly to be in the end, and this goal added scope to their education, which was otherwise designed essentially after the Ursuline fashion, as preparation for Christian motherhood, the vital and peculiarly female contribution to mankind's eternal salvation: "Young girls will reform their families, their families will reform their provinces, their provinces will reform the world." The inculcation of Christian values lay at the base of all instruction at Saint-Cyr, though, as with the Ursulines, this meant learning the Church's catechism and the habits of Christian living rather than theology or biblical exegesis: "I don't know anything about the scriptures," said Françoise, implying, perhaps, that her girls need not know anything about them, either. For the older girls, the "blues," lessons in Christian humility doubled with lessons in practical housekeeping: they were all obliged to help take care of the younger ones, and also, working on a roster system, to sweep out the dormitories and assist the *converses* (the servant sisters) in the laundry and refectory.

Naturally, all the girls learned to sew, not only to make and mend simple clothes and household linen, but also, innovatively, to work needlepoint tapestries for furniture. In this endeavour, one of the girls, or one of the dames, or possibly Françoise herself, a skilful practitioner, developed an especially robust new diagonal stitch, later to become famous as petit point (basketweave). Chairs and cushions worked in the useful new stitch subsequently made their appearance in all of Françoise's many apartments, and thence around the world.

Within the well-behaved Ursuline framework of Saint-Cyr, Françoise had introduced a number of very un-Ursuline activities for her 250 demoiselles. To begin with, there was dancing: "All girls learn the minuet. There are quite a number of minuets arranged for four, eight, twelve, or sixteen, and every class gives a performance once a year for the dames and the other girls." Every afternoon, classes adjourned for an hour-long promenade in the grounds, during which, or so Madame de Brinon assured Madeleine de Scudéry in a large and regular hand, "our young ladies read aloud from your own *Conversations*, delighting themselves and their companions." On Saturdays there were no classes at all, though there might be some revision of what had been learned during the week. And the girls were permitted games: pick-up sticks, bagatelle, even chess.

Every girl was taught to read music, and to sing plainchants and motets and other songs, both sacred and secular. But, possibly because of her own lack of musical training in girlhood, Françoise had decided there would be no instrumental teaching. "Madame de Maintenon thought it wasn't possible to teach music in general to young ladies as they do nowadays," one of her pupils, a subsequent teacher at Saint-Cyr, was to report in later years. "That's why they just learned the plainchant, which she regarded as much easier, and of course it was going to be useful for any of them who wanted to be nuns, but as it turned out, the girls were really bored with it, and it was useless anyway, a waste of time, because most of them wouldn't put any effort into learning it."

There was in fact only a single music teacher for all 250 girls. He was the organist Guillaume-Gabriel Nivers, a full-time member of the staff, recruited, perhaps significantly, by Madame de Brinon, and even he seems to have proved too much for the evidently unmusical Françoise. The religious services at Saint-Cyr, fewer than in the convent boarding-schools but all overseen by Nivers, contained more music than anything else; to such an extent, in fact, that by the end of the first year Françoise was complaining that "there are too many songs, too many ceremonies, too many processions: in a word, the organist forgets that most of our dames can't really sing, and anyway they need to save their voices for talking to the girls." This did not prevent various earnest composers producing songs of praise for the new Maison royale de Saint-Louis, songs in fact mostly in praise of its distinguished (and now well-to-do) founder:

Lord, conserve our only hope! She who leads us to the foot of your altars is the protector of innocence. Prolong her days for the benefit of mortals.

Thus the "Prayer for Madame de Maintenon," one of the many "spiritual airs" collected for the girls to sing when the plainchant lessons reached the limit of boredom.

The dames "need to save their voices for talking to the girls," Françoise had insisted, and talking to the girls was indeed important, for most of the lessons proceeded orally. Apart from among the youngest girls, there was surprisingly little reading or writing in the classes. Instead, instruction was given by way of "conversations" on social or moral questions, usually composed by Françoise herself, which would be read aloud by several of the girls, exemplifying the attitude or behaviour appropriate to each circumstance. Françoise had drawn the model for these from the popular *Conversations* of her friend Madeleine de Scudéry, for whom she had by now arranged a royal pension.

"Experience is the best teacher. I haven't so much learned through my intelligence as through what I've experienced myself," insisted Françoise, providing the girls with the benefits derived therefrom in her conversation, "Raising Oneself Socially":

EUPHROSINE: What does it mean when you say that a person wants to raise himself? I don't know whether it's praise or blame.

MÉLANIE: Yes, I've been wondering that for a long time.

AUGUSTINE: But what does it mean?

SOPHIE: I think it means having more courage than fortune, and wanting to raise yourself up through your own merit.

AUGUSTINE: What! You mean, raise yourself above your own father?

SOPHIE: Yes, and to place no limits on your ambition.

AUGUSTINE:　But that's useless. You'll always remain your fa-
　　　　　　ther's child. You can never be more than that.

SOPHIE:　　You can achieve a position that makes you greater
　　　　　　than your father.

MÉLANIE:　I must say your ideas are very fashionable these
　　　　　　days, when you see lackeys driving in coaches and
　　　　　　gentlemen going on foot. Would you say those
　　　　　　lackeys have raised themselves?

SOPHIE:　　Certainly, and a most praiseworthy thing it is.

HORTENSE:　I don't think so at all. I've always despised that
　　　　　　sort of person. I think their behaviour is insolent.

*Hortense, however, is eventually persuaded, and in the end pres-
ents a justification for Françoise's own elevation:*

HORTENSE:　I think one can genuinely raise oneself through
　　　　　　merit . . . If a common soldier earns the rank of
　　　　　　general through his own merit, and if some great
　　　　　　prince then berates him for being born in the
　　　　　　mud, he can say, Yes, it's true, I was born to noth-
　　　　　　ing, but if you'd been born where I was, you
　　　　　　wouldn't be where I am today.

EUPHROSINE:　That's rather a daring reply!

HORTENSE:　If there's anything that can raise us up to equal
　　　　　　those born above us, it's being more courageous
　　　　　　than they are.

The conversations were, in effect, a form of Socratic dialogue, with arguments presented on both sides, and in due course they were expanded into a collection of *"proverbes,"* actually one-act plays, also
written by Françoise, illustrating various common proverbs of the day
("Let sleeping cats lie"; "Nothing so proud as a newly dressed beggar"), and the moral lessons to be drawn from them. Amusing and col-
loquial in tone, with good and bad characters, they were acted in class,
like the conversations, by the girls themselves.

And there were "instructions" and "meetings" in the form of simple chats, and at times lectures, which Françoise held with the girls or the dames, with one of the latter serving as secretary, noting down particularly whatever was said by *Madame la fondatrice*.

It was an imaginative form of teaching, the result of Françoise's practical intelligence, and very likely also a legacy of her own early lessons with the chevalier de Méré. "Far better to awaken the intelligence than to fill the memory," he had said. "Self-confidence produces good results, provided it's well founded and not too obvious. It encourages one to do well, and *de bon air*, whatever one undertakes."

Françoise's conversations and proverbs were generally optimistic pieces, each no doubt written in an hour of particular exuberance. But alongside these lessons in ambition and self-confidence, the girls heard a very different message of resignation, sometimes bitter resignation, to their much more likely fates: "Reading is useful for men," Françoise told them. "From childhood, they begin to learn the things they will need in later life . . . whatever their work will require : . . But what does that have to do with us? All we'll have to do is obey, and hide ourselves away, lock ourselves up in a convent or within our families . . . Girls need to learn to prefer handiwork or housework to reading . . ."

If this was the result of experience, it also represented the most advanced pedagogical theory of the time, as evinced by the young educationalist, François Fénelon. A man of brilliance and imagination, Fénelon nonetheless espoused a quintessentially conservative view of the appropriate education for girls, certainly as compared with, for example, the mixed intellectual and practical education which Madeleine de Scudéry had received earlier in her uncle's house. "The world . . . is the sum of all its individual families, and who can oversee these with more care than women?" asked Fénelon rhetorically in his famous 1685 *Treatise on the Education of Girls*. "Apart from their natural authority and diligence in the house, women have the advantage of being born careful, attentive to detail, industrious, accommodating, and persuasive . . . Women's work is hardly less important to the public than men's. A woman has a household to manage, a husband to please, children to bring up properly . . ."

Fénelon served as spiritual director to the duc and duchesse de Beauvillier, members of Françoise's dévot circle at court and the parents of six (later eight) daughters. He had written his *Treatise* as a guide for the education of the Beauvillier sisters, whose background, though not poor, was similar in many ways to those of the girls at Saint-Cyr. It was through the Beauvillier family that Françoise had come to know Fénelon. She was later to involve him much more closely, and with disastrous consequences, in her own ambitious work at Saint-Cyr, but for now she was content to draw from his *Treatise* whatever she could use herself.

"Take care not to make young girls unhappy by teaching them to hope for things above their wealth and rank," Fénelon warned, in the timeless voice of the social conservative. "There are hardly any people who are not left disappointed by too-great expectations." There was truth enough in this to leave Françoise uncomfortable with her own pedagogical touchstone of personal experience.

But the contradictions in what her girls were now learning lay in that very fact. Françoise herself was the worst possible example for them. Her own experience of "Raising Oneself Socially," transformed and performed with such poignant enthusiasm, was in fact so wildly improbable as to be more of a fairy tale than a guide for future living. Few of her young charges possessed the maturity to make this distinction. Just as she had seen in them a chance to remake her own imperfect girlhood, so now they regarded their beautiful, powerful fifty-one-year-old foundress as an embodiment of their own future selves. Cruelly, inescapably, what each side saw in this distorted double mirror was only an illusion.

Madame de Brinon, first among the dames, was enormously admiring of Françoise's literary-pedagogic accomplishments. Not content with having composed some unsingable verses for the girls to accompany the music of master-composer Lully, she determined to attempt something of the proverbes ilk herself, indeed something rather more ambitious. Quite quickly, she produced a series of educational plays in the manner of the Jesuits, who had for many years made use of drama as a powerful pedagogical tool. Françoise admired Madame de Brinon's intentions, but the plays themselves she found, unfortunately, "execrable." Too sensible to think herself capable of more than the enjoyable and useful scenes of her conversations and proverbs, but persuaded of the Jesuits' theatre as an excellent method for advancing her own educational aims, she decided to appeal to talents of a higher order than her "very dear" Madame de Brinon could boast—talents, indeed, of the highest order, for directly at hand and already familiar with the constitutions of Saint-Cyr, or at least with their spelling, was the King's own historiographer and one of the greatest playwrights of the age, Jean Racine.

After the critical failure ten years before of his *Phèdre*, subsequently—though uselessly for its long-dead author— declared the masterpiece of the century, Racine had abandoned the theatre, devoting himself to the less demanding occupation of historiographer-royal to the King, a post he shared with the poet Nicolas Boileau-Despréaux. "I don't know whether M. de Racine will acquire the same reputation for history as he has for poetry," wrote Spanheim, "but I'm sure he'll be a truthful historian." Françoise knew Racine well and thought highly of him, as indeed he did of her. "She is just as she has always been," he wrote to Boileau-Despréaux at about this time: "full of intelligence, good sense, piety, and goodwill towards us."

Saint-Cyr had money, and the King's protection, and the interest of all the court. It would not be too much, Françoise thought, to request something from Monsieur Racine that her girls might study—indeed, perhaps even perform. What better advertisement of her own extraordinary accomplishment than to present to the King, to all the court, her rows of lovely demoiselles, rescued from poverty and oblivion, polished and primed, producing in their perfect new courtly accents the finest new poetry in the land? What gold would she not be said to have spun from this ragged provincial straw!

Racine was duly approached, but, though tempted at once, he hesitated. Drama belonged to his bruised past, and moreover it was of doubtful moral standing, or so he had been taught to think by his boyhood teachers at the seminal Jansenist school of Port-Royal. But on the other hand, as a young man he had chosen to ignore them, and though in middle age he had returned somewhat to their teachings, the urgency of his poetical gift once again proved stronger than the demands of his theology. He cast aside his Jansenist appellation of "public poisoner," and began looking about for a subject.

He did not have far to seek. Françoise had requested "something moral or historical, but there mustn't be any love in it, something with a lively action, where the music can fit in with the poetry." The absence of "love" was vital: the girls at Saint-Cyr had already proved only too interested in an earlier play of Racine's to which Françoise had introduced them: it was *Andromache*, a riveting exposition of a circle of endlessly frustrated passions: of Orestes for Hermione, of Hermione for Pyrrhus, of Pyrrhus for Andromache, and of Andromache for her dead husband, Hector.

In earlier days, Racine had generally drawn his subjects from the legends and tragedies of Greece, but this time the precedent would not serve: the Greeks talked constantly of "love." He turned instead to the Bible, and in the Old Testament Book of Esther he found exactly the subject he needed: during the Jewish captivity in Persia, Esther, the Persians' unwilling Queen and secretly a Jewess herself, risks her life to save her people, whom the King's wicked favourites, Aman and his wife Vasti, have plotted to destroy. "It is a story filled with lessons in the love of God," as the religious Racine reported, "and also," added his theatrical self, "I had no need to change even the smallest detail of the action as shown in holy Scripture, which would have been, in my view, a kind of sacrilege, so that I could write the entire play using only the scenes which God Himself, as it were, had provided."

It was a disingenuous claim, all the same, for into the scenes which "God Himself" had provided, Racine built his own element of subversion: his *Esther* is a parable of persecution in France—not of the Jews, however, nor even of the Huguenots, but of his own stubborn Catholic sect of Jansenists. "When Racine moved from the theatre to the court, he became a shrewd courtier," wrote Spanheim, and certainly the poet had been careful not to place the Persian King in the villain's role. That doubtful honour passed instead to Louis's hard-line Jesuit confessor, Père de la Chaise, who had led a recent charge against the Jansenists by forcing the closure of one of their schools. To Père de la Chaise, in parable, went the role of Aman, who ends, satisfyingly for the Jansenists, by acknowledging the superior theology of his enemies, before being led off to execution by the King's guards.

"I shall not regard Esther as completely finished, Madame, until I have received your own opinion of it," the poet wrote to Françoise. But she was delighted with it; the King—a few little observations notwithstanding—was delighted with it; and above all, the girls were delighted with it. Françoise sent six hundred livres to court composer Jean-Baptiste Moreau, who duly produced "music [to] fit in with the poetry." In due course, the King's own musicians arrived with their instruments; tailors arrived with fantastical eastern costumes; carpenters erected a stage in the entrance hall at Saint-Cyr; the parts were assigned among the older "green" and "blue" girls; Racine himself agreed to coach them, and rehearsals began.

Esther was performed for the first time on January 27, 1687, in the presence of the King and personally invited courtiers. "The play is extraordinarily lovely and there's no stupid gossiping in it . . ." wrote Liselotte, but if this was mild praise, it was more than enough to initiate a rush of courtly interest in the production, to such an extent, indeed, that further and then extra performances had to be scheduled to accommodate all those who wished to see it. "It was a delightful little divertissement for Madame de Maintenon's little girls," observed the pioneering novelist Madame de La Fayette, with a touch of patronization mixed in with her good sense, "but as the price of things always depends on who has made them, or who has commissioned them, Madame de Maintenon's involvement in this left everyone who saw it in ecstasies: nothing so charming had ever been seen before, the play was better than anything of the kind ever written, the actresses—even playing men—left all the famous ladies of the stage far behind." "Madame de Maintenon's involvement," and the courtiers' habit of applauding whatever the King applauded, had made *Esther* a sensation.

Incidentally to most of the fuss, Racine's poetry was admitted to be good. But although Racine himself was pleased with the play, in one respect he had failed. The successive audiences were quick enough to see the second dimension in the work, but, overlooking his intended Jansenist protest, they saw it instead as a parable of Françoise's rise, at Athénaïs's expense: the Persian King's first wife Vasti (Athénaïs) had been discarded in favour of the reluctant Esther (Françoise), "with this difference," added Madame de La Fayette, "that Esther was rather younger, and her piety a bit more genuine."

The production of *Esther* had achieved far more than even Françoise had intended. "This kind of artistic undertaking should have been very secondary at any girls' school. *Esther* showed the King, and the whole court, how unprecedented, how exceptional Saint-Cyr was"—and by inference, how exceptional was Françoise herself. "Madame de Maintenon's modesty . . . could not prevent her finding in the character of Esther . . . certain things flattering to herself," observed her niece Marthe-Marguerite. "Admire the wisdom, the rare piety, the prudence, the faith of this new Esther!" wrote the eighty-year-old Madeleine de Scudéry, in poetical homage to her former protégée.

"How could anyone resist such praise!" declared Madame de La Fayette, with a shake of her level head.

"I'm happier than I've ever been," said Françoise.

SIXTEEN

La Vie en Bleu

*I*f Françoise was happier than she had ever been, the same could by no means be said of her friends and relatives in Poitou, nor in any of the other Protestant regions of France. A single religion had been deemed vital for the country's political stability; no clique of religious sympathizers with France's Protestant enemies could be tolerated. All French Protestants were to be persuaded, or if necessary forced, to abjure their faith and become Catholic. Thus, and only thus, could absolute loyalty to the King and to France be assured. A peace treaty signed with the Habsburg Emperor in August 1684 had allowed Louis to turn his attention to possible sources of trouble at home, so that the following twelve months had seen the Huguenots deprived of almost all that had remained of their everyday rights and freedoms as his subjects, and within a few months more, they had found themselves at risk of their very lives.

In the terms of the day, discrimination in law, interference in private life, and even sentences of death were viewed without any particular horror. Already in 1681, Louis had been widely praised for issuing a royal declaration allowing Huguenot children of seven years and over to be taken by force from their parents for upbringing as

Catholics. But in 1685, with the support of almost all his priests and bishops, including, and most enthusiastically, his Jesuit confessor Père de la Chaise and the dévot preacher Bossuet, the King had initiated a new series of anti-Huguenot declarations of increasing severity. In April 1685, he forbade Huguenot sailors from praying in Protestant fashion while at sea. In June, Huguenot temples were demolished. In July, Huguenots were forbidden to employ Catholics as servants, and Huguenot lawyers prohibited from the practice of the law. In August, Huguenot physicians were prohibited from practising medicine and Huguenot teachers forbidden to teach. In September, Huguenots found practising their religion in secret were ordered to surrender half their property to those who had denounced them. In October, at the château of Fontainebleau, Louis signed an official Revocation of Henri IV's great Edict of Nantes; it was distributed publicly on the first day of November. In July 1686, a bounty of 1,000 francs was offered to those informing on any Huguenot attempting to leave the country. And from December of that year, anyone found helping Huguenots to leave the country was condemned to death, along with the Huguenots themselves.

This was Louis's battle, and the battle of the Catholic Church in France, against "the redoubtable monster of heresy." The "redoubtable monster" was requiring redoubtable means to subdue. The restraints and cruelties of the various royal declarations having proved insufficiently persuasive, Louis had at length agreed to a renewed campaign of *dragonnades*, the long-term billeting of Catholic soldiers on Huguenot families who refused to convert. The compulsory billeting of troops on local populations was a commonplace at the time, a form of taxation, effectively, to help pay for the country's periodic military endeavours. Even under the friendliest of circumstances, billeting meant extra expense and inconvenience for the host families, but in this case, where the ultimate purpose was not to spread costs, but to push families towards conversion, the dragoons had received special instructions to make themselves as troublesome as possible within the Huguenot households.

"If the King lives, there won't be a single Huguenot left twenty years from now." So Françoise had warned her apparently staunch Huguenot cousin Philippe in the spring of 1681. Now, after only five years, Louis seemed to be achieving his goal. Reports of conversions by the thousands, and by the tens of thousands, were read out weekly at the meetings of his ministers: In Protestant Béarn, in the southwest of the country, "600 people have converted . . . just from hearing that the army was on its way." From Françoise's native Poitou, another Huguenot stronghold, came the report: "We have just read the dispatch from Louvois to intendant Bâville announcing that the Asfeld regiment is arriving. There will be no need here . . . for any violence in His Majesty's name"—with the latter sentence subsequently crossed out. "With methods like these," Fénelon insisted to Bossuet, "one could convert all the Protestants to Islam: we'd only have to show them some dragoons."

But Fénelon, educationalist extraordinaire and firm friend of Françoise's dévot circle, belonged to a tiny, barely objecting minority. Louis's Revocation, and the harsh treatment of Protestants which had preceded it and which followed it now, proved overwhelmingly popular not only within the formal Catholic Church, but throughout the country at large. In Paris, mobs of people took it upon themselves to tear down the great Huguenot temple of Charenton, while the local illuminati looked on, adding their own, better-bred support: "Let the truth reign throughout France!" trumpeted La Fontaine. "Louis must banish this false, suspect, enemy cult from his kingdom!" shouted the moralist La Bruyère, with no hint, for once, of his celebrated satire. Even so moderate a Catholic as Madame de Sévigné was in lyrically enthusiastic vein, writing to her far-from-pious cousin, the comte de Bussy-Rabutin, only days after the signing of the Revocation: "You'll no doubt have seen the King's edict revoking the Edict of Nantes. There's nothing so fine as what he says there. No king has ever done nor ever will do anything more memorable . . . The dragoons have been very good missionaries up to this point; now it's up to the preachers to complete the work."

In fact, the dragoons had nothing "very good" about them. Ordinarily, the dragoon was simply a mounted infantryman, who travelled on horseback but fought on foot. His standard weapon was the fire-breathing "dragon," a short musket whence he drew his own name. The authorities commonly used dragoons against their own population, to quash city riots or smaller-scale seditious rebellions—Cardinal Richelieu and Louis's minister Colbert had both resorted to them in order to force reluctant peasants to pay their taxes. Lower on the social rung than the true cavalrymen, the dragoons shared the most unsavoury qualities of the poorly raised and often barbarous infantrymen. "The dragoons were mounted roughnecks," said one commentator succinctly, "to be avoided like the plague," an assessment confirmed by an eyewitness in these frightening days of the 1680s: "Several people in this town have been beaten up by the soldiers billeted with them," he reported. "[Other soldiers] raped the women in the presence of their husbands, and tied the children naked onto spits as if to roast them . . ."

Stories of the dragonnades, relayed by Huguenots who defied the threat of execution and managed to escape France, naturally produced outrage. In England, the diarist John Evelyn, himself smarting from the recent accession of the Catholic King James II in his Protestant land, recorded the following in his private pages:

This day was read in our church . . . a Brief . . . for relieving the French Protestants, who came here for protection from the unheard-of cruelties of the King . . . The French persecution of the Protestants raging with the utmost barbarity, exceeded even what the very heathens used; innumerable persons of the greatest birth and riches leaving all their earthly substance, and hardly escaping with their lives, dispersed through all the countries of Europe. The French tyrant abrogated the Edict of Nantes which had been made in favour of them, and without any cause; on a sudden demolishing all their churches, banishing, imprisoning, and sending to the galleys, all the ministers; plundering the common people; and exposing them to all sorts of barbarous usage by soldiers sent to ruin and prey on them; taking away their children; forcing people to the Mass; and then executing them as relapsers; they burnt their libraries, pillaged their goods, eat up their fields and substance, banished or sent the people to the galleys, and seized on their estates.

And at Versailles itself, one well-concealed Protestant heart was beating with indignation. Not daring to speak out, Liselotte had been reduced to railing about the Revocation in letters to her Aunt Sophie. "They compliment the King in every sermon for his persecution of the poor Huguenots. They think it's a great and wonderful thing, and anyone who wants to tell him any differently simply isn't believed," she wrote, before adding, with a mixture of good sense and jealousy, "It's really deplorable that no one taught him in his youth what religion is, properly speaking. He didn't understand that it was instituted to foster unity among men, not to make them torment and persecute one another. But how can anything good result when he allows himself to be governed by ambitious women and designing priests . . ."

Liselotte's insinuation, that at least part of the blame lay at Françoise's feet, was to be adopted, unfairly, by contemporary Protestants, and by later generations in France, as an anti-Maintenon refrain. But there was no truth in it. Indeed, if Françoise was able to sway the King in any way, it would certainly have been towards greater leniency. "Don't be harsh with the Huguenots," she had warned her brother Charles, as long before as 1672. "It's gentleness that draws people. Jesus Christ gave us that example . . ." Now, in 1687, she was passing on the same advice to her newly converted cousin Philippe, charged with the conversion of further Huguenot cousins. As resisters, they had been imprisoned, which, however, had done nothing to persuade them towards Catholicism. "I admit I'm not very happy, before God or before the King, about delaying these conversions," she sighed, ". . . but it's an infamous thing, to abjure without really being a convinced Catholic. Don't make your tolerance too obvious, though," she warned Philippe. "If you do that you'll be regarded here as a bad Catholic."

In fact, in her mildly devout heart, Françoise shared the King's conviction that Huguenots had "no good reason" to deprive themselves of the advantages enjoyed as of right by France's Catholics. Rarely among her compatriots, she had seen both Protestant life and Catholic life at first hand, and for many years together. In her view, both were equally capable of leading good people to salvation. Early anti-Huguenot measures taken in her home region of Poitou had left plenty of confiscated land, including the old d'Aubigné family estate of Surimeau, going cheaply: she had advised her brother to buy it. Religiously lukewarm, she was a pragmatist to her bones: God would not mind either way, so if the King did mind, it was best to follow the King.

Françoise's almost indifferent attitude to the Revocation stands in marked contrast to that of her friend Fénelon, who complained that "with methods like these one could convert all the Protestants to Islam." But Fénelon was out in the field, preaching in the Huguenot regions to those already converted through the terror of the dragonnades. He knew what was really happening, as Françoise, and indeed Louis, apparently did not. The King was kept regularly informed of the enormous numbers of new converts in town after town, but he was told little of the methods used to persuade them. Cynical enough to attribute the mass conversions to a normal human wish to advance in life, unable to empathize with any profound attachment to sectarian principle, it did not occur to him that any great force had been needed to effect the change he had sought. He had been content to leave the matter in the hands of his ministers of cloth and crown, and he was content now to accept the same ministers' account of it.

As early as 1671, before Françoise had even met the King, he had made up his mind what to do about "the great number of my subjects who are of the so-called reformed religion, an evil which I have always regarded . . . with great pain. I formed at that point the plan for all my conduct towards them . . ." At that time, as revealed in his *Mémoires* written for the young dauphin, Louis had dismissed the idea of converting the Huguenots by force. "It seems to me, my son," he had continued, "that those who want to use extreme and violent measures do not understand the nature of this evil . . . It must be allowed to die out very gradually, rather than to flame up again through strong opposition . . . And the best way of ensuring this is not to oppress them by any new restrictions . . . but also not to allow them any more new liberties . . . and to grant no favours at all to any of them . . . In this way, they will gradually realize, by themselves and without violence, that there is no good reason to deprive themselves of the advantages which my other subjects enjoy." In Louis's uncomplicated head, the Huguenots' religious convictions in themselves were self-evidently "no good reason" for resisting conversion to Catholicism.

The King's objections to violent measures had not changed markedly since his first anti-Huguenot plan of 1671. The savagery now, and the mild representation of it which Louis himself was receiving, were in fact both the work of the war minister, Louvois.

Louvois's name was a byword for brutality, and also for cynicism. Though himself Catholic, he had never evinced any particular personal antipathy towards the Huguenots. But the Peace of Nijmegen, at the end of Louis's Dutch wars in 1678, had left Louvois "floored," in Saint-Simon's expression, by the perverse weight of the absence of war. "Monsieur Louvois was afraid that all his wartime influence would dissipate, to the advantage of Monsieur Colbert's son, Seignelay," said Françoise's niece, Marthe-Marguerite, in later years. "Louvois was determined, at any price, to bring the army into a project that should have been founded on nothing but kindness and gentleness . . . It was he who asked the King for permission to send the dragoons into the Huguenot regions. He said the Huguenots would only need to see the dragoons, and that would be enough to persuade them to convert . . . And the King gave in, and in his name they carried out those cruelties that would have been punished if he had known of them. But Monsieur Louvois kept telling him every day how many people had converted, just at the sight of the troops, and the King was naturally so honest that he never imagined anyone could mislead him once he'd given them his confidence."

Louis had decided to do what his father and grandfather had deemed necessary "for the peace and security of the realm." "It was a most admirable project, and sensible politically, if you look at it apart from the methods they took to enforce it," said Marthe-Marguerite.

But, naïvely, "never [imagining] anyone could mislead him," Louis had left the management of his "admirable" project to others, and then, as Liselotte complained, simply refused to believe "anyone who wants to tell him any differently." "These new converts are about as Catholic as I am Mahometan," wrote Sébastien Vauban indignantly, but the King simply turned a deaf ear.

In later years, when the truth about Louvois's brutal dragonnades had been revealed and Louvois himself had died in disgrace, Françoise set down her reflections on the matter of the Huguenot conversions, in response to an apparently private *mémoire* which Vauban, a man of keen moral and political interests as well as a great military engineer, had sent for her personal consideration:

> If things were in the same state now [in 1697] as they were at the time of the Revocation, I would say without hesitation that it would have to be adhered to, but that it would be sufficient to abolish Protestant worship in public [so permitting liberty of conscience in private], and to exclude Huguenots gradually from public office, as the occasion arose, and to attempt, with patience and gentleness, to persuade them of the truth.
>
> . . . But things are different today. It seems to me that if liberty of conscience were to be reestablished, even without permitting public worship . . . this would reflect badly on France, as if France were nervous about the current state of affairs [war with the Protestant powers].
>
> . . . As for permitting the fugitive Huguenots to return to France, far from strengthening the state, some of them would only weaken it. It's only the most determined and stubborn of them, after all, who were able to leave behind all their property, leave their homeland and renounce their most basic responsibilities and even their legitimate sovereign, rather than accepting what was required of them. People like this are ready to risk anything . . . They would certainly be ready to incite others here

to renege on their conversions . . . and they would not be satisfied with liberty of conscience alone. They would want all their old rights and privileges back.

. . . And what of their children? If the parents had liberty of conscience, one would have to allow them to educate their children as Huguenots, and that would perpetuate a body of people whose interests, because of their religion, ran counter to those of the state. In time this could lead to civil war . . . We must not forget the lessons of history. Have not the Huguenots waged bloody war against our kings? Have they not several times brought in foreign armies? Even during the present reign, have we not discovered a secret plan of one of their synods to enlist the help of Cromwell?

. . . Moreover, the King took very strong measures against them, and for that he was both highly praised and harshly condemned . . . It would reflect very badly indeed on him to go back on what he has done, and it would also undermine confidence in any resolutions he may make in the future.

. . . For all these reasons, I think the best thing now is not to go back on what has been done, and to make no new declarations, either, but simply to treat the converted Huguenots more gently than they have been, and above all not to force them to commit sacrilege by taking the sacraments when they don't believe in them, nor to permit this dragging through the streets of the bodies of those who've refused to convert on their deathbeds, and also to stop trying to claim the assets of those who are now abroad. Those who initiate armed rebellion must be punished, and rigorously, but no reprisals should be carried out on those who are not rebels themselves.

. . . Vigilance should be maintained against those who form assemblies or who take a public stand on their religion, but we should close our eyes to those who don't go to mass or take the sacraments, and to how they die, and to all the other things we can choose not to see.

. . . The best thing would be to take their children from them [to educate them as Catholics], but that must be done with great delicacy.

. . . These things must all be entrusted to intelligent and devout people, who will keep the authorities properly informed of all the most important things, and proceed with the greatest care in everything else.

These are in no way the words of a fanatical anti-Huguenot. They are more measured and humane than those of all but the rarest Catholic commentators of the time. Those who were to accuse Françoise, after her death, of having instigated the Revocation and the dragonnades were never able to adduce any real evidence against her. But Liselotte's spiteful aside would prove enough to begin a harmful, and soon unquestioned, slandering of what Françoise had always held most dear: her own reputation.

The *réponse* concerning the Huguenots may be enough in itself to clear Françoise of these accusations, but it is revealing of her temperament in another respect as well: its tone is quite political; her arguments are not based on, for example, the demands of Christian charity or temperance, but rather on the security of the realm and on the need for the King to maintain his international standing. They suggest that Françoise may in fact have been more politically minded, in the traditional sense, than she was generally held to be, and that her public silence to date had been largely the result of the King's insistence that no woman at his court was to involve herself in politics. "A girl should recoil from worldly knowledge just as she does from vice," Fénelon warned the girls at Saint-Cyr.

France lost some 200,000 of its one million Huguenots during these years before and after the Revocation. Most of them fled at first to nearby Holland, and thence to England or the Protestant states of Germany. Obliged to leave their property behind them, the majority took nothing with them but their skills, of which their new homelands swiftly reaped the benefits. Ever-libellous Holland gained thousands of printers; women in Ulster rejoiced at the inflow of linen weavers, as did London's more elegant ladies at the arrival of the silk weavers in their new Spitalfields market. Some Huguenots had managed to smuggle a few jewels for immediate money on arrival, and from one or two refugee pockets appeared the precious, portable bulbs of Europe's newest and rarest flower, the tulip.

Nothing good in this world is absolutely good," wrote a sage and gloomy Madame de Sévigné to her cousin, Bussy-Rabutin. Life at court, at least, was certainly proving less than absolutely good. No one was happy. After a year in blooming health, the King was unwell, complaining of "a little tumour near the perineum, two fingerbreaths from the anus, quite deep, not sensitive to the touch, without pain or redness or throbbing, and not preventing any of his natural functions, nor horse-riding. However, it does seem to be hardening, and growing larger." This was the verdict of his prodding but unhelpful physicians, "and I won't be happy until he's out of their hands," Françoise fumed to Madame de Brinon. "They're killing me with worry: one day they say he's perfectly all right, the next day he's not doing well at all . . . I have no confidence at all in them." Days of lying in bed with hot and peppery poultices pressed against the tumour had proved to no avail, and indeed had induced both "pain and redness," and left the King walking with the greatest difficulty.

Liselotte was not happy, either, complaining to her aunt about not being "on the same footing with the King as I used to be," and blaming "his old prune" for the exclusion. Liselotte's grumpiness had a second cause, too. Now in her mid-thirties and more heartily built than ever, she had for the first time in her life begun to worry about her weight. "This slimming business is all well and good," she wrote, "but I haven't been able to manage it, since I can't stand fish, and I'm convinced there are nobler things to do than ruining my stomach by eating too much of it . . ." The gloom had lifted for her only temporarily, in church, where the famously long-winded abbé Bourdaloue had suffered a memory lapse in the middle of his sermon. "Catholic sermons are too long," she had sighed. "Bourdaloue is a famous Jesuit whose admirable sermons should render him immortal," retorted Saint-Simon with stern Roman piety.

Nor was Athénaïs happy. Resigned at last to the King's neglect, she had set off for the Paris convent of the Daughters of Saint-Joseph, there to seek out the celebrated dévote, Madame de Miramion, "to see if talking about nothing but God could make her forget men"—or rather, one man in particular.

The dauphine was unhappy, too. "She does everything she can to please the King, but she's mistreated every day, by order of the old bag," spat Liselotte. "She's spending her life between boredom and pregnancy."

Even the normally irrepressible Bonne was unhappy. Once "as beautiful as the day," now "as ugly as the devil," she had been insulted at a court ball by one of the dauphine's ladies-in-waiting. "You're a nice face to have at a party!" the girl had sneered. "She was right," commented Madame de Sévigné. "At a party you need a face that won't detract from the decorations."

Though the balls went on, the usual liveliness of the court had been rather dampened by the increased favour of Bossuet and his dévots, which Liselotte managed to blame entirely on Françoise. "Honestly, you'd cry laughing to see how things are at court at the moment," she wrote. "The King imagines he's being pious by making everything boring and tiresome . . . and he thinks he's living piously because he's not sleeping with any young woman. His entire fear of God consists in being finickety and in having spies everywhere accusing people left and right . . . and in tormenting the world in general. The Old Maintenon trout takes her pleasure in turning the King against all the members of the royal family and telling them what to do . . . For my part, I can't believe our Lord God can be served by nagging, fussy old women, and if that's the way to heaven, I'm going to have trouble getting there. It's a pitiful thing when a man can't rely on his own reason, and lets himself be led by manipulating priests and old courtesans."

And everyone, it seemed, had haemorrhoids—to such an extent, indeed, that Primi Visconti—"no physician and no astrologer"—nonetheless promised the King's brother to speak to the Venetian ambassador concerning a supposed secret remedy. Françoise, a regular sufferer, had her own preferred remedy, which she conveyed to her similarly afflicted brother:

> Believe me when I say I know more about it than the doctors. I didn't get well until I stopped taking all their remedies. Eat lots: indigestion is better than constipation; but don't eat anything salty or peppery or bitter. Stay in bed when your haemorrhoids are inflamed; travelling by coach is bad for them; only lying down will help. If the pain gets worse, bathe in warm water—the Abbé Testu has a very convenient chair where only your behind and your stomach are in the water. If you're constipated, take cinnamon and no other medicaments; don't have any enemas and don't take any other remedy you may be told of. Anything fatty or oily will make it worse. Follow what I say and you'll get well. Haemorrhoids are not to be treated lightly—that just makes them worse—but it will run its course and it won't last forever.

Haemorrhoids or not, life at court had lately come to seem rather tiresome. Twelve years after her first arrival and three years after her marriage, Françoise was worn down and worn out by the claustrophobic, incestuous, petty, false, crowded life at Versailles—so at least it felt. She could no longer even escape to her own château of Maintenon, since the King had invaded this once peaceful refuge with his mania for building: behind the lovely private park, with trees swaying classically in the breeze and swans gliding across the lake, thirty thousand men dug and pounded and hammered and sweated to build a vast aqueduct to service Louis's ever-thirsty fountains. Françoise had not wanted the aqueduct, did not care about the fountains, and, with Maintenon effectively a building site, now felt more trapped than ever at Versailles. Even Madame de Sévigné, hardly ever there if she could help it, had been complaining of the "insupportable martyrdom of being at court, all decked out and dressed up."

For Françoise, with her instinctive preference for simple clothes, the "decking out and dressing up" was a genuine trial. Her gowns were never extravagant, and in her own rooms she could resort to comfortable muslin, but for court evenings she was obliged to wear the usual damask or velvet or other heavy fabrics of the day, with her gowns weighing as much as sixty pounds. An obligatory ten-foot-long train, held up by her African page, Angola, indicated to everyone her standing as dame d'atour. In this respect, at least, Liselotte's superiority was apparent to all: as a duchess, she was entitled to a twenty-five-foot train.

If Liselotte took any comfort in this, she had none in the rest of her ordinary court attire. Beneath her sixty-pound gown, every lady wore three petticoats, and on top, a whalebone corset, which periodically snapped to stab its unsuspecting wearer. Her stockings, woollen or silk, were required to be either red, white, or blue, with a constant preference for the latter indicating intellectual pretensions on the lady's part. Her linen, extremely expensive, often imported from Holland, could at least be kept clean by being washed in boiling water and rubbed on wood or stone, but this sturdy method of laundering wore it out very quickly. Though muslin could be washed, too, the lady's heavier gowns were never washed at all, but simply sold after three or four wearings, to be cut up and remade into coverings for furniture.

The court lady could not even dress alone. She was helped into the various layers of her clothes by, typically, seven or eight maids, with her collar and sleeves added on at the end, and pins everywhere, a series of tiny threats making every movement hazardous. Her shoes were high-heeled, with the heels in the middle, a constant challenge to the lady's sense of balance, since, unlike the gentlemen at court, she could not use a cane to steady herself without being viewed as elderly. One little duchess, yet to master the high heels, was preceded at all times by three of her maids, to prevent her from toppling over.

Lully was dead, leaving the unfinished score of a new lyric tragedy behind him. The King's favourite composer, flagrant, obstreperous, wonderfully gifted, had more or less killed himself. During a performance of his own *Te Deum*, keeping time for the musicians with the regular thud of a heavy, pointed, six-foot staff, he had ended by piercing his own foot. The wound had turned gangrenous; the surgeons had advised amputation. But Lully was a dancer, too; though fifty-four years old, he had never stopped dancing; he could not live without both feet; he would die in possession of both of them. So he had declared to the surgeons, and so, two months later, he had done.

Lully's *Te Deum* was not a new work. He had written his one great hymn of praise, ironically, almost ten years before, at the height of his debaucheries. Lully had been a homosexual of the most flaunting kind, staging the wildest orgies known to the court, creating the greatest noise throughout the night and the greatest interest in the morning. For twenty years, his gift for the operas and ballets so loved by the King had protected him from retribution, despite personal admonishments and public sermons against his "ultramontain vice." But a few years before, the King's illegitimate son, the comte de Vermandois, not yet fifteen years old, had been seduced into "a villainous commerce with certain young men of the court, for which he was severely chastised by order of his father." The dauphin, too, had begun frequenting a group of flagrantly homosexual courtiers, with a certain outsized diamond ring being passed from one to the other as their affairs developed. "These vices are more Florentine than French," noted Primi Visconti, and indeed, given his customary outrageous indiscretion, it was the Florentine Lully who was held responsible. Though his wife had accepted the situation placidly, his mother-in-law had not. The King was petitioned, Père Bourdaloue preached a direful sermon, the police swooped on Lully's house, his beautiful page-boy was carted off to confinement in a monastery, and the composer himself became suddenly persona non grata.

Liselotte, no lover of the "bits of old Lully operas" so frequently played at the King's appartements, and whose husband, Monsieur, was himself homosexual, found it all deplorable, too, and blamed it on the court's too-pious Catholicism. "You wouldn't believe how blatant and wicked all these French people are, as soon as they turn twelve or thirteen . . . Their piety prevents the men from speaking openly with the women . . . and then once they're interested in boys, they don't care about pleasing anyone else, and the more dissolute and blatant and wicked they are, the more they like them . . . They say it was only a vice when there weren't very many people in the world, and so the sin lay in stopping the population from growing, but now that the world is fully populated, they say it's just a harmless pleasure . . . Among people of quality, it's perfectly acceptable to say that God hasn't punished anyone for these things since Sodom and Gomorrah . . . Where in the world can a man be found who simply loves his wife, and doesn't keep mistresses or boys on the side?" she added plaintively. The answer was in fact not far to seek, but thinking of Louis and Françoise did not make Liselotte any happier. "And as for that old whore," she concluded, "I wish her in hell, and may the Father, Son, and Holy Ghost lead her there!"

The "old whore" herself had felt obliged to raise the issue of the "ultramontains" with the King several years before, at the persistent urging of the curé of Versailles. Louis had conceded the scale of the problem, but, in consideration of his brother, had preferred to turn a blind eye. Françoise had evidently borne no ill will towards the "ultramontains." Indeed, in October 1685, after one of many altercations between composer and King, she had called Lully to her own rooms and suggested the means by which he could reestablish himself in Louis's good graces. "The King is just as angry with you as he was," she told him, apparently adding a few reproaches of her own, "but your own gifts can redeem you." Lully's *oeuvre de réconciliation*, on a theme suggested by Françoise herself, was *The Temple of Peace*, a full court ballet, completed in just one week.

But in the end, his continuing excesses had become impossible for the King to countenance. In the spring of 1686, Louis had indicated his final displeasure by failing to appear in the dauphine's apartments for a performance of Lully's newest and most accomplished opera, *Armide*. He had feigned illness, but the slight had been unmistakeable. Lully had responded with an anguished letter: "The praises of all Paris will not suffice. It is only to you, Sire, that I consecrate the fruits of my genius. Even this dangerous malady, which came upon me so suddenly, did not prevent me from completing this opera. It was to fulfill your own command, Sire, that I continued working . . ."

But Lully's passion, on paper as onstage, could no longer sway the King. Following his disgrace, there was a sharp decline in court entertainments of all kinds. The thrice-weekly performances in the King's apartments were reduced to a single performance per week, which may at least have pleased Liselotte. Newly favoured composers at court, notably the later famous Marc-Antoine Charpentier, were encouraged to turn away from profane operas and ballets, devoting their talents instead to sacred music. Though the change produced much that was lovely and lasting, it also increased the generally dampening effect of the new habits of piety at court. Alongside Lully, in his grave, lay the noonday glory of Louis's golden reign. The reprobate genius was to be long and sincerely mourned by his wife and his ten children, and by all the courtiers, newly garbed in the buttoned-up coats and plain stockings of the dévots, mourning no less the riotous old court of his heyday.

The King himself, though personally eschewing buttoned-up coats and plain stockings, also seemed, quite suddenly, past his heyday. He was now approaching fifty and, though still vigorous, was no longer the strikingly handsome man he had once been. He had lost most of his hair, pleasing at least the local wigmakers, since where the King went, so went the court; wigs had become fashionable, providing new employment, too, for street thieves, who quickly developed an innovative "fishing" technique to pluck them from the heads of passersby.

Less easy to take advantage of was the King's loss of teeth—most of his teeth, in fact—and even part of his jaw, removed by surgeons, whether intentionally or not, while attending to some rotted molars. Unable to chew, Louis now ate in gulps, wolfing down his food, and not infrequently bringing it back up again. Stuck in the various gaps inside his mouth, meaty pieces too often simply decayed there, rendering the royal breath foul even by the unwholesome standards of the day. And his famed dancer's legs were regularly swollen with gout, making walking and even riding near impossible: shortly after his forty-ninth birthday, he was obliged to take to a little wheelchair to do his pheasant shooting.

All of this Louis endured stoically, never complaining of pain, even during the gruesome operation on his jaw. His courage was matched by an equally reliable vanity: in 1685, Bernini's equestrian statue of Louis was unveiled at Versailles. The fruit of eight years of work, it was considered Bernini's masterpiece, but, "far from being able to appreciate it, when Louis saw it, he found it badly done and ordered it to be broken up." "He couldn't bear anyone else to be the object of public veneration," wrote Spanheim of the King.

"It's not pleasant to be mistaken, but it's much worse to be disillusioned," the chevalier de Méré had written. If Françoise had only too much reason to think now of her first tutor, she was wise enough to keep her disillusionment to herself. "The greatest man in the world" was proving only too human in his once magnificent physical person. Seldom ill herself apart from migraines and rheumatism, she was nonetheless a sympathetic and confident attendant at Louis's periodic sickbeds. Determined to keep her gaze fixed on the King's immortal soul, and accepting of suffering, like all her contemporaries, as an inevitable fact of life, she repeatedly proved more than worthy of his favourite epithet for her: Your Steadiness.

Steadiness was indeed the quality likely to prove more useful than any as the months of 1686 progressed. The King's "little tumour near the perineum" had been showing dangerous signs of ulceration; by the autumn his physicians had officially declared it "a fistula." An operation would be required to remove it.

Early in October the decision was made, in secret from the too-curious court, that the King would submit to "la grande opération." The tribe of royal physicians lacking the necessary skills, they sought help from outside the court. They found it in Dr. Félix, who had successfully treated Louis's dislocated elbow following his riding accident three years before. Dr. Félix assured them that he had perfected the required technique, which he had been practising for several months on corpses from the Paris hospitals. Félix was already noted for performing operations himself, in contravention of the usual practice, with the physician simply dictating what was to be done, and the lower-ranking surgeon carrying out the instructions.

"La grande opération" was performed on November 18. "Félix made two incisions with the scalpel and eight with scissors," reported the abbé de Choisy. "The King held his breath through the whole thing." "Félix's new instrument spared the King several more incisions with the scissors," recorded the marquis de Dangeau. "As soon as it was finished, the King sent word to the dauphin, who was out hunting . . . but as soon as he heard the news, he . . . came riding back at full speed, weeping." The royal physicians and the King's confessor, Père de la Chaise, had also been present throughout the ordeal, and Athénaïs, too, "had tried to get in, in her usual imperious way, but the guard at the door prevented her."

The news spread at once—"in a quarter of an hour," said the abbé—through the court and to Paris. "I can't express the effect of such astonishing news on the Parisians," he continued. "Everyone felt how precious the life of a good king was, and everyone was imagining himself in the same situation: the fear, the horror, the pity, it was all painted on every face. Every last person left his work to talk about it. *The King has just had la grande opération.* The very word was frightening. I heard with my own ears a litter-bearer saying—and he was crying— *They cut him twenty times with the scalpel, and he didn't say a word!*"

The King's wound began to heal, but unevenly, making it likely to open again in the future. On December 6, several further large incisions were made in an attempt to produce more durable scarring. "He was very jolly before and afterwards," noted Dangeau. Five days later, Françoise wrote to Madame de Brinon: "The King was in great pain for seven hours today. He suffered like a man broken on the wheel, and I'm afraid he'll be suffering again tomorrow."

On the same day, December 11, 1686, at eight o'clock in the morning, another courageous royal personage reached the end of his own mortal suffering. Louis's cousin, the generalissimo prince de Condé, le Grand Condé, had died, feverish and exhausted, at the age of sixty-five. Liselotte relayed the news to her aunt. "He was in torments, and he asked his physician if it would go on much longer . . . All his family were weeping around him, and he said to them, *For the last time, that'll do.. Let me think about the next world.* The poor prince died as bravely as he'd lived."

Through his agony, early on that same morning, Condé had written a final letter to the King. Hearing of his death, Louis acknowledged the loss of the greatest of his subjects. With Colbert dead, and Maréchal Turenne, Condé had been the last of Louis's giants laid to rest. Though a rebel in his youth, for thirty years he had proved an extraordinarily fine servant of his royal cousin. Louis's praise would have pleased him, but the old warrior would have been prouder yet of the eulogy escaping the lips of one of his toughest enemies in the field, the brilliant Dutch Prince Willem of Orange. "The greatest man in Europe has just died," declared Willem, and no one was heard to gainsay him.

"The King's wound is very much better this morning," wrote Françoise brightly, later in the month. "We must put our trust in God, since men don't know what they're doing or what they're talking about." Though one at least of the physicians had in fact done rather well, the King, for his part, had apparently decided in the end to put his trust in Françoise. The year's long trials had brought him to rely on her more than ever. From this time onwards, "he hardly moved from her apartments. He worked there, held his council meetings there, had plays and music performed there, dined there, and took his supper there."

On Christmas Day 1686, Françoise penned a relieved and slightly wicked letter to Madame de Brinon at Saint-Cyr. "Last night, the King attended part of the matins service," she wrote. "Today he heard three masses . . . This afternoon he heard a sermon, and then sat through a whole service of sung vespers. From all this you can see he's quite recovered . . . Madame [Liselotte] is very well indeed. Her delight at the King's recovery was painted all over her face. I'm sure you can well believe it."

—

ignon's military career was also progressing nicely. In 1682, at the age of twelve, he had been appointed governor of the southern region of Languedoc, a post long coveted by Monsieur, the King's brother and Liselotte's husband. Now, at sixteen, Mignon was on the point of becoming the King's General of Galleys, the fleet itself recently expanded by a large number of condemned Huguenots who had bravely resisted conversion.

Bonne's daughter Louise, two years older than Mignon, was safely married to the thirty-year-old marquis Jean-Françoise Cordebeuf de Beauverger de Montgon, himself well launched on the usual meteoric career of soldiers of noble birth. The long sought and finally captured Minette de Saint-Hermine, "threadbare demoiselle with all the provincialism of her origins," as the Versailles-born duc de Saint-Simon remarked snidely, had also been comfortably married off, to the twenty-five-year-old comte Louis de Mailly. "His family weren't at all happy about that," said Saint-Simon, "but Madame de Maintenon was all-powerful, so they just had to swallow it." Charles's two-year-old daughter, Françoise-Charlotte-Amable, was now living permanently at Versailles, already burbling greetings and compliments in the manner of a true-born courtier: her doting aunt found it "adorable."

Françoise could therefore claim a modest success in her clan-building efforts thus far, though one or two of her protégés, in fact one in particular, had recently been going dreadfully awry. Philippe's elder son, now aged twenty-two and comte de Mursay, was progressing in the army, too, but the light he had been reflecting back on Françoise was not entirely flattering. "He was unappealing, physically and mentally. He was brave, and not a bad officer, but gauche, clumsy in his speech, socially inept to the last degree. Even his valet made fun of him . . . His wife was ugly and stupid, and amazingly pious . . . She was constantly at her devotions, and wanted to sleep on her own. Mursay used to complain about it; he told everyone about his wife's *calendar* . . . Madame de Maintenon thought he was marvellous. He told her everything that was going on in the army, and he used to show her letters around, which shows how pathetically trusting he was . . . People made up to him because of her." Thus the duc de Saint-Simon, himself neither brave nor a good officer, nor indeed very appealing, physically or mentally.

But if Philippe de Mursay could at times be something of an embarrassment to Françoise, she was being driven almost to distraction by his sister, Marthe-Marguerite. Converted to Catholicism six years before through a mixture of force and guile, she had just celebrated her marriage to Jean-Anne de Thubières de Grimoard de Pestels de Lévis, comte de Caylus. Unfortunately for Marthe-Marguerite, her husband's name was by far the most impressive thing about him. He was young, and self-evidently from a very noble line, but his fortune was small, and his interests, far from stretching to his new wife, went no further than the nearest bottle of wine.

"I was not quite thirteen years old when I married," said Marthe-Marguerite, mistakenly, since she had in fact already turned fifteen. Six years of life at court had turned Philippe de Villette's little country girl, singing to herself in her kidnapper's coach, into a fascinating and delectable beauty. She was fun as well as beautiful, quick-witted, mischievous, and a wicked mimic, notoriously of the long and long-toothed dévote, Madame de Montchevreuil. "I must say I prefer the naughtier ones," Françoise confessed of her Saint-Cyr girls, and with Marthe-Marguerite, too, "she closed her eyes to the worst of her behaviour."

"You've never seen such an intelligent, sweet, expressive face, such freshness, such grace and wit, such liveliness and gaiety; there never was a more attractive creature," exclaimed the duc de Saint-Simon, with precocious appreciation, since he himself was only eleven years old at the time of Marthe-Marguerite's marriage. But the forty-two-year-old abbé de Choisy, an experienced admirer of the fair sex despite his transvestite habits, observed in her the same spirited grace: "It was constant delight whenever she was about. Her mental gifts were even more attractive than her lovely face. There was no chance of getting bored—you hardly had time to breathe. Her speaking voice was beautiful, far more so than those of the finest actresses . . ." "Her husband didn't notice any of it; he was in a daze from years of wine and brandy."

"She had everything a girl could need to marry brilliantly," sighed the abbé, and certainly the comte de Caylus had not been Marthe-Marguerite's only suitor. Foremost among them had been the illustrious Louis-François de Boufflers, forty-two years old, wealthy and charming, already a marquis and colonel-général of dragoons, with a dukedom and a maréchal's baton soon expected. His formal offer of marriage had been rejected on Marthe-Marguerite's behalf by Françoise herself, "in words fit to be engraved in letters of gold: *Monsieur*, she had told him, *my niece would not be a worthy match for you, though I am nonetheless touched by what you have offered for love of me, and in future I shall regard you as my nephew.*"

"Boufflers was devoted to Madame de Maintenon," wrote Saint-Simon. "Her door was always open to him," so that it may indeed have been partly "for love of me" that he had offered his hand in marriage to her barely noble niece from the modest château of Mursay. But the girl had had obvious attractions of her own, and after all, Françoise herself had married the King, if only in secret. If Marthe-Marguerite had been less than "a worthy match" for Boufflers, what was to be said of her own match with "the most glorious [king] in the universe"?

In fact it was probably Louis himself who had acted behind the scenes to prevent the marriage. He was fond of Boufflers and admired him, but, for reasons never clear, he had taken a strong disliking to Marthe-Marguerite. Perhaps, with her extraordinary charm, she outshone his own three daughters, all just a few years younger than she; perhaps, with her mischief and cleverness, he felt she was leading them astray, in particular his "Chubby," the thirteen-year-old Mademoiselle de Nantes; perhaps he was even a little bit in love with her himself. Or it may simply have been that a marriage with the popular and high-ranking Boufflers would have given Françoise's family too much prominence at court. The King had no wish to see an alternative court of influence and potential intrigue developing around his wife, such as had once existed around his powerful mother. "I got upset sometimes," Françoise later admitted, "because the King wouldn't grant

me what I asked for my family and my friends." If so, her declining of
the match, while a puzzle for Boufflers and perhaps a disappointment
to her niece, would have been above all a humiliation for her, a reminder of her status as an uncrowned queen, destined to remain effectively offstage.

Françoise consoled Boufflers, and reassured him of her friendship
by swiftly procuring for him the prestigious governorship of the territory of Luxembourg. "So being her adoptive nephew didn't do him
any harm," as the abbé de Choisy noted. Marthe-Marguerite, by contrast, sought consolation for herself in more serious mischief than the
mimicking of dévotes. She became a keen gambler, and soon began an
indiscreet affair with the marquis de Villeroy, son of Françoise's good
friend the duc de Villeroy. The marquis, charming and with a touch of
devilry about him, was thirty-three years old and himself recently
married, in fact to the daughter of the war minister, Louvois.

Within nine months of her wedding day, Marthe-Marguerite and
her husband were sufficiently at odds that Françoise was obliged to offer herself as an intermediary. "I am most impatient, Monsieur," she
wrote to the comte de Caylus in the week before Christmas of 1686,
"to make every effort I can to reconcile Madame de Caylus with you."
Reconciliation was equally needed between the comte and his recently
widowed mother, with whom he had also fallen out. Françoise does not
appear to have succeeded on either account, so that in the summer of
1687, Philippe de Villette himself decided to travel the three hundred
miles from Mursay to Paris, to do what he could to help his mismatched daughter. As usual, Françoise was not stinting in her advice:

> He has to make things up with his mother, and be on good terms
> with all his family . . . You have to make him see . . . the advan-
> tages of this, and also how bad it would be for him to quarrel
> with me, and what that would mean for him at court . . . Yester-
> day he was behaving like a madman, or rather like a drunkard:
> he wants to take his meals apart from his wife so that he can
> drink with fewer witnesses. Just between us, he's no good, but

no one knows that yet at court and there's still time for him to change. Couldn't you speak on my behalf to this abbé friend of his? You're a sensible man, and clever. Do something and help me; I really can't cope with managing both the husband and the wife.

The problem was too big, too intractable. No straightforward action from above could resolve it. While hoping for results from her "sensible and clever" cousin, Françoise could only address the simpler details of the case. In this same month of August 1687, she sent a pragmatic letter to the marquise de Caylus, Marthe-Marguerite's mother-in-law:

Do please send me the account of the comtesse de Caylus's debts, since we must know what the situation is and make some arrangements for the future: she hasn't a penny to her name. I've asked her husband to send me some money for her, so that I can manage it on her behalf. It distresses me to see her in her present state.

Marthe-Marguerite's debts could be taken care of, but her behaviour would be less easy to manage. Françoise, though admitting no responsibility of her own for the catastrophe of her niece's marriage, and still unreasonably hopeful of a decent outcome to it, decided to remove Marthe-Marguerite altogether from harm's way. "I'll send my coach tomorrow—no, on Monday, for you to take her to Sèvres," she wrote to Philippe. "I'd rather she were there than in Paris, where I'm afraid she'll do something foolish or let herself be led astray . . . and then you and I have to speak to the comte de Caylus, and do what we can to change him, but there's no time to lose. Adieu, my dear cousin. I have a thousand things to do." But her *obiter* to Philippe in the same letter reveals her desperation in the affair. The disgraceful situation had to be kept, as far as possible, from everyone at court, and there was little help to be expected from Louis, her own husband, for the wayward sixteen-year-old whom he so disliked. Close friends might sympathize, but in practical terms, she was alone with the problem—alone, that is, apart from Philippe. "It's really good to have you here and to be able to count on you in all this trouble Madame de Caylus is giving me; you're so reliable and thorough."

As Philippe knew perfectly well, "this trouble Madame de Caylus is giving me" had been brought about by Françoise's long-standing and too-confident assumption that she could do better for Marthe-Marguerite than he and his wife could do for her themselves. To his credit, Philippe made no accusations now, but set to, with all the reliability and thoroughness of which he was capable, to help his daughter out of her wretched situation. He proved no more successful than his cousin had been, and in the end, Françoise was obliged to appeal to the King. The comte de Caylus was packed off to the army, to remain permanently "on campaign"—that is, away from the court. "He was perfectly happy on the frontiers, anyway, provided he could keep drinking." And Françoise's ill-served, erring niece was sent to calm down at Saint-Germain, with toothy Madame de Montchevreuil as her chaperone, and, as Marthe-Marguerite herself remarked, "you can imagine how much fun that was."

SEVENTEEN

Crusaders

Far to the west, across the Channel, at the gigantic palace of Whitehall, the English court had been enduring troubles of its own, greater by far than any homosexual scandal or outbreak of haemorrhoids. At the base of it, however, was another ill-considered marriage, the 1673 match between James, then Duke of York, brother of Charles II, and the Italian princess Maria Beatrice d'Este, known to the English as Mary of Modena. Aged not quite fifteen, Mary had had no wish to be married off to the unknown, widowed, forty-year-old James in England. Though brought up in a fiercely unindulgent manner, she had, by her own admission, spent her last two days and nights in Italy "screaming and yelling" that she would not go.

She had gone, nonetheless, and though her louche royal husband had found her very much to his taste, in the country at large she had not been welcome. Young, talented, dazzlingly beautiful, Mary might have made a perfect consort but for her one unacceptable defect: she was Catholic. English Protestants high and low had ostracized and slandered her, declaring her a spy for the Pope, and even his natural daughter. In 1685, the discreetly Catholic Charles II had died, leaving a healthy brood of fourteen illegitimate children, but not a single one by his Queen. His brother James, staunchly and overtly Catholic despite being formally head of the Protestant Church of England, had ascended the throne. Of the five children born to Mary in the twenty years and more of her marriage, none had survived, but in June 1688 she had been safely delivered of a son, and the Protestant English had been obliged to confront the likelihood of a Catholic succession.

It was more than they could accept. By the end of the same month, on the initiative of the "immortal seven," a group of seven English nobles, the Protestant Prince Willem of Orange had been invited to capture the throne for himself. Willem was the husband of James's daughter Mary by his first wife; like her sister Anne, Mary was Protestant. In November 1688, Willem landed with a large mercenary force in what proved to be the first successful invasion of England since William the Conqueror's arrival in 1066. A month later, James and his Mary left the country, she in secret flight—"That flight will make a novel one day," observed Madame de Sévigné—and he firmly escorted out, to seek refuge with his cousin Louis at his safely Catholic court. The English and Scottish parliaments declared James's departure tantamount to abdication; a "Glorious Revolution" was announced, and James's daughter and her husband ascended the throne together, to reign jointly, if briefly, as William and Mary.

On the feast of the Epiphany, "the day of the Kings," January 6, 1689, James and Mary were installed at the château of Saint-Germain with their infant son James—the "Old Pretender," father of Bonnie Prince Charlie—still in his swaddling clothes. "And today it really is *la fête des Rois*," wrote Madame de Sévigné to her cousin, "a very satisfying one for the King who's providing asylum, and a very sad one for the King who needs it. Subjects and objects aplenty to reflect upon and talk about. The political people are having lots to say"—as, indeed, were the apolitical: "I've put a question to the Lord," Madame's friend Corbinelli added in a postscript to her letter. "I asked Him whether He's abandoning the Catholic religion, allowing the Prince of Orange, protector of Protestants, to prosper like this, and then I lowered my eyes . . ."

With two royal houses to consider, each accustomed to a different protocol, there was some to-ing and fro-ing over precedence. King James was formally presented to the dauphin and dauphine, then to Louis's brother, Monsieur, and Liselotte, but not to the humble dame d'atour, Françoise. The presentations to Queen Mary proved rather fraught, with the usual entitlements to armchairs and curtsys debated fiercely and at length—for four whole days, in fact, after which Louis's daughters and nieces agreed to wait upon Her Majesty. Françoise, being neither princesse nor duchesse, was again overlooked.

Even at the newly dévot French court, Queen Mary was swiftly declared to be far too pious, owing to her fussy Italianate devotions—"an infinity of petty little practices, useless anywhere, and surely particularly out of place in England," was the sage observation of eighteen-year-old Marthe-Marguerite, still in exile at Saint-Germain, which, with the arrival of the English couple, had turned quite suddenly from dreary royal outpost to the centre of all court interest. Mary was generally felt to be rather haughty as well as overly devout, "but she was intelligent and she did have good qualities, and that drew Madame de Maintenon to her . . ."

Liselotte was also an admirer of the beautiful thirty-year-old Mary, all the more so, perhaps, since Louis was clearly one, too, which occasionally appears to have rather piqued fifty-three-year-old Françoise. "You could say she had all the royal virtues," wrote Liselotte of Mary in later years. "Her only defect (no one's perfect) was to have pushed her piety to the extreme, but she paid dearly for that, since it was the cause of all her misfortunes."

James himself attracted less admiration than sympathy, and even amusement. He was an absolutist, which Louis naturally appreciated, and an exceptionally keen hunter, which the dauphin enjoyed as well. "Off he'd go to the chase, boldly, like a man of twenty without a care in the world," said Madame de La Fayette. And to the astonishment of the unintellectual Louis, James was able to quiz the royal astronomers at the famed Paris observatory, the first in the world: "The King possesses a naturally limited mind," the diplomat Spanheim observed coolly of Louis. But in the salons and appartements James cut a more equivocal figure, ceaselessly complaining of England's disloyalty in his uncontrollable stammer, every bit as bad in English as in his "very poor" French. "He'd thrown the seals of the kingdom [for authorizing royal documents] into the sea," Madame continued, "and we all had a good laugh about that, though it's true it did create some difficulty, because of their laws there . . . The Archbishop of Reims, Monsieur Louvois's brother, made fun of him coming out of church: *There's a fine fellow*, he said. *He's given up three kingdoms for the sake of a mass.* Very pretty words from the mouth of an archbishop!"

"The more you see of King James," concluded Liselotte, "the more you take the Prince of Orange's side."

Though the people of the lost three kingdoms, including "almost all the grandees," had generally reached the same conclusion, James and Mary had by no means given up hope of regaining the throne, and annoyed their French friends constantly with their apparent political indiscretions. "Every last plan for their reestablishment was known in England as soon as it was dreamed of at Versailles," said Marthe-Marguerite, a self-confessed "Jacobite" supporter of James, "but it wasn't really their fault. They were surrounded by people who betrayed them, even one of the Queen's own ladies . . . She would take letters from the King and Madame de Maintenon out of the Queen's pockets while Her Majesty was sleeping, and she would copy them, and send them to England." In February 1689, Françoise herself relayed to Père Gobelin King James's hopes of overturning the Protestant revolution in England through the back door of Catholic Ireland. "*Le milord* Tyrconnell is asking for arms and munitions. They're going to be sent. May God protect religion and our two kings; their piety has caused them plenty of trouble"—more, indeed, than her own had been causing her, given her recent neglect of the devotions prescribed by the reverend Père. "I couldn't make them," she insisted unconvincingly. "I had toothache."

In March 1689, only two months after his arrival in France, James set sail once again, not for England, however, but for Ireland, to join Tyrconnell and his "poorly disciplined and poorly armed militias," some of whom had taken advantage of the uprising to murder the families of their detested Protestant landlords. With his own best troops already on campaign in the Rhineland and half the powers of Europe arming against him, Louis's assistance to James had been small: four thousand men, since no more could be spared, "and officers of an exceedingly mediocre capacity," as Madame de La Fayette had noted. To no one's surprise, the Irish Jacobites met defeat a year or so later, in July 1690, at the Battle of the Boyne, whereupon James flew back to France. In Scotland, a Protestant victory at Cromdale in the same year was capped by the treacherous and soon legendary massacre of Glencoe, where Lowlands men of the English-backed Campbell clan murdered their Highland hosts of the Catholic clan Macdonald, marking "the onset of a war to the death between Lowlands and Highlands." It was to last half a century, until the Jacobites' final defeat in 1746, at the Battle of Culloden Moor.

Though William's staunch Protestantism had ensured him a genuine welcome in England, his Dutch bones had at first stuck in some English throats, prompting abusive pamphlets complaining about "foreigners" overrunning the "sceptr'd isle." His rescue had appeared in the unlikely person of a slender little Londoner, not five feet tall, with a hooked nose and a sharp chin, who pointed out that after the Romans and Vikings and Normans and Scots and everyone else, there was hardly any such thing as a "true-born Englishman" at all:

> From a mixture of all kinds began,
> That het'rogeneous thing, an Englishman . . .
> A true-born Englishman's a contradiction,
> In speech an irony, in fact a fiction.
> A metaphor invented to express
> A man a-kin to all the universe . . .
> Since scarce one family is left alive,
> Which does not from some foreigner derive.

The English, far from taking offence, had been hugely amused by this jab at their own mixed origins. The poem had become immensely popular and, as well as ensuring William's final acceptance, had made the name of its opportunistic author, the hack journalist, ex-convict, and thenceforth man of fame and fortune, Daniel Defoe.

William's capture of the English throne, in itself a triumph, was doubly valuable to him as a strengthening of arms in his ongoing battle with France. Since the Peace of Nijmegen in 1678, he had been intermittently roused, as indeed had the English, by French incursions into other European territories. But though England's pro-French Kings had been crossed by their anti-French parliament, the parliament itself, ever mindful of Dutch commercial competition, had not always stood reliably behind William. Now, as its King, he was far better placed to secure its support, though, unlike Louis, he could by no means take it for granted. Since the execution of Charles I in 1649, the authority of England's kings had been sharply circumscribed. And in fact, with the ousting of James and the assertion of a new "English ideology," the parliament in London had gained even greater power. No longer merely a rein on its King's wishes, it had itself assumed the despotic power of an absolute sovereign. With no countervailing force in the land, its wish, or its majority vote, had become the nation's command.

Fortunately for William, the wish of the English parliament now was to contest the power of Catholic France, and it was happy to vote the sums required for its new King's latest military venture against Louis. In May 1689, England joined William's great League of Augsburg, a coalition of mostly Protestant powers founded three years earlier to oppose and contain France; the League was renamed the Grand Alliance. Undeterred by the doubtful successes of his 1670s Dutch campaigns, in 1688 Louis had taken advantage of the vacant electoral throne of the Rhineland Palatinate to claim the territory for himself. The Elector of the Palatinate, Liselotte's brother, Karl Ludwig, had died leaving no heir; the territory lay on France's northeastern border; and Liselotte herself, or rather her marriage to Louis's brother and her own tenuous dynastic claim to the Palatinate, had provided the excuse for a French invasion. Ironically, Liselotte's marriage, eighteen years before, had been arranged as a form of security against possible French

attack; now, to her grief, it had served as the pretext for the devastation
of her homeland. Hearing the news of her brother's death, as Liselotte
herself had relayed to her Aunt Sophie in November 1688, "I wept
twice twenty-four hours without stopping . . . And, to add to my unhappiness, I have to listen all day to their plans to burn and bombard
the good city of Mannheim, which my late father built up with so
much care; it makes my heart bleed. And here they're offended that I
should be upset about it."

"The King has given orders that Mannheim is to be razed," the
marquis de Dangeau recorded, "not just the fortifications, but even all
the houses in the town as well as in the fortress, to stop the Germans
from using this [strategic] place . . ." "What distresses me above all,"
wrote Liselotte the following week, "is that they're using my name to
justify all this destruction . . . and that the King waited precisely until
I had begged him to spare Mannheim and Heidelberg before he went
ahead and destroyed everything." Liselotte had mistaken Louis's pitiless determination for personal spite, but there was no rationale, in any
case, that might have comforted her. While French soldiers rampaged
and burned their way through the towns and cities she had loved, their
supposed living justification passed a summer of melancholy days and
sleepless nights, "thinking of how it was there in my day, and what it
must be like now, imagining everything they've blown up . . ."

To the west, in Flanders, 35,000 others were also passing listless
days and nights "imagining everything they've blown up" in the
Palatinate, but with envy rather than distress. "Monseigneur's army is
very well occupied in Germany while we rot in idleness here," wrote
the duc du Maine to Françoise in the summer of 1689. Her "Mignon,"
now nineteen years old, had been appointed colonel-général of the
King's Swiss Guards, a post which had brought him an extra 100,000
livres a year. Under the overall command of the popular Maréchal
d'Humières and the detested Maréchal de Luxembourg (Primi Visconti's "deceitful little hunchback"), the army in Flanders lay waiting
to engage the troops of the Grand Alliance.

With time on his hands, Mignon was able to write to Françoise
every few days, relaying the boredom of camp life and his hopes for his

professional and personal future: "It's the same thing every day . . . I'm eating well, getting fatter even as you watch, and not drinking much . . . I still want to be made a brigadier, and I'm doing everything I can to learn what's necessary . . . I have learned something about the cavalry . . . I really want to be worth something . . . I'm willing to trade my post as General of Galleys for a cavalry command . . . Do please remember the Maréchal d'Humières. He and I both believe that if you support his advancement, it will happen in no time . . . I presume you were joking when you said you'd seen the object of my passion . . . I've no idea who you mean . . . I suppose though I'm not doing much here, it's more than I would be doing at court, where I do nothing but bumble about in front of people, getting on everyone's nerves . . ." In a measure which Françoise no doubt approved but the chase-loving King may have found unnecessary, an earnest Mignon decided to rein in his expenses as active young prince of the realm: "In time of war, of course, hunting is no more than an amusement for three or four months of the year, so I've decided, for my reputation before the King and the public, to reduce my hunting staff to one overseer, two lancers, two bloodhound keepers, five grooms, and seven dog-keepers."

At the beginning of July 1690, Colonel-Général Mignon wrote excitedly, and touchingly, to Françoise: "I'm thrilled, Madame. I've seen a battle. I'm so happy. I'm perfectly all right . . . I do hope the King will be satisfied with the services of this cripple . . ." Mignon's battle was in fact the famous Battle of Fleury, commanded by the "little womelette" Maréchal de Luxembourg, in which the French suffered 6,000 casualties and the army of the Grand Alliance 20,000—"carried off in wagons and carts." Mignon had gained his wish of a cavalry command, and had led several charges himself. Though his horse was killed beneath him and two of his aides-de-camp died at his side, he himself, "your poor puppet-leg," came through unscathed. "I'm embarrassed by all the congratulations I've been receiving," he wrote modestly. "What will people think of the French, when they praise a man to the skies for simply having done his duty! . . . You ask am I ambitious? I'm desperately ambitious! . . . Here I ask only to sacrifice my-self for the service of the King and the State, but at Versailles, you must be another me, and look after my interests there. Put yourself to work for your dear child . . . I can't wait to embrace you and to see the joy on the King's majestic face!"

Far from having nothing to do, Mignon was now most days in the saddle "from three in the morning until after midday, and I attend to the wounded, and stop the men quarrelling, and I've never done any harm to anyone, even the ones who've deserved it. And when I'm not fighting I go to mass, though it's true I haven't been doing much else in the way of devotions . . . In short, I flatter myself that I'm a decent man, especially for my age . . . I so cherish your affection for me . . . Don't believe those who speak ill of your *mignon* . . ."

In mid-July 1690, Colonel-Général Mignon's wish to see some-thing "blown up" was finally answered when his adored commanding officer, the Maréchal d'Humières, began the bombardment of the an-cient city of Brussels. At Versailles, Louis honoured a military hero of his own: "M. le Grand Prieur has received a diamond sword worth 1,500 pistoles," wrote the marquis de Dangeau, while the King's for-mer mistress, Madame de Soubise, rushed to the army camp, where a lesser hero, her own husband, lay "badly wounded."

England's entry into the Grand Alliance had overpainted Louis's ex-pansionist war in the Palatinate with a new, religious colour. Though the vast bulk of his army was operating aggressively in the east, or de-fensively elsewhere, his meagre support of James in Ireland allowed him to construe the fight now as a moral stand against the heresy of Protestantism. Louis himself understood very well the two separate issues which hung in the balance, but others at his court, including Françoise, persuaded themselves of the simpler alternative, closing their eyes to the fact that Catholic Spain had entered the lists against them. "It's the biggest war any king of France has ever had on his hands," declared the comte de Bussy-Rabutin, with the verve of his slippered seventy years. "The King augmented his infantry by fifty thousand men; he formed seventy militia battalions, and increased his cavalry by sixteen thousand, and his dragoons proportionately," wrote the duc de Saint-Simon, with equal noncombatant enthusiasm.

Françoise's own allegiance to Catholicism, and her personal friendship with Queen Mary, may explain her enthusiasm for the Jacobite cause in England—"No one should be surprised at that; we watched the little Prince of Wales grow up"—but it does not excuse her apparent silence on the ravaging of Liselotte's Palatinate. The savage and unprovoked invasion in the east had predated the half-hearted counter-attack in the west: if Françoise conflated them now into two aspects of the same war, as it seems she did, this suggests naïvety, or a fanaticism, or a wilful blindness, none of which reflect well on her. In fact, the latter is most likely: though her support of James's cause was no doubt sincere, there was nothing that Françoise could have said that might have prevented the Palatinate invasion or tempered its ferocity. "As soon as you permit a woman to speak to you of important matters," wrote Louis in his *Mémoires*, "it's inevitable that she will set you wrong." Throughout 1689 and 1690, Françoise's extant letters contain barely a mention of the war. Unable to justify Louis's actions, and equally unable to restrain them, she retreated into the apparently innocent everyday business of Saint-Cyr.

There is a clear beauty about Saint-Cyr in the autumn. The simple white stone stands dignified and assured with its graceful draping of golden leaves. But as the soft light darkens to a rainy sky or the lowering grey of snow, that assurance takes on a touch of menace, and the simplicity turns bleak.

Françoise was reconsidering her project. The hopeful early days of her grand and ambitious work had run only too swift a course. Within a handful of years, major problems had arisen, puncturing her bright confidence with worrying jabs of doubt.

She had been proven right, at least, in one respect: it had been unwise to build on swampy ground. Many of the girls had fallen ill with malarial fevers; not a few of them had died. The groundwater itself had proved of poor quality for drinking, and the long stone dormitories were damp and cold.

Most of the teachers had turned out to be incompetent, "the stupidest creatures I've ever set eyes on," as Françoise declared. Selected by a too-enthusiastic Madame de Brinon and a much too indulgent Père Gobelin, they had had to undergo instruction themselves before being released into the classrooms. But Françoise's own inconsistency had made things worse than the poorly trained dames could have done on their own. Months of steady and sincere effort on their part, and no doubt also on her own, would be undone in one bitter outburst or cruel change of heart. "There's no other school where young people have such fun," wrote Françoise of Saint-Cyr, "and even if there's a bit too much fun, that causes far fewer problems in the end than too much seriousness." Racine's earnest *Esther* had swiftly made way for the worldly plays of Molière and Madeleine de Scudéry's novels, all of them oozing "love." Some mornings, the girls would be awakened by the King's own musicians playing *en force* beneath the dormitory windows; a dancing monkey was brought over from Versailles to join their minuet and quadrille lessons; arithmetic classes were enlivened by an elephant plodding out the answers to simple sums with its huge, wrinkly feet. The standard whipping punishments of the day had been eschewed, with Françoise declaring, "Our maxim here is to begin with kindness," and by the way admitting, "In fact I prefer . . . the mischievous girls, wilful, temperamental, even a bit stubborn." When the bizarre French of a visiting Polish priest sent the girls into giggling fits during a chapel service, Françoise waved away the idea of any disciplining: "If you're going to punish anyone, you'll have to start with me," she told the girls' chaplain. "I was laughing harder than any of them."

The simple dames, most of them not long out of their own restrained convent schools, did their best to keep up with it all, while the girls quite naturally took advantage of it. But when some of her preferred "naughtier" girls, on kitchen duty as part of their training in household management, were found attempting to poison one of the less popular dames, Françoise turned on them with an alarming savagery. The culprits were hauled out and, far from being whipped, were "sentenced" to execution, for which purpose an actual scaffold was erected in the main courtyard of the school.

There were, of course, no executions, but if Françoise had succeeded in terrorizing the girls into subsequent good behaviour, she had also left them, and their teachers, in a state of real confusion. "We must have amusements for the girls," she would lecture the dames from the head of the main staircase, the usual place for their assemblies. "The theatre is good for them. It brings them a touch of grace, ornaments their memory, fills their heads with lovely things." But a few weeks later, the tone of the lecture would be unrecognizably different: "If they won't sit still in the places you've given them, you'll have to chain them up. I'm going to have chains made, and they'll be chained to the wall, shackled like dogs." "We're going to start treating you like slaves," she hurled at the girls, "like the wretched of the earth, like the galley-slaves on their forced marches." "Leave them in their rags," she spat, turning to the dames. "Leave them in their patched-up shoes, feed them plain food, get them used to all sorts of weariness. They're poor and they'll always be poor."

If any of the untutored dames possessed a grain of native astuteness, she might have heard, beneath the viciousness of these outbursts, the voice of a profound discouragement. Despite apparent omnipotence within the confines of the school and legendary influence at court, Françoise was at the end of her silken tether. The "weariness" to which the girls were to grow accustomed was not theirs, in fact, but hers. With the best will in the world, with careful planning, plenty of money, and endless attention to detail, Saint-Cyr was somehow not working as she had intended. Frustrated and only partly comprehending, she vented her feelings on the only people who could neither restrain nor oppose her. Françoise herself was more wilful and temperamental than any of her "naughty" girls. Always inclined to action, she could work indefatigably when the path to be followed lay clearly before her. But ambivalence disturbed her: when the path was not clear, she became confused, and her behaviour became erratic and aggressive.

"The best laid plans can go awry," observed Madame de La Fayette from the safe distance of her elegant house in Paris. "Now that we're all dévots, Saint-Cyr is supposedly the home of all virtue and piety. But it wouldn't take much to turn it into a place of absolute debauchery. When you think there are three hundred young girls there, up to the age of twenty, and at their very door there's a court full of eager young men . . . With so many of them so close to one another, it's hardly reasonable to think they won't be trying to climb over the walls . . ."

And, indeed, they were. Two of the older "blue" girls had been discovered in the grounds in the arms of their galants, who had quite literally climbed over the walls to meet them. A third had been abducted by a quick-thinking abbé following a performance of *Esther*. Even those who stayed the course through the colourful classroom grades were seldom finding the handsome young noblemen they had been led to expect as husbands. Noblemen, it seemed, whether handsome, young, or otherwise, did not want poor young noble girls for wives; they wanted rich bourgeoises of any description. Despite their guaranteed 3,000-livre dowries, most of Françoise's girls were marrying dreary old men, not even noblemen, but clumsy, ill-bred bourgeois. One of the luckiest of the girls, sixteen-year old Marie-Claire de Marsilly, had been plucked out of her place in *Esther*'s choir of Israelites to marry Françoise's own recently widowed cousin, Philippe, now aged a grandfatherly sixty-three. Philippe was at least a nobleman, with a proud record of naval service and, thanks to his cousin, a good income, but Françoise was embarrassed by the match, Philippe's daughter Marthe-Marguerite was horrified by it, and the feelings of young Marie-Claire can be only too well imagined.

The mismatched marriages and scandals of galanterie in fact lay at the heart of Françoise's deep discouragement. They were symptomatic of what was fundamentally wrong with Saint-Cyr, and of what, fundamentally, could not be changed. "Take care not to make young girls unhappy by teaching them to hope for things above their wealth and rank," Fénelon had warned. It was precisely what Françoise had been doing. Her poor but noble girls, her precious alter egos, were being left—were almost fated to be left—"disappointed by too-great expectations," great expectations that she herself had raised.

For whatever she said, or taught, or threatened, in the eyes of the

girls she herself was the ultimate model of the poor demoiselle raised
to glory. *"Is it true you're the Queen, Madame?* the girls would ask her.
And she wouldn't say no; she would just reply, *Don't mention that.
Who told you that?"* At Saint-Cyr, as in every other place, each blos-
soming sixteen-year-old could believe that she, among all others, was
destined for something special, until a gruff old wool-merchant came
knocking at the door, asking for her hand in marriage.

Madame de Brinon had gone from Saint-Cyr, dismissed by Françoise
following a "conflict of authority," in the words of Manseau, the administrative intendant. Père Gobelin was gone, too, gone from the
world, in fact, despite or because of "a book to divert him, wine to for-
tify him, peaches to refresh him, partridges to nourish him, and mel-
ons to contaminate the air in his room." Though he had remained in
her service for more than thirty years, Françoise had never taken Père
Gobelin very seriously as a spiritual guide, but now that he was gone,
and especially given her prominent position among the dévotes, she
was obliged to choose a new confessor. She approached the dévot
leader Bossuet, who advised her to choose François Fénelon, whose
educational maxims had formed the basis, and predicted the nemesis,
of her own endeavours at Saint-Cyr. But it seems that, after the pliable
Père Gobelin, Françoise was intimidated by Fénelon's hyperintelli-
gence and profound spirituality. Not wanting to engage him, but at the
same time not wishing to be seen to gainsay Bossuet, she shrewdly
asked Fénelon himself to nominate a confessor for her. He suggested
the abbé Paul Godet des Marais, whom Françoise knew from his work
on the Saint-Cyr constitutions.

Insofar as it went, Godet des Marais was irreproachable. A man of
wealthy background, a Sorbonne theologian, aged in his mid-forties,
he had given all his money to various charities, and now lived in
marked austerity, his possessions amounting to no more than one
rough bed, a wicker chair, a desk, a copy of the Bible, a map of Jeru-
salem, and, reassuringly for the less stringently devout, a clavichord,
upon which every evening he would tinkle away the stresses and
strains of his pious day. Godet des Marais was a stern man and rather

limited in his views, as Père Gobelin had been, but unlike him, he was a man of considerable strength of character. Where Gobelin had retreated before the force of Françoise's will or her simple determination to ignore him, Godet des Marais stood his ground, and in so doing he brought a definite change in Françoise's behaviour, and in the life of the girls and the dames at Saint-Cyr.

At first he had been a reluctant accomplice, regarding Françoise's "enterprise" as frivolous and even sinful. What was the purpose of a school for girls, he asked, unless it was a convent? What kind of women were teaching there, if they were not professed nuns? What was all this dangerous nonsense with plays and theatres, and what had it to do with instilling Christian virtues in the minds of future wives and mothers?

Françoise was in a sufficiently self-doubting frame of mind to allow herself to be persuaded. Very quickly, Godet des Marais's straight and narrow path became her own. The early years of the 1690s saw the end of her brief and lovely experiment in a freer, broader, happier education for girls. "We must rebuild our institution on foundations of humility and simplicity," she now declared, with all the determination of the newly converted. "We must renounce our airs of grandeur, and complacency, and pride, and self-importance. We must renounce our pleasure in things lively and refined, renounce our liberty of expression, our worldly joking and gossiping. We must renounce, in fact, most of the things we have been doing." Godet des Marais arranged a series of private interviews with the dames, giving each one the choice of taking the veil as a fully professed nun, with lifelong vows of poverty, chastity, and obedience, or of leaving Saint-Cyr altogether. Most departed, leaving their teaching ranks to be gradually replenished by their former pupils, who, for lack of much alternative, themselves began to take the veil in ever greater numbers. Within the space of barely a year or two, Françoise's Saint-Cyr became just one more rigid, dreary convent school, imbued with all the "miseries and pettiness" she had so wished to avoid.

Françoise's renunciations of pleasure on the girls' behalf were in fact only a reflection of her own attempt to lead, in Christian terms, a better life—certainly publicly, but also, though less successfully, in private. Though widely praised for her charity and her piety, she knew that, as to the latter at least, she was making no real progress. Her entry into the world of the dévots, more than a decade before, had been at least partly fraudulent: it had been a way of making herself necessary to the King. And though her belief was genuine, as was her desire to save her soul, when she turned her face towards God, she felt within her no real spirituality. Consequently, when she turned her face to the world, clad in her dévote robes, she felt that she lacked integrity. She felt, in a word, hypocritical.

> I take communion only out of obedience . . . I experience no
> union with God . . . Prayers bore me . . . I don't want to submit
> to the constraint of any pious exercises . . . I meditate poorly.
> Frankly, I see no reason at all to hope for salvation.

So she wrote to Père Godet des Marais, telling him the quintessential truth in utterly straightforward terms. And Père Godet des Marais, despite his forty-five years and his Sorbonne theology, failed to understand her. "Your hope of salvation is founded on the mercy of O.L.J.C.," he replied. "Saint Gregory says that the normal conduct of God towards the just is to leave them with some slight imperfections . . . so that they won't become too proud. If you really weren't conversing with God, you'd enjoy conversing with people on earth more than you do. There's nothing wrong with taking communion out of obedience."

And his letters continued with precisely the petty, restraining, pious exercises which Françoise, unconvinced by the moral economy underlying them, had always found so pointless. "I was informed yesterday evening, Madame, that you were suffering a good deal from the toothache: God be praised! He afflicts those whom He loves. Pain is His gift to His cherished children, and I rejoice to see you numbered among them."

"Sins just seem to get worse when you talk about them," sighed Françoise. And at that point she might have resigned herself to a surface piety, with no real "union with God," had it not been for the increasing presence of François Fénelon, at court, at Saint-Cyr, and in her own personal life.

Like Françoise, Fénelon came from a minor noble family fallen on hard times—"He was a man of quality who had nothing." The Church had given him his livelihood, though not, it seems, quite enough of a livelihood to satisfy him. Françoise had first met Fénelon at the house of the duc and duchesse de Beauvillier, where she dined two or three times every week. He was then in his late thirties, a thoughtful, even visionary man, concealing a passionate spirituality and a keen earthly ambition beneath an exterior of perfect, polished amiability, with a marked desire to please all who met him, high-born and low. He had a sound practical intelligence, too, and, as he had revealed in his *Treatise* for the guidance of the Beauvilliers' eight daughters, a first-class instinct for the education of the young. In short, despite a difference in age of sixteen years, he was a perfect soul mate for Françoise. The duc de Saint-Simon, in many respects antagonistic towards Fénelon, nonetheless described him in the following, greatly admiring terms:

> He was a tall, lean man, well made, with a pale complexion and a large nose, and eyes full of passion and intelligence. I've never seen anything to match his expression; and once you had seen it, you could never forget it . . . It was grave and yet elegant, serious but lively. You saw at once the scholar, the bishop and the grand seigneur, but more than anything, in his face and in his whole appearance, you saw refinement, intelligence, benevolence, discretion, and above all, nobility. You had to make an effort to stop looking at him.

In 1689, the dévot duc de Beauvillier, already well placed at court and keenly promoted by both Françoise and Bossuet, had been appointed governor of the dauphin's three sons, the little ducs de Bourgogne, Anjou, and Berry, aged seven, six, and three years old respectively. Beauvillier had at once invited Fénelon to become tutor to the eldest boy. It was a vital post, since, after his father, Bourgogne was second in line to the throne: Fénelon would be educating the future King of

France. He swiftly accepted, leaving the duchesse de Beauvillier to manage her own eight girls with the help of his now published *Treatise*.

Though not daring to make him her own confessor, Françoise had gradually fallen under the spell of the brilliant and insinuating Fénelon, and he, eager to advance his own interests at court, had by no means discouraged her. At the height of her worries about her demoiselles and dames, he had written to her, revealing what the duc de Saint-Simon called his "coquettish" manner with those who wielded influence:

> I am sorry I didn't know, before saying mass, that your name is *Françoise* . . . I've heard that you are unhappy about the way things are going at Saint-Cyr. God loves you and wants you to make Him loved. For that you need the holy intoxication of Saint François, which surpasses the wisdom of all the learned. When will the love of God be known and felt instead of this servile fear which disfigures religion?

"Saint François" was the recently canonized Bishop of Geneva, François de Sales, whose practical teachings had once guided the struggling Jeanne d'Aubigné through the many difficulties of her own life. Rejecting the fear of eternal damnation, François de Sales had embraced instead the idea of "God as love," and from this had developed a humanistic doctrine of salvation for everyday Catholics who neither claimed nor sought any special piety. Saint Francois's state of "holy intoxication"—spiritual ecstasy, perhaps, or even simply a pervasive feeling of peace and acceptance—was profoundly appealing to Françoise in her current spiritual state, paradoxically both tepid and overstrung. It was deeply reassuring to hear, after the harassing and thundering of Bossuet and his ilk, that ordinary people, without great learning or great piety, could arrive so readily at this blessed place.

Fénelon's understanding of the profound new message, and his eagerness to speak of it with her, contrasted keenly with Louis's matter-of-fact acceptance of the Church's stock teachings: "No one needs to know anything about these theological things," he had declared in his *Mémoires*. ". . . They're more to do with opinionated people getting carried away . . . and they're always connected with people's interests in the world . . ." An uncomplicated soul himself, Louis had no sense of the psychological yearnings which had produced such passionate new "theological things," and which made them so widely attractive; deeply self-satisfied, he could not empathize with those, like Françoise, who needed to achieve a measure of spiritual integrity in order to live at ease with themselves. Louis believed in God, and was afraid of hell, and was confident that he had stopped sinning in good time to cleanse his soul before he died—so much his marriage, and his faithfulness within it, had ensured. But in spiritual or psychological terms, he could venture no further, and because of this, his marriage with Françoise, though stable and useful on both sides, remained fatally limited. In the gap between them Fénelon had now presented himself, hinting at a closer marriage of minds than Françoise's own husband had been able to offer.

Though Saint François de Sales's teaching had received the formal imprimatur of acceptance in Rome, it had proved all too easy to dilute and misinterpret into spiritual laziness, neglect of conventional religious practice, and even straightforward sin. The leader of the derivative "quietist" movement, the Spanish priest Miguel de Molinos, was now languishing in a Roman prison, awaiting trial for alleged sins of the flesh, but in France the message was being spread anew by a forty-year-old widow from Orléans, mystic, preacher, and writer of theologically inflammatory tomes, Jeanne-Marie Bouvier de la Motte Guyon. The abbé de Choisy, himself a practising priest and, despite his penchant for women's clothing, a solidly orthodox theologian, described the basis of Madame Guyon's teaching as follows:

One gives oneself to God with all one's heart, without any formal ceremony, abandoning oneself entirely to the movements of the divine spirit, and then one is in a state of holy repose. While the soul is in this state, it pays no heed to what occurs in the imagination, or even what happens to the body . . . In the hearts of libertines, an idea like this can give rise to any number of scandalous disorders . . .

Madame Guyon had just been released from an obligatory eighteen-month sojourn in a Paris convent. But despite her doubtful reputation, her passionate spirituality had captured the hearts of Françoise's circle of dévot friends, notably the Beauvillier and Chevreuse families. Through them, it had reached Fénelon and then, rather too quickly, Françoise herself. Unconcerned with its evident byway to libertinage, she chose to understand it in terms of what she needed: salvation was possible after all without effort on her own part; the fate of her soul could be left in the hands of a loving God; she could stop fretting about the insincerity of her prayers and the moral value of toothache, and let herself relax at last in a state of "holy repose."

Listening to talk about Madame Guyon's controversial books— *The Short and Very Easy Road to Prayer* and *The Torrents of Pure Love*—but without troubling to read them, and ignoring a papal condemnation of the "blessed lady" herself, Françoise introduced her to Saint-Cyr, where her appealing ideas swiftly began to run riot, first among the novice nuns and then among the girls themselves. Within weeks, the older "green" and "blue" girls were to be found not in their classrooms or at their tasks, but "hiding in the attics with copies of *The Torrents*, sighing over each mention of *abandon* and *naked offerings*."

For a time, Françoise simply left it all running out of control, caught up in her own confusion of spiritual with earthly love. If she had not exactly fallen in love with the "coquettish" priest whom "you had to make an effort to stop looking at," she had at least fallen in love with the idea of him, and with his seductive spirituality, drawn from Madame Guyon, with its all-embracing, all-assuring divine love. In Fénelon, it seemed, she had finally found her platonic "other half," a perfect match, perfectly responsive to her. In 1690, without informing Père Godet des Marais, a cautious investigator of the "pure love" doctrine, Françoise rather boldly asked Fénelon for an analysis of her own spiritual character, in the manner of a confessor. If she had expected an indulgent, even flattering response in the usual way of Godet des Marais or, formerly, Père Gobelin, she was startled by Fénelon's lengthy reply. "I am hesitant to speak of your defects, Madame," he began, and then continued:

I'll tell you what I think, and you can make use of it as God wills. You are unaffected and natural, which means that you often do good, without having to think about it, to those whom you like and admire. But to those whom you don't like, you are cold and harsh, and that harshness can run to extremes . . . No one is allowed to have any faults at all . . . When you're hurt, you're deeply hurt.

You were born with far too much pride, by which I mean the need for respect . . . This is harder to correct than the simplest stupid vanity. You don't realize how deeply you still need to be respected . . . You like people to think that you deserve a higher place than you have.

You have not yet broken this idol, *myself*. You want to reach God, but not at the expense of *myself*; on the contrary, you seek *myself* in God . . . I hope that God will grant you the light to understand this better than I have been able to explain it . . .

. . . You need to make a long and careful examination of yourself . . . But you need not think you're a hypocrite. Hypocritical people never think they're hypocrites . . . Your piety is genuine. You have never had any of the world's real vices, and its lesser errors you gave up long ago . . .

Regarding affairs of state, you are far more capable than you think . . . but I think what you really want is a life of easy retirement . . .

You love your family as you should, without being blind to their defects . . . but you are far too attached to your friends. If you could really die to *myself*, you wouldn't care whether they were fond of you or not, any more than they were of the Emperor of China . . .

You use up all your strength on the exterior things of piety . . . If you want to correct your defects, you need to concentrate on the inner things . . .

In short, despite the supposedly easy doctrine of "pure love," Françoise appeared to have quite a way to go on the road to salvation.

Fénelon's perceptive portrait had struck directly home, and she was not at all pleased to read it. Madame Guyon, by contrast, seemed to be more or less a saint in his view, or at least a person of exceptional spirituality. Fénelon even regarded himself, in a sense, as her disciple. His letter had made things perfectly clear. Quite obviously, he thought more highly of Madame Guyon than he did of Françoise herself.

It was more than she was prepared to endure. Confirming Fénelon's view—"when you're hurt, you're deeply hurt . . . [and your] harshness can run to extremes"—Françoise decided that Madame Guyon would have to go, though Fénelon, somehow, must stay. The idea of "pure love" was to be cast out, yet its most seductive exponent must be retained. Thenceforth, Madame Guyon's too-saintly person was never again seen at Saint-Cyr, though Fénelon, concerned to maintain his connection with Françoise, continued to turn up almost every day. *The Short and Very Easy Road to Prayer* and *The Torrents of Pure Love* were banned from the premises, with Père Godet des Marais ferreting out every last copy, including an unexpected few hidden by the littlest "red" girls, all of them under twelve years of age. There was resistance, not only from the girls, but quite strongly from the dames as well, and for two years and more it persisted, with ambivalent support from Fénelon, until the last of Madame Guyon's acolytes had accepted the retraditionalized regime, and agreed to take the veil.

And there Françoise might have stopped. Madame Guyon was out; Fénelon was still in; the dames and demoiselles were under control again; Père Godet des Marais had formally declared Françoise superior for life at Saint-Cyr, and she had rewarded him with the bishopric of Chartres. Vitally, the whole muddled episode had been kept from the notice of the King, who, though without any interest in theological issues per se, instinctively opposed the unorthodox as tending towards indiscipline in the Church and a dangerous fractiousness in the body politic.

But Françoise could not stop there. Fénelon's clear admiration for Jeanne Guyon had been a challenge to her sense of herself as a spiritually superior person—admittedly with difficulties in the surface matters of daily devotion, but in essence one of creation's finer souls. Yet now, despite Françoise's complete rejection of Madame Guyon, despite the lady's personal eviction from Saint-Cyr and the abolition of her teachings on "pure love," Fénelon had refused to turn his back on the "blessed lady." Overlooking every question of theology, Françoise regarded this refusal as a simple choice of Jeanne Guyon over herself. The loss of the doctrine of "pure love," with its reassuringly easy path to salvation, may have been disappointing, but the prospect of losing Fénelon himself was more than she could countenance: his respect—and perhaps more than his respect—was absolutely necessary to her; additionally, and immaturely, it had to be exclusive. It was not a matter of agreement or disagreement: it was a matter of agreement or betrayal. Fénelon must renounce Madame Guyon, and all her works, and all her displays.

To this end, towards the end of 1693, Françoise arranged that Madame Guyon's writings be submitted to Bossuet for formal assessment. It seems that Fénelon himself may even have been behind this move, wishing to see the "blessed lady" confirmed as a light of the Church, while Françoise naturally wished to see her ideas condemned and Fénelon consequently obliged to renounce her; there was also the suggestion, reported by Bossuet's secretary, that "Madame de Maintenon wanted to clear Fénelon's name" from all association with the suspect new doctrine. Surprisingly, Bossuet, "the eagle of Meaux," with his famed, mighty theological intellect, was a complete ignoramus as far the Church's mystic tradition was concerned: it appeared that he had never read a word of Saint François de Sales or even of the great mystic theologian, Saint John of the Cross. Madame Guyon's ideas were in consequence quite new to him; he found them interesting, and thought the lady herself genuinely enlightened, observing at the same time that, as a member of "the weaker sex," she had stepped out of her place by seeking to "develop doctrine and teach." He suggested that the doctrine of "pure love" be examined formally by a circle of Churchmen, but for such an examination, the approval of the King would be required.

The examination began early in 1694, and continued until the end of the year. Madame Guyon's teachings were condemned, but the lady herself was exonerated of any heretical intention: she took herself off, apparently, to the spa at Bourbon. Outwardly at least, Fénelon submitted to the verdict with a good grace, and Françoise congratulated herself that the affair had been moved conclusively away from Saint-Cyr, with the King still unaware of the unorthodoxies formerly encouraged at her own personal domain.

During the course of the year, however, Louis had learned of a political tract critical of his rule, supposedly penned by Fénelon, his courage perhaps boosted by his recent election to the Académie Française. Written in the form of a personal letter to the King, it berated Louis harshly for neglecting his suffering and starving people in a continuing pursuance of martial glory against King William and his Grand Alliance. "Your Majesty's ministers have made your name hated," the letter declaimed. "This *gloire* . . . is dearer to you than justice . . . You do not love God," it concluded. "Your fear of Him is only that of a slave; it is Hell and not God that you fear. Your religion consists only of superstitions, in superficial little practices . . . You are scrupulous in small details, and hardened to horrible evils."

It is most unlikely that Louis actually saw this letter, at least at this time, since Fénelon continued in his post as tutor to the duc de Bourgogne, and even began to take the same role for the duc's younger brothers as well. And a few months afterwards, at Françoise's prompting, the King appointed him Archbishop of Cambrai, the wealthiest archdiocese in France. From Françoise's point of view, the archbishopric may have been a token of her continuing respect for Fénelon, or a bribe to keep him quiet about the "pure love" affair at Saint-Cyr, or even a means of keeping him safely out of the way for a time: the new appointment would require his absence from court for up to nine months of the year. In any event, she herself was evidently still in high favour with the King, benefiting from handsome new apartments at the château of Marly, Louis's favourite place of retreat. All seemed to be well.

A few weeks after Fénelon's consecration, which had taken place in the chapel at Saint-Cyr, the King recorded the death of the dissolute old Archbishop of Paris, Harlay de Champvallon, who had presided at his marriage to Françoise. The Archbishop, aged seventy-two, had apparently died of an apoplectic fit in the arms of his mistress, leaving most of the courtiers sniggering, and a pious few concerned about the possible content of his funeral eulogy. "The archbishop of Paris," began Spanheim, who, however, was not obliged to make his views quite public, "had all the advantages one could draw from a fortunate birth, an attractive exterior person, qualities of mind, a reputation for eloquence and learning, the dignity of his position, and not least, the favour and good graces of his king . . . One recalls, however, various circumstances concerning scandalous commerce . . . with the abbesses of Pontoise and d'Andely, and . . . a certain *présidente* of Bretonvilliers and other mistresses . . . in his charming house near Paris . . ."

The ambivalently pious Harlay de Champvallon was almost replaced as archbishop of Paris by the unassailable Bossuet, but Françoise managed to persuade the King to appoint a potential ally of her own instead. This was Monseigneur Louis-Antoine de Noailles, a man of illustrious family and modest ambition, having already declined the same archbishopric no fewer than three times already. But Louis, respecting Françoise's piety, accepted her suggestion.

It had not been Françoise's piety at all that had inspired her, however, on this occasion. She had really had to press Noailles, a provincial bishop known above all for his generosity to the poor, to accept the lordly appointment in Paris, insisting to him that the Jesuits were "declaring war on us on all sides." "What better cause could there be," she wrote, "than the King's salvation? Yes, you would have to endure the evils that others have created in the past, but think of how you could change things in the future! Monsieur," she urged, "you are young [he was forty-four], you are in good health. How can you prefer repose to work, when Providence has given us this opportunity without our even seeking it? But be careful to keep this letter secret . . ."

The Jesuits were not in fact declaring war on Noailles "on all sides," though they might have been had they known of his discreet Jansenist sympathies. But Harlay de Champvallon had been an ally of the King's Jesuit confessor, Père de la Chaise, and both had been not only staunch opponents of Fénelon, but also staunch opponents of any influence Françoise herself might claim over the King—including the indirect influence of a public declaration of the royal marriage itself. The "evils" which "others" had created may have been no more than the "superstitions [and] superficial little practices" of which Fénelon had accused the King in his unsent letter, and which the orthodox Père de la Chaise allowed to pass unchallenged, though Françoise may also have been referring to the King's continuing warmongering, which none of his chosen prelates had attempted to discourage, and which Bossuet, at least, considered vital for the nation's continuing earthly glory.

But above all, Françoise wanted to prove to herself, and no doubt to Fénelon as well, that at least in some sense she had kept the faith. The new Archbishop was the son of an old friend from the Marais, and, crucially, had himself been close to Fénelon since their student days together at the Sorbonne. Scion of an ancient noble family, he was a man of sincere and practical piety, though far from equal to his friend in intellectual terms. The King, who had never met Noailles, had appointed him purely on Françoise's recommendation. He had been a model pastor as bishop of Châlons, and Louis had concluded, trustingly, that he would very likely be the same as archbishop of Paris. With the adventure of "pure love" at Saint-Cyr an apparently certain secret, and now with the capture of Noailles, Françoise felt doubly, and prematurely, secure. But four months later, towards the end of 1695, she was jolted out of her composure by the sudden reappearance of Jeanne Guyon herself: far from taking the healthful waters at the Bourbon spa, since her trial in July she had been all the time in Paris, in hiding.

Madame Guyon was promptly arrested and escorted to the fortress of Vincennes for interrogation by the chief of police, Nicolas de La Reynie, happy to flex his investigatory muscles once again after the long period of relative calm which had followed the end of the Poisons Affair. The King, though not much interested in Madame Guyon, asked Père de la Chaise nonetheless to explain the matter to him. Père de la Chaise proceeded to explain not only Madame Guyon's personal form of "quietism," but also its popularity among certain prominent people at court, and its links—invented for the occasion—to certain political views which might be construed as seditious. Fénelon, as His Majesty knew, was a keen supporter of Madame Guyon, and an outspoken critic of certain of His Majesty's policies, including the forced conversion of Huguenots and the recent elevation of His Majesty's two legitimized sons, the ducs du Maine and Toulouse, to the status of princes of the blood. The ducs de Beauvillier and Chevreuse were also followers of Madame Guyon. Both held prominent posts; both had opposed the King's destruction of the Palatinate; both, though Père de la Chaise did not mention this, were his own enemies, seeking to create a more pious court, with a King less bent on warfare. And both, along with their wives, were members of Françoise's closest circle, and if the confessor did not mention this, it was because he did not need to.

Louis did not panic, and for the moment took no action: Beauvillier and Chevreuse were among his most trusted advisors, and his wife, undeclared or otherwise, was surely above suspicion. But he had been alerted. Jeanne Guyon, whom La Reynie had judged to pose no immediate threat to the state, was transferred from Vincennes to the less forbidding Bastille, while Bossuet and Fénelon, like two dogs fighting over a bone, refused to let the theological matter lie. "I would rather die than present so scandalous a scene to the public as to contradict Monsieur Bossuet," the latter insisted to Françoise, before proceeding to do exactly that, by publishing his opinions—"and to very bad effect," as she subsequently observed to Noailles. Bossuet, outraged by the impertinence of his brilliant former pupil, responded, unattractively, by publishing a series of personal and supposedly confidential notes which Fénelon had written him.

"The quietism affair is making more of a noise than I thought it would," Françoise recorded in the autumn of 1696. "A lot of people at court are quite alarmed about it." She herself, naturally, was among them, and her best protection lay, she felt, in persuading Fénelon to retract his support for Madame Guyon once and for all. But whether through principle or pride or longer-term ambition, he proved immoveable, as Françoise relayed to Noailles after Fénelon's parting visit in October 1696. "I have seen our friend," she wrote. "We had quite an argument, but very calmly. I wish I were so faithful and so attached to my duties as he is to his friend. He won't let go of her, and nothing will change his mind." Fénelon himself apparently felt there was nothing to be lost by nailing his colours to both masts: intransigent in his loyalty to Madame Guyon, or to her ideas, he nonetheless did his best to retain Françoise's support in a series of plaintive letters: "Why do you close your heart to us?" he wrote to her. "God knows how much I suffer in causing suffering to the person in the world for whom I have the most constant and sincere respect and attachment."

He continued to do so, all the same. In mid-1696, Bossuet had thrown down a final gauntlet in his new, as yet unpublished *Instructions on the States of Prayer*, to which, as he declared publicly, Fénelon would append his own signature of agreement. Fénelon picked up the gauntlet and sent it back to Bossuet unexamined. In January 1697 he thrust a gauntlet of his own at Bossuet's feet: a newly written, very Guyoniste, very quietist document entitled *An Explanation of the Maxims of the Saints on the Interior Life*—the "explanation" a little extra knock on Bossuet's large yet evidently uncomprehending theological head. In March, Bossuet published his *Instructions*, taking malicious care to present it to the King along with Fénelon's *Explanation* and, no doubt, an explanation of his own as to why he was right and Fénelon wrong.

For Louis, it was enough to know that Fénelon had been propounding unorthodox ideas. "If he's right," said one of Bossuet's shocked prelate friends, "we'll have to burn the whole of the New Testament and declare that Jesus Christ came into the world for the sole purpose of leading us astray." Even more importantly, as far as the King was concerned, was the threat posed by unorthodox religion to the state: like Jansenism, like Huguenotism, quietism was an encouragement to sedition. Fénelon was tutor to the King's own grandsons, among them the future King of France. And he was an archbishop. And he had been working closely at Saint-Cyr with—Madame de Maintenon.

"The King is watching me with suspicion," wrote a frightened Françoise to Noailles. "It isn't my fault, though I know I'll be blamed, all the same. The King hates anything unorthodox. I think God must want to humble Fénelon—he has gone too far along his own path . . . I was completely wrong in thinking he wouldn't write anything reprehensible," she continued, not quite convincingly. ". . . You can be certain that this affair is not going away, not in Rome, not in France, and not in the King's heart, and speaking of the King, he is concerned about the effect on the young princes. I am distressed and embarrassed about it, for the Church's sake, for your sake, for my own sake. I'm afraid of what might happen if these two great luminaries draw things out to the bitter end. I'm afraid of what the King will do, and how he will answer for it to God."

. In April 1697 Fénelon was instructed to submit his *Explanation* to Rome. "If he is condemned," Françoise wrote to Noailles, "it will be a stigmatization that he won't recover from easily, but if he isn't, he'll be a considerable protector for quietism." In mid-June, Fénelon was summoned to the King. "I have conducted an interview with the finest and most fantastical mind in my kingdom," Louis recorded. Evidently concluding that Fénelon, though quixotic, was essentially harmless, he sent him off to his archbishopric in Cambrai in northwestern France, without, however, removing him from the post of tutor to the young ducs. From Cambrai, Fénelon continued to write and publish further Guyoniste tomes, despite an official condemnation of his *Explanation*: though the examining prelates had in fact rather liked it, the Pope himself, attempting to curry favour with Louis, had insisted that it be condemned. "In France, anyway, no one cares what anyone thinks," Liselotte observed to her earnest Lutheran relatives. "Provided you don't publish anything, and you go to mass regularly and make your normal devotions, and you don't align yourself with any political group, you can think what you like, no one cares."

At Versailles, the victorious and unstoppable Bossuet carried on with his execrations of quietism, and Louis, shaken by the continuing denunciations, began to think again about its political ramifications. "The King is getting angry all over again about what we allowed Fénelon to do," wrote Françoise to Noailles. "He reproaches me greatly for it all . . . I've never seen him so stern, so defiant, so impenetrable. If I loved him less, I think he would have sent me away long ago. I've never been so close to disgrace," she continued, with the unsettling implication that it was her own devotion to Louis, and not his love for her, that had so far kept her safe.

"The old hag isn't the happiest woman in the world," noted Liselotte. "She cries all the time and talks about dying. But I think it's all just to see what people will say about it." It was not. Françoise was indeed very close to disgrace. Following the publication of yet another weighty tome of Bossuet's, Louis had actually mentioned that he might make her a duchesse, as he had made Louise de la Vallière, in her frigid convent, and Angélique de Fontanges, in her grave. Her flirtation with an improbably easy road to salvation, and her personal infatuation with Fénelon, had perversely metamorphosed into a seditious attempt to undermine the stability of the realm—not that Louis thought her guilty of anything so grave, but his confidence in her good sense, in her reliability, and in her honesty with him had been badly shaken. Throughout the summer of 1698, days on end would pass without his addressing a single word to her. She took to sleeping overnight at Saint-Cyr; when at Versailles, she would hide herself away, until the courtiers began to whisper that Madame de Maintenon was dying of cancer. "Pray for me," she wrote to Noailles, "but not for my health—for what I really need." Françoise's tears were genuine, and her talk of death, at the age of sixty-two, an ashamed and fearful wish for escape.

With Fénelon banished and Bossuet still ranting, it was steady, unspectacular Père Godet des Marais who thought of her now. Early in the autumn of 1698 he took it upon himself to write to the King, reminding him of Françoise's "tenderness and loyalty" towards him, and of her constant concern for his reputation among "all the self-serving and hypocritical" crowds at court. The letter did its work. Françoise may have been naïve and foolish; she may have involved herself with undesirable people—perhaps even, as Père de la Chaise had insinuated, with ambitious people who sought to manipulate her for their own ends—but Louis knew her too well to doubt that she had ever wished him anything but well.

"So, Madame," he said to her many sad evenings later, "are we going to see you die over this affair?" He had forgiven her, and just possibly, he had called himself to account as well, for maintaining her in an impossible position as his wife and yet not his queen. With formal status, acknowledged as his royal consort, with public duties of her own and unquestioned precedence at court, she might have had no need to cast about for influence, involving herself behind his back with dubious people and potentially dangerous ideas. But he had kept his proud and capable wife on a golden leash, and after fifteen years of humiliating duplicity, "Her Steadiness" had stumbled at last.

The duc de Bourgogne was sixteen years old, and in his honour Louis had commanded a vast series of military exercises at the camp of Compiègne, to the north of Paris. It took place in the middle of September 1698, a few days after the King's reconciliation with Françoise, and the two drove up, in separate carriages, to join the 60,000 soldiers and hundreds of courtiers and foreign diplomats assembled to pay homage to the young heir-but-one to the Bourbon throne. "There were so many men," wrote the duc de Saint-Simon, "that for the first time at Compiègne, the ducs had to share rooms." There was a great to-do among the ambassadors, since not all had been accorded the vital word "for" on the doors of their rooms. "No one knows how this *for* distinction came about," continued Saint-Simon, "and really it's idiotic. It just means that you have *for So-and-so* chalked on the door of your room, instead of just *So-and-so*. Princes of the blood, cardinals, and foreign princes all get a *for*, and some ducs and duchesses have got them, but it doesn't mean your room will be any better than anyone else's, and that's why I think it's idiotic . . ." concluded the duc, himself notoriously niggly about protocol, and incidentally *for*-less. The magnificence of the military exercises themselves knew no bounds, as he went on to explain:

> The King wanted to display all the images of war, so there was a siege, with lines, trenches, artillery, bridgeworks and so on . . . and an assault on an old rampart . . . and then on the plain beyond that were all the troops in formation . . . It was the most

marvellous thing to see, this game of attack and defence, and since it wasn't serious, no one had to worry about anything except the precision of all the movements.

But there was a spectacle of quite another sort which the King showed to everyone, to all his army and all this vast crowd of people from every country, and I'll be able to depict that spectacle in forty years' time as well as I can today, it struck me so forcibly. Madame de Maintenon was seated, facing the plain, in a litter chair with three window-panes . . . The King was standing to the right of her chair, and every second moment he would bend down to explain to Madame de Maintenon what was going on in the exercises. Each time, she would lower her window four or five fingerlengths . . . The King spoke to no one but her, other than to give out orders . . . Everyone was astonished and embarrassed and pretending not to notice, but they were watching this more attentively than anything the army was doing . . . The King put his hat on top of Madame de Maintenon's litter chair . . .

When Madame de Maintenon left, the King left less than a quarter of an hour later . . . Everyone was saying they could hardly believe what they'd seen, and even the soldiers who'd been on the plain were asking who it was that the King had kept leaning down to speak to . . . You can imagine the effect it made on the foreigners there. Soon they were talking about it all over Europe . . .

In terms of the baroque protocol of Louis's court, the fact that the King had spoken to no one but Françoise throughout the entire display—and above all, his "bending down" repeatedly to do so—could indicate only one thing: she was, de facto if not de jure, the Queen. There would be no announcement, no formal recognition, as was to be confirmed once and for all at a meeting of the High Council in October 1698, but the matter, from now on, could be regarded as an open secret. "They won't say whether she's the Queen or not," wrote Liselotte grumpily, "but she gets a queen's privileges, anyway."

Françoise, pulled back from the brink of disgrace, found her position paradoxically stronger than ever before. Louis had evidently been giving some thought to her previous exclusion from public affairs. It had caused mischief and might have proved genuinely dangerous, but her loyalty to him could not be in doubt, and there may even have been a trace of sympathy in his voice as he bent down to speak to her through the "four or five fingerlengths" of her window.

Whatever the case, from this point, at the King's invitation, Françoise was present at every meeting of his High Council. If formally she was to remain outside the royal circle, in practice her influence from now on was only to grow. Louis, now over sixty, wanted support and reassurance beyond the self-interested politicking inevitable at court among great and small. Increasingly, he came to rely on Françoise for advice—always presented with an exceeding, and very tactical, discretion. Once again, her protégés prospered: it was Françoise who chose the billiard-loving parlementary counsellor, Michel Chamillart, for the great Colbert's post of Comptroller-General of the nation's finances, and in the same year of 1699, she achieved for Archbishop de Noailles the coveted little red circle of a cardinal's hat.

In the autumn of 1697, with the signing of a series of treaties in the Dutch town of Rijswijk, Louis's war against William's Grand Alliance had at last come to an end. After nine years of fighting, no one had gained much. Hard-won territories were handed back; old and new regimes were grudgingly recognized. A time of peace had begun in Europe, but a wary, shaky peace, threatened by dislike and distrust and unsatisfied ambitions. Louis had been largely to blame with his Rhineland attack of 1688, and if he accepted peace for the moment, he had already begun to think of his next expansionist campaign.

There had been other endings and beginnings, too, during the years of the 1690s. After almost a decade of neglect and humiliation, Athénaïs had finally agreed to leave Versailles, on condition that it could be made to look as though she had done so voluntarily. No other lover had enlivened the days of her long decline at court. A healthy measure of vanity, and perhaps a residue of genuine love, had prevented her from seeking solace with any other man; indeed, had she done so, abandoning the game of protecting Françoise's reputation, Louis would almost certainly have dismissed her at once.

Athénaïs left Versailles with a pension of 240,000 livres per year in her pocket. The duc du Maine, ungallantly keen to take over his mother's apartment, began throwing her furniture out of the windows before she had even driven away—to begin sixteen years of penitence, apparently sincere, at the convent of Saint Joseph in Paris.

After years of ill health and unhappiness, the dauphine was dead. She had exceeded her dynastic duty in providing the dauphin with three healthy sons, and having spent most of her life at court in the seclusion of her sickroom, she was hardly missed at all.

The savage little Maréchal de Luxembourg had died at sixty-seven, having been living "the life of a twenty-five-year-old." His confrère in brutality, the marquis de Louvois, Minister of War, had also died, aged just fifty, from poisoning, it was rumoured, or suffocation, though no one really cared. An autopsy revealed that his lungs were full of blood, and his heart empty of it. Louvois's death prompted a nasty outburst from Liselotte, and not because of his destruction of her Palatinate homeland: "As far as I'm concerned," she declared, "I'd rather have seen a certain old turd finished off instead of him; she'll be more powerful than ever now."

Françoise's nephew, Henri-Benjamin de Villette, was dead, killed in battle at the age of twenty-four. And her old friend, lanky, loyal Madame de Montchevreuil was dead as well. "I know better than anyone how distressed you will be by her loss," wrote Mignon, who had himself been quite fond of the fussy and pious but good-hearted marquise. "Console yourself by reflecting on the virtue of our late friend: though death grieves the unbelieving, it must console good Christians: the death of a saint is precious to God . . . I beg you not to allow your grief to undermine your health." "Madame de Maintenon was dreadfully upset by the death of Madame de Montchevreuil," noted the duc de Saint-Simon, "and lots of other people pretended to be, too."

And lovely Madame de Sévigné was dead, at a perfectly elegant three score years and ten, despite the earlier plea of her adoring cousin, the comte de Bussy-Rabutin: "You are one of those people who should never die," he had written. "Madame de Sévigné [was] so amiable and such excellent company," wrote the duc de Saint-Simon with unusual generosity, before reverting to nasty form: "She died at Grignan at the house of her daughter, whom she idolized, and who didn't really deserve it."

There had been one major false alarm. Pseudo-news of King William's death had roused the people of Paris in the middle of the night, with officials shouting instructions to them to start celebratory bonfires, and wine being distributed freely to encourage dancing and singing outdoors. Discovered to be still alive, William was simultaneously discovered, at least by Liselotte, to be homosexual. "He changes favourites all the time," she wrote to her half-sister. "They say he's got another one now. It's not surprising that the Queen his wife had no rivals while she was alive. Men with that sort of taste make fools of plenty of women. I've learned so much about that in France, I could write books on it . . . "

Following his wife's death, the dauphin Louis had married his mistress, and like his father, morganatically. The new secret royal bride was Marie-Émilie de Choin, maid of honour to, and stealer of lovers from, the princesse de Conti. She was "a fat girl, squat, a brunette, ugly, with a flat nose," at least according to the duc de Saint-Simon. He allowed her to be intelligent, before condemning her directly afterwards for her "intriguing and manipulating mind." Even Françoise's niece, Marthe-Marguerite, described *La Choin* as a girl "of remarkable ugliness." But she was a keen hunter and evidently possessed a good appetite, two traits which were probably enough in themselves to endear her to the dauphin, blundering in from his wolf-hunting only to faint from over-indulgence at his supper.

Françoise's niece, Charles's fourteen-year-old daughter, Françoise-Charlotte-Amable, had made a brilliant match with the illustrious young duc de Noailles, nephew of the Archbishop, with the King himself providing a dowry of 800,000 livres for her. Mignon was married, too, to his first cousin once removed, the high-spirited granddaughter of le Grand Condé, already showing signs of her family's notoriously troublemaking blood.

The young duc de Bourgogne, Louis's grandson and heir, had married his own exquisitely charming cousin, eleven-year-old princesse Marie-Adélaïde of Savoy. Louis was immediately besotted by this granddaughter of his own illicit early love—his brother's first wife, the famously beautiful English princess Henrietta Stuart. Little Marie-Adélaïde was given into Françoise's care until the marriage could be consummated, after she turned fourteen, to Françoise's own overflowing delight: "She is perfect in every way," she rhapsodized to the girl's parents. "Madame [Liselotte] will tell you all of this, but I can't resist saying it myself. She's a prodigy. She'll be the glory of the age." Madame, however, had had other things to say about Marie-Adélaïde: "She hardly took any notice of her grandfather or me," she noted sulkily, "but she was all smiles for Madame de Maintenon . . . She's a real little Italian, as politically astute as a thirty-year-old. Her mouth and chin are Austrian, though"—a reference to the famously jutting Habsburg jaw.

Liselotte's bitterest complaint, all the same, had been for her own son, Philippe, duc de Chartres, who had been married to the fourteen-year-old Françoise-Marie, Mademoiselle de Blois, youngest daughter of Louis and Athénaïs, and, of course, illegitimate, the despised fruit, in Liselotte's eyes, of a disgraceful double adultery. Even a fabulous dowry of two million livres, provided by the King, had failed to cheer her. "My eyes are so thick and swollen that I can hardly see out of them," she wrote to her aunt. "I've spent the whole night weeping . . . Monsieur came to me yesterday at half past three and said, *Madame, I have a message for you from the King which you won't be very pleased to hear* . . ." Normally feisty Liselotte had acquiesced without a murmur, indicating the awe that Louis could inspire, even in his straightforward sister-in-law. "The King commanded me to come at eight o'clock and asked me what I thought about it," she continued. "I said, *When Your Majesty and Monsieur speak as my masters, as you have done, I can only obey* . . . The whole court came in to congratulate me on the wonderful event. I felt sick." Liselotte had gone home with a pounding headache, to pass another woeful night, consoled only by the reflection that at least "the limping bastard" (Mignon) had not been foisted on her daughter, as she had feared, and by the satisfaction of having given her son a good sound slap across the face in the presence of the entire court.

Across the Channel, there had been one particularly important beginning: in July 1694, the government in London had borrowed a million pounds from Scotsman William Paterson and a group of wealthy subscribers, together recently incorporated as "The Governor and Company of the Bank of England." And nearer to hand, in Paris, there had been one particularly important ending: the gentlemen of the Académie Française had at last presented their great *Dictionnaire*, the first in the French language, begun fifty-five years before. In August 1694, it was presented to the King by Jacques Tourreil, famed translator of Demosthenes and possessor of Armchair Number 40 in the Académie. Inspired by the presence of his sovereign and the historic nature of the occasion, Monsieur Tourreil gave no fewer than thirty speeches before finally handing over the volumes. "Messieurs," Louis is said to have responded, "we have been looking forward to the completion of this for a long time . . ."

~~~

EIGHTEEN

Castles in Spain

It had been more than twenty years since a kindly and unjoking
Liselotte had deposited her stepdaughter on the southward road,
"weeping and wailing" over her forthcoming marriage to the ghastly,
disfigured King of Spain. Ten years later, obese and profoundly depressed, the twenty-seven-year-old Queen had died, and now, at the
end of the 1690s, though not yet forty, Carlos II too was approaching
death. A second marriage with a German princess had proved no more
successful than his first, and the lack of an heir to the Spanish Empire
had become an issue of major importance throughout the courts of
Europe. The long-standing rivalry between France and the Austrian
Habsburgs, only recently calmed at the Peace of Rijswijk, looked
ready to flare up again, and Louis had been attempting to forestall it
by an arrangement with the Austrians' recent ally, King William of
England, formerly his own fiercest enemy. "That prince," the abbé de
Choisy had written, "had tried all sorts of ways to get the friendship of
[our] King, and failing that, he took the opposite path, saying *At least
I'll have his respect.*"

"I think . . . the King of Spain will outlive all those who are now
carving up his kingdom," observed Liselotte in mid-July 1700. But as

it turned out, she was mistaken: despite, or perhaps because of, the copious amounts of champagne administered to sustain him, Carlos died on November 1, 1700, leaving behind him a relieved widow, a vast empire in desperate straits, and a disastrously contentious will.

"We'll soon be hearing news of the King of Spain's death," Françoise wrote to the Cardinal de Noailles on Monday, November 8. "We've already heard he's in his last agony. Here's a great matter to be getting into." The news of Carlos's death in Madrid, and of his will, arrived at Versailles the following day. Louis was in the middle of a meeting of his finance council. He cancelled his scheduled afternoon hunt, and at three o'clock in the afternoon his High Council met in Françoise's apartments to discuss the vital new question. The dauphin had just arrived back from a morning's wolf-hunting. Though thirty-nine years of age, he was not formally a member of the Council, largely because of his own lack of interest in all things political. But, belatedly concerned about his son's future ability to rule effectively, Louis had recently begun encouraging him to take more part in affairs of state, and he was included in the meeting now. And as well, "Madame String-puller," as Liselotte observed peevishly, "was led in quite publicly by the King."

Louis had been the Spanish King's cousin and brother-in-law (Marie-Thérèse had been Carlos's half-sister), and in consequence Carlos had bequeathed his throne to Louis's younger grandsons. However, if the French princes were unable or unwilling to claim it, under the terms of the will, it was to be offered to the younger son of Carlos's Austrian Habsburg cousin, Leopold I of the Holy Roman Empire, and, failing him, to the infant son of the duc of Savoy, the small but strategic duchy on the southern border of France, homeland of Françoise's latest little protégée, future "glory of the age," Marie-Adélaïde. The feebleminded Carlos had hardly concluded the terms of the will himself: rather, it simply reflected the strength of the pro-French faction at his disordered court.

Each party had a good claim to the throne, since for generations everyone had been related to everyone else. But apart from the French, no one in Europe wanted to see the huge Spanish Empire combined with already too-powerful France, and apart from the Austrians, no one wanted to see it reunited with the Austrian Habsburgs, to dominate the continent as they had done during the sixteenth century. Vienna's dream was Versailles's nightmare, and vice versa. "Your Majesty's ministers have made your name hated, and the whole French nation intolerable to our neighbours," Fénelon's pamphlet had warned. If Louis accepted the will, the Spanish throne would pass to the dauphin's second son, the seventeen-year-old duc d'Anjou, whose elder brother, the duc de Bourgogne, was obliged to remain in France as his own country's heir. If Louis declined, it would pass to the fifteen-year-old Archduke Karl in Vienna, second son of the Emperor. Both parties wanted the throne, but after nine years of fighting during the 1690s, neither wanted to provoke a war over it now.

The meeting of the High Council on Tuesday, November 9, lasted four hours, until seven in the evening. There it was resolved that the terms of the will should be accepted. On Friday the twelfth, Louis met with the Spanish ambassador to inform him of the decision, and on Tuesday the sixteenth it was formally announced at court. "Gentlemen," said Louis, bringing forward the young duc d'Anjou, "I give you the King of Spain." "The Pyrenees have melted!" declared the ambassador, kneeling at the young man's feet, and kissing his hand after the Spanish custom. "And then he made him quite a long speech in Spanish," recorded the marquis de Dangeau in his journal of court life, "and when he'd finished, the King said to him, *He doesn't understand Spanish yet.*" The new King embraced his two brothers, the ducs of Bourgogne and Berry, whereupon "all three of them burst into tears." The dauphin, overjoyed, pointed out delightedly that he was "the only man I know of who can say, *My father the King,* and *My son the King* as well!"

"The duc d'Anjou will make a perfect King of Spain," wrote Liselotte. "He hardly ever laughs and he has always an air of gravity about him . . . It's going to be a bit awkward, though, given our King's treaty with England and Holland." "Everyone here seems thrilled about our new King of Spain," wrote Françoise to Cardinal de Noailles. "Lots of well informed people are saying that there won't be war at all now, whereas if we'd kept to the treaty [to partition the Spanish Empire], we would have been forced into a long and ruinous one. And the Emperor in Vienna has just confirmed that we have made the right decision, because he's refused to sign the treaty, anyway . . . The new King is taking three or four cooks along with him to Madrid, so that he can continue to eat in the French style . . . It will take them more than forty days to get there . . . "

Despite the anticipated length of his formal progress to Madrid, the new King Felipe V remained for the following three weeks at the French court, passing his days hunting and his evenings, "playing hide-and-seek in my room. I wish he'd gone already, and if I had any say in it," continued Françoise, "he'd have been off post-haste to take possession of so fine a throne . . . The King has asked me who I think should go to Madrid as his confessor, but I said I'd rather not say anything, since you're not here to advise me." He set off finally on December 4, accompanied by his lively former wet-nurse, his two brothers, and "any of the other young people who wanted to go along on the journey"—in fact, a retinue of more than a thousand—and armed with two provocative gifts from his grandfather: a collection of thirty-three articles, destined to guide him as King of Spain, and the assurance that regardless of the terms of Carlos's will and in defiance of all the European powers, he had not lost his right to succeed to the throne of France as well. "Be a good Spaniard," Louis told him, "but remember you're a Frenchman, too . . . That's the way to maintain a union between the two nations, and to keep the peace in Europe."

Maintaining a union between France and Spain, however, as Louis ought to have realized, was precisely not the way to keep the peace in Europe. France and Spain together were too powerful a bloc, and with Spain in chaos and the new King barely into manhood, the expansionist French King was clearly going to have the upper hand. In effect, Louis was still holding to a time when a single great power, richer and better-armed than all others, could dominate the whole of Europe. But since the terrible Thirty Years War of his childhood, since his incursions into Dutch territory and the inconclusive and costly Nine Years War which he himself had set in train, it was becoming gradually clearer that no one great power would ever have sufficient means to dictate terms across the entire continent, and that instead some balance of power would have to be reached among the premier nations.

Louis's vision, however, of Europe and power and kingship, was quintessentially backward-looking. "His passion for glory dominates him," wrote Spanheim. "He possesses it to excess, and it is the principal reason for the fatal events of our times . . . . He has gradually grown used to flattery and eulogy, and now he believes he deserves it." In contrast to himself, King William of England, the former Prince of Orange, was not of male royal blood—reason enough, in Louis's view, for his claim to the English throne to remain illegitimate. In January 1701, Louis similarly refused to recognize the newly crowned Friedrich I as King of Prussia: to him, Friedrich was not a king at all, but simply the Elector of Brandenburg, regardless of what clever diplomatic and financial arrangements he had made in order to have his powerful Prussian state declared a kingdom—a kingdom destined to play a perilous role in the history of Louis's own France. Louis's intractably static, unpragmatic views had seduced him into thinking that his Bourbon grandson could sit safely on the Spanish imperial throne. By his hasty acceptance of Carlos's disastrous will, he engendered an appalling conflict which would last for thirteen years, and splinter France's glory for almost a century.

Within six weeks of his grandson's departure from France, Louis had acknowledged that war could not be avoided. The other European powers, great and small, would not accept a Bourbon superpower stretching from the English Channel to Gibraltar, across Italy and the richest parts of the Netherlands, and controlling half the world's trade as well. Louis struck pre-emptively, giving orders for the raising of militias, pouncing on the Dutch garrisons to the west, and sending a hefty fleet out into the Channel.

In September 1701, the deposed King James II died at Saint-Germain. Louis, perhaps moved by his cousin's death, perhaps determined to avenge him, at once recognized his thirteen-year-old son as James III of England. It was an unwise and provocative act, and it revealed a sentimentality in Louis's judgement which would have been anathema to Colbert or Louvois—arch-pragmatists both who would not have thought for a second of favouring sentiment above self-interest. At the end of the month, representatives of the Grand Alliance (England, the Holy Roman Empire, and the United Dutch Provinces) reconvened in The Hague to sign a collective defence treaty against France, carving strategic pieces for themselves out of the territories of Louis's ally, Spain.

Though Louis had persuaded himself that he could recognize James without breaking the Treaty of Rijswijk, which had ended the Nine Years War, the Alliance had taken a different view. In England, earlier in the same year, the English parliament had restated its position concerning James by establishing a law of succession excluding all Catholics from the English throne, "and preventing English subjects themselves from practising the religion which has dominated England since the days of Queen Elizabeth," noted the abbé de Choisy indignantly, and not quite correctly. Consequently, William had been able to use Louis's recognition of James to persuade his unwilling parliament to vote him the money for a renewed war against France. The question of the Spanish succession, he had insisted, was a question of the English succession as well. Amid a public burst of Protestant patriotism, the parliament had accepted his argument, and preparations for the campaign had begun, only to be interrupted in early March 1702 by William's sudden death. Like Louis just after the death of Marie-Thérèse, William had taken a bad fall from his horse, breaking his collarbone. Unlike Louis, however, he did not escape the complications of the accident, only too serious in terms of the medical knowledge of the day: William died swiftly of pneumonia, at the age of just fifty-one. As his wife, Mary, had predeceased him, he was succeeded by his sister-in-law Anne—or rather, by Anne's clever and controlling favourite, Lady Sarah Churchill, whose husband John, Earl (later Duke) of Marlborough, now took command of the English armies—most of them, in fact, German mercenaries. In May 1702, Queen Anne declared war on France, by which time an imperial army was already doing battle, indecisively, against Spanish forces in Italy.

On July 3, 1702, Louis formally declared war on England, the Emperor, the United Provinces and all their allies—effectively, half of Europe, presenting it as a defensive war to preserve his grandson on his legitimately held Spanish throne. Most of his subjects appeared convinced, encouraged by an early victory at Luzarra over General Annibal Visconti—known to Liselotte as "Animal" Visconti.

But if it was a defensive war to the French, and no doubt also to the new King of Spain, to everyone else it looked like a continuation of Louis's long-evident will to European hegemony. The fighting spread through Dutch and German and Spanish territories, bringing Denmark and Savoy and several Italian states to the already mighty armies arrayed against Louis and his grandson. It spread into the English Channel, into the Atlantic, to Nova Scotia and Massachusetts, South Carolina and Florida, to the Caribbean colonies, to Rio de Janeiro and across to Chile and Peru, to the west coast of Africa, and into the poorly defended Spanish islands of the Pacific. The War of the Spanish Succession had become, in a sense, "the very first world war."

Françoise, like Louis and other "well informed people," had believed that accepting the Spanish throne would be the best way to avoid a "long and ruinous" war, but after the first years of fighting, with dozens of towns destroyed, scores of thousands dead, and young noblemen returning, maimed and blinded, to Versailles, she was more than convinced that it had been a terrible misjudgement. "At court, perhaps without even realizing it, Madame de Maintenon was encouraging defeatism, talking of prayer at a time which called for stiffened resolve and calling up every last reserve of strength. But the King didn't listen to her . . ." Beyond her distress at the human costs of the war, Françoise had begun to feel that France and Spain were destined, in any case, to lose it. "Our two Kings are fighting for religion and for justice, and they're failing. Our enemies are attacking both causes, and they're triumphant." It seemed to her useless and even wrong to remain defiant in the face of providence. "God is the master. We must submit to His will in everything," she concluded, while God-fearing generals on all fronts battled on.

Despite his impressive exploits in the Dutch wars of the 1670s, the King's brother had not been called to military service this time. Indeed, at sixty years of age, he was no longer well. On June 8, 1701, he was driven from his château at Saint-Cloud to dine with the King at Marly, looking so ill that Louis threatened to have him bled by force if he would not submit to the procedure of his own will. Monsieur refused, but later in the evening relented, calling in a physician to bleed him, in fact three times, and to administer as well an emetic purge— "*eleven ounces,*" recorded Liselotte, indignant, plus "two bottles of English drops." His condition worsened almost at once; within twelve hours, he was dead.

Liselotte panicked, fearing the classic banishment of the unwanted royal widow, and went sweeping through the halls of Versailles with cries of *No convent! No convent!* "The monastic life is not my *thing* at all," she insisted. " . . . If Monsieur had lived, I could have led a perfectly settled life . . . The poor man had begun to turn dévot; he was making amends; he wasn't misbehaving anymore . . ." But she was not pressed to leave the court, and in fact found her situation much improved, since Saint-Cloud and all the various residences of the late Monsieur passed on to her, and in addition, his generous personal pension was now to be paid to her directly. Liselotte, placated, dealt kindly with her late husband's memory: "If those in the other world know what's happening here, he will be very pleased with me," she wrote, "because I've been through all his things and found all the letters that his *mignons* wrote to him, and I burned them all, without reading them, to stop them falling into other hands . . ."

She might have done well to apply the same remedy to a different set of troublesome letters—a selection, in fact, of the indiscreet letters she herself had been sending with every ordinary post to her much-missed relatives in Germany. These had met the very fate from which she had saved Monsieur's billets-doux; they had been read by eyes never meant to see them and, far from being burned, had actually been copied and sent to the King, and the King had not been pleased to receive them. Politically incautious and personally offensive, the letters had roused his anger towards his unhappy sister-in-law. Because of this, she had been for many months almost persona non grata at Versailles, and though she had been laid low for some weeks now by a malarial fever, Louis had not sent to enquire after her, a deliberate discourtesy which caused her more distress than the fever itself. Still far from well, and now feeling the vulnerability of widowhood in a foreign land, she decided to take the opportunity afforded by Monsieur's death to attempt a reconciliation between herself and Louis.

According to Liselotte, writing to her Aunt Sophie, it was actually Françoise who set things in motion. "She sent a message through my son that this might be a good time to make things up with the King. So I sent a message back to her . . . asking her to come to me, since I was not well enough to go out. And she came at six o'clock . . . I admitted . . . that I'd always been against her because I thought she hated me and made the King think ill of me . . . but I said I was prepared to put all that behind me, if she would just agree to be my friend. She said lots of fine and eloquent things on that subject, and promised me her friendship, and then we embraced. Then I said she also had to help me get back into the King's good graces . . . and she advised me to speak to the King myself, quite openly . . ."

Liselotte had not in fact told her aunt the whole story of her interview with Françoise, but her lady-in-waiting, Madame de Ventadour, who had been present throughout, filled in the gaps for posterity by relaying every detail to the duc de Saint-Simon. According to the duc's rather different version, it was Liselotte herself who requested the interview by sending Madame de Ventadour to Françoise. The latter arrived, and Liselotte invited her to sit down, "which just shows how badly she needed to sit down herself," as the duc remarked. Liselotte began to complain of the King's treatment of her, "and Madame de Maintenon let her say all she wanted to say, and then replied that the King had instructed her to say that their recent mutual loss had effaced all anger in his heart, and that all would be forgiven, provided that Madame gave no further cause for offence . . . There were certain things, which he had not wished to mention, that were the real cause of his indifference during her recent illness." Liselotte, "thinking herself quite safe," responded with protestations of innocence, saying that she had "never done or said a thing" that could have displeased anyone. Riveted by his own retelling of the scandal, Saint-Simon continued:

And since she went on protesting, Madame de Maintenon took a letter from her pocket, and asked Madame whether she recognized the handwriting. It was a letter from Madame to her aunt in Hanover, and it was all about the King's relationship with Madame de Maintenon, whether they were married or simply living in concubinage, and then it went on all about the poverty in the kingdom that couldn't be alleviated . . . Madame looked as if she would drop dead on the spot. She began to cry, and Madame de Ventadour started wittering on all sorts of nonsense just to give her time to recover herself . . .

And then, thinking she was on safe ground this time, Madame began complaining that Madame de Maintenon had changed towards her, had dropped her all of a sudden, abandoned her, after she had been trying for so long to live amicably with her . . . And Madame de Maintenon let her carry on again . . . and in the end repeated to her a thousand things, every one more offensive than the last, that Madame had said to the dauphine about her, which the dauphine herself had relayed more than ten years before . . . At this second blow, Madame just stood there like a statue, and there was silence for a bit, until Madame de Ventadour started wittering on again to give Madame time to recover herself for the second time . . . She began to cry again, and admitted it was all true, and begged for pardon, clasping Madame de Maintenon's hands. Madame de Maintenon stood there coldly for quite a while, saying nothing, just letting her go on. It was a terrible humiliation for a haughty German . . . In the end, they embraced, and promised to forget the past, and be friends in future . . .

Three days after the interview, Liselotte met privately with Louis and, knowing she had nothing to hide from him now, spoke frankly, as Françoise had advised her. "I told him," her letter continued, "that, however badly he had treated me, I had always respected and loved him, and I said that it would have been a great joy for me if he had just allowed me to be near him. He embraced me and told me to forget what was past . . . and then I said to him, quite naturally, *If I hadn't loved you, I wouldn't have hated Madame de Maintenon so much* . . . And he laughed . . ."

Liselotte's admission, "quite natural" perhaps, but also touching and rather sad, was enough to bring her back into the fold. Louis had always been fond of her, and he had some sympathy for her injured sense of rank where Françoise was concerned. "I visited la Maintenon," she had written, "and found her . . . sitting in a big armchair behind a table, with all the other ladies on stools. She offered to have another stool brought in for me, but I assured her I was not too tired to stand. I had to bite my tongue—I nearly laughed out loud. How things have changed since the time when the King came to ask me whether I would allow Madame Scarron to eat with me just once so that she could cut the little duc du Maine's meat for him . . . Nowadays, when they take their promenades in the garden, she sits in a sedan chair with four fellows carrying her, and the King walks alongside like a lackey . . . The world is upside-down here . . ."

The court spent six black-clad, socially bereft months in mourning for Monsieur, and during that time and for a little while afterwards Françoise escaped further insult in Madame's letters. But in the end, Liselotte proved incorrigible. Four years later, the marquis de Torcy, grandson of the great Colbert and himself now Secretary of State, was still conveying her letters to the King, not copies now, but originals which Liselotte had imagined she had sent to Germany. "It's appalling, the way they deal with my letters," she had written, unwittingly or provocatively. "In Louvois' day, they would read them and then give them back to you. But since that little toad de Torcy's had control of the postal services, he's been really annoying me." "I'm sure his German pronunciation must be hilarious. Out of a hundred Frenchmen speaking German, there's hardly one you can understand, and they all think they know the language perfectly . . ." "This isn't actually a new joke . . . but I wanted to give M. de Torcy the pleasure of seeing I'd sent it. If he doesn't find it amusing, at least he can't complain *this time* on the pretext that it contravenes the interests of the State."

In March 1701, the new King Felipe V of Spain had married the princesse Marie-Louise of Savoy, twelve-year-old sister to the duc de Bourgogne's exquisite Marie-Adélaïde. If Louis had expected this second marriage to ensure Savoy's loyalty to French interests in the forthcoming battle for the Spanish crown, he was mistaken, though little Marie-Louise herself proved a remarkably staunch defender of her husband's claim.

She had been chosen as Felipe's consort by a friend of Françoise's from the days of her young widowhood, the politically minded Anne-Marie de La Trémoïlle-Noirmoutier, now known as the princesse des Ursins. Since her days in the salons of the Marais forty years before, Madame des Ursins had spent most of her time in Madrid and Rome, widowed, remarried, and widowed again. For years, her own sparkling salon in the Eternal City had served as an unofficial second embassy of France, where diplomats and cardinals inveighed and intrigued for the rival continental powers. Here, together with her close friend Porto-carrero, Cardinal-Archbishop of Toledo and Spain's ambassador to Rome, Madame des Ursins had promoted France's interests with skill and charm, and the keen delight of a born politico.

With young Marie-Louise's marriage to the new King of Spain arranged, Françoise had proposed her old friend for the influential position of *camarera mayor*: governess, tutor, lady-in-waiting, head of the Queen's household, political advisor, and, not least, *dueña* of the three hundred court ladies and their own one hundred chaperones. In April 1701, Françoise wrote to the duc d'Harcourt, son of her old Marais admirer and now, through her own auspices, ambassador extraordinary at the court of Spain: "As I am generally readier to give my opinion concerning the ladies rather than other affairs, I suggest

Madame des Ursins . . . She's intelligent, amenable, courteous, she's used to foreigners, and she's very well liked; she's a Grandee of Spain, she has no husband or children, and no awkward ambitions . . . She would be better than any of our ladies here." Never slow to promote herself, Madame des Ursins had in fact written much the same on her own behalf. "If I may say so," she had concluded, "I would be more suitable for the position than anyone else, since I have a great many friends in Spain . . . and I speak Spanish, too. I'm sure my appointment would please the whole nation." The duc d'Harcourt agreed, seeing in Madame des Ursins an excellent opportunity to rid the Alcázar palace once and for all of the "dwarves, clowns, parrots and monkeys, inquisitors, sorcerors, and priests disguised as physicians" plaguing the macabre Spanish court.

The precocious Marie-Louise, every bit as charming and astute— in Liselotte's word, every bit as "Italian"—as her sister at Versailles, accepted her sixty-year-old guide and companion with an easy grace. Her husband, inexperienced, naturally cautious, immature for his seventeen years, followed her direction. Madame des Ursins proved a perfect pillar for them both to lean on, and indeed, in the slow-moving gloom of the Spanish court, they had scarcely any other. On his arrival, young Felipe had been warned by the French ambassador of the local penchant for poisoning unwanted royals: His Majesty must never sniff a flower, nor indeed even touch one, nor use any perfume, nor open any letter with his own hands. As for Her Majesty, there were "a hundred ladies" complaining that her gowns, admittedly in heavy black fabrics, with bodices of lead, in the Spanish style, to flatten her pert adolescent breasts, were still scandalously short: her feet had once been seen while she was in the process of sitting down—certain local ladies had been stabbed by their husbands for this same fault. The trains of Her Majesty's gowns were evidently too short as well, allowing her to walk more quickly than the conventionally funereal Alcázar pace. The matter was referred to Louis for arbitration, with Madame des Ursins mounting a spirited defence: "The rooms in this palace are never cleaned," she wrote. "When the ladies turn around with these massive trains, they raise clouds of dust. They're dangerous for Her Majesty's chest, and they sound like rattlesnakes." Louis, seated one evening in Françoise's apartment, turning over the Spanish-dressed doll which the indignant camarera mayor had submitted as evidence, returned a verdict of compromise: Marie-Louise should wear the long trains occasionally, though she need not do so as a matter of course. The Spanish must be won over gradually to the idea of change. Their new Bourbon King and his wife should do nothing to alarm their ossified sub-Pyrenean sensitivities.

One Grandee, at least, had felt prompted towards a humble gesture on the side of innovation, as Felipe's French attendant, the marquis de Louville, relayed to the head-shaking courtiers at Versailles. "It was in the middle of a five-hour-long ceremony," he said. "The King was enclosed in a kind of elaborate cupboard, and the Grandee realized that after such a length of time, the King might wish to address a particular corporeal need, so he passed in his beaver hat—it was brand new—with a respectful note inviting His Majesty not to restrain himself."

With the priests and dust clouds and five-hour ceremonies, there might have been enough to do at the court in Madrid, but the new King and Queen, together with their *éminence française*, had weightier matters pressing in on them. By the time they had even arrived in Spain, Marie-Louise's own relative, the generalissimo Prince Eugene of Savoy, imperial commander-in-chief, was raising a force against them in Italy. In the spring of 1702, seeking to boost morale by his own royal presence, Felipe set off in person for Naples, to join the French army led by the brilliant Maréchal Vendôme. Marie-Louise remained behind in Madrid, missing her young husband, but eager to further his cause and her own political education: at thirteen years of age, she had found herself, quite suddenly, Regent of the Spanish Empire.

The King of Spain had ridden off to the wars in the south, and to east and west were his father, the dauphin of France, his brothers, Bourgogne and Berry, and his half-brothers, du Maine and Toulouse. And in the summer of 1706, the duc d'Orléans set off for Italy, "to command as generalissimo. I can't describe my son's joy," wrote Liselotte to her aunt. "He's standing up straighter and he seems to have grown three thumbs higher." Conspicuous in his absence from the lists, however, was the twenty-seven-year-old duc de Saint-Simon, a titular colonel, who had requested permission to leave the service, supposedly because of his poor health. "As I had had various health troubles, and had been advised to take the waters," he wrote, "I spent three years with no troops and nothing to do. The King didn't seem to be bothered," he added petulantly, or perhaps with relief. "M. le duc de Saint-Simon, peer of France, governor of Blaye, bailiff and governor . . . captain . . . colonel of cavalry . . ." began Spanheim, adding the duc's name in a mere four-line appendix to his memoirs: "No one pays any attention to him," he concluded.

As expected, the loss of the duc's services made no difference to Louis's armies. Though Turenne and Luxembourg and le Grand Condé had long since passed into legend, France could still boast some formidable military names: Vendôme; Villars; sixty-year-old Maréchal Boufflers, Françoise's "nephew" who had once proposed marriage to Marthe-Marguerite; and, until his death in 1707, Sébastien Vauban, now in his seventies and still Europe's master of military engineering. Leading the forces against them were Marlborough and Prince Eugene of Savoy, two of Europe's best military commanders, and working against them, too, was one of their own "commanders," the twenty-six-year-old duc de Bourgogne.

The maréchal-duc de Vendôme, known as *le Grand Vendôme*, was among the very finest of all Louis's generals, worshipped by his men, with an impressive string of military glories to his credit—though the duc de Saint-Simon wrote snidely that "if you count up all the men Vendôme says he's killed and taken prisoner, you'll find it's the entire enemy army." Sixteen years younger than the King—Louis liked to call him "my nephew," though he was more properly a cousin of sorts—Vendôme was a quintessential soldier, a drinker, curser, and fornicator (though only with men) of the first water. Bourgogne, by contrast, Louis's grandson and heir-but-one, was a priggish young man, devoted to his mass book and to his enchanting wife, Marie-Adélaïde, who did not reciprocate his passion—indeed, even his slow-witted father, the dauphin, found him dull.

Unwisely, in the spring of 1708, Louis had sent the two to command the French army in Flanders. While the young Bourgogne deferred to Vendôme's far greater experience, all progressed well, but when the pair entered combat with both Marlborough and Prince Eugene together at Oudenarde in July, Bourgogne's arrogance and cowardly incompetence cost France the battle, along with the lives of some 10,000 men—five times allied losses—and Louis's cause was swept decisively backwards.

Vendôme and Bourgogne returned in disgrace to Versailles, to private audiences with their irate King. Louis had understood the nature of the case, but too late, and, putting pride ahead of policy, he opted to support his grandson. Vendôme was relieved of his command for two years, though so valuable a commander could not easily be spared. Louis tried to distract attention from Oudenarde with the public celebration of a lesser victory in Catalonia, but no one was deceived. New songs were heard in the streets of Paris, berating Bourgogne, who had at one point been relaxing behind the lines with a game of shuttlecock while his soldiers faced the enemy.

Vendôme had at least managed to capture Ghent and Bruges before his forced retirement, partly with the help of a population disaffected with their own goverment, but the French were no more welcome for all that. Liselotte relays the story of a local man in Ghent, who "dropped his pants and presented his behind [to one of our soldiers]. The soldier took offence and fired his musket right at the presented behind. The man dropped dead. One of his friends avenged him by killing the soldier, and that was the end of the war . . ."

For a time, it seemed that that might indeed be the end of the war. The disaster of Oudenarde in 1708 left France, in most eyes, finished. It had been preceded, in 1704 and 1706, by the two great battles of Blenheim in Germany and Ramillies in the Spanish Netherlands, both dazzling victories for the brilliant Duke of Marlborough over the French. Blenheim had cost France 40,000 of its 60,000 men fighting there; Ramillies had left the allies in command of the whole of the Spanish Netherlands, obliging Louis to transfer troops from Spain and Italy, leaving the French armies in the south undermanned and, soon, defeated. From Madrid, Madame des Ursins had written sarcastically to Françoise about "the loss of the Kingdom of Naples, though that's no more than might have been expected, since they received no reinforcements."

The friction between Vendôme and Bourgogne was in fact symptomatic of a continuing problem for France's entire military enterprise on land. While Marlborough had enjoyed, at least until this point, unequivocal overall command of the allied armies and the general strategy of the war, France had suffered from too frequent changes and too little clarity in the army chain of command; this had muddied larger-scale plans and hampered tactics in the field. In addition, the French armies were inadequately supplied, leading to hesitant planning by the commanders and mass desertions among the rank and file.

The fault was Louis's. The death of the unloved marquis de Louvois had left the Ministry of War in the hands of his incompetent son, Barbezieux, and on Barbezieux's death, early in 1701, Louis had appointed Michel Chamillart as his replacement. Chamillart was one of Françoise's protégés, a former bursar at Saint-Cyr. In 1699 she had arranged his promotion to the post of Comptroller-General of the kingdom's finances, once the fief of the great Colbert. He was still holding this office when Louis, pleased with Chamillart and seeking to favour him further, appointed him Minister of War as well, over his own protestations and against Françoise's advice. "They say he owed his post to his talent for billards . . . [and his] honesty, modesty and strict piety . . . [but] these qualities aren't enough when one . . . has to be a Colbert and a Louvois at the same time . . ." But Louis insisted, revealing, as many had noted, that in his years of assiduous attention to public affairs, fixed on counting individual trees, Louis had never really mastered the business of government, and too often failed to see the forest as a whole.

The misguided new experiment proved only that Chamillart and Françoise had been right: it was impossible to run the two vital ministries of finance and war effectively at the same time. Though Chamillart had devolved ever more of his work onto subordinates, nothing had been done well, as he himself was quick to admit. By the time of his resignation, in June 1709, the nation's finances were in hopeless disarray; military supply lines were failing; and in the absence of firm direction from the War Ministry, commanders all over western Europe had taken to harassing Françoise in an attempt to secure the King's support for their own, uncoordinated ideas, including the detailed plans for individual battles. Even when these were—always tardily— approved, there was no guarantee that a commander would have the necessary troops at his disposal. "There are deserters in all the armies," as Liselotte noted. Though defeat on the field accounted for some desertions, the main problem was the lack of regular pay for the soldiers. In a time of "relentless increase in the financial demands of war," setting strategy and battle plans and personal bravery aside, it was money that was making the difference. As the French were to realize only far into the future, the allied victories were in fact "a triumph for the new regime in England over the old regime typified in France." England's reformed political system had engendered a new capitalistic financial system, with money being raised in commercial markets and interest paid in stable currency; this in its turn was determining, ever more clearly, who would win and who would lose. Following the victory celebrations for the battle of Blenheim, for example, a loan to the government of almost a million pounds, "an impressive sum in those days," was fully subscribed within two hours of its floating in the City of London, by "large numbers of persons eager to prove their confidence in the national cause at 6⅔ per cent." After the battle of Oudenarde, a further City loan, this time guaranteed by the Whig government, itself comprising many City merchants, raised two and a quarter million pounds, and the confident British parliament itself voted the money to raise an extra 10,000 troops.

Louis, by contrast, was dependent on his creaking feudal system of taxation by royal decree, supplemented by loans to the crown (to be repaid, if at all, in devalued coin) and the sale of offices, with the national economy being gradually stifled as people did all they could to keep their money, often physically, in their own hands. As an absolute monarch, Louis was able, quite simply, to announce new taxes for any purpose he chose, and to impose them upon any particular group of his subjects: his nobles, for instance, were typically exempt, whereas the townsfolk and, especially, the peasants generally bore the heaviest tax burden. "I have found everywhere an extreme poverty," reported one tax-collecting intendant in southern France. "The great majority of the people have no seed to sow their land with," reported another, from the west. "The nation's finances are so exhausted that one can promise nothing for the future," Chamillart had told Louis. "The revenue for 1708 has been eaten up in advance, and credit is exhausted." Some areas of the country were in conditions of actual famine. In Paris, the hungry townsfolk took to rioting over the exorbitant price of bread— to which the Cardinal-Archbishop de Noailles responded by perversely calling for a general fast to placate the Lord into ending the shortage. A major rebellion of Huguenots in the south, urged on by the successes of the Protestant allied forces, swiftly developed into a full-scale peasant revolt against the impossibly heavy taxes which Louis had imposed to finance the war, now ongoing for more than seven years. And a bitter new prayer was heard in the streets of French towns:

> Our Father which art at Versailles, thy name is no longer hallowed, thy kingdom is not so great, thy will is no longer done on earth or sea. Give us this day our bread which we lack on all sides. Yield not to the temptations of la Maintenon, and deliver us from Chamillart. Amen.

"The maréchal de Villars has told me," wrote Françoise to Madame des Ursins, "that four days ago, he requisitioned eight or ten thousand sacks of wheat from people who had great need of it themselves. He was not happy about doing so, but he said he had no other way of putting his army in the field: the soldiers had no food . . . The people are dying of hunger. And there's everything to fear from them. They're saying that the King is taking all the grain and enriching himself by selling it to them at the highest prices."

Chamillart, impossibly overworked, had abandoned his office of Comptroller-General in June 1708. It passed it to Nicolas Desmarets, a nephew of Colbert promoted by Françoise at Chamillart's own request. Desmarets was quickly overwhelmed by the enormity of the nation's financial difficulties. He fell back on the old ruses of devaluing the currency, postponing repayment of crown loans, and selling offices. "Rents, new offices, tax exemptions were . . . created, sold, suppressed, recreated, resold." It was even considered that recent ennoblements might be revoked, "so forcing the new nobles to pay for their titles a second time." Where possible, the wealthy moved money abroad, some of it ending up in the hands of bankers in enemy Amsterdam— seldom filtering down, however, to the poorer Dutch folk living in "penuriousness."

As for loans, as Chamillart had reported before his resignation, credit was exhausted. Among the bourgeoisie and some of the nobles there was in fact still plenty of money in the country, but Louis, and consequently his armies, now had no access to it. From Madrid, itself in a state of destitution, Madame des Ursins sent fuming letters to Françoise, insisting that France was full of "sleeping wealth," and berating the lack of patriotism among the French: "I'm so angry, my blood boils when I think of . . . all the money the business people have, and they won't release it for the good of the state." From her quiet room at Saint-Cyr, Françoise replied, "As for the money here, that's still hidden. Everyone agrees there's more in the kingdom than before the war, but it's not circulating, and you know, Madame, when the blood stops circulating, it means death."

Instead of circulating, particularly in the form of loans to the crown, the hidden wealth of France was "sleeping" in the form of ever more valuable objects in the households of the rich—fabulous silverware, table services made of gold, even high-quality furniture—in short, anything that was less likely to lose its value than the actual coin of the realm. Even the Church kept most of its money hidden: the parish of Saint-Eustache in Paris had had made a gigantic silver candelabra, weighing two hundred pounds instead of the usual twenty. In a hopeless measure to combat the problem, the Comptroller-General introduced new restrictions on the utilization of precious metals: they could no longer be used for soufflés or cooking pots or grills, but lest the gently bred be too incommoded, gold and silver might still be used for "chamber pots, soap basins, chocolate, tea, and coffee pots, pocket candlesticks, and the tops of walking sticks." The Saint-Eustache candelabra, however, was confiscated and melted down for the purchase of food for the poor, and the fasting Cardinal-Archbishop de Noailles added a large sum of money from his own personal resources.

"This question of wheat makes me dizzy," complained Françoise. "In every market you see more than you've ever seen, and yet the cost of it rises and rises." Profiteering was rampant, and there was hoarding, but genuine dearth was recurrent, too. In the summer of 1709, the relics of Sainte Geneviève were exposed in Paris in supplication for divine assistance in the city's terrible need. And in Madrid, as Madame des Ursins relayed, "they're holding a big procession carrying the relics of Saint Isidore and his beatified wife. Saint Isidore was a labourer and the people here are very confident that he'll protect their crops. That's all very admirable, but I'm more concerned about this plague of grasshoppers that's descended on the fields . . ."

In this year of processions and plague, the year of 1709, France reached its nadir. "A great many of the poor have died," wrote Françoise at the end of January, "in Paris and in the countryside. Entertainments have stopped, the colleges are closed, the craftsmen do no work. The result of all this is great hardship." The city's hôpital-général was besieged by 14,000 destitute people seeking food and shelter; 4,000 of the sick were crammed into the hôtel-Dieu. At a single Paris orphanage, 2,500 babies had been left—only one in ten would survive. "Madame de Maintenon redoubled her alms that year," her secretary recorded. "She sent out bread, broth, blankets and clothes, and often she went out herself to distribute the things . . . In that same year she took sixteen poor Versailles families into her particular care, going to see them and taking medicines when they were sick and so on . . . But in general she concealed her identity wherever possible. She said to me, I don't like it at all that everyone knows how little good I do. Yet every year she gave away 54,000 or 60,000 livres in charity. She never thought of piling up money . . . I often saw her weeping over the wretchedness of the poor, especially if they were nobles . . ."—an empathy no doubt born of Françoise's own humiliations as an impoverished girl of modestly noble birth.

At Versailles, Françoise's Mignon and his brother, the comte de Toulouse, led the younger nobility in donating their gold and silver possessions to be melted down for the sustenance of the army. The King gave his gold services, too, and even promised the crown jewels as security for further loans, should they be forthcoming. Marie-Adélaïde, the young duchesse de Bourgogne, agreed "quite willingly to dress more simply," but most ladies at court preferred to keep up appearances. "The women here are very well turned out, given the degree of poverty there is," wrote Françoise to her niece Marthe-Marguerite in Paris. "They all complain, and they go on ruining themselves. No one has any money, and no one has a single skirt the less."

But by the middle of the year, with France in a desperate financial situation and threatened with invasion, Louis had been forced to sue for peace. The allies responded positively, but the terms for France were harsh: Louis was to recognize the Emperor Karl as the rightful King of Spain and, if need be, turn France's armies against his grandson to force him from the Spanish throne. Louis was to abandon his support for the young James Stuart and recognize Queen Anne as the legitimate sovereign of Britain. France was to be barred from trading in the vast Spanish colonies, and was to admit British commerce within its own territories on especially advantageous terms. The French were to relinquish the seven barrier fortresses in Holland which they had captured at the beginning of the war, and a large part of the Spanish Netherlands was to be handed over as well, to provide a further buffer for the Dutch against any future French incursion. Such were the demands of the British and Dutch. The German princes were to present their own terms at a later peace conference. "You'll have heard the news of our present situation, Madame, and of the insolence of our enemies," Françoise wrote to Madame des Ursins in the first week of June. "The French are no longer French if they're not offended by such indignities. It's made me ill . . . I don't want to talk about it any more."

Madame des Ursins, by contrast, was only too eager to "talk about it," and she replied with a series of spirited accusations: "How can anyone buy peace at such a price? How can the King's subjects not be ready to sacrifice everything they have to avoid such a disgrace for France? . . . I leave you to imagine the situation of Their Catholic Majesties . . . The King is completely occupied with plans for his own defence, in case the King his grandfather should withdraw the support he has been giving him, and without which it will be exceedingly difficult to hold the kingdom."

Before her letter had even crossed the Spanish border, Madame des Ursins had received the response, half-heroic, half-tragic, which came in urgent dispatches from France. The King's subjects were indeed ready to sacrifice everything they had; there would not be any bargaining for peace. But continuing the war on the western and eastern fronts meant abandoning the south, abandoning Spain and Louis's grandson and his claim to the Spanish throne. Madame des Ursins's reply to Françoise, her friend of forty years' standing, was a model of politesse, shot through with the bitterest irony: "The King of Spain has received a letter from the King, Madame, informing him that he is no longer able to avoid abandoning him, and that all French troops are to be withdrawn: the matter is settled as has long been expected. It is my hope that His Majesty draws all that he desires from this abandonment and that since, through the sacrifice of Their Catholic Majesties, he is now at liberty to conclude a peace, his enemies will prove more tractable and that France will once again find the money and the wheat which have been so sorely lacking. Your own anxieties, Madame, so well founded, will no longer be so great, and you will begin to enjoy the repose that has been so troubled for so many years, and of which you are in so great need . . . I expect your enemies will require the King to exhibit joy if his grandson is dethroned . . ."

Madame des Ursins was not quite correct: a few French troops were to be left in Spain, after all, a "compromise" force of twenty-five battalions. And His abandoned Catholic Majesty was in fact to do rather better with his own army than he had done with the help of his grandfather's. But for the moment, the glory belonged to France—not for any battlefield success, but for the outpouring of patriotic stoicism which met Louis's appeal to his people for a continuation of the war. On June 12 it was sent out to every town in the country, to be posted up in every market square and read out before the sermon at every mass. Every French subject was to know why, after more than seven years of war, no peace had yet been agreed. They were all to understand "the impossible condition of forcing Louis . . . to make war upon his own grandson." To provincial governors throughout the land, Louis sent the following:

> The hope of peace has been so widespread in my kingdom that I believe, given the fidelity of my people throughout the course of my reign, that I owe them the consolation of knowing the reasons which prevent their now enjoying the repose which I had sought to procure them . . . My enemies have made it clear that their intention is to strengthen the neighbouring states of France . . . so that they may penetrate into the interior of the kingdom whenever in the future it should be in their interests to begin a new war . . . I say nothing of their demands that I should join my forces to those of the Alliance to dethrone the King my grandson . . . It is unbelievable that they should even have thought of demanding such a thing . . . My tenderness for my people is no less than that I feel for my own children; I share all the sufferings which the war has brought upon so faithful a people . . . All Europe knows that I seek peace for my people, but I am persuaded that they themselves would not accept it under conditions so unjust and so contrary to the honour of the FRENCH name . . . Had it been a question of my will alone, my people would have rejoiced in a peace, but it can only be achieved through renewed efforts . . .

It was an extraordinary appeal, and indeed the very fact of it was extraordinary. An absolute monarch, accountable to no one, with no parlement to constrain him and no threat to his power within the land, a man exceedingly proud of his throne and greatly ambitious for his nation, had circulated what was in effect an explanation of the frightening situation as it stood, and a plea for the support of his people to carry on, in defiance of the extra hardship for themselves which would almost certainly ensue.

Louis's representation of himself as, in effect, the father of his people, who loved them as he loved his own children, was a master-stroke of public relations, as was his call to their emerging sense of a common nationality as Frenchmen. In this Churchillian call avant la lettre, Louis identified himself with his people as sharing their suffer-ings, offering, as it were, his own blood, toil, tears, and sweat. But it was not a cynical call. Louis was as devoted to his people as he was to France and to his throne: he had understood that the three were interdepen-dent, and, arguably, he made no conceptual distinction between them.

Louis took no blame upon himself—so much could not have been expected—but in his soon legendary appeal of June 12 he revealed that he had at last, and crucially, learned that France could not remain strong and his own throne secure through the obedience of his people alone: he needed their support as well.

In its own way, Louis's appeal was a revolutionary document. The very fact of its existence was an admission of the limits of absolutism, an indication that the King had grasped the lesson that James II had failed to learn in England, and that William of Orange had understood only too well—the lesson that, except by force, a people cannot long be governed against its will. In June of 1709, in response to a heartfelt ap-peal from their King, the people of France—soldiers, peasants, towns-folk—rallied their forces for determined resistance in a moment of great peril. It was to prove their finest hour.

"Advices from the *Hague* of the 14th instant say . . . that the Allies [have] strong Resentments against the late Behaviour of the Court of *France*; and the *French* [are] using all possible Endeavours to animate their Men to defend their Country against a victorious and exasperated Enemy." So Joseph Addison and Sir Richard Steele circulated the news in their *Tatler* through the coffee-houses of London in that same June of 1709. After three months of defensive manoeuvres, Villars's troops finally gave battle to "Marlbrouk" on September 9, at Malplaquet, near Mons, a fortress vital for the defence of France itself. This terrible battle, the bloodiest in the whole of the eighteenth century, was a victory for Marlborough. At the cost of some 20,000 men, twice as many as the French lost, the allies managed to hold the terrain. Maréchal Villars, badly wounded, ceded command to Maréchal Boufflers, Marthe-Marguerite's rejected suitor. "Nothing is equal to what he achieved," declared Françoise proudly. After six hours of savage fighting, Boufflers conducted an orderly French retreat, with the allied troops too exhausted to pursue.

In military terms, it was a defeat for the French, but they had acquitted themselves valiantly, and the national pride was intact, though from court Françoise wrote pitifully of "all the ladies crying out for their husband or their sons." At Malplaquet, no prisoners had been taken on either side. "The duc de Guiche was wounded in a cannonade. The duchesse . . . left as soon as she heard. She had her husband and two sons there. The marquis de Coëtquen was wounded in the same cannonade; they have cut off his leg . . . Madame de Dangeau's son has had his leg cut off . . . M. de Pallavicino and M. de Chermerault have been killed . . . Madam d'Epinoy's . . . son is out of danger . . ."

France was saved, but in the end, less through the talent of her generals or the strength of her defences or the determination of her people than through the unexpected death in 1711 of the Emperor Joseph, who had succeeded his father's throne of the Holy Roman Empire in 1705. Joseph, only thirty-two years old, had died of smallpox, leaving two small daughters but no sons: in consequence, his throne devolved to his brother, the Archduke Karl—the same Karl who was fighting to claim the Spanish throne from Louis's grandson. The massive alliance of European powers, who had until now been supporting Karl, suddenly found themselves in the paradoxical position of fighting to bring about precisely what they had been trying to avoid: the concentration of too much power in too few hands. In October 1711, Karl was elected Holy Roman Emperor; if the war were to conclude in the allies' favour, he would soon control the vast Spanish Empire as well. Led by the Dutch and English, the allies agreed that the time was ripe for diplomacy. By the end of the year, plans were being drawn up for a peace conference in the Dutch town of Utrecht, and in January 1712 it began.

"And what about the peace?" wrote Françoise in May of that year to her friend Madame de Dangeau. "Doesn't M. de Dangeau think it will be agreed, and soon?" There was good reason to believe so, although the fighting was to continue, in ever smaller theatres, for two further years and more. Throughout 1711, the armies of the Alliance had held the advantage, but despite this, the newly elected Tory government in England, land-owning opponents of the pro-war city-based Whigs, had begun negotiations with Louis in "a greedy and treacherous desertion" kept secret from its allies and even from Marlborough, its own (Whig-sympathizing) commander-in-chief; in July 1712, England signed a separate peace with France. Towards the end of the same year, having suffered particularly heavy losses in the campaigns of the autumn, the Dutch agreed to a peace as well; they were quickly followed by the smaller allied powers. With one empire now in his hands, Karl himself might have been expected to be less concerned to win a second; after the death of his brother, in 1711, he had left Barcelona, his last Spanish stronghold, to claim the imperial throne in Vienna. But in fact he proved the most determined of all the Alliance leaders. His imperial armies battled on through 1713, until their final defeat by the French in the first months of the following year.

The peace was thus more than two years in the making, with concessions and compromises extracted from all parties even as the fighting went on. Karl was obliged to abandon his claim to Spain, but his Holy Roman Empire regained almost all of its German territories, and acquired large areas of Italy as well. Spain itself, which had effectively been waging a civil war over the two contenders for the throne, became, for the first time, a formally united country—once the Catalans had been massacred for their support of the losing side. From his decayed capital in Madrid, the now thirty-year-old Felipe proceeded to impose by force a French-style centralized government on his kingdom, ignoring the greater wealth and vibrancy of provinces other than Castilla. In so doing, he ensured the survival of strong regional resentments which were to cripple the economic and political development of the country for almost three hundred years.

In return for recognition as the rightful King of Spain and its extensive empire, Felipe had been obliged to renounce his rights to the throne of France. This he had done, and similarly, his brother, the duc de Berry, and his uncle, the duc d'Orléans, had formally abandoned their own right to the Spanish throne, so apparently ensuring that there would be no Bourbon superpower in Europe. Doubts remained of the legality in French law of Felipe's renunciation, but Louis was in no position now to dictate terms. In London, Queen Anne was dying. "I reckon the City [merchants] will not easily be persuaded to declare a popish French King shall be master of all their riches . . ." observed her former favourite, Sarah Churchill, wife of the Duke of Marlborough. She was right, and Louis, too, was obliged to accept this truth, making no further protest against the "Protestant Succession" law excluding Catholics from England's throne.

The war was over, and "for all this waste of wealth and loss of blood," France had gained next to nothing. But Louis was now seventy-five years old. The world was to be spared any further ravages inspired by his insagacity. In his final, prolonged battle to extend French influence in Europe and its colonies, he had unwittingly brought to birth a great new power which he had barely considered part of Europe at all: "perfidious Albion," the real victor of the War of the Spanish Succession.

England—or rather, Great Britain, since an Act of Union in 1707 had joined that country formally with Scotland—had certainly gained territory from the conflict: a hefty piece of French Canada now became British, as did the Caribbean island of Saint-Christophe (St. Kitts), where an eleven-year-old Françoise had long ago dined on manioc and pineapple at the governor's residence. Britain also gained two small but strategically important territories from Spain: the island of Minorca in the eastern Mediterranean, and the rocky promontory of Gibraltar to the south. For an adventuring naval power, these were excellent acquisitions, and the British gained further from the Dutch loss of trading rights in the Mediterranean and in South America, which ultimately reduced what had been the greatest of her commercial rivals to "no more than a sloop in the wake of the ship of England." France was obliged to accept Britain as her own favoured trading nation, and to dismantle the defences at Dunkirk which might have threatened

British trade through the Channel. And, vitally, Britain won from Spain the notorious *Asiento*—an exclusive right to provide slaves, some 20,000 every year, to the many Spanish colonies of South America.

In the end, the British proved more dangerous as allies than as enemies, particularly to the Dutch, who had also lost territory to the Empire and—thanks to the secret treaty of 1711—a long line of fortifications to the French. The Treaty of Utrecht stripped the British of all credibility with their former friends in the Grand Alliance, but it brought them so much in other respects that they could afford not to care. "England wishes to become master of the world's trade," Louis had observed, and indeed, helped substantially if inadvertently by his own actions, through the course of the eighteenth century, England was to become precisely that. The Europeans, meanwhile, after decades of exhausting hegemonic militarism, and with the worrying new power of Peter the Great's Russia to the east, agreed to settle instead for something closer to a balance of power on the continent. It was to last until the appearance of another expansionist Frenchman, ninety years later, in the person of Napoléon Bonaparte.

The dauphin is shorter than average, of compact build, with a handsome, full face . . . His greatest love [is] wolf-hunting . . . and he is keen to learn about soldiering." So Spanheim had recorded, more than two decades before. The dauphin was now in his fiftieth year, content in his second, morganatic marriage, still serving in the army, still riding and hunting wolves with a royal passion. Never much interested in politics or strategy, he had had to be prodded towards his expected future duty as sovereign, pushed into council meetings, pressed into taking a stand on the issues of the day. Apart from his lack of interest in government, he had given no other cause for concern other than by persistently overeating—unrepentant even after the alarming evening on which he had lost consciousness after indulging himself with particular enthusiasm. But even his large frame and healthy constitution had proved no match for the ravaging diseases of the age: in April 1711 he had contracted smallpox, and on the fourteenth of the month, he died. "The King has so humbled himself to the will of God, you can't imagine it," wrote Liselotte to her half-sister Luise. "He talks so piously, it goes straight to your heart; it made me weep all day yesterday . . ." The dauphin's valets had work to make them weep, too, as the duc de Saint-Simon records: the outsized corpse had to be "trampled down" so that it might fit into its coffin.

The dauphin himself had been the father of three sons, which had boded well for France's royal succession. All born within four years, they had remained on good terms as they grew to adulthood. The dauphin's eldest son, the duc de Bourgogne, now became dauphin in his turn: with his lovely wife Marie-Adélaïde, he too had had three sons, and though the eldest of these had died very young, there were still two healthy little boys to inherit the throne in due course.

On February 5, 1712, Marie-Adélaïde herself had fallen ill with the measles; remorselessly bled and purged by the royal physicians, by the twelfth of the month, she was dead. On the eighteenth, Bourgogne, the new dauphin, afflicted with the same malady and subjected to the same treatment, died, too. "You will understand the excess of my grief," the King wrote to his grandson in Spain, "when you learn that the dauphin has died. Within only a few days it has pleased God to make two terrible trials of my submission to His will. I pray that He keep Your Majesty safe for me, and that He grant us consolation in these miseries . . ."

On March 7, Marie-Adélaïde's eldest son, the third dauphin, just five years old, fell ill with measles in his turn. Bled by the relentless physicians, he died the next day. His two-year-old brother, the duc d'Anjou, now the fourth dauphin, had also fallen ill. "Misfortune . . . overwhelms us," wrote Liselotte. The child was cured, ironically, through lack of medical care. His sensible governess, outraged by the physicians' treatment of the rest of his family and blaming them roundly for three unnecessary deaths, spirited the little boy away and cared for him herself in the homeliest way, without recourse to medicines or purgatives or bleedings.

Two years later, in May 1714, Louis's youngest grandson, the duc de Berry, fell from his horse while hunting, and died soon afterwards

from internal injuries, "vomiting violently . . . green stuff, then black . . .
It was found to be blood clots . . . They thought him out of danger . . ."
said Liselotte, with Françoise, now seventy-eight, writing, "I feel
lethargic in the extreme and I think I'm going to die of it. I feel exhausted in a way that I've never felt before . . ."

A handful of years earlier, Louis had been able to rejoice in an apparently secure succession: a son, three grandsons, and four great-
grandsons—the King of Spain and Marie-Louise already had two little
boys of their own. Now, given the terms of the peace, the Spanish
princes could not inherit the throne of France: defiance of this agreement would almost certainly mean a resumption of war. And of the
French princes, all but one were dead, with the future of the fleur-de-
lys throne of the Bourbons now resting on the tiny, orphaned shoulders of the four-year-old dauphin Louis.

They were not strong enough to ensure Louis's peace of mind, and
his fears persuaded him now towards a step of doubtful legality. After
the duc de Berry's death, he signed a royal edict declaring that in default of legitimate male heirs, his legitimized sons could inherit the
throne. The edict was hugely controversial, prompting Chancellor Pont-
chartrain, Colbert's distant successor, to resign in protest. Ignoring
rumours that all the young princes had been poisoned by Liselotte's
son, the duc d'Orléans, Louis proceeded with his own undignified work,
"violating the constitution [and] trying to change the fundamental
laws governing the succession."

Françoise no doubt knew this, too, but nonetheless she welcomed
the edict. It placed her beloved Mignon fourth in line to the throne, after Liselotte's son, the duc d'Orléans, and his own eleven-year-old
Louis, duc de Chartres. Liselotte herself was not so indignant about
this affront to untainted blood as she would once have been. As she explained, "Since the sister of the duc du Maine and the comte de
Toulouse married my son, and she became part of our family, I've preferred to see them raised up rather than set lower." By now, the duc
d'Orléans and his wife, Athénaïs's hotheaded daughter, had six living
children, and as Liselotte pointed out, "du Maine and Toulouse are
their uncles, just the same . . ."

The duc de Saint-Simon, himself of a fairly recent line and a fanatical stickler for the niceties of rank, was very much less relaxed about it all. Steam rises from the pages of his memoirs as he describes being summoned to hear "this news which would not allow a moment's delay, which couldn't even be written down, which was of the most extreme importance." Saint-Simon sneaked out of his own house in the night: "My wife was away . . . No one saw me get into my carriage, and I made for Paris at top speed . . . The King had declared his two bastards, and their heirs male in perpetuity, to be true princes of the blood, able to inherit the crown. I had not expected any such news . . . I was very angry . . ." He was courtier enough, all the same, to pay swift compliments to the "limping" Monsieur du Maine on his new rank. "And I said the same the next day to Monsieur de Toulouse and to Madame la duchesse d'Orléans. She was already imagining her brothers crowned. She's a hundred times more of a bastard than they are . . . Monsieur du Maine cultivated a modest and solemn air for the sake of appearances. Monsieur de Toulouse is a beneficiary of this monstrous affair, though he had nothing to do with it himself. It was all arranged by the duc du Maine and his all-powerful protectress."

Saint-Simon, a persistent enemy of Françoise, was no doubt overstating the case. A careful plot, or even an opportunistic plot to raise Mignon to the position of heir to the throne—and in fact only fourth heir, after the dauphin and d'Orléans and the latter's young son—is less than unlikely. All the same, Françoise was happy to see Mignon so recognized: in dozens of little ways, all bitterly enumerated by Saint-Simon, he would from now on be treated with the deference to which she felt he was entitled. "Look at the King," she had said to him, almost forty years before. "He never makes a fuss about what's due to him." "Ah, but Madame," Mignon had replied, "the King is sure of his position, while I cannot be sure of mine." Now, at last, it seemed that he could, and if some in France foresaw the troubles this princely elevation was soon to cause, Françoise does not appear to have been among them.

~~~~~

NINETEEN

All Passion Spent

*T*he King was very well until the 14th of the month of April [1711], when he was overtaken by an inconceivable sadness at the death of Monseigneur . . . Since that day . . . his sadness has been ever present . . . He has headaches . . . He complains of . . . tiredness . . . partly caused by *the quantity of peas that he generally eats . . .*"

Thus Louis le Grand, France's Sun King, now in his mid-seventies, still hunting and still a crack shot, but these days jumping no ditches, charging across no open ground, just rattling alongside the horses in a little three-wheeled chariot, gritting his remaining teeth against the intractable pain of his gout. His zest for the life of the body was still strong: Françoise can be found in these years of her seventies asking her confessor whether she must carry on accepting the King's embraces every afternoon. "Yes, my dear daughter, you must," came the reply. "You must accept this subjection, and view it as the asylum of a weak man who would otherwise be lost in impurity and scandal. It is part of your vocation." The King's enormous appetite for food was also intact: Liselotte describes a regular supper as "a whole pheasant and a partridge after four plates of different kinds of soup, a large dish of salad, two great slices of ham, mutton served with gravy and garlic, a plate of sweet cakes and, on top of that, fruit and hard-boiled eggs."

The years were telling, all the same. And if the long war had revealed France's decline, it had revealed as well the decline of France's King. Louis had not recovered from the strain of it, nor from his grief at the loss of so many of his heirs. Many afternoon and evening hours he now spent alone with Françoise, weeping inconsolably. At night, undressing at his formal bedtime ceremony of *coucher*, "he looked like a corpse," said a saddened courtier. By the time the last treaty was signed, in September 1714, brokers in London were taking bets that he would not last the year, and though he did, it was not by much.

Seven years before, the King had set off on a long, solitary walk in his ever-blooming gardens, to think of la belle Athénaïs, who had died in her Paris convent at the age of sixty-five, "her skin like a bit of screwed-up paper, her whole face red and covered with little wrinkles . . . and her lovely hair white as snow . . ."

"Old age is terribly sad," said Françoise. "You feel you're paying for the pleasures of youth." Most of her old Marais friends were no longer living: her beloved and undeserving brother Charles was gone, and cousin Philippe, a lieutenant-général at the end, and impossible Bonne, and even Ninon de Lenclos, Paris's most celebrated courtesan, who had "corrupted" Françoise with the marquis de Villarceaux more than fifty years before. In the early years of the war, Françoise had in fact invited Ninon to come and live with her and Bonne at Versailles, but Ninon had declined, preferring to remain at the centre of her still delightful salon in Paris, celebrating her eightieth birthday, or so it was said, by taking a new lover in the person of her abbé. In her charitable will she had left one thousand francs to a clever young friend "to buy books," and the boy, François-Marie Arouet, better known as Voltaire, later relayed the story for posterity with a touch of eighteenth-century ebullience: "I was about thirteen when I saw her," (he was ten) "and she was eighty-five" (eighty-two). "She left me two thousand francs" (in fact one thousand). "She was dried up like a mummy." Perhaps.

"I'm sure you don't have as many wrinkles as I do," Liselotte had written to her Aunt Sophie, "but that doesn't bother me. I've never been a beauty, so I haven't lost much." The Electress Sophie, in her mid-eighties and herself a great beauty long faded, had in fact narrowly missed becoming Queen of England. Her death in 1714, only weeks before that of Queen Anne, had brought her eldest son, George, to the throne in her stead, to sire a long German dynasty in Defoe's land of men "a-kin to all the universe." The arrival of the Hanoverians in London had not seemed without danger for those watching from France, but on the whole they were mistaken. Eighteenth-century Britain was to turn its gaze away from military conquest on the continent and out onto a wider horizon, "to become master of the world's trade," as Louis had foreseen.

But that was all for a new age, which the Sun King himself would not know, an age which, in France, for half a century and more, was to define itself simply as an aftermath of his own. The fates permitted Louis a final burst of splendour in February 1715, with the reception of the ambassador of Persia in the Hall of Mirrors at Versailles. The King himself wore a "heavy and sumptuous suit of black and gold, embroidered in crown diamonds valued at 12,500,000 livres. He appeared at the balcony . . . before the crowd of curious people who had invaded the courtyards . . ." The ambassador's gifts were regarded as shockingly disappointing by contrast: "a hundred and six little pearls, a hundred and eighty turquoises and two jars of embalming ointments. The public were scandalized; they started to speak every infamy under the sun about the ambassador, and most people, even people of the first consideration, decided that the ambassador was an impostor . . . who had never been to the court of the King of Persia."

In the end it was not disappointment at his presents or the strain of government or the desperation of grief that killed Louis, nor was it even simple old age, but his old ailment of the gout, excruciating, debilitating, and half-comical all at once. His premier physician, Fagon, standing by old supposed remedies, kept the King's throbbing leg wrapped tightly in plasters, sweating, immobile, the blood unable to circulate. Its condition worsened daily. In mid-August, with Louis still working a little and even attending a musical soirée in Françoise's apartments, Fagon suggested he might be helped by spa water brought from Bourbon. By August 20, he was unable to be moved even to Françoise's nearby rooms, "so he sent for her," recorded the duc de Saint-Simon; indeed Louis was never to leave his own chamber again. Françoise's niece Marthe-Marguerite de Caylus and her friend Madame de Dangeau were admitted shortly afterwards, "to help keep the conversation going." Fagon "proposed a meeting of the principal physicians in Paris and at court," and Saint-Simon's wife paid a brief, respectful visit to Louis. "She was the last of the court ladies to whom he spoke," wrote the duc, "since I don't count . . . Mesdames . . . Dangeau and . . . Caylus . . . they were only familiars of . . . Madame de Maintenon."

On August 21, a quartet of physicians examined the King, "taking care to pronounce nothing but praises of Fagon," who then prescribed medicines of quinine water and ass's milk. The following day, Louis chose some clothes which he intended to wear when he felt better. "It's because men never want to die," said Saint-Simon, "so they pretend as much and as long as possible." But a further examination of the now badly swollen leg, during which Louis fainted, revealed "gangrene through the whole foot and in the knee."

The King lived ten more days, during which time, as the duc de Saint-Simon relates, "Monsieur d'Orléans's apartments, deserted before, were now absolutely crowded" with courtiers making haste to ingratiate themselves with France's probable new Regent—"and what could the dying Jupiter do? . . . But the King's ministers didn't dare approach Monsieur d'Orléans. Monsieur du Maine was watching everything and they were still afraid of Madame de Maintenon and terrified of the King . . . There was just enough life left in him to dismiss them from their posts, and then they would have had to go to Orléans on their knees . . ."

Apart from his physicians and priests, Louis saw few people during these final days: Mignon was often with him, and Françoise constantly; the duc d'Orléans was admitted once or twice every day, Liselotte hardly at all, and she left the royal apartments "weeping and wailing so loudly that everyone thought the King must have died already." Mignon's wife, the duchesse du Maine, turned up—"Until now she hadn't taken the trouble to move from her château at Sceaux, with all her friends and her amusements . . ."—but if she was late to arrive at her father-in-law's bedside, once there she proved kind and helpful. The little dauphin was brought in by his governess, and the King received him very tenderly, with the valets recording his words of counsel, the first and the last that the boy was to receive: "My child," said Louis, "you are going to be a great king. Do not imitate me in my love of building, nor in my taste for warfare. On the contrary, try to remain at peace with your neighbours. Render to God what you owe Him . . . and make your subjects honour Him . . . Try to comfort your people, as, unhappily, I have been unable to do. And don't forget what you owe to your governess . . . My dear child, I give you my blessing with all my heart."

Most of the courtiers remained milling outside the doors of the King's apartments, now and then being allowed a brief entry. "The King could swallow nothing but liquids," said Saint-Simon, and, seeing his now too-evident weakness, "I noticed that he didn't like being watched. He asked the courtiers to leave the room."

The duc himself went in as often as he was permitted, and what he did not observe in person, he gleaned later from the King's valets, reporting it all with his customary spite where those he disliked were concerned. "The King paid Madame de Maintenon a compliment which didn't please her at all; she didn't say a word in reply. He said that his consolation in leaving her was the hope that, given her age, they would soon be joined again." In fact, Françoise herself repeated this "compliment" proudly to her secretary, seeing in it, as indeed did Mademoiselle d'Aumale, not an insult to her near-eighty years, but an indication of the King's love for her after almost thirty-three years of marriage. "The King said to Madame de Maintenon that he'd heard it was difficult to accept one's death, but that . . . he hadn't found it so difficult. She replied," continued Saint-Simon, revealing more of himself than of Françoise in what was very probably a pure fabrication, "that it was much harder when one was attached to people, and had hatred in one's heart, and still wanted vengeance."

Françoise was often to speak of the King's last days with Mademoiselle d'Aumale, who had been with her for much of the time—"I was a witness of almost everything he said to her," she confirmed, and indeed Françoise herself was to retell the story as part of her own last will and testament. The King had asked for a room to be made up next to his own, where the two could spend the nights rather than returning to their own apartments. Françoise had not prayed that His Majesty's life be spared, she said, but rather that his soul should be saved. In his confessor's presence, "she reminded him of several faults that she had seen him commit, and he confessed these, and thanked her for reminding him." Together they went through various papers and letters, most of which were burned on the King's instructions. "We won't need these lists of guests for weekends at Marly anymore," he said, "and burn those documents, too, otherwise there'll be two of my ministers at each other's throats." Taking his rosary beads, he gave them to her with a smile: "They're not a saintly relic," he said, "just a souvenir."

On August 27, the King appeared to rally, eating some soup and even a little biscuit. Courtiers hastened back from the duc d'Orléans's apartments, ready to acknowledge their revived master. "If the King eats another mouthful," quipped the astute duc, "I'll have no servants left." But it was not to be. On the last day of August, the priests began to recite the prayer for the dying: "Now and at the hour of our death . . ."

"The King was constantly putting his hands together, and saying prayers, or beating his breast with a confiteor," said Saint-Simon. "He noticed his valets weeping, and he said to them, *Why are you crying? Did you think I was immortal? I never thought so, and given my age, you should have been prepared to lose me . . .*"

Françoise, frequently weeping herself, took care nonetheless that the King should not see this, stepping out of the room "whenever she felt she could not hold back her tears." Three times he seemed to be on the point of death, and three times he bade Françoise farewell. "I have no regrets," he said the first time, "other than in leaving you, but we'll soon see each other again." The second time, he asked her pardon for the difficulties she had endured in living with him. "Forgive me, Madame," he said. "I know I didn't make you happy, but I did love you and I did respect you," revealing that if he had not been able to meet her needs, he had at least understood them. And he began to weep.

At the third farewell, he asked her anxiously, "But what will become of you, since you have nothing?" "I am nothing," she replied. "Think only of God."

But she had gone "only two steps" from the bed when she turned back, herself stricken by a sudden anxiety "about the uncertain treatment I might expect from the princes, and I asked the King to ask Monsieur le duc d'Orléans to have some consideration for me."

It is Françoise's own admission, affixed to her will, and it is clear testimony that, the brilliance of her position notwithstanding, the fears of her earliest life, fears of exclusion, of humiliation, of poverty, had never really left her. "What will become of you," Louis had asked, "since you have nothing?" "I am nothing," she had said—or at least, nothing without you. So she had realized, turning from what she had thought to be Louis's very last words, and she had turned back in fright.

Louis lived one more day. On the first morning of September, he heard the bell of his late-finished chapel ring out the hour: a quarter past eight o'clock. Then the great Sun King, ever magnificent, ever glorious, gave a sigh, and two little hiccups, and died.

"He surrendered his soul without effort," wrote the marquis de Dangeau, "like a candle going out."

Françoise, cloaked and hooded, "and perfectly dry-eyed," noted Saint-Simon meanly, had already fled Versailles. No longer needed, with the King unconscious and his death imminent, she had driven away in Villeroy's carriage, escorted by the maréchal-duc's guards. "She had asked me to make sure to have some other carriage waiting for her, and not her own," wrote Mademoiselle d'Aumale. "She was afraid of being treated as she had seen other favourites treated, once they'd lost everything. And she was afraid there would be people shouting insults at her on the road to Saint-Cyr. Monsieur de Villeroy had posted guards along the route to make sure this didn't happen, but there was really no likelihood of it; he just wanted to reassure her."

In the carriage with Mademoiselle d'Aumale, Françoise spoke of her grief, "a calm grief, she said, because the King had made a perfectly Christian death, and if she was weeping, her tears were tears of tenderness, and her heart was tranquil . . . But when we arrived at Saint-Cyr, she began weeping more than ever. *I don't want anything now, except God and my children*, she said . . . All the girls were waiting for her, and it was the saddest thing in the world. Madame de Maintenon absolutely broke down, and all the girls were sobbing, even the littlest ones . . . *I hope I'll be able to see you soon without tears*, she said to them, *but today I just can't help it*."

France's new king, Louis XV, had made his transition from baby gowns to trousers only a year before, pattering in to see his great-grandfather with a tiny sword at his side. He was now five years old, and the kingdom was officially in the hands of his forty-one-year-old cousin Philippe, Liselotte's son, the duc d'Orléans, now Regent of France. Despite warning his sons and nephews to avoid dangerous disagreement within the royal family such as he had known during the days of the Fronde, the dying Louis had made conflict almost inevitable by the terms of his own last will and testament.

In the final days of his life, Louis had added to the will a secret codicil, which the duc de Saint-Simon blamed roundly on Françoise and Mignon, acting with the connivance of the maréchal-duc de Villeroy. "The King had paper and ink by him, and since they felt he hadn't done enough for the duc du Maine in his will, they wanted to fix this with a codicil, which shows how enormously they abused the King's weakness in this extremity . . ."

The King's weakness, however, was not a weakness of mind, as the forgetful Saint-Simon himself had very recently recorded. Seeing quite clearly through the wiles of his confessor, Père Tellier, for instance, Louis had refused to be persuaded into making any last-minute clerical appointments, "that's to say, to leave them in Père Tellier's own gift . . . The worse the King became, the more Père Tellier pressed him . . . but he didn't succeed. The King said he had enough to do making his accounts with God, and told him to stop it once and for all . . ." Louis had remained in possession of his faculties to the last. Neither Françoise nor Mignon nor Villeroy could have persuaded him on his deathbed, any more than they had ever been able to persuade him during his active life, to do anything that was against his own inclination.

All the same, the will had been changed. Only hours after Louis's death, his nephew, the duc d'Orléans, Regent of an absolutist state, with no legal restraint whatsoever on his power, found that in the codicil, his legitimized cousins, du Maine and Toulouse, together with others of their supporters, had been named members of the Regency Council. Orléans wasted no time in having the late King's will overturned. The very next day, he convoked a *lit de justice*, an exceptional session of the Paris parlement with the little King in formal attendance, and there ensured the disallowing of the troublesome codicil. Mignon and his brother scarcely minded, neither being of a strongly political disposition, as Orléans evidently realized: having proved his point and ensured his control of the regency, he at once appointed Mignon superintendent of the little King's education, with his friends Villeroy and Bishop André-Hercule de Fleury, both former protégés of Françoise, the boy's governor and tutor respectively.

If Orléans was satisfied, the duc de Saint-Simon was not. In his view, present control of the little King's education implied future power in the land: influence in the framing of policy and the choosing of ministers. The regency would last only until the King attained his formal majority in 1723, at the age of thirteen, still too young by far to have escaped the thrall of his childhood governors. Ministers would be appointed, powerful and lucrative posts would be assigned, and Saint-Simon himself, a long-standing enemy of both Mignon and Villeroy, would be left, he feared, empty-handed.

With this prospect before him, the ambitious forty-year-old Saint-Simon set to undermining Mignon in the eyes of his cousin, the Regent. Orléans himself, with a mixture of his father's wild flair and his mother's down-to-earth common sense, had begun his regency with a series of practical reforms and a relaxing of the stiff formal protocols of his uncle's day. He had abandoned Versailles for the Palais-Royal in Paris, bringing government back to the capital, and in the process rejuvenating both city and court: in place of Louis's tediously ceremonious *petit lever*, his official waking-up each morning, courtiers now sought *l'admission au chocolat*—the right to attend the Regent as he sat up in bed, sipping an early cup of hot chocolate. But though intelligent, farsighted, and widely popular, Orléans was enjoying no great success as Regent. After only two years, his liberalization of the Paris parlement, permitting the parlementaires to raise objections to his own decrees, had, unsurprisingly, begun to turn to his disadvantage; his bold economic reforms were foundering, and the difficulties of repaying the late King's vast debts seemed insurmountable. He fell into a great lethargy, from which Saint-Simon spent months attempting to rouse him, with Liselotte complaining to her half-sister that "if my son's mistresses really loved him, they'd be taking better care of him, but these Frenchwomen, they don't care about anything but themselves and their own pleasures . . ."

In the late summer of 1718, Saint-Simon finally achieved his goal of removing Mignon from power. Though he had half-persuaded Orléans, the Regent remained "irresolute," so that Saint-Simon was obliged to join forces in the venture with Orléans's cousin, the prince de Condé, himself, unlike the upstart Mignon, an unquestionably legitimate prince of the blood, and evidently happy to overlook all family liabilities which might attend his action: his own wife, Louise-Françoise, the former Mademoiselle de Nantes, was Mignon's sister "Chubby," and his sister, Louise-Bénédicte, was the duchesse du Maine, Mignon's wife.

Saint-Simon, informed by a helpful valet of his best chance of capturing Condé's undivided attention, turned up at the prince's residence in Paris just as he was getting out of bed. The prince dressed quickly, and the two sat down together "in armchairs of equal size" to plot in egalitarian comfort. "I asked him how he intended to strike at the duc du Maine," said Saint-Simon, "and he told me, by removing

him from the King's education." Saint-Simon concurred, adding, improbably but self-justifyingly, that "such a blow to the duc du Maine
now" would be "the surest way of avoiding civil war in the future."

The blow was struck on August 26, and indeed succeeded beyond
Saint-Simon's fondest hopes. By the Regent's decree at a specially con-
vened *lit de justice*, Mignon not only lost "the education" of eight-
year-old Louis, but he and his brother, the comte de Toulouse, lost
their always controversial status as princes of the blood, and with this,
their right to inherit the throne. Toulouse, the younger brother and evidently regarded as less of a potential threat than Mignon, was permitted to retain the honours of his former rank in terms of hats, bows, and
the ever vital armchairs, but for Mignon it was a reduction to the ranks
of an ordinary peer.

He accepted the demotion mildly, though the same could by no
means be said of his diminutive but superebullient wife, Louise-
Bénédicte. Granddaughter of le Grand Condé and, like most of her
family, a constitutional troublemaker, Louise-Bénédicte, "no taller
than a ten-year-old," was popularly known as "Madame Gunpowder." Declaring that "she would set the whole kingdom ablaze to keep
du Maine's right to the throne," she stormed into Orléans's rooms and
abused him "very loudly indeed . . . which her timid husband hadn't
dared to do himself."

As for Saint-Simon, it is a wonder he survived hearing the news:
"I was dying of joy. I really feared I was going to faint. My heart was
beating madly; it was bursting out of my chest, but I couldn't stop listening, it was such delicious torment . . . I had triumphed over the
bastards, I had revenge at last, I was swimming in my revenge, overjoyed by the final accomplishment of the most violent and constant
desires of my life . . ."

As required by the 1714 Treaty of Utrecht, which had concluded the
long War of the Spanish Succession, Louis had renounced the right of
his grandson, the King of Spain, to succeed to the French crown. In
Madrid, Felipe himself had renounced any pretensions of his own to
France's throne. Even at the time, peers and counsellors had ques-

tioned the legality of this step under French law. Now, less than four years later, the cynicism, or treachery, that Louis had instilled in his heirs was to drag Bourbon France once again into war—this time, perversely, with Bourbon Spain.

Louis XV was still only eight years old and his health was by no means robust; in the perilous, disease-ridden eighteenth century, there was no guarantee that he would survive to adulthood. His brothers were both dead, his father and Uncle Berry as well. Now that the bastards du Maine and Toulouse had been struck from the line of succession, in case of the little King's death the throne would pass to the Regent, Orléans. But in Madrid, the French-born Felipe had three living sons already, and a second wife, the German-Spanish Elizabeth Farnese, who was still only twenty-six years of age. He and his sons were the direct descendants of Louis XIV, with a far better claim to his throne—if the Utrecht treaties were disregarded—than the Regent, merely the late King's nephew. Encouraged by his hugely ambitious First Minister, Cardinal Alberoni, Felipe decided to seek the regency for himself, so that in the event of little Louis's death, he or one of his sons might take the throne of France.

Over the course of 1718, the plans were laid: Orléans was to be captured during one of his many journeys outside Paris, Felipe was to be declared the new Regent, and the whole coup was to be sustained by a landing of Spanish forces in the west of France. Within the country itself, the Spanish ambassador Cellamare was to lead the conspiracy, assisted by various disaffected French nobles resentful of their own exclusion from power, with Mignon's wife, Louise-Bénédicte, "Madame Gunpowder," prominent among them.

Abetting her in this treasonous exercise were a halfhearted Mignon and his sister Françoise-Marie, duchesse d'Orléans—the wife, no less, of the Regent himself: twenty-six years and eight children after the marriage which had so upset her, Liselotte once again was to have cause for outrage. Françoise-Marie's motive appeared to be simple hatred of her husband, admittedly a man of flagrant infidelities. In her younger days, together with her sister "Chubby," she had caused endless scandal at court with her wild behaviour, which included sitting up half the night with unsuitable friends, smoking and getting drunk. But now at forty, Françoise-Marie was scarcely to be seen moving from her sofa. "Her laziness is beyond belief," wrote mother-in-law Liselotte. "She's had a chaise longue made especially to lie on when she's playing cards. She gambles on it, eats on it, reads on it . . . She's just had the colic again from having eaten too much; that woman can eat the most enormous quantities of food—she gets that from her father and mother. Her daughters are exactly the same; they eat until they make themselves sick, and then they start eating again. It's disgusting . . ."

Françoise-Marie had in any case moved, or been moved, sufficiently to take some part in Cellamare's plot, which gathered in pace towards the autumn of 1718. The duc de Saint-Simon "persuaded" himself, by his own admission, that from her cloister at Saint-Cyr, Françoise was involved as well: "It doesn't take too much to persuade oneself that she knew all about what her Mignon was up to, all his plans," he later wrote. "The hope of his success had been sustaining her . . ."

But by the beginning of December there were clear indications that all had been discovered, and at the end of the month Mignon and Louise-Bénédicte were arrested, along with 1,500 co-conspirators scattered throughout the provinces. At Saint-Cyr, Françoise heard only vaguely of the arrests. "She knew something had happened, but she didn't know what," said Mademoiselle d'Aumale, "so she sent out for more information . . . When she learned the news, she was really grief-stricken."

The Regent repaid his treacherous family with more generosity than they had deserved. Escaping a possible sentence of death, Louise-Bénédicte, though one of the principal plotters, was exiled to the province of Burgundy. Françoise-Marie went unpunished apart from a baptism of slander: thenceforth her husband was to refer to her only as "Madame Lucifer." The reluctant conspirator Mignon was imprisoned in the grim northern fortress of Doullens, in the Somme. His disgrace left Françoise "dreadfully afflicted"—"It was Death's first strike at her," said Saint-Simon. She was never to see Mignon again.

Louise-Bénédicte eventually returned to her château of Sceaux to a brilliant salonnière life, with the young Voltaire one of her most frequent and adoring guests. On Mignon's release from prison in 1720, he took up a gentlemanly existence in the country, and for the rest of his days lived quietly, apolitically, and determinedly far from his wife.

The following year, the duc de Saint-Simon was appointed France's ambassador to the court in Madrid. There he contracted smallpox, which he survived, counting himself well compensated by his subsequent promotion to the rank of Grandee of Spain.

D'Orléans died in 1723, shortly after the young King reached his majority. Liselotte's son had proved a good regent for his cousin, if not wholly for France. But over the first twenty years of Louis XV's personal reign, things improved considerably, largely owing to the intelligent direction of André-Hercule de Fleury, now a cardinal and, in the time-honoured tradition of éminences rouges, prime minister of France. Fleury had been first set on the road to prominence by Françoise, a fact which Saint-Simon, returning from Spain to seek accommodation with the new regime, swiftly took care to forget.

O f all the political upheavals which beset the early days of the regency, Françoise saw nothing. Since her arrival at Saint-Cyr on the day of Louis's death, she had not left it, nor was she ever to do so. "She'd had the good sense to declare herself dead to the world," declared the duc de Saint-Simon, ungenerously. Though she had never been on good terms with the duc d'Orléans, as Regent of France he had treated her kindly, maintaining her annual pension of 48,000 livres and assuring her of his personal attention should she ever be in further need. But Françoise was almost eighty years old. There was little left for her now, as she said, but "to think of my salvation and to do good works."

She dismissed her household of servants, enumerated by Mademoiselle d'Aumale as follows: one stable manager, three household valets, one maître d'hôtel, one functionary, one assistant functionary, one cook, one assistant cook, one coachman, one postillion, one groom, three lackeys, one porter, two litter-bearers, two or three chambermaids, one serving-woman, and one kitchen-boy. Of the entire retinue she retained only two maids "for inside the house" and a valet "for outside." To Marthe-Marguerite in Paris, she sent instructions to sell her carriage, with an afterword reminding her that it was "very well made, the seats well stuffed, the windows of beautiful glass, very comfortable, and the damask good for another four or five years"—all prompted by the reflection that her niece was likely to let it go too cheaply, since "you don't have the right look for haggling."

Françoise had no wish, and no need, to raise money now for her own expenses. They were minimal, and indeed declining. Her two private rooms at Saint-Cyr were enough for her own use; all her visitors were received there, or if the weather was fine, they would stroll about together in the gardens. Once at Saint-Cyr, in fact, she became ever more concerned—almost obsessed, in fact—with giving things away. Everything spare was put to immediate use, not only money and every kind of clothing, but bread, meat, and salt; wine and sugar for the sick; sheets and blankets and layettes for babies. These days, however, she did not go about the town distributing things herself, but remained at Saint-Cyr, soliciting alms from those of her visitors who had something to spare, and passing them on to those who had not.

Her own clothes and more decorative personal items were swiftly turned into alms as well. Abandoning her colourful court gowns, she took to wearing "very simple, not to say rough" black dresses with plain linen—to such an extent, in fact, that by the summer of 1717 her maids were having to press her to buy herself a few new blouses. "They tell me I'm almost out of them," she wrote to Marthe-Marguerite, "but I don't feel like buying things at the moment. Could you have half a dozen made for me? The fabric doesn't have to be anything very fine."

Though eighty years old, she had still been using perfumes and lotions for her hands and her hair. These she now relinquished, saying, "The man I used these things for is gone." At table, armed with a single napkin—"Isn't that all I need?"—she ate one dish only, and though she had been accustomed to taking a cup of hot chocolate every evening, she now gave this up, "not wishing to introduce any delicacies into Saint-Cyr." Her table linen, "floral muslin, the most beautiful I'd ever seen," she gave away, "and she returned to me [Mademoiselle d'Aumale] a basket which I'd given her for emptying her pockets into at the end of the day. *It's too pretty for me now,* she said."

Most of Françoise's royal pension of 48,000 livres was spoken for each year by the many schools and workshops she supported. The rest was spent, almost to the last penny, on casual charity as the need arose. She barely regarded it as charity at all: "God will have to be very good indeed to reward us for this," she said, "since as far as I'm concerned, it already gives me more pleasure to do it than I deserve." Memories of her hard early days were no doubt always with her, along with a strong consequent empathy for the poor, but she may have felt as well a touch of guilt at even the modest comfort of her own present life. She was apparently much taken by the parable of Dives and Lazarus, noting that it was not for any crime that Dives was to be punished in the next world, but rather for the life of ease that he had lived on earth while the poor at his gate went hungry. If in her younger life she had played the role of Lazarus, she was anxious not to play Dives now in the years remaining to her.

Closeted with the demoiselles and nuns at Saint-Cyr, divested of all worldly goods and cares, Françoise, in her eighties, had imagined she would simply fade away, without any fuss, into the next world. "I have found the pleasantest retreat that I could desire," she had written to Madame des Ursins a few days after her arrival. "My life will be short now. I have nothing to complain of . . ." But the lure of company and correspondence proved too great, and besides, the present world kept breaking in. In the two years before his arrest, Mignon had been a regular visitor, as the duc de Saint-Simon reported, informed by one of the former demoiselles—"who was always fond of la Maintenon, although she'd given her nothing . . . And her 'Mignon' was always welcomed with open arms, although he really stank"—only in the duc's nostrils, however.

Charles's daughter, Françoise-Charlotte-Amable, now duchesse de Noailles, came often with her husband, the duc, himself a close friend of Françoise's; she had given the pair her château of Maintenon, with its unfinished aqueduct already decaying into ivy-clad romantic ruin. There were clergy, of course, including "several obscure and fanatical bishops," as Saint-Simon described them, and, one evening every week, Mary of Modena, impoverished widow of the former King James II of England. The quondam Queen, still a beauty at almost sixty, would set out from the dreary retreat of her convent at Chaillot "in an extraordinary equipage, a coach and six emblazoned with a splendid but darkening coat-of-arms, with a drunken-looking crown inclining on the top of its dome-shaped roof." Thirty years before, "it had been the height of elegance; now it was a source of embarrassment." Mary would spend the evening dining and chatting with Françoise, nibbling on sweets and pastries provided by an admiring clergyman, and both equally seated, to Saint-Simon's indignation, in a proper chair with a back and arms.

One monarch very far from decline paid a visit to Françoise, too, rather to her surprise, in fact. Installed at her own marble Trianon at Versailles, in the middle of his second grand tour of Europe, was Peter the Great, Tsar of all the Russias, "with some girl in tow, scandalizing everyone." Six feet eight inches in height, the ruthless great Westernizer had acquired an unsought admirer during his soujourn in France. No doubt unaware of Peter's propensity to dispose of unwanted royal females in the nearest ice-cold convent, Liselotte wrote excitedly to her half-sister in the middle of May 1717:

> Dearest Luise, I've had a great visit today, from my hero, the Tsar. He's a really good man, by which I mean he's not the least bit affected and doesn't stand on ceremony. He's very intelligent and speaks broken German, but he wasn't hard to understand, and he understood me perfectly. He's polite to everyone and everyone likes him . . . Our Great Man here used to laugh when people talked about the Tsar working with carpenters and shipbuilders in Holland, but I think a man who knows fourteen trades is never going to die of hunger . . .

Talk of the Tsar's extended visit to France was constantly swirling about Saint-Cyr as well. Though Françoise had declared her own "hero" to be Peter's now-vanquished enemy, King Karl XII of Sweden, she was prepared to accept the victor of the northern wars on his own terms. "The Tsar seems to me to be a very great man," she wrote cheekily to Marthe-Marguerite in Paris, "now that I've heard he's been asking after me." It was almost a month, all the same, before she met him in person, and even then, though neither party was personally fond of ceremony, it was a most unusual meeting for the Tsar of all the Russias and the widow of a Bourbon King. On an afternoon in June, just as Françoise was about to add her signature to one of her regular letters to Marthe-Marguerite, a servant entered to inform her that "he" wanted to pay a visit after dinner—"*he* being the Tsar. I didn't dare say no and I'm just going to wait for him here in my bed . . . I don't know whether he expects some kind of formal welcome, whether he wants to see the building, or the girls, or whether he'll go into the chapel—I'll leave it all to chance." Françoise's postscript described the bizarrely informal meeting: "The Tsar arrived at seven o'clock. He sat down beside my bed and asked me if I was ill. I said yes. He asked me what was the nature of my illness. I told him great age and a weak constitution. He didn't know what to say to that . . . Oh yes, I forgot to say, he pulled back the curtains at the foot of my bed so as to get a better look at me. Naturally, he was perfectly satisfied!"

Star-struck Liselotte herself came to visit Françoise once, offering to bring along other court ladies to pay their compliments in the future, but Françoise declined. She had no wish, and now no need, to serve as an object of politesse or curiosity. Life at Saint-Cyr, with nothing left to prove and Louis's daily demands at an end, was now a life of quiet happiness. "Men are tyrannical. They're not capable of friendship as women are," she remarked to her secretary, as they sat together in amicable indolence. Mademoiselle d'Aumale had been reading to her from the marquis de Dangeau's informative but rather stiffly written journal of life at Louis's court. "I'm enjoying it very much," she wrote to Marthe-Marguerite in Paris. "It's just a pity he doesn't write as well as we do."

Her women friends, among them several of the dames, and above all the presence of the demoiselles, graced the peacefulness of Françoise's sanctuary with a tranquil daily joy. "She always loved children," said

Mademoiselle d'Aumale. One little visitor, observing the motherly tenderness with which she spoke to various of the 250 demoiselles making their way to the chapel, remarked to her in astonishment, "You have a great many children, Madame."

Among them was one special little girl, plucked from among the youngest demoiselles rouges, perhaps for her mischief—"I must say I prefer the naughtier ones"—one Mademoiselle de la Tour, seven or eight years old, Françoise's last little second-self. She was brought to live in Françoise's own rooms, to keep her company, perhaps, but more likely just to be spoiled and petted as Françoise had never been by her own unloving mother. Unlike the other demoiselles, who called Françoise "Madame," the little de la Tour was invited to call her "*maman*." Françoise taught her to read, rehearsed her catechism with her, and, one day, gave her a silver tea service to play with. "I'm a bit hesitant to let her play with it," she said, but then, thinking, perhaps, of another little girl and another little tea service in the prison at Niort so many years before, she added, "Let her have it. Silver is what she'll need to help her in the future."

"I'm well, but I'm going," replied Françoise to a visitor's enquiry after her health. At eighty-three, she was preparing for death. Divested, of her own will, of almost all her possessions and money, she began to burn all the letters she had received in more than sixty years of constant correspondence. Copies of the letters and notes which she herself had written—some 60,000, it is thought—were also burned, and though Mademoiselle d'Aumale and the other dames did what they could to save some, the most personal among them, and particularly those from Louis—"a great many"—were all destroyed by Françoise's own hand. "Now I can no longer prove that I was ever in the King's good graces," she said, "or that he ever did me the honour of writing to me." And she added, "We should leave as little of ourselves behind us as we can."

Towards the end of March 1719 she fell ill with a violent fever, a remnant, perhaps, of the long-ago malarial fever which had so nearly taken her life on board ship for the Americas. On April 4, she took to her bed. Though the spring flowers had arrived, the weather remained bitter, and Françoise, always sensitive to the cold, had her room rearranged to give more protection against the chill draughts, sending for some of the littlest girls to be brought in from their freezing dormitory to sleep within her warmer walls. Thinking, perhaps, of the bleak months she had spent so long ago in La Rochelle with Charles and Constant and Maman in their unheated attic room, she also sent money to the village for the purchase of firewood for the poor.

Marthe-Marguerite came from Paris to see her, and stayed eight days, from morning till evening, talking and reading to her. Marthe-Marguerite was now a widow, the drunkard comte de Caylus having died during the last war—"probably the only gentlemanly thing he'd ever done for his wife"—and the mother of a very promising son, Anne-Claude, destined to become famous as one of Europe's first scientific archaeologists.

On April 12, Françoise's fever abated somewhat, though she seemed weaker. She was bled, but only once, and after a great deal of protest. A sudden craving for goat's milk took her, but she found she could not drink it after all. On April 13, she read again her last will and testament, making some small changes—"and you see my handwriting's still firm," she said. But she had given away already almost all she had possessed, leaving so little to be bequeathed that, as she remarked, "People will make fun of this." And she crossed out the too grand title, "Will and Testament," overwriting it with a simple "Distribution of What She Had." Little Mademoiselle de la Tour, seeing her making her will, insisted on making one of her own. It was placed in a small box together with Françoise's, but later removed. "Take it out," said Françoise to Mademoiselle d'Aumale. "It will make mine look ridiculous by comparison."

On April 14, her pulse grew suddenly stronger. "Yes, I do feel better," she said to those at her bedside, "but I'm still going." "She was full of chat and witticisms right to the very end," said Mademoiselle d'Aumale.

The spring storm that had been gathering for days broke that night, and Françoise's fever worsened. A mass was said in her room; she took Communion, with the priest offering to hear her confession, but no, she said, there was nothing troubling her conscience that she needed to confess. And seeing the various people standing expectantly around her bed, she flung them an instruction to go: "Am I in my last throes that you're all standing there?" she said.

But in the morning, when the storm had cleared, her confessor decided it was time to administer the last rites. Françoise, drowsy and very weak, told him that she had been expecting him. When he asked her to bless her demoiselles, she replied that she was not worthy to do so, and when he insisted, she raised her hand in a blessing, but had no further strength to speak a word. Later in the day, Françoise-Charlotte-Amable and her husband visited her for the last time. The duc kissed her hand. "How are you?" he asked. "Not too bad," she replied, before falling asleep once again.

"It seems that God wanted to spare her the horrors of death," wrote Mademoiselle d'Aumale. "She was almost three hours in her last agony, but it was just like a very tranquil sleep; there was nothing frightening about it. Her face looked more beautiful and more noble than ever . . ." At five o'clock on that spring evening of April 19, 1719, she died.

Françoise had expressed the wish to be buried as an ordinary sister, in the cemetery alongside the chapel at Saint-Cyr. But, following the dames' wishes, the duc de Noailles agreed that her body should be buried within the chapel itself. The heart was not removed for separate keeping in a place of special affection to the deceased, as was usual before a noble's burial, "because we preferred to have the entire treasure in the same place"—her old childhood haunt of Mursay perhaps excepted, there was in any case no place of greater affection in Françoise's heart. Though the body was embalmed, "it was not opened for the embalming, but simply covered in all kinds of aromatic ointments."

The body was laid in a lead coffin, which itself was placed in an outer casing of oak. For two days, the body lay exposed in Françoise's old room, while the dames and demoiselles filed past, "in such a state of grief that none of us could do anything but weep." On the evening of April 17, the coffin was closed and carried to the chapel, with the dames processing behind it, and the 250 demoiselles with lighted torches in their hands. A grave had been prepared at the front of the chapel, between the girls' benches and the sisters' stalls, and into this the coffin was laid, while a bishop recited a restrained prayer above it. The Lazarist priests, chaplains at Saint-Cyr, sang the office of the dead. There was no funeral oration, and no one from the court was present, as Françoise herself had wished. "What a noise this event would have made throughout Europe, if it had happened a few years ago!" declared the duc de Saint-Simon. But Louis the Sun King had been four years in his grave, and, out of sight of the great world in perfect seclusion, his secret widow had faded quietly out of mind.

On the following day, a requiem mass was said in the chapel for the repose of Françoise's soul, and here the clergy excelled itself with a lengthy and florid oration on the exceptional qualities of the deceased, praising and lamenting "our wise, modest, gentle foundress, most noble of birth, the like of which we shall seek again in vain, mother to the poor, refuge of the unfortunate, unwavering in her goodness, faithful in the exercise of piety, tranquil amidst the turmoil of the court, simple amidst its grandeur, humble though crowned with honours, revered by Louis the Great, bathed in glory, a second Esther in royal favour, a new Judith in prayer and contemplation, loving and beloved through all the years of her long and illustrious life, now ended in a saintly death."

"Such a prodigious elevation, from such depths!" sniffed the duc de Saint-Simon.

"The old hag's croaked at last," wrote Liselotte.

Some time after Françoise's funeral, a plaque of black marble was placed over her place of burial, engraved with the superlaudatory words of the oration delivered in her honour. Had she known of it, she would no doubt have protested that it was far more than she deserved, and indeed, in its extravagance, not even to her taste. And certainly, a plainer epitaph would have been more in keeping with the modest face she had chosen to present to the world, and more in keeping, too, with her straightforward religious faith.

"Saint Paul declares it's terrible to fall into the hands of the living God. Well, I don't believe that," she had stated roundly to Mademoiselle d'Aumale. "I can't think of anything sweeter than to fall into the hands of God." Françoise had said "more than a hundred times" that she could not believe she would be damned, after all the blessings God had given her in this life. Mademoiselle d'Aumale had said that, as for herself, she lived in fear of the Last Judgement, afraid she'd be sent to hell. "*Ah, mon Dieu!*" Françoise had exclaimed in response. "I've never considered that for a second. It's true I've been no saint, but I've done my best. That's all God asks. No, that's impossible. I won't be going to hell."

In these last tranquil years at Saint-Cyr, Françoise had acquired a perfect peace of mind—very near, in her own understanding, to a religious state of grace. Her old anxieties about spiritual pride and inability to pray had long been laid aside. She had returned to the practical Christianity of her happy childhood years at Mursay, and by these simplest of religious lights, she had succeeded: she had been good to her family, generous to the poor, devoted to her difficult husband. There was nothing on her conscience and no sin on her soul. "I've done my best," she had said. "That's all God asks." For this, by the terms of the believer's great bargain, she was entitled to expect a reward. The reward that Françoise expected was not sainthood, nor glory, but simply the meeting at last of her deepest needs, the needs which had kept her striving through more than eighty extraordinary years: a measure of recognition, and a lasting safety.

Epilogue

The body of Madame de Maintenon had not been laid to any final rest. Seventy years later, in the summer of 1789, rioting in Paris signalled the beginning of the great Revolution that would shatter forever the life of the old regime that had been Françoise's own.

In the anticlerical frenzy of the Revolution, all "houses of religion" were suppressed. In November 1793, Saint-Cyr was declared a military hospital, and its chapel converted to a hospital ward. As the stalls in the choir were being removed, the marble gravestone beneath them was revealed. Seeing the noble name engraved on it, the workmen broke the stone, hauled out the coffin, and forced open first the layer of oak, then the interior lead case. The embalmed body inside was still perfectly preserved. They pulled it out and tied a rope around its neck, dragging it outside into the courtyard and then through the streets of the town. If not for an officer's intervention, the body would then have been set alight in a mock witch-burning, but the workmen were persuaded to delay the "execution" until the following day. During the night, accompanied by a former Saint-Cyr servant, the officer returned: the two stole the body, replaced it in its lead coffin, and buried it beside a quiet path in the garden of the institution.

Nine years later, in 1802, the body was exhumed from the garden and reburied, with considerable ceremony, in the "Maintenon" courtyard at Saint-Cyr. A tombstone was erected, and a grille placed around the grave. But the site proved too central for a working military hospital; the courtyard was needed for other things. In 1816, the body was exhumed again, and for more than twenty years it lay undisturbed among the army stores at Saint-Cyr, by now a military academy.

In 1836, the academy's administrative council decided to accord it a further burial. A sarcophagus of black marble was constructed, and into this, alongside the body, they placed the things that had been found with it: pieces of the shroud, an ebony cross, shreds of parchment, a few herbs, and a lady's shoe. The old oak coffin, broken and decayed, was buried with the marble sarcophagus in the original site in the chapel. The lead coffin was sold as scrap metal.

In 1890, restoration work in the chapel required the grave to be opened again. The pieces of the oak coffin were carefully collected. Five years later, amid rumours that the remains buried in the grave were not in fact human, the marble sarcophagus was disinterred, and a post-mortem performed by two military physicians, on what was now no more than a huddle of bones. In the presence of the academy's commandant and several officers, the physicians declared the bones to be "incontestably" those of Madame de Maintenon. A chaplain recited the prayers for the dead, and the bones, replaced in the marble sarcophagus, were reinterred in their chapel grave.

In the summer of 1944, Saint-Cyr was badly damaged in an Anglo-American bombing raid. The chapel floor was destroyed and the marble sarcophagus ripped open, exposing the bones amid the rubble. They were removed to Versailles, and buried in the chapel there.

And in April 1969, 250 years after Madame de Maintenon's death, her remains were returned to Saint-Cyr for a sixth burial. The site, in the central aisle of the rebuilt chapel, was marked by a black marble gravestone, outlined in bronze, bearing a plain Latin cross and the simplest of inscriptions: *"Françoise d'Aubigné, Marquise de Maintenon, 1635–1719."* It would have pleased her well.

NOTES

One: Doubtful Origins

5 *private cell*: There has been some debate about the exact place of birth of the baby Françoise. The Niort Conciergerie (the prison buildings), where Constant was incarcerated, adjoined the Palais de Justice (law courts), the whole being part of the large Hôtel Chaumont. Nothing of this Hôtel now remains. In his *Françoise d'Aubigné: Étude Critique*, Gelin claims that the baby was born not in the prison itself, but in one of the buildings surrounding the prison courtyard, basing his evidence on a phrase contained in a letter of July 23, 1642, from Françoise's mother, Jeanne, in Paris, to her sister-in-law: in response to a complaint that she has moved into a convent and is too far away from her imprisoned husband in Niort, Jeanne replies that she is no further away now than she was "in the courtyard of the Palais de Justice." Gelin takes this to refer to the courtyard of the Conciergerie of the Palais de Justice in Niort, and hence as proof that she was living there seven years previously, at the time of Françoise's birth. However, at the time of writing this letter, Jeanne had just moved from lodgings in the courtyard of the Palais de Justice in Paris, and it seems much more likely that it was to this Paris courtyard that she is referring in the letter. In addition, three of Françoise's biographers, all of whom knew her personally (Madame de Caylus, Mademoiselle d'Aumale, and the Archbishop Languet de Gergy), claim that she was born in the prison. Prisoners' families commonly lived with them in the prison, and it seems on balance likely that Françoise was indeed born there.

6 *Huguenot gentry*: The "Huguenots" were France's Calvinists. This overall term also included a small number of Lutherans.

6 *"spectacularly un-Christian"*: Davies, Norman, *Europe: A History* (Oxford: OUP, 1997), 506.

6 *into the bargain*: Henri's first wife was Marguerite de Valois (1553–1615), also known as *la Reine Margot*. Exceedingly beautiful and cultured, but also promiscuous and ambitious, she was the last member of the Valois dynasty. Henri divorced her in 1699; they had lived apart for most of their marriage and had no children.

6 *Catholic France*: Not all credit for the Edict should be laid at Henri's feet. Most of its terms
   had in fact been suggested by his predecessor, Henri III, but had been rejected by Catholic
   extremists. The Edict did not apply to Jews and Muslims, of whom the latter were expelled
   from France in 1610.

7 *Catholic King*: In England, by contrast, public officials were obliged to swear an Oath of Supremacy to the sovereign as head of both state and Church. In Germany, the principle of *cuius
   regio eius religio* (whose region, his religion) permitted each local ruler to choose his confession, and required all his subjects to follow it. As far as most Europeans of the time were concerned, religion *was* politics. The only other states to possess any form of official religious
   cohabitation were Transylvania and Poland-Lithuania, the latter then Europe's largest state.
   Henri III of France (then duc d'Anjou) had been obliged to accept religious pluralism as a
   condition of his acceptance of the Polish-Lithuanian throne; he reigned there only from 1573
   to 1574.

7 *"my spiritual children"*: D'Aubigné, Agrippa, *Sa vie à ses enfants*, ed. Gilbert Shrenk (Paris:
   Nizet, 1986), 220 ff. The greatest of d'Aubigné's works, his *Tragiques*, is a relation of the conflict provoked by the Paris Saint Bartholomew's Eve massacre of 1572, in which some 5,000
   Huguenots were killed at the hands of Catholic mobs. *Les Tragiques*, begun in 1577, was completed and first published in 1616.

8 *bitterest enemies*: The Habsburg dynasty had been divided into two separate houses, Austrian
   and Spanish, by the Holy Roman Emperor Charles V in 1521. By 1610 both were Catholic
   powers of vast extent. The Austrian Habsburg Empire stretched from Poland to the Czech
   lands and from Bavaria to Croatia, and the Spanish included Portugal, parts of the present-
   day Netherlands, Italy, and central Europe, as well as overseas territories in East Asia, Africa,
   and the Americas. For the Austrian Habsburgs, see Evans, R. J. W., *The Making of the Habsburg Monarchy, 1550–1700: An Interpretation* (Oxford: OUP, 1984). For the Spanish, see
   Elliott, J. H., *Imperial Spain, 1469–1716* (New York: Mentor, 1966). For the early history of the
   dynasty, see Wheatcroft, Andrew, *The Habsburgs: Embodying Empire* (London: Penguin, 1996).

8 *"Indian gold"*: See Christopher Marlowe, *The Massacre at Paris*, Act I, scene ii, ll. 60–61.
   Marlowe based his play on the events of Saint Bartholomew's Eve, 1572.

8 *Henri's death*: A truce between the two countries had been signed in 1598 (the Peace of
   Vervins), but Henri had continued hostilities in a kind of "cold war," by supporting Spain's
   enemies.

8 *Habsburg influence*: The sudden loss of French prestige after Henri's death was most
   clearly seen, then as now, by the cancelled attack on Spanish-held Milan. See Bertière, Simone, *Les Reines de France aux temps des Bourbons: Les deux régentes* (Paris: De Fallois,
   1996), 80 ff.

9 *prince de Bourbon-Condé*: Henri II de Bourbon Condé, duc d'Enghien (1588–1646), father of
   Louis II, *"le Grand Condé."*

9 *livres*: One *livre* at this time was roughly equivalent to one English shilling; twenty livres
   would therefore be about one pound.

9 *once again repelled*: The French Catholic Church had maintained a formal degree of independence from Rome at least since the Bologna Concordat of 1516. In 1616, this was strength-
   ened by France's refusal to publish the Tridentine dictates, that is, the dictates of the Council
   of Trent (1545–63), a central feature of the Catholic Counter-Reformation. See the sections
   on Gallicanism in MacCulloch, *Reformation*.

9 *"I do not like you"*: Quoted in Garrisson, Janine, *L'Édit de Nantes et sa révocation* (Paris: Seuil,
   1985), 59.

10 *death as a traitor*: Belatedly, for his support of the Protestant cause against Marie de' Medici. In his *Sa vie à ses enfants* (220), Agrippa suggests that Constant agreed to turn Catholic in order to have his gambling debts paid off.

10 *seventeen years*: Nathan is believed to have been born in 1601 to a Jacqueline Chayer. Françoise does not appear to have ever met or corresponded with this illegitimate uncle, who later practised medicine in Geneva under the name of Nathan Engibaud, the surname an anagram of d'Aubigné.

10 *Maillezais*: Now known as Coulonges-sur-l'Autize.

10 *"Father, forgive them"*: Agrippa d'Aubigné's second wife, whom he married in 1623, was the fifty-five-year-old Italian Renée Burlamacchi, widow of a César Balbani. Segrais nonetheless later described her as "very young"; the story of the lesson is taken from Segrais, Jean Regnault de, *Segraisiana, ou mélange d'histoire et de littérature* (Amsterdam: Compagnie des libraires, 1722), I, 111–12.

10 *the same dagger*: Constant's first wife was Anne Marchand, widow of Jehan Courrault, a minor nobleman. They were married in La Rochelle on September 3, 1608. There were no children from the marriage. Anne's lover was one Lévesque, son of a Niort lawyer. Both were killed in that town on February 6, 1619.

10 *"furiously writing prose"*: D'Aubigné, 223.

11 *Holy Roman Empire*: The Holy Roman Empire of the German Nation was a loosely linked archipelago of hundreds of principalities and estates, cities, and bishoprics, both Catholic and Protestant. It was by no means exclusively German; territories as far afield as Lombardy had allowed it to claim its "Roman" title, and it had once encompassed even the papal states. For generations, the Holy Roman Emperors had been successively elected from the Catholic Austrian House of Habsburg, but since the beginning of the Reformation, the Empire's tenuous cohesion had been threatened by growing Protestant objections to the rule of a Catholic Emperor. Of the Empire's seven Electors, three were Catholic bishops, three Protestant princes, and the seventh was the elected King of Bohemia, in recent decades always Catholic and always a member of the Habsburg family. But following the death of the childless Emperor Matthias, Bohemian Protestants elected Friedrich, the Calvinist Elector of the Palatine, neither Catholic or Habsburg, as their new King, and effectively the new Emperor. The Habsburgs retaliated in what came to be seen as the first battle of the Thirty Years War of 1618–48. See Wedgwood, C. V., *The Thirty Years War* (London: Pimlico, 1992). France was not yet officially involved in the war.

11 *Cardinal Richelieu*: Armand Jean du Plessis de Richelieu, Cardinal-Duc de Richelieu (1585–1642), prime minister from 1624 until his death, he was effectively the architect of absolutism in France.

11 *La Rochelle Huguenots*: In 1625, Buckingham had offered to help Richelieu in his fight against the Huguenots, in return for French help against the Spanish. Nothing came of these negotiations, and in June 1627 Buckingham led an eighty-strong English fleet to aid the Huguenots besieged by Richelieu at La Rochelle; he failed disastrously.

11 *"the treacherous soul"*: Quoted in Desprat, Jean-Paul, *Madame de Maintenon, ou le prix de la réputation* (Paris: Perrin, 2003), 22.

12 *"gentleman landowner"*: Pierre de Cardilhac was entitled "Sieur de Lalonne," that is, gentleman landowner of Lalonne. His wife came from the family Montalembert, of the Essarts family branch. Besides Jeanne, they had several other children, of whom little is known.

13 *Gaston d'Orléans*: Gaston Jean Baptiste de France, duc d'Orléans (1608–60). Married, he became the father of the duchesse de Montpensier, *la Grande Mademoiselle*.

13 *of course, himself*: This 1630 rebellion was led by Henri II de Montmorency (1595–1632), who was finally defeated at Castelnaudary in 1632; he was subsequently executed for treason.

14 *nothing at all*: Françoise's godfather was the nephew of the first duc de La Rochefoucauld, former governor of Poitou, and the son of Benjamin, the baron d'Estissac, at this time only a *mestre de camp*, but later governor of La Rochelle. Her godmother's mother, Madame de Neuillant, was related by marriage to the d'Aubignés through the family Laval-Lezay. Her father was the brother of the comte de Parabère, governor of the province of Poitou from 1633. Godmother Suzanne married in 1651 the future maréchal-duc de Navailles.

14 *near Geneva*: The château of Crest, rebuilt by Agrippa d'Aubigné in the early seventeenth century, is still standing and is now a wine domaine.

15 *since died*: Marie de Caumont d'Adde (1581–1625).

15 *"ugly, vulgar spendthrift"*: The verdict of Caumont d'Adde's superior, the governor of Maillezais, quoted in Desprat, 20.

15 *years' income*: See Cornette, Joël (ed.), *La France de la Monarchie absolue, 1610–1715* (Paris: Éditions du Seuil, 1997), 281 ff.

15 *lands attached*: The château de Mursay is still standing, though in a state of near ruin. However, in 2002 it was purchased by a local Niort authority for the modest sum of 12,000 euros. Consolidation and preservation work is now underway at the expense of the French government. The château will not be fully restored but will be maintained as a type of "romantic ruin."

16 *"little lap desk"*: Rapley, Elizabeth, *The Dévotes: Women and the Church in Seventeenth-Century France* (Montreal and Kingston: McGill-Queen's University Press, 1990), 161.

17 *"I love a big fire"*: Letter to Mr d'Aubigné, February 10, 1680, in Madame de Maintenon, *Lettres*, ed. Langlois, Marcel, Vols II–V (Paris: Letouzy et Ané, 1935–59), II, no. 207, 335–41.

18 *"I'm a lady"*: D'Aumale, Marie-Jeanne, *Souvenirs sur Madame de Maintenon: Mémoire et lettres inédites de Mademoiselle d'Aumale*, 2e ed. (Paris: Calmann-Levy, 1902), 15.

18 *"You were my father"*: Letter from Madame Scarron in Paris to Benjamin de la Villette at Mursay, December 7, 1660, in Langlois (ed.), *Lettres* II, no. 6, 28.

18 *"painting some good"*: Letter from Pierre Sansas de Nesmond to Caumont d'Adde, dated Pentecost 1642, quoted in *Correspondance générale de Madame de Maintenon*, ed. Lavallée, Théophile, 4 vols (Paris: Charpentier, 1866) I, 1e partie, 15 ff. Subsequent quotations from Nesmond in this paragraph are taken from the same letter.

19 *"The smallest gift"*: See the letters from Jeanne d'Aubigné of June 12, 1641, and January 26, 1642, in ibid., nos I and II, 11–15. Despite his lack of enthusiasm for the cause, Benjamin de Villette did visit Jeanne at least once after this, in March 1642, during her battle with Sansas de Nesmond.

19 *"I feel so sorry for him"*: Letter of July 14, 1642, in ibid., no. III, 17–18.

19 *"I acknowledge"*: Constant's note of August 14, 1642, quoted in Lavallée, Théophile, *La Famille d'Aubigné et l'enfance de Madame de Maintenon* (Paris: Henri Plon, 1863), 74.

20 *"for the trouble"*: Letter of July 14, 1642, in Lavallée (ed.), *Correspondance générale* I, 1e partie, no. III, 17–18.

20 *"having abandoned, against all"*: From Constant's *requête* to the tribunal at Niort, quoted in ibid., 22 ff.

20 *"bit of misbehaviour"*: Quoted in ibid., 19.

20 *"cast aside your sisterly passion"*: Letter of July 23, 1642, in ibid., no. IV, 20–2.

22 *"one of our Catholic authors"*: Letter of July 14, 1642, in ibid., no. III, 18.

22 *"Widows should not"*: Ibid.

22 *political amnesties*: The duc de La Rochefoucauld suggested that "a sentiment of piety" may also have motivated the King to declare the amnesties. See La Rochefoucauld, *Mémoires* (Paris: La Table Ronde, 1993), 99.

Two: America!

24 *half-brother, Nathan*: In June 1643, Constant, then in Lyon, wrote to his half-brother Nathan in Geneva that he was in the direst financial straits and thinking of seeking a provincial retreat in Provence.

24 *"only twice"*: D'Aumale, Marie-Jeanne, *Souvenirs sur Madame de Maintenon: Mémoire et lettres inédites de Mademoiselle d'Aumale*, 2e ed. (Paris: Calmann-Levy, 1902), 18.

24 *"My mother brought us up"*: Desprat, Jean-Paul, *Madame de Maintenon, ou le prix de la réputation* (Paris: Perrin, 2003), 262.

26 *the difficulties which his bad behaviour*: Letter of July 23, 1642, in *Correspondance générale de Madame de Maintenon*, ed. Lavallée, Théophile, 4 vols (Paris: Charpentier, 1857), I, 1e partie, no. IV, 19.

26 *"She did not like to talk"*: D'Aumale, 15.

27 *in Spanish possession*: In 1493, after Columbus's first voyage, Valencia-born Pope Alexander VI had issued a papal bull according Spain and Portugal (but mostly Spain) sovereign rights over all the New World territories. Surprisingly, the two countries between themselves had subsequently managed to work out a more equitable arrangement, without bloodshed, which was approved in 1506 by Alexander's successor, Pope Julius II (an Italian).

27 *"Gentlemen's Association"*: L'Association des Seigneurs de la Colonisation des îles de l'Amérique received its letters patent on October 31, 1626.

28 *"in good silver écus"*: Quoted in Merle, Louis, *L'Étrange beau-père de Louis XIV: Constant d'Aubigné 1585–1647, le père de Madame de Maintenon* (Paris: Beauchesne, and Fontenay-le-Comte: Lussaud, 1971), 118. The écu was a coin worth three livres.

28 *"roots or leaves"*: Bates, E. S., *Touring in 1600* (London: Century, 1987), 78.

29 *"Some of the engagés"*: Maurile de Saint-Michel, Le Père, *Voyage des îles Camercanes, en l'Amérique* (Au Mans: H. Olivier, 1652), Preface.

29 *"detestable pudding"*: The shocked Chevalier d'Arvieux, sailing to Egypt on an English ship in 1658, quoted in Lewis, W. H., *The Splendid Century: Life in the France of Louis XIV* (New York: Morrow, 1954), 227.

30 *"Most of our passengers"*: Maurile de Saint-Michel, 9.

30 *"all of a heap"*: Quoted in Bates, 77.

30 *"One doesn't return"*: This was Georges d'Aubusson de la Feuillade, Bishop of Metz, whom Madame de Sévigné described as "a courtier to outdo all other courtiers." See the letter of July 20, 1679, to the comte de Bussy-Rabutin and Madame de Coligny, in Sévigné, Marie, marquise de, *Lettres*, 3 vols (Paris: Pléiade, 1960), II, no. 574, 435. The Bishop's remark is quoted in d'Aumale, 16. Merle places this incident on the return voyage to France, on the assumption that Françoise must have caught a tropical fever while in the islands. Françoise Chandernagor, in *L'Allée du Roi: Souvenirs de Françoise d'Aubigne, marquise de Maintenon, épouse du Roi de France* (Paris: France Loisirs, 1981), also places it on the return voyage.

30 *Fort Royal*: Renamed Fort-de-France by Napoleon in 1801, despite being under English occupation at the time. The town is still known by this latter name.

30 *been established*: Guadeloupe was claimed for France on June 28, 1635, by Captain Charles Lyénard de l'Olive and Jean du Plessis. See Lara, Oruno, *La Guadeloupe dans l'histoire* (Paris: Harmattan, 1979), 20 ff.

31 *the island outright*: On September 4, 1649, Houël bought the island from the *Compagnie des îles de l'Amérique*, for 73,000 livres, payable in silver and sugar. This purchase included Marie-Galante and several other small islands, dependencies of Guadeloupe. With the land were sold the islands' buildings, plantations, and slaves. See Lara, 31.

31 *"naked savages"*: Moreau, Jean-Pierre (ed.), *Un Flibustier français dans la mer des Antilles* (Paris: Payot & Rivages, 2002), 105.

31 *later to be*: The infamous *Code Noir* (Black Code) was introduced only in 1685, by Louis XIV, greatly restricting the activities of slaves and introducing much new cruelty in their treatment. The Code also regulated relations between slave and owner, and required all Jews to be "chased from the islands." Guadeloupe's first African inhabitants had in fact been born in the Christian households of Seville and brought to the island at the beginning of the sixteenth century as supposed middlemen/evangelists to the Carib Indians. It was not until the 1660s that serious sugar cultivation began on Guadeloupe (and also Martinique). As this crop required more labour to grow than most others in the tropics, it was at this point that the number of slaves began to outpace the number of colonists.

32 *"I loved oranges"*: D'Aumale, 17.

33 *"how a clever girl"*: Caylus, Marthe-Marguerite, comtesse de, *Souvenirs*, ed. Bernard Noël (Paris: Mercure de France, 1965 et 1986), 23.

33 *"Assured of your loyalty"*: Quoted in Merle, 123. At this period, the French trading Companies, as distinct from those in England, were typically founded and funded by the government. See Rich, E. E. and C. H. Wilson (eds), *The Cambridge Economic History of Europe*, Vol IV: *The Economy of Expanding Europe in the Sixteenth and Seventeenth Centuries* (Cambridge: Cambridge University Press, 1967), 240 ff.

35 *new-bought slaves*: Mademoiselle d'Aumale records hearing Françoise, in later life, say that her mother had "up to 24 maids" in Martinique. See d'Aumale, 14.

36 *Greeks and Romans*: The *Parallel Lives* had been rediscovered during the Italian Renaissance after centuries of obscurity. Its first French translation appeared in 1559.

36 *"If you want to be happy"*: D'Aumale, 18.

36 *"My brother insisted"*: "Instruction aux demoiselles de la classe bleue," in Leroy, Pierre-E. et Marcel Loyau (eds), *Comment la sagesse vient aux filles: Propos d'éducation* (Paris: Bartillart, 1998), no. 18, 93–4.

36 *"There is an extreme pleasure"*: Maurile de Saint Michel, Preface.

36 *"I imagined"*: D'Aumale, 17.

37 *"I had just put my doll"*: Ibid., 17–18.

38 *"Let him eat up"*: Letter of June 2, 1646, quoted in Lavallée, Théophile, *La Famille d'Aubigné et l'enfance de Madame de Maintenon* (Paris: Henri Plon, 1863), 80–2. It is surprising that Jeanne found the food so bad, given the general profusion of easily available fruits and birds, etc., on the island at this time. Perhaps her slaves were new to the Caribbean and did not know how to prepare the local food, or perhaps they had all been sold by now, leaving Jeanne and her French maid to (mis)manage the cooking alone.

39 *"a very hard thing"*: D'Aumale, 17.

40 *"two or three types of parrot"*: The descriptions of food in the Caribbean islands are from Moreau (ed.), 115–57. The anonymous buccaneer spent ten months in the islands between

1618 and 1620. Many foods now considered native to the Caribbean were in fact introduced later in the century by Europeans travelling from Asia or from elsewhere in the Americas.

41 *"When the sea waves rise"*: Maurile de Saint-Michel, 8.

42 *up for sale*: M. S. Anderson writes that "the seas swarmed, in peace as well as wartime, with actual or potential corsairs, many of whom were hardly distinguishable from outright pirates," and notes, for example, that "the remains of the English royalist fleet degenerated from the later 1640s into little more than a gang of pirates." See Anderson, M. S., *War and Society in Europe of the Old Regime 1618–1789* (Guernsey, Channel Islands: Sutton Publishing, 1998), 57.

42 *"At least if we're captured"*: D'Aumale, 16.

Three: Terra Infirma

43 *"You're a fine fellow"*: Letter to the comte de Bussy-Rabutin, March 15, 1648, in Sévigné, Marie, marquise de, *Lettres*, 3 vols (Paris: Pléiade, 1960), I, no. 6, 99.

44 *"some little allowance"*: Letter of June 10, 1647, quoted in Merle, Louis, *L'Étrange beau-père de Louis XIV: Constant d'Aubigné 1585–1647, le père de Madame de Maintenon* (Paris: Beauchesne, and Fontenay-le-Comte: Lussaud, 1971), 133 ff.

45 *"Pastors and Elders"*: The consistory's certification of January 9, 1650, is quoted in ibid., 135 ff.

45 *William II*: Prince of Orange (1626–50) and father of William III of England (1650–1702).

45 *islands in 1644*: Benjamin de Villette's letter of April 12, 1647, is referred to in Merle, 128.

45 *"I knew for a reasonable certainty"*: Tallemant des Réaux, writing on October 1, 1647, quoted in ibid., 136.

45 *"went to England"*: Esprit Cabart de Villermont, quoted in Boislisle, M. A. de, "Paul Scarron et Françoise d'Aubigné," *La Revue des questions historiques*, juillet–octobre 1893, 127.

46 *"a thorny discussion"*: Desprat, Jean-Paul, *Madame de Maintenon, ou le prix de la réputation* (Paris: Perrin, 2003), 41. In Langlois, Marcel, *Madame de Maintenon* (Paris: Plon, 1932), the author suggests that during this autumn the family was taken to the home of their Parabère relatives in Angoulême, and later to the Magallan family, but it seems rather that it was only later, in 1648, that Charles went to the Parabère family (in fact in Poitiers), and Constant would have gone to the Magallan family, had he survived, 6. Langlois also suggests that it was a M. d'Alens, a Huguenot, who took Françoise to Mursay.

47 *in the land*: The English Civil War(s), which also involved Scotland and Ireland, lasted from 1642 to 1651, including two periods of uneasy peace. The causes were a mixture of constitutional and religious grievances. In Norman Davies's summary, "Catholics and High Church Anglicans felt the greatest loyalty for the King, whose monarchical prerogatives were under attack. English Puritans and Calvinist Scots provided the core support of Parliament, which they saw as a bulwark against absolutism." See Davies, Norman, *Europe: A History* (Oxford: OUP, 1997), 551. The Commonwealth was initiated after the execution of Charles I in January 1649; Cromwell became Lord Protector in 1653. The monarchy was restored in 1660.

47 *"subtle and full of trickery"*: La Rochefoucauld, *Mémoires* (Paris: La Table Ronde, 1993), 101. Subsequent quotations in this paragraph are from ibid., 120. Cardinal Mazarin (1602–61), born Giulio Mazzarini, became prime minister of France in 1643, at the beginning of the reign of Louis XIV and the regency of his mother, Anne of Austria. Mazarin had formerly been a protégé of Cardinal Richelieu's.

48 *Battle of Rocroi*: On May 19, 1643, at Rocroi, in the Ardennes, Condé (then duc d'Enghien and aged just twenty-one) defeated the Spanish Habsburg army under Don Francisco Melo. See Pujo, Bernard, *Le Grand Condé* (Paris: Albin Michel, 1995), 59 ff. Davies (565) writes that Rocroi "ended the Spanish military supremacy which had lasted since . . . 1525." The battle was part of the Thirty Years War of 1618–48, which the French had entered formally in 1635.

48 *felt himself entitled*: In fairness to the young prince, it should be noted that at this time "the distinction between military and naval commands was still blurred." See Anderson, M. S., *War and Society in Europe of the Old Regime 1618–1789* (Guernsey, Channel Islands: Sutton Publishing, 1998), 57.

48 *"the pittance"*: Langlois, 6. In Bonhomme, Honoré (ed.), *Madame de Maintenon et sa famille: Lettres et documents inédits . . .* (Paris: Didier, 1863), the author writes (226) that "[s]ome Jesuits came here some time ago saying that in her childhood Madame de Maintenon was so poor that she would go with a bowl to get soup which was being distributed at a particular place . . ." However, Bonhomme did not believe this.

49 *"gallows meat"*: See Rapley, Elizabeth, *The Dévotes: Women and the Church in Seventeenth-Century France* (Montreal and Kingston: McGill-Queen's University Press, 1990), 78. The secret group of the *Compagnie du Saint-Sacrement* (Company of the Holy Sacrament) was known to its enemies as the *cabale des dévots*. See Chill, E., "Religion and Mendicity in Seventeenth-Century France," *International Review of Social History* 7, no. 3 (1962): 400–25.

49 *only turnips*: See the *Instruction pour le soulagement des pauvres*, produced by the chapter of Notre-Dame, quoted in Saint-Germain, Jacques, *La Reynie et la police au grand siècle* (Paris: Hachette, 1962), 256.

50 *"All her tenderness"*: D'Aumale, Marie-Jeanne, *Souvenirs sur Madame de Maintenon: Mémoire et lettres inédites de Mademoiselle d'Aumale*, 2e ed. (Paris: Calmann-Levy, 1902), 16.

51 *"and I wasn't revolted"*: "Instruction aux demoiselles de Saint-Cyr. Sur les amitiés," May 1714, in Leroy, Pierre-E. et Marcel Loyau (eds), *Comment la sagesse vient aux filles: Propos d'éducation* (Paris: Bartillart, 1998), no. 3, 42.

52 *"the meanest and most avaricious pair"*: The genealogist Guillard, quoted in Boislisle, 95.

52 *Madame de Neuillant's brother*: It is in fact not certain whether Pierre Tiraqueau, baron de Saint-Hermant, was the brother or the cousin of Madame de Neuillant.

53 *"Everyone knows what money-grubbers"*: The genealogist Guillard, quoted in Boislisle, 95. Suzanne became *demoiselle d'honneur* to the duchesse de Montpensier, later known as *la Grande Mademoiselle*. Suzanne's husband was the duc, and later maréchal, de Navailles.

54 *"They had been intending"*: Wicquefort, A. de, *Chronique discontinue de la Fronde, 1648–52*, ed. Robert Mandrou (Paris: Fayard, 1978), 101.

55 *their own capital*: For eyewitness accounts of *la Fronde du Parlement* (1648–49) and *la Fronde des Princes* (1650–53), see Wicquefort; La Rochefoucauld; Retz, Paul de Gondi, Cardinal de, *Mémoires* (Paris: Garnier, 1987); Patin, Guy, *La France au milieu du XVII siècle, 1648–1661* (Paris: Armand Collin, 1901); Montpensier, Anne Marie Louise d'Orléans, duchesse de, *Mémoires de la Grande Mademoiselle*, ed. Bernard Quilliet, 2 vols (Paris: Mercure de France, 2005).

55 *"doing without everything"*: Montpensier I, 108.

55 *"a jealous, unthinking"*: Leca, Ange-Pierre, *Scarron: Le malade de la reine* (Paris: KIMÉ, 1999), 82.

55 *"Since Cardinal Mazarin"*: Wicquefort, 113–14.

56 *a few days later*: The Peace of Rueil was signed on March 11, 1649, and was ratified by the parlement on April 1.

57 *"a lot of wretched fields"*: Lewis, W. H., *The Splendid Century: Life in the France of Louis XIV* (New York: Morrow, 1954), 242.

57 *young girls*: See Rapley, and see Jégou, Marie-Andrée, *Les Ursulines du Faubourg Saint-Jacques à Paris 1607–1662: Origine d'un monastère apostolique* (Paris: Presses Universitaires de France, 1981), Appendix 1, *Le contrat de fondation.*

58 *"reading, writing, needlework"*: From a papal bull addressed to the Ursulines of Toulouse, quoted in Dubois, Elfrieda, "The Education of Women in Seventeenth-Century France," *French Studies* 32, no. 1 (1978), 4.

58 *"Young girls will reform"*: See Rapley, 157.

58 *"confine her intellect"*: Re Mère Madeleine in 1646. See Jégou, 135.

58 *"The girls got up at 6"*: Drawn from a Grenoble Ursuline convent in 1645. See Dubois, 4. Jégou describes the almost identical daily routine at the Ursuline convent in the rue Saint-Jacques in Paris, where Françoise later stayed, 148ff.

59 *"Well of course"*: D'Aumale, 22–3.

60 *"I loved her more"*: *"Instruction aux demoiselles de Saint-Cyr. Sur les amitiés,"* May 1714, quoted in Leroy, Pierre-E. et Marcel Loyau (eds), *Comment la sagesse vient aux filles: Propos d'éducation* (Paris: Bartillart, 1998), 41.

60 *"the girls liked me"*: Ibid.

60 *"Little by little"*: D'Aumale, 23.

61 *"I thought I'd die"*: *"Instruction aux demoiselles de Saint-Cyr. Sur les amitiés,"* May 1714, quoted in Leroy et Loyau (eds), 42.

61 *"They gave us big sticks"*: Ibid., 39.

61 "Changeable are the blessings:" Guy du Faur de Pibrac (1529–84), quoted in Maugin, Georges, *La Jeunesse mystérieuse de Madame de Maintenon* (Vichy: Wallon, 1959), 24. In his *Sganarelle* of 1660, Act I, scene i, Molière pokes fun at "Pibrac, et [autres] doctes tablettes."

62 *"The girl was a relative"*: Tallemant des Réaux, Gédéon, *Les Historiettes de Tallemant des Réaux: Mémoires pour servir à l'histoire du XVIIe siècle*, 6 vols (Paris: Bibliothèque Nationale Française, 1995), V, 259–60.

63 *"with very beautiful black eyes"*: D'Aumale, 36, note 1.

63 *Blaise Pascal*: (1623–62). Forbidden as a boy to study mathematics owing to his delicate health, Pascal became one of the greatest of all mathematicians. At the age of eighteen he invented an "arithmetical machine," the forerunner of the computer; his contributions to geometry and probability theory were equally remarkable. In his late twenties he underwent a religious conversion, becoming one of the leading lights of the controversial Catholic Jansenist movement and a fierce opponent of the Jesuits.

63 *Pierre de Fermat*: (1601–65). A lawyer by profession, Fermat insisted on remaining an "amateur" mathematician, generally refusing to publish his work or to provide proofs of his theorems. He is nonetheless regarded as the founder of number theory and a major contributor to the development of modern calculus. His famous "last theorem" remained unproven for 358 years, until 1995.

63 *probability theory together*: Their correspondence was first published in 1654. See Pascal, Blaise, *La Correspondance de Blaise Pascal et de Pierre de Fermat: La géometrie du hasard ou le calcul des probabilités* (Fontenay-aux Roses: École Normale Superieure, 1983).

64 *"She understood Spanish"*: D'Aumale, 189.

64 *"If you were simply"*: Letter to Mademoiselle*** [d'Aubigné], undated, in Chamaillard, Edmond, *Le Chevalier de Méré, rival de Voiture, ami de Pascal, précepteur de Madame de Maintenon* (Niort: Clouzot, 1921), 2e partie, 22–4.

64 *"I would really like her"*: Letter to Madame la duchesse de Lesdiguières, probably 1652, in ibid., 24–6.

64 *"the first to give you"*: Quoted in Madame de Maintenon, *Lettres*, ed. Langlois, Marcel, Vols II–V (Paris: Letouzy et Ané, 1935–59), II, note 233, 381–2.

65 *"between the hard-boiled eggs"*: Magne, Émile, *Scarron et son milieu*, 6e ed. (Paris: Émile-Paul Frères, 1924), 177.

65 *"before anyone could tell me"*: Desprat, 49.

66 *"beaten you to it"*: D'Aumale, 23.

66 *"I think God will change His mind"*: Ibid., 16.

66 *Palais d'Orléans*: Built in the earlier seventeenth century by Marie de' Medici, mother of Gaston, duc d'Orléans, this is now the Palais du Luxembourg, the seat of France's Senate.

Four: Burlesque

67 *"Paris . . . is . . . one"*: Evelyn, John, *The Diary* (London: Macmillan, 1908). Entry for December 24, 1643, 29–30. Evelyn arrived in Paris in mid-November 1643 and remained there until April 19, 1644, before setting off for the French provinces and Italy. His diary entries for these months contain detailed descriptions of the city as he saw it.

68 *"All the same"*: Gui Patin's letter of October 18, 1650, to Charles Spon, in Patin, Guy, *La France au milieu du XVIIe siècle, 1648–1661* (Paris: Armand Collin, 1901), 96. Patin was a famous opponent of the theory of the circulation of the blood.

68 *a hundred years of building*: The original Louvre, a fortress constructed between 1190 and 1202 by King Philippe Auguste, was demolished early in the fifteenth century before being rebuilt by François I and Henry II in the sixteenth century. The exterior of the palace as it is today was not completed until the mid-nineteenth century.

69 *"most unpleasant for those on foot"*: Saint-Germain, Jacques, *La Reynie et la police au grand siècle* (Paris: Hachette, 1962), 10, quoting Locatelli's *Voyage de France* of 1664–65.

69 *"not to spit inside"*: See Castiglione, Baldassar, *Le Livre du Courtisan* (Paris: Flammarion, 1991). First published in 1580, it remained popular reading for courtiers and gentlefolk in France until the eighteenth century.

71 *"Monsieur Scarron's house"*: D'Aumale, Marie-Jeanne, *Souvenirs sur Madame de Maintenon: Mémoire et lettres inédites de Mademoiselle d'Aumale*, 2e ed. (Paris: Calmann-Levy, 1902), 26.

72 *"My body, it's true"*: Letter to the comtesse de Brienne, August 7, 1657, in Scarron, Paul, *Oeuvres*, 7 vols (Paris: Bastien, 1786), I, 195–6.

72 *"This is for you"*: From the *Portrait de Scarron, fait par lui-même, au Lecteur, qui ne m'a jamais vu*, in Scarron I, 129–31.

73 *"To look him in the face"*: Tallemant des Réaux, Gédéon, *Les Historiettes de Tallemant des Réaux: Mémoires pour servir à l'histoire du XVIIe siècle*, 6 vols (Paris: Bibliothèque Nationale Françoise, 1995), V, 258.

73 *had begun*: This story may have originated with biographer and editor la Beaumelle in the eighteenth century. One of Scarron's contemporaries attributed his condition simply to a *maladie des garçons* (venereal disease), but at the time there was no consensus as to its cause.

75 *"admired by all"*: From Scarron's *Epitre à Mademoiselle de Neuillant*, in Scarron VII, 102–4.

75 *Mademoiselle, I had my suspicions*: Undated letter, probably written during the summer of 1651, to Françoise d'Aubigné, in ibid., I, 170–1.

75 *"I should have been more wary"*: Undated letter to Françoise d'Aubigné, in ibid., 179–82.

76 *"You say,"* he writes: La Beaumelle, Laurent Angliviel de, *Lettres de Madame de Maintenon,* nouvelle édition, 9 vols (Amsterdam: Pierre Erialed, 1758), I, 10.

76 *"white, plump, naked body"*: Undated letter to Françoise d'Aubigné, in Scarron I, 179–82.

76 *"Come back"*: Ibid.

76 *"little tigress"*: La Beaumelle (ed.), *Lettres* I, 8.

77 *"where the earth yields wealth"*: From Scarron's *Réflexions politiques et morales,* quoted in Leca, Ange-Pierre, *Scarron: Le malade de la reine* (Paris: KIMÉ, 1999), 127.

77 *"my own dear town"*: Ibid.

77 *"the fruit of seventeen years"*: Mazarin's librarian Gabriel Naudé, quoted in Pujo, Bernard, *Le Grand Condé* (Paris: Albin Michel, 1995), 201.

78 *young Queen*: See Buckley, Veronica, *Christina, Queen of Sweden* (London: Fourth Estate, 2004).

78 *"five hundred écus"*: Scarron VII, 339–40.

78 *"Richelieu's monkey"*: La *Mazarinade* of February 10, 1651, in Scarron I, 283 ff.

78 *"In a month's time"*: Letter to Scarron's friend, the poet Sarrazin, written during the winter of 1651–52, in ibid., 169–70.

79 *"a badly behaved woman"*: Letter to the poet Gilles Ménage, quoted in Desprat, Jean-Paul, *Madame de Maintenon, ou le prix de la réputation* (Paris: Perrin, 2003), 54.

79 *"damned his soul"*: Undated letter to Françoise d'Aubigné, in Scarron I, 179–82.

79 *"She's caused me"*: Letter to Monsieur de Marillac, quoted in Magne, Émile, *Scarron et son milieu,* 6e ed. (Paris: Émile-Paul Frères, 1924), 188, note 1.

80 *10,000 livres*: See Rapley, Elizabeth, *The Dévotes: Women and the Church in Seventeenth-Century France* (Montreal and Kingston: McGill-Queen's University Press, 1990), 181 and passim.

81 *"very low figure"*: From Furetière's *Dictionnaire,* quoted in Duchêne, Roger, *Être femme au temps de Louis XIV* (Paris: Perrin, 2004), 117.

82 *"I preferred to marry him"*: Tallemant des Réaux V, 259.

82 *"She'll be the most useless"*: See the undated letter from the chevalier de Méré to la duchesse de Lesdiguières, in Chamaillard, Edmond, *Le Chevalier de Méré, rival de Voiture, ami de Pascal, précepteur de Madame de Maintenon* (Niort: Clouzot, 1921), 2e partie, 24–6.

Five: Marriage of True Minds

83 *"the lady Jeanne"*: Boislisle, M. A. de, "Paul Scarron et Françoise d'Aubigné," *La Revue des questions historiques,* juillet–octobre 1893, 138. The *procuration* was dated February 19, 1652.

84 *"for fear they should bring"*: Jégou, Marie-Andrée, *Les Ursulines du Faubourg Saint-Jacques à Paris 1607–1662: Origine d'un monastère apostolique* (Paris: Presses Universitaires de France, 1981), 151.

84 *"before the King's notaries"*: Boislisle, 141 ff.

84 *"two big eyes"*: Quoted in Desprat, Jean-Paul, *Madame de Maintenon, ou le prix de la réputation* (Paris: Perrin, 2003), 58.

84 *"one thousand livres"*: Boislisle, 141 ff.

85 *"setting the courtiers' hearts on fire"*: For Scarron's poem in praise of Marie-Marguerite, see Scarron VII, 102–4.

85 *"He liked teasing"*: Segrais, Jean Regnault de, *Segraisiana, ou mélange d'histoire et de littérature* (Amsterdam: Compagnie des libraires, 1722), I, 139.

85 *"Why, Father,"* replied Scarron: Desprat, 59.

85　*"He really was"*: Segrais I, 87.

85　*"He couldn't even turn"*: Letter of 1691 to Madame de Lesdiguières, quoted in Magne, Émile, *Scarron et son milieu*, 6e ed. (Paris: Émile-Paul Frères, 1924), 197.

86　*"Scarron said of his wife"*: Segrais I, 87.

86　*"someone would have had to"*: Tallemant des Réaux, Gédéon, *Les Historiettes de Tallemant des Réaux: Mémoires pour servir à l'histoire du XVIIe siècle*, 6 vols (Paris: Bibliothèque Nationale Française, 1995), V, 258–9. However, Segrais said that Scarron's family made over his inheritance to him on his marriage. See Segrais I, 140.

86　*"You can't satisfy a woman"*: Segrais I, 140. Unbeknown to him, Segrais's anecdotes of the 1690s, related at the home of a friend, were being regularly recorded by a scribe hidden behind a tapestry. It is from these anecdotes that the *Segraisiana* was eventually compiled.

87　*"their taste is a cross"*: Ibid., 183.

87　*"She and her mother"*: Ibid., 135.

87　*"seven hundred men"*: From a verse of the satirist Loret in *La Muze historique* of May 19, 1652, quoted in Leca, Ange-Pierre, *Scarron: Le malade de la reine* (Paris: KIMÉ, 1999), 126.

88　*family lands*: These were the estates of Fougerets and La Rivière. See Magne, 200, note 2.

88　*"It's a good enough work"*: Scarron's verse quoted in Desprat, 68.

89　*It isn't true*: From a verse of the satirist Loret in *La Muze historique* of October 5 and November 9, 1652, quoted in Magne, 202, note 2.

90　*"because there are twelve"*: Segrais I, 78. And see Leca, 59.

90　*"in the Marais fashion"*: Segrais I, 78–9.

90　*"a pleasant temperament"*: Boislisle, 111. Saumaise (1588–1653) was one of the period's most distinguished humanist scholars.

90　*"She likes men"*: Segrais I, 78.

91　*She was tall*: Desprat, 63.

91　*"They weren't really"*: Segrais I, 213. Molière's celebrated play was first performed in November 1659 by the troupe belonging to the King's brother.

92　*"Take every chance"*: *"Instruction aux demoiselles de la classe jaune,"* quoted in Leroy, Pierre-E. et Marcel Loyau (eds), *Comment la sagesse vient aux filles: Propos d'éducation* (Paris: Bartillart, 1998), 1155 ff.

92　*"If you've made yourself"*: Chamaillard, Edmond, *Le Chevalier de Méré, rival de Voiture, ami de Pascal, précepteur de Madame de Maintenon* (Niort: Clouzot, 1921), 1e partie, 155.

93　*"her advice"*: Segrais I, 112–13.

93　*"I've always been a bit lazy"*: From the *Portrait de Scarron, fait par lui-même, au Lecteur, qui ne m'a jamais vu*, in Scarron, Paul, *Oeuvres*, 7 vols (Paris: Bastien, 1786), I, 129–31.

93　Roman Comique: Part I was published in 1651 and Part II in 1657. Scarron never completed Part III.

94　*rue Neuve-Saint-Louis*: The house is still standing, though the street has been renamed. It is on the corner of the present rue Villehardouin and the rue de Turenne, in the Marais.

94　*"praying to the Lord"*: From the *Stances Chrétiennes*, in Scarron VII, 244–6.

94　*"I support my ills"*: From the *Portrait de Scarron*, 129–31.

95　*"That yellow damask"*: Segrais I, 114.

95　Saint Paul: Poussin's *Ravissement de Saint Paul*, painted in 1649–50, is now in the Louvre in Paris.

95　*"The best way of conducting oneself"*: Chamaillard, 1e partie, 154.

96　*"It's the one where people talk"*: Letter to the comte de Vivonne of June 12, 1660, in Scarron I, 198–200.

96 *"It's one of the miracles"*: Tallemant des Réaux V, 257.

97 *"Scarron's house was the meeting place"*: Segrais I, 114.

97 *"so extraordinarily ugly"*: From Furetière's *Roman bourgeois*, quoted in Leca, 133.

97 *"a little man"*: Ibid., 133–4.

98 *"since my husband"*: Duchêne, Roger, *Ninon de Lenclos: ou la manière jolie de faire l'amour* (Paris: Fayard, 2000), 247.

98 *"as good as cheeses can be"*: Letter to d'Albret of December 2, 1659, in Scarron I, 213–14.

99 *"One foolish statement"*: Chamaillard, 1e partie, 126.

99 *"Don't talk too much"*: "Avis à une demoiselle qui sortait de Saint-Cyr," quoted in Leroy et Loyau (eds), 163 ff.

99 *"Don't try to keep up"*: "Instruction aux demoiselles des deux grandes classes" and "Lettre aux demoiselles de Saint-Cyr," quoted in ibid., 189 ff. and 225 ff.

100 *"And what I admire"*: Lettre à Madame la duchesse de Lesdiguières, probably 1652, in Chamaillard, 2e partie, 24–6.

101 *"And I have to admit"*: D'Aumale, Marie-Jeanne, *Souvenirs sur Madame de Maintenon: Mémoire et lettres inédites de Mademoiselle d'Aumale*, 2e ed. (Paris: Calmann-Levy, 1902), 26.

101 *"that her friends were ashamed"*: Ibid., 27.

101 *"What I don't like"*: Lettre à Madame la duchesse de Lesdiguières, probably 1652, in Chamaillard, 2e partie, 24–6.

101 *"But I wasn't doing these things"*: D'Aumale, 27.

101 *"He shouldn't have come"*: Ibid., 28.

101 *"never turning her wit"*: Lettre à Madame la duchesse de Lesdiguières, probably 1652, in Chamaillard, 2e partie, 24–6.

101 *"my idols"*: Letter to the maréchal d'Albret of October 13, 1659, in Scarron I, 206–8.

Six: End of the Beginning

102 *I'm not going to attempt*: Letter of August 27, 1660, in Madame de Maintenon, *Lettres*, ed. Langlois, Marcel, Vols II–V (Paris: Letouzy et Ané, 1935–59), II, no. 2, 18 ff.

102 *"I bring Your Majesty"*: From Madame de Motteville's *Mémoires*, quoted in Fraser, Antonia, *Love and Louis XIV: The Women in the Life of the Sun King* (London: Weidenfeld and Nicolson, 2006), 40. The Treaty of the Pyrenees between France and Spain was signed on November 7, 1659.

103 *"She has very white skin"*: See the *Notice* to the *Oraison de Marie-Thérèse d'Autriche*, in Bossuet, Jacques-Bénigne, *Oraisons Funèbres* (Paris: Hachette, 1898), 214.

104 *"Scarron laughed at those"*: Tallemant des Réux, Gédéon, *Les Historiettes de Tallemant des Réaux: Mémoires pour servir à l'histoire du XVIIe siècle*, 6 vols (Paris: Bibliothèque Nationale Française, 1995), V, 262.

105 *"Up to this point"*: Ibid.

105 *"Beauty can be"*: "Instruction aux demoiselles de Saint-Cyr," quoted in Leroy, Pierre-E. et Marcel Loyau (eds), *Comment la sagesse vient aux filles: Propos d'éducation* (Paris: Bartillart, 1998), no. 4, 43, ff.

105 *"months on end"*: The memoirist La Fare, quoted in Duchêne, Roger, *Ninon de Lenclos: ou La manière jolie de faire l'amour* (Paris: Fayard, 2000), 244.

106 *"I can play the man"*: Letter to Boisrobert, quoted in ibid., 245 and passim.

106 *"They had no reason"*: Ibid., 245.

107 *"I might have guessed"*: Quoted in Magne, Émile, *Scarron et son milieu*, 6e ed. (Paris: Émile-Paul Frères, 1924), 261.

107 *"My wife is most unhappy"*: Letter to Monsieur de Villette of November 12, 1659, in Scarron, Paul, *Oeuvres*, 7 vols (Paris: Bastien, 1786), I, 263–4.

107 *"I find my wife"*: Letter to the maréchal d'Albret of October 13, 1659, in ibid., 206–8.

108 *"I'm afraid that débauchée"*: Quoted in Duchêne, *Ninon de Lenclos*, 246.

108 *"well known for her love of women"*: Tallemant des Réaux V, 264.

108 *"I've always been a bit greedy"*: From the *Portrait de Scarron, fait par lui-même, au Lecteur, qui ne m'a jamais vu*, in Scarron I, 129–31.

108 *"To my wife I bequeath"*: From *"Testament de Scarron, en vers burlesques,"* in ibid., 133–4.

109 *"Come on, then, Monsieur"*: Quoted in Desprat, Jean-Paul, *Madame de Maintenon, ou le prix de la réputation* (Paris: Perrin, 203), 100.

109 *"I'll never make you weep"*: Quoted in ibid.

109 *breathing his last*: Scarron died in the night of October 6–7, 1660, not on October 14, as is often stated. See Leca, Ange-Pierre, *Scarron: Le malade de la reine* (Paris: KIMÉ, 1999), 186, note.

109 *This man knew every pain*: *Épitaphe*, in Scarron I, 141.

110 *"the first thing I did"*: Segrais, Jean Regnault de, *Segraisiana, ou mélange d'histoire et de littérature* (Amsterdam: Compagnie des libraires, 1722), I, 134.

110 *Pierre Mignard*: This Mignard drawing has since been lost.

111 *"a furious number of people"*: Tallemant des Réaux V, 263.

111 *"I have been so overwhelmed"*: Letter to Mme de Villette of October 23, 1660, in Langlois (ed.), *Lettres* II, no. 3, 23.

112 *Monsieur Scarron has left*: Letter to M. de Villette of November 1660, in ibid., no. 4, 25.

112 *"They've staged a comedy"*: Letter to M. de Villette of December 7, 1660, in ibid., no. 6, 27.

113 *"But what is there"*: Letter to Mme de Grignan, June 24, 1676, in Sévigné, Marie, marquise de, *Lettres*, 3 vols (Paris: Pléiade, 1960), II, no. 437, 130.

Seven: The Merry Widow

115 *"I'm a widow, thank God"*: See Florent Carton Dancourt's *Le Chevalier à la mode* of 1687; Molière's *Le Misanthrope* of 1666; and Madame de Sévigné's *Lettres*. All three quotations are from Duchêne, Roger, *Être femme au temps de Louis XIV* (Paris: Perrin, 2004), 249 ff.

116 *rue des Tournelles*: Ninon de Lenclos's house at no. 36 is still standing.

117 *"Quite tall, a brunette"*: Taillandier, Madame Saint-René, *La Princesse des Ursins: Une grande dame française à la cour d'Espagne sous Louis XIV* (Paris: Hachette, 1926), 4.

117 *"something majestic in her whole bearing"*: Saint-Simon, Louis de Rouvroy, duc de, *Mémoires*, 7 vols (Paris: Pléiade, 1953), I, 924.

118 *"Maréchal d'Albret and all the other gentlemen"*: Caylus, Marthe-Marguerite, comtesse de, *Souvenirs*, ed. Bernard Noël (Paris: Mercure de France, 1965 et 1986), 27–8.

118 *"frighteningly tall"*: Saint-Simon I, 327.

118 *"a bit mad, always herself"*: Caylus, 67.

119 *"She met Madame de Montespan"*: Montpensier, Anne Marie Louise d'Orléans, duchesse de, *Mémoires de la Grande Mademoiselle*, ed. Bernard Quilliet, 2 vols (Paris: Mercure de France, 2005) I, 322.

119 *"blonde, with big azure blue eyes"*: Visconti, Primi, *Mémoires sur la Cour de Louis XIV, 1673–1681* (Paris: Perrin, 1988), 16.

119 *"of respectable conduct"*: Caylus, 37.

119 *"You could have heard it"*: The chevalier d'Arvieux, quoted in the Notice to *Le Bourgeois Gentilhomme*, in Molière, Jean-Baptiste Poquelin de, *Oeuvres Complètes*, 2 vols (Paris: Gallimard, 1971), II, 697.

120 *"Her appearance was charming"*: René de Saint-Léger, quoted in Desprat, Jean-Paul, *Madame de Maintenon, ou le prix de la réputation* (Paris: Perrin, 2003), 101.

120 *"Widowed a day"*: "La jeune Veuve," in La Fontaine, Jean de, *Fables*, ed. René Radouant (Paris: Hachette, 1929), Livre VI, no. 21, 219.

122 *"A widow is a most dangerous thing"*: Quoted in Duchêne, *Être femme au temps de Louis XIV*, 254.

122 *"Three months in love"*: Letter to Vassé, quoted in Duchêne, Roger, *Ninon de Lenclos: ou la manière jolie de faire l'amour* (Paris: Fayard, 2000), 165. Ninon frequently accepted a lover for three months' duration, "infinity as far as I'm concerned." See ibid., 114.

123 *"Madame Scarron went that spring"*: Tallemant des Réaux, Gédéon, *Les Historiettes de Tallemant des Réaux: Mémoires pour servir à l'histoire du XVIIe siècle*, 6 vols (Paris: Bibliothèque Nationale Française, 1995), V, 263–4.

123 *"Ninon wasn't at all concerned"*: Quoted in Duchêne, *Ninon de Lenclos*, 242. Bret was Ninon's first biographer.

124 *"Don't the three of you"*: Ibid., 244.

124 *"I often let Villarceaux"*: Ibid.

125 *"as poor as church mice"*: Saint-Simon I, 45.

125 *"Montchevreuil was a very good fellow"*: Ibid., 45–6. Saint-Simon did not know the Montchevreuils at this time, having still fourteen years to wait until his own birth. His words are probably exaggerated in any case by his personal resentment of Françoise.

125 *"She would start talking about vespers"*: D'Aumale, Marie-Jeanne, *Souvenirs sur Madame de Maintenon: Mémoire et lettres inédites de Mademoiselle d'Aumale*, 2e ed. (Paris: Calmann-Levy, 1902), 49.

126 *"There is nothing so fine"*: Chamaillard, Edmond, *Le Chevalier de Méré, rival de Voiture, ami de Pascal, précepteur de Madame de Maintenon* (Niort: Clouzot, 1921), 1e partie 148.

126 *"There's no greater pleasure"*: "Instruction aux demoiselles de la classe bleue," quoted in Leroy, Pierre-E. et Marcel Loyau (eds), *Comment la sagesse vient aux filles: Propos d'éducation* (Paris: Bartillart, 1998), no. 5, 48–9.

126 *"The pleasure of doing good"*: Chamaillard, 2e partie, 151.

126 *"No one has ever established"*: Cordelier, Jean, *Madame de Maintenon* (Paris: Club des Éditeurs, 1959), 51.

127 *"A debauched girl"*: From the treatise *L'Honnête fille* of 1639, quoted in Duchêne, *Être femme au temps de Louis XIV*, 121.

127 *"I wasn't seeking the esteem"*: "Entretien particulier avec Mme de Glapion," *Portraits-Souvenirs* no. 1, in Leroy et Loyau (eds), 38.

128 *"a bit mad"*: Caylus, 67.

128 *"as beautiful as the day"*: Saint-Simon I, 327.

128 *"perhaps pushed by the maréchal"*: Caylus, 87.

128 *"or so the gossips say"*: Ibid.

128 *"The King . . . is only too susceptible"*: Spanheim, Ezechiel, *Relation de la cour de France, faite au commencement de l'année 1690* (Paris: Renouard [pour la Société de l'histoire de France], 1882), 10–11.

128 *"During all these affairs"*: Saint-Simon VII, 355.

129 "Man shall not quite be lost": Milton, *Paradise Lost*, II, 173–5. Milton's great poem was first published in 1667.

130 *"She's desperate to make me"*: Choisy, Abbé François-Timoléon de, *Mémoires pour servir à l'histoire de Louis XIV, et Mémoires de l'abbé de Choisy habillé en femme*, ed. Georges Mongrédien (Paris: Mercure de France, 1966), 266.

131 *"She was fond of Madame de Montespan"*: Caylus, 82–3.

131 *"She so much enjoyed"*: Visconti, 16.

131 *"hardly saying hello to her"*: Choisy, 267.

131 *"expressed my affection"*: Louis XIV, *Mémoires, suivi de Réflexions sur le métier de Roi* (Paris: Tallandier, 2001), 247.

131 *"though La Vallière complained"*: Visconti, 16.

131 *"Only then did it seem"*: Quoted in Dunlop, Ian, *Louis XIV* (London: Chatto and Windus, 1999), 67.

132 *"to which everyone swore"*: The abbé de Choisy, quoted in Cornette, Joël (ed.), *La France de la Monarchie absolue, 1610–1715* (Paris: Éditions du Seuil, 1997), 266.

132 *"The ministers of kings"*: Louis XIV, *Mémoires*, 247.

133 *"He had come to work"*: Letter to Anne of Austria of September 5, 1661, quoted in Déon, Michel, *Louis XIV par lui-même* (Paris: Gallimard, 1991), 295.

133 *"brilliant," though not altogether*: Saint-Simon I, 668.

133 *"I left him to investigate"*: Louis XIV, *Mémoires*, 86.

134 *"Colbert had his own interests"*: Choisy, 142.

134 *"Colbert's ferociously active"*: Visconti, 130.

134 *Spanish Netherlands*: The southern part of the "low countries," they comprised, broadly, today's Belgium and Luxembourg, plus the Lille region of northern France.

134 *"When you act in contravention"*: Louis XIV, *Mémoires*, 65.

134 *"perhaps the first genuine one"*: Anderson, M. S., *War and Society in Europe of the Old Regime 1618–1789* (Guernsey,Channel Islands: Sutton Publishing, 1998), 100.

135 *"Madame de la Vallière"*: Letter to Madame de Grignan, February 20, 1671, in Sévigné, Marie, marquise de, *Lettres*, 3 vols (Paris: Pléiade, 1960), I, no. 84, 199–203.

Eight: City of Light

136 *Trois-Pavillons*: Now the rue Elzévir in the Marais district of Paris.

137 *"a very fashionable fabric"*: Desprat, Jean-Paul, *Madame de Maintenon, ou le prix de la réputation* (Paris: Perrin, 2003), 111, and see d'Aumale, Marie-Jeanne, *Souvenirs sur Madame de Maintenon: Mémoire et lettres inédites de Mademoiselle d'Aumale*, 2e ed. (Paris: Calmann-Levy, 1902), 50–2.

137 *"highly esteemed"*: D'Aumale, 50.

137 *"Why, you have a really beautiful bust"*: Ibid.

137 *"But, monsieur," she protested*: Ibid., 52.

138 *"to try to bore everyone"*: Ibid., 51.

138 *"The diocese would have to be"*: Duchêne, Roger, *Ninon de Lenclos: ou la manière jolie de faire l'amour* (Paris: Fayard, 2000), 270.

138 *"Really, Madame," he told her*: D'Aumale, 51.

139 *"every morning at seven o'clock"*: See Saint-Germain, Jacques, *La Reynie et la police au grand siècle* (Paris: Hachette, 1962), 72–8 and passim.

140 *"they're much more skilled in love"*: The traveller Locatelli, quoted in ibid., 11.

141 *"It is the King's mission"*: A March 1672 letter patent of Louis XIV, quoted in ibid., 141.

141 *"My lazy Muse"*: From the "Remerciement au Roi" of 1663, in Molière, Jean-Baptiste Po-quelin de, *Oeuvres Complètes*, 2 vols (Paris: Gallimard, 1971), I, 631.

141 *"I am so constitutionally inclined"*: Quoted in Cornette, Joël (ed.), *La France de la Monarchie absolue, 1610–1715* (Paris: Éditions du Seuil, 1997), 274. The "labouring ox" quotation is from the great nineteenth-century French historian Jules Michelet.

141 *"trumpets for the King's virtues"*: A. Viala quoted in Guy Thewes, "Peintre, théâtre et propa-gande" in Musée des Beaux-Arts de Dijon et Musée d'Histoire de la ville de Luxembourg, *À la gloire du Roi: Van der Meulen, peintre des conquêtes de Louis XIV* (Imprimerie Nationale, 1998), 263.

143 *"It's the machinery"*: Quoted in Saint-Germain, 141.

143 *"some gentlemen singing along"*: This was the naturalist and physician, Martin Lister. See ibid., 141 ff.

144 *"a magnificent confirmation"*: Louis XIV, *Mémoires, suivi de Réflexions sur le métier de Roi* (Paris: Tallandier, 2001), 277.

144 *"every person of quality"*: Montigny, J. de, "La feste de Versailles du 18 juin 1668," in *Recuil de diverses pièces faites par plusieurs personnes illustres* (The Hague: Jean et Daniel Steucker, 1669), 4.

144 *"strictly forbidden every sort"*: Ibid., 4–5.

145 *"in heroic harmony"*: Scudéry, Madeleine de, *La Promenade de Versailles*, ed. Marie-Gabrielle Lallemand (Paris: Honoré Champion, 2002), 257 and see passim.

145 *"and you know he is"*: Ibid., 256.

Nine: Duty Calls

148 *"She became thin"*: Caylus, 39.

148 *"the fight against debauchery"*: Saint-Germain, Jacques, *La Reynie et la police au grand siècle* (Paris: Hachette, 1962), 26.

148 *"Praise the Lord"*: Quoted in Hilton, Lisa, *The Real Queen of France: Athénaïs and Louis XIV* (London: Abacus, 2003), 88.

150 *"Jupiter had a son"*: "Pour Monseigneur le duc du Maine," in La Fontaine, Jean de, *Fables*, ed. René Radouant (Paris: Hachette, 1929), Livre XI, no. 2, 418.

151 *"scared to death"*: Lauzun relayed this story himself to La Grande Mademoiselle. See Desprat, Jean-Paul, *Madame de Maintenon, ou le prix de la réputation* (Paris: Perrin, 2003), 132.

151 *"Don't abuse my secret"*: Letter to the comte de Bussy-Rabutin, April 16, 1670, in Sévigné, Marie, marquise de, *Lettres*, 3 vols (Paris: Pleiade, 1960), I, no. 59, 166. The portrait appeared in his satirical *Histoire Amoureuse des Gaules*, in which his cousin appeared as Madame de Cheneville.

152 *The duty of a wet-nurse*: From Audiger's *La Maison réglée* of 1688 and 1692, quoted in *La Vie de Paris sous Louis XIV*. See Franklin, Alfred, *La Vie privée d'autrefois: Arts et métiers, modes, moeurs, usages des Parisiens, du XIIe au XVIIe siècle, d'après des documents originaux ou in-édits*, 27 vols (Paris: E. Plon, Nourri, 1887–1902), XXIII, 78–9.

152 *"a wet-nurse must be able"*: Quoted in Desprat, 131.

152 *"and other little sums"*: Letter to Père Gobelin of March 2, 1674, in Madame de Maintenon, *Lettres*, ed. Langlois, Marcel, Vols II–V (Paris: Letouzy et Ané, 1935–59), II, no. 31, 76–8.

153 *"and Madame d'Heudicourt gave her"*: Caylus, Marthe-Marguerite, comtesse de, *Souvenirs*, ed. Bernard Noël (Paris: Mercure de France, 1965 et 1986), 39.

154 *"like a good courtier"*: Saint-Simon, Louis de Rouvroy, duc de, *Mémoires*, 7 vols (Paris: Pléiade, 1953), I, 327.

154 *"the most awful things"*: Letter to Madame de Grignan of February 6, 1671, in Sévigné, Marie, marquise de, *Lettres*, 3 vols (Paris: Pléiade, 1960), I, no. 79, 191.

154 *rue des Tournelles*: An unpublished letter of September 20, 1669, from Madame du Bouchet to the comte de Bussy-Rabutin (Madame de Sévigné's cousin) reveals the details. See Caylus, 180.

154 *"in absolute despair"*: Letter to Madame de Grignan of February 9, 1671, in Sévigné I, no. 80, 192–3.

154 *"I was quite distressed"*: Letter to Mr de Villette, April 14, 1675, in Langlois (ed.), *Lettres* II, no. 71, 126.

154 *"Send me news"*: Letter to Mr de Villette, April 19, 1675, in ibid., no. 74, 130.

155 *"It's quite hard to get"*: Lettre à Madame*** [Scarron], undated, in Chamaillard, Edmond, *Le Chevalier de Méré, rival de Voiture, ami de Pascal, précepteur de Madame de Maintenon* (Niort: Clouzot, 1921), 2e partie, 26–8.

155 *"climbing up ladders"*: "Entretien particuler avec Madame de Glapion" of October 18, 1717, quoted in Leroy, Pierre-E. et Marcel Loyau (eds), *Comment la sagesse vient aux filles: Propos d'éducation* (Paris: Bartillart, 1998), no. 6, 52–4.

156 *rue Vaugirard*: The house does not survive; its location is now on the boulevard du Montparnasse, at number 25.

156 *"far more than the real mother"*: Caylus, 40.

157 *"The dauphin became like an idiot"*: Visconti, Primi, *Mémoires sur la Cour de Louis XIV, 1673–1681* (Paris: Perrin, 1988), 148. One of the dauphin's governors, the duc de Montausier, served as model for the character of the miserable Alceste in Molière's play *The Misanthrope*.

158 *"in between mathematics"*: Letter to Madame de Maintenon, probably December 1683, in *Correspondance générale de Madame de Maintenon*, ed. Lavallée, Théophile, 4 vols (Paris: Charpentier, 1857), II, no. CCCXLV, 338–9.

158 *"I couldn't bear it"*: Letter of 1686 or 1687, quoted in Hilgar, Marie-France, "Madame de Maintenon et le duc du Maine," in Niderst (ed.), *Autour de Françoise d'Aubigné, marquise de Maintenon*, Actes des Journées de Niort, Mai 23–25, 1996, Albineana 10–11, 2 vols (Niort: Albineana-Cahiers d'Aubigné, 1999), II, 264–5.

158 *"He couldn't stand her"*: Choisy, Abbé Françoise-Timoléon de, *Mémoires pour servir à l'histoire de Louis XIV, et Mémoires de l'abbé de Choisy habillé en femme*, ed. Georges Mongrédien (Paris: Mercure de France, 1966), 262.

158 *"She knows how to love"*: Caylus, 40.

158 *"A king must distinguish"*: *Instructions au duc d'Anjou*, in Louis XIV, *Mémoires, suivi de Réflexions sur le métier de Roi* (Paris: Tallandier, 2001), 284.

158 *"so delightful and such good company"*: Letter of Madame de Coulanges to Madame de Sévigné of March 20, 1673, quoted in Desprat, 141.

159 *"Madame Scarron is charming"*: Letter to Madame de Grignan of January 13, 1672, in Sévigné I, no. 184, 453.

159 *"But I don't regard this"*: Letters to Mr d'Aubigné of September 19 and 27, 1672, in Langlois (ed.), *Lettres* II, nos 24 & 25, 63–6.

Ten: L'Arrivée

160 *"With the King giving"*: Solnon, Jean-François, *La Cour de France* (Paris: Fayard, 1987), 282–5.

162 *"I saw some samples"*: Letter to Charles d'Aubigné of October 31, 1673, in Madame de Maintenon, *Lettres*, ed. Langlois, Marcel, Vols II–V (Paris: Letouzy et Ané, 1935–59), II, no. 30, 73–5. The relatives in question are not named, but Françoise gave financial help to both her father's and her mother's families and also to the extended Scarron family.

163 *"like a prison rack"*: Desprat, Jean-Paul, *Madame de Maintenon, ou le prix de la réputation* (Paris: Perrin, 2003), 142.

164 *"stretched out naked"*: Visconti, Primi, *Mémoires sur la Cour de Louis XIV, 1673–1681* (Paris: Perrin, 1988), 1;17.

164 *"with a back and arms"*: Ibid., 169.

165 *"excessive expense"*: Letter from Louis XIV to Colbert, June 8, 1675, quoted in Déon, Michel, *Louis XIV par lui-même* (Paris: Gallimard, 1991), 288.

165 *"She'd play the entire evening"*: Petitfils, Jean-Christian, *Louis XIV* (Paris: Perrin, 2002), 304.

165 *"Le hocca is forbidden"*: Quoted in Saint-Germain, Jacques, *La Reynie et la police au grand siècle* (Paris: Hachette, 1962), 133.

166 *"This means it will certainly spread"*: Ibid.

166 *"your clever friend"*: D'Aumale, Marie-Jeanne, *Souvenirs sur Madame de Maintenon: Mémoire et lettres inédites de Mademoiselle d'Aumale*, 2e ed. (Paris: Calmann-Levy, 1902), 55.

167 *"Ah, no! Not Madame Scarron"*: Desprat, 148.

167 *"Half the court was living"*: Visconti, 35.

167 *"her stupidity"*: Saint-Simon, Louis de Rouvroy, duc de, *Mémoires*, 7 vols (Paris: Pléiade, 1953), II, 412.

167 *"That whore will kill me"*: Hilton, Lisa, *The Real Queen of France: Athénaïs and Louis XIV* (London: Abacus, 2003), 218.

168 *"She's no beauty"*: Visconti, 26.

168 *"so terrifically big"*: Letter to the Herzogin Sophie, August 5, 1673, in Liselotte von der Pfalz, *Briefe* (Ebenhausen bei München: Langewiesche-Brandt, 1966), 18.

168 *"The King invites me:"* Letter to the Herzogin Sophie of December 14, 1676, in ibid., 29.

169 *"running and jumping about"*: Letter to Frau von Harling of November 23, 1672, in ibid., 15.

169 *"Catholic sermons"*: Letter of March 19, 1693, in ibid., 118–19.

170 *"You're very particular"*: D'Aumale, 61.

170 *"The old parliamentary resistance"*: Quoted in Goubert, Pierre, *Louis XIV et vingt millions de Française* (Paris: Hachette, 1977), 116.

171 *"Monsieur Colbert said"*: Letter to the Kurfürstin Sophie, September 23, 1699, in Liselotte von der Pfalz, *Briefe*, 163.

172 *much of it, Dutch*: See Goubert, 50 ff. Goubert notes that between 1601 and 1750, during a period of phenomenal advance elsewhere, there was not a single treatise on agriculture written in France.

172 *United Provinces of the Netherlands*: Also called the Republic of the Seven United Provinces. The republic was formed in 1648, having won a final independence from Spain at the end of the Thirty Years War. It comprised the northern provinces of Holland, Zeeland, Gelderland, Utrecht, Friesland, Overijssel, and Groningen. Holland was the largest and most important of the provinces, hence the frequent use of its name alone for all seven.

173 *"tired of these [commercial] insolences"*: Quoted in Schama, Simon, *The Embarrassment of Riches: An Interpretation of Dutch Culture in the Golden Age* (London: Fontana, 1991), 271. In fact, the only commerce being blocked was that of French wines and spirits, which the Dutch had attempted to ban from their country in response to Colbert's imposition of tariffs on all Dutch goods a few years previously. As for the Huguenots, though many in the mostly Calvinist republic felt some solidarity with them, a third of its people were actually Catholic, and if some Dutchmen were printing pamphlets declaring Protestant solidarity, this was not owing to any grand plan on the part of the republic, but rather to the decentralized nature of Dutch authority, which was simply "without the machinery for the suppression of opinion" (Schama, 268). A Dutchman could print, more or less, whatever he liked.

173 *"When a Prince is wounded"*: From Stubbes's *Justification of the Present War Against the United Netherlands* of 1672, quoted in Schama, 271.

173 *Triple Alliance*: The Treaty of Dover of June 1670 took the English secretly out of the Alliance. See Fraser, Antonia, *King Charles II* (London: Phoenix, 2002), 350 ff. and passim. The Swedes, encouraged by cash payments from France, renounced the Alliance early in 1672. Other German states also received money in return for their promise of neutrality. In 1671, the Holy Roman Emperor had also agreed to remain neutral in the event of a Franco-Dutch conflict.

174 *their advantage*: At the Peace of Westphalia, which ended the Thirty Years War, the United Provinces of the Netherlands finally gained their independence from the Spanish Habsburg Empire. Moreover, the city of Amsterdam won its own important victory by forcing the end of free navigation on the Scheldt River, so diverting trade away from Spanish Antwerp northwards to its own wharves.

174 *"most theatrical form of warfare"*: Thewes, in Musée des Beaux-Arts . . . , 265.

174 *so enjoyed*: Siege warfare was "[possibly] the biggest engineering operation known to the age" and "a striking example of unproductive investment." It required not only trench-digging but also the building of elaborate defensive lines which often required the conscription of locals, including, most harmfully, peasants at harvest time. See Anderson, M. S., *War and Society in Europe of the Old Regime 1618–1789* (Guernsey, Channel Islands: Sutton Publishing, 1998), 40 ff., 87 ff., and 140 ff. The fortified towns of Vesel, Burick (Büderich), Orsoy, and Rheinberg were attacked simultaneously, and all taken in the first two weeks of June 1672, as were the smaller towns of Emmerich and Rees.

175 *"I can't understand how they managed"*: Letter to the comte de Bussy-Rabutin of June 19, 1672, in Sévigné, Marie, marquise de, *Lettres*, 3 vols (Paris: Pléiade, 1960), I, no. 229, 571. The King in fact crossed the Ijssel river, a distributary of the Rhine. For details of the crossing, see Pujo, Bernard, *Le Grand Condé* (Paris: Albin Michel, 1995), 312 ff. For the artworks pertaining to the Rhine crossing and the Dutch campaign in general, see Musée des Beaux-Arts . . . , and also Burke, Peter, *The Fabrication of Louis XIV* (New Haven and London: Yale University Press, 1994), Chapter VI. For art propaganda on the Dutch side, see Schama, 270 ff.

175 *imperial territory*: Both the Archbishopric of Cologne and the Bishopric of Münster, France's German allies bordering the Rhine, were states of the Holy Roman Empire and hence owed allegiance in some degree to Leopold.

176 *"the depth of their contrition"*: Schama, 273–5.

177 *"men for the Dutch"*: Quoted in Pujo, 319.

177 *"What do you think"*: Letter of July 15, 1673 to the comte de Bussy-Rabutin, in Sévigné, Marie, marquise de, *Lettres*, 3 vols (Paris: Pléiade, 1960), I, no. 249, 603.

179 *"[U]nder Vauban's direction"*: Thewes, in Musée des Beaux-Arts . . . , 265.

179 *"encouraging the troops"*: Ibid., 246.

179 *"resolved to die for the King of Spain"*: Ibid.

179 *"on a parterre strewn"*: Sabban, Françoise, et Silvano Serventi, *La Gastronomie au Grand Siè-cle: 100 recettes de France et d'Italie* (Paris: Stock, 1998), 85. The Franche-Comté was finally ceded to France at the Treaty of Nijmegen in 1678.

179 *"Kings should enjoy"*: *Réflexions sur le métier de Roi*, in Louis XIV, *Mémoires, suivi de Réflexions sur le métier de Roi* (Paris: Tallandier, 2001), 279.

Eleven: The Course of True Loves

181 *"Her chambermaid threw herself"*: Letter to Madame de Grignan of December 15, 1673, in Sévigné, Marie, marquise de, *Lettres*, 3 vols (Paris: Pléiade, 1960), I, no. 276, 653.

181 *"who had great influence"*: Saint-Simon, Louis de Rouvroy, duc de, *Mémoires*, 7 vols (Paris: Pléiade, 1953), I, 709 & II, 255.

182 *"I command you all"*: From Charles Perrault's *Mémoires*, quoted in Tiberghien, Frédéric, *Versailles: Le Chantier de Louis XIV, 1662–1715* (Paris: Perrin, 2002), 77.

183 *"A public apology"*: Bertière, Simone, *Les Femmes du Roi Soleil* (Paris: de Fallois, 1998), 212.

183 *"but she's dead to me now"*: Ibid., 216.

183 *"She's too useful an example"*: Ibid., 214.

184 *"I'll be sure to pass it on"*: Letter to Madame et Monsieur de Grignan of April 29, 1676, in Sévigné II, no. 416, 80.

184 *"would have given themselves"*: Visconti, Primi, *Mémoires sur la Cour de Louis XIV, 1673–1681* (Paris: Perrin, 1988), 164.

185 *"My sufferings"*: Letter to Père Gobelin of March 2, 1674, in Madame de Maintenon, *Lettres*, ed. Langlois, Marcel, Vols II–V (Paris: Letouzy et Ané, 1935–59), II, no. 31, 76.

186 *"He didn't understand"*: Letter to Père Gobelin of July 1674, in ibid., no. 36, 83.

186 *"to remove myself"*: Letter to Père Gobelin of March 6, 1674, in ibid., no. 32, 78.

186 *"If he were walking"*: Letters to Charles d'Aubigné of May 21 and Pére Gobelin of July 24, 1674, in ibid., nos 35 & 40, 81–2 & 87–8.

187 *"How could you know better"*: Quoted in Desprat, Jean-Paul, *Madame de Maintenon, ou le prix de la réputation* (Paris: Perrin, 2003), 153.

187 *"Madame de Montespan and I"*: Letter to Père Gobelin of about July 26, 1674, in Langlois (ed.), *Lettres* II, no. 41, 90–1.

188 *"I spoke to Madame"*: Letter to Père Gobelin of August 6 or 7, 1674, in ibid., no. 43, 93–4.

188 *"[Françoise] was born with nothing"*: D'Aumale, Marie-Jeanne, *Souvenirs sur Madame de Maintenon: Mémoire et lettres inédites de Mademoiselle d'Aumale*, 2e ed. (Paris: Calmann-Levy, 1902), 60.

189 *"She and Madame la duchesse"*: Letter to Père Gobelin of July 24, 1674, in Langlois (ed.), *Lettres* II, no. 40, 87.

189 *"We've had a horoscrope"*: Letter of November 16, 1674, in *Lettres de Madame duchesse d'Orléans, née Princesse Palatine, 1672–1722*, ed. Olivier Ameil (Paris: Mercure de France, 1985), 42.

189 *"So you see how the French"*: Visconti, 61.

190 *"You may have heard"*: Letter to Mr d'Aubigny of November 10, 1674, in Langlois (ed.), *Lettres* II, no. 56, 109–10. The château de Maintenon, in the town of Maintenon, forty miles west

of Paris, dates from the thirteenth century. From 1698 to 1981 it was owned by the Noailles family, and since then has belonged to the Foundation du Château de Maintenon.

190 *"The King fucks them"*: Quoted in Bluche, *Louis XIV* (Paris: Hachette, 1986), 399.

191 *"I am sure, Madame"*: See Fraser, Antonia, *Love and Louis XIV: The Women in the Life of the Sun King* (London: Weidenfeld and Nicolson, 2006), 167.

191 *"He liked almost all women"*: Caylus, Marthe-Marguerite, comtesse de, *Souvenirs*, ed. Bernard Noël (Paris: Mercure de France, 1965 et 1986), 82.

192 *"berating Louis"*: Letter of August 7, 1675 to Madame de Grignan, in Sévigné, Marie, marquise de, *Lettres*, 3 vols (Paris: Pléiade, 1960), I, no. 328, 792. It was customary for the French aristocracy to take their titles from the names of their estates.

192 *"a sweet and simple girl"*: Visconti, 169.

192 *"As beautiful as an angel"*: Choisy, Abbé Françoise-Timoléon de, *Mémoires pour servir à l'histoire de Louis XIV, et Mémoires de l'abbé de Choisy habillé en femme*, ed. Georges Mongrédien (Paris: Mercure de France, 1966), 267.

192 *"all dressed up"*: Letter to Madame et Monsieur de Grignan, March 6, 1680, in Sévigné II, no. 638, 634–5.

192 *"Her astonishing beauty"*: Choisy, 207.

192 *"No amount of good qualities"*: Chamaillard, Edmond, *Le Chevalier de Méré, rival de Voiture, ami de Pascal, précepteur de Madame de Maintenon* (Niort: Clouzot, 1921), 1e partie, 143.

194 *"For her sake"*: Visconti, 175–6.

194 *"who had been paying her"*: Ibid., 176.

194 *"stumbling block"*: Quoted in Desprat, 162.

194 *"Madame de Montespan had had a dream"*: Visconti, 66.

195 *"Madame de Montespan and I"*: Desprat, 173.

195 *"No, it wasn't me"*: Letter to Mr l'abbé Gobelin of March 30, 1675, in Langlois (ed.), *Lettres* II, no. 67, 122–3.

196 *"provided she was"*: Cordelier, Jean, *Madame de Maintenon* (Paris: Club des Éditeurs, 1959), 87.

196 *"From now on"*: Letter of July 3, 1675 to Madame de Grignan, in Sévigné I, no. 318, 754.

196 *"It took less time"*: Letter to Mr de Villette of June 23, 1675, in Langlois (ed.), *Lettres* II, no. 79, 137.

196 *"a place more frightful"*: Letter to Mr d'Aubigny of July 8, 1675, in ibid., no. 80, 138–9.

196 *"My dear, here's a turn"*: Letter to Madame de Grignan, August 7, 1675, in Sévigné I, no. 328, 792.

196 *"It seems a thousand years"*: Letter to Mr l'abbé Gobelin of May 8, 1675, in Langlois (ed.), *Lettres* II, no. 75, 131.

197 *"he's walking"*: Letter to Mr d'Aubigny of October 16, 1675, in ibid., no. 82, 143.

197 *"my little angel"*: Letter to Philippe de Villette (son of her cousin Philippe) of November 11, 1675, in ibid., no, 84, 147.

197 *"People bring up children"*: Letter of September 14, 1675, in *Lettres de Madame duchesse d'Orléans, née Princesse Palatine, 1672–1722*, ed. Olivier Ameil (Paris: Mercure de France, 1985), 44.

198 *"calmly taking precedence"*: Letter of July 3, 1675 to Madame de Grignan, in Sévigné I, no. 318, 755.

198 *"Remember, Madame"*: Caylus, 59.

198 *"The King's attachment"*: Letter of July 31, 1675 to Madame et Monsieur de Grignan, in Sévigné I, no. 325, 779.

198 *"They're all good enough"*: Quoted in Petitfils, 304.

198 *"only too happy"*: Letter of August 21, 1675 to Madame de Grignan, in Sévigné I, no. 334, 820.

198 *"They say she's happy"*: Letter of August 26, 1676 to Madame de Grignan, in Sévigné II, no. 455, 182.

199 *"and it was almost as fat"*: Visconti, 117.

199 *"I've had Monsieur"*: Letter to Madame de Villette of April 7, 1677, in Langlois (ed.), *Lettres* II, no. 123, 193.

200 *"I hope you didn't"*: Letter to Mr d'Aubigny of February 28, 1678, in Langlois (ed.), *Lettres* II, no. 149, 224.

200 *"and if you don't"*: Letter to Mr d'Aubigny of February 27, 1678, in ibid., no. 148, 223.

200 *"Don't let her"*: Letter to Mr d'Aubigny of February 28, 1678, in ibid., no. 149, 224–9. This long letter has been compressed here.

202 *"that poor creature Garé"*: Letter to Mr d'Aubigny of July 11, 1683, in ibid., no. 316, 502.

202 *"he was still sitting"*: Visconti, 107.

203 "The brazen throat": Milton, *Paradise Lost*, ll. 713–18.

204 *"This year has been"*: Vallot, d'Aquin, et Fagon, *Journal de la Santé du Roi Louis XIV de l'année 1647 à l'année 1711, écrit par Vallot, d'Aquin et Fagon*, ed. Le Roi, J. A. (Paris: A. Durand, 1862), 141.

204 *"sceptre"*: See Fraser, 95.

204 *"The Queen of Spain"*: Letter to Madame de Grignan, September 15, 1679, in Sévigné II, no. 581, 445.

204 *"The Spanish ambassador"*: Visconti, 134.

204 *"horribly muddy in winter"*: Villars, Pierre de, *Mémoires de la Cour d'Espagne de 1679 à 1681*, ed. M. A. Morel-Fatio (Paris: Plon, 1893), 4. Madrid had been the capital of united Spain only since 1561, following a planned temporary move from Toledo.

205 *a thousand conquistadores*: See Elliott, J. H., *Imperial Spain, 1469–1716* (New York: Mentor, 1966), 62 and passim.

205 *"soporific mental climate"*: Ibid., 366.

205 *"very few tradesmen"*: Villars, 4.

205 *"living death"*: Elliott, 365.

205 *"The King of Spain is shorter"*: Villars, 8–11.

205 *"a rachitic and feeble-minded weakling"*: Elliott, 355–6.

206 *"A daughter must obey"*: Molière, *Le Tartuffe ou l'Imposteur*, Act II, scene iii, 925.

206 *"The people are saying"*: Letters to Madame de Grignan of September 18, 20, 22, and 27, 1679, nos 582–4 and 586, in Sévigné II, 445 ff.

206 *"The Queen of Spain was rather"*: Villars, 11.

Twelve: The Poisons Affair

207 *"enemy of the human race"*: Somerset, Anne, *The Affair of the Poisons: Murder, Infanticide and Satanism at the Court of Louis XIV* (London: Phoenix, 2004), 1 and passim, chapter 1.

207 *"It's over at last"*: Letter to Madame de Grignan, July 17, 1676, in Sévigné, Marie, marquise de, *Lettres*, 3 vols (Paris: Pléiade, 1960), II, 145.

208 *"an elaborate raised pie"*: Somerset, 14.

208 *"extraordinary fits of vomitings"*: Ibid., 13.

209 *"no man with four millions"*: Visconti, Primi, *Mémoires sur la Cour de Louis XIV, 1673–1681* (Paris: Perrin, 1988), 157.

209   *"the repression of blasphemers"*: Saint-Germain, Jacques, *La Reynie et la police au grand siècle* (Paris: Hachette, 1962), 26.

210   *"that the abbé Brigalier"*: Segrais, Jean Regnault de, *Segraisiana, ou mélange d'histoire et de littérature* (Amsterdam: Compagnie des libraires, 1722), I, 54.

210   *"Madame de La Fayette is drinking"*: Letter to Madame de Grignan, October 20, 1679, in Sévigné II, no. 594, 480.

211   *"In my job"*: Extract from *La Devineresse* by Thomas Corneille and Jean Donneau de Visé, quoted in Saint-Germain, *La Reynie*, 108.

211   *"Though I pretended not to be"*: Visconti, 38 and passim.

211   *"the King stood guarantee for me"*: Ibid., 162,

212   *"Men's lives are up for sale"*: Hilton, Lisa, *The Real Queen of France: Athénaïs and Louis XIV* (London: Abacus, 2003), 247.

212   *"rare that it has extracted"*: Somerset, 21.

212   *"to have the question"*: Evelyn, John, *The Diary* (London: Macmillan, 1908), March 11, 1651.

212   *"interspersed with her shrieks"*: Somerset, 287.

213   Place de Grève: A common place of public execution in Paris during the ancien régime, it is now the Place de l'Hôtel de Ville. During the seventeenth century, it was also a common place for unemployed day labourers to assemble, between four and six in the morning, hoping to be selected for a day's work.

213   *"They say the repercussions"*: Letter to Monsieur et Madame de Grignan, February 23, 1680, in Sévigné II, 617.

213   *"fat and sweaty-palmed"*: Primi Visconti quoted in Richardt, Aimé, *Louvois, le bras armé de Louis XIV* (Paris: Tallandier, 1998), 154.

213   *"the chiefest places in trust"*: The English ambassador, quoted in Somerset, 224.

213   *"His low stature was not"*: Spanheim, Ezechiel, *Relation de la cour de France, faite au commencement de l'année 1690* (Paris: Renouard [pour la Société de l'histoire de France], 1882), 340.

213   *"A deceitful little hunchback"*: Visconti, 84.

214   *"the ugliest person alive"*: Ibid., 84.

215   *"He's not a man"*: Letter to Madame de Grignan and Mademoiselle Montgobert, January 31, 1680, in Sévigné II, no. 627, 593.

216   *"provided he got his share"*: Ibid., 71, for both quotations here.

216   *"Yes, I have," she retorted*: Ibid., 160.

216   *"All those involved"*: Letter from Louis XIV to Colbert of June 28, 1676, quoted in Déon, Michel, *Louis XIV par lui-même* (Paris: Gallimard, 1991), 289.

217   *"all the terrors of torture"*: Somerset, 314.

217   *"You couldn't trust your friends"*: Visconti, 162–3.

217   *"Where on earth"*: Letter to Madame et Monsieur de Grignan, October 25, 1679, in Sévigné II, no. 597, 484.

217   *"If all the bad cooks"*: Quoted in Somerset, 406.

217   *"and I can assure you"*: Visconti, 155.

218   *"cunning and ingenious"*: Somerset, 315.

218   *"a strange cast of mind"*: Ibid., 314.

218   *"to free herself"*: Somerset, 333.

219   *"The Chambre Ardente"*: Visconti, 155.

220   wounded On His Majesty's Service: Letter to Madame de Grignan, July 14, 1680, in Sévigné II, no. 680, 777.

220   *"[P]eople viewed [it] as a private court"*: Visconti, 165.

220 "It's all prejudice": "Les Devineresses," in La Fontaine, Jean de, *Fables*, ed. René Radouant (Paris: Hachette, 1929), Livre VII, no. 15, ll. 4–5, 260.

220 *"[t]hey never found so much as"*: Visconti, 158.

221 *"whether it's because of the climate"*: Ibid., 165.

221 *"incapable of abusing"*: Choisy, Abbé Françoise-Timoléon de, *Mémoires pour servir à l'histoire de Louis XIV, et Mémoires de l'abbé de Choisy habillé en femme*, ed. Georges Mongrédien (Paris: Mercure de France, 1966), 205.

Thirteen: Madame de Maintenant

225 *"No Spring, nor Summer"*: John Donne, Elegie IX, *The Autumnall*, ll. 1–2.

225 *"still attractive"*: Choisy, Abbé Françoise-Timoléon de, *Mémoires pour servir à l'histoire de Louis XIV, et Mémoires de l'abbé de Choisy habillé en femme*, ed. Georges Mongrédien (Paris: Mercure de France, 1966), 262.

225 *"No one knew what to think"*: Visconti, Primi, *Mémoires sur la Cour de Louis XIV, 1673–1681* (Paris: Perrin, 1988), 150.

226 *"The most beautiful women"*: Chamaillard, Edmond, *Le Chevalier de Méré, rival de Voiture, ami de Pascal, précepteur de Madame de Maintenon* (Niort: Clouzot, 1921), 1e partie, 161.

226 *"Madame de Maintenon was good-natured"*: Choisy, 262 & 265.

226 *"She has shown him"*: Letters to Madame de Grignan, July 17 & 7, 1680, in Sévigné, Marie, marquise de, *Lettres*, 3 vols (Paris: Pléiade, 1960), II, nos 682 & 678, 785 & 770.

226 *"The King doesn't like to see"*: Visconti, 124.

226 *"He gives her more care"*: Letter to Madame de Grignan, July 17, 1680, in Sévigné II, no. 682, 785.

226 *"I'm naturally impatient"*: Quoted in Langlois, Marcel, "Madame de Maintenon, ses oeuvres complètes, la légende et l'histoire," *Revue Historique*, Vol. 168, September–December 1931, 298.

228 *"His Majesty often spends"*: Letters to Madame de Grignan, April 6, June 30, September 11, and June 9, 1680, in Sévigné II, no. 649, 670; no. 675, 762; no. 700, 845; no. 668, 736.

228 *"Not all the ladies responded"*: Spanheim, Ezechiel, *Relation de la cour de France, faite au commencement de l'année 1690* (Paris: Renouard [pour la Société de l'histoire de France], 1882), 11, 17–19.

229 "God has sent Madame de Maintenon": See the *Notice* to the *Oraison de Marie-Thérèse d'Autriche*, in Bossuet, Jacques-Bénigne, *Oraisons Funèbres* (Paris: Hachette, 1898), 217.

229 *"to relax from the cares of state"*: Choisy, 262.

229 *"I've told [your manservant]"*: Letters to Mr d'Aubigny, March 1679 & July 3, 1680, in Madame de Maintenon, *Lettres*, ed. Langlois, Marcel, Vols II–V (Paris: Letouzy et Ané, 1935–59), II, no. 184, 301, & no. 212, 345.

229 *"Madame de Maintenon is the machine"*: Letter to Madame de Grignan, July 7, 1680, in Sévigné II, no. 678, 770.

231 *"The King has no galanteries"*: Letter to Mr de Villette, August 14, 1681, in Langlois (ed.), *Lettres* II, no. 241, 395.

232 *"I pray for a moment"*: Letter to Mr l'Abbé Gobelin, January 8, 1680, in ibid., no. 205, 329.

233 *"The duc de Vendôme"*: Letter to Madame et Monsieur de Grignan, October 25, 1679, in Sévigné II, no. 597, 485.

234 *"to deprive the faithful"*: Quoted in Langlois (ed.), *Lettres* II, note 207, 339.

234 *"a saint, but not very bright"*: D'Aumale, Marie-Jeanne, *Souvenirs sur Madame de Maintenon: Mémoire et lettres inédites de Mademoiselle d'Aumale*, 2e ed. (Paris: Calmann-Levy, 1902), 81.

235 *"Did she think"*: Letter to Madame de Grignan, July 7, 1680, in Sévigné II, no. 678, 770.

235 *"be careful what you say"*: Letters to Mr d'Aubigny, July 3 & 6, 1680, in Langlois (ed.), *Lettres* II, nos 212 & 213, 346–7.

235 *"She was almost unhinged"*: Choisy, 205.

235 *"She told her, in the clearest terms"*: Ibid., 205–6, 265 & 248.

235 *"suffocating in black bile"*: Ibid., 206.

235 *"was only fond of Madame"*: Caylus, Marthe-Marguerite, comtesse de, *Souvenirs*, ed. Bernard Noël (Paris: Mercure de France, 1965 et 1986), 67.

236 *"If my enemies fail"*: Letter to Mr d'Aubigny, July 6, 1680, in Langlois (ed.), *Lettres* II, no. 213, 347.

236 *"The King wasn't ashamed"*: Saint-Simon, Louis de Rouvroy, duc de, *Mémoires*, 7 vols (Paris: Pléiade, 1953), I, 38–9.

236 *"I am not a dame d'atour"*: Letter to Mr d'Aubigny, December 15, 1679, in Langlois (ed.), *Lettres* II, no. 200, 322–3.

237 *"The light of her intelligence"*: Spanheim, 49–51.

237 *"The dauphin accepted his wife"*: Visconti, 148.

237 *"even if I saw him"*: Letter of May 11, 1685, in *Lettres de Madame duchesse d'Orléans, née Princesse Palatine, 1672–1722*, ed. Olivier Ameil (Paris: Mercure de France, 1985), 97.

237 *"He was a terrific eater"*: Saint-Simon I, 886–7.

237 *"and if she thinks:"* Letter to Madame de Grignan et Mademoiselle Montgobert, February 14, 1680, in Sévigné II, 609.

237 *"They were all talking"*: Visconti, 151.

238 *"Madame la dauphine has"*: Letter to Mr d'Aubigny, June 25, 1684, in Langlois (ed.), *Lettres* III, no. 365, 54–5.

239 *"I asked you to buy"*: Letter to Mr de Guignonville, November 7, 1681, in ibid., II, no. 251, 411–12. Angola had been "presented" to Françoise by her cousin Philippe de Villette. He eventually went into the army, where he served until his death in 1704.

239 *"And she thought just as much"*: Saint-Simon, Louis de Rouvroy, duc de, *Mémoires*, 7 vols (Paris: Pléiade, 1953), I, 316.

240 *"fourteen hundred thousand livres"*: Caylus, 85.

240 *"Madame de Montchevreuil was a woman"*: Ibid., 69–70.

240 *"The position wasn't so much"*: Ibid., 71.

241 *"a very rich cousin"*: Letter to Madame de Grignan of September 21, 1676, in Sévigné II, no. 464, 208.

241 *"And besides"*: Segrais, Jean Regnault de, *Segraisiana, ou mélange d'histoire et de littérature* (Amsterdam: Compagnie des libraires, 1722), I, "Sa Vie," iv.

241 *"You need to reason"*: Letter to Mr le marquis de Montchevreuil, April 27, 1681, in Langlois (ed.), *Lettres* II, no. 226, 369–70.

241 *"Mademoiselle de Laval"*: Caylus, 71 ff.

241 *"She's too good"*: Letter to Mr le marquis de Montchevreuil, May 2, 1681, in Langlois (ed.), *Lettres* II, no. 227, 371.

242 *"Madame d'Heudicourt is here"*: Letter to Mr d'Aubigné, February 20, 1682, in ibid., no. 258, 422.

242 *"How ridiculous"*: Letter to Madame de Grignan of July 17, 1680, in Sévigné II, no. 682, 786. This letter is possibly a composite.

242 *"She never opens her mouth"*: Caylus, 67 & 89.

243 *"to stand up straight"*: Letter to Mr de Villette, between April 1 & 5, 1678, in Langlois (ed.), *Lettres* III, no. 156, 241.

243 *"like an affected little idiot"*: Letter to Mr d'Aubigny, March 1679, in ibid., II, no. 184, 301.

243 *"Here he comes"*: Charles d'Aubigné as the character Théodecte, in La Bruyère, Jean de, *Les Caractères ou les moeurs de ce siècle* (Paris: Hachette, 1935), 33.

243 *"No, don't move to Paris"*: Letter to Mr d'Aubigny, June 18, 1684, in Langlois (ed.), *Lettres* III, no. 364, 51.

244 *"perfectly healthy"*: Letters to Mr d'Aubigny, May 19, 1681 (interposed) & July 11, 1683, in ibid., II, no. 231, 375–7, & no. 316, 501–3.

244 *for his maintenance*: See, for example, the letters to Mr l'abbé Gobelin, July 24, September 28, & December 8, 1674, in ibid., no. 40, 87–90; no. 49, 100–1; & no. 59, 112–3. Langlois speculates, without providing convincing evidence, that Toscan was in fact the illegitimate son of Françoise herself and the maréchal d'Albret. See "Madame de Maintenon, ses oeuvres complètes . . ."

244 *"a boy of twelve or thirteen"*: Letter to Mr l'Abbé Gobelin, May 17, 1681, in ibid., no. 230, 374–5.

245 *"I was in transports"*: Letter to Mr de Villette, February 26, 1676, in ibid., no. 96, 161–2.

245 *"I've told the King"*: Letter to Mme de Villette, June 7, 1676, in ibid., no. 103, 170.

245 *"but Seignelay said"*: Letter to Mr de Villette, about August 2, 1679, in ibid., no. 190, 313.

246 *"all naval officers"*: Quoted in Villette, Philippe Le Valois, marquis de, *Mémoires* (Paris: J. Renouard, 1844), 177, note.

246 *"either by supplying"*: Quoted in ibid., 180, note.

247 *"choking in little gulps"*: Garrisson, Janine, *L'Édict de Nantes et sa révocation* (Paris: Seuil, 1985), 119 ff. The figure of one million, about 5 percent of the population, is for 1670, and includes both Huguenots (strictly, Calvinists) and Lutherans. See ibid., 46.

247 *"There's no knowing"*: Letter to Mr de Villette, about February 9, 1678, in Langlois (ed.), *Lettres* II, no. 147, 222.

248 *"only a thirty-six-cannon vessel"*: Villette, 52.

249 *"but we need not be:"* Letter to Mr l'Abbé Gobelin, November 14, 1680, in *Correspondance générale de Madame de Maintenon*, ed. Lavallée, Théophile, 4 vols (Paris: Charpentier, 1857), II, 2e partie (suite), no. CCXXV, 135.

249 *"Our little nephew"*: Letter to Mr d'Aubigny, December 8, 1680, in Langlois (ed.), *Lettres* II, no. 217, 351.

249 *"Monsieur de Saint-Hermine arrived"*: Letter to Mr d'Aubigny, December 19, 1680, in ibid., no. 218, 352–3.

249 *"God, who knows everything"*: Quoted in Desprat, Jean-Paul, *Madame de Maintenon, ou le prix de la réputation* (Paris: Perrin, 2003), 201.

250 *"They were astonished"*: Caylus, 31.

250 *"Although I'm quite sure"*: Letter to Mme de Villette, December 23, 1680, in Langlois (ed.), *Lettres* II, no. 219, 353–6.

251 *"Your letter makes me"*: Letter to Mme de Villette, December 25, 1680, in ibid., no. 220, 356.

252 *"obligingly"*: Ibid.

253 *"Don't tell him"*: Letter to Mr l'Abbé Gobelin, January 15, 1681, in Lavallée (ed.), *Correspondance générale* II, 2e partie (suite), no. CCXXXIV, 150.

253 *"to the infinite glory"*: Caylus, 31.

253 *"They're all leaving"*: Letter to Mr d'Aubigny, February 5, 1681, in Langlois (ed.), *Lettres* II, no. 223, 361.

253 *"I've been making her"*: Letter to Mme de Villette, January 25, 1681, in ibid., no, 221, 358.

254 *"My father's letters"*: Caylus, 31.

254 *"I'm not even going to"*: Letter to Mr de Villette, April 5, 1681, in Langlois (ed.), *Lettres* II, no. 225, 367.

254 *"Madame de Maintenon had only asked"*: Caylus, 31.

255 *"If the King lives"*: Letter to Mr de Villette, April 5, 1681, in Langlois (ed.), *Lettres* II, no. 225, 367.

Fourteen: Uncrowned Queen

256 *"The year 1678"*: Dunlop, Ian, *Royal Palaces of France* (London: Hamish Hamilton, 1985), 122.

256 *"this house is more"*: Letter from Colbert to Louis XIV of September 28, 1663, quoted in ibid., 120.

257 *"It abounds with stags"*: Evelyn, John, *The Diary* (London: Macmillan, 1908), March 7, 1644, 36–7.

257 *"rats' holes"*: Quoted in Dunlop, 112.

257 *"a heap of chimneys"*: Quoted in ibid., 167.

258 *"Paris being the capital"*: Quoted in ibid., 112.

258 *"the heights of Chaillot"*: Quoted in ibid., 213. This is broadly the area of today's Trocadero and Eiffel Tower. Part of the Tuileries garden still exists.

259 *"the most sad"*: The duc de Saint-Simon, quoted in ibid., 135.

259 *"It will not be possible"*: Ibid.

259 *"and don't do anything"*: Letter from Louis XIV to Louvois of November 8, 1684, quoted in Tiberghien, Frédéric, *Versailles: Le Chantier de Louis XIV, 1662–1715* (Paris: Perrin, 2002), 74.

259 *"I heard Monsieur"*: Visconti, Primi, *Mémoires sur la Cour de Louis XIV, 1673–1681* (Paris: Perrin, 1988), 152. A hundred million francs was about thirty-five million livres.

259 *"22,000 men and 6,000 horses"*: Entry for August 27, 1684, in Dangeau, Philippe de Courcillon, marquis de, *Journal de la cour de Louis XIV, avec les additions inédites du duc de Saint-Simon*, 19 vols (Paris: Firmin-Didot Frères, 1854–60), I, 48.

260 *"We have two teams"*: Letter from Colbert to Louis XIV of May 22, 1670, quoted in Tiberghien, 149.

260 *for centuries*: See ibid., 141.

260 *"Consider how many"*: Louis XIV, *Mémoires, suivi de Réflexions sur le métier de Roi* (Paris: Tallandier, 2001), 89.

261 *"teetering constantly"*: Bernard, Leon, *The Emerging City: Paris in the Age of Louis XIV* (Durham, North Carolina: Duke University Press, 1970), 119 and passim. See also Tiberghien, 124 and passim.

262 *"So we can perish in symmetry"*: See Lewis, 40.

262 *"so overpowering"*: Saint-Simon, quoted in Solnon, Jean-François, *La Cour de France* (Paris: Fayard, 1987), 319.

262 *"with six little dogs"*: Letter to the Herzogin Sophie, December 4, 1701, in Liselotte von der Pfalz, *Briefe*, 194.

263 *"which are better housed"*: See Dunlop, 122.

264 *"an open-air extension"*: Ibid., 135.

264 *"a place naturally without water"*: Ibid., 137.

265 *"The water is putrid"*: Visconti, 152.

265 *"feeling very well indeed"*: Letter to Charles d'Aubigné, August 22, 1680, in Madame de Maintenon, *Lettres*, ed. Langlois, Marcel, Vols II–V (Paris: Letouzy et Ané, 1935–59), II, no. 216, 350.

265 *"fifteen rolling chairs"*: Louis XIV, *Manière de montrer les jardins de Versailles* (Paris: Réunion des musées nationaux, 2001), 10.

265 *"The King . . . has ordered"*: Dangeau, marquis de, Journal entry for November 16, 1704, quoted in Louis XIV, *Manière de montrer les jardins de Versailles*, 13.

265 *"he preferred to watch"*: Bouchenot-Déchin, Patricia, *Henry Dupuis, jardinier de Louis XIV* (Versailles: Perrin, 2001), 169. Marly was an elegant château that had been built as a country retreat for Madame de Montespan, near Versailles.

266 *palace of Alcázar*: Alcázar was destroyed by fire in 1734. The palace of Buen Retiro (Pleasant Retreat) was originally outside the city of Madrid. It was destroyed during the Napoleonic Wars. Its site is now a large public park within the city. The "planet" epithet of Felipe IV in fact referred to the sun, then deemed to be the fourth "planet" in the solar system.

266 *"The King admits himself"*: Letter of November 5, 1699, in *Liselotte von der Pfalz, Lettres de Madame duchesse d'Orléans, née Princesse Palatine, 1672–1722*, ed. Ameil, Olivier (Paris: Mercure de France, 1985), 268.

267 *"Let's not make fools"*: D'Aumale, Marie-Jeanne, *Souvenirs sur Madame de Maintenon: Mémoire et lettres inédites de Mademoiselle d'Aumale*, 2e ed. (Paris: Calmann-Levy, 1902), 69.

268 *"Madame de Montespan and I"*: Letter to M. le marquis de Montchevreuil, May 27, 1681, in Langlois (ed.), *Lettres* II, no. 233, 380. And see Desprat, Jean-Paul, *Madame de Maintenon, ou le prix de la réputation* (Paris: Perrin, 2003), 193–4.

268 *"in the afternoon"*: Letter to the Herzogin Sophie, August 1, 1683, in Liselotte von der Pfalz, *Briefe*, 61.

268 *"a cruel and malignant fever"*: Vallot, d'Aquin, et Fagon, *Journal de la santé du Roi Louis XIV de l'année 1647 à l'année 1711, écrit par Vallot, d'Aquin et Fagon*, ed. Le Roi, J. A. (Paris: A. Durand, 1862), 157.

268 *"In the twenty-three years"*: Quoted in Bouchenot-Déchin, 127.

268 *"She died quite quickly"*: Letter to the Herzogin Sophie, August 1, 1683, in Liselotte von der Pfalz, *Briefe*, 61.

269 *"Let them," he said*: Saint-Germain, Jacques, *La Reynie et la police au grand siècle* (Paris: Hachette, 1962), 189.

269 *"With too little intelligence"*: Spanheim, Ezechiel, *Relation de la cour de France, faite au commencement de l'année 1690* (Paris: Renouard [pour la Société de l'histoire de France], 1882), 155.

269 *"This is no time"*: D'Aumale, 78–9. And see Caylus, Marthe-Marguerite, comtesse de, *Souvenirs*, ed. Bernard Noël (Paris: Mercure de France, 1965 et 1986), 84.

269 *"The King doesn't need"*: Caylus, 84.

269 *"And I can't promise"*: Ibid., 84–5, and see note 1 on 175–6.

270 *"Madame de Montespan wept"*: Ibid., 84.

270 *"You're quite right"*: Letter to Mr d'Aubigny, August 24, 1683, in Langlois (ed.), *Lettres* II, no. 323, 514.

270 *"In all my troubles"*: Letter to the Herzogin Sophie, August 1, 1683, in Liselotte von der Pfalz, *Briefe*, 61.

270 *"We were all very concerned"*: Letter of October 1, 1720, quoted in Langlois (ed.), *Lettres* II, 503, note 316.

270 *"more touched than afflicted"*: Caylus, 83.

271 *"very moved to see her die"*: Letter of October 1, 1720, quoted in Langlois (ed.), *Lettres* II, 503, note 316.

271 *"No, you can't come"*: Letter to Mr d'Aubigny, August 7, 1683, in ibid., no. 318, 505–7.

272 *"I ask your prayers:"* Letter to Mme de Brinon, August 12, 1683, in ibid., no. 320, 509.

272 *"There's nothing at all"*: Letter to Mme de Brinon, August 22, 1683, in ibid., no. 322, 513.

272 *"the most illustrious kingdom"*: "Oraison funèbre de Marie-Thérèse d'Autriche," in Bossuet, Jacques-Bénigne, *Oraisons Funèbres* (Paris: Hachette, 1898), 203 ff.

273 *"because, according to"*: Letter to the Raugrave Amélie-Élisabeth, May 13, 1705, in *Liselotte von der Pfalz, Lettres de Madame*, 357.

273 *"All salvation comes from"*: "Oraison funèbre de Marie-Thérèse d'Autriche," in Bossuet, 262–3.

273 *"We've hardly got over"*: Letter to Mr d'Aubigny, September 7, 1683, in Langlois (ed.), *Lettres* II, no. 325, 516.

273 *"completely dislocated"*: Vallot et al., 159–60.

274 *"a very fine capture"*: André Zysberg, *L'ascension de Colbert*, in Cornette, Joël (ed.), *La France de la Monarchie absolue, 1610–1715* (Paris: Éditions du Seuil, 1997), 269–70.

275 *"But the King couldn't do"*: Choisy, Abbé Françoise-Timoléon de, *Mémoires pour servir à l'histoire de Louis XIV, et Mémoires de l'abbé de Choisy habillé en femme*, ed. Georges Mongrédien (Paris: Mercure de France, 1966), 262.

275 *"the attchment to her"*: Spanheim, 18–25.

275 *"beyond the age"*: Choisy, 262.

276 *"the greatest of all men"*: "Oraison funèbre de Marie-Thérèse d'Autriche," in Bossuet, 227.

276 *"as if the thing hadn't yet"*: Choisy, 263.

276 *"It was rumoured"*: Spanheim, 20.

277 *"the best valet ever"*: Choisy, 183.

277 *"He had the King's"*: Saint-Simon, Louis de Rouvroy, duc de, *Mémoires*, 7 vols (Paris: Pléiade, 1953), I, 826.

277 *"as capable as anyone"*: Caylus, 90.

278 *"When I think of all"*: Lettre à Mademoiselle *** [d'Aubigné], undated, in Chamaillard, Edmond, *Le Chevalier de Méré, rival de Voiture, ami de Pascal, précepteur de Madame de Maintenon* (Niort: Clouzot, 1921), 2e partie, 22–4.

278 *"The King loved dignity"*: Saint-Simon, Louis de Rouvroy, duc de, *Mémoires*, 7 vols (Paris: Pléiade, 1953), II, 412.

279 *"Will you look at Madame"*: Molière, *Le Bourgeois gentilhomme*, Act III, scene xii, 755–6.

280 *"Madame de Maintenon would never have"*: D'Aumale, 81–2.

280 *"and after her death"*: Caylus, 68.

280 *"Owing to her modesty"*: Ibid.

280 *"He'll quite happily go"*: Letter to the Herzogin Sophie, July 23, 1699, in Liselotte von der Pfalz, *Briefe*, 160.

281 *"I knew I had nothing"*: Quoted in Bertière, Simone, *Les Reines de France aux Temps des Bourbons: Les deux régentes* (Paris: De Fallois, 1996), 503.

281 *"He knew that Madame"*: Choisy, 205.

281 *"to make it habitable"*: Solnon, 315.

281 *"and one most remarkable pearl"*: Ibid.

Fifteen: La Vie en Rose

282 *"Think about your pleasure"*: Letter to Mr d'Aubigny, quoted in Cordelier, Jean, *Madame de Maintenon* (Paris: Club des Éditeurs, 1959), 150.

282 *"I'm dying to see you"*: Letter to Madame de Brinon, October 11, 1683, in *Madame de Maintenon, Lettres*, ed. Langlois, Marcel, Vols II–V (Paris: Letouzy et Ané, 1935–59), III, no. 333, 5.

282 *"hadn't touched the tip"*: Choisy, Abbé Françoise-Timoléon de, *Mémoires pour servir à l'histoire de Louis XIV*, et *Mémoires de l'abbé de Choisy habillé en femme*, ed. Georges Mongrédien (Paris: Mercure de France, 1966), 206.

283 *"You ask whether"*: Letter to the Herzogin Sophie, May 13, 1687, in Liselotte von der Pfalz, *Briefe*, 79.

284 *"She was so charming"*: Caylus, Marthe-Marguerite, comtesse de, *Souvenirs*, ed. Bernard Noël (Paris: Mercure de France, 1965 et 1986), 28.

284 *"It's the same stuff"*: Letter to the Raugrave Amélie-Élisabeth, November 9, 1709, in *Lislotte von der Pfalz, Lettres de Madame*, 419.

284 *"and I can still sing them"*: Letter to the Herzogin Sophie, May 31, 1692, in Liselotte von der Pfalz, *Briefe*, 112.

284 *"Add to that"*: The Mercure Galant news sheet, quoted in Dunlop, Ian, *Royal Palaces of France* (London: Hamish Hamilton, 1985), 125.

284 *"I don't like these French dances"*: Letter to the Raugrave Amélie-Élisabeth, March 4, 1706, in Liselotte von der Pfalz, *Briefe*, 225.

284 *"I much prefer English food"*: Letter to the Raugrave Amélie-Élisabeth, July 24, 1699, in *Liselotte von der Pfalz, Lettres de Madame*, 262–3.

285 *"In any other country"*: From Justus Zinzerling's 1616 *Itinerarium Galliae*, quoted in Sabban et Serventi, 23.

285 *"roast or fried meat"*: See ibid., 68.

285 *"skinned and washed"*: See Bonnefons, Nicolas de, *Les délices de la campagne, suite du "Jardinier français,"* où est enseigné à préparer pour l'usage de la vie, tout ce qui croît sur terre et dans les eaux, 2e ed. (Amsterdam: Raphaël Smith, 1655), 346.

285 *"but lightly, so as not to"*: See Sabban et Serventi, 63.

286 *"The saga of the peas"*: Letter to the Cardinal de Noailles, May 18, 1696, in *Correspondance générale de Madame de Maintenon*, ed. Lavallée, Théophile, 4 vols (Paris: Charpentier, 1857), IV, 3e partie, CDXI, 98.

286 *"Last week it gave me colic"*: Letters to Madame de Grignan of May 13 & 25, October 1671, in Sévigné, Marie, marquise de, *Lettres*, 3 vols (Paris: Pléiade, 1960), I, no. 114, 290–1 and no. 161, 408–9. The quotations from these letters are mixed together.

287 *"The winter has passed"*: Letters to Mr d'Aubigny of March 1 & October 25, 1685, in Lavallée (ed.), *Correspondance générale* II, 3e partie, no. V, 354 & no. XLIV, 430. Letter to Mr le marquis de Montchevreuil, May 2, 1681, in Langlois (ed.), *Lettres* II, no. 227, 371.

287 *"I'm really desperate"*: Letter to the abbé Gobelin, January 6, 1684, in Lavallée (ed.), *Correspondance générale* II, 3e partie, no. 1, 347–8.

287 *"the extremities of the Universe"*: Choisy, 225.

288 *"who never thought much"*: Ibid., 233. The abbé de Choisy had been part of a diplomatic mission to Siam (Thailand). His engaging *Mémoires* contain a description of it. See also his *Journal du voyage de Siam fait en 1685 et 1686* (Paris, 1687).

288　*"You'll easily believe"*: Letter to Mr d'Aubigny, September 19, 1683, in Langlois (ed.), *Lettres* II, no. 328, 520.

288　*"The baby clothes"*: Letter to Mr d'Aubigny, March 1, 1684, in ibid., III, no. 355, 39.

288　*"Don't be concerned"*: Letter to Mr d'Aubigny, April 7, 1684, in ibid., no. 359, 43.

288　*"I already feel a kind of tenderness"*: Letter to Mr d'Aubigny, May 5, 1684, in ibid., no. 362, 47.

289　*"I'm sorry to hear about this"*: Letter to Mr d'Aubigny, June 25, 1684, in ibid., no. 365, 53–4.

290　*"Don't give in"*: Letter to Mr d'Aubigny, July 11, 1684, in ibid., no. 366, 57.

291　*"The King has agreed"*: Letter to Mr l'Abbé Gobelin, March 8, 1684, in ibid., no. 357, 41.

291　*"It often happens"*: Letter to Mme de Brinon, February 15, 1684, in ibid., no. 353, 37.

292　*"Please give the curé"*: Letter to Mr de Guignonville, August 10, 1683, in ibid., II, no. 319, 507; Letter to Madame de Dangeau, in Leroy, Pierre-E. et Marcel Loyau (eds), *L'Estime et la tendresse: Correspondances intimes* (Paris: Albin Michel, 1998), no. 169, 200; Letter to Madame de Caylus in ibid., no, 31, 107.

292　*"It would take too long"*: D'Aumale, Marie-Jeanne, *Souvenirs sur Madame de Maintenon: Mémoire et lettres inédites de Mademoiselle d'Aumale*, 2e ed. (Paris: Calmann-Levy, 1902), 162.

292　*"I'm sending you the fifteen pistoles"*: Letters to Mr d'Aubigny, March 1679, April 2, 1678, July 3, 1680, April 9, 1678, in Langlois (ed.), *Lettres* II, no. 184, 301; no. 157, 242; no. 212, 340; no. 158, 245.

292　*"one brown satin skirt"*: Letter to Mr d'Aubigny, April 1679, in ibid., no. 187, 306–7.

292　*"I'm really sorry to be"*: Letter to Mr d'Aubigny, July 11, 1679, in ibid., no. 189, 310–11.

294　*"You can't think highly enough"*: Letter to Mr l'Abbé Gobelin, January 17, 1686, in Lavallée (ed.), *Correspondance générale* III, 3e partie (suite), no. XLIX, 4.

294　*"We mustn't lose"*: Letters to Mme de Brinon, probably November 6, 1683, & December 2, 1683, in Langlois (ed.), *Lettres* III, no. 337, 11, & no. 340, 15.

294　*"Keep what wood you need"*: Letters to Mme de Brinon, December 7, 1683, January 25, 1684, January 28, 1684 (note added on January 29) & November 13, 1683, in ibid., no. 341, 17; no. 345, 23; no. 348, 28; & no. 339, 13.

295　*"It's true that I like the Ursulines"*: Letter to Mme de Brinon, August 29, 1681, in ibid. II, no. 243, 398.

295　*"I'm sending her back"*: Letter to Mme de Brinon, about February 19, 1684, in ibid. III, no. 354, 38.

296　*"the talent that I have"*: Letter to Mme de Villette, December 25, 1680, in ibid. II, no. 220, 356.

296　*"Today the King signed"*: Entry for June 6, 1686, in Dangeau, Philippe de Courcillon, marquis de, *Journal de la cour de Louis XIV, avec les additions inédites du duc de Saint-Simon*, 19 vols (Paris: Firmin-Didot Frères, 1854–1860), I, 346–7.

297　*"It was all built so quickly"*: Choisy, 214.

297　*"a fine big building"*: Letter to the duchesse de Hanovre, June 11, 1686, in *Liselotte von der Pfalz, Lettres de Madame*, 100.

297　*"the great increase"*: Letter to Mr l'Abbé Gobelin, April 7, 1686, in Lavallée (ed.), *Correspondance générale* III, 3e partie (suite); no. LV, 15.

297　*"Madame de Maintenon entered into"*: Choisy, 214.

298　maladie des directions: Langlois, "Madame de Maintenon," in *Revue Historique*, 296.

298　*"Sister Martha is to share"*: Letters to Mme de Brinon, July 21, March, July 21, May 1, May, August & March 1686, in Lavallée (ed.), *Correspondance générale* III, 3e partie (suite), no. LXX, 34; no. LIII, 11–12; no. LXX, 34; no. LX, 22; no. LXV, 28; no. LXXIV, 41; & no. LIII, 11.

298　*"Now that was a waste of time"*: D'Aumale, 184.

298 *"The King is very much occupied"*: Letter to Mme de Brinon, February ?7, 1686, in Lavallée (ed.), *Correspondance générale* III, 3e partie (suite), no. LII, 9.

299 *"We're working very hard"*: Letter to Mme de Brinon, April 1686, in ibid., no. LVIII, 19.

299 *"Do keep working"*: Letter to Mr l'Abbé Gobelin May 1686, in ibid., no. LXVI, 28–9.

299 *"They're correcting the spelling"*: Letter to Mme de Brinon, April 1686, in ibid., no. LIX, 20.

300 *"I myself was never kissed"*: D'Aumale, 18, and see Desprat, Jean-Paul, *Madame de Maintenon, ou le prix de la réputation* (Paris: Perrin, 2003), 262.

301 *"Young girls will reform their families"*: See Rapley, Elizabeth, *The Dévotes: Women and the Church in Seventeenth-Century France* (Montreal and Kingston: McGill-Queen's University Press, 1990), 157.

301 *"I don't know anything about the scriptures"*: Quoted in Desprat, 264.

301 *"All girls learn the minuet"*: Quoted in ibid., 267.

302 *"our young ladies read aloud"*: Letter of August 3, 1688, in Rathery, Edmé-Jacques-Benoît, et Boutron, *Mademoiselle de Scudéry: Sa vie et sa correspondance, avec un choix de ses poésies* (Paris: Léon Techener, 1873), 479–80.

302 *"Madame de Maintenon thought it wasn't possible"*: Madame de Pérou, quoted in Ramière de Fortanier, Arnaud (directeur), *Les Demoiselles de Saint-Cyr. Maison royale d'éducation, 1686–1793* (Versailles: Archives départementales de Yvelines; Paris: Somogy, éd. d'art, 1999), 175.

302 *"there are too many songs"*: Letter to Mme de Brinon, December 26, 1686, in Lavallée (ed.), *Correspondance générale* III, 3e partie (suite), no. LXXXV, 56.

303 *"Lord, conserve our only hope"*: "Prière pour Madame de Maintenon," in *Recueil d'airs spirituels à une, deux et trios voix sans accompagnement, de différents autheurs* (Bibliothèque municipale de Versailles, BMV MS musical 65, 2), 901–2.

303 *"Experience is the best teacher"*: Quoted in Desprat, 264.

303 *"Raising Oneself Socially"*: Maintenon, *Comment la sagesse vient aux filles*, Conversation 59, 232–4.

305 *"Self-confidence produces"*: Chamaillard, Edmond, *Le Chevalier de Méré, rival de Voiture, ami de Pascal, précepteur de Madame de Maintenon* (Niort: Clouzot, 1921), 1e partie, 130–2.

305 *"Reading is useful for men"*: Quoted in Duchêne, *Être femme au temps de Louis XIV*, 316, 324.

305 *"Apart from their natural authority"*: Fénelon, François de Salignac de La Mothe, *Traité de l'éducation des filles* (Paris: Kincksieck, 1994), Chapter 1, 38.

306 *"Take care not to make"*: Ibid., Chapter XII, 93.

307 *"I don't know whether"*: Spanheim, Ezechiel, *Relation de la cour de France, faite au commencement de l'année 1690* (Paris: Renouard [pour la Société de l'histoire de France], 1882), 403.

307 *"She is just as she has"*: Letter to Boileau, August 4, 1687, in Boileau, Nicolas and Jean Racine, *Lettres d'une amitié: Correspondance 1687–1698*, ed. Pierre E. Leroy (Paris: Bartillat, 2001), no. 7, 43–7.

308 *"public poisoner"*: The phrase is from the 1671 *Essais de Morale* of Pierre Nicole, one of Racine's teachers at Port-Royal.

308 *"something moral or historical"*: Desprat, 267.

308 *"It is a story filled"*: Preface to *Esther*, in Racine, Jean, *Théâtre et Poésies* (Paris: Gallimard, 1950), 812.

308 *"When Racine moved"*: Spanheim, 402.

309 *"I shall not regard"*: Racine, Jean, *Oeuvres Complètes* 7 (Paris: Garnier Frères, 1869–77), Lettre LXIV, 1688, 439.

309 *"The play is"*: Letter of July 12, 1715, in *Lettres de Madame duchesse d'Orléans, née Princesse Palatine, 1672–1722*, ed. Olivier Ameil (Paris: Mercure de France, 1985), 514. Liselotte is here writing of both *Esther* and *Athalie*.

309 *"It was a delightful little divertissement"*: La Fayette, Madame de, *Mémoires de la cour de France, pour les années 1688 et 1689*, nouvelle édition (Paris: GALIC, 1962), 68. Marie-Madeleine de La Fayette's *La Princesse de Clèves*, first published in 1678, is generally regarded as the first example of the novel in French.

310 *"with this difference"*: Ibid.

310 *"This kind of artistic undertaking"*: Anne Piéjus, in Ramière de Fortanier, *Les Demoiselles de Saint-Cyr*, 181.

310 *"Madame de Maintenon's modesty"*: Caylus, 95.

310 *"Admire the wisdom"*: Quoted in Rathery et Boutron, *Mademoiselle de Scudéry*, 521.

310 *"How could anyone resist"*: La Fayette, 68.

310 *"I'm happier than I've ever been"*: Letter to Mr l'Abbé Gobelin, September 22, 1686, in Lavallée (ed.), *Correspondance générale* III, 3e partie (suite), no. LXXVI, 44.

Sixteen: La Vie en Bleu

312 *"the redoubtable monster"*: Letter from the Bishop of Uzès to Louis XIV, quoted in Garrison, Janine, *L'Édict de Nantes et sa révocation* (Paris: Seuil, 1985), 146.

313 *"600 people have converted"*: Journal entry for April 18, 1685 of Nicolas Foucault, quoted in Garrisson, 219. And see passim, chapter 6.

313 *"We have just read"*: Response to Louvois's dispatch of March 1685, quoted in Garrisson, 220.

313 *"With methods like these"*: Letter from Fénelon to Bossuet of March 8, 1686, quoted in Richardt, Aimé, *Fénelon* (Paris: Éditions In Fine, 1993), 59.

313 *"Let the truth reign"*: Quoted in Richardt, *Louvois*, 206.

313 *"You'll no doubt have seen"*: Letter to the comte de Bussy-Rabutin, October 28, 1685, in Sévigné, Marie, marquise de, *Lettres*, 3 vols (Paris: Pléiade, 1960), III, 113.

314 *"The dragoons were mounted"*: Historian Pierre Miquel, quoted in Richardt, *Louvois*, 195.

314 *"Several people in this town"*: Quoted in Garrisson, 216.

314 *"This day was read"*: Evelyn, John, *The Diary* (London: Macmillan, 1908), November 3, 1685; March 29 & April 25, 1686, 384, 389–90.

315 *"They compliment the King"*: Letter to the duchesse de Hanovre, May 13, 1700, in *Liselotte von der Pfalz, Lettres de Madame*, 273.

315 *"Don't be harsh"*: Letter to Mr d'Aubigné, September 27, 1672, in Madame de Maintenon, *Lettres*, ed. Langlois, Marcel, Vols II–V (Paris: Letouzy et Ané, 1935–59), II, no. 25, 65.

315 *"I admit I'm not very happy"*: Letter to M. de Villette, September 4, 1687, in *Correspondence générale de Madame de Maintenon*, ed. Lavallée, Théophile, 4 vols (Paris: Charpentier, 1857), III, 3e partie (suite), no. CX, 91.

315 *"no good reason"*: Louis XIV, *Mémoires, suivi de Réflexions sur le métier de Roi* (Paris: Tallandier, 2001), 75–7.

317 *"Monsieur Louvois was afraid"*: Caylus, Marthe-Marguerite, comtesse de, *Souvenirs*, Bernard Noël (Paris: Mercure de France, 1965 et 1986), 28–9. Saint-Simon is quoted in Richardt, *Louvois*, 193.

317 *"It was a most admirable project"*: Quoted in Dunlop, *Royal Palaces of France*, 234–5.

318 *"These new converts"*: Quoted in Dunlop, *Louis XIV* (London: Chatto and Windus, 1999), 277.

318 *"If things were in the same state"*: Réponse a un mémoire touchant la manière la plus convenable de travailler à la conversion des Huguenots, in Maintenon, *Comment la sagesse vient aux filles*, 201–6. The *réponse* is generally dated 1697, though this date is not certain.

320 *"A girl should recoil from worldly knowledge"*: Quoted in Lewis, 245.

321 *"Nothing good in this world"*: Letter to the comte de Bussy-Rabutin, July 20, 1679, in Sévigné II, no. 574, 434.

321 *"a little tumour"*: Vallot et al., 167.

321 *"and I won't be happy"*: Letters to Mme de Brinon, February 27 & April 12, 1686, in Lavallée (ed.), *Correspondance générale* III, 3e partie (suite), no. LII, 9; & no. LVI, 16.

321 *"on the same footing"*: Letter to the duchesse de Hanovre, August 2, 1688, in *Liselotte von der Pfalz, Lettres de Madame*, 117.

321 *"This slimming business"*: Letter to the Raugrave Amélie-Élisabeth, March 30, 1704, in ibid., 329.

321 *"Bourdaloue is a famous Jesuit"*: Saint-Simon, Louis de Rouvroy, duc de, *Mémoires*, 7 vols (Paris: Pléiade, 1953), I, 211.

322 *"to see if talking"*: Choisy, Abbé Françoise-Timoléon de, *Mémoires pour servir à l'histoire de Louis XIV, et Mémoires de l'abbé de Choisy habillé en femme*, ed. Georges Mongrédien (Paris: Mercure de France, 1966), 206.

322 *"She does everything she can"*: Letter to the duchesse de Hanovre, August 11, 1686, in *Liselotte von der Pfalz, Lettres de Madame*, 103.

322 *"You're a nice face"*: Letter to Madame de Grignan, July 22, 1685, in Sévigné III, no. 794, 94.

322 *"Honestly, you'd cry laughing"*: Letter to the Herzogin Sophie, August 11, 1686, & October 1, 1687, in Liselotte von der Pfalz, *Briefe*, 77, 79–80.

322 *"no physician and no astrologer"*: Visconti, Primi, *Mémoires sur la Cour de Louis XIV, 1673–1681* (Paris: Perrin, 1988), 53.

323 *"Believe me when I say"*: Letter to Mr d'Aubigny, December 15, 1679, in Langlois (ed.), *Lettres* II, no. 200, 323.

323 *"insupportable martyrdom"*: Letter to Madame de Grignan, March 1, 1680, in Sévigné II, no. 636, 629.

325 *"a villainous commerce"*: Spanheim, Ezechiel, *Relation de la cour de France, faite au commencement de l'année 1690* (Paris: Renouard [pour la Société de l'histoire de France], 1882), 101.

325 *"These vices are more"*: Primi Visconti, quoted in Solnon, Jean-François, *La Cour de France* (Paris: Fayard, 1987), 286. And see Visconti, 13.

325 *"You wouldn't believe how blatant"*: Letters to the Kurfürstin Sophie, February 6 & 13, 1695, in Liselotte von der Pfalz, *Briefe*, 126–7. And see Lebrun, François, *La vie conjugale sous l'Ancien Régime* (Paris: Armand Colin, 1978), 93.

326 *"The King is just as angry"*: Haymann, *Lulli*, 243.

326 *"The praises of all Paris"*: Ibid., 246–7.

328 *"far from being able"*: Chantelou, Paul Fréart de, *Journal du Voyage du Cavalier Bernin en France, avec Préface de G. Charensol* (Paris: Delamain et Boutelleau, 1930), 12. Reworked by Girardon, the statue was kept in the park at Versailles until it was damaged by vandals in 1980. A copy now stands outside the Louvre, while the repaired original remains in storage.

328 *"He couldn't bear anyone"*: Spanheim, 7–8.

328 *"It's not pleasant"*: Chamaillard, Edmond, *Le Chevalier de Méré, rival de Voiture, ami de Pascal, précepteur de Madame de Maintenon* (Niort: Clouzot, 1921), 1e partie, 54.

329 *"Félix made two incisions"*: Choisy, 253–4.

329 *"Félix's new instrument"*: Entry for November 18, 1686, in Dangeau, Philippe de Courcillon, marquis de, *Journal de la cour de Louis XIV, avec les additions inédites du duc de Saint-Simon,* 19 vols (Paris: Firmin-Didot Frères, 1854–1860), I, 417–8.

329 *"had tried to get in"*: Choisy, 253.

329 *"He was very jolly"*: Dangeau I, December 6, 1686, 424.

329 *"The King was in great pain"*: Letter to Mme de Brinon, December 11, 1686, in Lavallée (ed.), *Correspondance générale* III, 3e partie (suite), no. LXXIX, 49.

330 *"He was in torments"*: Letter to the duchesse de Hanovre, December 11, 1686, in *Liselotte von der Pfalz, Lettres de Madame,* 107.

330 *"The greatest man in Europe"*: Pujo, Bernard, *Le Grand Condé* (Paris: Albin Michel, 1995), 385.

330 *"The King's wound"*: Letter to Mme de Brinon, December 1686, in Lavallée (ed.), *Correspondence générale* III, 3e partie (suite), no. LXXXII, 52–3.

330 *"he hardly moved"*: Solnon, 321.

330 *"Last night, the King attended"*: Letter to Mme de Brinon, December 25, 1686, in Lavallée (ed.), *Correspondance générale* III, 3e partie (suite), no. LXXXIV, 54–5.

331 *"His family weren't at all"*: Saint-Simon I, 39–40.

331 *"He was unappealing"*: Ibid. II, 672–3.

332 *"I must say I prefer"*: Desprat, Jean-Paul, *Madame de Maintenon, ou le prix de la réputation* (Paris: Perrin, 2003), 265.

332 *"she closed her eyes"*: Saint-Simon II, 411.

332 *"You've never seen"*: Ibid.

332 *"It was constant delight"*: Choisy, 193–4.

333 *"Her husband didn't notice"*: Saint-Simon II, 411.

333 *"in words fit to be engraved"*: Choisy, 194.

333 *"Boufflers was devoted"*: Saint-Simon III, 178, 182.

333 *"I got upset sometimes"*: Quoted in Langlois, "Madame de Maintenon," in *Revue Historique,* 298.

334 *"So being her adoptive nephew"*: Choisy, 194.

334 *"I am most impatient"*: Letter to M. le comte de Caylus, December 21, 1686, in Lavallée (ed.), *Correspondance générale* III, 3e partie (suite) no. LXXXI, 51–2.

334 *"He has to make things up"*: Letter to M. de Villette, August 2, 1687, in ibid., no. CVI, 85–6.

335 *"Do please send me"*: Letter to Mme la marquise de Caylus, August 30, 1687, in ibid., no. CIX, 89–90.

335 *"I'll send my coach"*: Letter to M. de Villette, August 19, 1687, in ibid., no. CVIII, 87–9.

336 *"He was perfectly happy"*: Saint-Simon II, 411.

336 *"you can imagine"*: Caylus, 107.

Seventeen: Crusaders

337 *"screaming and yelling"*: See Oman, Carola, *Mary of Modena* (London: Hodder and Stoughton, 1962), 20.

338 *"That flight will make"*: Letter to Mme de Grignan, December 13, 1688, in Sévigné, Marie, marquise de, *Lettres,* 3 vols (Paris: Pléiade, 1960), III, no. 891, 275. Madame de Sévigné describes the details of Queen Mary's flight in a further letter to her daughter of December 24, 1688. See ibid., no. 899, 287–9. King James's separate progress to France is described in the subsequent letters.

338 *William and Mary*: Mary II died in 1694. William III continued to reign alone until his death, in 1702. As they had no legitimate issue, they were succeeded by Mary's sister, Anne (r. 1702–14).

338 *"And today it really is"*: Letter to the comte de Bussy-Rabutin, January 6, 1689, in Sévigné III, no. 905, 305–6.

339 *"but she was intelligent"*: Caylus, Marthe-Marguerite, comtesse de, *Souvenirs*, ed. Bernard Noël (Paris: Mercure de France, 1965 et 1986), 105.

339 *"You could say she had"*: Letter of June 15, 1718, quoted in ibid., 198.

339 *"Off he'd go to the chase"*: La Fayette, Madame de, *Mémoires de la cour de France, pour les années 1688 et 1689*, nouvelle édition (Paris: GALIC, 1962), 64–5.

339 *"The King possesses"*: Spanheim, Ezechiel, *Relation de la cour de France, faite au commencement de l'année 1690* (Paris: Renouard [pour la Société de l'histoire de France], 1882), 7.

340 *"The more you see"*: Letter to the duchesse de Hanovre, September 13, 1690, in *Liselotte von der Pfalz, Lettres de Madame*, 138–9.

340 *"almost all the grandees"*: La Fayette, 65.

340 *"Every last plan"*: Caylus, 105.

340 *"Le millord Tyrconnell"*: Letter to M. l'abbé Gobelin, February 14, 1689, in *Correspondance générale de Madame de Maintenon*, ed. Lavallée, Théophile, 4 vols (Paris: Charpentier, 1857), III, 3e partie (suite), 170–1. The Irish uprising of 1689, led by Richard Talbot, first Earl of Tyrconnell, followed Jacobite rebellions in the Scottish Highlands. The Irish Jacobites finally conceded defeat in October 1691 at the Treaty of Limerick.

340 *"poorly disciplined"*: La Fayette, 66.

341 *"and officers of an exceedingly mediocre"*: La Fayette, 72.

341 *"the onset of a war"*: Davies, Norman, *Europe: A History* (Oxford: OUP, 1997), 632. The Battle of Culloden Moor, which preceded the Highland clearances, was the last battle to be fought on British soil.

341 "From a mixture of all kinds": Daniel Defoe, *The True Born Englishman* (1701), ll. 279–80, 317–21, 333–4. Defoe wrote the poem in response to William Tutchin's *The Foreigners: a Poem* (1700), an attack on William III's foreign birth.

342 *absolute sovereign*: By contrast, most countries of the West today base their parliaments on the later doctrine of the sovereignty of the people, drawn from the eighteenth-century models of revolutionary France or the United States, with "a formal constitution governing all branches of the polity." See Davies, *Europe*, 631.

343 *"I wept twice twenty-four hours"*: Letter to the Herzogin Sophie, November 10, 1688, in Liselotte von der Pfalz, *Briefe*, 88–9.

343 *"The King has given orders"*: Dangeau, Philippe de Courcillon, marquis de, *Journal de la cour de Louis XIV, avec les additions inédites du duc de Saint-Simon*, 19 vols (Paris: Firmin-Didot Frères, 1854–1860), II, November 26, 1688, 218.

343 *"What distresses me"*: Letter to the Herzogin Sophie, March 20, 1689, in Liselotte von der Pfalz, *Briefe*, 90–1.

343 *"Monseigneur's army"*: Letter to Madame de Maintenon, July 24, 1689, in Lavallée (ed.), *Correspondance générale* III, 3e partie (suite), 183–4. Monseigneur (the twenty-nine-year-old dauphin) held only honorific command of the armies in the Rhineland. They were in fact commanded by the Maréchal de Lorge.

344 *"It's the same thing"*: Letters to Madame de Maintenon, May 22 to October 31, 1689, in ibid., nos CLXVI–CXCIII, 174–204.

344 *"I'm thrilled, Madame"*: Letters to Madame de Maintenon, July 3 to August 20, 1690, in ibid., nos CCXII–CCXXVI, 233–49.

345 *"M. le Grand Prieur"*: Dangeau III, July 19 and 20, 1690, 174.

345 *"It's the biggest war"*: Quoted in Bluche, François, *Louis XIV* (Paris: Hachette, 1986), 626. Catholic Spain, outraged by Louis's pseudo-legal seizures, known to the French as *réunions*, of several of her smaller territories during the 1680s, had joined the otherwise Protestant Grand Alliance in an attempt to restrain him now. Through the réunions, France had gained some 160 small territories on its northern and eastern borders, notably Strasbourg and Luxembourg, mostly at the expense of Spain. To arrange this, Louis had set up quasi-legal courts to enforce the supposed claims of the Treaty of Westphalia of 1648, which had ended the Thirty Years War.

345 *"The King augmented"*: Saint-Simon, Louis de Rouvroy, duc de, *Mémoires*, 7 vols (Paris: Pléiade, 1953), I, 888.

346 *"No one should be surprised"*: Caylus, 105.

346 *"As soon as you permit"*: Louis XIV, *Mémoires, suivi de Réflexions sur le métier de Roi* (Paris: Tallandier, 2001), 259.

347 *"the stupidest creatures"*: Desprat, Jean-Paul, *Madame de Maintenon, ou le prix de la réputation* (Paris: Perrin, 2003), 266.

347 *"There's no other school"*: Ibid., 269.

347 *"Our maxim here"*: Ibid., 265–70.

348 *"If they won't sit still"*: Ibid., 269.

348 *"The best-laid plans"*: La Fayette, 67.

350 *"Is it true you're"*: D'Aumale, Marie-Jeanne, *Souvenirs sur Madame de Maintenon: Mémoire et lettres inédites de mademoiselle d'Aumale*, 2e ed. (Paris: Calmann-Levy, 1902), 97–8.

350 *"a book to divert him"*: Letter from Françoise to Madame de Brinon, quoted in Desprat, 280.

351 *"We must rebuild"*: Ibid., 282.

351 *"miseries and pettiness"*: Ibid., 282.

352 *"I take communion only"*: See Letter XLVII, *Sur les découragemens de la Dirigée*, in Godet des Marais, Paul, *Lettres de messire Paul Godet Des Marais, Évêque de Chartres, à Mme de Maintenon, recueillies par l'abbé Berthier* (Paris: J. Dumoulin, 1980), 137–41.

352 *"Your hope of salvation"*: Ibid., 137–41. "O.L.J.C.": Our Lord Jesus Christ.

352 *"I was informed yesterday"*: Letter XLIV, *Sur la douleur*, in ibid., 131–2.

352 *"Sins just seem to get worse"*: Letter to Mme de Brinon, July 21, 1686, in Lavallée (ed.), *Correspondance générale* III, 3e partie (suite), no. LXX, 34.

353 *"He was a man of quality"*: Saint-Simon I, 256.

353 *"He was a tall"*: Ibid. IV, 606.

354 *"I am sorry I didn't know"*: Letter of October 4, 1688, in Lavallée (ed.), *Correspondance générale* III, 3e partie (suite), 117–18.

354 *"No one needs to know"*: Louis XIV, 35. Louis is here writing of the Jansenist controversy within the Catholic Church, but he maintained the same attitude towards other unorthodox movements.

355 *"One gives oneself to God"*: Choisy, Abbé François-Timoléon de, *Mémoires pour servir à l'histoire de Louis XIV, et Mémoires de l'abbé de Choisy habillé en femme*, ed. Georges Mongrédien (Paris: Mercure de France, 1966), 202–3.

356 *"hiding in the attics"*: Desprat, 299.

356 *"I am hesitant to speak"*: Letter of 1690, in Lavallée (ed.), *Correspondance générale* III, 3e partie (suite), 259–74.

359 *"Madame de Maintenon wanted to clear"*: Desprat, 309.

359 *"develop doctrine and teach"*: Ibid.

360 *"Your Majesty's ministers"*: Paraphrased from Levi, Anthony, *Louis XIV* (London: Constable, 2004), 237–8.

361 *"The archbishop of Paris"*: Spanheim, 244–7.

361 *What better cause*: Letters to the Évêque de Châlons, August 13 & 18, 1695, in Lavallée (ed.), *Correspondance générale* IV, 3e partie (suite), nos CCCLIII & CCCLIV, 12.

363 *"I would rather die"*: Letter from Fénelon to Madame de Maintenon, September 1696, in Lavallée (ed.), *Correspondance générale* IV, 3e partie (suite), no. CDXXXII, 119.

363 *"and to very bad effect"*: Letter to M. l'Archévêque de Paris, August 7, 1698, in ibid., no. XXVII, 245.

363 *"A lot of people at court"*: Quoted in Desprat, 317.

363 *"I have seen our friend"*: Letter to M. l'Archévêque de Paris, October 7, 1696, in Lavallée (ed.), *Correspondance générale* IV, 3e partie (suite), no. CDXXXIV, 121.

364 *"Why do you close your heart"*: Letters of March 7 & September 1696, in ibid., nos CCCXCIV, 68 & CDXXXII, 118–20.

364 *"If he's right"*: Saint-Simon I, 504. The speaker was Dom Jacques de la Cour, abbé de la Trappe.

364 *"The King is watching me"*: Letter to M. l'Archévêque de Paris, February 21 & April 3, 1697, in Lavallée (ed.), *Correspondance générale* IV, 3e partie (suite), nos CDL, 145–6 & CDLVI, 152. And see Desprat, 325.

365 *"If he is condemned"*: Letter to M. l'Archévêque de Paris, August 7, 1698, in ibid., 4e partie, no. XXVII, 245.

365 *"In France, anyway"*: Letter to the duchesse de Hanovre, August 31, 1698, in *Liselotte von der Pfalz, Lettres de Madame*, 240.

365 *"The King is getting angry"*: Desprat, 320–4.

366 *"The old hag isn't the happiest"*: Letter to the duchesse de Hanovre, November 18, 1698, in *Liselotte von der Pfalz, Lettres de Madame*, 240.

366 *"Pray for me"*: Letter to M. l'Archévêque de Paris, September 3, 1698, in Lavallée (ed.), *Correspondance générale* IV, 4e partie, no. XXIX, 247.

366 *"tenderness and loyalty"*: Quoted in Desprat, 326.

366 *"So, Madame"*: Desprat, 326.

367 *"There were so many men"*: Saint-Simon I, 550–7.

368 *"They won't say whether"*: Letter to the duchesse de Hanovre, July 19, 1699, in *Liselotte von der Pfalz, Lettres de Madame*, 261.

370 *"the life of a twenty-five-year-old"*: Somerset, Anne, *The Affair of the Poisons: Murder, Infanticide and Satanism at the Court of Louis XIV* (London: Phoenix, 2004), 299.

370 *"As far as I'm concerned"*: Letter to the duchesse de Hanovre, August 10, 1691, in *Liselotte von der Pfalz, Lettres de Madame*, 144.

370 *"I know better than anyone"*: Letter from the duc du Maine to Madame de Maintenon, October 25, 1699, in Lavallée (ed.), *Correspondance générale* IV, 4e partie, no. LIX, 292–3.

370 *"Madame de Maintenon was dreadfully upset"*: Saint-Simon I, 678.

371 *"You are one of those people"*: Letter of July 4, 1679, quoted in Sévigné II, 1050.

371 *"Madame de Sévigné"*: Saint-Simon I, 228.

371 *"He changes favourites"*: Letter of October 12, 1701, in *Lettres de Madame duchesse d'Orléans, née Princess Palatine, 1672–1722*, ed. Olivier Ameil (Paris: Mercure de France, 1985), 305.

371 *"a fat girl"*: Saint-Simon I, 191.

371 *"of remarkable ugliness"*: Caylus, 79.

372 *"She is perfect"*: Letter to Their Royal Highnesses of Savoy, November 5, 1696, in d'Aumale, 124–5.

372 *"She hardly took any notice"*: Letters to the Kurfürstin Sophie of November 8 & 22, 1696, in Liselotte von der Pfalz, *Briefe*, 137.

372 *"My eyes are so thick"*: Letter to the Herzogin Sophie, January 10, 1692, in Liselotte von der Pfalz, *Briefe*, 109–10.

Eighteen: Castles in Spain

374 *"That prince"*: Choisy, Abbé François-Timoléon de, *Mémoires pour servir à l'histoire de Louis XIV, et Mémoires de l'abbé de Choisy habillé en femme*, ed. Georges Mongrédien (Paris: Mercure de France, 1966), 176.

374 *"I think . . . the King of Spain"*: Letter to the duchesse de Hanovre, July 17, 1700, in *Liselotte von der Pfalz, Lettres de Madame*, 275.

375 *"We'll soon be hearing"*: Letter to M. le Cardinal de Noailles, November 8, 1700, in *Correspondance générale de Madame de Maintenon*, ed. Lavallée, Théophile, 4 vols (Paris: Charpentier, 1857), IV, 4e partie, no. XCVIII, 341.

375 *"Madame String-puller"*: Letter to the duchesse de Hanovre, November 10, 1700, in *Liselotte von der Pfalz, Lettres de Madame*, 282.

376 *"Gentlemen," said Louis*: Dangeau, Philippe de Courcillon, marquis de, *Journal de la cour de Louis XIV, avec les additions inédites du duc de Saint-Simon*, 19 vols (Paris: Firmin-Didot Frères, 1854–1860), November 16, 1700, VII, 418.

376 *"The duc d'Anjou will make"*: Letters to the duchesse de Hanovre, November 13 & 10, 1701, in *Liselotte von der Pfalz, Lettres de Madame*, 282.

376 *"Everyone here seems thrilled"*: Letters to M. le Cardinal de Noailles, November 17 & 25, 1700, in Lavallée (ed.), *Correspondance générale* IV, 4e partie, nos XCIX, 344–5 & C, 347–8. The cardinal was in Rome to attend the papal conclave which eventually elected Clement XI Albani.

377 *"playing hide-and-seek"*: Letter to M. le Cardinal de Noailles, November 25, 1700, in ibid., no. C, 348.

377 *"Be a good Spaniard"*: Dangeau VII, November 16, 1700, 418.

378 *"His passion for glory"*: Spanheim, Ezechiel, *Relation de la cour de France, faite au commencement de l'année 1690* (Paris: Renouard [pour la Société de l' histoire de France], 1882), 25.

379 *"and preventing English"*: Choisy, 177.

380 *"Animal" Visconti*: Letter of August 8, 1702, in *Lettres de Madame duchesse d'Orléans, née Princesse Palatine, 1672–1722*, ed. Olivier Ameil (Paris: Mercure de France, 1985), 320.

380 *"the very first world war"*: Davies, Norman, *Europe: A History* (Oxford: OUP, 1997), 625. In North America, it was known as Queen Anne's War.

380 *"At court, perhaps without"*: Déon, Michel, *Louis XIV par lui-même* (Paris: Gallimard,1991), 144–5.

380 *"Our two Kings"*: Letter to Madame des Ursins, June 5, 1706, in Truc, Gonzague (ed.), *Lettres à d'Aubigné et à Madame des Ursins* (Paris: Bossard, 1921), Part 2, 8.

381 "eleven ounces": Letter to the Kurfürstin Sophie, June 12, 1701, in Liselotte von der Pfalz, *Briefe*, 183.

381 *"The monastic life"*: Letters to the duchesse de Hanovre and the Raugrave Amélie-Élisabeth, July 15 & 7, 1701, in *Liselotte von der Pfalz, Lettres de Madame*, 302 & 301–2.

381 *"If those in the other world"*: Letter to the duchesse de Hanovre, June 30, 1701, in ibid., 301.

382 *"She sent a message"*: Letter to the duchesse de Hanovre, June 12, 1701, in ibid., 299–300.

382 *"which just shows how badly"*: Saint-Simon, Louis de Rouvroy, duc de, *Mémoires*, 7 vols (Paris: Pléiade, 1953), I, 917–19.

384 *"visited la Maintenon"*: Letter to the Herzogin Sophie, July 22, 1699, paraphrased from Bryant, *Françoise d'Aubigné, Marquise de Maintenon*, 153. Use of an armchair was a mark of precedence in rank. Liselotte, as a duchess, would normally have been entitled to an armchair rather than a stool. However, in Françoise's apartments, since the King entered frequently and without formal warning, no armchairs were made available for guests.

384 *"It's appalling"*: Letter to the Raugrave Amélie-Élisabeth, February 19, 1705, in Liselotte von der Pfalz, *Briefe*, 217–18.

384 *"I'm sure his German"*: Letters of September 29, 1702 and July 16, 1702, in *Lettres de Madame*, 323–4 and 320.

385 *"As I am generally"*: Letter to M. le duc d'Harcourt, April 16, 1701, in Lavallée (ed.), *Correspondance générale* IV, 4e partie, no. CXXXVIII, 423–4.

386 *"If I may say so"*: Taillandier, Madame Saint-René de, *La Princesse des Ursins: Une grande dame française à la cour d'Espagne sous Louis XIV* (Paris: Hachette, 1926), 52.

386 *"dwarves, clowns, parrots"*: Ibid., 36 and passim.

386 *"The rooms in this palace"*: Paraphrased from ibid., 67–8.

387 *"It was in the middle"*: Paraphrased from ibid., 68–9.

387 *"to command as generalissimo"*: Letter of June 24, 1706, in *Lettres de Madame*, 370. D'Orléans was replacing the brilliant Vendôme, himself transferring to Flanders after the resignation of Villeroy following the May defeat at Ramillies, where the French lost some fifteen thousand men.

388 *"As I had had various"*: Saint-Simon II, 26.

388 *"M. le duc de Saint-Simon"*: Spanheim, 423.

388 *"if you count up all"*: Saint-Simon II, 330.

389 *"dropped his pants"*: Letter of July 11, 1708, in *Lettres de Madame*, 393.

390 *"the loss of the Kingdom"*: Letter of August 10, 1707, in Geoffroy, M. A. (ed.), *Lettres inédites de la Princesse des Ursins* (Paris: Didier, 1859), 316.

390 *"They say he owed"*: Goubert, Pierre, *Louis XIV et Vingt Millions de Français* (Paris: Hachette, 1977), 288–9.

391 *"There are deserters"*: Letter of August 9, 1702, in *Lettres de Madame*, 321.

391 *"relentless increase"*: Anderson, M. S., *War and Society in Europe of the Old Regime 1618–1789* (Guernsey, Channel Islands: Sutton Publishing, 1998), 142.

391 *"a triumph for the new regime"*: Rothstein, Andrew, *Peter the Great and Marlborough: Politics and Diplomacy in Converging Wars* (London: Macmillan, 1986), 33.

391 *"an impressive sum"*: Sir Winston Churchill, quoted in ibid., 33.

392 *"I have found everywhere"*: Quoted in ibid., 112.

392 *Our Father which art at Versailles*: Quoted in ibid., 112.

392 *"The maréchal de Villars has told me"*: Letters of May 26 & June 10, 1709, in Loyau, Marcel (ed.), *Correspondance de Madame de Maintenon et la Princesse des Ursins, 1709: une année tragique* (Paris: Mercure de France, 2002), 189 & 199.

393 *"Rents, new offices"*: Goubert, 290.

393 *"penuriousness"*: The Englishman Joseph Addison in 1707, quoted in Rothstein, 158.

393 *"I'm so angry"*: Letter of July 1, 1709, in Loyau (ed.), 215.

393 *"As for the money here"*: Letter of August 10, 1709, in ibid., 243.

394 *"chamber pots"*: Saint-Germain, Jacques, *La Reynie et la police au grand siècle* (Paris: Hachette, 1962), 151.

394 *"This question of wheat"*: Letter of August 10, 1700, in Loyau (ed.), 243.

394 *"they're holding a big procession"*: Letter of May 26, 1709, in ibid., 186.

394 *"A great many of the poor"*: Letter of January 27, 1709, in Loyau (ed.), 94.

394 *"Madame de Maintenon redoubled her alms"*: D'Aumale, Marie-Jeanne, *Souvenirs sur Madame de Maintenon: Mémoire et lettres inédites de Mademoiselle d'Aumale*, 2e ed. (Paris: Calmann-Levy, 1902), 153–4.

395 *"quite willingly"*: Letter of June 10, 1709, in Loyau (ed.), 199.

395 *"The women here"*: Letter to Mme de Caylus in Paris, June 12, 1706, in Leroy, Pierre-E. et Marcel Loyau (eds), *L'Estime et la tendresse: Correspondances intimes* (Paris: Albin Michel, 1998), 105.

395 *"You'll have heard"*: Letter of June 3, 1709, in Loyau (ed.), 194.

396 *"How can anyone buy peace"*: Letter of June 10, 1709, in ibid., 196.

396 *"The King of Spain has received"*: Letter of June 10 or 11, 1709, in ibid., 201.

397 *"the impossible condition"*: Rothstein, 115.

397 *"The hope of peace"*: Petitfils, *Louis XIV*, 635–6. Petitfils notes the Churchillian nature of Louis's appeal.

398 *"Advices from the* Hague*"*: Addison, Joseph and Sir Richard Steele, *Selections from The Tatler and The Spectator*, ed. Robert J. Allen, 2nd ed. (New York: Holt, Rinehart and Winston, 1970), 23.

399 *"Nothing is equal"*: Letter of September 14, 1709, in Loyau (ed.), 277.

399 *"all the ladies"*: Ibid., 277–8.

400 *"And what about the peace"*: Letter to Madame de Dangeau of May 21, 1712, quoted in Leroy et Loyau (eds), *L'estime et la tendresse*, no. 212, 236.

400 *"a greedy and treacherous desertion"*: Sir Winston Churchill, quoted in Rothstein, 151. Marlborough was the victim of domestic political intrigues. His opponents sought to present him as a would-be "second Cromwell" (Rothstein, 154). His preference for maintaining the general interests of the Alliance had been superseded in parliament by a decision to maintain the exclusive interests of Great Britain, particularly against the Dutch.

401 *"I reckon the City"*: Letter to Charlotte Clayton of January 1614, quoted in Field, Ophelia, *The Favourite: Sarah, Duchess of Marlborough* (London: Hodder & Stoughton, 2002), 335.

401 *"for all this waste"*: Milton, Sonnet XI, l. 451.

401 *"no more than a sloop"*: Lavisse, quoted in Rothstein, 196.

402 *"England wishes to become master"*: Paraphrased from ibid., 196.

402 *"The dauphin is shorter"*: Spanheim, 40, 46.

403 *"The King has so humbled"*: Letter of April 16, 1711, in *Lettres de Madame duchesse d'Orléans, née Princesse Palatine, 1672–1722*, ed. Olivier Ameil (Paris: Mercure de France, 1985), 449.

403 *"You will understand"*: Letter from Louis XIV to Felipe V of February 21, 1712, quoted in Déon, Michel, *Louis XIV par lui-même* (Paris: Gallimard, 1991), 300–1.

403 *"Misfortune . . . overwhelms us"*: Letter of March 10, 1712, in *Lettres de Madame*, 468.

404 *"vomiting violently"*: Letter of May 3, 1714, in ibid., 499–500.

404 *"I feel lethargic"*: Letter to the duc de Richelieu, April 30, probably 1713 (unpublished ms).

404 *"violating the constitution"*: Bluche, François, *Louis XIV* (Paris: Hachette, 1986), 865.

404 *"Since the sister"*: Letter to the Raugrave Luise, September 2, 1714, in *Liselotte von der Pfalz, Lettres de Madame*, 507.

405 *"this news which would not allow"*: Saint-Simon IV, 341–5.

Nineteen: All Passion Spent

406 *"The King was very well"*: Vallot, d'Aquin, et Fagon, *Journal de la Santé du Roi Louis XIV de l'année 1647 à l'année 1711, écrit par Vallot, d'Aquin et Fagon*, ed. Le Roi, J. A. (Paris: A. Durand, 1862), 344–5. Italics in the original.

406 *"Yes, my dear daughter"*: Quoted in Desprat, Jean-Paul, *Madame de Maintenon, ou le prix de la réputation* (Paris: Perrin, 2003), 340.

406 *"a whole pheasant"*: Quoted in Fraser, Antonia, *Love and Louis XIV: The Women in the Life of the Sun King* (London: Weidenfeld and Nicolson, 2006), 201–2.

407 *"her skin like a bit of"*: Letter to the duchesse de Hanovre, December 29, 1701, in *Liselotte von der Pfalz, Lettres de Madame*, 313.

407 *"Old age is terribly sad"*: Letter to Madame des Ursins, August 26, 1709, in Loyau (ed.), 255.

407 *"I was about thirteen"*: Duchêne, Roger, *Ninon de Lenclos: ou la manière jolie de faire l'amour* (Paris: Fayard, 2000), 336.

407 *"I'm sure you don't have"*: Letter to the duchesse de Hanovre, December 29, 1701, in *Liselotte von der Pfalz, Lettres de Madame*, 313.

408 *"heavy and sumptuous suit"*: Castellucio, Stéphane, "La Galerie des Glaces: Les réceptions d'ambassadeurs," *Versalia, La Revue de la Société des Amis de Versailles*, no. 9, 2006, 41.

408 *"a hundred and six"*: Le baron de Breteuil, quoted in ibid., 43.

409 *"so he sent for her"*: Saint-Simon, Louis de Rouvroy, duc de, *Mémoires*, 7 vols (Paris: Pléiade, 1953), IV, 887–8, and to 939 for subsequent paragraphs.

409 *"Monsieur d'Orléans's apartments"*: Saint-Simon, Louis de Rouvroy, duc de, *Mémoires*, 7 vols (Paris: Pléiade, 1953), IV, 889–91, and to 939 for quotations in subsequent paragraphs.

411 *"I was a witness"*: D'Aumale, Marie-Jeanne, *Souvenirs sur Madame de Maintenon: Mémoire et lettres inédites de Mademoiselle d'Aumale*, 2e ed. (Paris: Calmann-Levy, 1902), 200, and see 198–202.

411 *"If the King eats"*: Quoted in Petitfils, Jean-Christian, *Louis XIV* (Paris: Perrin, 2002), 694.

411 *"The King was constantly"*: Saint-Simon VI, 934.

411 *"whenever she felt she could not"*: D'Aumale, 198–202.

412 *"He surrendered his soul"*: Quoted in Petitfils, 695.

412 *"She had asked me"*: D'Aumale, 203–4, and note to 209.

413 *"a calm grief"*: Ibid., 205.

413 *"The King had paper and ink"*: Saint-Simon IV, 925.

414 *"that's to say, to leave them"*: Ibid., 923.

415 *"if my son's mistresses"*: Letter to the Raugrave Luise, December 14, 1717, in *Liselotte von der Pfalz, Lettres de Madame*, 532.

415 *"I asked him how"*: Saint-Simon VI, 35–7.

416 *"she would set the whole kingdom"*: Ibid., 15–16.

416 *"I was dying of joy"*: Quoted in Gourdin, Jean-Luc, *La Duchesse du Maine: Louise-Bénédicte de Bourbon, Princesse de Condé* (Paris: Pygmalion, 1999), 222.

418 *"Her laziness is beyond belief"*: Letters to the Raugrave Luise, April 7 & 17, 1718, in *Liselotte von der Pfalz, Lettres de Madame*, 539.

418 *"It doesn't take too much"*: Saint-Simon VI, 336.

418 *"She knew something had happened"*: D'Aumale, 223.

418 *"dreadfully afflicted"*: Saint-Simon VI, 336.

419 *"She'd had the good sense"*: Ibid., 332.

419 *"to think of my salvation"*: D'Aumale, 204.

420 *"very well made"*: Ibid., 188–9, 211–12. The letter to Madame de Caylus is of February 16, 1716.

420 *"They tell me I'm almost"*: Letter of August 23, 1717, in ibid., 213 & 216, note 1.

420 *"The man I used these things for"*: Ibid., 213–15.

421 *"God will have to be"*: Ibid., 163.

421 *"I have found the pleasantest retreat"*: Letter of September 11, 1715, in ibid., 224.

421 *"who was always fond of"*: Saint-Simon VI, 332–3.

422 *"in an extraordinary equipage"*: Oman, 228.

422 *"with some girl in tow"*: Letter to Madame de Caylus, June 11, 1717, in Leroy, Pierre-E. et Marcel Loyau (eds), *L'Estime et la tendresse: Correspondances intimes* (Paris: Albin Michel, 1998), 416–17.

422 *"Dearest Luise, I've had"*: Letters to the Raugrave Luise and the Kurfürstin Sophie, May 14, 1717 & September 18, 1697, in Liselotte von der Pfalz, *Briefe*, 283 & 147.

423 *"The Tsar seems to me"*: Letters to Madame de Caylus, May 14 & June 11, 1717, in Leroy et Loyau (eds), *L'Estime et la tendresse*, 416–17.

423 *"Men are tyrannical"*: D'Aumale, 97.

423 *"I'm enjoying it"*: Letter of June 19, 1716, in ibid., 217, note 1.

423 *"She always loved children, Madame"*: Ibid., 110.

424 *"I'm a bit hesitant"*: Ibid., 221.

424 *"Now I can no longer prove"*: Ibid., 112.

425 *"probably the only gentlemanly thing"*: Bernard Noël in his introduction to Caylus, Marthe-Marguerite, comtesse de, *Souvenirs*, ed. Bernard Noël (Paris: Mercure de France, 1965 et 1986), 13.

425 *"and you see my handwriting's"*: D'Aumale, 233–4.

425 *"She was full of chat"*: Ibid., 223–7.

426 *"Am I in my last throes"*: Ibid., 235.

426 *"How are you"*: Ibid., 236.

426 *"It seems that God"*: Ibid.

426 *"because we preferred"*: Ibid., 237.

426 *"in such a state of grief"*: Ibid.

427 *"What a noise"*: Saint-Simon VI, 332.

427 *"our wise, modest, gentle foundress"*: D'Aumale, 239–40.

427 *"Such a prodigious elevation"*: Saint-Simon I, 437.

427 *"The old hag's croaked"*: Desprat, 462.

428 *"Saint Paul declares"*: D'Aumale, 182–3.

428 *"Ah, mon Dieu"*: Ibid., 228–9.

BIBLIOGRAPHY

Unpublished Sources

Brinon, Madame de, *Lettre à Mlle de Scudéry concernant le théâtre de Racine*, 1688 (Archives départementales des Yvelines, J3326).

Maintenon, Madame de, *Les Petits Cahiers secrets*, 8 vols (Bibliothèque municipale de Versailles, BMV MS P 36 à 42, et BMV MS P 98).

———, *Proverbes* (Bibliothèque municipale de Versailles, BMV MS M 57).

———, Letter of July 14, 1708, to Mme la comtesse de Caylus (Amsterdam University Library, Died 35 Ah.1).

———Letter of December 29, 1708, to an unidentified gentleman (Amsterdam University Library, Died 35 Ah.2).

———, Letter of February 22, year unknown, to Mme des Marets (Amsterdam University Library, Died 35 Ah.3).

———, Letter of April 30, probably 1713, to the duc de Richelieu (Sotheby's Paris, auction of June 15, 2005, lot no. 42, letter 2).

Lettres adressées à Madame de Maintenon à la suite de la mort de Louis XIV (Bibliothèque municipale de Versailles, BMV G 328).

Recueil d'airs spirituels à une, deux et trios voix sans accompagnement, de différents auteurs (Bibliothèque municipale de Versailles, BMV MS musical 65, 2).

Primary Sources

Addison, Joseph and Sir Richard Steele, *Selections from The Tatler and The Spectator*, ed. Robert J. Allen, 2nd ed. (New York: Holt, Rinehart and Winston, 1970).

À Kempis, Thomas, *Of the Imitation of Christ* (New Canaan, Connecticut: Keats Publishing, 1973).

d'Aubigné, Théodore-Agrippa, *L'Histoire universelle du sieur d'Aubigné* (Maillé: J. Moussat, 1616–1620).

———, *Mémoires*, ed. Ludovic Lalanne (Paris: Librairie des bibliophiles, 1889).

———, *Sa vie à ses enfants*, ed. Gilbert Schrenk (Paris: Nizet, 1986. First published in 1729).

d'Aumale, Marie Jeanne, *Souvenirs sur Madame de Maintenon: Mémoire et lettres inédites de Mademoiselle d'Aumale, publiés par le comte d'Haussonville et G. Hanotaux, avec une introduction par le comte d'Haussonville*, 2e ed. (Paris: Calmann-Lévy, 1902).

Boileau, Nicolas and Jean Racine, *Lettres d'une amitié: Correspondance 1687–1698*, ed. Pierre E. Leroy (Paris: Bartillat, 2001).

Bonhomme, Honoré (ed.), *Mme de Maintenon et sa famille: Lettres et documents inédits publiés sur les manuscripts autographes originaux, avec une introduction, des notes et une conclusion* (Paris: Didier, 1863).

Bonnefons, Nicolas de, *Les délices de la campagne, suitte du "Jardinier françois," où est enseigné à préparer pour l'usage de la vie, tout ce qui croît sur terre et dans les eaux*, 2e ed. (Amsterdam: Raphaël Smith, 1655).

Bossuet, Jacques-Bénigne, *Oraisons funèbres* (Paris: Hachette, 1898).

———, *Correspondance 1651–1704*, Vols 1–15 (Paris: Hachette, 1909–25).

———, *Oeuvres complètes* (Paris: L. Vivès, 1865–75).

Castellucio, Stéphane, "La Galerie des Glaces: Les réceptions d'ambassadeurs," *Versalia, La Revue de la Société des Amis de Versailles*, no. 9, 2006.

Castiglione, Baldassar, *Le Livre du Courtisan* (Paris: Flammarion, 1991. First published in 1580).

Caylus, Marthe-Marguerite, comtesse de, *Souvenirs*, ed. Bernard Noël (Paris: Mercure de France, 1965 et 1986. First published in 1770).

Chantelou, Paul Fréart de, *Journal du Voyage du Cavalier Bernin en France, avec Préface de G. Charensol* (Paris: Delamain et Boutelleau, 1930).

Choisy, Abbé François-Timoléon de, *Mémoires pour servir à l'histoire de Louis XIV, et Mémoires de l'abbé de Choisy habillé en femme*, ed. Georges Mongrédien (Paris: Mercure de France, 1966).

Colletet, François, *Journal de la ville de Paris, contenant ce qui se passe de plus mémorable pour la curiosité et avantage du public* (Paris: Mille de Beaujeu, 1676).

Dangeau, Philippe de Courcillon, marquis de, *Journal de la cour de Louis XIV, avec les additions inédites du duc de Saint-Simon*, 19 vols (Paris: Firmin-Didot Frères, 1854–60).

Depping, G. B. (ed.), *Correspondance administrative sous le règne de Louis XIV, entre le cabinet du roi, les secrétaires d'État, le chancelier de France et les intendants et gouverneurs de province*, 4 vols (Paris: Imprimerie nationale, 1850–55).

Des Ursins, Anne-Marie de La Trémoïlle, princesse, *Lettres inédites*, recueillies par M. A. Geffroy (Paris: Didier et Cie, 1859).

———, *Lettres de la Camarera mayor* (Paris: H. Gautier, undated).

———, *Lettres inédites . . . à M. le maréchal de Villeroi, suivies de sa correspondance avec Mme de Maintenon*, ed. Léopold Collin (Paris: 1806).

———, *Madame Des Ursins et la succession d'Espagne, fragments de correspondance*, ed. Louis de La Trémoïlle, 6 vols (Nantes: E. Grimaud et fils and Paris: H. Champion, 1902–07).

———, *Lettres inédites de la Princesse des Ursins, avec une introduction et des notes de M. A. Geof-froy* (Paris: Didier, 1859).

Dufour, Philippe Sylvestre, *Traitez nouveaux & curieux du café, du thé et du chocolate: Ouvrage également nécessaire aux médecins & à tous ceux qui aiment leur santé* (Lyon: Jean Girin & B. Riviere, 1685).

Evelyn, John, *The Diary* (London: Macmillan, 1908. First published in 1818).

Fénelon, François de Salignac de La Mothe, *Correspondance*, Vols 1–5 (Paris: Klincksieck, 1972–76); Vols 6–17 (Geneva: Droz, 1987–9).

———, *Les Aventures de Télémaque* (Paris: Classiques Garnier, Dunod, 1994).

———, *Traité de l'éducation des filles* (Paris: Kincksieck, 1994. First published in 1685).

Forbin, Claude de, *Mémoires du comte de Forbin*, publiées par son secrétaire Simon Reboulet (Paris: Mercure de France, 1993).

Gelin, Henri, *Francoise d'Aubigné: Étude critique* (Niort: Bureaux du Mercure Poitevin, 1899).

Godet des Marais, Paul, *Lettres de messire Paul Godet Des Marais, Évêque de Chartres, à Mme de Maintenon, recueillies par l'abbé Berthier* (Paris: J. Dumoulin, 1980).

Guiffrey, Jules (ed.), *Comptes des Bâtiments du Roi*, 5 vols (Paris: Imprimerie nationale, 1891).

Guyon, Jeanne-Marie, *La vie par elle-même, et autres écrits biographiques*, ed. Dominique Tronc (Paris: Honoré Champion, 2001).

———, *Correspondance*, 3 vols, ed. Dominique Tronc (Paris: Honoré Champion, 2003).

Hébert, François, *Mémoires du curé de Versailles* (Paris: Les Éd. de France, 1927).

La Bruyère, Jean de, *Les Caractères ou les moeurs de ce siècle* (Paris: Hachette, 1935).

La Fayette, Madame de, *Mémoires de la cour de France, pour les années 1688 et 1689*, nouvelle édition (Paris: GALIC, 1962).

La Fontaine, Jean de, *Fables*, ed. René Radouant (Paris: Hachette, 1929).

La Rochefoucauld, *Mémoires* (Paris: La Table Ronde, 1993).

Liselotte von der Pfalz, *Die Briefe der Liselotte von der Pfalz: Ein Frauenleben am Hofe des Sonnenkönigs* (München: Goldmann, 1960).

———, *Briefe* (Ebenhausen bei München: Langewiesche-Brandt, 1966).

———, *Lettres de Madame duchesse d'Orleans, née Princesse Palatine, 1672–1722*, ed. Olivier Ameil (Paris: Mercure de France, 1985. First published in 1843).

Locatelli, Sébastien, *Voyage de France, moeurs et coutumes françaises (1664–65)*, ed. A. Vautier (Paris: A. Picard et fils, 1905).

Loret, Jean, *La Muze historique*, nouvelle éd. (Paris: 1857).

Louis XIII, *Édict du Roy sur la Pacification des Troubles de ce Royaume, donné a Nantes au mois d'avril 1598 . . . avec les articles particuliers. Ensemble autres Édicts et Déclarations des Roys Henry IV, Louys XIII, et Louys XIV* (Paris: Anthoine Estienne, 1644).

Louis XIV, *Acte royal 1710–05–01 Marly: Ordonnance du Roy pour empescher que les officiers des troupes de ses armées ne répètent les cavaliers, dragons et soldats déserteurs de leurs compagnies, qui pourroient se rencontrer dans les régimens qui sont revenus d'Espagne* (Paris: F. Léonard, 1710).

———, *Manière de montrer les jardins de Versailles* (Paris: Réunion des musées nationaux, 2001).

———, *Mémoires, suivi de Réflexions sur le métier de Roi* (Paris: Tallandier, 2001).

Louville, Marquis de, *Mémoires secrets sur l'établissement de la maison de Bourbon en Espagne: Extraits de la correspondance du marquis de Louville, gentilhomme de la chambre de Philippe V*, 2 vols (Paris: Maradan, 1818).

Maintenon, Françoise d'Aubigné, marquise de, *Lettres*, ed. Laurent Angliviel de La Beaumelle, nouvelle édition, 9 vols (Amsterdam: Pierre Erialed, 1758).

————, *Lettres historiques et édifiantes adressées aux dames de Saint-Louis*, ed. Théophile Lavallée, 2 vols (Paris: Charpentier, 1856).

————, *Conseils et instructions aux demoiselles pour leur conduite dans le monde*, ed. Théophile Lavallée, 2 vols (Paris: Charpentier, 1857).

————, *Lettres et entretiens sur l'éducation des filles*, 2e édition, ed. Théophile Lavallée, 2 vols (Paris: Charpentier, 1861).

————, *Correspondance générale de Madame de Maintenon*, ed. Théophile Lavallée, 4 vols (Paris: Charpentier, 1866).

————, *Extraits sur l'éducation*, 3e édition, ed. Oct. Gréard (Paris: Hachette, 1885).

————, *Lettres à d'Aubigné et à Madame des Ursins*, avec introduction et notes de Gonzague Truc (Paris: Bossard, 1921).

————, *Lettres*, ed. Marcel Langlois, Vols II–V (Paris: Letouzy et Ané, 1935–39). Volumes I and VI of this scholarly edition are currently being prepared for publication at the Université de Paris IV Sorbonne.

————, *Comment la sagesse vient aux filles: Propos d'éducation*, choisis et présentés par Pierre E. Leroy et Marcel Loyau (Paris: Bartillart, 1998).

————, *L'estime et la tendresse: Correspondances intimes*, réunies et présentées par Pierre E. Leroy et Marcel Loyau (Paris: Albin Michel, 1998).

————, *Correspondance de Madame de Maintenon et la princesse des Ursins: 1709, Une année tragique*, ed. Marcel Loyau (Paris: Mercure de France, 2002).

Mancini, Hortense et Marie, *Mémoires*, ed. Gérard Doscot (Paris: Mercure de France, 1987).

Marteilhe, Jean, *Mémories d'un galérien du Roi-Soleil*, ed. André Zysberg (Paris: Mercure de France, 1989).

Maurile de Saint Michel, Le Père, *Voyage des îles Camercanes, en l'Amérique, qui font partie des Indes occidentales, et une relation diversifiée de plusieurs pensées pieuses et d'agréables remarques tant de toute l'Amérique que des autres pays, avec l'établissement des RR. PP. carmes réformez de la province de Touraine esdites isles et un discours de leur ordre* (Au Mans: H. Olivier, 1652).

Mercure galant, 1678–1714 (Paris: au Palais, 1678–1714).

Montespan, Françoise-Athénaïs de Rochechouart de Mortemart, marquise de, *Lettres de Madame de Montespan, de sa famille et de ses amis*, contenu dans Clément, Pierre, *Madame de Montespan et Louis XIV, étude historique*, 2e ed. (Paris: Didier, 1868).

————, *Trois lettres inédites de Madame de Montespan, 1700–1701*, ed. P. Moulard (Le Mans: E. Lebrault, 1881).

Montigny, J. de, "La feste de Versailles de 18 juin 1668," in *Recueil de diverses pièces faites par plusieurs personnes illustres* (The Hague: Jean and Daniel Steucker, 1669).

Montpensier, Anne Marie Louise d'Orléans, duchesse de, *Mémoires de la Grande Mademoiselle*, ed. présentée et annotée par Bernard Quilliet, 2 vols (Paris: Mecure de France, 2005).

Moreau, Jean-Pierre (ed.), *Un Flibustier français dans la mer des Antilles: Relation d'un voyage infortuné fait aux Indes occidentales par le capitaine Fleury, 1618–1620* (Paris: Payot & Rivages, 2002).

Pascal, Blaise, *La Correspondance de Blaise Pascal et de Pierre de Fermat: La géométrie du hazard ou le calcul des probabilités* (Fontenay-aux-Roses: École Normale Supérieure, 1983).

————, *Les Provinciales* (Paris: Gallimard, 1987).

Patin, Guy, *La France au milieu du XVII siècle, 1648–1661* (Paris: Armand Collin, 1901).

Pérou, Madame du, *Mémoires sur Madame de Maintenon* (Paris: Fulgence, 1846).

Retz, Paul de Gondi, Cardinal de, *Mémoires* (Paris: Garnier, 1987).

Sales, Fançois de, *Introduction à la vie dévote* (Paris: Nelson, 1947).

————, *Les Femmes mariées* (Paris: Éditions du Cerf, 1967).

Scarron, Paul, *Oeuvres*, 7 vols (Paris: Bastien, 1786).

Scudéry, Madeleine de, *Clélie: Histoire romaine*, 10 vols (Paris: Augustin Courbé, 1660).

————, *Lettres de mesdames de Scudéry, de Salvan de Saliez et de mademoiselle Descartes* (Paris: L. Colin, 1806).

————, *Conversations nouvelles sur divers sujets* (The Hague: A. Arondeus, 1685).

————, *Pellisson, Paul et leurs amis, Chroniques du Samedi suivies de pièces diverses, 1653–1654*, ed. établie et commentée par Alain Niderst, Delphine Denis et Myriam Maître (Paris: Honoré Champion, 2002).

————, *La Promenade de Versailles*, ed. Marie-Gabrielle Lallemand (Paris: Honoré Champion, 2002. First published by Claude Barbin in 1669).

Segrais, Jean Regnault de, *Segraisiana, ou mélange d'histoire et de littérature* (Amsterdam: Compagnie des libraires, 1722).

Sévigné, Marie, marquise de, *Lettres*, 3 vols (Paris: Pléiade, 1960).

Spanheim, Ezechiel, *Relation de la cour de France, faite au commencement de l'année 1690* (Paris: Renouard, [pour la Société de l'histoire de France], 1882).

Tallemant des Réaux, Gédéon, *Les Historiettes: Mémoires pour servir à l'histoire du XVIIe siècle*, 6 vols (Paris: Bibliothèque Nationale Française, 1995. First published in Paris by A. Levavasseur, 1834).

Taphanel, Achille, *Mémoires de Manseau, intendant de la Maison royale de Saint-Cyr*, publiés d'après le manuscrit autographe (Versailles: L. Bernard, 1902).

Vallot, d'Aquin, et Fagon, *Journal de la Santé du Roi Louis XIV de l'année 1647 à l'année 1711*, écrit par Vallot, d'Aquin et Fagon, ed. J. A. Le Roi (Paris: A. Durand, 1862).

Villars, Pierre de, *Mémoires de la Cour d'Espagne de 1679 à 1681*, ed. M. A. Morel-Fatio (Paris: Plon, 1893).

Villette, Philippe Le Valois, marquis de, *Mémoires* (Paris: J. Renouard, 1844).

Visconti, Primi, *Mémoires sur la Cour de Louis XIV, 1673–1681* (Paris: Perrin, 1988).

Wicquefort, A. de, *Chronique discontinue de la Fronde, 1648–52*, ed. Robert Mandrou (Paris: Fayard, 1978).

Secondary Sources

Ackerman, Simone, "Madame de Maintenon et la lettre d'amour glacial(e)," Niderst (ed.), *Autour de Françoise d'Aubigné* I, 217–27.

Anderson, M. S., *War and Society in Europe of the Old Regime 1618–1789* (Guernsey, Channel Islands: Sutton Publishing, 1998).

Audiger, "*La Maison réglée,*" *L'Art de la cuisine française au XVIIe siècle* (Paris: Payot 1995. Originally published in Paris by Pairs in 1692).

Bates, E. S., *Touring in 1600* (London: Century, 1987. First published in 1911).

Beaussant, Philippe, *Versailles, Opéra* (Paris: Gallimard, 1981).

Bernard, Leon, *The Emerging City: Paris in the Age of Louis XIV* (Durham, North Carolina: Duke University Press, 1970).

Bertière, Simone, *Les Femmes du Roi Soleil* (Paris: De Fallois, 1998).

————, *Les Reines de France au temps des Bourbons: Les deux régentes* (Paris: De Fallois, 1996).

Biet, Christian, *Les Miroirs du Soleil: Le roi Louis XIV et ses artistes* (Paris: Gallimard, 2000).

Bluche, François, *Louis XIV* (Paris: Hachette, 1986).

———— (ed.), *Louis XIV vous parle* (Paris: Stock, 1988).

Boislisle, M. A. de, "Paul Scarron et Françoise d'Aubigné," *La revue des questions historiques*, juillet–octobre 1893, 86–144.

Boles, Laurence Huey, *The Huguenots, the Protestant Interest, and the War of the Spanish Succession, 1702–1714* (New York: P. Lang, 1997).

Bouchenot-Déchin, Patricia, *Henry Dupuis, jardinier de Louis XIV* (Versailles: Perrin, 2001).

Bryant, Mark, *Françoise d'Aubigné, Marquise de Maintenon: Religion, Power and Politics—a Study in Circles of Influence During the Later Reign of Louis XIV, 1684–1715* (Unpublished Ph.D. thesis, University of London, 2001).

Buckley, Veronica, *Christina, Queen of Sweden* (London: Fourth Estate, 2004).

Burguière, André et Jacques Revel, *Histoire de la France: Les conflits* (Paris: Éditions du Seuil, 2000).

Burke, Peter, *The Fabrication of Louis XIV* (New Haven and London: Yale University Press, 1994).

Busson, Henri, *La Religion des Classiques, 1660–1685* (Paris: Presses Universitaires de France, 1948).

Cambier, Maurice, *Racine et Madame de Maintenon: Esther et Athalie à Saint Cyr* (Bruxelles: Durendal et Paris: Lethielleux, 1949).

Campbell Orr, Clarissa (ed.), *Queenship in Europe, 1660–1815: The Role of the Consort* (Cambridge: Cambridge University Press, 2004).

Castelot, André, *Madame de Maintenon: La reine secrète* (Paris: Perrin, 1996).

Chaline, Olivier, *Le Règne de Louis XIV* (Paris: Flammarion, 2005).

Chamaillard, Edmond, *Le Chevalier de Méré, rival de Voiture, ami de Pascal, précepteur de Madame de Maintenon: Étude biographique et littéraire suivie d'un choix de lettres et de pensées du chevalier* (Niort: Clouzot, 1921).

Chandernagor, Françoise, *L'Allée du Roi: Souvenirs de Françoise d'Aubigné, marquise de Maintenon, épouse du Roi de France* (Paris: France Loisirs, 1981).

———— et Georges Poisson, *Maintenon, le château* (Paris: Norma, 2001).

Chill, E., "Religion and Mendicity in Seventeenth-Century France," *International Review of Social History* 7, no. 3 (1962), 400–25.

Collins, James, "The Economic Role of Women in Seventeenth Century France," *French Historical Studies*, 16 (1989), 435–70.

Cordelier, Jean, *Madame de Maintenon* (Paris: Club des Éditeurs, 1959).

Cornette, Joël (ed.), *La France de la Monarchie absolue, 1610–1715* (Paris: Éditions du Seuil, 1997).

Courtin, Antoine de, *Nouveau traité de la civilité qui se pratique en France parmi les honnestes gens* (Paris: H. Josset, 1671).

Couton, Georges, *La Chair et l'âme: Louis XIV entre ses maîtresses et Bossuet* (Grenoble: Presses universitaires de Grenoble, 1995).

Davies, Norman, *Europe: A History* (Oxford: Oxford University Press, 1997).

Dawson, Robert, "The Sieur de Villette's Love-Letters to Louise d'Aubigné," *Studies in French Fiction in honour of Vivienne Mylne*, ed. Robert Gibson, 89–102 (London: Grand and Cutler, 1988).

Déon, Michel, *Louis XIV par lui-même* (Paris: Gallimard, 1991).

Desprat, Jean-Paul, *Madame de Maintenon, ou Le prix de la réputation* (Paris: Perrin, 2003).

Donne, John, *Poems of Love* (London: Folio, 1979).

Dubois, Elfrieda, "The Education of Women in Seventeenth-Century France," *French Studies* 32, no. 1 (1978), 1–19.

Duchêne, Roger, *Naissances d'un écrivain: Madame de Sévigné* (Paris: Fayard, 1996).

————, *Ninon de Lenclos ou la manière jolie de faire l'amour* (Paris: Fayard, 2000).

———, *Les Précieuses ou comment l'esprit vint aux femmes* (Paris: Fayard, 2001).

———, *Être femme au temps de Louis XIV* (Paris: Perrin, 2004).

Dunlop, Ian, *Royal Palaces of France* (London: Hamish Hamilton, 1985).

———, *Louis XIV* (London: Chatto and Windus, 1999).

Elliott, J. H., *Imperial Spain 1469–1716* (New York: Mentor, 1966).

Evans, R.J.W., *The Making of the Habsburg Monarchy, 1550–1700: An Interpretation* (Oxford: Oxford University Press, 1984).

Félibien, André, *Relation de la feste de Versailles du dix-huitième juillet mil six cens soixante-huit* (Paris: Pierre Le Petit, 1668).

Félibien Des Avaux, Jean-François, *Description sommaire de Versailles ancienne et nouvelle, avec des figures* (Paris: A. Chrétien, 1703).

Field, Ophelia, *The Favourite: Sarah, Duchess of Marlborough* (London: Hodder and Stoughton, 2002).

Fondation du Château de Maintenon, *Louis XIV, Mme de Maintenon: Tricentenaire du marriage*, Exposition 7 avril–novembre 1984, 2 vols (Maintenon: Fondation du Château de Maintenon, 1984).

Franklin, Alfred, *La vie privée d'autrefois: Arts et métiers, modes, moeurs, usages des Parisiens, du XIIe au XVIIIe siècle, d'après des documents originaux ou inédits*, 27 vols (Paris: E. Plon, Nourrit, 1887–1902).

———, *Les anciennes bibliothèques de Paris: Églises, monastères, collèges, etc.*, 3 vols (Paris: Imprimerie impériale, 1867–73).

Fraser, Antonia, *King Charles II* (London: Phoenix, 2002).

———, *Love and Louis XIV: The Women in the Life of the Sun King* (London: Weidenfeld and Nicolson, 2006).

Frey, Linda and Marsha Frey (eds), *The Treaties of the War of the Spanish Succession: An Historical and Critical Dictionary* (Westport, Connecticut and London: Greenwood, 1995).

Garrigues, Dominique, *Jardins et jardiniers de Versailles au Grand Siècle* (Seyssel: Champ Vallon, 2001).

Garrisson, Janine, *L'Édit de Nantes et sa révocation* (Paris: Seuil, 1985).

Garros, Madeleine, *Madame de Maintenon et la musique*. Extrait des rapports et communications de la Société française de musicologie. Série spéciale no. 1, janvier 1943 (Abbeville: F. Paillart, 1943).

Genlis, Stéphanie-Félicité Du Crest, comtesse de, *Madame de Maintenon, pour servir de suite à l'histoire de la duchesse de la Vallière* (Paris: Maradan, 1806).

Gibson, Wendy, *Women in Seventeenth Century France* (London: Macmillan, 1989).

Goubert, Pierre, *Louis XIV et vingt millions de Français* (Paris: Hachette, 1977).

———, *La Vie quotidienne des paysans français au XVIIe siècle* (Paris: Hachette, 1982).

Gourdin, Jean-Luc, *La Duchesse du Maine: Louise-Bénédicte de Bourbon, Princesse de Condé* (Paris: Pygmalion, 1999).

Gutton, Jean-Pierre, *Domestiques et serviteurs dans la France de l'Ancien Régime* (Paris: Aubier Montaigne, 1981).

———, *Dévots et société au XVIIe siècle: Construire le ciel sur la terre* (Paris: Belin, 2004).

Haldane, Charlotte, *Madame de Maintenon: Uncrowned Queen of France* (London: Constable, 1970).

Haymann, Emmanuel, *Lulli* (Paris: Flammarion, 1991).

Hedin, Thomas and Folke Sandgren, "Deux voyageurs suédois visitent Versailles," *Versalia, La Revue de la Societe des Amis de Versailles*, no. 9, 2006, 86–113.

Hilgar, Marie-France, "Madame de Maintenon et le duc du Maine," Niderst (ed.), *Autour de Françoise d'Aubigné*, II, 259–67.

Hilton, Lisa, *The Real Queen of France: Athénaïs and Louis XIV* (London: Abacus, 2003).

Hoog, Simone, *Le Jardin de Versailles* (Versailles: Artlys, 1999).

Jasinski, René, *Autour de l'Esther Racinienne* (Paris: A.-G. Nizet, 1985).

Jeanmougin, Bertrand, *Louis XIV à la conquête des Pays-Bas espagnols: La guerre oubliée 1678–1684* (Paris: Économica, 2005).

Jégou, Marie-Andrée, *Les Ursulines du Faubourg Saint-Jacques à Paris 1607–1662: Origine d'un monastère apostolique* (Paris: Presses Universitaires de France, 1981).

Kamen, Henry, *Philip of Spain*, 2nd ed. (New Haven and London: Yale University Press, 1998).

Langlois, Marcel, *Le Journal du ministre Chamillart, ou les Mémoires attribués au marquis de Sourches*, Extrait des Comptes rendus de l'Académie des sciences et politiques (Paris: F. Alcan, 1925).

———, "Madame de Maintenon, ses oeuvres complètes, la légende et l'histoire," *Revue Historique*, Vol. 168, September–December 1931, 254–99.

———, *Madame de Maintenon* (Paris: Plon, 1932).

———, "Madame de Maintenon et le Saint-Siège," *Extrait de la Revue d'histoire ecclésiastique* (Louvain: Bureaux de la Revue, 1929).

Lara, Oruno, *La Guadeloupe dans l'histoire* (Paris: Harmattan, 1979).

Lavallée, Théophile, *Mme de Maintenon et la maison royale de Saint-Cyr (1686–1793)*, 2e ed. (Paris: Henri Plon, 1862).

———, *La Famille d'Aubigné et l'Enfance de Mme de Maintenon, suivi des mémoires inédits de Languet de Gergy, archevêque de Sens, sur Mme de Maintenon et la cour de Louis XIV* (Paris: Henri Plon, 1863).

La Varenne, François Pierre, dit *Le Cuisinier françois* (Paris, Montalba 1983. Originally published in Paris in 1651).

Le Blanc, J., *Scarron aparu à Madame de Maintenon et les reproches qu'il lui fait sur ses amours avec Louis le Grand* (Cologne: J. Le Blanc, 1694).

Lebrun, François, *La Vie conjugale sous l'Ancien Régime* (Paris: Armand Colin, 1978).

Leca, Ange-Pierre, *Scarron: Le Malade de la reine* (Paris: KIMÉ, 1999).

Le Roy Ladurie, Emmanuel and Jean-François Fitou, *Saint-Simon, ou Le système de la cour* (Paris: Fayard, 1998).

Letrouit, Jean, "Une lettre inédite de Malebranche à Madame de Maintenon contre Fénelon, Paris, 2 Octobre 1697," *XVII Siècle* 227 (2005 no. 2), 333–48.

Lewis, W. H., *The Splendid Century: Life in the France of Louis XIV* (New York: Morrow, 1954).

Louis XIV, Mme de Maintenon: Tricentenaire du mariage, Exposition, 7 avril–4 novembre 1984 (Maintenon: Fondation du Château de Maintenon, 1984).

MacCulloch, Diarmaid, *Reformation: Europe's House Divided 1490–1700* (London: Allen Lane, 2003).

Magne, Émile, *Scarron et son milieu*, 6e ed. (Paris: Émile-Paul Frères, 1924).

Mansel, Philip, *Dressed to Rule: Royal and Court Costume from Louis XIV to Elizabeth II* (New Haven and London: Yale University Press, 2005).

Maral, Alexandre, *La Chapelle Royale de Versailles sous Louis XIV: Cérémonial, Liturgie et Musique*, Coll. Études du Centre de Musique Baroque de Versailles (Sprimont: Mardaga, 2002).

Marchand, Louis, *Nouveaux principes d'écriture italienne suivant l'ordre de Mme de Maintenon pour les demoiselles de Saint-Cyr* (Paris: Collombat, 1721).

Marlowe, Christopher, "The Massacre at Paris," *The Complete Plays and Poems* (London: Everyman, 1976).

Mauguin, Georges, *La Jeunesse mystérieuse de Mme de Maintenon* (Vichy: Wallon, 1959).

Merle, Louis, *L'Étrange beau-père de Louis XIV: Constant d'Aubigné 1585–1647, le père de Madame de Maintenon* (Paris: Beauchesne, and Fontenay-le-Comte: Lussaud, 1971).

Molière, Jean-Baptiste Poquelin de, *Oeuvres Complètes*, 2 vols (Paris: Gallimard, 1971).

Munck, Thomas, *Seventeenth-Century Europe: State, Conflict and the Social Order in Europe, 1598–1700*, 2nd ed. (Basingstoke: Palgrave Macmillan, 2005).

Musée des Beaux-Arts de Dijon et Musée d'Histoire de la ville de Luxembourg, *À la gloire du Roi: Van der Meulen, peintre des conquêtes de Louis XIV* (Imprimerie Nationale, 1998).

Newton, William Ritchey and Jean-Pierre Babelon, *L'Espace du roi: La cour de France au château de Versailles 1682–1789* (Paris: Fayard, 2000).

Niderst, Alain (ed.), *Autour de Françoise d'Aubigné, Marquise de Maintenon*, Actes des Journées de Niort, mai 23–25, 1996, Albineana 10–11, 2 vols (Niort: Albineana-Cahiers d'Aubigné, 1999).

Noailles, Paul, duc de, *Histoire de Madame de Maintenon et des principaux événements du règne de Louis XIV*, 4 vols (Paris: Comptoir des Imprimeurs unis, 1848–58).

Oman, Carola, *Mary of Modena* (London: Hodder and Stoughton, 1962).

Petitfils, Jean-Christian, *Louis XIV* (Paris: Perrin, 2002).

Phillips, Henry, *Church and Culture in Seventeenth-Century France* (Cambridge: Cambridge University Press, 1997).

Pin, Marcel, *Madame de Maintenon et les Protestants. Contribution à l'étude de la révocation de l'Édit de Nantes* (Uzès: H. Peladan, 1943).

Plattard, Jean, *Agrippa d'Aubigné: Une figure de premier plan dans nos Lettres de la Renaissance* (Paris: Boivin, 1931).

Portemer, Jean, "Reflexion sur les pouvoirs de la femme selon le droit francais au XVIIe siècle," *XVIIe Siècle* 144 (July September 1984), 189–99.

Porter, Roy, *The Greatest Benefit to Mankind: A Medical History of Humanity from Antiquity to the Present* (London: Fontana, 1999).

Prévot, Jacques, *La Première institutrice de France, Madame de Maintenon* (Paris: Belin, 1981).

Pujo, Bernard, *Le Grand Condé* (Paris: Albin Michel, 1995).

Racine, Jean, *Oeuvres Complètes*, 8 vols (Paris: Garnier Frères, 1869–77).

———, *Théâtre—Poésies* (Paris: Gallimard, 1950).

Ramière de Fortanier, Arnaud (directeur), *Les Demoiselles de Saint-Cyr, Maison royale d'éducation, 1686–1793* (Versailles: Archives départementales des Yvelines; Paris: Somogy, ed. d'art, 1999).

Rapley, Elizabeth, *The Dévotes: Women and the Church in Seventeenth-Century France* (Montreal and Kingston: McGill-Queen's University Press, 1990).

Rathery, Edmé-Jacques-Benoît, et Boutron, *Mademoiselle de Scudéry: Sa vie et sa correspondance, avec un choix de ses poésies* (Paris: Léon Techener, 1873).

Ribardière, Diane, *La Princesse des Ursins: Dame de fer et de velours* (Paris: Perrin, 1988).

Rich, E. E. and C. H. Wilson (eds), *The Cambridge Economic History of Europe, Vol. 4: The Economy of Expanding Europe in the Sixteenth and Seventeenth Centuries* (Cambridge: Cambridge University Press, 1967).

Richardt, Aimé, *Fénelon* (Paris: Éditions In Fine, 1993).

———, *Louvois: Le bras armé de Louis XIV* (Paris: Tallandier, 1998).

Robert, Marie, "Inventaire des livres de musique de l'institut Saint-Louis de Saint-Cyr," *XVIIe siècle*, no. 34, mars 1957.

Rorive, Jean-Pierre, *Les Misères de la guerre sous le Roi-Soleil: Les populations de Huy, de Hesbaye et du Condroz dans la tourmente du siècle de malheur* (Liège: Université de Liège, 2000).

Rothstein, Andrew, *Peter the Great and Marlborough: Politics and Diplomacy in Converging Wars* (London: Macmillan, 1986).

Ruppert, Jacques, *Le Costume: Époques Louis XIV et Louis XV* (Paris: Flammarion, 1990).

Sabban, Françoise et Silano Serventi, *La Gastronomie au Grand Siècle: 100 recettes de France et d'Italie* (Paris: Stock, 1998).

Saint-Germain, Jacques, *Samuel Bernard: Le Banquier des Rois* (Paris: Hachette, 1960).

———, *La Reynie et la Police au Grand Siècle* (Paris: Hachette, 1962).

Saint-Simon, Louis de Rouvroy, duc de, *Mémoires*, 7 vols (Paris: Pléiade, 1953).

Saule, Béatrix, *La Journée de Louis XIV: novembre 16, 1700* (Arles: Actes Sud, 2003).

Schama, Simon, *The Embarrassment of Riches: An Interpretation of Dutch Culture in the Golden Age* (London: Fontana, 1991).

Sée, Camille, *L'Université et Mme de Maintenon*, 2e ed. (Paris: L. Cerf, 1894).

Solnon, Jean-François, *La Cour de France* (Paris: Fayard, 1987).

Somerset, Anne, *The Affair of the Poisons: Murder, Infanticide and Satanism at the Court of Louis XIV* (London: Phoenix, 2004).

Taillandier, Madame Saint-René, *La Princesse des Ursins: Une grande dame française à la cour d'Espagne sous Louis XIV* (Paris: Hachette, 1926).

Tiberghien, Frédéric, *Versailles: Le Chantier de Louis XIV, 1662–1715* (Paris: Perrin, 2002).

Voltaire, *Le Siècle de Louis XIV*, ed. M. J. Zeller (Paris: C. Delagrave, 1892).

Wedgwood, C. V., *The Thirty Years War* (London: Pimlico, 1992. First published in London by Jonathan Cape, 1938).

Wheatcroft, Andrew, *The Habsburgs: Embodying Empire* (London: Penguin, 1996).

Williams, E. N., *The Ancien Régime in Europe: Government and Society in the Major States, 1648–1789* (London, Pimlico, 1999).

Wilson, Derek, *All the King's Women: Love, Sex, and Politics in the Life of Charles II* (London: Hutchinson, 2003).

INDEX